# AFRICAN
## DREAM
## MACHINES

ANITRA NETTLETON

# AFRICAN DREAM MACHINES

*Style, Identity and Meaning of African Headrests*

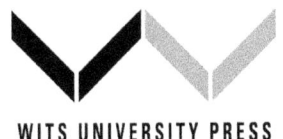

WITS UNIVERSITY PRESS

Published in South Africa by
Wits University Press
1 Jan Smuts Avenue
Johannesburg
http://witspress.wits.ac.za

© Anitra Nettleton 2007

First printed 2007

ISBN 978-1-86814-458-7

All rights reserved. No part of this publication may be reproduced, stored in a retrieval system, or transmitted in any form or by any means, electronic, mechanical, photocopying, recording or otherwise, without the prior permission of the copyright holder.

Edited by Alex Potter
Indexed by Marina Pearson
Cover and book design by Lisa Platt, Hothouse South Africa

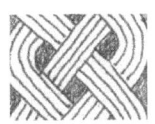

# Contents

| | | |
|---|---|---|
| Preface | | vii |
| Acknowledgements | | ix |
| Notes on the Use of African Ethnic Names and Country and Place Names | | xi |
| References to Illustrations in the Text and Notes on Illustrations | | xiii |
| CHAPTER 1: | Headrests and Art<br>*Figures 1–3* | 1<br>21 |
| CHAPTER 2: | A Matter of Style, or, Why Style Matters<br>*Figures 4–26* | 23<br>47 |
| CHAPTER 3: | Methodology, Position and Limitations | 59 |
| CHAPTER 4: | The Geographical and Chronological Distribution of the Columned Headrest<br>*Figures 27–108* | 69<br>95 |
| CHAPTER 5: | Authenticity and History<br>*Figures 109–179* | 131<br>160 |
| CHAPTER 6: | East African Headrests: Identity, Form and Aesthetics<br>*Figures 180–261* | 187<br>217 |

| | | |
|---|---|---|
| CHAPTER 7: | Tracing Histories: Central and Southern African Connections | 245 |
| | *Figures 262–432* | 274 |
| CHAPTER 8: | Not Just a Curious Beauty: The Anatomy of Meaning in Useful Objects | 341 |
| | *Figures 433–465* | 373 |

| | |
|---|---|
| Notes to Chapters | 387 |
| Bibliography | 425 |
| List of Illustrations | 445 |
| Index | 463 |

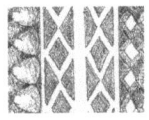 Preface

This book has been in the making for a total of fifteen years. The research started with my PhD on the traditional woodcarving of the Shona- and Venda-speaking peoples of Zimbabwe and South Africa (Nettleton 1985). Among the artefacts made by Southern African peoples, headrests were the best known, and they formed the centre of what I was to write about the art of the Shona. I spent a year in Europe in 1975-1976 researching all forms of woodcarving among Southern African peoples and discovered museum stores full of unacknowledged 'masterpieces' made by speakers of numerous Southern African languages. Many of these were headrests. In investigating headrests closely, I became aware of contexts of use and distributions of form which allowed me to use headrests to investigate a number of problems that face anyone who wishes to use art-historical methodologies to understand form, style and content in African art objects. A Council Fellowship from the University of the Witwatersrand in 1990 to 1991 enabled me to hunt down more headrests from across the African continent held in museum collections across Europe, and to develop an archive in the form of notes on, and photographs and sketches of each headrest I encountered. Where I was permitted, I also consulted museum registers for histories of these objects and made notes on that material in order to establish a particular context for each.

Armed with this research I returned home to begin its compilation, and began the process of drawing every headrest which I intended to illustrate in the book. Some of the drawings were made between 1980 and 1983, as illustrations for my PhD thesis, but the vast majority were executed between 1992 and 2005. Many examples from South African collections were added at this time, expanding the field vastly. Initially I started the drawings because I was obstructed from taking photographs in two museums, once in

Zimbabwe in 1981, and once in Belgium in 1991. However, I soon discovered that drawings enabled me to present information that would have been completely impossible with single views of each object such as those offered by the conventional face-view photograph. The process of drawing then became a tool of analysis as much as it was a means of presenting visual information. So, while the drawings started out as mere accompaniments to a text whose research dimension was vast, they have become a major part of the project in their own right.

The text in this book examines objects whose functional utility might, in the past, have prevented them from being taken seriously as forms of art. The book therefore starts with a chapter which examines the processes whereby such objects have been incorporated into a discourse of aesthetics and meaning and thus of 'art'. That is followed by a chapter in which the notion of 'style' is interrogated in relation to a single, albeit contested, 'ethnic' group, the Tellem. Chapter three is a short explanation of methodological issues underlying the research and the use of the drawings. In the next two chapters I track the distribution of a single form of headrest, those which use single or multiple columns as supports, across the continent and across time on the continent, and in the process I trace similarities among widely dispersed forms. This distribution study is also used to challenge notions of 'authenticity'. I then turn to discussing headrests in regional categories, starting with East Africa, looking mostly at forms made by people speaking Cushitic and Nilotic languages. The following chapter looks at headrest forms made by Bantu speakers, which are quite different from those made by the East African groups and which are tracked here in relation to histories of collection and marketing. These two chapters also look at the ways in which identity has been assigned to particular headrests. In the final chapter I discuss the making, use and meanings of African headrests on a number of different levels, using examples from across the continent, and contextual material. In this chapter a number of photographs are used to provide the reader with a visual context into which to place the drawings and textual exegesis.

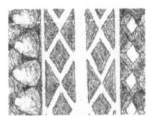 # Acknowledgements

This book would not have been possible without the generous support I have received over the years from the University of the Witwatersrand, including not only a publication grant from the University Research Committee in 2006, but also, earlier, a University Council Research Fellowship that enabled me to spend 12 months in Europe in 1990–91 researching this material, and a smaller research grant in 2005 that enabled me to wrap up research at some other museums. The book also draws on research that was funded by the Ernest Oppenheimer Memorial Trust in 1975–77.

In my research, I was dependent on the goodwill of many staff members at a variety of museums, and I thank them for their help and generosity in allowing me into their stores and making their archives available to me. Among these were staff at the following institutions: the British Museum Department of Ethnography, London, where I was given free reign in the African stores as a curatorial assistant; the Pitt Rivers Museum, Oxford; the World Museum, Liverpool; the Powell-Cotton Museum, Birchington on Sea; the Manchester University Museum, Manchester; the Royal Scottish Museum, Edinburgh; the Musée Royal de l'Afrique Central, Tervuren; the Staatlisches Museum für Völkerkunde, Munich; the Museum für Völkerkunde, Frankfurt am Main; the Museum für Völkerkunde, Hamburg; the Musèe de Ville, Neuchâtel; the Musée d'Ethnographie, Geneva; the Museum Rietberg, Zurich; the Koninklijke Museum voor Volkerkunde, Leiden; the Johannesburg Art Gallery; MuseumAfrika, Johannesburg; the Iziko South African Museum, Cape Town; and the National Culture History Museum, Tshwane (Pretoria).

Some of the people who have consistently maintained an interest in my work and whom I would like to thank for this are (in no particular order): John Mack and John Picton, whom I first met in 1975 at what was then the Museum of Mankind, and who saw me through the initial research on Shona headrests that formed a substantial part of my PhD and of this project; Sandra Klopper, whose work on Zulu art has contributed to this study, as has that of Rayda Becker; Allen Roberts, who read a draft of the final chapter and made invaluable comments via an extended e-mail correspondence; Jane Taylor, who responded to a version of the final chapter in a seminar at the Wits School of Arts with great enthusiasm and insight; Elizabeth Rankin, who was a mentor of note through the first 8 of the 17 years consumed by this project; Julia Charlton and Fiona Rankin-Smith, whose patience with my colonisation of facilities in the University of the Witwatersrand Art Galleries and my use of the collection was boundless; and David Hammond-Tooke, who introduced me to anthropological ways of thinking.

Finally I have to thank my family, Paul, Luke, Natalie and Matthew, who have shared so much of their lives with this project.

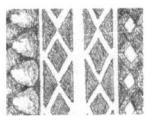

# Notes on the Use of African Ethnic Names and Country and Place Names

## AFRICAN ETHNIC NAMES

This study of African headrests includes pieces made by or attributed to members of a large number of different ethnic groups across the continent. Identifying these groups in an English-language text forms a major challenge. This text does not use complex forms of orthographic marking, but uses the simplest recognisable name for each ethnic group. Because French and English have been the main languages in which studies of African peoples have been published, there remain a number of differences in spelling of names of some groups. I have decided to use English forms wherever that makes most sense.

In some instances, ethnic names indicate small groups that are in turn classified as belonging to larger groups; two examples are as follows:
1. The Tiati Pokot are a sub-group of the Pokot (sometimes spelt Pakot), who, in turn, have been classified as Suk, and as part of a larger group called Kalenjin.
2. The Gwamba and Ronga are sub-groups of the Tsonga (sometimes spelt Tonga/Thonga).

In old European practice, ethnic groups among the speakers of the Bantu languages were identified by a form of their names that indicates 'persons of' (Ba/Ma). This form of identification often appears in the museum registers and in older anthropological literature. In line with current practice, I have identified these groups by the name stem rather than the plural, e.g.
- BaLuba — Luba;
- BaKuba — Kuba;
- MaShona — Shona: sub-groups include the Kalanga (MaKalanga), Zezeru, (MaZezeru), Korekore (MaKorekore), Karanga (MaKaranga) and Ndau (MaNdau);
- AmaZulu — Zulu, and so forth.

I have kept these names constant when I have referred to languages as well. So, instead of using the more correct term isiZulu-speaking, or tshiTsonga-speaking, I have, for greater ease of comprehension, avoided these prefixes.

In cases where confusion may arise, footnotes at the first appearance of a name indicate the possible variations in form/spelling.

## COUNTRY AND PLACE NAMES

Country and place names have changed over the years. Generally, for clarity, the modern name is used, e.g. Democratic Republic of the Congo for the area once known as the Belgian Congo and later as Zaire; or KwaZulu-Natal for the South African province once known as Natal. Such usage cannot be absolute, and may change in a particular context (for example, it sounds strange to talk of a nineteenth century collector acquiring items in the Democratic Republic of the Congo), but indication of this is given where it is thought necessary.

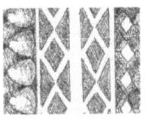 # References to Illustrations in the Text and Notes on Illustrations

References to the figures in the illustrations are always given separately in the text of the book, e.g. 'in figures 23 and 24' or (figs. 23 & 24), to avoid confusion with figures from other works referred to, which are always connected to a particular work, e.g. (Maes, pl. I, fig. 23, 24).

Entries in the notes to the illustrations are generally standardised as follows: Museum/author of publication, museum number/publication source, collected by/donated by/source, country and attribution to ethnic group, indigenous name where known, material and height where known.

I can't claim all notes as direct running quotes from register entries, as different museums do it differently, but the following applies:
- Italics indicate exact histories, provenances, or attributions from a book or museum register.
- Occasionally the modern version of the terms and names appears in brackets after the entry of a term or name, or there is an indication of whether a name is a district, region, province, etc.
- "Double quotation marks" indicate problematic terms or names.
- 'Single quotation marks' indicate attributions made in museum registers some time after the original attribution.
- No quotes appear for the parts that I have synthesised.
- Where publication sources are given, the full details of the publication are given in the Bibliography.

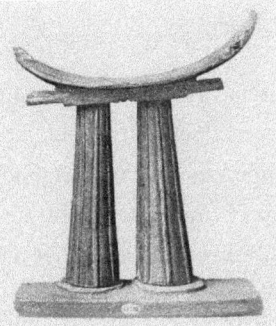

# 1 | Headrests and Art

> [ART] OBJECTS ARE not there to fulfill a technical or even aesthetic function, but quite simply to symbolize that function and solemnize it by their age, to which their patina bears witness. Being defined as the instruments of a ritual, they are never questioned as to their function or convenience (Bourdieu 1980:313).

African headrests, as members of a class of objects that have been assimilated into the mystical realm of art, have been subject to the processes of transfiguration outlined by Bourdieu in the quotation above. They have become synecdochic metaphors of not only a class of functional, yet more than utilitarian objects, but also of groups, identities and personal histories. The headrest in the African context is thus clearly not the same object as the headrest in the 'art' collections of the modern West. Its metamorphosis, to use Malraux's not unproblematic notion,[1] has been among the most recent of a set of conjuring acts to be performed by the discipline of art history on the ritual and functional objects of African and other peoples' material culture. Similar transpositions of items of material culture from across the world have allowed the emergence of the study of 'World Art', as opposed to the more narrowly defined forms of Western 'High Art' in the increasingly challenged discipline of art history. In many ways, this study, which encompasses only one kind of object, from one continent, is counter-intuitive to the kind of study that the advocates of the discipline of 'World Art' might envisage, largely because it challenges, and ultimately rejects the idea that categories such as art and craft have any relevance outside studies of post-Renaissance Western art.[2] This study is not so much, then, about how we recognise things as 'art', but how we deal with things that have been included into a pre-existing canon with some dis-ease.[3]

The study of human-made objects from Africa and other regions outside the West has only recently been included as part of the larger project of art history, mostly from the mid-twentieth century onwards.[4] Prior to this, most studies of those African, native American and Oceanic objects that were later warped into the dimension of art were either ethnological (and these were rather thin on the ground), appreciative or aesthetic in the most general of senses, but rarely were they 'critical'.[5] Fry's (1925) appreciation of African objects on the basis of their formal structures and non-mimetic qualities laid the foundation from which English-language art history was to initially approach the 'art' of Africa. Most of the early studies of African art objects were grounded in a modernist formalism that saw as its main project the definition of grand stylistic divisions and smaller sub-divisions, all of which were predicated on formal stylistic grounds and then assigned 'ethnic' identities following the nomenclature used to designate the peoples who had made and/or used them. Such formalism is evident in works such as Kjersmeier's *Centres de Style de la Sculpture Negre Africaine* (1935–38), Lem's *Sculptures Soudanaises* (1948), Olbrechts' *Plastiek van Congo* (1946)[6] and Fagg's *Tribes and Forms in African Art* (1965), and clearly has its base in other comparable projects, such as Berenson's classificatory projects in Renaissance art (Berenson 1952).[7] African art studies did not, however, benefit from other art-historical methodologies: no paradigms of development or stylistic changes were adumbrated, individual artists were ignored[8] and values of 'authenticity' were prescribed; while styles were defined, confined to one group and frozen in a static or cyclical time frame. There was no history of African art, and still is none, and it is questionable, for a number of reasons, whether there ever could be one,[9] or for that matter, whether there could ever be a global history of 'art'. One of the major factors is the genealogical line of art historical discourse on 'other' art traditions.

It is possible to trace the methodological trademarks of writing on non-Western art to the lead set by the ahistoricist approach of cultural and social anthropology of the early twentieth century. Anthropological studies of African material objects lagged behind American studies of Native American arts (e.g. Boas 1955 [1927]; Bunzel 1972 [1929]) and, when Africanist studies did start, largely from the 1950s onwards, they followed many of the same paradigms: the ethnographic present, the ethnic fixity and the frozen time frames.[10] From the 1950s onwards, such studies grounded their objects in an analysis of social practices, something that art historians in general only recognised as an appropriate praxis for 'historical' societies in the 1960s,[11] but which has become the norm in the discipline. Africanist art history has, likewise, followed the lead set by anthropology in its examination of contexts, but has retained in most instances a formalist system of analysis and categorisation. That this formalism is grounded in an acknowledgement of aesthetic value in African works is not in question, but how the aesthetic dimension is defined is, in most instances, problematically glossed over, or simply assumed to stand.

In the study of African art, art historians and anthropologists have deemed worthy of notice those objects whose form is figurative and whose representational emphasis apparently overshadows their functional nature. This preference would appear to be entirely in line with the kind of traditionalist Kantian aesthetics argued by Crowther (2004) to be universally based in forms of figuration across the world's art, and therefore recognisable across cultures.[12] Most of the general reference works on African art include utilitarian objects, such as headrests, only when they have figural sculpture as part of their form (e.g.

Leuzinger 1972; Trowell 1967; Willett 1971; Koloss 1990). The divide is thus not merely between the utilitarian and the non-utilitarian, as Shiner (1994:226–27) has suggested; the anomalies that arise in our classification of any so-called 'primitive' object as 'art' also result from the separation of figurative representational images (or objects) from non-figurative, and (apparently) therefore non-representational, objects. This follows from the fact that the canonical Western view of 'art' proposes that it is *essentially* about representation, based on a form of mimesis, and, according to Crowther (2004), it *necessarily* entails a series of renewals through innovations in its formal aesthetic sense.[13] Berlo and Phillips (1998) note a similar tendency to concentrate on figural works in the history of writing on native North American art studies, but they tie this to questions of the gender of the makers — men make figural arts and women don't, and men's art is generally more easily recognised within the Western art paradigm than women's. Yet the problem is the same — the figurative, the representational is isolated from all other production, and the same definition is reproduced in studies of world art such as that edited by Onians (2004) and that by O'Riley (2001),[14] in spite of the fact that there is some degree of emphasis on architecture, in which the figurative cannot be supposed to be the touchstone of the 'art-ness' of the object.

Figural sculpture from Africa, North America or Oceania is, on the surface, quite easily reconcilable with the contemporary category of 'high art', while other objects from these societies have been equated with the lesser category of 'craft', because they are seemingly non-representational. Of course, it is also possible to oppose the term *high art* to a broader, generic notion of 'art' as any aesthetic activity/practice, as do Berlo and Phillips in defining a work of art as 'an object whose form is elaborated (in its etymological sense of "worked") to provide visual and tactile pleasure and to enhance its rhetorical power as a visual representation' (Berlo & Phillips 1998:7).

But this definition, while it widens the notion of 'representation', simply reinforces the superiority of one kind of object over the other, by means of an appeal to the 'aesthetic' as 'elaboration', in the same way as 'art' is ranked higher than 'craft' (see Shiner 1994:25).[15] This is possibly most graphically illustrated by a cursory survey of the objects included in the essays in the catalogue for the Primitivism in Twentieth Century Art exhibition in New York in 1985 (Rubin & Varnedoe 1985). Here the overwhelming majority of non-Western objects included in the illustrations and in the exhibition were recognisably figurative masks and three-dimensional figure carvings with which early twentieth century artists purportedly had some ineffable 'affinity' (Rubin & Varnedoe 1985:15–17). That it was these artists' responses to so-called 'primitive' art that allowed African sculpture to be considered as art is little debated (see Steiner 1994:4; Rubin & Varnedoe 1985:11).[16] According to Firth, even anthropologists were liberated by the new vision created by the early modernists and started to consider these objects as art (Firth 1992:19). Yet this liberation occurred entirely within the boundaries of a Western definition in which mimesis was the prime mode of representation, and thus of art making.

It has been argued that modernist primitivism revealed an interest in the 'primitive' art of 'primitive' others, not in copying it, for those involved were not interested in the social contexts in which it was generated, but rather in reinventing it as 'art', albeit as an art that they thought stood as a foil to the cul-de-sac of the Western traditions.[17] But it is more plausible to argue that this art acted as a foil to Western naturalism, not only because of its formal differences, but because it carried with it a subliminal reminder of its supposed magical and ritual origins. Steiner suggests that for the early modernists, '[i]tems which were thought to speak across cultural barriers were judged as works of art, whereas those considered as impervious to cross-cultural interpretation, remained locked in the artifact class' (Steiner 1994:180).

It seems that the objects cited as sources for Picasso and Matisse (among others) were able to 'speak' because they were almost exclusively carved wooden masks and figures.[18] The common perception of the formal and aesthetic radicalism of these artists might, therefore, be tempered by the fact that they seem to have concentrated to a large extent on representational images, albeit from exotic places.[19] Transformed into art works in their own right, African, native North American and Oceanic figures and masks were found to be similar to the early twentieth century artists' own inherited practices of *representation*,[20] and were thus seen as 'art' works. Their insertion into the canon of art could be argued to have been dependent on what 'innovations' they added to the possible range of representational modes known to the artists of the West in the early twentieth century.[21] Their classificatory similarity was sufficient to allow the formal potential offered by such objects to be harnessed in a challenge to the naturalistic tradition to which the early modernists were the uneasy heirs. So, even at the dawn of developments in the European art tradition that led to a disavowal of representational modes, 'art' from Africa was defined in terms of a Western paradigm as constituting a set of representational images.[22]

Steiner takes a commonly held position that Picasso, Braque and Matisse may have had no interest in these African objects beyond what they could see:

> For artists like Picasso and Braque, the products of African art were silent, not only because they lived in lands that were oceans away, nor simply because they communicated in unfamiliar tongues, but, more profoundly, because their world-view was stifled, quite conveniently, by the West's summary dismissal of whatever constituted 'authentic' African culture (Steiner 1996:214).23

But it must be remembered that this notion of an 'authentic' culture was based, at least in the minds of the early European modernists, on romantic notions of the primitive 'purity' of the 'other'. It was to be found in images redolent with traces of magical and ritual activity, to which these modernist artists were likely to have subscribed, and which would have allowed them to project their own varying notions of primal creativity onto the unknown makers of 'other' objects and onto the objects themselves.24 The subsequent conservation and study of and writing about so-called 'primitive' art by art historians and anthropologists insisted on the frozen ethnographic present and the purity of unchanging historical tradition as two touchstones against which modernism itself, with its valorisation of innovation, via the individual 'genius' artist and the notion of an avant-garde, could be measured.25 As Elkins (2006:205) states: 'There is no sense to modernism without the privileging of innovation and the avant-garde: the terms cannot be subtracted away without dismantling the very idea of modernism.' These notions are further addressed in this study of headrests in unpicking the notion of ethnic purity and exclusive stylistic identification of objects as signs of ethnic identity.

It is important, given the modernist and primitivist roots of art history's interest in African and other peoples' objects, to explore the development of the representation of their carvings as works of art, and the relegation of other objects to the craft category, within a broader framework of colonialism and imperialism. In his discussion of the discourse that frames the colonised subject, Bhabha suggests that the colonial process is adumbrated on the idea that the civilising mission is based on the notion of mimicry in which 'the reformed, recognizable Other [is desired] *as a subject of difference that is almost the same, but not quite*' (Bhabha 1984:126; emphasis added). Given that African art studies arise out of the colonial expropriation of African territories and cultures, one might suggest that the objects appropriated into Western 'art' discourse were those that were, similarly, 'almost the same, but not quite', since, in both the imaginations of the early modernists who drew on these forms, and in the epistemologies of the art historians and anthropologists who wrote these forms' histories, their ritual functions, however vaguely perceived, remained a persuasive reminder of their difference. As Bhabha further elaborates: 'The success of colonial appropriation depends on a proliferation of inappropriate objects that ensure its strategic failure, so that mimicry is at once resemblance and menace' (Bhabha 1984:127).[26]

Thus, although, as Coombes (1985) points out, Africans were, even in the late nineteenth century, seen by Europeans as having 'art' and thus also the potential for being civilised, their near similarity but definitive difference was maintained through the metonymy of their presence in the inappropriately non-naturalistic carved and cast figures that were recognised as their 'art'. The threat that Bhabha suggests to be inherent in the colonised 'other' is tamed through the capture and closure of the African object's 'otherness' by divorcing it from its non-art functions.[27]

This process of divorce and closure was referred to by Malraux (1974) as a 'metamorphosis', a euphemism that, because it negates the presence of an agent, naturalises a complex process. This euphemism legitimates the valorisation of particular kinds of objects and their removal from the real world of material culture into a world of special commodities and class structures in which a moneyed elite has become their privileged and largely exclusive proprietor. This removal is most emphatically illustrated by Varnedoe's contention that 'modernist primitivism ultimately depends on the autonomous force of objects — and especially on the capacity of tribal art to *transcend the intentions and conditions that first shaped it*' (Varnedoe 1985:x; emphasis added).

The autonomous force that Varnedoe refers to here is not the animism that early commentators on 'primitive' art first postulated,[28] but is some imagined aesthetic quality inherent within works that appears to be not only independent of their makers and users, but also discernible only by those with particular sensibilities. However, such aesthetic and ascetic qualities are, it might be argued, precisely not what we expect of 'primitive' art — we want it to repeat the fact of its difference through both its appearance and its contexts of usage. Miller suggests that in Western societies,

> [i]n constructing itself as ideology, art will always tend to control, as far as possible, the image of that which it defines itself in opposition to. Thus art will attempt, from time to time, to enter, represent, and define popular culture, kitsch and folk traditions and also the *representations* made by other societies (Miller 1991:60; emphasis added).

Thus African art was characterised as anti-naturalistic and fixed as European art's 'other', in both formal and functional terms. But the nature of art as primarily representational, or at least figurative, was something seen to obtain in African art as much as it did in other of the world's multifarious art traditions.

This emphasis on the representational/figurative in the definition of art gave headrests with figures supporting their platforms entry into the 'family of art',[29] a family that was to be increasingly a shared domicile for artists, dealers, anthropologists and art historians. Steiner suggests that a shift in market demand from the 'classic' forms of African art, defined as figures and masks, occurred from the 1950s onwards, as more functional items were included by West African traders in their shipments of 'art' to Western Europe (Steiner 1994:7). But the apparently non-figural images created by the makers of headrests, who might have been the same persons as those who made the free-standing figures,[30] are not as easily recognised as art objects: they do not have the same necessary familiarity or 'affinity' with the West's representation-based forms to allow for their inclusion. Their difference is paramount, and the similarity demanded by Bhabha's 'almost the same' cannot in this case be invoked, because at first glance these objects are above all functional, and apparently only marginally — if at all — representational. In fact, they were and are used in a variety of ways, and this study explores some of their range of signification, but their non-Western strangeness remains at the centre of many readings of their significance.

It may be possible to explain the fascination that such aesthetically pleasing, but obviously functional objects have had for the outside observer, and thus their subsequent inclusion in the art category, in terms of the relationship between the technological expertise apparent in their making and our expectations of their makers. Gell suggests that

> the attitude of the spectator towards a work of art is fundamentally conditioned by his notion of the technical processes which gave rise to it, and the fact that it was created by the agency of another person, the artist. The moral significance of the work of art arises from the mismatch between the spectator's internal awareness of his own powers as an agent and the conception he forms of the powers possessed by the artist (Gell 1992:51–52).

Gell argues that the observer is in some way 'obliged' to perceive in this an agency whose creative powers are greater than his/her own. However, when a 'Western' viewer approaches objects made by those whom he/she may construe as 'inferior' or 'other', the mismatch between his/her perception of the culture that produced the object and his/her intuitive appreciation of the object must affect the ways in which his/her attitude to and classification of the object are set.[31] Headrests can become art objects only because, in this disjunction, it is the appeal to technical mastery and aesthetic formations that dominates. But, although their functionality is never forgotten, it is not understood in its own terms, or in terms of its original context. As Geertz reminds us, 'one can no more understand aesthetic objects as concatenations of pure form than one can understand speech as a parade of syntactic variations, or myth as a set of structural transformations' (Geertz 1983:98).

Yet functional objects from societies across the world that have been identified as aesthetically pleasing are defined as art because of their visual and formal qualities rather than because of the ways in which they allow observers and admirers to reflect on aspects of their social and cultural significance (or, in fact, prevent them from doing so).

As Dewey (1993:16) notes, the emphasis on free-standing figural carvings began to change in academic African art studies only after Sieber published his catalogue *African Furniture and Household Objects* in order to awaken scholars and the public to the 'aesthetic' qualities of African functional objects (Sieber 1980:13).[32] Shiner, however, has criticised this move to widen the term *art* so inclusively as a form of 'double-tracking', whose effect is 'to allow them to describe the practices of small-scale "traditional" societies according to the generic concept of art while telegraphing to the reader the spiritual and status connotations that go with modern aesthetic conception' (Shiner 1994:226).[33]

The inclusion of useful objects in the art category is here suggested to be possible not merely by the objects' loss of their functions, but also by virtue of the documented, perceived or projected spiritual content of the art object itself. This is well illustrated in two sets of examples: the first is found in studies of stools among the Asante (Patton 1979; 1981; Sarpong 1971; Cole & Ross 1977) and among the Lega (Biebuyck 1977), and of chairs among the Cokwe (Kauenhoven-Janzen 1981): the second is in the studies of Southern African headrests (Nettleton 1985; 1990; Wanless 1985–1990; Dewey 1993; Klopper 1991; Becker 1991). In all these cases, the delineation of an 'iconography' for these objects appears to lift them out of the purely functional category of furniture into the realm of art. This latter development is particularly significant in the light of the fact that objects from the geographical region of Southern Africa were not, before this, generally included in general surveys of African art, presumably because little was known of any figurative free-standing sculpture from this region. However, in some of the general books on African art published between 1967 and 1972, apparently non-figurative headrests were used to represent the art of Shona speakers in Zimbabwe and of Zulu speakers in KwaZulu-Natal.[34] This attitude to functional objects may have been stimulated by Western anthropological studies of the art of the 'other' in which, Firth notes: 'many simple iconic forms can bear a strong semantic load, which puts them alongside more elaborate ritual forms to which the designation "art" would be given' (Firth 1992:26).

Geertz (1983) had already argued that art (including objects that were not figurative) could only be understood as meaningful if it were studied as part of a cultural or social system, a position similar to that taken by Baxandall (1972) in his pursuit of meaning in Italian Quattrocento art. But here 'meaningful' is situated beyond the understanding of the generation of aesthetic form that seems to be at the heart of contemporary studies of world art, and is to be found in the realm of the cultural and the personal.

Thus entered the headrest (among a number of other types of object whose iconography was not obvious), by virtue not only of its aesthetic 'quality', but also of its claim to 'meaning', as a possibly legitimate art form in a scholarly publication of 1980, and Southern Africa had arrived as an art-producing area on the sculpture maps of Africa.[35] Because of the variety and intricacy of headrest forms from Southern Africa, emphasis could be laid on stylistic regions and aesthetic and formal characteristics, and this subsequently led to iconographic studies of their forms. Similar emphases have emerged in the study of East African headrests that have entered the disciplines of art history, and anthropological studies of material culture,[36] as well as the operations of commercial markets, as objects of investigation, objects for collection and objects for contemplation.[37] That is, they have become, or are becoming 'works of art', part of a Western aesthetic continuum that validates and underpins scholarly interest in such objects by art historians. Given the more anthropological emphasis that has been evident in the study of headrests in East Africa as elements of material culture, this raises the question of what the consequences of such an opening up of categorical divisions between 'art' and 'material culture' have been. Firth's (anthropologist's) definition of art is illuminating in this regard: 'Art is a product of human commitment, determined by man's social existence. It is essentially form; but only when form is mobilized for human purposes, given meaning in human terms by comparative associations, can one properly speak of art' (Firth 1992:18).

Such a view opens up the field for any object of material culture to become 'art', as long as its form is significant[38] and as long as there are no forms produced by that culture that more obviously conform to the canons of 'art'.[39]

Here Danto's (1981) notion of art as a process of the 'transfiguration of the commonplace' is useful. Although Danto is largely concerned with art as representation and therefore as mimetic, his discussion of the distinction between works of art and 'mere real things' is central to the way in which utilitarian objects may be said to carry both an aesthetic and an iconographic load. Further, Preziosi's (1989: 81–121) discussion of art works as loci for signifying practice has direct relevance to the analysis of the status of objects such as headrests as art works, as opposed to their status as objects of mere utility. Gell's (1998) proposition that objects can be considered art objects in so far as they have agency in relation to their audiences, however, takes the discussion out of the arena of semiotics and into a territory in which the 'art-ness' of the object is contingent on its power to affect and effect. This agency is, however, still something, Gell argues, that is supernumerary, not linked to the object's mundane functions (Gell 1998).[40]

African headrests have, in fact, been on the 'high' art market for a considerable period of time, i.e. in the economic superstratum constituted by 'upmarket' commercial galleries and auction houses. Between 1973 and 1975, Shona headrests, for example, featured in sales catalogues from Southeby, Parke Bernet in New York, during which time only one example from New Guinea[41] appeared for sale. Significantly, none of these was illustrated, because, presumably, they were not considered as important as the figurative items of sculpture that dominated in the sales and which were more elaborately described and illustrated, with really important pieces being reproduced in colour. In volume 7 of the *Antique Collector*, an article by Donne (1980) entitled, significantly, 'African art or African craft?', in which he hoped to open the eyes of European collectors to the merits of African stools and headrests as desirable objects, started with the following statement:

> Europeans make a false distinction between African 'art' and African 'craft'. Carved wooden bowls, spoons, forks, beakers, game boards, drums, door-locks, as well as stools and headrests, form just as integral a part of the African art tradition as ancestor figures (Donne 1980:56).[42]

The general sentiment expressed in this article is similar to the views expressed by Sieber (1980), although Sieber cautions against too great an emphasis on the aesthetic aspect, and Donne, on his part, elides all of African art into a single monolithic 'art' tradition. Donne's article is illustrated with photographs of largely non-figurative stools and headrests from West, East and South Africa, objects that it would be difficult to class as 'art' or even as 'sculpture' within the generally accepted limits of those terms. Yet they were clearly being appropriated into the category of 'high art', at least on the commercial markets, from the early 1970s. This appropriation, however, was paralleled by a contemporary interest in the semiotic and aesthetic loads carried by material culture evidenced in the work of anthropologists such as Geertz (1983), who rejected a division between art and craft. He argued that besides aesthetic discourse, there is, everywhere else in the world, other sorts of talk 'whose terms and conceptions derive from cultural concerns art may serve, reflect or challenge, or describe, but does not in itself create, [and which] collects about it to connect its specific energies to the general dynamic of human experience' (Geertz 1983:96).

Of course, headrests had been collected as curiosities, as synecdoches of 'primitive' practices, for many years prior to their inclusion as works of art in private collections and public art museums, the latter being the last to open their doors to these objects. Headrests were better known both in European and American museums and in their colonial clones in Africa as artefacts, parts of material culture that were more at home in ethnological or archaeological museums.[43] So the largest concentrations of headrests are to be found in such museums as the British Museum in London; the Museums für Völkerkunde in Berlin, Hamburg and Frankfurt; the Musée de l'Homme in Paris (now the Musée Quai Branly); and the Musée Royal de l'Afrique Central in Tervuren, although there are also significant private collections of headrests that have been published, such as the Joss Collection (Dewey 1993). There are other unique collections such as the Jaques Collection in the Johannesburg Art Gallery (see Wanless 1985–90; Becker 1991), which contains a significant number of headrests from a single geographical area, and the more recent collection including a large number of headrests displayed on the Tervuren exhibition *Aethiopie, Objets d'Ethiopie* (Van der Stappen 1996a).

The earliest examples of African material culture to enter these European museums were precisely those that were least secret and most accessible to early explorers and missionaries, objects used openly and apparently simply in day-to-day living.[44] Headrests and stools, bowls for milk and platters for meat, staffs, spears and axes are all among these early acquisitions.[45] In the British Museum, the headrests with the earliest accession dates were almost all collected in Southern Africa. Many objects, including headrests, were sent back to England as examples of 'natural history', and they ended up in natural history museums, in this case at Kew Gardens. Two headrests from Natal (i.e. KwaZulu-Natal) are examples; although their date of collection is unknown, possibly they were imported for the International Exhibition of 1862 in London, but they passed from the collections at Kew Gardens to the British Museum, and thus from *nature* to *culture* in 1866.[46] This reclassification of the material culture of the peoples who lived on the periphery of the colonial world,[47] the work of so-called 'primitive' peoples, rested on a recognition of their humanity, to some extent as a result of recognising that they possessed culture, and their potential for salvation (via Christian missionary activity) and exploitation, as well as on a growing base in anthropological studies of the differences between peoples as members of different racial categories.[48] It is not the intention here to discuss the various discourses that have emerged on the subject of the construction of 'otherness' over the past ten years. Nevertheless, these constructions are undoubtedly of signal relevance to what follows in this discussion of African headrests, and many of the arguments about representations of 'others' inform my discussion of the headrests of Africa. It is important to understand that, in the second half of the nineteenth century, these objects were collected and then displayed as partial representations of the people from whom they had been taken[49] — of these 'primitive others' — and not as items of interest in their own right, as they might have been for the cabinets of curiosities of the seventeenth and eighteenth centuries in Europe.

The collections of objects from Africa included in cabinets of curiosities between 1500 and 1800 probably all came from areas of Africa that were in direct contact with European traders and explorers, and thus would not have included many examples from the interior of Central or Southern Africa.[50] The objects listed by Bassani and McLeod (1985) in their overview of this subject bears this out, as most objects in their study were from the Gold Coast (i.e. Ghana), coastal Nigeria, and the Atlantic coastal regions of the Democratic Republic of the Congo (DRC) and Angola. Jones's analysis of the *kunst- und naturkammer* of Christian Wieckmann illustrates this point clearly (Jones 1994). Virtually all the African objects in Wieckmann's collection came from West Africa and the Atlantic coast of Central Africa.[51] But Jones suggests other reasons for the inclusion of objects in such collections:

> Objects were collected not so much because they were 'beautiful' (or ugly), but because they were 'wondrous'. Those who referred to their curiosity value were not necessarily denigrating African art .... Had Wieckmann been insensitive to the merits of African artistry, it is doubtful that he would have bothered to make such a collection (Jones 1994:43).

Further, as recent research has shown, no claims could be made for the collections in cabinets of curiosities as representative of the cultures whose objects they assembled. These collectors appear to have selected their objects on the basis of arbitrary personal preferences in the creation of a 'universal' picture of humans and their activities, or in terms of the extraordinariness of the objects themselves, and not in terms of a scientific schema such as was to become prevalent in nineteenth century collections.[52] Jones suggests that two criteria were at work in the selection of ethnographic objects: the real or imagined socio-political importance of particular objects, and/or their ability to elicit wonder and surprise from the viewer (Jones 1994:43). Headrests would appear to fit both these categories, but, while it has been shown that African objects in European collections prior to the end of the eighteenth century were mostly portable, including textiles, baskets, items of dress, musical instruments and a couple of isolated representational carvings, it nevertheless remains to be shown whether African headrests or any headrests from other sources featured in any curiosity cabinets.

Headrests have been collected largely in East, Central and Southern Africa (Van Dantzig & Jones 1987, cited in Falgayrettes 1989:122),[53] and few, if any, appear to have made their way to Europe prior to the mid-nineteenth century,[54] although at the beginning of the seventeenth century, Pieter de Marees described the use of small stools as headrests on the Gold Coast,[55] indicating that some Europeans were aware of the existence of such forms in sub-Saharan Africa. It may be suggested, then, that the apparent lack of headrests in early European collections may have been the result of their limited availability, or — and this would seem more probable — to the lack of interest that they offered to a collector of things memorable or extraordinary when they were divorced from their seemingly exotic functions. For example, two Angolan representational wood carvings collected between 1690 and 1695 in the Kwango region of the DRC by a Capuchin friar made their way first into the private collection of Antonio Vallisnieri in Padua, and ultimately into the Museo Pigorini in Rome (Bassani & McLeod 1985: 250), but, although the region is rich in headrest forms, both figurative and abstract

(Baumann 1935; Bastin 1961), none of these appears to have been collected early in the encounters between Europeans and Africans, nor do any headrests appear to have survived as curiosities from these contexts.

In the nineteenth century, however, collected objects that originated in the 'distant lands' of what we now call the 'Third World' were seen to be part of a 'scientific' project of both representing the 'other' through his/her products, and of allowing the observer to draw distinctions between the different 'others' who were represented. This project was guided by the emergent discipline of anthropology. Fabian suggests that the aim was

> to explain, or account for, the culture history of mankind (in the case of diffusionism) or the law-determined emergence of cultural variation (in the case of evolutionism) by means of the comparative method whose primary datum was the distribution or dispersion of culture traits in space (Fabian 1991:197).

He goes on to stress that spatio-temporal distance was a 'necessary assumption, a conceptual category involved in the constitution of the Other' (Fabian 1991:197). It is according to this comparative method, using difference constructed in terms of the 'primitive' as both early/original and as removed, that objects were acquired for the major collections of ethnology in Europe.

A passage from the *Manual of Ethnological Enquiry* (Royal Society 1852),[56] from a section dealing with the arts, demonstrates, however, that there were overtly imperialist motives underlying the supposed scientific interest in 'primitive' artefacts:

> When a people display their ingenuity by the extent or finish of their works of art, it will not only be desirable to describe what these are, but also the materials of which they are constructed, the mode in which these materials are obtained, the preparations which they undergo when any is required, and the instruments by which they are wrought. Such particulars will not only throw light on the character and origins of the people, but will directly or indirectly, influence the commercial relations which may profitably be entered into when commerce alone is looked to. When colonization is contemplated, the facts obtained ... *will point out the material advantages which might be obtained by preserving, instead of annihilating the aboriginal population* (Royal Society 1852:68; emphasis added).

A survey of headrests and other non-figurative objects from Southern Africa acquired by the British Museum in the second half of the nineteenth century reveals that a number of these entered the collections immediately after the Great International Exhibition in London in 1862. The exhibition displayed different artefacts from the colonies in Africa: from the Cape of Good Hope,[57] 'specimens of aboriginal industry', from Natal,[58] 'kaffir manufactures illustrating native industry etc.' (Her Majesty's Commissioners 1862:16, 28). The descriptive catalogue for Natal, written by Robert Mann, starts with a lengthy description of contemporary developments in Natal, including industries of settler origin, but spends most time on 'native' manufactures, including sleeping mats, headrests, meat plates, milk bowls, spoons and kieries, all of wood, weapons made of wood and metal, bone snuff-spoons and some clay artefacts (Mann 1862:3–23).

Mann's description of the contents of the 'Brobdignagian beehives' (Mann 1862:16), the epithet he uses for Natal grass-house constructions, emphasises the sleeping arrangements, particularly headrests, and thus demonstrates clearly how such objects came to be succinct synecdochic representations:

> Lying near these may, or may not, be some low blocks of wood with a pair of crossed legs at either end. These are the Kaffir's pillows. The Kaffir lies, in sleep, extended upon his back, on his unrolled mat, and with the nape of his neck supported on one of these wooden props, in order that the elaborate coiffure of his head may not be deranged by rough contact. A glance at the photographic portrait of Udamsu (photograph no. 19-13) will indicate the urgent need of some such contrivance as this to take the place of the nightcap and the feather pillow (Mann 1862:17).

Here Mann moves from the sleeping arrangements to the image of the man, the first term apparently standing as a mnemonic for the second. He shows no real appreciation of the artistry of the headrest as an object, nor of the coiffure. Only some clay figurines made by children approached the station of 'art' by virtue of their being representational; as Mann observes:

> Some Kaffir children show considerable power of observation and imitation in modelling figures out of clay. This is illustrated in the images marked 308K, which represent oxen, dogs, cats, bucks, a wagon and a white driver, all made by a boy from the Umvoti, twelve years old (Mann 1862:23).[59]

But any suggestion to Mann and his contemporaries that these objects might be classifiable in the same category as works by the Italian Renaissance 'masters' such as Raphael Santi would undoubtedly have been considered absurd. These objects were possibly as close as he came to something that transcended the level of the decorative, as he and his contemporaries saw abstract patterns engraved into wooden objects or moulded on clay vessels.

Mann (1862) claims that carved patterning, the single 'aesthetic' element that could be divorced from utility in functional objects, occurred in relation to the prestige of the object's user/owner. He records that abstract forms were found on the headrests of important Zulu-speaking persons only, and he describes the use of large decorated wooden pots among important members of Natal groups for drinking beer. Yet a survey of objects collected at the time from Natal and the Zulu kingdom, and those that are still in European collections, reveals the fact that most domestic objects were decorated with relief carvings of varying complexity. In spite of his limited exploration of the forms of decorative wood carving among Zulu speakers, Mann was nevertheless able to wax lyrical about the inventiveness of line used by the Natal indigenes in making and decorating snuff-spoons (Mann 1862:21).[60] This appreciation of the inventiveness of the decorative qualities of such 'primitive' instruments allows for the objects to be considered as 'artistic', if not as 'art'. This appreciation, in addition, clearly marked the honourable Dr Mann as a member of his generation: one has only to think of the major works on the evolution of decoration by Jones (1910), Stolpe (1927) and Haddon (1895), as well as scholars such as Grosse (see Eitner 1970:195), where ornament was considered as one of the first steps to 'art' on an evolutionary scale from abstraction to naturalism.[61]

A similar appreciation of the decorative qualities of the objects, not just African ones, shown at the International Exhibition in London in 1862 is to be found in a manuscript by a Victorian woman, Leila Hawkins, and Henry Christy, eloquently and perhaps significantly titled, *Gleanings of Aboriginal Ornament from the International Exhibition, 1862: Drawings and Handwritten Text for Henry Christy Esq.* Christy was a gentleman collector, dealer and connoisseur through whom the British Museum acquired large amounts of ethnographic material, and he acquired objects such as the large carved bowls in fig. 387 from the International Exhibitions himself, some of which he sold and some of which he later bequeathed to the British Museum, along with an acquisitions fund that only ran out in 1940 (Braunholtz 1970:38ff.). The manuscript, which he appears to have commissioned, includes water-colour sketches by Hawkins, about whom we have absolutely no information, except that, from the drawings themselves, we can sense that she had a genuine interest in the aesthetic qualities of these objects. There is an uneven distribution of the number of plates devoted to each of the four regions 'covered' by the drawings: British Columbia (ten plates), Australia (four plates), British Guiana (i.e. Guyana), (eight plates) and Natal — the only African region represented in the manuscript — (nine plates). The descriptions in the manuscript dwell largely on the physical characteristics and formal composition of the objects themselves, but nevertheless betray an attitude that marks their author as a follower of evolutionist paradigms. The title of the manuscript, starting with the word *Gleanings*, suggests a sense of the search among things 'primitive' for rather meagre reward. The only headrest included here is described thus:

> 'Isicamela' A native pillow carved in black wood with a small jar with cover attached to each end and the whole appears to have been cut out of one piece of wood, the vessels and their lids are covered with a carved pattern representing closely plaited rushes. This pillow or support for the head appears to have been carved for the same purpose as those used by the Ethiopians and ancient Egyptians to preserve the elaborately dressed hair from derangement and thus showing that the ancients were as much in the habit of sacrificing the interior of the head to outside show as any votary of fashion (Hawkins & Christy 1862, pl. 10).

The drawing itself concentrates on the details of the carving and the intricacy of its decoration, and clearly shows an interest in the technical achievements of the object. So there appears to be a tension between, on the one hand, the admiration for aesthetic complexity achieved in the object itself and, on the other hand, the notion of the backwardness of the people who made and used these objects, whose artistic talents had to be 'gleaned', and placed in the same paradigm as ancient civilisations and North Africans.

This tension is clearly evident in commentaries made on African sleeping practices and coiffures by European observers for over a century. In 1892 Theodore Bent published one of the first written descriptions of Great Zimbabwe and of some of the Shona-speaking peoples of present-day Zimbabwe. Included in the story of his progress through unfamiliar territory were illustrations of objects that Bent collected on his travels. Bent deposited headrests that he had acquired in Africa in the British Museum in 1892, with minimal documentation.[62] However, in *Ruined Cities of Mashonaland*, in the first chapter, aptly titled 'First impressions of Mashonaland', Bent gives the following account:

> The natives ... are unaccustomed to postures of comfort, reclining at night on a grass mat on the hard ground with their necks resting on a wooden pillow, curiously carved; they are accustomed to decorate their hair so fantastically with tufts ornamentally arranged and tied up with beads that they are afraid of destroying the effect, and hence these pillows.
>
> These pillows are, many of them, pretty objects and decorated with curious patterns, the favourite one being the female breast, and resting on legs which had evidently been evolved out of the human form. They bear a close and curious resemblance to the wooden headrests used by the Egyptians in their tombs .... They are common all over Africa and elsewhere among savage tribes where special attention is paid to the decoration of the hair (Bent 1892:34–35).

Situated on the same page as this written text is a lithographically reproduced illustration of one of these 'curiously carved' pillows (fig. 1). It is fitted into the same discourse on headrests from Africa that had its origins with the great exhibitions in Europe from 1862 onwards, a discourse that emphasises the curious/exotic nature of both the objects and Africans' hairstyling and sleeping practices.[63] Dewey suggests that the subsequent continual cross-reference made between African headrests and the habitual elaboration of coiffures among African peoples 'has become a truism' (Dewey 1993:21). He suggests that the purpose of hairstyling in marking gender, age and status is overlooked in these accounts. But the need for such explanations may stem from a continuing fascination with the 'otherness' of such practices. This 'othering' is further evident in another passage from Bent, where he refers to the relationship between patterns on the headrests and those in female scarification among Shona speakers (Bent 1892:45),[64] (fig. 2), thus calling up further notions of exoticism and savagery. He pursues the headrest as a synecdochic trophy of difference, marking out the savage from the civilised, but also inscribing the potential for civilisation within the primitive. This potential is contained in an originary meaning that is discovered through relating the Shona headrest to an Ancient Egyptian headrest, which he illustrates overleaf (fig. 3). For all the stylistic and formal and iconographic differences between the two, he nevertheless implies that there is an Ancient Egyptian origin for the Shona work. The headrest then becomes partial evidence, along with European incredulity at the suggestion that the Shona might have built Great Zimbabwe, that allows Bent to suggest a Semitic origin for the Shona themselves (Bent 1892:54).[65]

Such cross-referencing to Egypt becomes a trope where African headrests are concerned, and is repeated after Bent and Hawkins by others such as Jaques (1941), through to Falgayrettes (1989) and to the African stores of the British Museum collections,[66] where an Egyptian headrest is kept separately from those in the main Egyptian collections for purposes of comparison. This comparison may be seen further as an attempt at the legitimation of the African forms via the fact that they seem to be related to that civilisation from which the West traces its ultimate origin. In this the circle of closure on African headrests is completed, their functions and meanings filtered through discourses of difference and origins. The headrest becomes another art object and stands for an 'other' culture, but also for a universal origin.

The chapters that follow will pursue many of the issues outlined in this introduction, but always with an eye to understanding each headrest as an object in its own right, as well as a manifestation of particular sensibilities and relations within a social matrix, or many social matrices. In subjecting African headrests to close scrutiny, the book will be looking at aspects of history and authenticity and the ways in which their historical path to 'art-hood' has informed our understanding of the significance of these objects in contemporary art worlds.

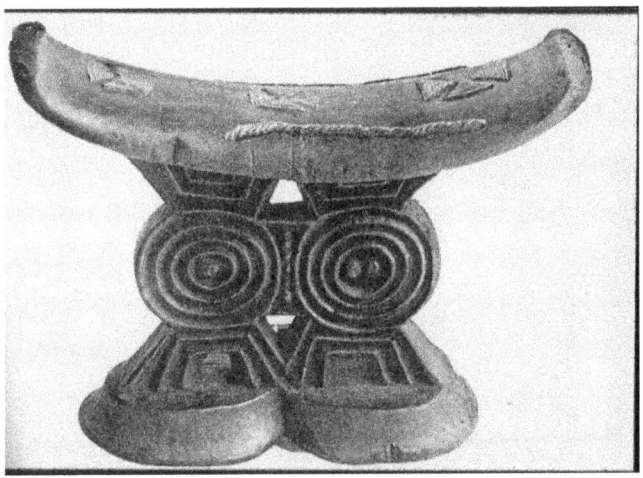

1   Bent (1892:35), *Wooden Pillow*, Mashonaland, Mashona.

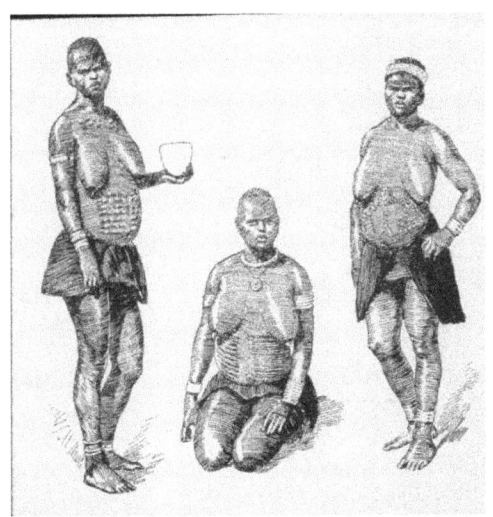

2   Bent (1892:45), *Tattooed Women from Chibi's, Gambidgi's and Kunzi's Countries*, Mashonaland, Mashona.

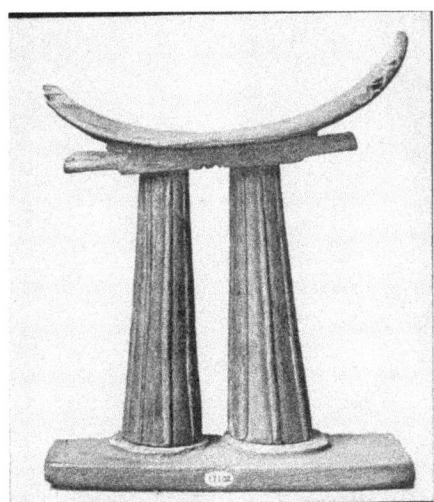

3   Bent (1892:46), *Egyptian Pillow*, Ancient Egypt.

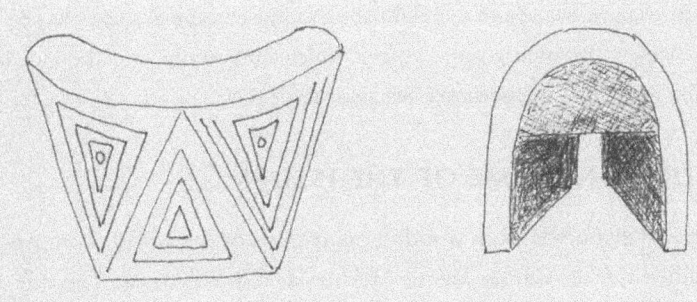

# 2 | A Matter of Style, or, Why Style Matters

BUT STYLE IS, above all, a system of forms, with a quality and a meaningful expression through which the personality of the artist and the broad outlook of a group are visible. It is also the vehicle of expression within a group, communicating and fixing certain values of religious, social and moral life through the emotional suggestiveness of forms. It is, besides, a common ground against which innovations and the individuality of particular works may be measured (Schapiro 1957:287).[1]

## INTRODUCTION: SOME OF THE ISSUES

Headrests have been made from wood in many parts of the world, from Ancient Egypt to Africa, Southeast Asia, China, Japan, Melanesia and Polynesia. There is a remarkable degree of formal similarity among these headrests, all of which fall within a fairly narrow band of possible structural arrangements. In the catalogue entitled *Support des Rêves*, which accompanied an exhibition at the Dapper Museum in Paris, Falgayrettes (1989) arranged the illustrations according to the *formal* resemblances visible among headrests from provenances geographically, spatially and chronologically far distant from one another, thus creating a series of comparative tableaux of this 'affinity' of form.[2] The existence of visibly recognisable similarities in formal elements among so many different examples of this single object type from such widely separated social and historical origins can only be explained in terms of the limitations imposed by the function of these objects in relation to human anatomy and the contexts of their original use.[3] Height, size and stability would have been primary constraints, as would relative comfort and durability. The height of the headrest would be constrained by the length of the human neck and the degree of the angle to which it could be elevated comfortably above the shoulders of the sleeping person. The headrest would have to be relatively stable to support the head in the relaxation of sleep, and the curvature, width, and length of the platform or upper surface, although more variable, would be important in providing comfort. The general everyday/-night use of the headrests would suggest that they should be durable, and in many instances, portable. As most of these headrests are made from wood, there would also have been many similarities in the technological possibilities and constraints present in the processes of their conceptualisation and execution. However, even where other materials, such as ceramic, ivory, stone and metal, are used to make headrests, their structural principles and formal arrangements remain fairly constantly within the same range as those encountered in wooden headrests, suggesting that structural constraints arising from considerations of utility were more determinant than technological/material ones, or that wood was the material used to 'think the forms', no matter what substance was used in their actual execution.[4]

There are, nevertheless, clearly visible, divergent formal and structural arrangements among headrests, which scholars have used to distinguish stylistic categories, not only among continents or among the inhabitants of various regions within continents, on the basis of linguistic and/or ethnic categories, but also among villages and, even more minutely, among individuals within these broader social and political frameworks. Such stylistic variations may be established through analysis of both the formal and structural arrangements used in the construction of the headrests and their decorative embellishments. The result is the identification of a multiplicity of differences, often at their most complex in headrests associated with peoples who lived in close proximity to one another.[5] This suggests that stylistic choices were not determined, except in the most basic ways, by structural necessity, and that, because form was not therefore dictated by the primary use of the objects as pillows, other explanations for such variations must be sought. In this study of headrests from sub-Saharan Africa, I have taken on the programme of establishing the significance of each object as an instance of practice, a practice that includes not only the production and use of functional objects, but also the production and use of aesthetic dimensions and their contribution to meaning. It is the formal properties of objects that lead us most directly to the aesthetic, and it is only through mapping of specific forms that we can achieve an understanding of the changing faces of formal and aesthetic traditions. In order to facilitate this mapping of African headrest forms, reliance has been placed on an old art historical tool, what Elkins (1997:11–13) refers to as one of the modes of 'normal art history', namely formal analysis, to distinguish different *styles*, something that will follow through in a number of chapters. For this reason, an analysis of the notion of style has been outlined below in some detail.

## DEFINITION OF TERMS: WHAT IS STYLE?

In much of the literature on African art and material culture, there have been continuing attempts to link the variations of formal styles of material objects to particular ethnic or cultural groups: the 'one-tribe-one-style' syndrome discussed by Kasfir (1984). Kasfir suggests that the dominant model used in art-historical research is an anthropological one, with the notion of the group being fixed in terms of the 'tribe', a term now shunned by most anthropologists and art historians (Kasfir 1984:163). But the problem may equally be an archaeological and art-historical one, and may be taken back to Schapiro's now canonical definition of style quoted at the start of this chapter.[6] For in this short quote lies a veritable quagmire of problems, some of which are referred to by Kasfir *vis-à-vis* African art, but many of which are embedded at the very roots of formalist art history. As a working tool,[7] the notion of style involves the examination of the forms used in any culture's material production both for abstracting their common characteristics to establish a series of types and for outlining how the formal characteristics defined as typical of one culture's objects may be differentiated from those of other cultures.[8] Gell suggests that what objects that are stylistically related have in common is not just external formal elements, but something integral to their standing as 'expressions' of 'the culture' in the wider sense: common stylistic attributes are associated, via a basic scheme transfer, with shared 'cultural values' in a community (Gell 1998:155–56).

This view is close to Schapiro's (1957), and is ultimately linked to the kind of *Zeitgeist* theory posited by Worringer (1957) and Winckelmann (1972) in the later nineteenth century, and to Hegel's notion of art as an expression of a *Weltanschauung*,[9] both of which informed Herbert Read's (1967) theories about art and society in the twentieth century, but which are so troublesome when applied to actual cultures. In both archaeology and art history, the definition of ethnic or cultural art styles takes as its starting point the notion of the social group.[10] In this scenario, the definition of style is based on the assumption that each group/culture is an homogeneous entity, whose members share beliefs, customs and language and which thus will produce an homogeneous form of art. Such homogeneously defined arts/styles have been seen as reproducing and/or producing particular ideologies, and, by concentrating on similarity, scholars have denied any recognition of contesting ideologies in art production.[11] This is evident in much anthropological literature in its definition of culture: an example is found in Geertz's essay 'Art as a Cultural System', in which he claims that when one studies an aesthetic or formal system, one is engaging with a sensibility that is shared within a social collective (Geertz 1983).[12] An essentially art-historical dimension of this notion of culture is entered in the delineation of wider historical groupings along largely linguistic lines, only in the delineation of very broad and sweeping categories, for example, that the Italian (read

'Romance language') Renaissance painting is separated from the northern (read 'Germanic language') Renaissance painting by cultural factors. So Alpers[13] characterises Dutch artists' way of approaching the world as essentially optical/visual, and thus opposes them to the intellectual/rational approach taken by artists of the Italian Renaissance. In doing this she sets up meta-categories that transgress other linguistic and ethnic divisions. Preziosi argues that such concern for identity (national or ethnic) is embedded within the discipline of art history at its very foundation:

> From its beginnings, art history was a site for the production and performance of regnant ideology, one of the workshops in which the idea of the folk and the nation state was manufactured. Today, the extension of its disciplinary horizons to all places and all times essentially continues this programme of identifying, manufacturing and sustaining selfhood and solidarity (Preziosi 1989:32).

By the same terms, however, it could be argued that art history has also been, and is still concerned with manufacturing and sustaining 'otherness' and separation. This is evident in the area of art history outside the West and that branch of anthropology that concerns itself with the art of 'others'. Here, because 'cultures' are always identified with linguistic or ethnic divisions, political and structural divergence within the larger ambit of a linguistic group is ignored, and the diversity of relations both within and among such linguistic groups is not accounted for.

This use of linguistic markers appears to be predicated on an anthropomorphic model for defining cultures, in which a specific culture replaces the individual as the artist.[14] The culture is seen as having particular traits in terms of beliefs, norms and practices: something that parallels the psychology of the individual. In some instances, the culture is also seen as having a history, a biography like that of the artist, and, in most art-historical discourse, notions of development and influence are applied undifferentially in the analysis of the productions of both artists and cultures. In this way, the notions of 'spirit' and 'tradition' are adumbrated into formal style studies. Foucault admonishes us to rid ourselves of these notions, suggesting that the notion of spirit 'enables us to establish between the simultaneous and successive phenomena of a given period, a community of meanings, symbolic links ... which allows the sovereignty of the collective unconscious to emerge as the principle of unity and explanation' (Foucault 1972:21).

It therefore makes sense to be wary of such formulations of style as those outlined by both Gell (1998) and Schapiro (1957). Not only does Schapiro see art styles as systems, and thus as homogenous or tightly coherent means of expression practised by groups or communities/cultures, he also, and in some senses contradictorily, allows for style to be a manifestation of an individual psyche, enabling the observer to identify the 'hand' of a particular master (Schapiro 1957). But this rather peculiar formulation of the relationship between artist and connoisseur, in terms of hand vs. eye, is in itself rather unequal. It seems to demote the activity of the artist (the hand) in opposition to the contemplation of the viewer/connoisseur (the eye), and tends to thereby negate the eye of the artist as he (and occasionally she) refers or defers to, or changes, a visual canon in the process of production.[15] The tracing of such reference/deference on the part of individual artists had, of course, been common practice in Western art connoisseurship and history, possibly from Vasari,[16] but definitely from Winckelmann onwards. It is revisited by Wolheim (1987) in his discussion of painting as art as an opposition between the activity of the artist and the seeing by the viewer, and where the artist becomes at some point a conscious viewer of his/her own product.[17] Interestingly, however, in African art studies, while an individual artist's works may be differentiated by a variety of measures centred on stylistic analysis, as can be seen from work on Yoruba and Luba art (Abiodun, Drewal & Pemberton 1994; Neyt 1994), identifying the social/cultural group becomes more problematic, precisely because, in Schapiro's terms, the group that produced a particular style must be demonstrated as having (or having had) fixed or fixable 'values of religious, social and moral life' (Schapiro 1957:287),[18] rather than simply identifiable common formal stylistic traits. The eye is thus suggested to be less important for identifying works that are made following communally agreed formulae than it is for isolating those that are attached to individual hands.

Holly suggests that the way in which we organise elements in explaining art works may be legislated by the 'rhetorical features of a period's consciousness' (Holly 1996:81) rather than discovered within or recovered from the works. To what extent these 'rhetorical features' might be seen to correspond to Schapiro's notion of shared values is not clear, but a community is implied, especially as Holly gives primacy to the object as the locus of expression rather than to the connoisseur as the reader of meaning, to a voice rather than to a contemporary hand or a later eye. Eldridge's analysis of Althusser's notion of culture is similar in its conclusions: that the apparently 'individual and intentional acts which are assumed to make up culture, are entirely reliant on the possibilities which their cultures have made available to them' (Eldridge 1993:193). Hence it remains incumbent on the historian to isolate and identify the cultural possibilities, and, as this is most likely in art history to be done via reference to the works, the project becomes hopelessly circular, self-referencing and self-reinforcing.

There are other problems that arise out of the linking of style with identity, particularly with the lack of analysis of time as a factor within the classifications of styles in African and other world arts. Kasfir puts this lack down to the adoption of anthropological ethnographic present/s within the writing on African art (Kasfir 1984:169), but it might with greater justification be laid at the door of the notion of style itself. As Kubler points out:

> Historically every work of art is a fragment of some larger unit, and every work of art is a bundle of components of different ages, intricately related to many other works of art, both old and new, and these interrelations across time and space constitute the study of historical style, which is called stylistic analysis (Kubler 1985:386).

This leads him to the conclusion that '[t]he idea of style is best adapted to static situations, in crosscut or synchronous section. It is an idea unsuited to duration which is dynamic, because of the changing nature of every class in duration' (Kubler 1985:390).

In European art history, style is almost always constructed in terms of a period, a place and a people for which and for whom a coherent structure can be claimed or (re)constructed, and in which a development from a supposed beginning to a proposed end can be traced. The construction of a specifically 'Western' art history generally finds its basis in the notion of the 'development' of a naturalistic tradition (via a series of 'innovations', original and individually driven to the point that they are located in the works of single famous artists) in painting and sculpture.[19] This chronological narrative of increasing naturalism runs from the Italian Primitives in the fourteenth century to an end at the point in the twentieth century where Fauvist or Cubist works broke from their strictures via the inspiration provided by traditions beyond the West. Development and style are consequently two of the notions of which Foucault suggests we must rid our discourse, because: '"tradition" makes it possible to rethink the dispersion of history in the form of the same', and because '"style" allows one to homogenise statements according to the manner of their making'. He suggests that we need to rather 'characterise and individualise ... the coexistence of these dispersed and heterogeneous statements' (Foucault 1972:21–24).

In African art-historical studies, traditions are constructed as completely homogenous within 'tribal' boundaries, despite fragmentation of styles within these boundaries. They are also in some instances fragmented by 'tribal' boundaries, especially where these are drawn despite stylistic similarities that occur across their imaginary lines. This fragmentation of style is only synchronically conceived across the sub-Saharan regions of the continent, with the inevitable result that it is ahistorical. Underlying this syndrome of synchronic narrative is the fact that within single, apparently homogeneous artistic traditions in Africa (with some exceptions in Nigeria and Ghana), periodisation is highly problematic,[20] because the objects that one would need to analyse across a diachronic range, in Kubler's terms, are almost entirely lacking. Africanist art historians have thus constructed taxonomies of style according to a notion of the producing group as a static ethnic and linguistic entity, although some have attempted to assign historical depth to specific sculptural traditions, without, however, attempting to trace an historical development of styles.[21] While the value of histories of art styles, the bread and butter of Elkins' 'normal art history' is moot, the usefulness of synchronic divisions has been cast into doubt, because it reflects Western ideas about the supposedly 'primitive' other. Kasfir's examination of Idoma art does much to challenge the validity of such static ethnic divisions in African art studies (Kasfir 1984), but she has nevertheless been accused of being party to the construction of a 'new mythology' (Dutton 1995).

Dutton, in comparing what he calls the 'old mythology' and the 'new mythology', points to the problems inherent in the ways in which Western scholarship has constructed other societies, particularly pre-industrial ones outside Europe, and the ways in which contemporary theory deconstructs these notions: 'In the Old Mythology, precontact tribal societies were seen as largely isolated, unchanging, coherent and unbroken in their cultural tradition' (Dutton 1995:35), while '[t]he New Mythology asserts to the contrary that these societies never were isolated, were not necessarily "unified" or "coherent" and underwent profound breaks in their traditions before European contact' (Dutton 1995:36).

While Dutton's argument on methodologies has been debated (Miller 1991; Steiner 1996; Kasfir 1992), his critique of contemporary orthodoxies (authordoxies?) is possibly a salutary warning. Perhaps there *were* isolated societies such as those he outlines, and to some extent defends, for the 'Old Mythology', but recent historical research has revealed a much more fluid past for African societies, and it would be very difficult to give examples of pristine 'primitive' African societies. It is interesting, in relation to these arguments, to recall Elkins's (2006) suggestion that the most fruitful of possible futures for the discipline of history of art/art history may lie in the abandonment of both the modernist/positivist and postmodern/relativist positions in favour of a discourse embedded in local concepts of the visual, in which all concepts of style would probably fall away, as the categorical schemas of Western classification would no longer be regnant.[22] While this might enable us to deal with objects more closely to their own terms, it would, however, leave us without any understanding of why we were bothering to study the objects at all, because if we study them as 'art', we have already categorised them according to a Western discourse. What this study will do is to provide a critique of Western categorisations and suggest ways in which some of them might themselves be retooled.

## HEADRESTS AS STYLES IN THE LITERATURE ON AFRICAN ART

Within the field of African art history, the study of headrests has focused almost exclusively on those headrests that include figurative elements in one form or another, and can thus be accommodated within the more general stylistic categories set up for African sculpture. The publications on African headrests include both generalised coverage and specific focus on either ethnic or regional types. In all of these, the main concerns have been 1) the classification of ethnic 'styles', and 2) the decoding of iconographic content in the headrest forms. This has resulted in the creation of a meta-text of stylistic classifications in which headrests are flattened as parts of a system of signification that emphasises form as *the* index of ethnic difference and function as a prime index of supposed 'primitiveness'.

General references to African headrests can be found in a number of publications. It is not possible to list all of these here, but the main trends within these publications will be outlined. In the general reference works on African art, headrests appear for the most part only when they have as part of their support a figural sculpture.[23] In all these surveys of 'art' from a vast continent, and, in the case of Falgayrettes (1989), of the world, a straight correlation between styles and ethnic groups is simply accepted: headrests as part of a sculptural corpus stand as exemplars of ethnically defined identity in material production. Most of this classification is based in a study of figurative sculpture and very little literature exists that focuses on headrests from Africa *per se*.

Graebner's (1927) article was a pioneering formal survey of types of African headrests arranged into an ethnic taxonomy that included examples from East, Central and Southern Africa. The catalogue *Support des Rêves* (Falgayrettes 1989), which accompanied the exhibition of headrests at the Dapper Foundation in Paris, encompassed headrests from Asia, Africa and Oceania, and stylistic categorisation of these was again made according to 'ethnic' groups for African and other non-Western examples. However, because of its catholic inclusiveness, this assemblage ultimately raised more questions than it answered, especially as the Egyptian and Chinese examples were placed according to a period classification. The bias in the text of the catalogue is towards psychological explanations of formal qualities, along with much-abbreviated accounts of specific cultural practices associated with the headrests of particular peoples. By contrast, William Dewey (1993), in his catalogue of the African headrests of the Jerome L. Joss Collection,[24] organised the individual entries according to broad geographical regions, but almost every headrest is, nevertheless, assigned an ethnic classification. This is done with careful consideration of ethnographic 'evidence' on the production, use and indigenous meaning of each form. It is interesting to note, however, how often these attributions carry queries in cases where there are no figural or other stylistic elements to allow for more 'secure' attributions (in the inevitable absence of documentation in an originally private collection), suggesting that outlining stylistic characteristics here may only problematically be assigned to the promotion of difference.[25] While Dewey clearly delineates problems encountered with some of the ethnic terminology used, and extends his sources for interpretation beyond strict ethnic boundaries, as is the case for his use of Ngoni ethnography in the interpretation of Swazi and Zulu headrests, he nevertheless does not attempt a classificatory system that might transgress ethnic boundaries or amplify relationships beyond them.

The large majority of African headrests are non-figurative in form, and this poses problems for taxonomic classification quite different from classification of figurative sculptural elements on other headrests. Such a taxonomy was attempted by Maes's (1929) classification of Congolese[26] headrests in the Musée Royal de l'Afrique Central in Tervuren into five major regional groups. Maes organised these headrests within a stylistic framework, where the formal similarities among specific examples, established through analysis of the shapes and composition of elements such as bases, supports and platforms, could theoretically cut across strict ethnic boundaries. Maes's arrangement of his material is, however, a little inconsistent. Although, for the most part, he arranged the images of the headrests so that formally similar examples are grouped together, there are times where, because he gave each headrest a specific ethnic label, he nevertheless felt constrained to keep objects associated with particular ethnicities together.[27] Despite some problematic attributions, his work remains a major contribution to the study of this form of cultural production. The ethnic attributions made by subsequent scholars of Congolese headrests[28] have rested heavily on this base (e.g. see Dewey 1993:53), and his catalogue is used extensively in this research, although there are numerous instances where the present book will suggest alternative ways of classifying pieces.

Similar formally based analyses of stylistic categories are found in other early literature on Central African headrests. Baumann's (1935) account of Lunda and Cokwe[29] headrests attempts to arrange the headrests according to three formal types, with a further sub-typology proposed for the Luimbi peoples (Baumann 1935). Baumann further noted the dual functionality of many Lunda and Cokwe headrests, which may at times be used as stools, and thus raised problems of categorisation of function that arise with headrest types from other regions. Bastin (1961) gives a number of examples of Cokwe headrests, with both non-figurated and figurative supports, but examines them within the framework of formal and iconographic readings of Cokwe decorative art as a whole, and not within a typology of headrest forms. Both these authors thus use the ethnic group as the core classificatory genre, with stylistic analysis as the tool for determining ethnic styles, and both separate headrests from other forms of sculpture. Even though both Baumann and Bastin illustrate examples with figurative sculptural elements, the similarities between these and some figurative headrests provenanced among the Yaka is not remarked on.

Bourgeois (1984), too, does not consider the possibilities of a larger stylistic conglomerate: his brief account of the headrests of the Yaka and Suku discusses only the figurated forms, and thus falls into a type of analysis of style that concentrates only on 'masterworks' — on objects that appear to be art. He does not mention the many examples of non-figurative headrests attributed to the Yaka, many of which are kept in the Musée Royal de l'Afrique Central in Tervuren. A similar pattern is followed for most of the sculpture-producing peoples of the Congo basin, where the non-figurative headrests are ignored, and stylistic analysis is based on the stylistic elements of the figurative supports, to the exclusion of all other elements (e.g. Cornet 1971; Olbrechts 1946). In his catalogue on Luba art for the Musée Dapper in Paris, Neyt (1994) concentrated on the figurative headrests produced by the 'Kikondja workshop' — the master of the 'cascade' hairstyle — which are all extraordinary by any standards, he but illustrates only a few others without explaining the bases of his attribution of their workmanship to particular workshops.[30] In most of these publications, the separation of headrests that include figurative elements from those that are without obvious figurative forms is never problematised, and in all of them there is an implicit acceptance both of the style–ethnic group correlation and of the figures-equal-art equation (where 'figures' equal representation or depiction).

No cohesive studies of headrests from the regions of East Africa have been attempted, apart from the recent publication by Van der Stappen (1996a) on Ethiopia, and the exhibitions on Turkana and Somali arts hosted by the Smithsonian Institution at the National Museum of African Art in Washington, DC.[31] Information on these headrests is scattered: Schweinfurth (1875) and Stuhlmann (1910) are early sources for drawings and descriptions of East African hairstyles, stools and headrests; Zach (1986) outlines the headrest types used in ancient Sudan, again with the inference that modern headrests used by other groups in East Africa have 'spread' from this origin; and Trowell and Wachsmann (1953), in their study of the arts and crafts of Uganda, attribute particular headrest types to specific ethnic groups. The only fully formed iconographic study of an East African headrest type is Prins's (1965) very speculative analysis of a Boni headrest, which questions the attribution of this headrest type to ethnic groups other than the Cushitic Boni, despite its very wide distribution that can be clearly demonstrated through provenanced examples, an issue discussed in greater depth in chapter 6. Otherwise, most of the information available on East African headrests is scattered through numerous articles in colonial anthropological journals. Hodder's work on material culture in the East African region raised a number of questions about the use of objects as ethnic markers, as headrests there were often cited as indexical signs of identity (Hodder 1977). A major contribution to the documenting of headrests in the region appeared in the form of Van der Stappen's (1996a) catalogue *Aethiopie*, where firmly attributed examples of recently collected examples of headrests from Ethiopia are illustrated. But, once again, these headrests are grouped under ethnic labels, and the resultant image is one of ethnic categories. A perusal of the examples in this catalogue reveals not only the stylistic and structural variation of headrests attributed to a single ethnic group, but also the number of headrest styles shared among different ethnic groups. However, no concerted effort appears to have been made to correlate information about different headrest types and particular ethnic groupings within the larger East African context.[32] Chapter 6 attempts to provide such a correlation, but also tries to destabilise the notion that there are clear-cut boundaries, because historical factors have clearly smudged the dividing lines.

The literature on Southern African headrests is more extensive than that for both Central and East Africa. On of the earliest publications is Müller and Snelleman's (c. 1892) portfolio of numerous drawings, including some headrests from south-east Africa. These drawings help establish an historical base-line for panoptic studies of such objects, although little specific information accompanies the headrests published there. While Müller and Snelleman were content with a geographical classification 'Zambèze',[33] later publications, such as those by Battiss, Junod and Grossert (1958), use a classificatory system that links headrest types to specific, and often inaccurate, ethnic groupings.[34] But specifically 'ethnic' studies have been published more recently, all of which deal with both spatial distribution of headrests and their iconographic content. Extensive analyses of Shona headrests in terms of typologies of form and decoration, and iconographic content have been conducted by both Dewey (1991; 1993) and Nettleton (1985),[35] while Becker (1991; 1999) has analysed the types and variations in the corpus of Tsonga headrests, taking into account the problems involved in the classification of ethnic and language groupings. She concludes that one should talk of a single, inclusive regional style complex rather than numerous styles based on atomised ethnic groups. Klopper's (1991) discussion of the headrests made and used in Zululand and KwaZulu-Natal concentrates on aspects of patronage and use, but she does not attempt a stylistic taxonomy of Zulu headrests, citing the problems inherent in such a taxonomy.[36] Nevertheless, particular styles of headrests have been claimed as part of a pan-Zulu heritage in a catalogue for an exhibition at the Local History Museum in Ulundi, situated in the heart of KwaZulu and in the capital of the Zulu kingdom.[37] This exhibition was put together as part of a process of building awareness of ethnic rather than national identity, something that ups the stakes in any consideration of the use of style as a marker of difference in contemporary social contexts. This will be discussed in more detail in chapter 7.

Style and ethnicity can thus be demonstrated as forming the major classificatory categories within the metatexts of African art historical writing. Within the broader category of African sculpture, headrests can be — and have been — treated as a sub-genre in determining style and ethnic categories, as postscripts to more impressive and less obviously functional forms, or as substitutes for the latter. The intention in this study is to place headrests at centre stage and to shift at least one of these tools to one side, to treat ethnicity as *only one* of the formative or critical dimensions in the determination of stylistic categories, and to follow other trajectories in understanding how forms circulated historically.

## TELLEM/DOGON HEADRESTS: A CASE STUDY OF ETHNIC STYLE

Tellem/Dogon headrests serve as a very good example of the problems inherent in the use of style as an index of social or ethnic homogeneity. The headrests attributed to the Tellem and their successors in the Bandiagara cliffs region of present-day Mali are among the comparatively few examples known from West Africa. In the most recent literature, some of them have been called Dogon (Dewey 1993:96, 97); however, the Dogon[38] do not make headrests now, and may not have made them in the past, although it has been suggested that they may have reused Tellem examples (Dewey 1993:97).

The majority of the headrests attributed to the Tellem and Dogon that are held in private and public (museum) collections have been classified on the basis of style and age, or via a comparison with the relatively few examples that were retrieved from burial contexts in caves within the Bandiagara region in the course of archaeological investigation.[39] These cave sites are associated by the Dogon with earlier inhabitants of the cliff region, most often referred to in the literature as the Tellem.[40] Whether the 'Tellem' can be seen as ethnically and culturally distinct from the Dogon is not clear, even though Bedaux suggests that they were genetically distinct populations (Bedaux 1977:78). The existence of a Tellem style of sculpture as distinct from a Dogon style is equally debated (Bedaux 1988:45). But most of the headrests labelled 'Dogon' do not appear to have been made by the Dogon, and thus 'Tellem' might be more appropriate, if we accept it as a tag for all predecessors of the Dogon in the area (Bedaux 1988:45). The issue is further complicated by the fact that the name 'Tellem' has been promoted for a number of artefacts from the Dogon region because of the age that its use implies. Tellem occupation of the Bandiagara area has been dated between the eleventh and the fourteenth centuries, as opposed to the Dogon occupation, which began in the fifteenth century.[41] The consequent — assumed — antiquity of objects so labelled has been adumbrated to their value in terms of the notion of an authentic and unspoilt Africa.[42] If any group could be shown to correspond to the notion of the isolated tribe, then the Tellem should answer, because the Tellem have been constructed as standing at the beginning of a particular cultural stream that flows relatively seamlessly into the Dogon. But Bedaux (1977:78) suggests that the Tellem people might have had a more southerly origin,[43] and any migration would have brought them into contact with others, just as Dogon migration to the Bandiagara cliffs brought them into contact with this earlier culture.

However, simply labelling all these headrests as 'Tellem', or even 'Dogon', is itself problematic, as there appears to be no structural stylistic coherence among the different headrests associated with these groups. Attribution of the headrests to the category Tellem, even those examples recovered from archaeological deposits associated with this group, thus has not relied on structural stylistic features alone, but has taken into account both the age — or the appearance of age — adduced through the degree of patination of the object, and the ways in which decorative motifs are deployed on the object. In fact, these headrests are so diverse structurally that they match a large number of the structural headrest types/styles made and used by diverse populations across East, Central and Southern Africa. Examples of such correspondences of form with other African headrest styles range from headrests with a vertical orientation, often using single or multiple columns for support, to those that have a horizontal orientation, with a wide range of variables in the plan, profile and elevation of platforms, bases and supports and their combinations. An analysis of the headrests attributed to the Tellem, from both museum and private collections, bearing in mind that these attributions are not all equally well founded, yields approximately four structural styles that can be isolated as distinct from one another.

Tellem headrests with vertical orientation (figs. 4–15 & 18) almost all have bases and platforms separated from the supports, which may be single (figs. 1–10) or multiple (figs. 11–15 & 18), rectangular or cylindrical, and some have handles projecting from their sides.[44] The bases of these headrests range from rectangular blocks to oval or lobed shapes, and the platforms have a similar degree of difference, from rectangular to oval, shield or butterfly shapes, all with varying degrees of curvature, many with small projections from the short ends and one with triangular lugs on the undersides of the ends. On some of the headrests with handles there is an almost equine, head-like projection (Ezra 1988:102), which might suggest some correspondence with the headrests of the second type.

The iron headrests appear to belong to the same structural stylistic corpus as the vertical wooden examples, but with a greatly restricted range of forms and structural solutions. Bedaux (1977:50, 52) illustrates two examples of these iron headrests: one illustration shows only the top surface of the platform, which is decorated with engraved chevron and herringbone patterns and a circular knob at its centre at the point at which the iron rod support is attached. The second shows the whole headrest, with a long rectangular base, single iron rod support and shaped platform, at the ends of which are sharp extensions, which Bedaux identifies as snake heads. Another example in the Musée Royal de l'Afrique Central (fig. 5) has an almost square base, an iron rod support and a wide platform, rounded at the ends and slightly constricted in the middle. At the ends of the platform are two small rounded projections, each with a single hole through it. An example illustrated by Ross (1994), (fig. 20) has three supports on an oval base with an iron clapper attached to each of the lateral supports. While these examples illustrate the apparently restricted range of design in the iron headrests, there are exceptions, such as the one provisionally attributed to the Tellem by Falgayrettes (1989:27), (fig. 19), which has a support formed by an arc, below which two spirally wound extensions curve to form at their ends two flat vertical spirals.

Headrests of the second, horizontal type mostly have multiple supports, with the base and platform integrated into the support, and sometimes a greater degree of surface decoration than is evident on the examples of the vertical type. Some of these horizontal examples could be viewed as variations of the vertical ones, where the platform is encased by lateral supports, as is evident from the following examples. Figure 17 shows an example where the base remains articulated as an independent element, but where the support, a central column flanked by two lateral elements of a square profile, encompasses the ends of the platform. Like many examples of the vertical type, it has a long handle projecting from one side. In figure 18, the central support is rectangular, and two further supports of rather indeterminate shape join the platform to the base, thus integrating all the elements into a clearly vertical form, however. Two examples are illustrated by Falgayrettes (1989:26, 47). One (fig. 21) has two central supports, flanked on one side by a large strut joining base and platform, and, on the other side by a projecting handle, like those on the vertical headrests, which branches at its centre to link the base and the support. It has traces of circle and dot motifs on the surface of the support elements and chevron designs on the lateral strut.

On the second (Falgayrettes 1989:47),[45] the central support with chevron designs on its vertical axis has been supplemented by a fretwork of chevrons linking the base and the platform. In these two examples, a process of elaboration of elements around a central support, possibly in a search for greater stability or for a different aesthetic, seems to have resulted in a distinct type, with an emphasis on the horizontal and an emphasised element of asymmetry.[46] Another example in the Musée Royal de l'Afrique Central (fig. 22) is extraordinary in that it has been structured with two lateral supports flanking a thick central column that opens through the top of the platform so that the column forms the mouth of the bowl. The surface is extremely worn, and the bowl section of the platform is broken, but it is difficult to imagine that this object ever actually functioned as a headrest, unless the bowl had a lid. It has decoration on the surfaces of the platform and the bowl in the form of engraved lines, and may have had similar decoration on the lateral supports as well. Although the base and the platform are not joined by the supports, its length provides a very strong horizontal emphasis, and again an element of asymmetry is introduced through the equine, head-like form pendant from the underside of one of the ends of the platform.

More clearly distinct from these are headrests that have multiple supports, mainly rectangular, arranged at regular intervals along the rectangular base with ends to their platforms, which might be read as figurative.[47] Dewey (1993:96–97) suggests that these might be equine forms similar to those found on other Dogon objects, such as troughs. He concludes that, on the basis of this iconographic detail and the forms of decoration that correspond quite closely to Dogon sculpture, this type might be more correctly ascribed to the Dogon, although at least one example of this type is known to be from a Tellem archaeological site (Bedaux 1977:54), and appears to have a far greater degree of patination and a use of surface decoration of circle and dot motifs that set it apart from the examples published by Dewey and relate it to others of the vertical type (figs. 8, 11 & 17). Bedaux, however, notes that because no vertical stratigraphy was discernible within the archaeological record (Bedaux 1988:45), it is possible that objects made after the disappearance of the Tellem might have been deposited in the caves at a later date, and these might have been Dogon deposits.

A third type of headrest associated with the Tellem is almost completely block-like, sometimes with the thickness of the block hollowed out along the length of the support. Two examples in the Musée Royal de l'Afrique Central[48] (figs. 23 & 24) are attributed to the Dogon.[49] One of these has projections from the short ends, one larger than the other, again suggestive of animal imagery and again introducing an element of asymmetry.

Bedaux identified another object type as headrests: these are composed of a broad rectangular to square platform[50] with a slightly concave upper surface on a low, truncated cone support, often hollowed out underneath (figs. 25 & 26). The platforms of these objects almost all have projections from their ends and geometric decoration on their surfaces, which is very reminiscent of the kind of decoration one sees on Dogon granary doors and door locks. Ezra (1988:103) also illustrates one of these objects, but raises questions about its function, suggesting, following Sieber, that they may have been boards used by women for carrying loads on their heads.[51] These putative headrests were found in association with female skeletons, and Bedaux (1977:75) suggests that there was a gender differentiation in the use of the headrests, with men using the vertical type. Furthermore, the examples of these low 'headrests' in the Musée Royal de l'Afrique Central do not appear to have an extensive sacrificial patina, although one (Musée Royal de l'Afrique Central, no. 62.21.28) had traces of both red and white pigment in stripes across the top of the platform. This may suggest that they did indeed function quite differently from the taller headrest forms that are often covered with a thick, encrusted paste of various substances.

There does not appear to be much predictability to the choice of decorative motifs used on any particular headrest type. Patterns employed on the earlier wooden headrests range from rows of dots or circles, or circle and dot motifs, to more linear designs of engraved chevrons, crosses, herringbone, squares, diamonds or triangles, and their use continued in the iron headrests (Bedaux 1977:50). In some examples, this patterning appears to anticipate similar decorative forms associated with some — probably later — Dogon sculpture. This linkage is further suggested by the presence of equine 'heads' on some of the headrests, particularly those of the horizontal type.

While many African societies employed stylistically and structurally differentiated categories of headrests to mark particular status, or used particular patterns to publicise ethnic, status or gender affiliations, the same degree of stylistic variation as that found in the headrests attributed to the Tellem does not appear to have been common within other single ethnic/cultural groupings, and its presence here could be interpreted in different ways. It might be constructed as an index of fairly extensive, local and pre-Dogon, cultural differences; or as a signifier of social stratification or gender differentiation; or as an index of Dogon borrowing of the horizontal structure from Tellem prototypes. One is thus led to the conclusion that there must have been as great a degree of what Roe (1995:45) has termed 'protected deviance' within Tellem stylistic norms as there appears to have been in Dogon, if not in Tellem, sculpture.[52]

Unfortunately, the distribution of the Tellem headrests in their original contexts is not known, because many have been plundered from these caves and have ended up in private and some public collections with little or no documentation. Bedaux notes the use of carbon dating to ascertain the ages of the figurative sculptures recovered by the 1964 expedition, but, perhaps indexical of their lesser status in Western value systems, no dates for the wooden headrests have been published (Bedaux 1977:19, 77). The headrests are thus aligned with the dates attributed to the particular caves in which they were found. Bedaux suggests that the wooden headrests were in use before the votive iron headrests. The wooden headrests found *in situ* that he lists in the catalogue *Tellem* (Bedaux 1977:83) were all found in different caves,[53] and thus have derived dates of the eleventh–twelfth centuries, whereas all the iron 'votive' headrests listed in the catalogue appear to have come from a single cave that has a derived date of the fourteenth century. Whereas other iron objects appear to have been distributed widely across other caves, this concentration of iron headrests in a few caves may suggest that they had a site-specific function, or that they were used in preference to wooden headrests for burial purposes in the fourteenth century. A notable feature of the material from the caves listed by Bedaux (1977) is the relative paucity of crafted wooden objects from caves dated to the thirteenth century, including headrests. Bedaux also notes that the iron headrests may have been used for votive purposes only, a conclusion based on their small size and their apparent structural and material unsuitability for actual use as supports for the head. In none of the iron examples does it appear possible that it could have actually supported the head of a sleeping person, or even that of a corpse. The more limited variation in style in the iron headrests compared to the wooden examples could possibly be read as a function of their material construction, but possibly also as a result of either a change in function, or a greater social and artisanal homogeneity among the producers of the headrests. While wooden headrests might have been made by quite a wide range of craftsmen, the production of iron headrests would, presumably, have been limited to a few iron-working specialists. A further dimension might be that of social stratification, with only some members of the group able to access iron votive headrests — objects whose lack of functionality would indicate some form of ostentatious consumption.

Thus, between the twelfth and the fourteenth centuries in Tellem burial contexts, iron headrests, which could not have been used as supports for the heads of living persons, completely replaced wooden ones that could have been used in sleep. However, many of the vertically oriented wooden headrests appear to have an encrusted patina of sacrificial materials, as do some of the horizontal examples, particularly those that appear to be hybrids of the vertical form. This encrustation at times obscures the relief carvings on the surfaces, thus suggesting that the headrests functioned not only as supports for the head, but also as sites for ritual activity. This is particularly evident in the example that includes a bowl/column at its centre (fig. 22). It might thus be suggested that the headrests in burial contexts thus always had a votive function.[54] There is some similarity in style between some earlier vertical-type wooden headrests and the later iron ones, and there appears to have been some correspondence in their usages at some point of their biographies. However, there is a greater disjunction in structural style between the iron headrests and most of the horizontal-type wooden headrests, many of which have 'heads' at the ends of their platforms and do not appear to have much patination, and thus may not have served a specifically ritualistic purpose. Some of these horizontal headrests might belong to a Dogon reworking of Tellem forms, and this might account for the stylistic similarities they display with other forms of Dogon sculpture.

As no further conclusions appear to be forthcoming from the archaeological records, largely because of a paucity of archaeological research on, or carbon/thermoluminescence dating of, Dogon material culture (Dewey 1993:97), it is impossible to suggest a history of stylistic development (as opposed to a history of its ruptures) for the different Dogon/Tellem headrest styles as an explanation of their variety. Yet many of the headrests found in the contexts of cave burials within the Bandiagara region, and those associated with them stylistically, appear to share at least one idiosyncratic feature that is less immediately apprehended. This is an apparent tendency to formal asymmetry. In the headrest in figure 6, the upward curve of the platform has been deliberately extended on one side, a feature also visible in figure 4, although less emphasised. In figure 7, the platform ends have different shapes, with decoration at one end only, while the platform of the headrest in figure 8 has a projection from only one end, echoing the handle that projects from the support on the same side. In examples where a handle extends from one side, itself inherently productive of asymmetry, there is often a compensation of weight in the base (fig. 8) or in the extension and curvature of the platform (figs. 10 & 15). In the horizontal example illustrated by Bedaux (1977:54), there is a head at one end only, and the fretwork in the example illustrated by Falgayrettes (1989:47) is not symmetrically designed. Similar asymmetries can be seen in figures 21 and 22. The block-type headrests have this asymmetry in a number of features, figure 23 having decoration on only one of its vertical faces and extensions of different size at its ends, while the headrest in figure 24 has different decoration on its two vertical sides and bands of different motifs in the decoration at each of the two short ends of the platform.

Thus the features that might, in the absence of concrete evidence on dating and provenance of many of these headrests, nevertheless be seen to unite them into a coherent category, are not necessarily elements of style that can be easily isolated. It appears that stylistic coherence here is insecure, not attached to the listing of formal, structural features: perhaps it is caught only in the ways in which this variety has been manipulated, in the insubstantiality of manipulation of forms, and in the material accretions of elements such as patina and other traces of usages. Identification, then, relies on the trained eye, on the panoptic gaze that subjects all examples of the same type to a particular surveillance. Thus, the identity of a Tellem style is constructed; it belongs to the writers of art history, to the realm of categories; it does not touch on style as a bearer of meaning within the context of the usages of these headrests by the long-gone Tellem.

## SOME CONCLUSIONS ON STYLE

It is perhaps necessary to acknowledge that ethnic or linguistic groupings have been useful, and are probably still inescapable, in establishing a taxonomic base for the study and understanding of the diverse arts of African peoples. Yet Hodder's (1977; 1978; 1982) ethno-archaeological studies suggest other parameters for dealing with the questions of the distribution of material culture and its relation to particular ethnic groupings. In particular, Hodder (1977) has shown that as identities fluctuate, the items that are used to mark those identities are subject to equivalent fluctuations in type and form. Faris's linking of cultural production and its styles to the politics of indigenous social relations can further amplify the path taken by Hodder (1977; 1978) in explaining the persistence of some stylistic forms over others (Faris 1988). Faris's contention that style and aesthetic elaboration can be explained through an analysis of the social relations of production, furthermore, can be used to analyse the validity of long-held anthropological notions that societies that produce rudimentary forms of material culture necessarily express more numerous social relations through fewer objects (Evans Pritchard 1969).[55] While these authors touch on the question of ethnicity, the issue is more fully discussed outside the realm of art-historical studies and, occasionally, within it.[56] Many of these studies question the fixity of ethnic identity, and, working with the notion that identities are constructed and situational, it may thus be possible to uncover other networks in which material objects in particular styles may have been manipulated as indices of other political affiliations.

The 'trained eye' of the hypothetical observer, of whatever ethnic origin or gender, is able to distinguish Yoruba art from Dogon, or Luba sculpture from the DRC, not only in terms of the forms and types of objects, but also in terms of styles of carving, i.e. in the manner of statement making to which Foucault objects. This accepted, one nevertheless has to keep in mind that these ethno-linguistic units are useful only in so far as they denote abstractions. For there is not, and probably never was any such thing as 'the Yoruba', or 'the Luba', or 'the Zulu', or 'the Shona', even though all Yoruba- or Luba- or Zulu- or Shona-speaking people may have shared language, often in distinct dialects, and numerous other cultural traits.[57] Nevertheless the 'trained eye' can distinguish not only regional differences in style and object types for any one of these apparently unitary cultures, but can even detect the hands of particular masters in many instances.[58] Thus, Kasfir's self-confessed failure to find a replacement for the 'tribal model' (Kasfir 1984) suggests that ethnically based typology may have its functions, as long as it is not treated as a means of rigid and watertight encapsulation of one art style in opposition to another, and as long as we do not succumb to the temptation to define 'centres' and 'peripheries' within stylistic complexes. For centres imply fixed social, and particularly political, relationships within static and stable societies that would produce a canonical style against which those of the peripheries might be measured. Thus, as the peripheries themselves might be centres of other ethnic or political alignments, the perspective from which one establishes putatively normal 'canons' becomes extremely problematic, as will emerge in a more detailed discussion of headrest styles.

This caveat must be amplified through the acknowledgement that styles are in themselves constructed, not necessarily only by the people who made the objects of African art, but also by those who used them, and, on a wider scale, by those who collected and those who display them. For it is only through the function of surveys of large numbers of objects that a distillation of common stylistic traits can be achieved. Preziosi (1989) likens this process to that outlined by Foucault for the surveillance of prisoners in Bentham's Panopticon, but the panoptic survey of African art objects, like that of the societies from which they originated, was intended to aid in exact compartmentalisation of peoples so as to allow for greater colonial control. Stylistic analysis in this context was not entirely innocently used; however, it may have been conceived and executed.[59]

Even if we accept the existence of group styles, we are nevertheless left with a number of problems, not least of which is how individual artists within the producing societies related their own works to those of the 'tradition', something that has been discussed with producers in only a few instances.[60] In these studies, there is some emphasis on the ways in which carvers are trained in the workshops of their mentors, although there are a number of instances where artists claim to have been self-taught. The transmission of style through an apprenticeship system is thus predicated on the model of emulation.[61] The fact that many of these artists claimed originality and individuality for their work suggests that such individuality might be seen in terms of Roe's notion of 'realms of protected deviance' (Roe 1995:49), which he predicates upon the notion of an '*aesthetic imperative*' (Roe 1995:50; emphasis added). In societies without stratified apprenticeship and production systems, such as that described by Fernandez (1973) for the Fang, the transmission of style does not appear to have the same coherence, although Perrois' (1990) work on the styles and sub-styles of Fang figurative sculpture and Chaffin and Chaffin's (n.d.) catalogue on the Kota suggest that there must still be a fair amount of emulative practice among carvers within the region of Gabon. If style is passed through a system of emulation or replication, as Kasfir (1987, citing Vansina) suggests, and if replications inevitably drift ever further from the 'original model' (if such a thing can be postulated without replicating a Platonic notion of an 'idea'), then from a certain point onwards, as the originals are lost, stolen or destroyed, emulation can only take place in relation to replicas, all of which are different and all of which will contribute to the changes within stylistic categories.

Virtually all the studies of workshops and apprenticeships in African art history have been concerned with the notion of the *artist* as author of figurative works of art, and the artist as producer of utilitarian objects such as headrests is almost entirely ignored. In the following analyses of a variety of different headrests from far-flung parts of the African continent, the initial emphasis will be on a challenge to the notion of the supremacy of group or ethnic authorship, but I shall also be raising both the issue of individual authorship and the issue of changes over time, where sufficient information and examples are available. For the headrest is as much the product of an 'artist' as a free-standing figure sculpture is, and it is executed in a particular style and made at a particular time, all of which confer on the object a very specific individual identity.

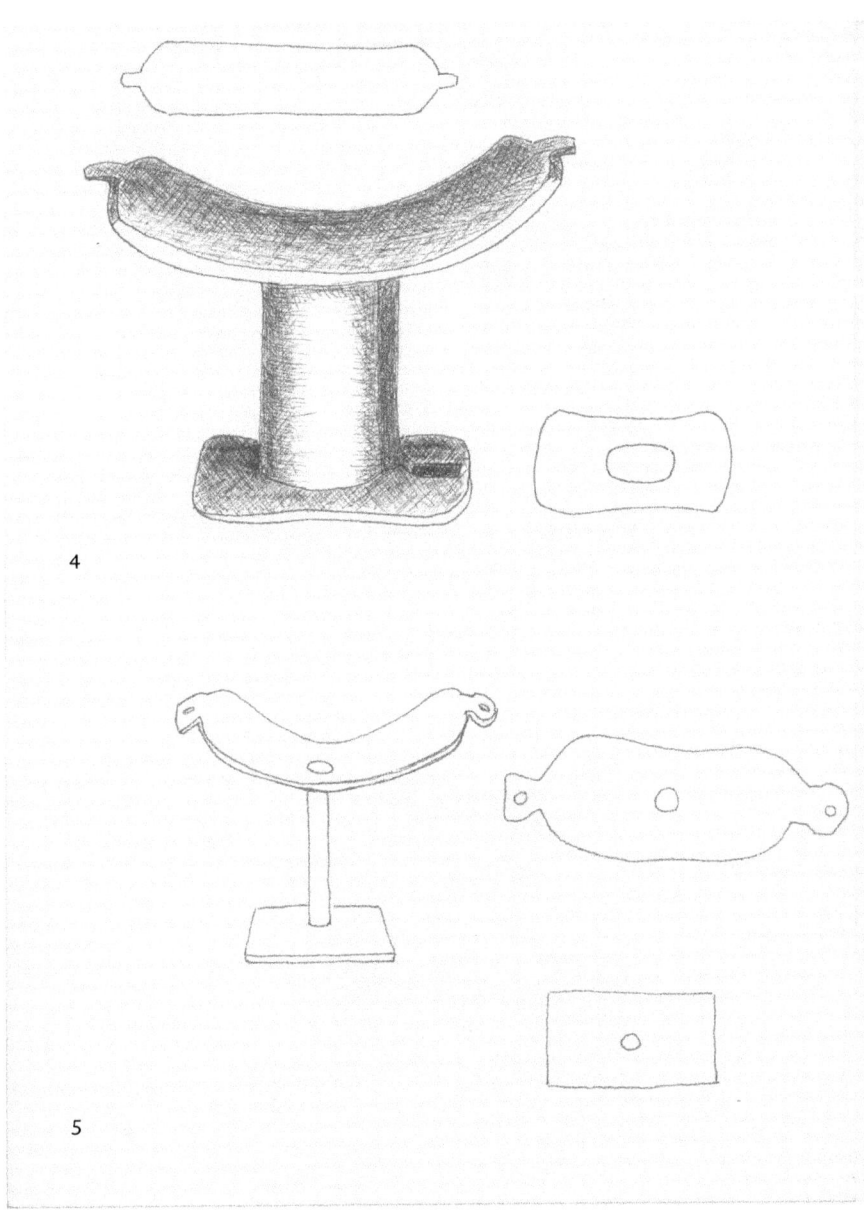

4   Musée Royal de l'Afrique Central (no. 66.14.10), *Mali*, "*Tellem*", wood.
5   Musée Royal de l'Afrique Central (no. 67.19.1), *Mali*, "*Tellem*", iron.

**48** | AFRICAN DREAM MACHINES

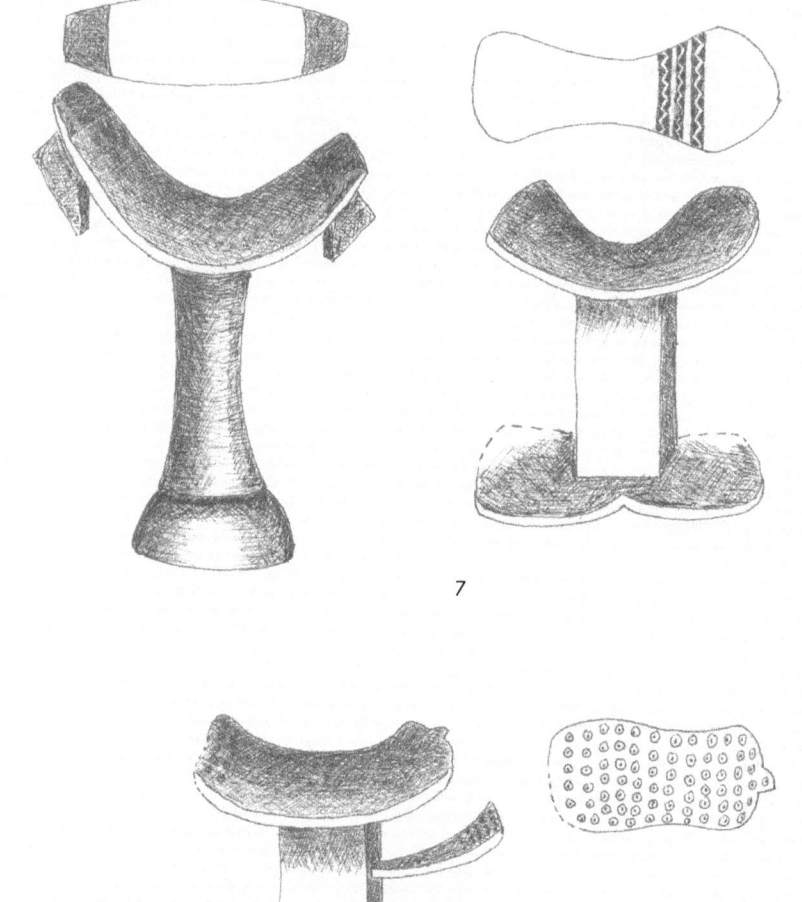

6
7
8

6    Musée Royal de l'Afrique Central (no. 78.15.1), *Mali*, "*Tellem*", wood.
7    Musée Royal de l'Afrique Central (no. 78.16.9), *Mali*, "*Tellem*", wood.
8    Musée Royal de l'Afrique Central (no. 78.17.6), *Mali*, "*Tellem*", wood.

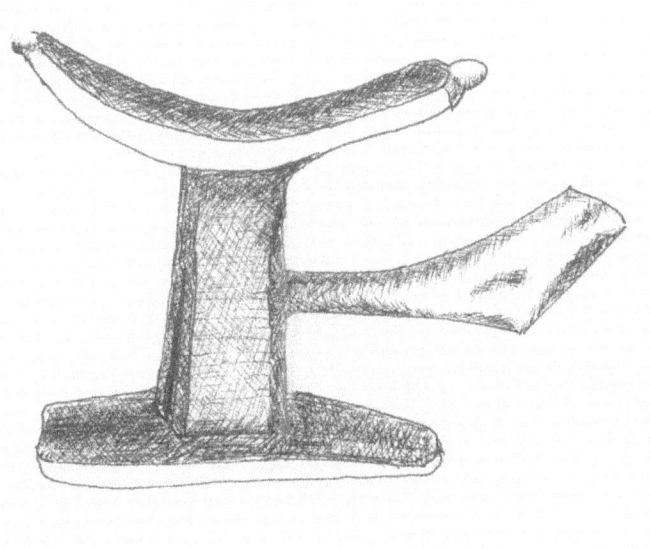

9

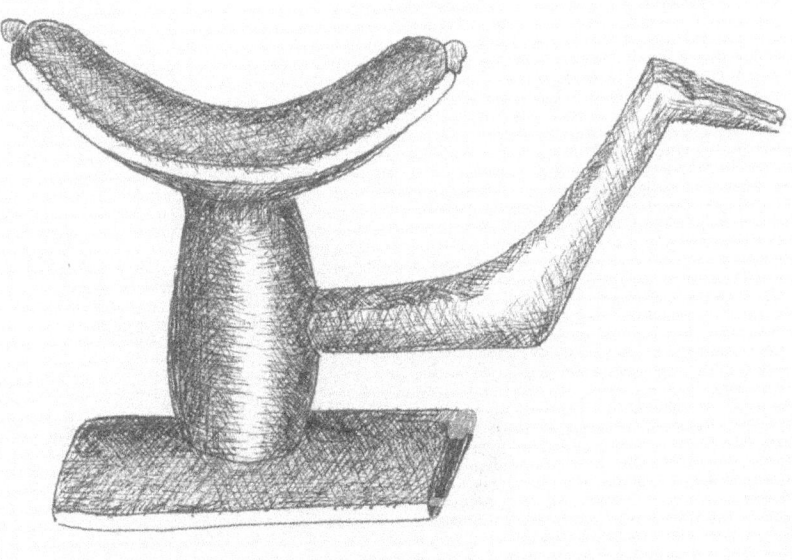

10

9   Bedaux (1988:44, no. 20), *Mali*, *"Tellem"*, wood.
10  Ezra (1988:102), *Mali*, *"Tellem"*, wood.

50 | AFRICAN DREAM MACHINES

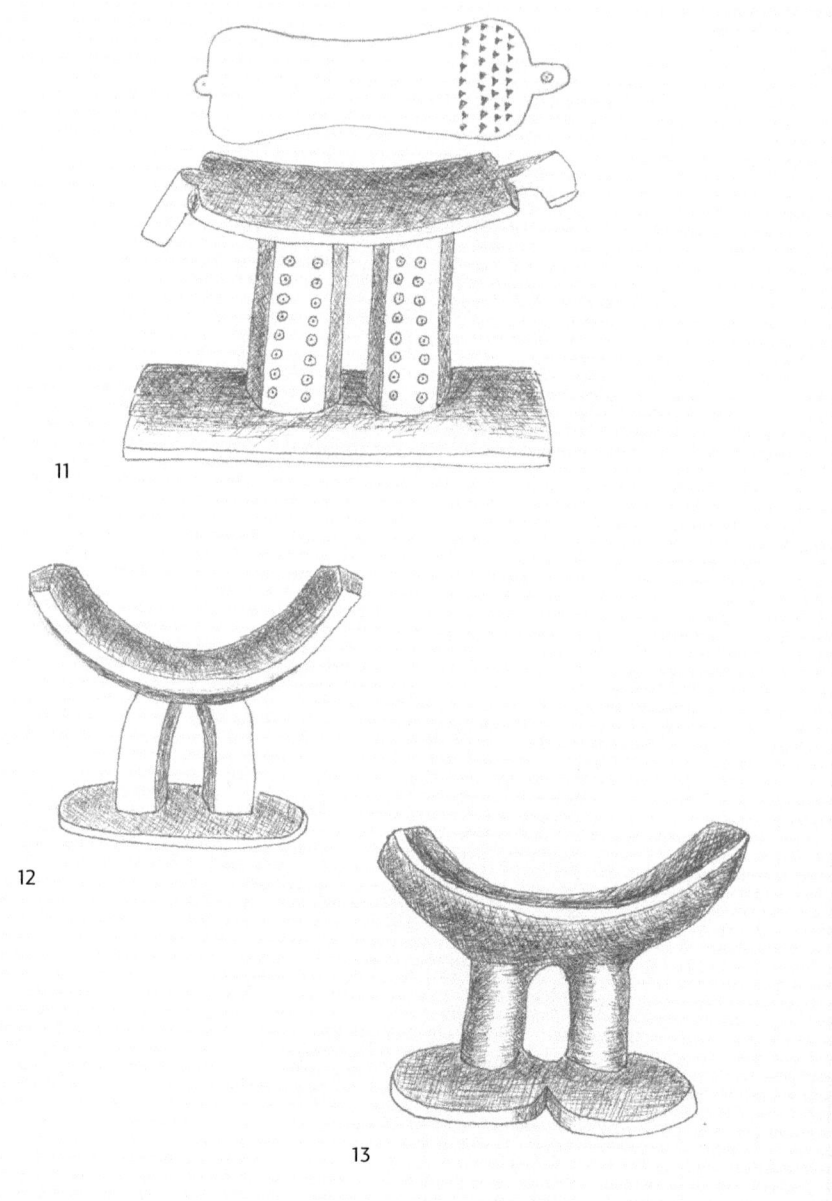

11  Musée Royal de l'Afrique Central (no. 78.17.7), *Mali*, "*Tellem*", wood.
12  Dewey (1993:95), *Mali*, "*Tellem*", wood.
13  Falgayrettes (1989:27), *Mali*, "*Tellem*", wood.

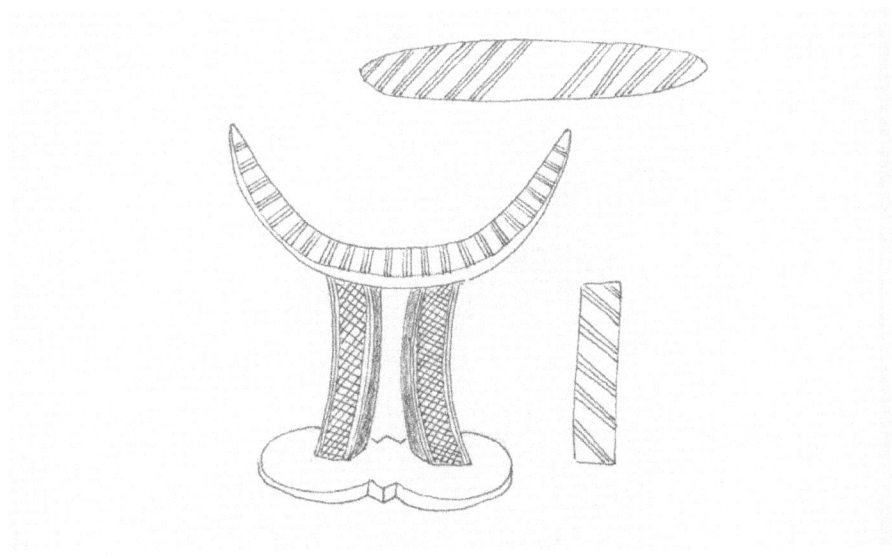

14   Falgayrettes (1989:27), Mali, "Tellem", wood.

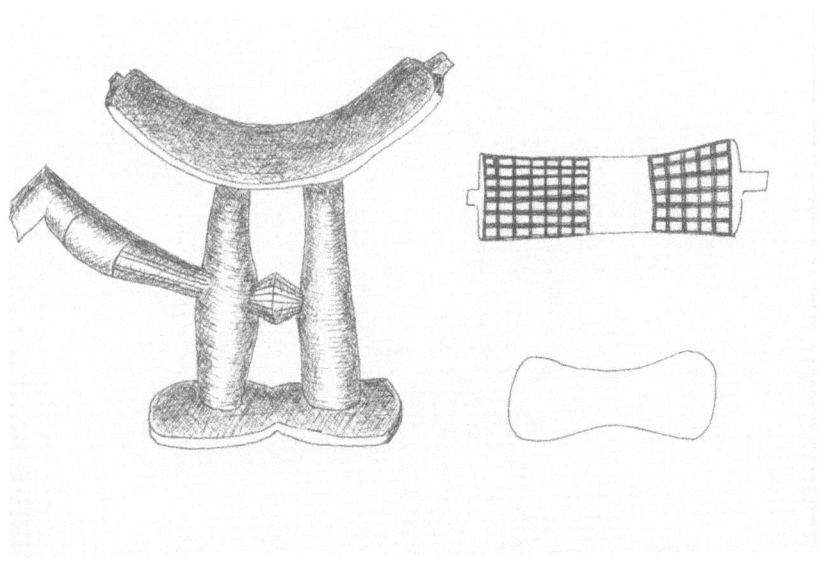

15   Musée Royal de l'Afrique Central (no. 73.30.1), Mali, "Tellem", wood.

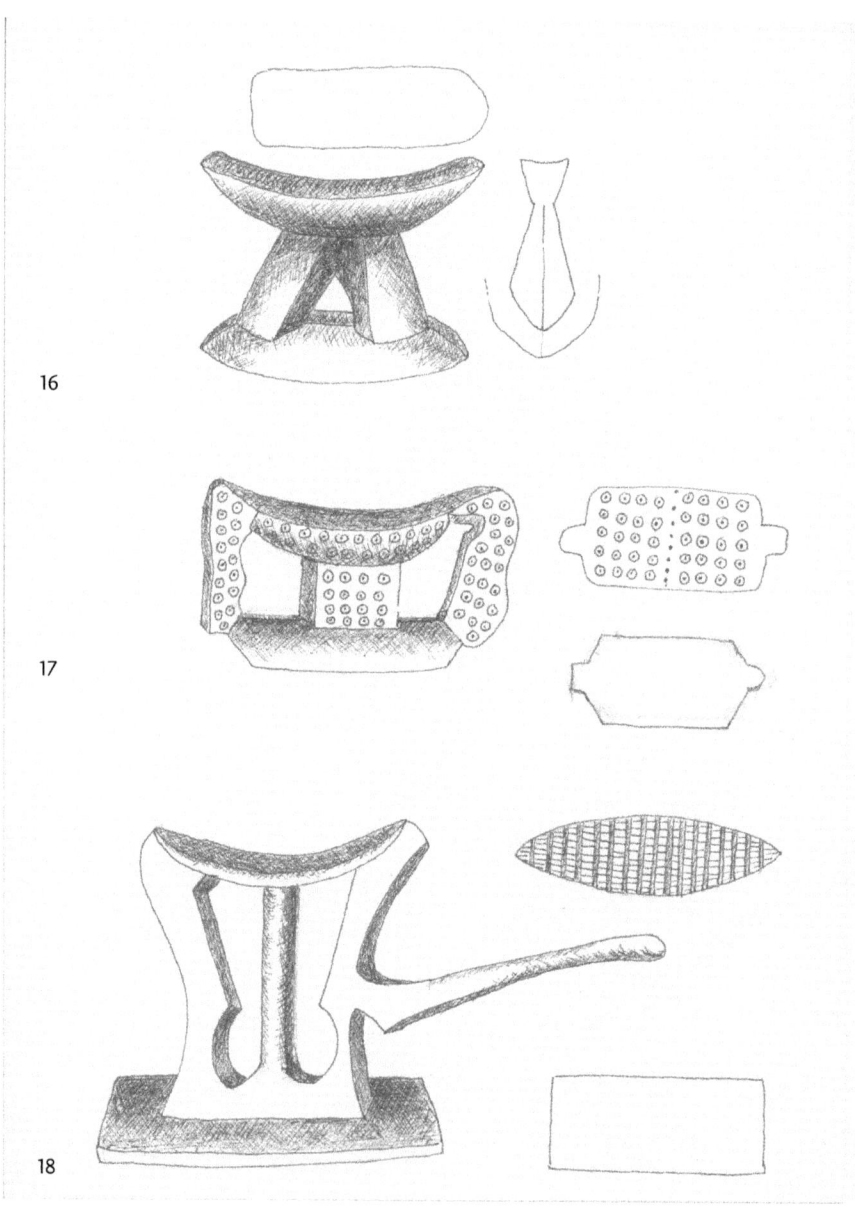

16   Musée Royal de l'Afrique Central (no. 78.16.8), *Mali*, "*Tellem*", wood.
17   Musée Royal de l'Afrique Central (no. 66.16.3), *Mali*, "*Tellem*", wood.
18   Musée Royal de l'Afrique Central (no. 79.20.4), *Mali*, "*Tellem*", wood.

CHAPTER 2 *Illustrations: figures 4-26* | 53

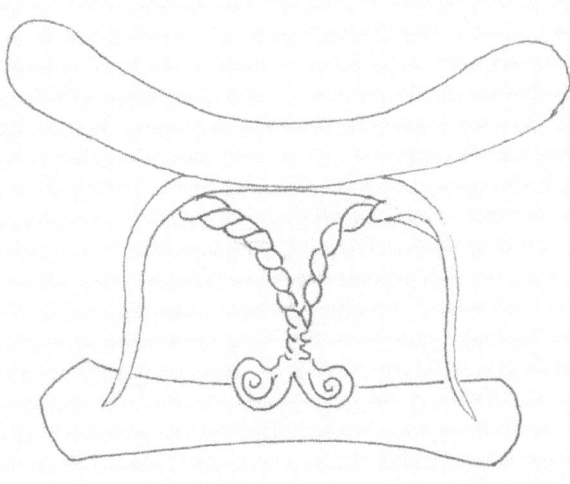

19

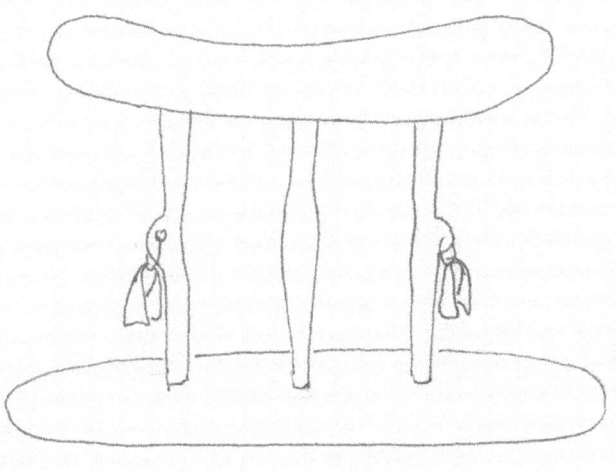

20

19   Falgayrettes (1989:27), *Mali*, "*Tellem*", iron.
20   Ross (1994, fig. 7), *Mali*, "*Tellem*", iron.

## 54 | AFRICAN DREAM MACHINES

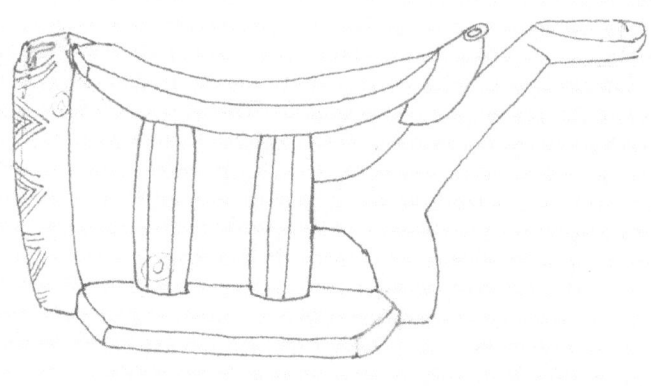

21

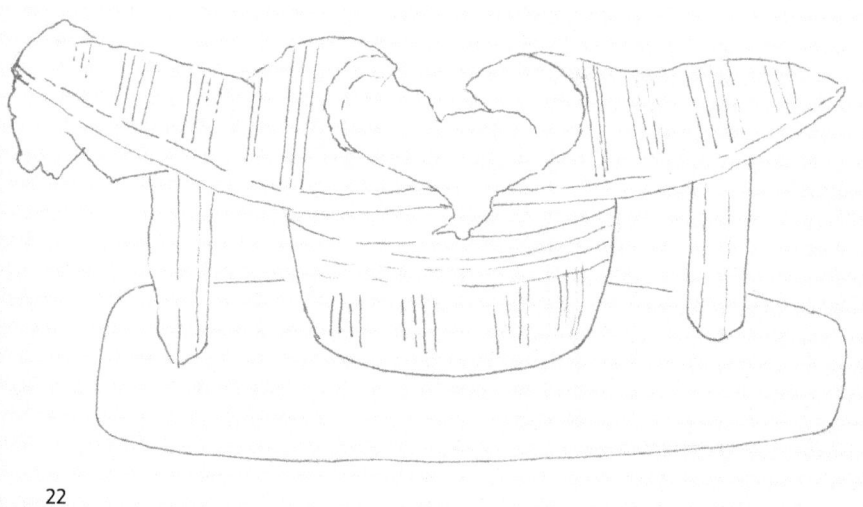

22

21   Falgayrettes (1989:26), *Mali*, "*Tellem*", wood.
22   Musée Royal de l'Afrique Central (no. 63.15.1), *Mali*, "*Tellem*", wood.

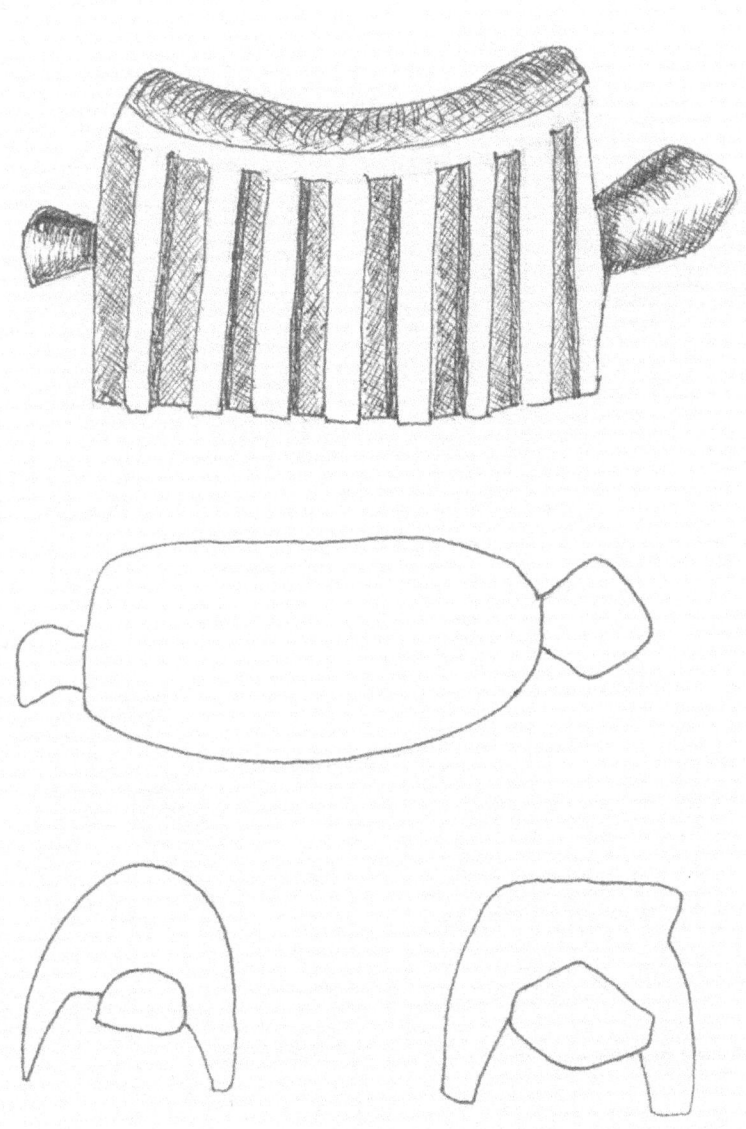

23  Musée Royal de l'Afrique Central (no. 78.73.2), *Mali*, *"Tellem"*, wood.

**56** | AFRICAN DREAM MACHINES

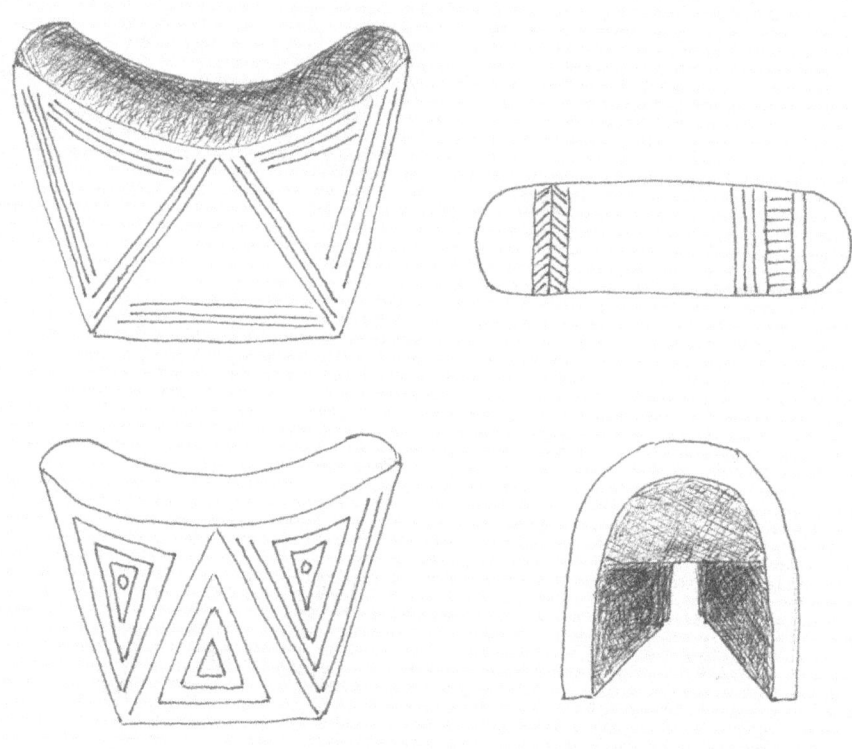

24   Musée Royal de l'Afrique Central (no. 79.20.8), *Mali*, *"Tellem"*, wood.

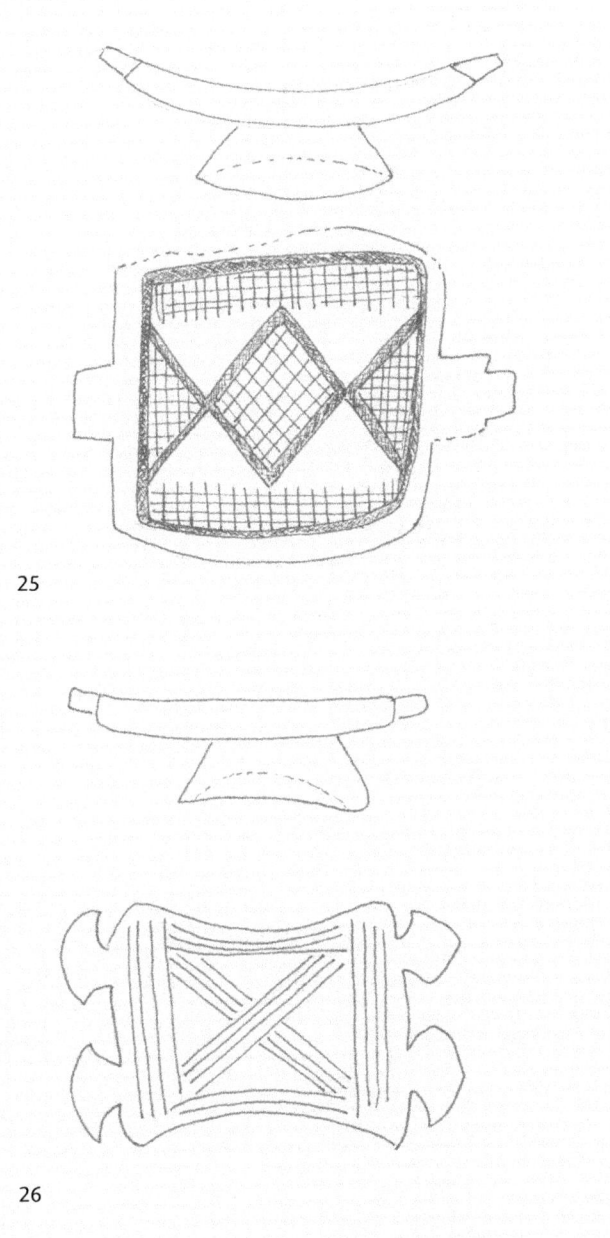

25  Musée Royal de l'Afrique Central (no. 78.73.3), Mali, "Tellem", "headrest"/board, wood.
26  Musée Royal de l'Afrique Central (no. 79.20.9), Mali, "Tellem", "headrest"/board, wood.

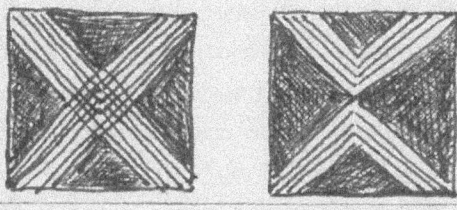

# 3 | Methodology, Position and Limitations

NOTWITHSTANDING KASFIR'S DOUBTS about the value of the study of object types (Kasfir 1984), this study chooses to continue an earlier approach to the study of African headrests as object types.[1] Because headrests are so widely distributed in Africa, they slip, for the large part, between the cracks of conventional art-historical enquiry. The lack of overtly figurative elements in most African headrests allows their stylistic features to be articulated easily, both in terms of functional/technical considerations and in terms of aesthetic dimensions divorced from notions of representation; i.e. they transcend the narratives of iconographic studies and enter into different kinds of textual formations. And, because they were not necessarily always produced by skilled carvers, they can be shown to transgress the limits set to stylistic analysis by the notion of the mastery of specific modes of representation, linked either to specific ethnic categories or to particular artists and ateliers.

The contention underlying the analyses that follow in the next four chapters is that headrests made in Africa may be categorised morphologically into distinct types that are differentially distributed across the geographical areas of Southern, Central and East Africa, with a significantly small number recorded from West Africa. Using an analysis of headrest forms, from those that have a single column or multiple columns as their supporting element to those that are horizontally oriented with multiple legs, the study traces a distribution of headrest types that does not rely on ethnic or tribal categories as its primary organisational principle, and thereby destabilises the idea that spoken or verbal language is at the core of visual stylistic difference. From this it should be possible to establish whether there are formal types that are confined to particular ethnic groups, or to find those instances where particular ethnic groups have managed to establish a peculiar stylistic identity within the broad formal type that separates them from others of the same type.

On the one hand, headrests constitute a visible manifestation, a concrete statement and a knowledge statement, which, following Foucault (1972:39), can be used to map distributions, differences and interrelations. But, on the other hand, each headrest is the product of an individual maker and an individual user, and, in some instances, of the first user's descendants and legitimate local or colonial heirs. As such, each headrest has its own identity and history, something that the study tries to convey through the inclusion of large numbers of illustrations and details of collection. The reading of the headrests is partly about establishing the identity of each, but, more than that, it is about establishing the limits of possibility in making headrests and the boundaries of interpretation of headrests as objects of interest. The study is interested in understanding how we make sense of objects that are no longer themselves, but are synecdoches for something else, including 'art'.

Because the research for this study was almost entirely archival, drawing on museum collections, published ethnographies and unpublished reports, with field work limited to the Southern African region, the research could not encompass an examination of the dynamics of headrests as they are currently made (or no longer made) and used within different African societies. In this sense, the study is profoundly unanthropological. Thus, the following chapters are as much concerned with the processes of categorisation and the assumptions that underlay those processes as they are with the actual objects.

African headrests are found in almost all the major ethnographic museums in Europe, and in a number of minor ones as well.[2] Research for this book was done in some of these museums, as well as in South African and Zimbabwean museums.[3] Approximately 900 headrests were examined in total in these museums, with the greatest number being recorded as from the Southern African region, the second largest group from Central Africa, and the smallest number from East Africa,[4] and a further 700 have been researched in reproductions in books and catalogues. With the exception of examples of archaic Dogon headrests, an insignificant number were found that could with any certainty be provenanced to West Africa.[5] Examples of headrests in museum collections have been compared with others in private collections, although here significant documentation is almost entirely lacking, as it is for most published examples, including the Joss Collection published by Dewey (1993), to date the most comprehensive publication on African headrests. Some examples of Ancient Egyptian headrests were included as comparative material.[6]

In the absence of extensive field work on the production and functions of headrests, as well as their exact location of collection, the data obtained from museum sources had, in most instances, severe limitations. Museum collections are extremely varied in the amount of documentation that accompanies the objects. Some objects are more fully documented with regard to their provenance, authorship and usage than others. In some instances, attributions made on the basis of style were in apparent conflict with fairly detailed and accurate documentation of provenance. In other instances, details of provenance could be called into question owing to various factors, generally concerning the movement of collectors (missionaries, explorers, military personnel, anthropologists, settlers, etc.) within Africa and the accuracy of their records or the particular museum's transfer of these records. In many cases, no accurate documentation of provenance was available to museum curators, and attributions have been made purely on the basis of comparison with documented examples of headrests or other carvings in similar styles, as is the case with the vast majority of headrests in private collections. It was interesting in this context to note how, in some instances, attributions were made on the basis of assumptions about style and ethnicity rather than on a full examination of provenance, with the result that curators and collectors between them have constructed bodies of works attributable to single ethnic groups.

In any discussion of stylistic distributions or type distributions within a broad geographical area, an attempt must be made to establish the historical dimensions of the production, distribution and collection of particular headrest types. But here very little direct documentation was available. Museums' acquisition dates merely establish a date before which the object was accessioned. In some instances, precise dates can be established for the collection of single examples of particular types of headrests, either through museum records or through published travellers' or missionaries' accounts. The start of the tourist trade in items such as headrests, and the stylistic parameters of the headrests made for this trade, can be traced through catalogues of the great exhibitions of the nineteenth century in London and Paris, as well as through sales house catalogues and their correlation with objects in museum holdings, and these may throw light on the chronological development of some headrest types and styles.

In order to control the variables in the information that was gathered, headrests from various museum collections were compared and contrasted, both in terms of their provenance/attribution and their date of collection/acquisition. Using this process, it was possible to build up a picture in which the accuracy of attributions made on the basis of styles could be measured in terms of the acceptance of formal, stylistic conventions associated with particular ethnic groups. In some instances, headrests whose provenance was not documented were measured against those whose provenance was securely recorded; attributions could be substantiated or discarded, while boundaries of distribution of particular styles could be expanded or contracted. Secure dates of collection and acquisition could be used to establish periods within which particular headrest types were made and used.

The medium used in the manufacture of the vast majority of African headrests is wood, although some ivory and iron examples have been collected. The notion that the medium may affect the style of the work is one accepted widely in art-historical studies, and has been used in the analysis of Igbo Ikenga sculptures (Boston 1977), but it is almost impossible to distinguish the types of wood used in the making of African headrests with any accuracy. While quite detailed analysis of the types of wood used for making headrests is available for Democratic Republic of the Congo examples (Dechamps 1970; 1971; 1974a; 1974b; 1975; 1976; 1982), no such information is available for the Southern and East African areas. Information regarding methods of carving is likewise patchy, and is to be gleaned largely from anthropological literature. As a result of these limitations on data and information, the research was concerned as much with the way in which the history of African headrests (and, by extension, other African carving traditions) has been constructed as it was with a set and unchanging taxonomy of African headrest forms.

## AN APOLOGIA: DRAWINGS VS. PHOTOGRAPHS

During research in museums in Europe and Southern Africa, it was not always possible to photograph the headrests being studied. In the process of examining the headrests, I made copious sketches, a process that enabled me to understand intellectually, visually and somatically the structural and stylistic principles that had gone into their making and use. One of the most commonly asked questions about the headrests is whether they *can* be slept on, the contemporary viewer generally finding it difficult to relate to the apparent discomfort the headrests imply in their somatic cognition of sleeping [dis]comfort. Apprehending the headrests as functional objects is, in this sense, quite different from understanding their structural principles and aesthetic qualities. The sketches have provided me with a personal archaeology of headrest forms, and have facilitated a process of understanding their structural principles, and thus their aesthetic and functional dimensions. Translating these sketches into more formal drawings has further enhanced that process, and it is for this reason that the majority of headrests illustrated here are in this particular graphic form of reproduction. This procedure was somewhat different from that which Elkins (1997) advocates for art historians (and he is largely concerned with Western art history), namely, to copy works by masters (he only deals with male artists in the Western tradition) in order to understand the processes of painting, sculpting, drawing or engraving. This, he suggests, would enable art historians to have a better understanding of the non-linear reason and somatic experience of such forms of making, and indeed, attempting to carve a headrest from a block of wood with no preliminary drawings, but only a mental template, is very different from making a drawing of the existing object. But the process followed in the present research involved an engagement with the objects, including trying to sleep on one, which allowed me to build up a different experience of their being.

While I acknowledge that there is some erasure of the original aesthetic of the headrest that might be more easily apprehended from photographic reproductions, the drawings also erase some of the seductions of lighting, added colour and dramatic contrast that appear to be fashionable in much photography of African art objects. Some photographs have been included to give the reader an idea of the 'real' appearance of some types, but this realism is limited, because most published photographs of headrests have been shot in vertical elevation only, either frontally or at a slight three-quarter view, and rarely from the top or from the short end elevation, or in any position other than standing. While in many instances the plan shape of the platforms and bases may be crucial in establishing types among similar structural styles, this is not provided by photographic reproductions of these three-dimensional objects. Further, the photographic bias towards the vertical and frontal view establishes the headrest as an art object, in contrast to the way they are handled, carried, used and stored. In instances where drawings have been made from published photographs, details of decoration are not provided, because the single photographic image cannot encompass all the decorative elements.

The drawings are reproduced as a means of conveying information ancillary to spoken or written language. I do not claim the drawings as realistic portraits, nor can they be taken as reproductions of the headrests that they are used to analyse, but that claim cannot be made for written descriptions, or even for photographs: reproducing three-dimensional objects in a two-dimensional form is something for which it is impossible to claim veracity anyway. The drawings may also be seen as a form of appropriation[7] of the headrests into a realm of academic games, floated upon a page as ciphers for a particular function, another form of writing, but this is a justifiable risk in relation to the analyses in which they are used.

At the same time, a few photographs of a few headrests have been used to provide 'illusionistic' reproductions: the illusion rests in the fact that they are more easily apprehended as realistic views of the objects. However, this realism is inevitably limited to those intellectual spaces of art history and ethnology, where headrests are removed from any context other than their presentation as aesthetic objects, this constituting a more violent form of appropriation. Thus the use of photographs in the research process was conditioned by a number of factors. Some of the photographs show the headrests in other than frontal or side view, either to emphasise aspects of structure or function, or their present status as specimens within museum collections. Thus, in some examples, labels were left on the objects, or they were photographed in groups, and those that do not necessarily stand on their own were photographed lying flat, as were others whose detailing includes elements not seen from frontal or side views. In using these strategies of visual representation, the changing nature of these objects, from three-dimensional utilitarian tools and ritual accessories that were handled and used in different ways to specimens of particular types, and/or to aesthetic objects for contemplation or as subjects requiring particular forms of description, is communicated in a meta-text that is different from the verbal analyses of style and functions.

## MORPHOLOGY AND TAXONOMY

The morphology of African headrests can be discussed within a geographical framework, rather than a purely ethnographic one in which styles are linked with specific linguistically or ethnically differentiated peoples or cultures. In the chapters that follow, the reasons for this will become apparent, as it will be clear that headrest styles often cross not only narrowly defined ethnic cultural boundaries, but are found as echoes across enormous distances on the African continent, echoes that cannot be ascribed to ethnic affiliation or historical contexts of contact or migration.

In delineating the morphological syntax of headrests' construction and establishing taxonomies of headrest types, I have found certain features to be more important than others, and have therefore delineated particular criteria in separating the major headrests types from one another. While this process may to some extent be arbitrary, it may also be argued, following Holly (1996:82–83), that one can assume a 'match' between the needs of the narrator and the 'formal ideology' of the work itself. Holly suggests that this can be assured by 'making what will forever be a provisional metaphoric construction at least partially consonant with that made visible in the reigning artistic metaphors of the period' (Holly 1996:83).

Although the project does not deal with a single period, it does seek to expose common formal ideologies within the headrest genre that cut across assumed ethnic boundaries within the genre of headrests in African societies. In choosing to detail particular formal criteria, the study in some senses follows a formalist tradition in French scholarship on African art from Olbrechts (1946), to Neyt (1977), Perrois (1990), and Chaffin and Chaffin (n.d.), but I hope to demonstrate through detailed analysis that each headrest has its own identity as a complete formal solution to particular problems of design and expression.

For the purposes of this study, a number of features that are common to most headrests have been used to delineate a number of different formal and stylistic solutions to the design problem posed by the making of these objects as beautiful functional pieces:

- the shape of the platform (the top section of the headrest), and its structural relationship to the support — either separately articulated or integrated;
- the presence or absence of a base and the shape that it takes, and its structural relationship to the support; and
- the number and shapes of the supporting elements between the platform and the base, or the ground, if there is no base.

The first two, i.e. the platform and the base and their structural relationship to the supports, are generally more significant as indices of particular styles than the third, as there is often quite a wide variety of supports within any given type of headrest, even at the micro level of a very narrow geographical and ethnic distribution. This is clear from comparisons of columned headrests with those that have figurative supports in place of columns, where attributions to ethnic groups are made on the basis of the sculptural style of the figures rather than on the structural relationships of the various parts of the headrest. In some instances, it is the decoration applied to those headrests that follows a single formal structure, which allows one to make narrower, ethnic attributions, but in others it is the use of particular proportions or combinations of all of these that are significant. Here, the important factors in the formation and classification of stylistic criteria are not the individual elements of the decoration, which would constitute a different level of 'close reading' (Elkins 1997), but the patterns according to which they have been assembled and the points at which they have been deployed. This discussion defers the investigation of what headrests 'mean' on a wider scale of reading to the last chapter. In the next two chapters, the delineation of different stylistic and structural features is linked to a larger discussion of issues of ethnic attribution, formal distribution, history and notions of 'authenticity'. The subsequent three chapters will outline selected examples of headrest types attributed to single ethnicities, in an attempt to demonstrate the complexities of headrest manufacture and usage within single groups. But these will also be related to visually presented outlines of structural form across ethnic groups, continuing the kind of analysis presented below for columned headrests. The final chapter moves from the strictures of formal analysis to look at other ways in which headrests can be contextualised into meaning.

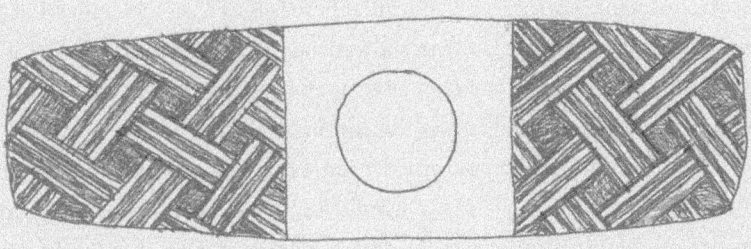

# 4 | The Geographical and Chronological Distribution of the Columned Headrest

THIS CHAPTER SETS out to examine the distribution of a single headrest type, the columned headrest, but does not follow set geographical imperatives, even though it uses a progression from north to south similar to that used in many studies of art from the African continent. The typology outlined here is based on the analysis of formal elements in particular objects, and it traces the occurrence of similar individual features and combinations of constituent elements in the headrests made and used among ethnic groupings widely dispersed across the continent.

The distribution of the columned headrest across Africa could be approached from two angles. On the one hand, it would be an attempt to trace a continuous master narrative of the diffusion of this headrest type across African from an originary point — a genealogical line punctuated by entries and exits of the kind posited by Kubler (1985).

It is, however, doubtful that a clear linear historical development could ever be traced for all African columned headrests. A logical place to seek origins for African headrest types would appear to be in the forms used in Ancient Egypt, where some columned headrests, especially those made of alabaster (figs. 3 & 27), were fluted, following the classical format of temple architecture. These are quite different from those other, mostly wooden, Ancient Egyptian headrests (figs. 28 & 29) that appear to belong to the same type as some nineteenth and twentieth century Sudanese examples (figs. 208 & 209) and some of the Tellem examples discussed in the previous chapter (figs. 4, 6 & 9). But while this observation may be made on a formal level, it cannot be accepted at face value without implying the direct descent from Ancient Egypt claimed for later African forms by Theodore Bent discussed in chapter 2, because there is no way of tracing such a simple genealogy. Although some headrests have been recorded from archaeological contexts, such as those found at Sanga in the Congo (now the Democratic Republic of the Congo or DRC) by William Burton (University of the Witwatersrand Art Galleries 1992), there are insufficient instances to allow for such a reconstruction across two millennia.

A second means of tracing the distribution of this headrest type would be to try to match the pattern of distribution of headrests to that of broader culture types among African peoples, on the assumption that all pastoralists within the same geographical region would have used the same headrest types, and all agriculturalists within the same region, or distributed across different regions, would have had headrests of types that differed from the pastoralists. From this research, and as demonstrated by my analysis of Tellem headrests, it is evident that a single group may have used more than one type of headrest. This study demonstrates that headrest types can also not be strictly correlated with the distribution of language groups (e.g. Nilotic vs. Bantu) or political or ethnic groupings, although there are some examples in which these do coincide. Finally, it also becomes quite clear from this study that while certain elements of formal style are consistently employed by successive generations in making headrests, there was a large degree of borrowing and adaptation of forms across language and culture boundaries.

This chapter proceeds by examining different formal variations of the columned headrest types, starting with examples from north-east Africa (Ethiopia and Somalia) and traversing the continent in a southerly direction. The examples used here to demonstrate variations within the range of columned headrests, which represent the single structural solution to the functional and aesthetic problem posed for headrest makers with the widest spread in Africa, are drawn from headrests in museum collections, but also include salient provenanced, published examples that were not seen in the 'flesh'/wood. For each specific example examined, the museum number has been given, and published examples that were not encountered in museums are referenced to the sources from which they were taken.

Two major divisions were identified within the generic category of columned headrests, but there are numerous variations within these, constituted of small differences. These variations are discussed in two separate chapters in order to understand aspects of distribution, history and the value implied in the notion of 'authenticity'. The case has been built through the examination of specific objects, both in terms of their individual forms and in terms of their collection and acquisition, and their provenances and dates. For it is only through the panoptic analysis of individuals lined up together, not in the flesh, because of their physical dispersion across the globe, but captured in the form of illustrations, that one is able to construct categories that both encompass and surpass the individual instances of the use of particular forms. That this follows a somewhat conservative art-historical model is acknowledged, but it is necessary for establishing the grounds on which other kinds of observations can be founded.

## COLUMNED HEADRESTS: THE LIMITATIONS OF ETHNIC ATTRIBUTION

Headrests with columnar supports are commonest in north-east and Central Africa, although significant numbers are known from across Southern Africa. They can be divided according to two main geographical zones, north-east and East Africa, and Central and Southern Africa, although there are correspondences between these mega-regions. I have divided these columned headrests into two main structural types, depending on the formal arrangement of base, column and platform in relation to one another. A third category, of multiple-columned headrests, is structurally linked to the second of these main types. While the fact that headrests in which the support is primarily constituted of a cylindrical column have spread across Africa from Sudan, Ethiopia and Somalia southwards to the Tropic of Capricorn is potentially suggestive of an African aesthetic and African connectivity, the lack of recorded use of headrests west of the Benue River excludes most West African societies. The correspondences that McGaffey (2000) seeks to establish, via an examination of cosmological structures and divination systems between Central and West African societies, thus find no reflection here. Further, while headrests using columns as their supports were made by peoples speaking Nilotic, Sudanic, Amharic and Bantu languages, other headrest types, such as the tied-leg types from East Africa discussed in chapter 6, are found among various peoples speaking related languages, but are at the same time exclusive to these larger language groups.

The headrests grouped together in this category and discussed in this and the following chapter have been chosen because they display the following common characteristics:

a) *A platform*, which, being clearly articulated from the support, curves upwards (at varying degrees of steepness) at its ends, and generally has either a flat or convex upper surface plane. The shape of the platform in plan may vary from a keloid with tapering ends, to a rectangle with curved ends, or a butterfly shape with either straight or curved ends. Generally, platforms with marked crescent-shaped curves are found mainly on north-east and East African headrests, while exaggerated butterfly shapes are more common in platforms of Central and Southern African headrests than those from elsewhere. Pendant forms on the platform of the headrest are known from both Central and Southern African examples, and some Ethiopian ones.

b) *A base* on which the headrest stands. The bases of the headrests in this type vary, from flat circular or rectangular forms, to conical, domed, oval, pyramidal, lobed and cotton-reel shapes. The shapes of the bases are used in my analyses as constant elements in delineating the characteristics of one of the two main sub-styles of columned headrests. In other words, while headrests from a single sub-style within the larger type may well vary in their use of different platforms, in the taxonomic arrangement proposed here, the bases and supporting columns have a relatively constant and narrow range of variation. Circular and conical bases are most common on East and Central African headrests, but lobed bases are almost exclusively found on Southern African ones, particularly Zimbabwean and Mozambican headrests, although there are some Tellem, Teke and Luba examples with this feature. Rectangular and pyramidal bases are most common in Central Africa, while conical bases are common in both north-east African and Central African examples, and can be seen in a few examples from the Southern African region.

c) *A support*, which is clearly demarcated from both its base and the platform that it carries. The supports of these headrests vary in form, but to a far lesser extent than the platforms. They include single columnar or pillar-like forms, and columns articulated into cotton-reel shapes or with spherical bosses, while some headrests have multiple columns. In some instances, the supports are augmented or replaced by figurative carvings of humans and animals, and it is largely within the formal typology of columned headrests that such figurative carving occurs, although there are a few instances of this occurring in the other headrest types. The use of figures as supports is generally restricted to Central African examples, with a small, but nevertheless significant, number traceable to the Southern African region. In a few cases where animal figures form the supports in this headrest type, the base is dispensed with, although this is not the case with those where human figure sculptures support the platform. There is generally a greater degree of uniformity in the combination of support and base in any single sub-style of the headrests of this type than there is in the combination of base shapes with platform, or of platform with support.

d) *Decorative elements* are found on most of these headrests, created either by relief carvings on the surfaces of the supports, base and/or platform, or by the addition of other materials, such as metal strips or studs and sometimes beads or leather. The use of metal strips and studs as decorative elements on headrests is most commonly found on Central African examples, but beads are added to headrests in East, Central and Southern Africa.

## COLUMNED HEADRESTS WITH CONICAL/DOMED BASES

This section discusses those headrests with a circular, conical or domed base, above which is a column supporting a platform of generally rectangular or tapering shape, although some have butterfly-shaped platforms, and some have flaps turning downwards from the ends of the platform. In some cases, the bases are almost as tall as the columns that they support, and in others the column is omitted, so that the base forms the support. Thus, in all of these examples, the distinction between base and support is somewhat blurred, either because the two are not demarcated, or because they are proportionally skewed towards the dominance of the base. Engraved decoration is found on examples from both East and Central Africa, and sculpted figurative elements are found on some Central African examples.

## Laying out the basics: Figures 30–42

The following examples are used here to establish the basic elements of the type. They all have a column that is taller than the base. Their recorded provenances range across Ethiopia, Sudan, Egypt (Ancient and modern) and Somalia, but their compositional simplicity makes it difficult to support clear ethnic attributions. Most of these examples have early museum acquisition dates, but many have not been attributed to specific ethnic categories.

One of the earliest examples (fig. 30), which was collected by J. T. Bent before 1893 in Ethiopia, has a circular/conical base sloping gently upwards towards the column at its centre. The base is slightly concave on its underside. The column is articulated at its centre by a flattened spherical knob, a feature that is found in one example collected by Van der Stappen (1996a:66) in Ethiopia a century later, but is not repeated in other examples. These two headrests and another of Van der Stappen's (1996a:62) have platforms shaped very similarly to a simpler example collected by Seligman (fig. 31),[1] who recorded its provenance as 'Upper Egypt'. Here the column is taller than the conical base, and the use of a tenon to join platform to column is reminiscent of the construction of both Ancient Egyptian and more recent Ethiopian examples.

Figure 32 has a flaring conical base with a column articulated at the points at which it joins the base and the platform. The platform tapers towards its ends and its upper surface, and the edges of the base are decorated by rows of small engraved diagonal marks. Collected at an unknown date by one Brigadier Matthews,[2] and accessioned by the British Museum in 1972, it is provenanced to Somalia. Another example almost identical to this, accessioned by the Liverpool Museum in 1921, has a secure provenance to Ethiopia.[3] Examples collected by Dr S. F. Nadel in the Jebel District of the Nuba Hills in Anglo-Egyptian Sudan c. 1938 (fig. 33) and by Van der Stappen (figs. 35 & 36) in 1996, respectively, all have columns with entasis; two have, in addition, a raised ring at the centre. The Nuba example has a two-tiered base and a relatively short platform whose upper surface has a minimal curve. These examples do not have surface decoration, and their conical bases are small in proportion to the columns. Van der Stappen's (1996a) examples are all 'Ethiopian', but some have more specific attributions. For example, the headrest in figure 36, attributed to the Oromo peoples, has a column articulated by a raised ridge at the points where it joins both the base and the platform. Its base is almost as tall as its column, but these raised ridges clearly mark the column as a separate element.

The headrests in figures 37–39 belong to the same stylistic and structural category, but they are provenanced to Kenya and Tanzania, with museum acquisition dates of 1912, 1914 and 1928, respectively. Figure 37 shows an early example whose collector is not recorded, but which is attributed to the 'Matengo'. It has a single column support with a slight entasis separating a conical, unevenly domed base from the platform, which is slightly wider at its centre than its ends. There is no surface decoration. Very similar are the examples in figures 38 and 39, both of which are from German East Africa/Tanganyika (now Tanzania), the former collected in 1914 and attributed to the 'Wagowa', and the latter given both an ethnic attribution, 'Namalengo', and the vernacular name for headrest, '*msamiro*'. In these examples, short columns separate the slightly domed, unevenly carved conical bases from heavy rectangular platforms, which curve quite steeply inwards. Only one example of this type in the British Museum, accessioned in 1934, is provenanced to Kenya (fig. 40), but its proportions are quite different, with a slightly domical base, a tall, plain column and a butterfly-shaped platform with minimal curvature.

All of these headrests can be viewed as following generic forms, whose recurrence is not linked to particular ethnic affiliations, although in some cases, very small details may serve to distinguish one ethnic style from another. This may be demonstrated by reference to two headrests in the Brighton Museum (figs. 41 & 42), both relatively early examples of this type, one of which was attributed to the Luba and the other to the Shona. Both have round conical bases with single columnar supports, one with a tapering platform, and the other with a butterfly shape. Although the two are similar, there are tell-tale signs that distinguish them quite clearly from one another. Figure 41 shows a headrest that most resembles Ethiopian examples (figs. 34 & 35), although its accession notes record it as having been collected by A. G. Mumford, who had travelled through the DRC and made 'copious notes' on his collected objects,[4] this one being recorded as 'Luba, Katanga'. The second example, accessioned in 1913 (fig. 42) has a propeller-shaped platform and a column with a spiral in relief around it. It is provenanced to the Shona, Mashonaland, having been collected by Rev. Dr Polly, who had collected other Shona objects, but is quite unlike any other Shona examples, and quite like some DRC ones. These examples thus suffice to show that this headrest form has a widespread geographical distribution and a history traceable back to the late nineteenth century at least. Thus, narrower ethnic attributions could only be made on the basis of more consistent and possibly micro-scale differentiations of style; this will be demonstrated via a detailed examination of examples from different centres of production of this type of headrest. We start with examples from Ethiopia, because they present particular problems that can be carried over into a discussion of other regions.

## Ethiopian examples: Figures 43–60

### Early acquisitions: Figures 43–46

Headrests of this type from East Africa are scarce in the European collections studied for this research. Prior to the publication of the catalogue *Aethiopie* (Van der Stappen 1996a), few of the examples from Ethiopia in European museum collections consulted for this study were attributed to specific ethnicities. Almost all of these museum examples follow the pattern outlined for discussion in this section, i.e. a conical base with a column supporting the platform, in most cases a rectangle tapering towards its ends, and the base generally being as tall as, or taller than the column. One of the remarkable features to emerge from the publication of the *Aethiopie* catalogue is the enormous diversity of headrests contained by this restricted structural range within a relatively small geographical region within Ethiopia.

An early example of this type in the Staatlisches Museum für Völkerkunde in Munich, accessioned in 1914 (fig. 43), has engraved lines around the lower perimeter of the base, and on the column where it joins the base and the platform.[5] An example in the British Museum (fig. 44), made before 1954 (its acquisition date), and which is not clearly provenanced,[6] has a truncated conical base and column, both of which are covered with a beadwork dress consisting of a tight-fitting neck around the column and a loose-fitting skirt around the base. The beadwork patterns consist of stripes, lozenges and diamonds, with a colour range of mustard yellow, red, white and deep blue colours that are evident on a stained example from the same collection (fig. 45). This example has, however, a tiered conical base, from which a very short column is separated by a raised ring. There is engraved decoration on the base and the column, and in both examples the bases are hollowed out. This pattern is replicated in another unattributed example from the Musée Royal de l'Afrique Central (fig. 46), which has a similar structure and red and yellow colouration, but this example has two flap-like extensions from the ends of the platform, with engraved and coloured patterns on their outer surfaces. A further example, published by Falgayrettes (1989:25), with a similarly tiered base and column, is attributed to the Oromo, with a query, but it is not dated.[7]

These early examples suggest that this headrest type has been made in Ethiopia for at least 100 years, and, on the evidence presented by Van der Stappen's (1996a) contemporary collection, that these forms may not have changed radically in that period. Other examples that appeared on the exhibition Ethiopia: Traditions of Creativity, curated by Silverman (1999),[8] bear this out, as one exhibited example had pristine engraved designs coloured on a tiered base of the same kind. This example also has flaps from the end of the platform, but is documented as having been made by Gebre Wolde Tsadik, and as being Gurage[9] in style. Further examples in the University of the Witwatersrand Art Galleries were acquired at about the same time as Van der Stappen's and show the same range of variation, but no collection data from the field are available for these.

The limits of ethnic specificity: Van der Stappen and the headrests of the Oromo, Gurage, Arsi and Afar (figures 49–60)

None of the headrests of this type published by Van der Stappen (1996a) appears to be coloured, and, as all were collected between 1991 and 1995, they may therefore be assumed to be more recent than the museum examples discussed above. Nevertheless, there is a clear continuity in the structural and decorative elements between these two groups of headrests.

There are some curiosities in Van der Stappen's attributions to ethnicities, where he distinguishes between a simple attribution such as 'Oromo' and 'collected in the country of the Oromo language' (Van der Stappen 1996a:58–59). But in the introductory text, he lists 'Oromo' as a language with sub-groupings, in which it appears that the Arsi, whose headrests he distinguishes from the category of 'Oromo', are Oromo speakers of the south (Van der Stappen 1996a:11). Huntingford (1955:12–15) lists six major territorial districts into which the Oromo can be divided within Ethiopia, with numerous 'tribes' distinguished within these areas,[10] and he places the Arsi within the southern geographical area. One therefore has to question the distinction made by Van der Stappen between the generic 'Oromo' and the Arsi. Further, Hassen (1990:21–22) notes that the Oromo 'tribes', through their institutionalised process of adoption of Cushitic and Semitic speakers as serfs, were always fluid groupings, in which 'Oromisation' occurred very easily. Van der Stappen (1996a:11) lists the Arsi with the Borana, but Huntingford (1955:15.25) distinguishes the Arsi from the Borana, although both are pastoralist groups. Thus, the use of the names Oromo and Arsi as indices of identity should also be done very cautiously, as it clearly denotes only a language division and not necessarily either an homogeneous cultural or an historical entity.[11] The distinctions among the headrests of these peoples are not very marked, and it may make some sense to speak of Oromo as a style.

Van der Stappen attributes examples of this headrest type to the Gurage, Oromo and Arsi. One of his Oromo examples has a beaded dress (Van der Stappen 1996a:59, no. 120) like the early one in the British Museum (fig. 44), as does one Arsi example (Van der Stappen 1996a:71, no. 167), although the beads on the latter are large plastic ones, itself an index of a more recent date of decoration, if not of manufacture. The groups among which Van der Stappen collected the headrests do not appear to be linguistically or culturally homogeneous. The headrests of the largely agriculturalist Oromo and Gurage in the Kaffa area, south of Addis Ababa, are almost impossible to attribute definitively to any one group or region without very specific collection data, which is not always given by Van der Stappen. The Arsi, the southern pastoralists, use headrest types that are stylistically clearly related to those of the Oromo and Gurage, but that appear better documented in Van der Stappen's catalogue (1996a).

Many of the headrests attributed to these three 'ethnic' groups have elaborate engraved decoration around their conical bases. These designs generally take the form of straight lines or chevrons around the circumference, and seem to mark out East African examples of this type from those found elsewhere. Some of the Oromo examples (figs. 47 & 49), (Van der Stappen 1996a:59, no. 119) are made in two parts, with the platform joined to the column by a tenon, suggesting echoes of some Ancient Egyptian headrests. The headrests in figures 47 (listed as Oromo) and 48 (listed as Arsi) are very similar, but that in figure 48 is differentiated by the inclusion of flaps from the ends of the platform, something that is present in three of the four examples of this type that Van der Stappen attributes to the Arsi, and that may be seen to be one of the distinguishing marks of Arsi style. This headrest (fig. 48) is also the only example published by Van der Stappen that has a tiered base, thus suggesting that the earlier examples in the British Museum (fig. 45), the Musée Royal de l'Afrique Central (fig. 46) and the one published by Falgayrettes (1989:25) may be attributable to the Arsi. It (fig. 48) is one of a number for which Van der Stappen notes a differentiated gender use, but it is impossible to establish from this whether there is any coherent stylistic differentiation between women's and men's headrests.[12] Furthermore, Gurage examples, many of which were and still are made by Fuga craftsmen of a lower caste status, are identical to some Oromo and Arsi ones, but more colourful, so it is almost impossible to work with an idea of separate structural and stylistic features as exclusive ethnic markers.[13]

Some examples from Ethiopia, in which the base is bell-shaped with a relatively short column linking it to the platform, are attributed by Van der Stappen to both the Arsi (Van der Stappen 1996a:70, no. 166) and the Oromo (fig. 49). Another variation on this headrest type is that in which the base and column merge or the column is omitted from the structure. One example of this columnless type was recorded in the Musée Royal de l'Afrique Central (fig. 50), but, unlike the majority of Van der Stappen's examples, it has fairly extensive surface decoration on its base and some lines engraved at the ends of its platform. Its use of decoration is paralleled in an example published by Van der Stappen (fig. 51), which has a flaring conical base and virtually no column, but this he attributes to the 'Guragué(?)', (i.e. Gurage). He attributed two others of the same style to the Oromo, one with a flared base, the other with a domical base (Van der Stappen 1996a:58, no. 118; 59, no. 122).

There are also numerous headrests of this type that Van der Stappen (1996a:92, no. 93) collected among the Afar, but which are much cruder in execution and more robustly conceived.[14] Their use of the basic structural elements of the type varies enormously. The Gurage example in figure 52 follows the 'Oromo/Arsi' pattern, but has very different proportions, with a short conical base, a fat column and a relatively flat platform, all articulated from one another by roll mouldings. In this, it is also different from the other Afar examples published by Van der Stappen, where base and column are not clearly distinguished. The Arsi example in figure 53 has a conical base split by a V-shaped indentation, and the 'column' above it has two tiers that flare outwards (cf. also Van der Stappen 1996a:94, no. 240), while in figure 54, an Afar example, the base merges into a thick, conical-shaped support, so that the two are not separated in any way. Finally, in the

Afar example in figure 55, the base is eliminated completely, with the conical support given two tiers, as though the flared conical base has been extended upwards and the column abandoned. This pattern is also found in examples attributed to the Oromo, one having a flaring conical base (Van der Stappen 1996a:58, no. 118) and the other a domed base (Van der Stappen 1996a:59, no. 122). Although some Afar examples are decorated, this embellishment, like the proportions and execution, is less refined than that used on headrests attributed to the other Ethiopian groups in question.

Afar are transhumance pastoralists who inhabit the more easterly regions of Ethiopia, stretching to the Red Sea coast of Eritrea (Lewis 1955:155). Their language is related to Somali, and, like Somali and Oromo, belongs to the Southern Cushitic group (Lewis 1955:11). Van der Stappen (1996a:13) suggests that the restricted range of their moveable objects is probably a result of their nomadic lifestyle, although their social and political organisation was fairly complex, with a split being maintained between nobles (Asaimara) and commoners (Adoimara) (Lewis 1955:156). The less-finished appearance and stockier proportions of their headrests may be a result of their lifestyle and a lack of artisanal specialisation,[15] and it is perhaps these factors that explain the discrete nature of their use of the structural elements of this headrest style.

While Lewis claims that Afar material culture appears to be poorer than that of the Somali to which it 'is similar in most respects' (Lewis 1955:162), the headrests published by Van der Stappen as Afar are more clearly related to the Ethiopian examples discussed above than to most Somali ones. Lewis's and Van der Stappen's assessments of Afar artisanal output contrast Afar with Oromo: the highly finished quality of many of the Oromo headrests discussed here suggests a degree of artisanal specialisation. Hassen (1990:130–31) explains the place of artisanal groups (*ogessa*) within the Oromo kingdoms of the Gibé region, suggesting that it was only as the originally pastoralist Oromo became sedentary that a demand for crafted goods increased. Such *ogessa* were relegated to a low social caste called *hiru*, and were distributed among Oromo clans, without being assimilated into them. Thus, the more integrated stylistic features and finished aesthetic quality of Oromo headrests may be ascribable to specialisation in wood carving by their makers and to the fact they belonged to a single class spread out among the dominant Oromo kingdoms. A similar explanation may be put forward for the Gurage headrests, as they appear to have been made by the lower caste, i.e. endogamous Fuga who lived sparsely interspersed among the Gurage. Shack (1964; 1966) suggests that their workmanship was highly valued by the Gurage. The similarities between Gurage and Oromo/Arsi forms may thus owe as much to the existence of specialist crafts groups as to any putative ethnic similarities. On the other hand, Van der Stappen's Afar examples were collected in Ethiopia and follow a formal arrangement shared by other Ethiopian groups. It may be that Afar examples from areas bordering more closely on Somali territory, where Afar live alongside Issa[16] groups, would show closer affinity with so-called 'Somali' headrest styles.

An explanation for these stylistic similarities and modifications across ethnic boundaries that uses the principle of centre and periphery may be applicable here. If one sees the settled Oromo, Arsi and Gurage forming a kind of stable centre, the Afar of Ethiopia, who, according to the figures presented by Lewis (1955:157), formed the bulk of this linguistic group, could be seen as moving on the periphery, replicating and modifying the style elements of the headrest carving of the centre. In some senses, one could look at Afar style in Ethiopia as involving some inversions of the others' headrest styles through such elements as the tiering of the column rather than the base (fig. 53), and inversions might be seen as a stylistic strategy that could be used to back up the centre–periphery model. In addition, the lack of a technical skill in those Afar headrests, which are comparable to Oromo and Arsi forms, fits a differentiation between the technically skilled and aesthetically advanced centre[17] vs. the aesthetically unskilled and technically backward periphery, although such relations could not so easily be posited for the Afar in relation to the Issa Somalis. All the headrests attributed to the Afar by Van der Stappen appear to have been used by men, while two of his four Arsi examples were used by women, and gender inversions may be present in Afar usage of these forms. But such differentiation between centre and periphery suggests particular kinds of power relations and systems of exchange among the groups concerned, where the Afar would necessarily be in a position of inferior influence. The model of centre and periphery also suggests a process of borrowing: that the Afar might have started to make such headrests only after coming into contact with the other groups, something that cannot be substantiated without clear historical pointers.

Van der Stappen also illustrates three examples (two attributed to the 'Oromo' and one to the 'Afar') that can be regarded as variants on the structural theme isolated in this headrest type, where two lateral supports link the ends of the plateau to the conical base, thus framing the central column. In figure 56, two side supports bend from the ends of the platform inwards towards the flaring conical base that supports a very minimal column. By contrast, the headrest in figure 57 has a conical base distinct from the column, with the platform ends joined to the junction of the column and base by curved arms framing the column. It has finely engraved decoration on the base and on the top end surfaces of the plateau, similar to that on other 'Oromo' examples (cf. fig. 47). A similar variant example attributed by Van der Stappen to the Afar (fig. 58), which has two rounded supports connecting the ends of the platform to the base, but no engraved decoration, is also much more compressed in its proportions than the other two. Two headrests in the British Museum (figs. 59 & 60) have a shape and engraved decoration very similar to these variant Oromo examples, but are provenanced respectively to the 'Belgian Congo' (i.e. DRC), (fig. 59) and 'Ethiopia/Somaliland' (fig. 60). On the basis of stylistic similarities and the Somali provenance of one, it is tempting to conclude that these are both Ethiopian, and that they provide examples of variant types collected earlier than those published by Van der Stappen. It could then be suggested that experimentation with basic canonical forms was a well-established practice among Ethiopian headrest makers.

These variant headrests clearly demonstrate the complexities inherent in stylistic categorisation in the face of the wide distribution of a single stylistic theme among disparate peoples, although it must be remembered that the Oromo, Afar and Somali belong to the same larger linguistic grouping, and that a final explanation for both similarities and differences in this headrest form may lie in common origins[18] as much as in processes of diffusion, borrowing and adaptation among linguistically related and neighbouring groups.

Headrests of another related variant have domical oval bases and tapering platforms linked by multiple supports, thus integrating the structural elements so that neither the base nor the platform projects beyond the supports, and the headrest has a more block-like appearance. Van der Stappen collected examples among the same Ethiopian groups (mainly Gurage and Arsi) as those making the headrests with conical bases (Van der Stappen 1996a:43, 44, 61, 62, 73). These are discussed later,[19] but it must be borne in mind that there are examples in every category, which, because they appear to be hybrid, suggest the fluidity of stylistic forms and the permeability of stylistic/structural boundaries.

## Somali versions: Figures 61–69

Two other headrests (figs. 61 & 62) further emphasise the problematics of too close a definition of stylistic parameters in ethnic attributions. These two have domical bases hollowed out beneath, with single columns narrowing towards their platforms, which are small, with a moderate upwards curve, tapering towards their ends. Both examples have engraved lines around the circumferences of their bases and columns. One (fig. 61) was collected by 'Balfour' in Aden before 1905, the other (fig. 62) by Major Powell-Cotton in Addis Ababa in 1900, both of which records can be regarded as fairly secure.[20] While these two are very similar in style, they are also different from Ethiopian examples discussed above, and from the forms commonly associated with Somali style (see figs. 180–195). The differences in their recorded provenances could be explained in different ways, but the most likely interpretation may be that they were made either in Somaliland or Ethiopia by Somali craftsmen and exported from the point of manufacture, probably for sale. Neither example shows any significant signs of wear, the one in the British Museum (fig. 62) having a broken platform that has been glued together, and either, or both, might have been bought as unused specimens of a type by interested gentlemen collectors — an early form of tourist art that was paralleled elsewhere, at an earlier date. The ethnic certainty of these examples is thrown into doubt, however, by a third example, collected by Jean Brown among the Walamo of Korale (near Soldo) in Ethiopia (Pitt Rivers Museum, no. 1973.14.40). According to her documentation, this type, called *bareota*, was made by 'Walamo carpenters, *hilancha*', and was used by both men and women. The later date of acquisition (1971) of this example does not allow us to draw any conclusions about the origin of the type, but it does allow us to question the notions of the stasis and exclusivity of ethnically defined styles.[21]

A headrest from 'French Somaliland' (fig. 63), provenanced to the 'Esa (Issa) tribe/Rahale?', is one of a few from this area that follows the Ethiopian pattern of a conical base with a single column, but this one has finely carved geometric interlace patterns covering the surface of both the column and the underside of the platform. It is this use of interlace, the shallow base, the broad column and the deep crescent shape of the platform that clearly distinguishes it from Ethiopian headrests of the same type: the pattern corresponds with those on other Somali headrests. Further examples of this type, attributed to the Somali, demonstrate a much more idiosyncratic treatment of the platform and the column. In these, the platform has a very pronounced curvature, resulting in a crescent-shaped elevation (figs. 64 & 65), and it tapers towards its ends, which are either pointed, carved with W-shaped notches, or with short extensions on each of the long sides. The conical base flows directly into the column, which is shallowly cut back in triangular relief sections on the front and back, to give the impression of ridges or pointed leaf shapes extending down the column and over the base to its edge. In figure 65, the upper surface of the platform has engraved decoration, while figure 67 shows engraved decoration on the undersides of the platform. The fifth and possibly later example of this variant type (fig. 68), however, has much more extensive decoration along the edges of the platform, on its undersides and on the ridges that extend down the column. There are traces of red and yellow pigmentation on all four in figures 64–67, and none have their bases hollowed out.

The headrests in figures 64, 65 and 67 have relatively securely recorded provenances to British Somaliland,[22] and can be used to establish a stylistic genre that is definable at least in terms of a geographical area[23] and possibly a limited time span, i.e. before 1934. There is, of course, a problem in these attributions, as Somali is here used as a mega-ethnic classification that does not reflect the diversity of peoples and political groupings in the region, a diversity that is discussed in the section on Somali headrests in chapter 6. The collection information given with the examples collected by 'Lieutenant Colonel Alden' (figs. 64 & 65) 'that they are of an ordinary type, in everyday use' also establishes a notion of hierarchical difference among headrest types among the Somali, and these examples do differ from other Somali headrests, which use single supports and circular bases of quite different structural design, as well as those others that use two curved triangular supports.[24]

Evidence for these other types of headrests made and used by the Somali, particularly from the British Museum, the Powell-Cotton Museum and the Pitt Rivers Museum (see figs. 180–195) suggests that different Somali groups may have shared headrest forms with one another and with surrounding groups. From the evidence to hand, it appears that the conical based form may have been restricted to the area of the former British Somaliland, or it could be that this type was one of the more stable, broad-based examples that Dewey, following Puccioni, says was used by women (Dewey 1993:40). This view is reinforced by information recorded by Powell-Cotton in relation to the Somali headrests of this type that he collected in Somaliland. Alternatively, these headrests may have been used by younger men, following both Dewey's (1993:40) citing of Brandt's information that younger and elder men used different kinds of headrests, and the information that this was the ordinary type 'in everyday use' (figs. 64 & 65). These examples add to the known repertoire of Somali headrests and suggest that there has been too tight a definition of Somali headrest styles, and that the issue of gender identity has largely been overlooked.

In fact, the breadth of styles from the region can be demonstrated by another example

CHAPTER 4 *The Geographical and Chronological Distribution of the Columned Headrest* | 85

(fig. 69), which was on the Paris exhibition of 1878, where it may have been identified as 'Neam Neam' (Azande), but, much later, Margaret Carey reassigned it to the Somali. It is one of the earliest headrests acquired by the British Museum, and it shows practically no signs of use, yet its variation on the conical base, but with a flat support covered by finely carved geometric decoration, is curiously similar to the forms encountered on securely documented Somali headrests (see figs. 186 & 193), but not on any known Azande forms,[25] although some Turkana/Karamojong examples (see fig. 220) have similar base shapes, and all together indicate the fluidity of stylistic features.

### Dinka/Bari? and Sudanese variants: Figures 70–74

Headrests of this type have also been provenanced to the Sudan, but there are a number of variations in the ways in which the basic elements are used. This can be seen in three examples from the British Museum (figs. 70 & 71)[26] which are identical in form, but whose provenancing raises a problem of ethnic attribution. These examples all have a conical base cloven into four or five segments on the underside, forming pads like an animal paw/hoof. This base flows directly into a single column, which supports a wide, rectangular platform with a concave upper surface. At the top of the column in all three examples, a rectangular protrusion with a hole through its thickness has a wound leather or string handle attached to it, joined to the base through a hole. One (fig. 70) has engraved decoration on the upper surface of the platform.

The provenancing of these headrests to the Sudan and Kenya–Uganda is not as problematic as the ethnic attributions that are adduced alongside their geographical placing.[27] Trowell and Wachsmann do not illustrate any headrests even vaguely like these in their drawings of Ugandan headrest types, but the rectangular to butterfly-shaped platforms of these headrests, together with their breadth and convex curvature, are more similar to those of many headrests with flattened hour-glass-shaped supports used in the regions of southern Sudan, Ethiopia and Uganda than they are to those recorded columnar headrests from the same region. Further, the attachment of a handle to the headrest in the form of a circular arm also brings to mind similarities with Pokot and Turkana examples, where leather or string handles are integrated into the overall design of the headrest (see figs. 249 & 250). To complicate the matter, the collection records of another example with a conical base, a strong upward-curving platform and a composite column, which is attributed to the Dinka (fig. 72), suggests that this attribution might be as tenable as the Bari one. Again, the relatively early museum acquisition dates of the British Museum examples suggest that these may either represent headrest forms that have subsequently fallen out of use, or, given the small number of recorded examples, that they may have been the work of a single artist working for a small clientele.

Both the cases of the Somali and these Dinka/Bari columnar headrests suggest that one must tread very carefully in the waters of ethnic attribution. Sudanese variants on this theme include examples such as one (fig. 73) securely provenanced to the 'Koalit tribes, Ko'aub' of the Nuba Hills, and another (fig. 74) whose only provenance is to the Anglo-Egyptian Sudan. These examples, however, are so isolated that it is impossible to build up any picture of particular ethnic usage. Thus, the classification of headrests according to structural types throws up many of the anomalies that go hand in hand with over-determined ethnic or broader cultural classifications. Pastoralists, sedentary agriculturalists and nomadic peoples can all be shown to use headrests of this type in the north-east African region. Furthermore, headrests of this type are also found, although on a more restricted scale of distribution, among peoples of Central and Southern Africa.

## Democratic Republic of the Congo and Angola: Figures 75–102

Headrests of this type have been recorded from the DRC, largely from the south-west, in the Kwango-Kwilu region, but also from the north-east and from Angola and Namibia. The main ethnic groupings in the Kwango-Kwilu region with whom this type of headrest is associated are the Teke and Yaka, although others have been attributed to the Hungana[28] and Holo.[29] The Angolan examples were collected among the Wila,[30] and the Namibian examples among the Himba.[31]

Three examples, collected by Emil Torday and accessioned by the British Museum in 1907 (figs. 75–77), follow the pattern of a tall, truncated conical base supporting a column and a curved plateau: one (fig. 75) with a simple plateau, is attributed to the 'Huangana' (i.e. Hungana), while the other two, both of which have butterfly platforms with ends with pendant flaps, are provenanced to the 'Kwango-Kwilu region' and attributed to the 'Northern Bambala/KotoKoto' (i.e. Mbala/Kotokoto),[32] (fig. 76) and the 'Northern Bambala' (i.e. Mbala), (fig. 77). The rather subtle differences in design, particularised in the platforms, form one of the bases for attribution of styles to specific ethnic groups. Maes

(1929) did not illustrate any examples of the variants that have end flaps on their platforms, and the examples of this type that he did illustrate (Maes 1929, pl. I, figs. 10–16) are, with two exceptions,[33] attributed to the Teke. These examples have different proportions in the height of the base relative to the column, and their platforms are simply rectangular, as can be seen in figures 78, 79[34] and 80.[35] None of them has any decoration, unlike two other examples (figs. 81 & 82) in the Musée Royal de l'Afrique Central, where brass studs are abundant and the platforms pronouncedly butterfly in shape.

One of these (fig. 81) has a row of brass studs at the juncture of the base and the column, and a single row of studs round the entire circumference of the base, with another immediately above it running only half-way round, thus marking one face of the headrest more clearly than the other. It also has a metal casing around the column and a mirror embedded in the underside of its base, features not encountered on other examples in museum collections. This example was collected between 1890 and 1899 and is attributed to the Teke. The other example (fig. 82), collected by Albert Maesen half a century later, is very similar, but here the studs are arranged around the base in groups of three and four, and three studs mark the juncture of the platform and the column, while its carrying string is still attached. Its provenance to the Teke is secure, and a photograph showing it being carried by its owner has been published (Van Wassenhove 1996:65, pl. 47). In all the examples of this type attributed to the Teke, the bases are tall in proportion to the columns and flare outwards, a pattern repeated in most examples attributed to the Yaka.

A number of examples attributed to the Yaka are held in the Musée Royal de l'Afrique Central, but none of these appears in Maes's 1929 catalogue, the earliest having been collected/accessioned only in 1931. These examples (figs. 83–87) consistently use flaps at the ends of the platforms, which often include figurative elements, most commonly faces, on their outer surfaces or on the conical base (fig. 86).[36] In figure 83, the faces are engraved into the surface with minimal modelling and schematised features, while those on the flaps in figure 85 are fully modelled, one having the protuberant, upturned profile associated with so much Yaka figure carving (see Bourgeois 1984). The headrest in figure 84 has different carvings on the two platform flaps, set against engraved geometric designs. On one there are three birds carved as if viewed from above, the central one larger than the others, and facing vertically downwards, while the two flanking it face upwards. On the other flap are two kneeling human figures, legs intertwined and facing each other, one with an elaborate coiffure and the other with breasts. This example is also different from the others in its degree of decorative elaboration, from the diamonds engraved into the vertical surface of one of the long sides of the platform, to the central sphere, divided into keloid-shaped segments, that divides the column from the base and the number of brass studs that encircle the upper section of the base itself. Such a degree of formal aesthetic elaboration and figuration suggests that this example was extraordinary and was probably made for a person of some status.

These examples can be distinguished from those attributed to the Teke, both by their use of platform flaps and their figurative elements. But the minutiae of such attributions has to be treated with caution, as they might lead to an atomisation of what should be a single stylistic group, in which individual differences correspond to personalised details. The complexities can be demonstrated by an analysis of a similar example from the British Museum (fig. 87). With no recorded provenance, and accessioned only in 1949, it has a row of brass studs in the vertical edges on the long sides of the platform and a face carved on each of the platform flaps. On the basis of the sculptural and structural elements, William Fagg identified this as 'Bayaka' (i.e. Yaka), an attribution that appears reasonable on stylistic grounds.[37] It is, however, different from others of this type attributed to the Yaka in its use of engraved lines encircling the base and stained bands encircling the column, which is itself stepped. The relief on the platform end flaps is similar to that on the flaps in figures 76, 77 and 83, in that it is very shallow and schematised, whereas the faces used in this position in figure 85 are more three-dimensionally conceived.

A similar rotundity is evident in another example, published by Dewey (1993:59, fig. 47), where the flaps are carved almost as three-dimensional heads. This example Dewey attributes to the Holo, presumably on the basis of the style of the carving of the heads, for in all other respects, from its flaring base to its butterfly platform, it is like the Yaka examples discussed above. It also uses brass studs very liberally, as do both the examples attributed to the Yaka and the Teke. The presence of flaps on the ends of the platforms of these headrests might be taken as an index of their origin among the Yaka (or possibly the Holo), but there are a number of problems associated with this. The structural similarity among all the examples attributed to the Yaka and the two attributed to the Northern Mbala (figs. 76 & 77) suggests that the presence of flaps is not a reliable index of either ethnic affiliation or of a shift in style across time. Further, in an example of this headrest type from the British Museum (fig. 88), where two heads face outwards from the crudely carved and squat conical base, parallel to the platform, the figurative carving style is classifiable as Yaka (or possibly Cokwe?). Yet here the platform is without end flaps, possibly because they would have interfered with a view of the figurative carving. Assuming that the attributions of these particular headrests to the Hungana, Northern Mbala, Teke, Yaka and Holo are reliable,[38] one can postulate that there was a regional style, crossing ethnic boundaries, in which differences may well occur on the level of individual makers and users, rather than on the grounds of ethnic identities.

The idiosyncrasies of each headrest in this group do not allow for any grouping other than the most general ones. Maes placed his examples of this headrest type in the Middle Congo/DRC region (Maes 1929:4–6), but Biebuyck (1985) separates the people to whom these headrests have been attributed into smaller sub-regions. In this scheme, the Hungana are grouped with the Pindi and Tsaam as '[p]eople submerged between the Kwango and the Kwilu' (Biebuyck 1985:150–60), the Mbala and the Ngongo make up the '[p]eople between the Lower Kwango and the Lower Kwilu' (Biebuyck 1985:161–72), while the '[p]eople of the Middle and Upper Kwango-Kwilu divide' include the Yaka, Nkanu, Suku and Holo (Biebuyck 1985:173–219). The Teke are not included in this scheme, although Biebuyck acknowledges that they, with the Kongo, belong in the region of south-western Congo/DRC (Biebuyck 1985:51). He further remarks of this region:

> Here the map of cultural distributions has been profoundly affected by common origins of groups, local migration, diversification and specialization, political fragmentation and internal scission, incorporation and assimilation .... Specific populations and culture areas can, of course, be recognized, but no sharp boundaries can be traced because of continuities across tribal cultures and culture units (Biebuyck 1985:57).

Biebuyck further acknowledges that the exclusion of the Lunda–Cokwe culture clusters from the region is artificial (Biebuyck 1985:51–52). It thus appears that the distribution of this headrest type and its classifications into ethnic sub-types within the region of south-west DRC and Angola has to be very broadly conceived. There is also no evidence from the dating of headrests that any major development of style happened between 1900 and the 1960s.

One headrest of this type in the Musée Royal de l'Afrique Central (fig. 89), which is given no attribution, has somewhat stockier proportions and a shallow, flattish platform combined with very long flaps. The carved faces on the flaps are in a style that is reminiscent of Cokwe or Lunda reliefs. Bastin illustrates one of these in her work on

Cokwe decorative arts (Bastin 1961, fig. 151), also taken from a headrest, but one that is structurally quite distinct from these. On the base of this headrest there is a figure composed of diamond-shaped head and body with linearly rendered, long, bent limbs engraved into the surface. As a whole, this example does not show the sculptural finesse evident in the Yaka and Teke examples, and in much other Cokwe–Lunda figurative carving, but both the figure's style and the rectangular shape of the platform suggest Cokwe–Lunda manufacture.[39]

A further southwards extension of this headrest type is evidenced through four headrests collected by the Misses Powell-Cotton (figs. 90–93) in southern Angola among the Wila in 1936–37.[40] Two of these (figs. 90 & 91) have their conical bases clearly demarcated from the supporting column, and oval platforms that curve nominally upwards to their ends, but which have a pronounced curvature on the transverse axis. Three examples have engraved decoration on the base (figs. 90, 92 & 93). One of these (fig. 92) has an almost-tiered base, separated into two horizontal sections, a very clearly delineated, but fat, collar-like column and a curved platform. The third example (fig. 93), however, is the only one that does not have a delineated column: the base flows directly into the platform, which has a flat upper surface.[41] All these examples are hollowed out underneath, and in one (fig. 94), there are traces of a white fatty substance in the hollow. Significant, perhaps, both to the cruder execution of these headrests and their function, is the fact that they were carved from what appears to be a much softer and more porous wood than the Yaka or Teke examples of the same type, and than two other headrests collected by the Misses Powell-Cotton in southern Angola among the Wila. These are solid, heavy, hard-wood block forms, documented as 'men's headrests, *otchintiamino*', with the remark that 'women's headrests are of a different form'.[42] It is probable that the examples with conical bases are women's headrests, reflecting a gender differentiation in the style of headrests similar to that recorded among Ethiopian and Somali groups. Further support for this supposition comes from a recent set of these headrests acquired by the University of the Witwatersrand Art Galleries in 2003, whose accompanying documentation identifies them as women's headrests.

Headrests of this type collected among the Himba of Namibia and Angola also have some recorded gender differentiation, but here it is not certain what the markers of gender are. The earliest accessioned example found in this research, in MuseumAfrika (Johannesburg), dates to before 1951. It has a very short column, a hollow bell-shaped base covered with incised and blackened geometrical decoration, and a rectangular platform covered with incised lines (Wanless 1985:231). Two examples in the University of the Witwatersrand Art Galleries (figs. 95 & 96) have cylindrical bases without columns, but with clearly articulated platforms. One (fig. 95) has a 'tiered' base/support, with the lower section divided into panels of alternating designs, using engraved lines and small round dots arranged in lines. A similar design is found on the underside of the platform, which is shield-shaped. The other example is completely plain, with the conical base flattening towards the juncture with the platform, which is markedly butterfly-shaped. Both examples are hollowed out under the base. The plain example (fig. 96) is recorded as being a man's headrest, so here the gender differentiation could be construed as resting on the presence or absence of decoration on the headrest rather than on its structural qualities.[43]

Another example of a closely related form (fig. 97), albeit an isolated one, suggests that this type was known further eastwards, possibly among Luba speakers. Acquired by the British Museum from the Wellcome Collection, it was recorded as having been collected by 'Steans' in 1907 and attributed to the 'BaLuba [i.e. Luba]/Nyangire'. The documentation suggests that it was 'used also as a cup',[44] presumably referring to the hollowed-out, bell-shaped base, which supports the butterfly-shaped platform without an intervening column. It has a carved decorative band of chevron/interlace around the lower end of the base and herringbone designs in panels on the ends of the platform, both of which, together with the form of the platform, suggest a Songye/Luba origin. These decorative elements are executed with a far greater degree of technical refinement than the Wila examples collected by the Misses Powell-Cotton or the later Himba examples.

One of the features common to most western Central African examples of the larger category of columned headrests, the three-dimensional sculptural embellishment of the base and the column, is not found in the Wila and Himba examples discussed above, and this clearly separates them from other DRC and Angolan examples of this type. In fact, their closest relatives are forms found in Ethiopia, e.g. figures 44, 50, 51 and 55. While acknowledging that drawings tend to create a particular kind of unity, this comparison nevertheless reveals particular structural similarities. They contrast quite strongly with another group of headrests from north-eastern and central-south-eastern DRC which, while following the same overall pattern, show a much greater elaboration of both base and column than either the Angolan/eastern DRC or Ethiopian examples.

For example, the headrests in figures 98 and 99 are distinguished by the greater height of the column in proportion to the base. The earliest recorded example is illustrated by Maes (1929, pl. I, fig. 16), (fig. 98), who suggests that it has the attributes of the 'Bateke [i.e. Teke]-Bayanzi', although it is documented as having been collected in 1912 'among the Mangbetu' in the 'Ituri district'. It is also quite different from the Teke examples he published (e.g. figs. 78–80) in its degree of elaboration of both base and column. A similar example, also from the Musée Royal de l'Afrique Central (fig. 99), with tiered base, elaborate column and similarly shaped platform, with a convex upper surface, is given a provenance of 'Kasai, Sapo-Kanwamba'. The height of the conical base in these two examples is matched in only a few others of this type that can be securely provenanced to Kasai or Shaba. Two of these, in the Musée Royal de l'Afrique Central, appear to have quite diverse origins. One (fig. 100) has a tiered base with an elongated, cotton-reel-shaped column, a butterfly platform with decorated ends, and an attribution to 'Kwango Popokabaka', while the other (fig. 101), with a flaring conical base, a double-cotton-reel column and a butterfly platform, is provenanced to 'Shaba, Kinda Kamina'. A third (fig. 102), quite extraordinary example has a tiered base with raised relief decoration of diamonds within triangles, a column articulated into cotton-reel shapes and bulbous rings, with some elements of the base and column stained a darker colour. The ends of the butterfly platform are carved with herringbone relief designs similar to those on many Songye and Luba headrests discussed in the next chapter. Collected with a large group of other headrests in 1952, this example appears to have come from the region 'Kasai Kapanga', with a possible attribution to the Songye.[45]

These three examples have, by virtue of their articulated columns and elaborate platforms, a close affinity to headrests of the second category of columned headrests. However, in the second category, the base is clearly articulated from the column, always following relatively circumscribed manners of elaboration on the constant themes of the circular base and the articulated column.[46] That they are distributed across a large area of the DRC encompassing the Kasai, Kwango and Katanga regions suggests that the stylistic distinctions that one can draw by separating the various formal elements of the headrest from one another will inevitably become very fragile. Placing of all these headrests under a single type, with sub-sections, rather than separating them into distinct categories is therefore a consequence of the recognition that all of them are based in the same design template.

CHAPTER 4 *The Geographical and Chronological Distribution of the Columned Headrest* | 93

## Southern Africa: Challenging the category: Figures 103–108

That examples of columned headrests with conical bases were made relatively early in South Africa can be established through reference to Müller and Snelleman's publication of a group of headrests from what they called the 'Zambèze' region[47] (*c.* 1892, pl. XIV, no. 10), in which the columnar support flares outwards to its base without any clear demarcation between the two. Its distinguishing feature is the platform with pendant flaps from the short ends, something that is very common on, but not exclusive to, some headrests from the south-east African region.

Six Southern African examples, which may be fitted into either of the present study's columnar categories quite comfortably, can therefore also be used to challenge these categories quite strongly. Of these, four follow the conical base pattern closely; one is attributed to the Shona (fig. 103), the second is firmly provenance to Shona territory (fig. 104), the third was collected in 'Southern Rhodesia' (i.e. Zimbabwe) and is attributed to the 'Mashona?' (i.e. Shona), (fig. 105), and the fourth is placed in the ubiquitous, inaccurate and opprobrious ethnic category 'Kaffern' (fig. 106). The first three all have relatively short conical bases, with the base and column clearly articulated from each other in three of the four, and in each case the column is elaborated with three-dimensional protrusions or relief patterns. The platforms are butterfly-shaped, and all but one have pendant flaps from the undersides of their short ends, something that is found on many Shona and Tsonga headrests.[48] In all of these examples, the proportions of the bases might allow them to be placed in the first category of columned headrests, but other features, such as the articulation of the column, would suggest that they belong rather among the columned headrests discussed in chapter 5.

Another example that may have corresponded closely to these in its column and platform elements was destroyed in the Second World War, but is known from a drawing in the Hamburg Museum für Völkerkunde register (fig. 107). But it has two distinctive features that might place it fairly firmly in the second category: the domical base is distinctively lobed — i.e. it is not a circle in plan and is definitely not conical. Like many other Southern African objects accessioned early in this museum, it was attributed to the 'Betschuaan' (i.e. Tswana),[49] but it may have been of Kalanga (Shona) origin, there being a significant Kalanga presence in Botswana. The issue of attribution of these headrests to one or other of the ethnic groups in the area of Zimbabwe, Mozambique and the north-eastern parts of South Africa has been addressed by Dewey (1991; 1993), Becker (1990; 1999) and Nettleton (1985;

1991), and is far from resolved. The fact that there was a fair degree of interchange of forms within the general area has been suggested by Becker (1999), and this seems to be the most promising route to follow. Although most of the Southern African examples of the columned type appear to fall onto the Shona side of the ethnic divide between Shona and Tsonga, this is by no means a fixed relation. An example published by Müller and Snelleman (c. 1892, pl. XV, no. 3), which has a flat circular base with its edge carved as a rim of triangular prismatic projections — a pattern repeated vertically on the boss encircling the centre of the column — would possibly fit best into the next category of headrests (the columned type discussed in chapter 5), because of the explicit differentiation of base and column, but would be most comfortably distinguished as Tsonga because of its flat base. Similarly, the headrest in figure 108, which has a lobed base, a very fat column with raised conical bosses alternating with relief ridges of diamond shapes in vertical panels on one side and horizontal rows of zig-zag patterns on the other, is probably identifiable as Shona by virtue of its chamfered, lobed base with its central triangular projection, and the distinctive relief patterns on the upper surface of the platform.

This does, however, demonstrate that, in examples from the headrests type with conical base and column supports, elements that may be used to link them with a particular ethnic or linguistic grouping are rarely found in the structural composition of the headrest itself, but rather in such details as decorative designs, the presence or absence of platform flaps, and, in some instances, a particular proportion of base to support, or shape of platform. The differences in structural conformation *between* these two categories of columned headrests are thus more immediately evident than the differences that occur *within* the categories themselves, and are even less noticeable at the level of individual examples of both sub-types that may be attributed to a single ethnic group. This level of differentiation will be further examined in the next chapter, which takes the second of the categories of headrests with column supports as the objects through which to further examine questions of authenticity and history.

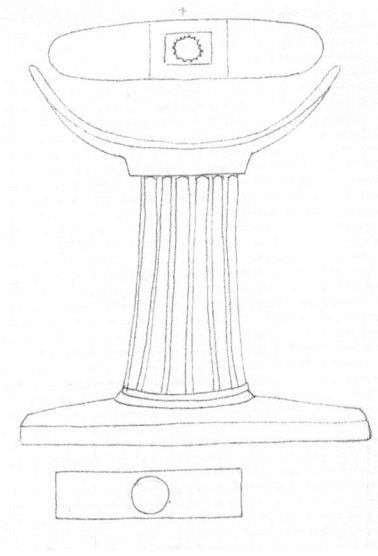
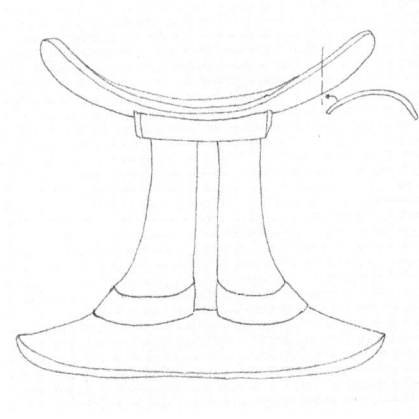

27  Brussels, Musée des Arts et Histoire, Ancient Egypt, *headrest of a contemporary of Pharaoh Pepi I, Old Kingdom*, alabaster, c. 2200 BCE.

28  Brussels, Musée des Arts et Histoire, Ancient Egypt, *headrest, Old Kingdom*, wood, metal, 14 cm h.

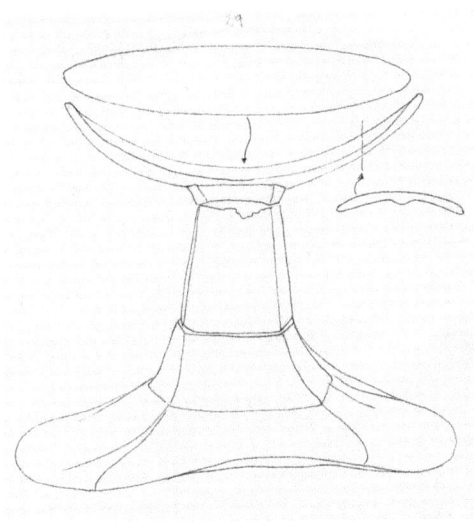

29  British Museum (no. 1949.46.689), Oldman Collection, *Ancient Egypt, Old Kingdom*, wood, 13 cm h.

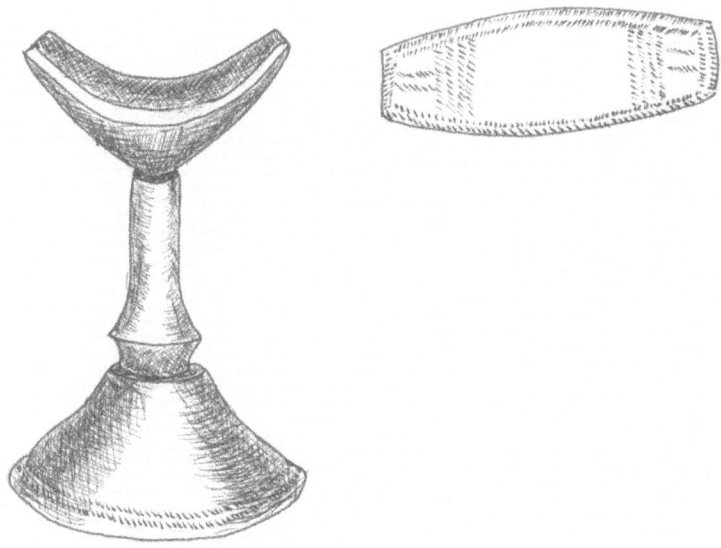

30  British Museum (no. 1893 7.15.16), collected by J. T. H. Bent, *Ethiopia*, wood, 15.5 cm h.

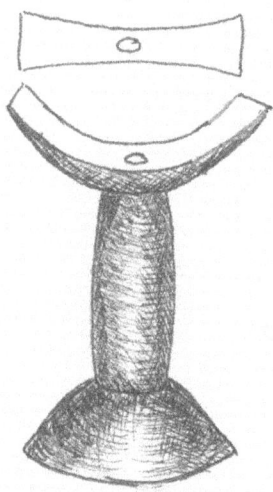

31  Oxford, Pitt Rivers Museum (no. 1940.12.532), collected by Charles G. Seligman, *Upper Egypt, Bisharin(?) near Assuan*, wood, 15 cm h.

CHAPTER 4  *Illustrations: figures 27–102*  |  **97**

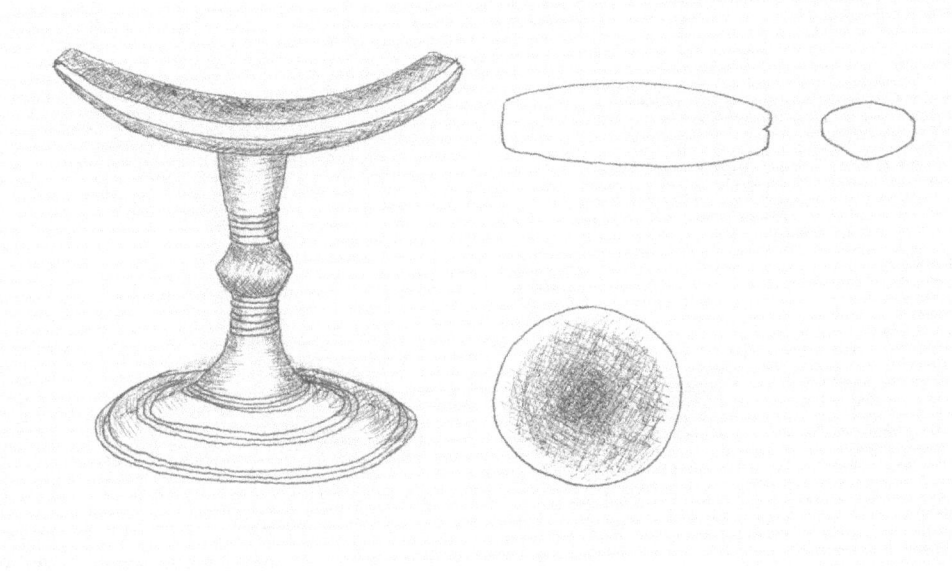

32   British Museum (no. 1972 Af11.5), collected by Brigadier General Matthews, donated by Mrs Collins, *Somalia*, wood, 16.5 cm h.

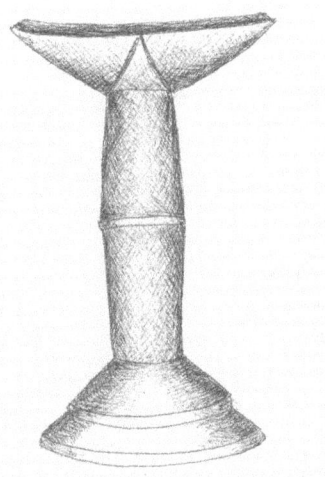

33   British Museum (no. 1939 Af30-42), collected by Dr S. F. Nadel, *c.* 1938, *Anglo-Egyptian Sudan, Jebel District, Nuba Hills, Ko'aub*, wood, 13.75 cm h.

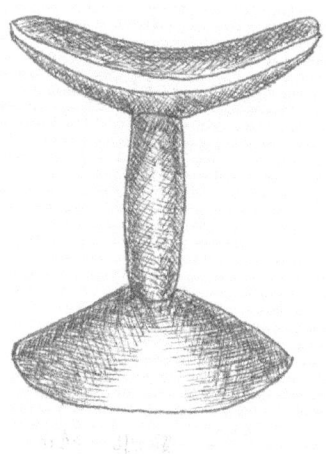

34  Van der Stappen (1996:41, no. 62), *Collected 1995*, 'Ethiopia', wood, 17 cm h.

35  Van der Stappen (1996:42, no. 66), *Collected 1994*, 'Ethiopia', wood, 14 cm h.

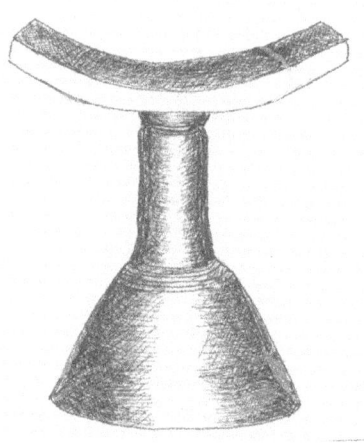

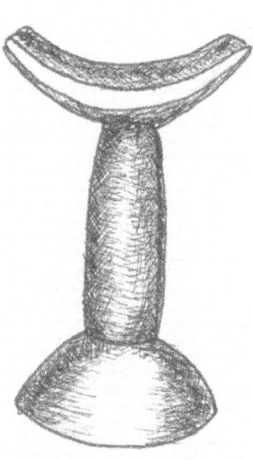

36  Van der Stappen (1996:58, no. 117), *Collected 1993*, 'Ethiopia', 'Oromo', wood, 14 cm h.

37  Munich, Staatlisches Museum für Völkerkunde (no. K D 12), *Tanzania/Zaire, Matengo*, wood, 15 cm h.

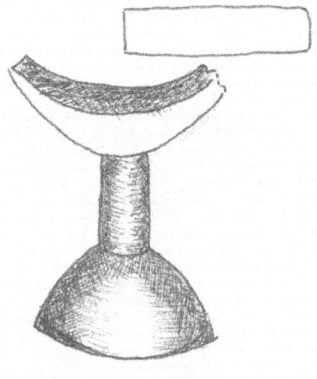 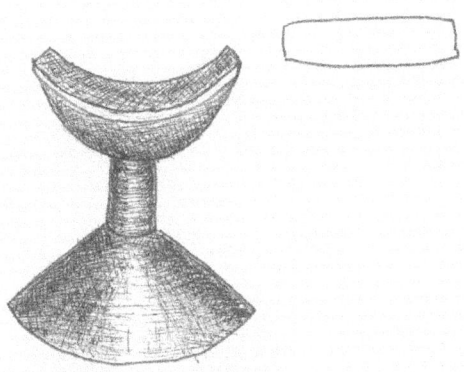

38  Munich, Staatlisches Museum für Völkerkunde (no. 14.4.36), acquired from Rattwinkel, 1914, *German East Africa, Wagowa,* wood, fibre, 13 cm h.

39  Munich, Staatlisches Museum für Völkerkunde (no. 28.1.111), acquired from Küsters, *Tanganyika (Tanzania), Namalengo (1928), msamiro,* wood, 11.5 cm h.

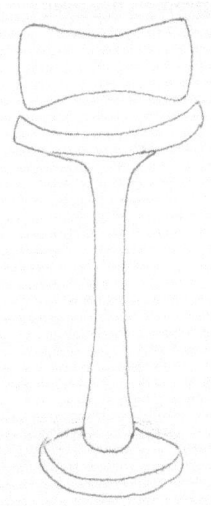 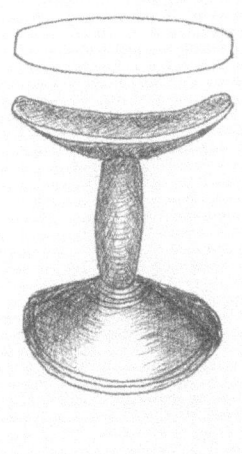 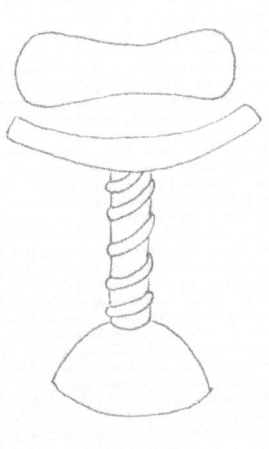

40  British Museum (no. 1934 05076), collected by Major Hinde, 'Kenya', wood, 14 cm h.

41  Brighton Museum (no. R844/54), collected by A. G. Mumford, accessioned 1908, *Mumford travelled through the Belgian Congo and made copious notes on the objects he collected,* Democratic Republic of the Congo, *Katanga, Luba,* wood, 16 cm h.

42  Brighton Museum (no. R1437/3), collected by Rev. Dr Polly, accessioned 1913, *Zimbabwe(?) Mashonaland/Shona,* wood, 14 cm h.

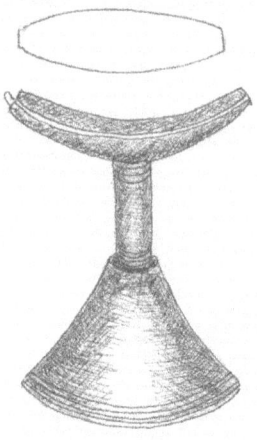
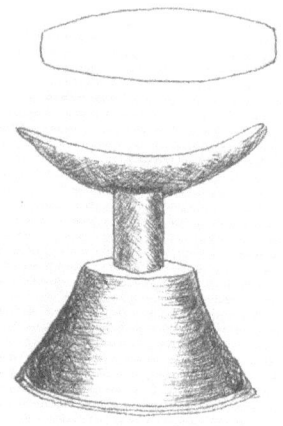
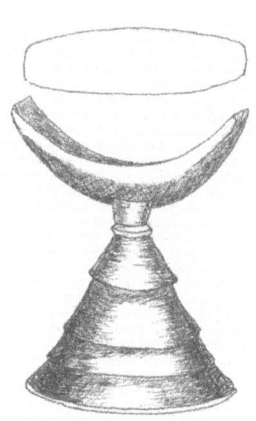

43 Munich, Staatlisches Museum für Völkerkunde (no. 13.68.14), 'Ethiopia', wood, 16 cm h.

44 British Museum (no. 1954 Af23 TB 182), (Wellcome Collection, no. 41391 A), 'Ethiopia', wood, beads, 14 cm h.

45 British Museum (no. 1954 Af23 TB 182), (Wellcome Collection, no. 41391 B), 'Ethiopia', wood, pigment, 17 cm h.

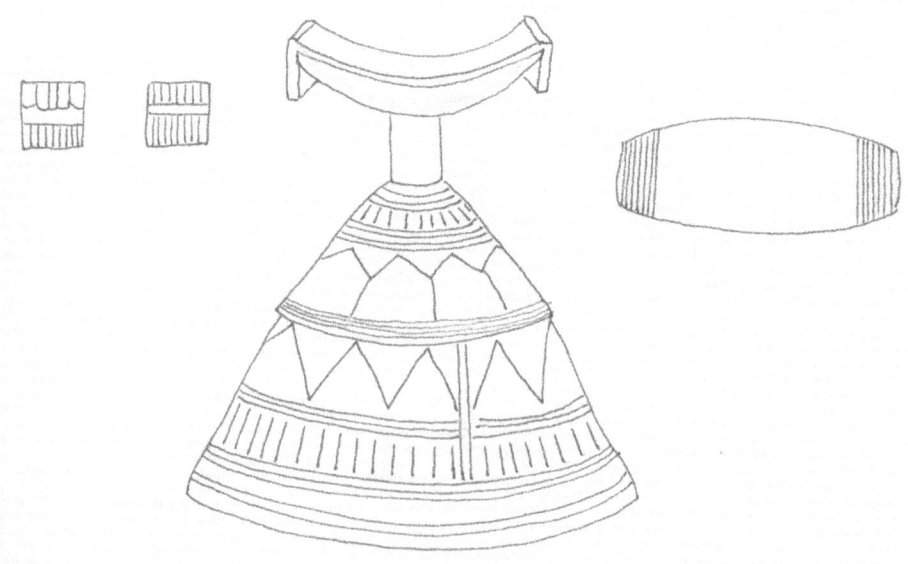

46 Musée Royal de l'Afrique Central (no. 73.65.1), 'Ethiopia', wood, 16 cm h.

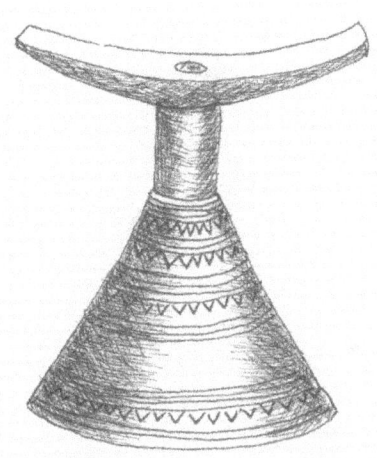

47 Van der Stappen (1996:60, no. 123), *Collected 1993 in the country of the Oromo language*, Ethiopia, Oromo(?), wood, 17 cm h.

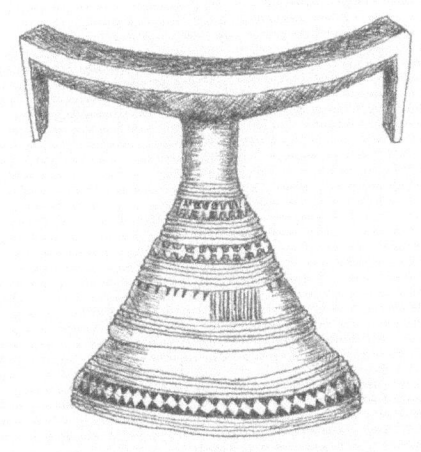

48 Van der Stappen (1996:70, no. 165), *Collected 1991 in the Lake region, used by women*, Ethiopia, 'Arsi', wood, 18 cm h.

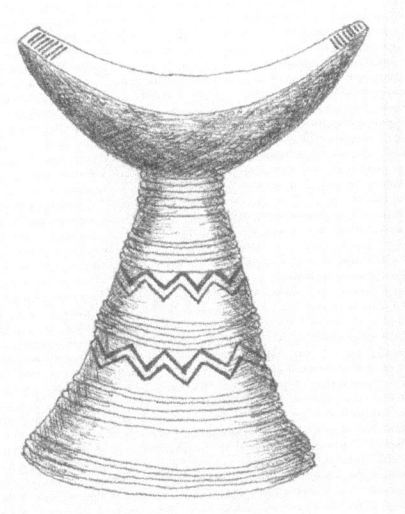

49 Van der Stappen (1996:58, no. 116), *Collected 1994*, Ethiopia, 'Oromo', wood, 13 cm h.

**102** | AFRICAN DREAM MACHINES

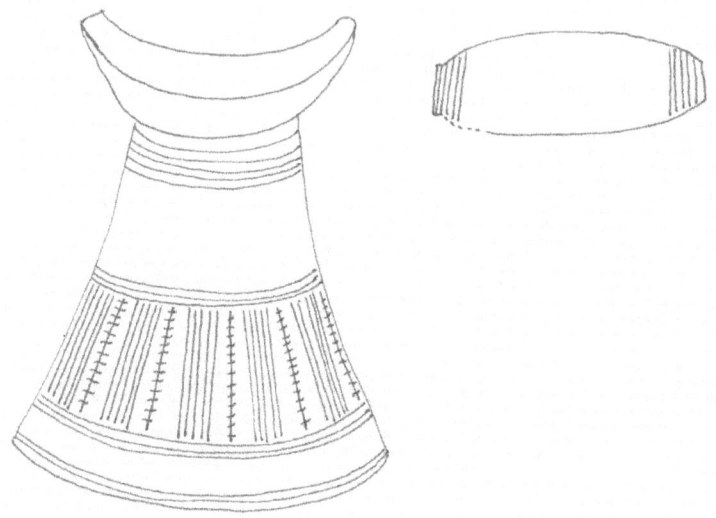

50   Musée Royal de l'Afrique Central (no. 74.57.3), 'Ethiopia', wood, 17 cm h.

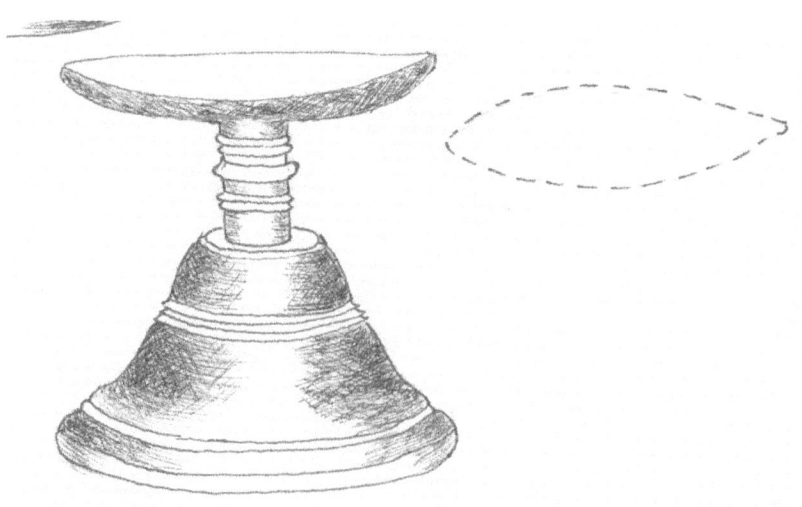

51   Van der Stappen (1996:44, no. 74), *Collected 1991*, 'Ethiopia', 'Guragué' (Gurage), wood, 19 cm h.

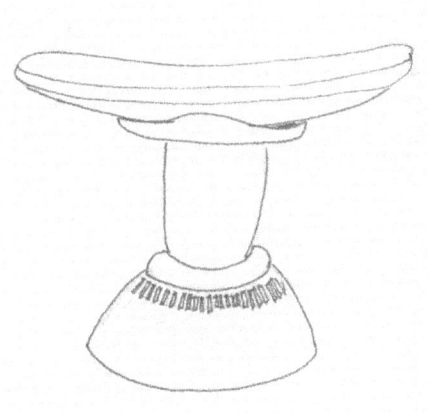

52  Van der Stappen (1996:94, no. 243), *Collected 1995 (Wassero Village), fidéna ... only used by men*, Ethiopia, 'Guragué' (Gurage), wood, 15 cm h.

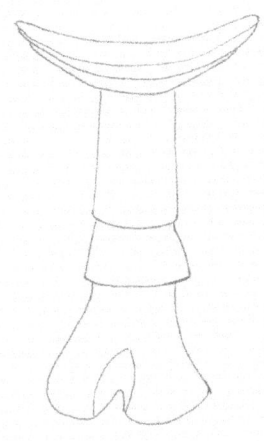

53  Van der Stappen (1996:93, no. 237), *Collected 1995 (Wassero Village), fidéna ... only used by men*, Ethiopia, 'Afar', wood, 17 cm h.

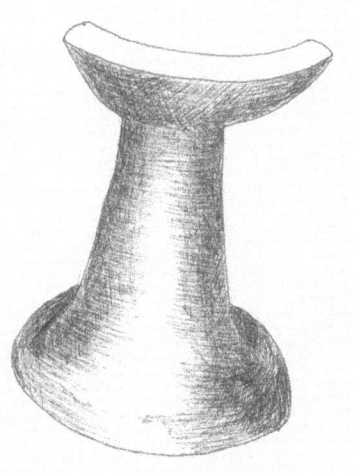

54  Van der Stappen (1996:94, no. 241), *Collected 1995 (Wassero Village), used by men*, Ethiopia, 'Afar', wood, 16 cm h.

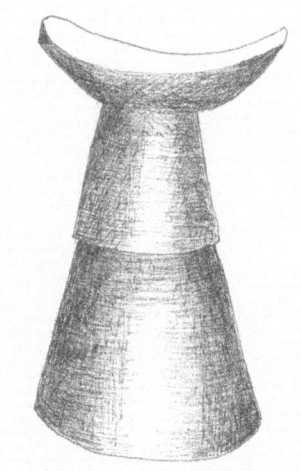

55  Van der Stappen (1996:93, no. 239), *Collected 1995 (Wassero Village)*, Ethiopia, ' Afar', wood, 16 cm h.

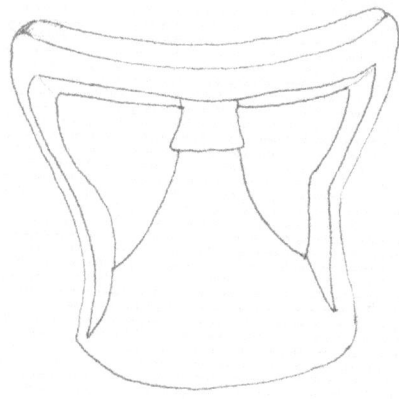

56 Van der Stappen (1989:61, no. 127), *Collected 1993*, Ethiopia, 'Oromo(?)', wood, 16 cm h.

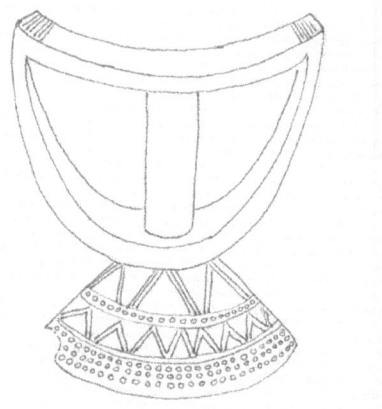

57 Van der Stappen (1996:61, no. 128), *Collected 1993*, Ethiopia, 'Oromo(?)', wood, 17 cm h.

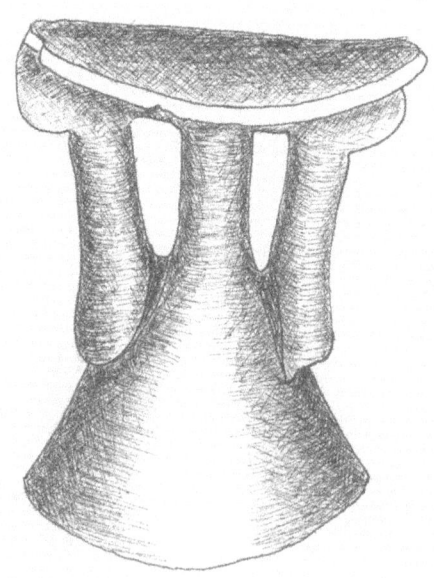

58 Van der Stappen (1989:92, no. 234), *Collected 1991 in the village of Ali Bete, used by men*, Ethiopia, 'Afar', wood, 14 cm h.

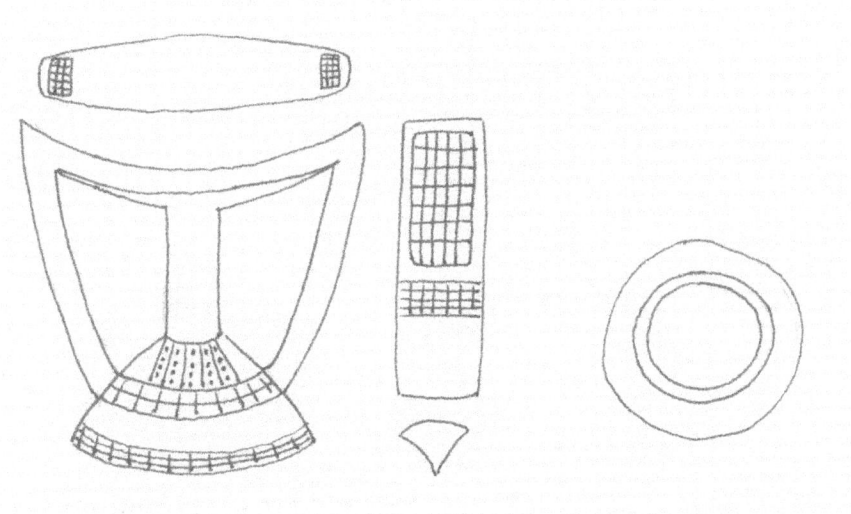

59  British Museum (no. 1949 Af46.739), *Belgian Congo* (Democratic Republic of the Congo), wood, 16.2 cm h.

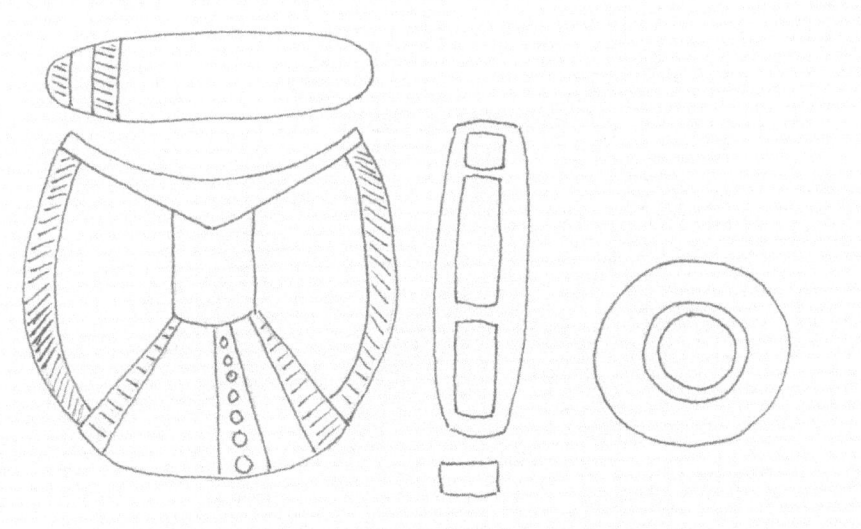

60  British Museum (no. 1954 Af23), (Wellcome Collection, no. 31628 [TB 181]), *Ethiopia/Somaliland*, wood, 18.2 cm h.

**106** | AFRICAN DREAM MACHINES

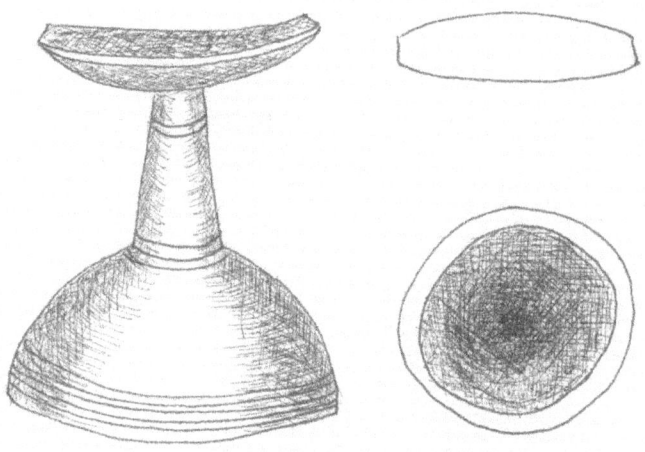

61   Oxford, Pitt Rivers Museum (no. Balfour I.35.III.168), *Collected by Balfour in Aden, donated 1905*, 'Somali?', wood, 13 cm h.

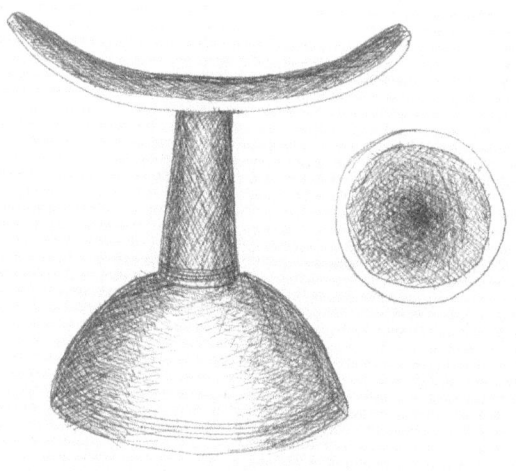

62   British Museum (no. 1928 3.3.17), collected by Major Powell-Cotton *in Addis Ababa on 27th January 1900, bought by the British Museum in 1928*, Ethiopia, wood, 18.6 cm h.

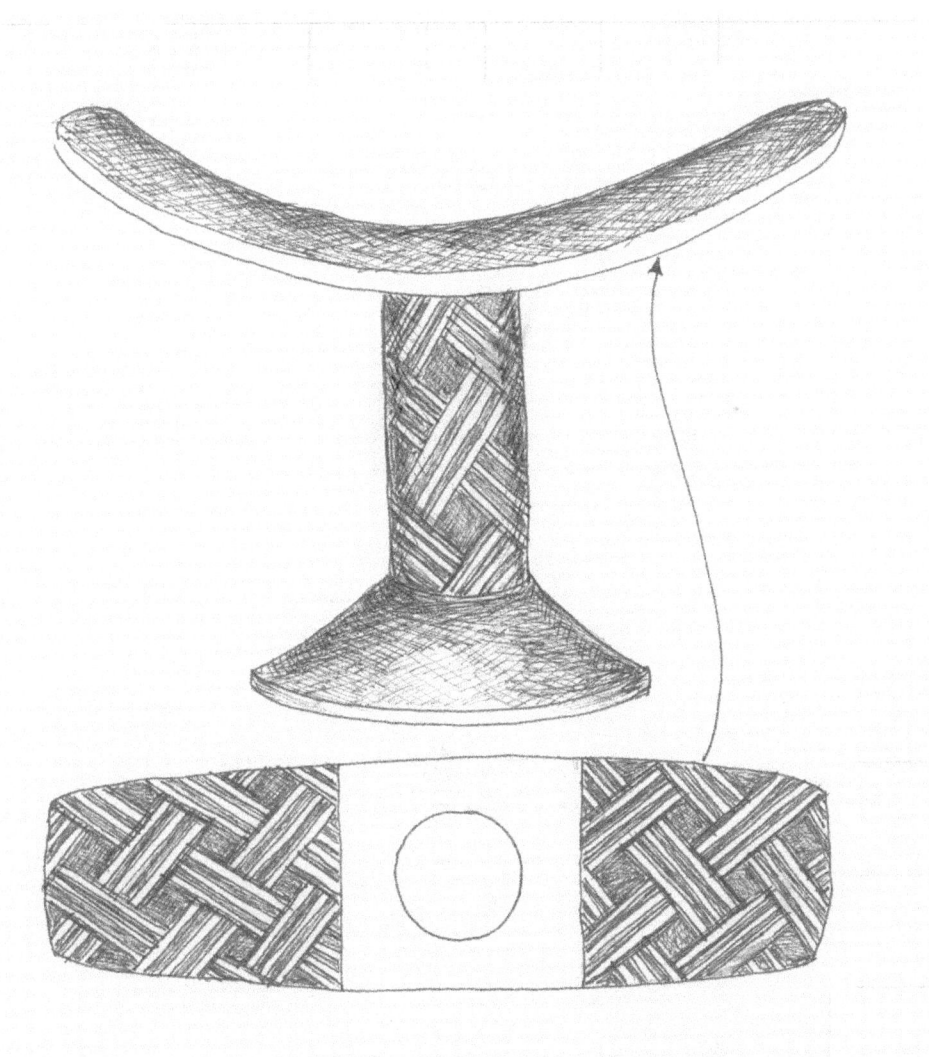

63   British Museum (no. 1934 7-17.45), collected by T. Culle, *French Somaliland/Ethiopia Border, Esa* (Issa) *Tribe/Rahale?*, wood, 14.5 cm h.

**108** | AFRICAN DREAM MACHINES

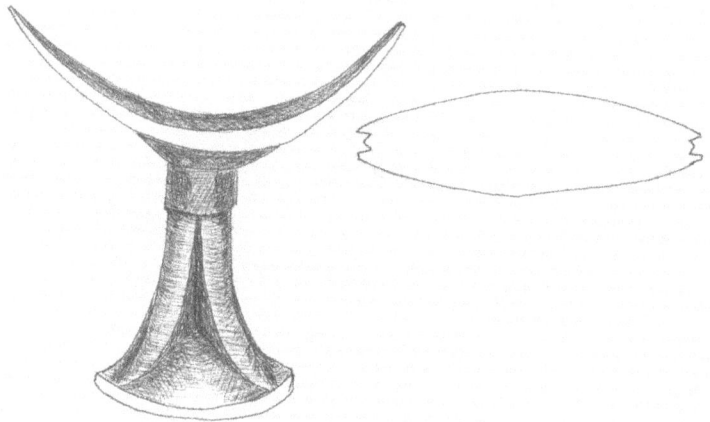

64  British Museum (no. 1928 5.9.1), collected by Lieutenant Colonel P. E. Alden, *Obtained 1923 from the Somali — ordinary type in general use*, 'British Somalia', wood, pigment, 19.5 cm h.

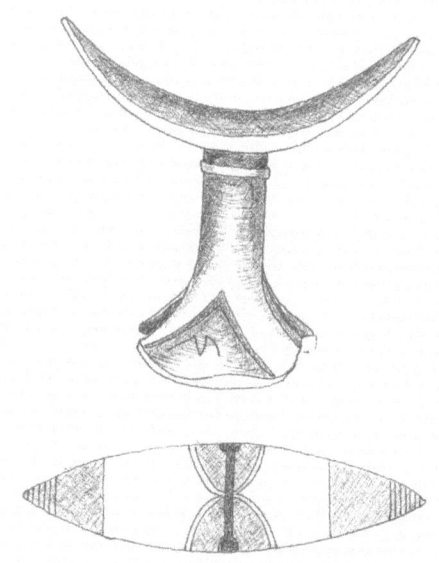

65  British Museum (no. 1928 5.9.3), collected by Lieutenant Colonel P. E. Alden, *Obtained 1923 from the Somali — ordinary type in general use*, 'British Somalia', wood, pigment, 15.2 cm h.

CHAPTER 4 *Illustrations: figures 27–102* | 109

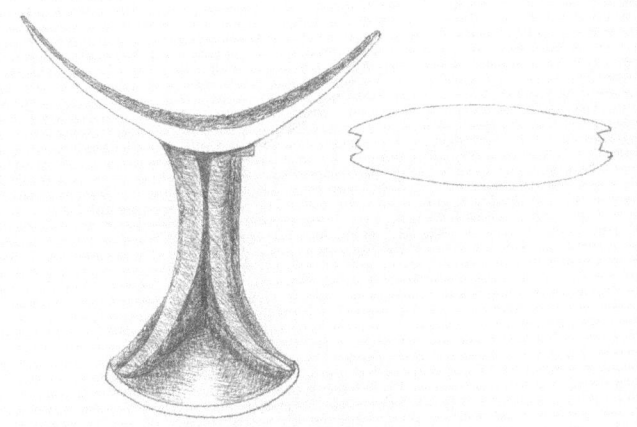

66  British Museum (no. 1934 605 145), donated by Captain Blaine, *Somali, Somali Republic (Kenya? Ethiopia?)*, wood, pigment, 21 cm h.

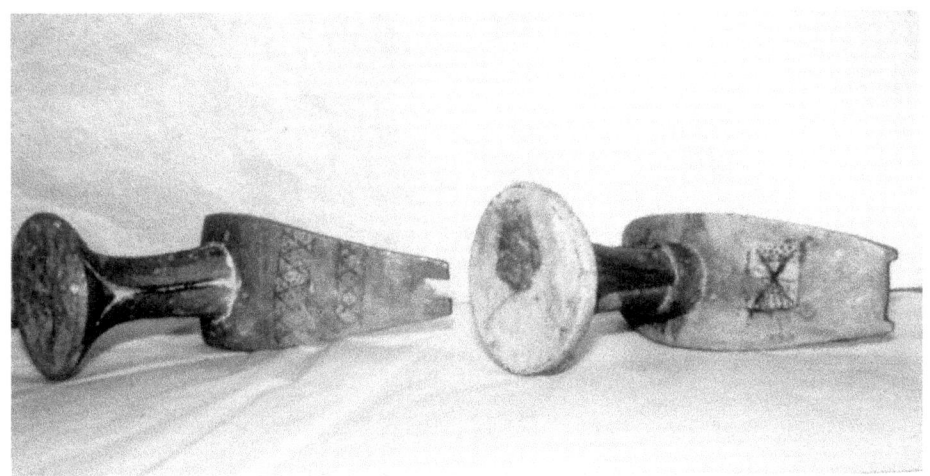

67  British Museum (no. 1935.11.08.14), collected by Major Powell-Cotton, *NE Africa, Somaliland*, wood, pigment, 17.9 cm h.

110 | AFRICAN DREAM MACHINES

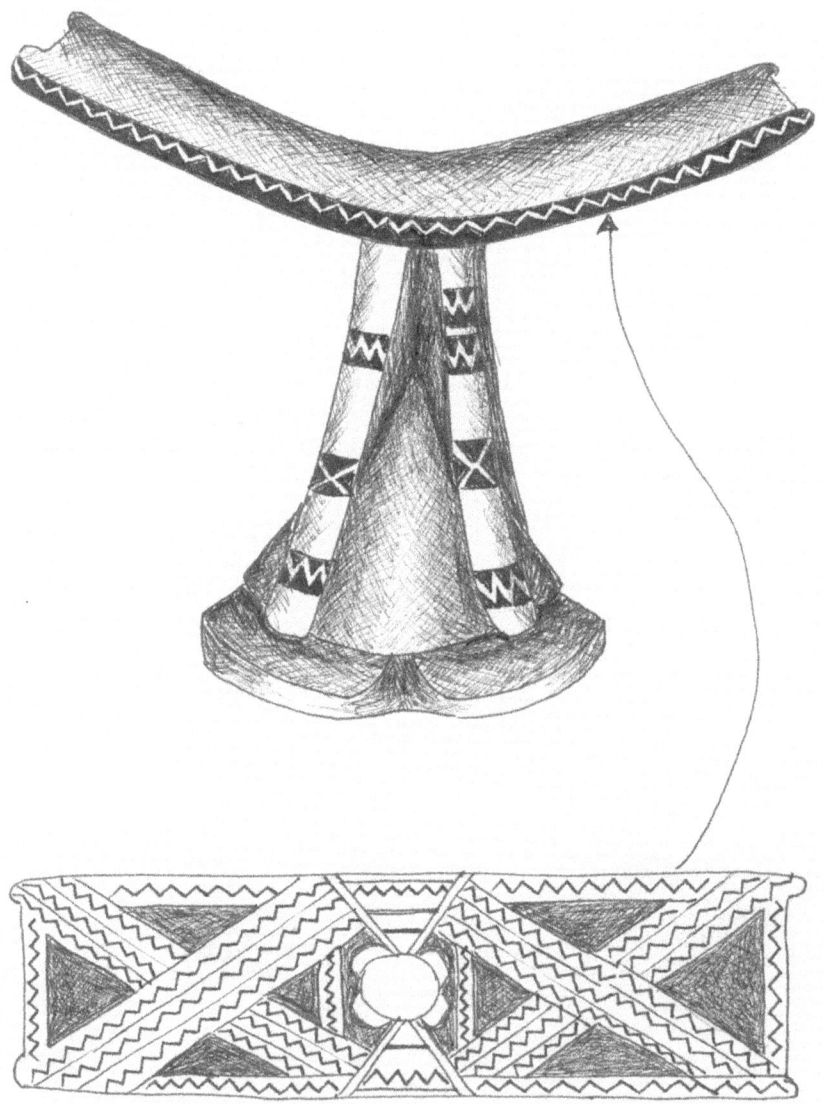

68    British Museum (no. 1954 Af23), (Wellcome Collection, TB 1800, no. 15154, B. Wells), 'Somali', wood, pigment, 16.1 cm h.

CHAPTER 4  *Illustrations: figures 27–102* | **111**

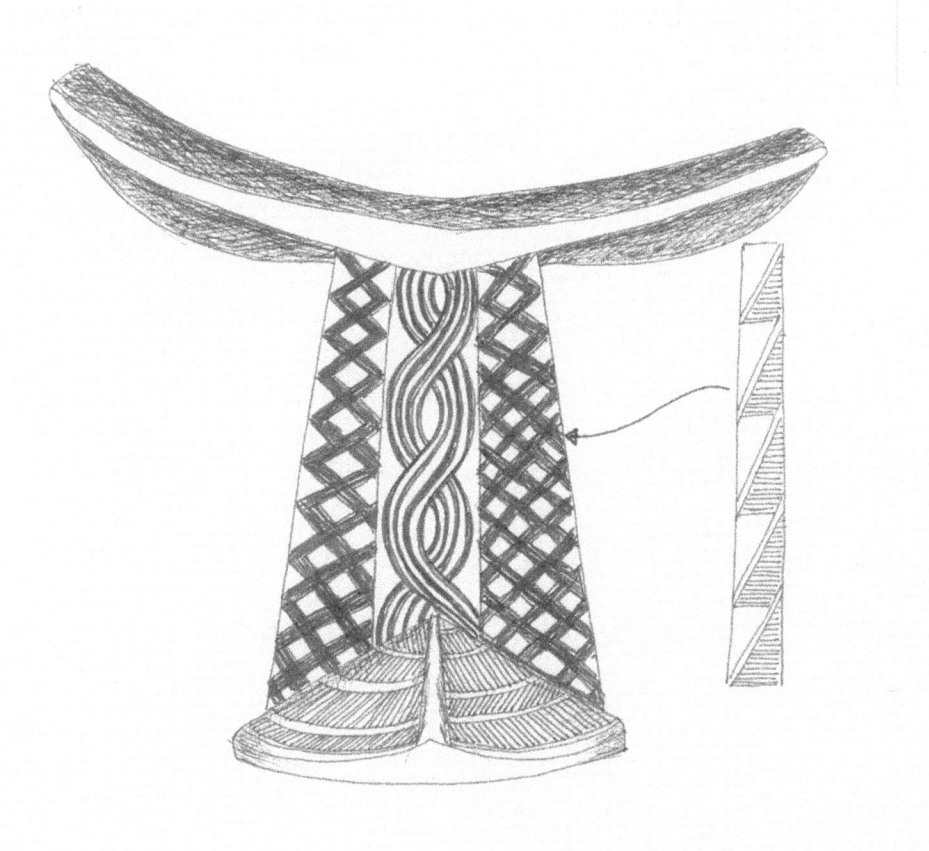

69  British Museum (no. +990), *Presented by Khedive of Egypt 1-12-78, Paris Exhibition 1878* (register entry), *Nile, Congo "Azande Tribe"* (label). *NE Africa, "Neam Neam"*, 'Somali' (attributed by M. A. Carey), wood, burning, 14 cm h.

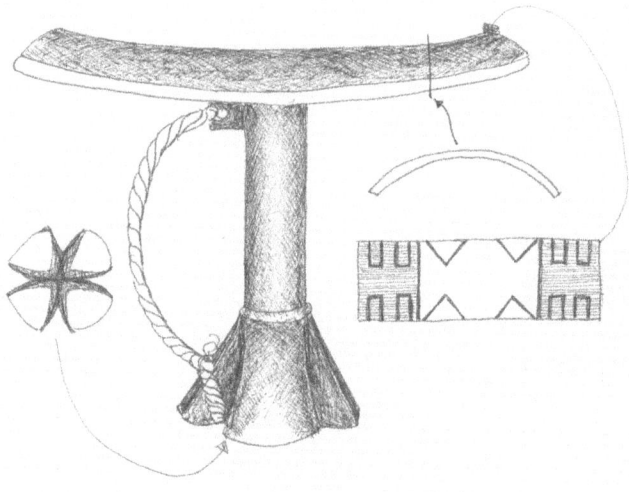

70   British Museum (no. 1923.0710.22), collected by Dr Crispin, *NE Sudan, Dinka*, wood, fibre, burning, 14 cm h.

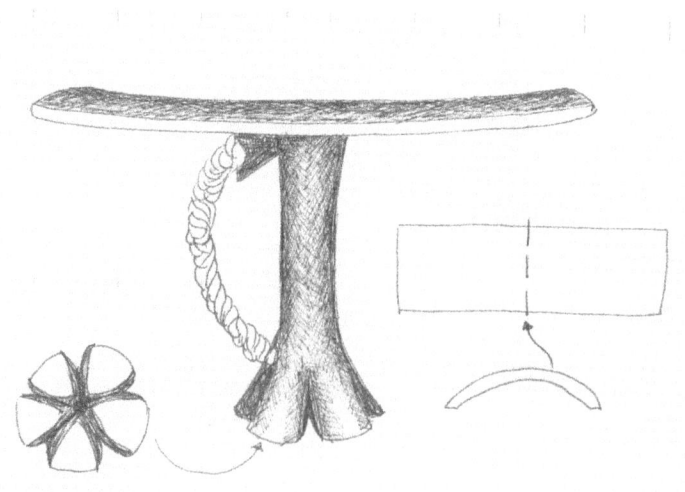

71   British Museum (no. 1954 Af23), (Wellcome Collection, no. 22497, 1902), *Uganda, Bari, Gondokoro*(?), wood, fibre, 16 cm h.

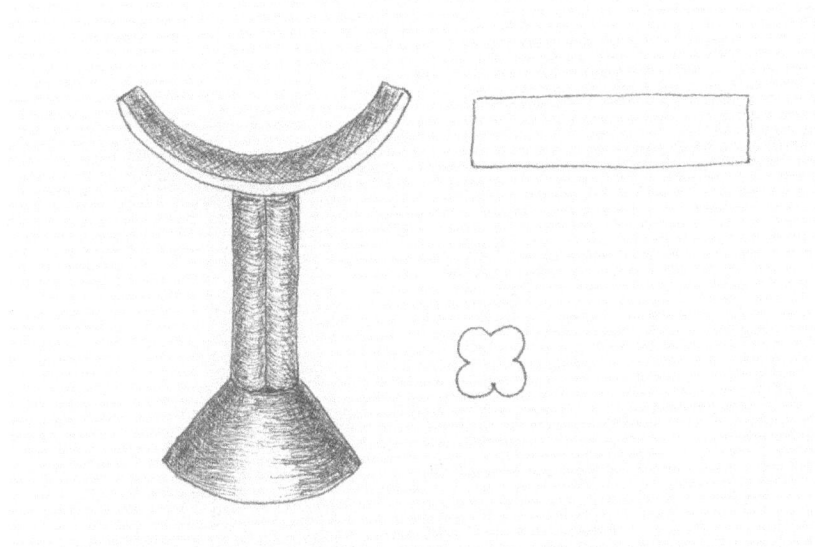

72  Munich, Staatlisches Museum für Völkerkunde (no. 26-T-1975), acquired from Theresa Prins, *Sudan, Dinka*, wood, 21 cm h.

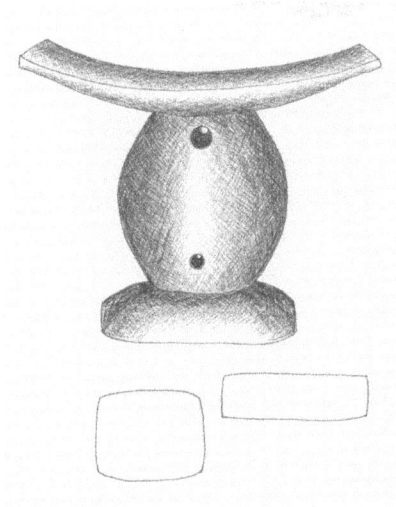

73  British Museum (no. 1935 Af30-42), collected by E. E. Evans Pritchard, *Anglo Egyptian Sudan, Eastern Jebel District, Nuba Hills, Koalit Tribes, Koa'ub*, wood, 18 cm h.

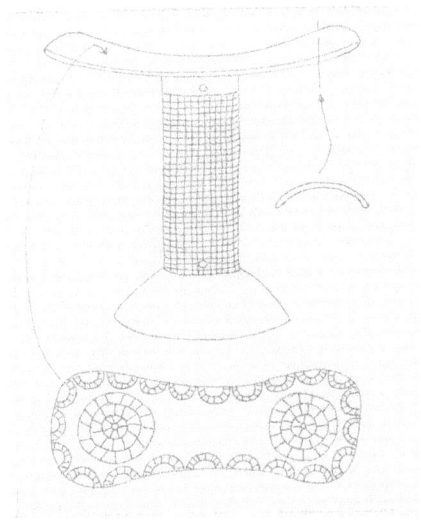

74  British Museum (no. 1934 6.5.65), collected by Captain G. Blaine, *Anglo Egyptian Sudan*, wood, 12.5 cm h.

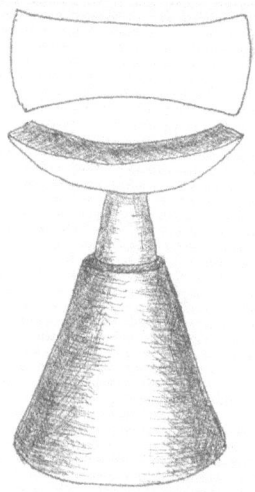

75   British Museum (no. 1907.5.28.15), collected by Emil Torday, Democratic Republic of the Congo, 'Huangana' (Hungana), wood, 20 cm h.

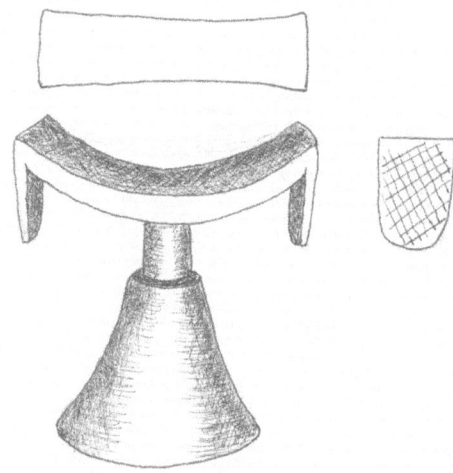

76   British Museum (no. 1907.5.28.16), collected by Emil Torday, Democratic Republic of the Congo, *Kwango-Kwilu* (region), *Northern Bambala/KotoKoto* (Northern Mbala/Kotokoto), wood, 16.4 cm h.

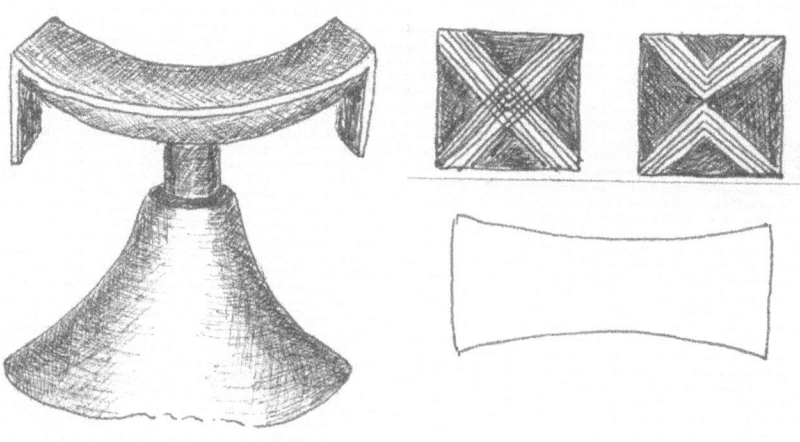

77   British Museum (no. 1907.5.28.158), collected by Emil Torday, Democratic Republic of the Congo, *Kwango-Kwilu* (region), *Northern Bambala* (Mbala), wood, 18.3 cm h.

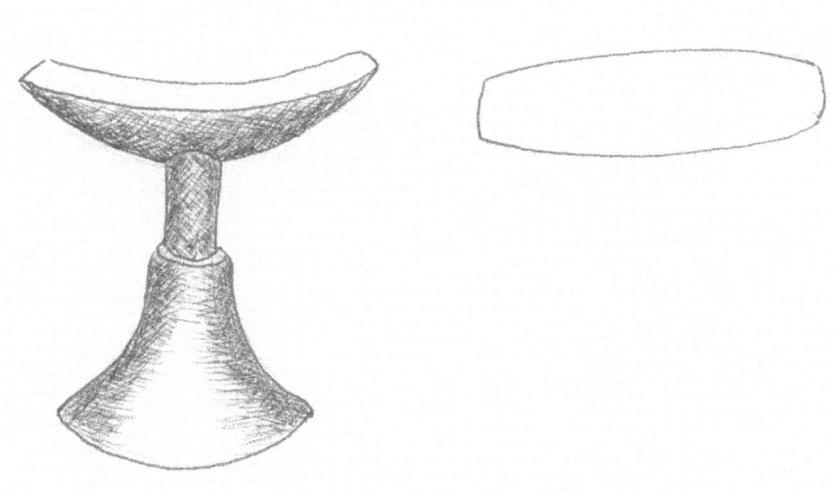

78   Musée Royal de l'Afrique Central (no. 17217), (Maes 1929, pl. I, fig. 14), Democratic Republic of the Congo, *Cataract region*, *BaTeke* (Teke), wood, 15 cm h.

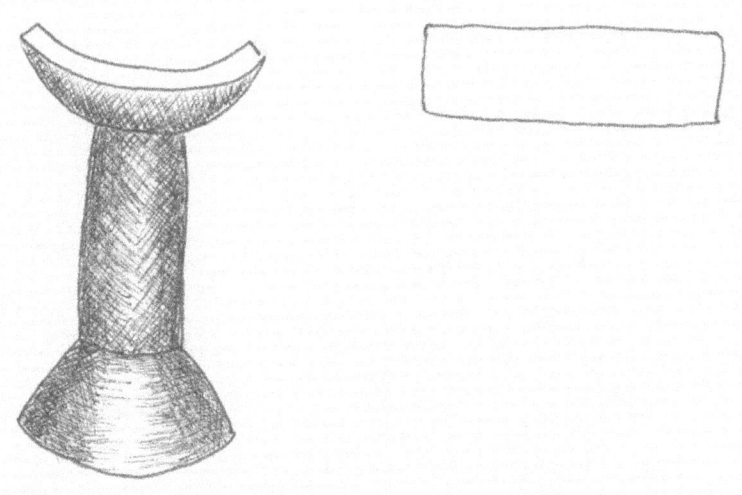

79   Musée Royal de l'Afrique Central (no. 17248), (Maes 1929: pl. I, fig. 11), Democratic Republic of the Congo, *Stanley-Pool region, Léopoldville*, *BaTeke* (Teke), wood, 17.5 cm h.

116 | AFRICAN DREAM MACHINES

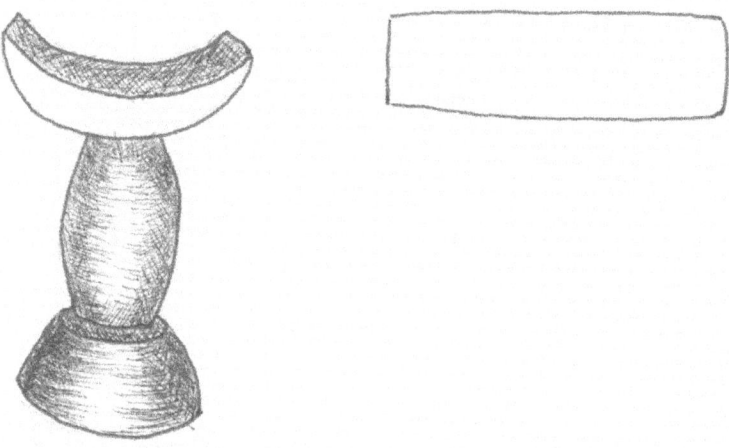

80   Musée Royal de l'Afrique Central (no. 30535), (cf. Maes 1929, pl. I, fig. 13), Democratic Republic of the Congo, 1929, *BaTeke* (Teke), wood, 15 cm h.

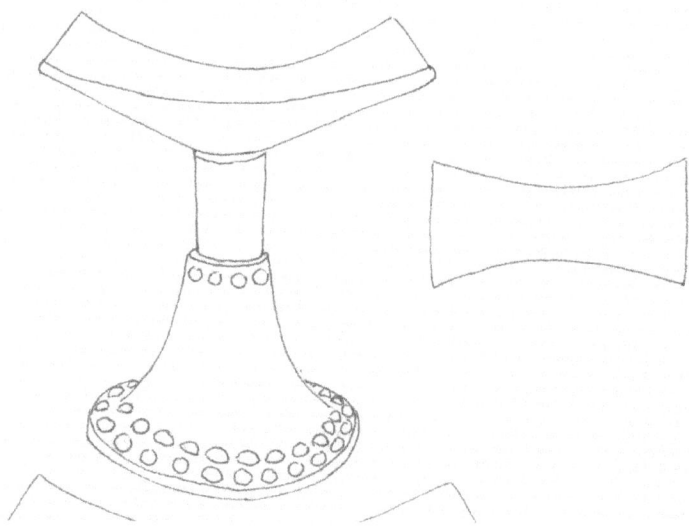

81   Musée Royal de l'Afrique Central (no. 37385), Democratic Republic of the Congo, *BaTeke* (Teke), (1890–99), wood, metal studs, 17.7 cm h.

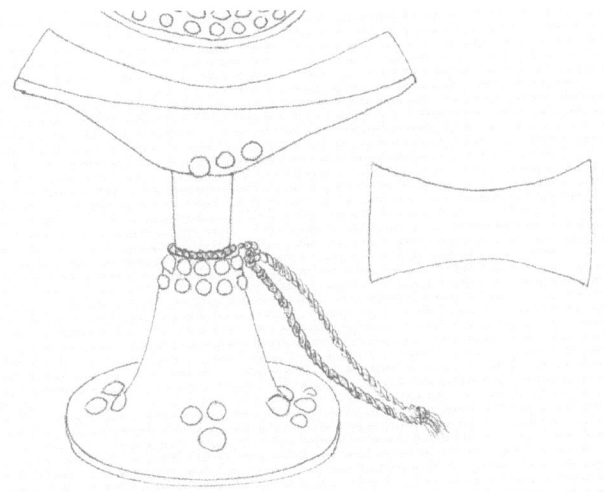

82  Musée Royal de l'Afrique Central (no. 53.74.3301), collected by Albert Maesen, *acquisitioned 1954*, Democratic Republic of the Congo, *Kingala, village of Bandundu, Bandundu, Teke*, wood, metal studs, fibre, 13.9 cm h.

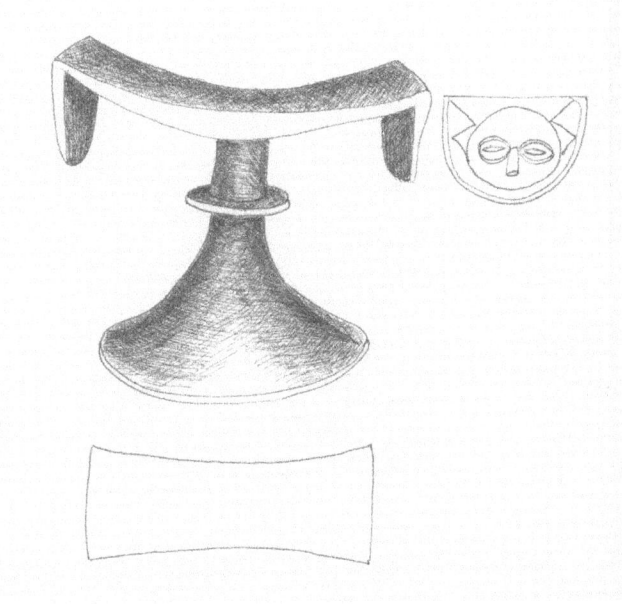

83  Musée Royal de l'Afrique Central (no. 33171), 1931, Democratic Republic of the Congo, Kwango (region), 'Yaka', wood, 12.2 cm h.

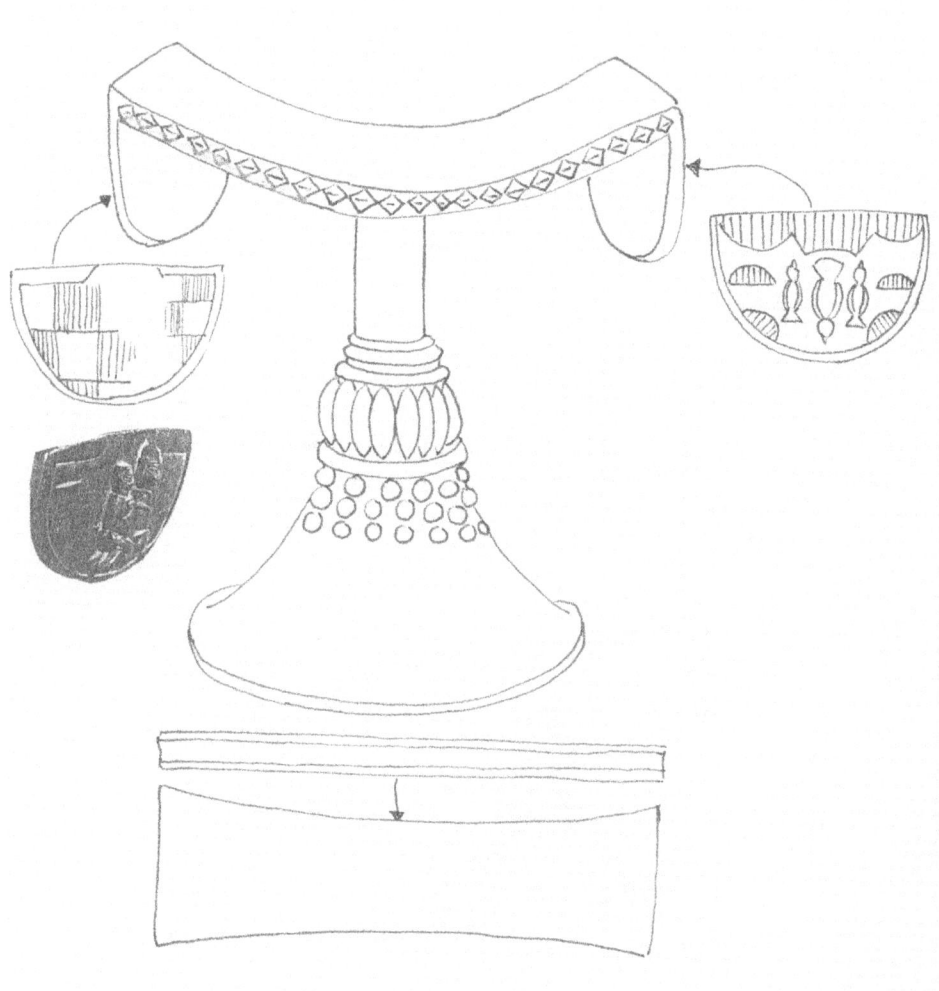

84  Musée Royal de l'Afrique Central (no. 44555), 1945, Democratic Republic of the Congo, Kwango (region), 'Yaka', wood, metal studs, 13.3 cm h.

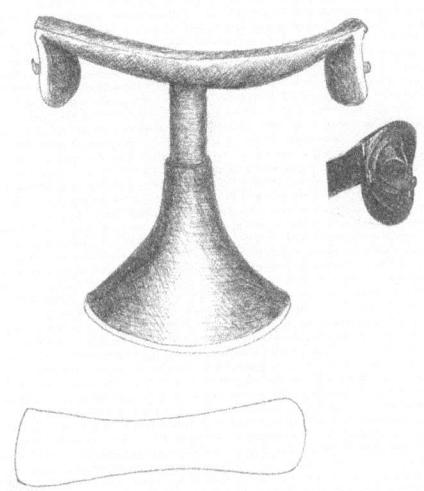
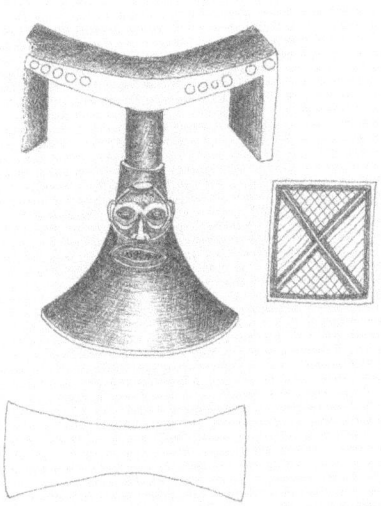

85 Musée Royal de l'Afrique Central (no. 60.39.1030), Democratic Republic of the Congo, Kwango (region), 'Yaka', wood, 15.5 cm h.

86 Musée Royal de l'Afrique Central (no. 56.10.10), Democratic Republic of the Congo, Kwango (region), 'Yaka', wood, metal studs, 15.5 cm h.

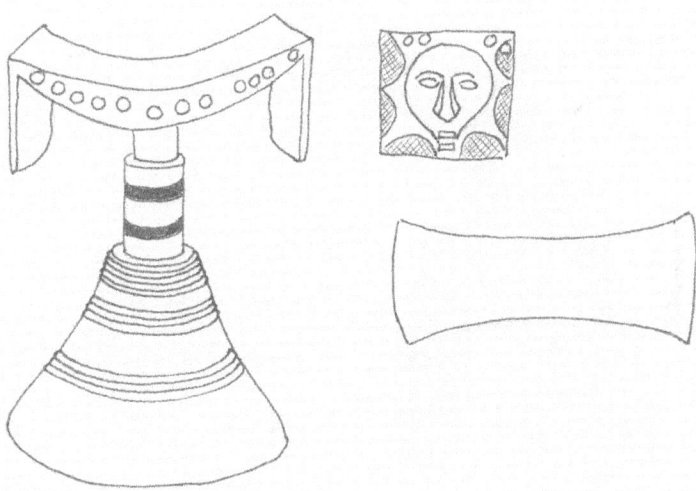

87 British Museum (no. 1949 Af43.352), Democratic Republic of the Congo, Oldman Collection, 'Yaka' (attributed by William Fagg), wood, metal studs, 14.8 cm h.

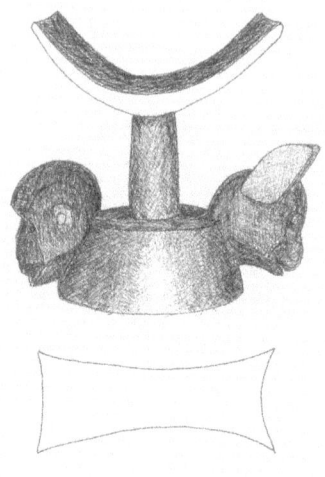 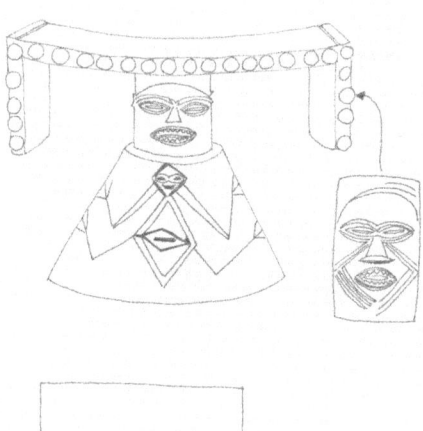

88 British Museum (no. 1954 Af23.1832), (Wellcome Collection, no. 8584), Democratic Republic of the Congo, 'Yaka', wood, metal studs, 18 cm h.

89 Musée Royal de l'Afrique Central (no. 40544), (no museum attribution), 1945, Democratic Republic of the Congo/Angola? Cokwe/Lunda?, wood, metal studs, 11.3 cm h.

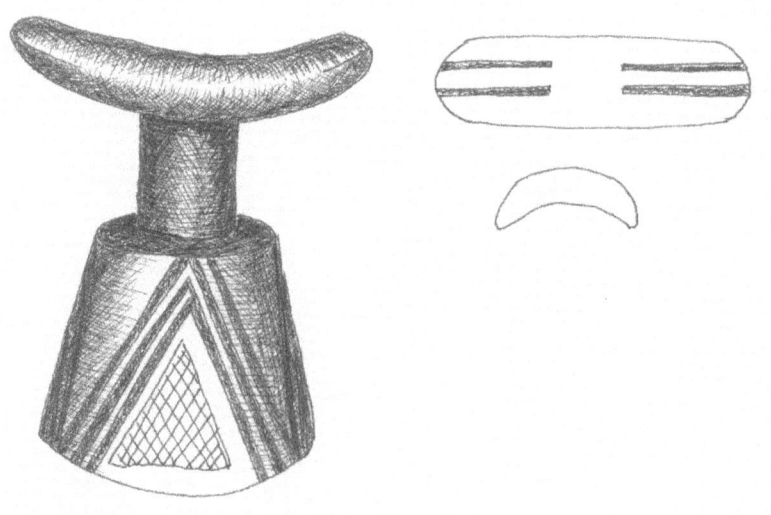

90 British Museum (no. 1979 Af1.2119), collected by Misses A. and D. Powell-Cotton, 1936, *Angola, Mwila* (Wila), *Mucanka*, wood, 15 cm h.

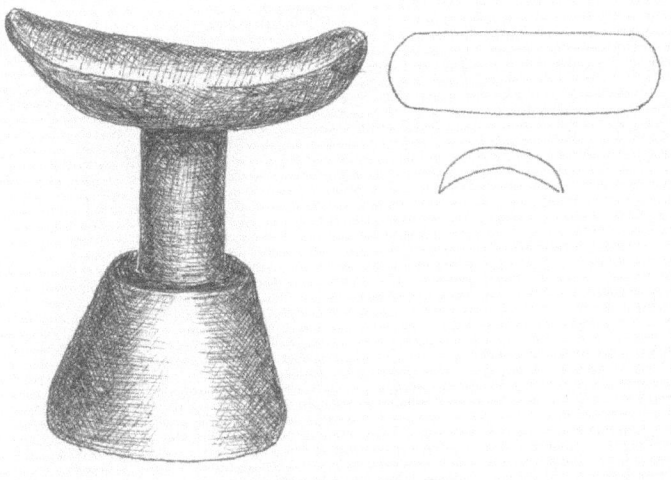

91  Oxford, Pitt Rivers Museum (no. 1940.7.231) (37.268), collected by Misses A. and D. Powell-Cotton, 1937, donated 1940, Angola, *Mwila* (Wila), wood, 14 cm h.

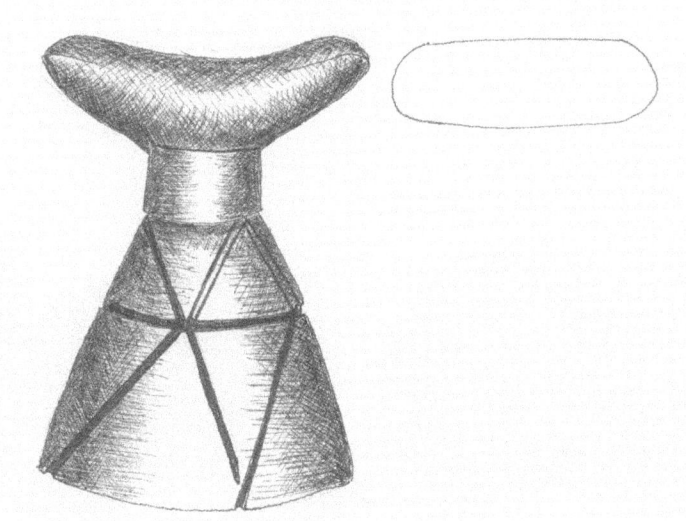

92  British Museum (no. 1979 Af1.2006), collected by Misses A. and D. Powell-Cotton, Angola, *Mwila* (Wila), 1936, wood, 17 cm h.

**122** | AFRICAN DREAM MACHINES

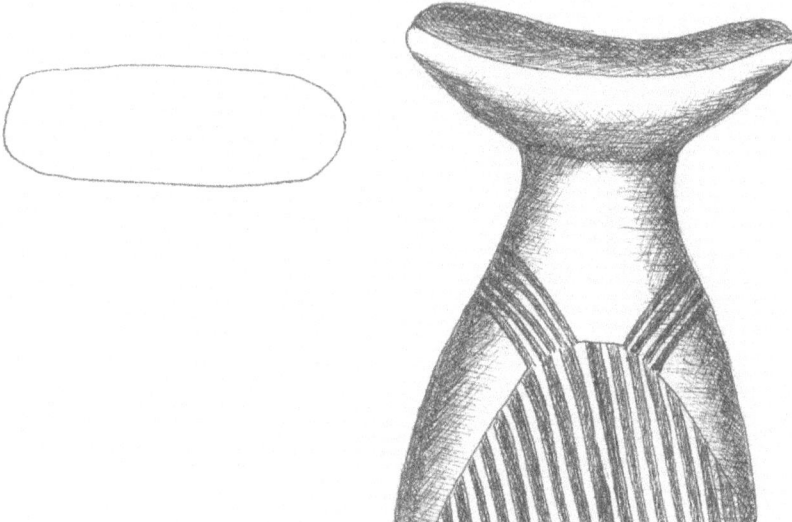

93  Oxford, Pitt Rivers Museum (no. 1940.7.232) (37.268), collected by Misses A. and D. Powell-Cotton, 1937, donated 1940, Angola, *Mwila* (Wila), wood, 15 cm h.

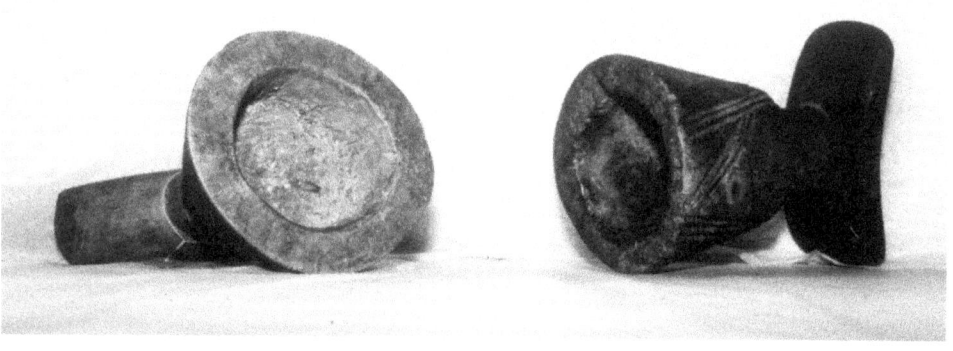

94  Bottom view of headrests in figures 90 and 91.

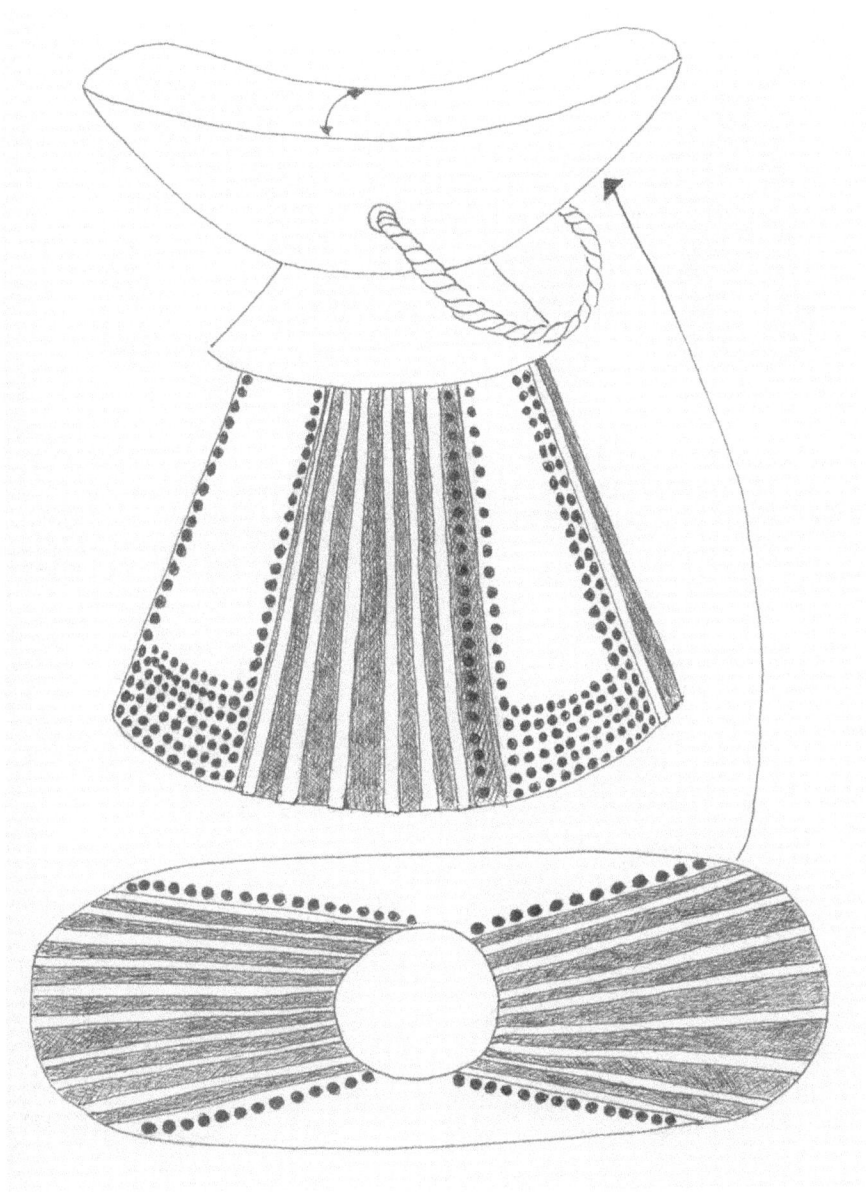

95  University of the Witwatersrand Art Galleries (no. 89 4505), Angola, *Ovahimba* (Himba), wood, 17 cm h.

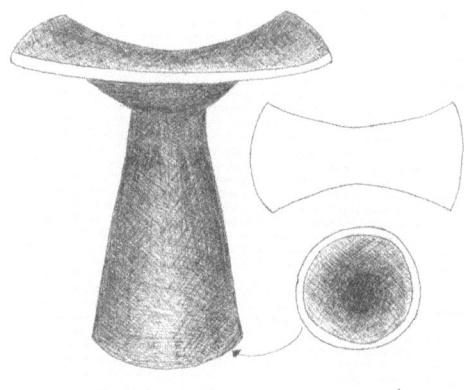 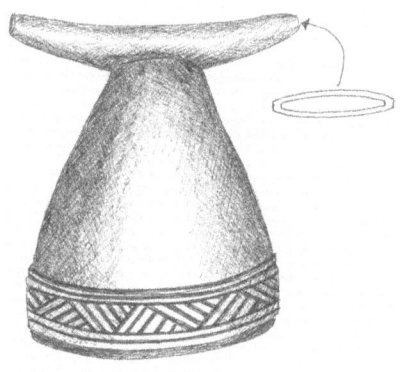

96  University of the Witwatersrand Art Galleries (no. 89 4411), Angola, north-east Namibia, *Ovahimba* (Himba) *men's headrest, opuwo,* wood, 17 cm h.

97  British Museum (no. 1954 Af23), (Wellcome Collection, no. 232216), collected by Steans, 8 January 2007, Democratic Republic of the Congo, *BaLuba?* (Luba), *Nyangire,* wood, 16.2 cm h.

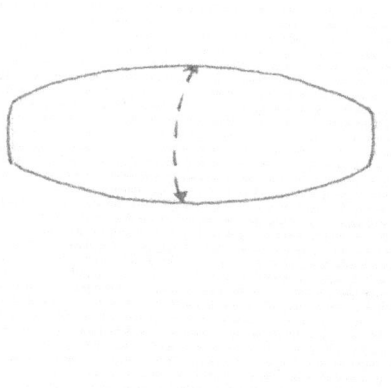 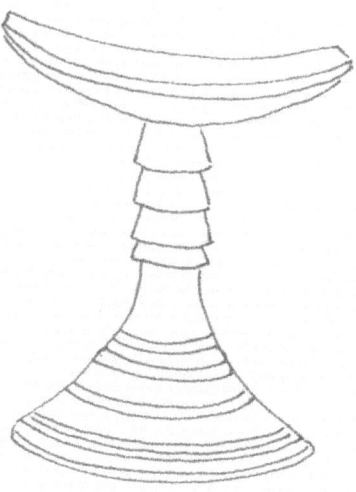

98  Musée Royal de l'Afrique Central (no. 6567), (Maes 1929:6, pl. I, fig. 16), donated by M. Janssens of the Musées Royaux du Cinquantenaire, Democratic Republic of the Congo, *Ituri district, Mangbetu,* wood, 15.5 cm h

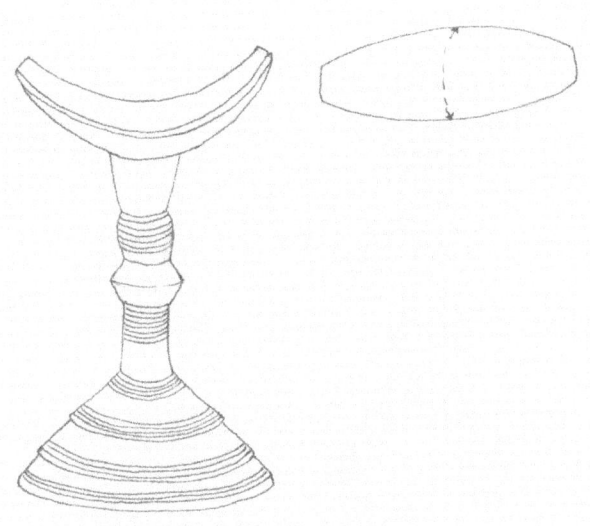

99   Musée Royal de l'Afrique Central (no. 35927), (cf. 6567, 1912), Democratic Republic of the Congo, 'Kasai' (region), *Sapo-Kanwamba*, wood, 17 cm h.

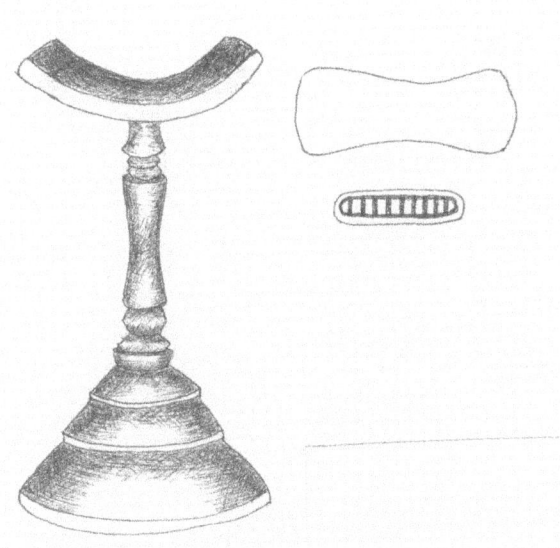

100  Musée Royal de l'Afrique Central (no. 40561), Democratic Republic of the Congo, 'Kwango' (region), *Popokabaka 'district'*, wood, 14 cm h.

**126** | AFRICAN DREAM MACHINES

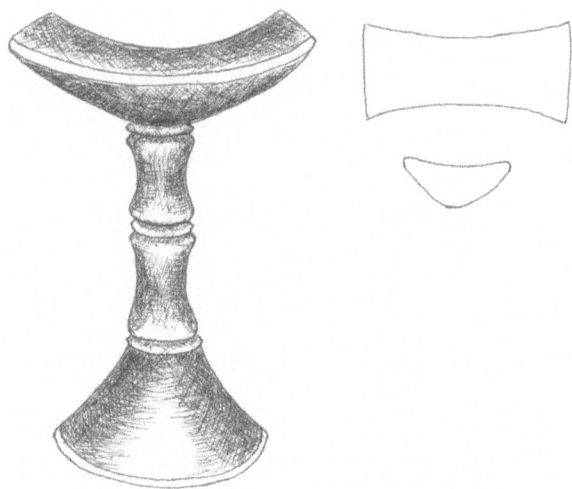

101  Musée Royal de l'Afrique Central (no. 57.53.19), Democratic Republic of the Congo, 'Shaba' (province), *Kinda Kamina* (region), wood, 16.3 cm h.

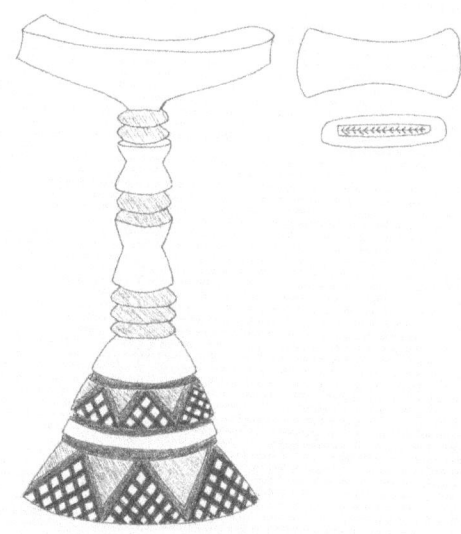

102  Musée Royal de l'Afrique Central (no. 52.48.98), Democratic Republic of the Congo, Kasai (region), *Kapanga* 'district', wood, 16 cm h.

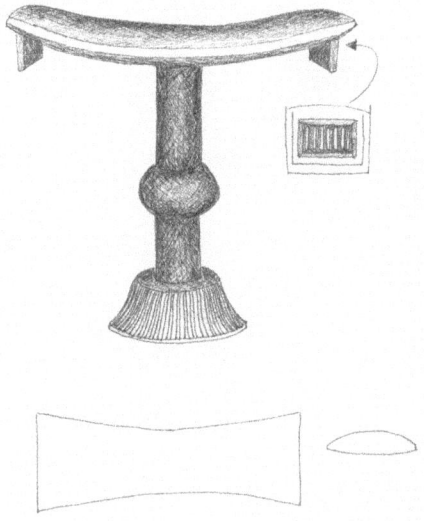

103  British Museum (no. 1949 Af46.629), Oldman Collection, *Southern Rhodesia(?) (Zimbabwe), Mashona* (Shona), wood, 15.4 cm h.

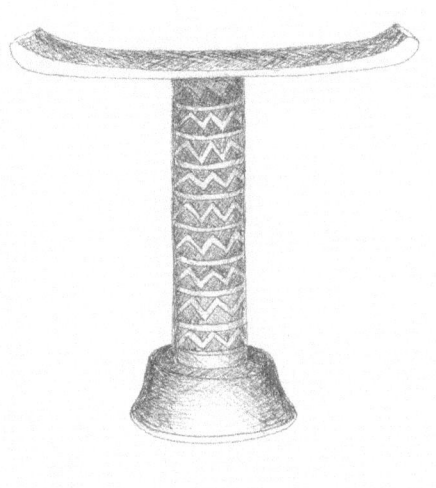

104  British Museum (no. 1902.107), collected by H. F. Tomalin, *Southern Rhodesia (Zimbabwe), between Salisbury (Harare) and Tete on the Zambesi,* Mashona?, wood, 14.1 cm h.

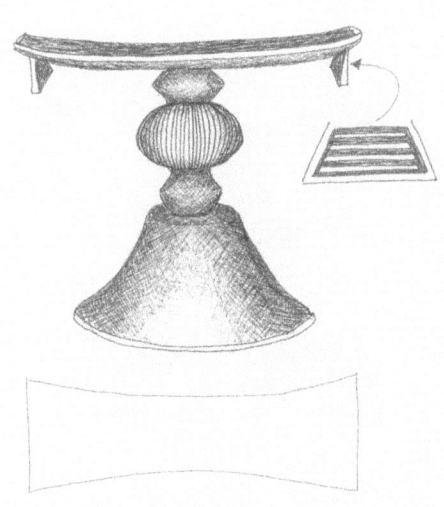

105  British Museum (no. 1952 Af26.42), collection by Main and Williams, *Southern Rhodesia, Zimbabwe? Mashona?*, wood, 14.1 cm h.

**128** | AFRICAN DREAM MACHINES

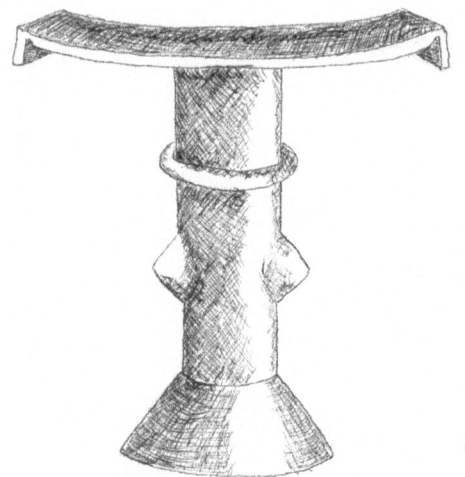

106  Frankfurt, Museum für Völkerkunde (no. NS 26675), *Collected by Frobenius? South Africa, "Kaffern"*, wood, 12.5 cm h.

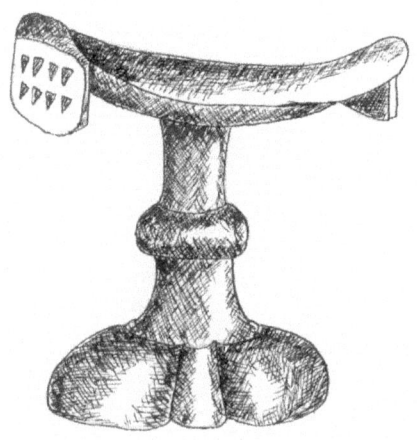

107  Hamburg, Museum für Völkerkunde (no. 13.174:30), bought from *"Kowietzko", Destroyed in World War II*, *"Betshuaan"* (Tswana), 'Kalanga?', wood, 14.6 cm h.

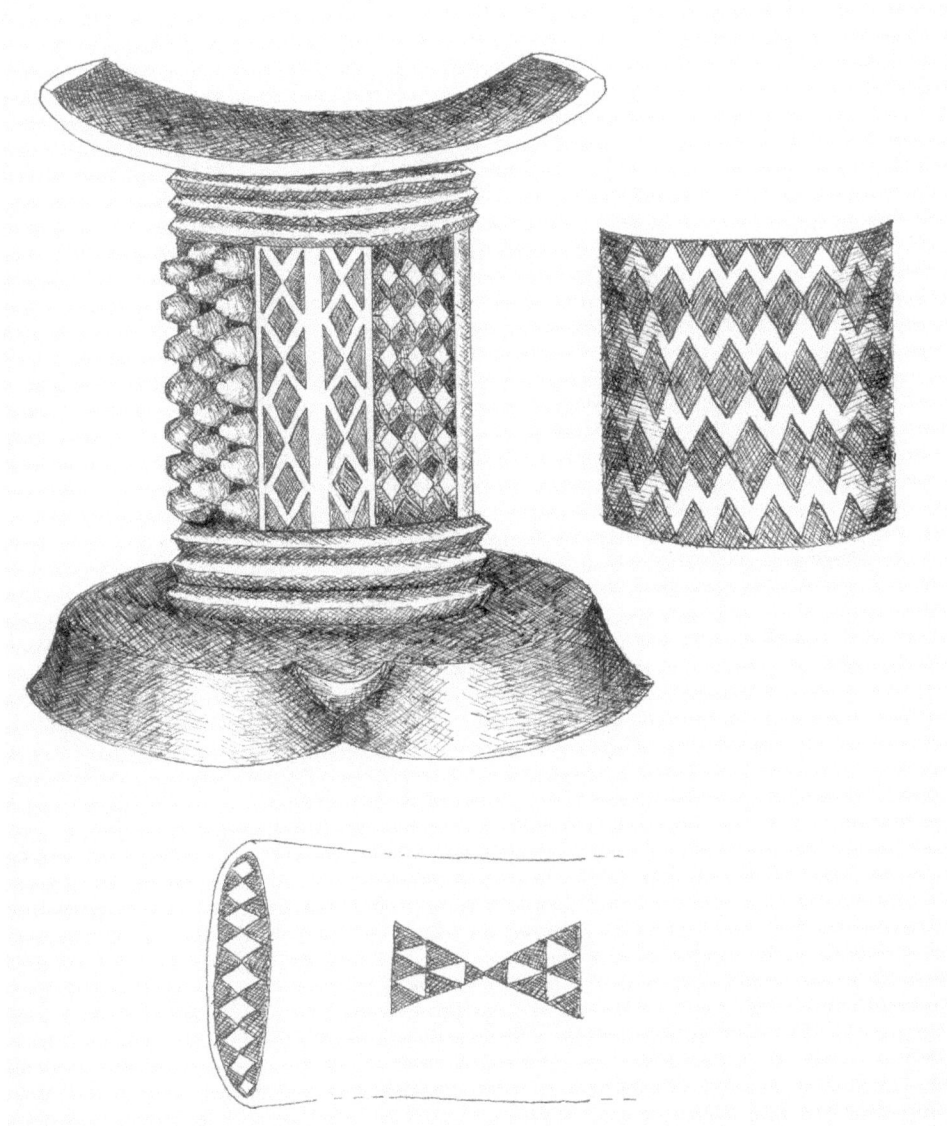

108  British Museum (no. 1954 Af23), (Wellcome Collection, no. 221010), *Southern Rhodesia* (Zimbabwe), 'Shona', wood, 14.6 cm h.

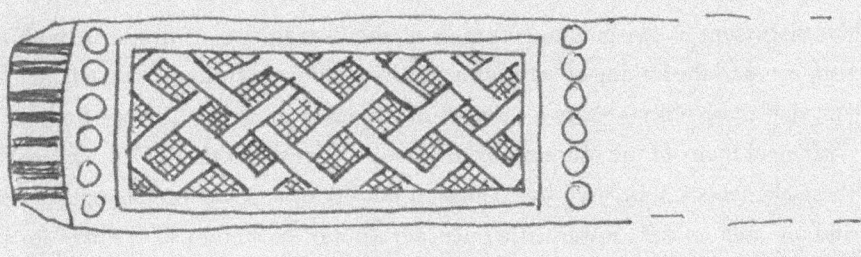

# 5 | Authenticity and History

THIS CHAPTER INTERROGATES some historical problems of attribution in order to unpick and, it is hoped, destabilise some notions of ethnic identity and authenticity in relation to headrests with column supports that were collected in particular regions at specific historical moments, but which all share the same basic structural traits. This follows from the discussion in the previous chapter of the distribution of headrests with columnar supports and the linking of style with ethnicity. The contention in this chapter is that the fact that these objects share a number of elements across a number of ethnic divisions challenges many of the more problematic aspects of the notion of 'authenticity'. Because these elements can be used to establish a fluidity of stylistic interchange among groups and an open attitude towards the incorporation of new and useful forms for particular purposes, they can also be used to undermine the idea that 'authentic' African art work is necessarily ethnically exclusive in terms of both style and iconography. By examining the circumstances of collection of each headrest in relation to its stylistic forms, it is possible to suggest some of the historical dimensions of the 'ownership' of particular styles.

A headrest in the (South African) National Culture History Museum in Tshwane (Pretoria) illustrates the difficulties involved in the division of headrests with columnar supports into different categories, such as those proposed here, as well as those based on notions of ethnic styles. This example has a truncated, flaring conical base with a convex top surface into which an articulated column 'fits' (fig. 109). The column is articulated into two sections: the lower section has a spiral design carved in deep relief; the upper section is plain. The platform is slightly butterfly-shaped, with the upper short edges flattened and decorated with a geometrical design. From the underside of the platform, two pendants (one broken), also with relief designs, are placed parallel to the short ends. In its formal arrangement of column and base, this example clearly demonstrates features associated with headrests predominantly associated with Ethiopian and Democratic Republic of the Congo (DRC) examples, while the arrangement of the platform and its pendants point to a provenance in south-east Africa, probably in either Tsonga or Shona territories, which overlap significantly.

Further, the formal articulation of elements in figure 109 is one that defies the division that I have made between headrests with conical bases that merge with their columns and those with bases clearly articulated from their columns. That this headrest is of a type that was of some antiquity in the area of south-east Africa is borne out by a similar example published in Müller and Snelleman (*c.* 1892), (fig. 110). Like the latter, the example in figure 109 is of apparently impeccable provenance, having been collected by H. P. Junod in the then Transvaal in the 1940s, and thus each of the two constitutes what many would consider to be 'authentic' objects. But the question of authenticity cannot simply rest in its provenance; this merely makes it authentic as a headrest collected by Junod in Tsonga territory, or in Sotho territory from a Tsonga-speaking vassal, at a particular time. The exact composition of elements in this example is not often found in Tsonga headrests, although it is echoed in other Tsonga headrests with columnar supports and in examples from a number of other Southern and Central African locations.

Many different peoples produce and use headrests in which the base, column and platform are all articulated as clearly separate elements. Bases are circular or rectangular, in some cases pyramidal, and columns are round, and for the most part single. Platforms vary from rectangular, to oval shield shapes with tapering ends, to butterfly shapes with flaring ends. In many of these examples, the columns and the bases are sculpted with a degree of intricacy not seen in the columned headrests with conical bases discussed in the previous chapter, and the proportion of the column to the base is generally such that the column is emphasised by its relative height. In its simplest form, this type of headrest consists of a shallow circular base, a plain circular column and a plain platform, but, at its most elaborate, it can have a pierced, cotton-reel-shaped base, spiral column and elaborately engraved platform surface. Headrests that can be placed in this category are provenanced to regions from Ubangi in the north to the lower Congo/Kasai in the DRC, with some examples of multiple-columned supports from south-east Africa, mainly Zimbabwe, Mozambique and the north-eastern parts of South Africa. The vast majority of headrests with figuratively carved supports can be fitted into this category by virtue of the types of bases and platforms they exhibit, and most of them are from the Central African region.

## DEMOCRATIC REPUBLIC OF THE CONGO

This region boasts the greatest variety of headrests of this structural sub-type, ranging from the equatorial region of Ubangi in the north, through the central region of Kwango-Kwilu to Katanga–Shaba in the east, and including a large number of ethnic groups. While some headrest forms are clearly attributable to specific ethnic groups, others appear to have been made and used by a number of different ethnic groups with minimal modifications of the basic theme. A glance at the pages of illustrations in Maes's catalogue of headrests from the DRC (Maes 1929, pls. II, IV, V), of which a large proportion belongs to this type, clearly demonstrates this ethnic interchangeability, but it can be more fully explored by comparative analysis of a number of examples. The vast majority of headrests listed here are in the Musée Royal de l'Afrique Central, whose holdings of DRC headrests are unparalleled elsewhere and allow for immediate cross-referencing between individual instances. Unfortunately, however, the documentation of these headrests is not even, the earlier examples listed by Maes (1929) being the best documented. Headrests accessioned later in this museum, particularly those from the 1950s when the end of colonial rule was becoming imminent and collecting less discriminating, are, with some exceptions, much less carefully documented, and so examples from other museums become important comparative points.[1]

The simplest form within this type is one in which the headrest is composed of a flat, disc-shaped base, a plain column, and a rectangular or butterfly-shaped platform. Headrests of this pattern are widely distributed with various modifications throughout the southern DRC region. The headrest used by Maes (1929, pl. I, fig. 1) as his first example represents the form very clearly (fig. 111). Its only decoration is the single engraved line at the outer circumference of the upper surface of the base. This is provenaned to 'Bangoi (Giri)region, Bangala district, BaLoei' (i.e. Loei), while a second, rather fatter example (Maes 1929, pl. I, fig. 7), with brass tacks around the vertical surfaces of both base and platform, is provenanced to the Teke in the area of Stanley Pool.[2] The only other example of this type showing such extreme simplicity illustrated by Maes (1929, pl. IV, fig. 15) has a domical circular base, a very thin, elongated column and a butterfly-shaped platform. It has a provenance documented as 'Katanga', and it is attributed to the Luba. Two similarly structurally simple examples, each with a circular, mildly domical, two-stepped base, a pronouncedly butterfly platform with brass studs at the ends of the upper surface, and a column with concave sides (fig. 112)[3] in the Musée Royal de l'Afrique Central are provenanced to Kasai, Sapo Kanwamba and Kasai, Kapanga.

### The question of Luba 'abstract' headrests

Examples with so few distinguishing markers establish a basic structural type, but do not allow for a clear demarcation of stylistic boundaries. More complex structural and stylistic features could allow for a narrower set of definitions of stylistic categories. For example, Dewey suggests that there is some question as to what non-figurative Luba headrests look like, because of a paucity of examples with certain, documented provenances (Dewey 1993:66). The problematic question of 'Luba' as an ethnic category has been discussed by Jewsiewicki (1989), and Roberts and Roberts (1996), among others. In the final chapter of *Memory: Luba Art and the Making of History*, Roberts and Roberts give an overview of the problems inherent in the creation of the Luba as a 'supertribe' (Roberts & Roberts 1996:251–52), but seek to establish a difference between, on the one hand, colonial and post-colonial notions of Luba identity as inclusive and, on the other hand, pre-colonial Luba identity as (implicitly) more exclusive and pure. Even if we accept that the people in the Luba 'heartland' in the nineteenth century could have been seen as constituting an homogeneous linguistic entity, there was, as Roberts and Roberts (1996:12) point out, little political or economic centralisation. The multiplicity of figural styles produced within the Luba heartland suggests that there are at least as many ways of interpreting and presenting Luba iconography as there were kingdoms. This may partly answer Dewey's question about the existence of a Luba style of abstract headrests — there is not one; there are many; and they may not necessarily be exclusively Luba.

Simple headrests of this type attributed to the Luba have disc-shaped bases, columns that are carved either as spirals or as a vertical series of slightly bulbous rings (fig. 113) and, generally, butterfly-shaped platforms. One ivory example in the British Museum (fig. 114), from the Wellcome Collection, appears to have documentation pointing to the area of Luluabourg as provenance,[4] but this has been overridden in the museum's attribution in favour of the larger ethnic attribution of Luba. Two others (fig. 115),[5] collected by Torday, are both provenanced to Lake Mweru and attributed to the Luba. A double-columned example collected by Torday in the same region (fig. 116) follows the same pattern, and is matched by one published by Maes (1929, pl. V, fig. 30), but has a lobed base, one lobe for each column,[6] and is provenanced to the Luba in the region of Luluabourg.

Dewey (1993:72, fig. 67) published an example with a very similar column that has, however, two heads sculpted facing outwards from the column parallel to the platform. This he identifies as Luba, presumably on the basis of the figurative carving of the heads, but the general configuration of the base, column and platform may be as clear an index of authorship. Another, very similar example, in this case with five heads around the column, in the Museum für Völkerkunde in Berlin (Krieger 1978, pl. 272) was bought from Frobenius in 1904, and is provenanced to 'Urua' and attributed to the Luba (Koloss 1990:21–22). Although this example was not collected personally by Frobenius, its attribution to the Luba acquires a particular gloss in the light of Biebuyck's critique of Frobenius' approach to collecting

> as a strange blend of carelessness and superficiality and, contrastingly, as an attempt at precise localization of objects (without differentiating between places where they were collected and places where they were made, but often indicating subgroups, restricted areas, villages, or chiefs and headmen) (Biebuyck 1985:7).

Nevertheless, if we assume that the attribution is correct, even only in hindsight and by comparison with others from better-documented sources, it can be argued that these headrests, together with Torday's examples from Lake Mweru,[7] provide examples that have an apparently secure provenance to Luba territory. While one explorer-anthropologist's opinion does not make an ethnicity certain, it nevertheless establishes some sort of baseline from which to build. For, as in the case of how many swallows it takes to make a summer, one of the major problems in giving any object an identity beyond its functional use rests in deciding how many securely provenanced examples would be necessary to establish an ethnic style. A further corollary to this is raised in Biebuyck's assessment of Frobenius: does one assign an ethnic identity to the object by virtue of the identity of the maker or the user, or by the ethnically defined or geographical provenance? In the case of these headrests, stylistic identity is probably the least secure of all markers of ethnic origin, and geographical provenance does not necessarily coincide with a secure ethnic attribution, especially as there is some distance between Lake Mweru–Urua (Torday's and Frobenius' examples) and Luluabourg (British Museum/Wellcome Collection example), a distance that is both spatial and, possibly, temporal.

Many of the wooden headrests assumed to be Luba in style have relief decoration around their bases, and on some there is similar relief patterning on the vertical faces of the platform ends (figs. 113, 115 & 116). It may be that these elements could be used more significantly as diagnostic tools when attributing headrests to ethnicities, carvers and workshops in the regions of Kasai, Sankuru and Katanga than the structural elements and their combinations. The question of what Luba headrests might have looked like is thus beggared by its own assumption of ethnic homogeneity, and it will be dealt with in the context of a wider analysis of headrest styles that used columnar supports in this region, which was, by the time headrests started to be collected, very heavily destabilised by colonial incursions.

## In search of the melting pot: Lusambo and environs

The area encompassed by the towns of Lusambo, Luebo and Luluabourg, between the Lulua and Sankuru rivers, is the provenance given for a large number of examples of this generic columned headrest type in Maes's catalogue (1929:24–27), and for some collected by Torday. Of these three towns, Lusambo, situated on the Sankuru River south of its junction with the Lubefu, is the provenance most frequently listed by Maes (1929) for headrests of this type (and for some others). It raises some pertinent questions as to the ways in which styles have been assigned to ethnic groups and/or developed as markers of identity by the people who used them. There appears to have been a great fluidity of style in the construction of headrests provenanced to this area, but in the sample of headrests that use columns on articulated round bases, the majority fall within a restricted range of formal possibilities, where the marking of ethnic differences may lie only in the subtlest of changes in decoration or proportion, if indeed such marking exists at all.

Emil Torday, on his collecting expedition for the British Museum, spent a few weeks at Lusambo, arriving at the end of February 1908 (Mack 1990), and was impressed with both the size and (rather negatively) polyglot complexion of the town's population:

> Lusambo is one of the great towns of the Kasai district; the population cannot be much less than 40,000. Here all tribes meet and the Sunday market is one of the most picturesque sights that can be imagined. Bakuba, Batetela, Basonge, Babinji, Bakwamputu, Bakwam-Kosh and many other tribes are represented (Torday 1910:31).

He continues with a description of the degeneration of the morals of the inhabitants, and concludes his description of the town with the following: 'Where so many tribes meet it is not possible to study the ethnography of the people; *a mixture of habits and customs is evolved which is very misleading*' (Torday 1910:32; emphasis added). It is precisely this melting pot character of Lusambo that could be used to explain the structural similarities and detailed differences that appear in the headrests of this type that are provenanced to this area.

For Lusambo to have reached a population size estimated by Torday in 1908 to stand at 40,000, there must have been a large influx of people from quite a wide area, and, as Torday notes, from many different ethnic groups. Vansina, discussing the movement of populations in the formation of the Kuba kingdom, suggests that in the eighteenth century, the Kuba 'lost the Isambo, who were the Pyaang who followed Mashaal to Lusambo' (Vansina 1978:165). The Isambo[8] of Lusambo ultimately formed one of the outer reaches of the trade routes from the Kuba kingdom along the Sankuru River to the Songye (Vansina 1978:193). Presumably this trade route, from its inception some two to three hundred years ago, would already have introduced separate polities to their neighbours. But, at the end of the nineteenth century, Lusambo's cosmopolitan nature was given a boost. The Congo Free State was founded in 1885, and in 1890 a military post was founded by Le Marinel and Gillain at Lusambo to stop the advance of Ngongo Luteta, who, with a Songye following, was raiding the Luba of southern Kasai and trading in slaves with the 'Arabs'.[9] At the same time, the Luba of Kasai were being attacked by Cokwe raiders who traversed Kaniok territory (Vansina 1966: 162). The military post at Lusambo was built as one of a number of fortified camps both to stop 'Arab' drives and to make offensive moves against them, and Ngongo Luteta was defeated at Lusambo in 1890 and surrendered to the colonial forces under Dahnis (Fabian 1996:23) at Lusambo in 1892 (Tourist Bureau for the Belgian Congo and Ruanda-Urundi 1956:13, 305).[10] The relative safety against slave traders offered by a military post must have drawn people to Lusambo from the surrounding districts.

Lusambo remained a large town into the 1920s: when Fraser, travelling through the Sankuru region, visited Lusambo it had large wireless masts, which he rather disparagingly refers to as 'signs of civilization', visible from the steamboat on the river. He ascribes the large size of the town to a regulation put in place by the Belgian administration in the Sankuru district that prohibited the erection of factories except in designated commercial centres, ostensibly to encourage the formation of large towns and also to encourage competition (Fraser 1927:187). Some eight kilometres from the town, he visited an oil plant owned by the Compagnie de Niengélé, which was producing soap for the local market (Fraser 1927:188), while in the town itself he visited an industrial school founded by Catholic priests where tailoring, carpentry and bricklaying were taught (Fraser 1927:190). Not only was Lusambo by then a bustling centre of colonial industry, accessible along the river, which linked it to Port Franqui (opposite Basongo) at the juncture of the

Sankuru and Kasai rivers, it was only 134 kilometres away from the railway line that ran from Port Franqui to Kamina and Elizabethville by 1927 (Frederick & Gielen 1950:433).

Vansina (1966:163) remarks that by 1950, Lusambo was 'the equivalent of two villages', which suggests that the town had shrunk, and population figures given for larger towns by Gille (c. 1950:736) back this up, with Lusambo having a figure of only 1,600 in 1950, although it is seems that this figure includes only white settlers. Compared to Torday's estimate of 40,000, this is very small. The settler town of Luluabourg was founded after 1944,[11] and may have attracted people away from Lusambo, being only 134 kilometres distant. Luluabourg is also listed as a source for headrests of the type under discussion, as is Luebo: together with Lusambo, they define a territory from the Lulua River eastward across the Sankuru River, to which these headrest types are most commonly provenanced.

Apart from the ethnic groups listed by Torday as being in Lusambo in 1908 (see above), among which are some familiar from literature on the art history of the Congo, maps of the region suggest that there may well have been other well-known producers of wood carving involved in this stylistic complex. Maes's map (1929) shows both 'Bena Lulua' (i.e. Lulua) and Luba in territories not too far south of Lusambo, and Bankutshu and Basongo Meno north and down-river. A simplified map of a smaller region reproduced in Mack (1990:53) shows Isambo, the group for whom Lusambo was named, as well as Nkutshu to the north, and many of the groups named by Torday and cartographically marked by Maes. Vansina, however, does not include the Isambo in his 1966 map of the region, but shows Lusambo surrounded by Luba (Kasai) and Songye (Vansina 1966:163), and he further points out that the Lulua only came by this name very late, being part of the Luba Kasai complex (Vansina 1966:162). Furthermore, bordering on this central point of Lusambo are the Kuba, whose territory stretched as far south as Luebo on the Lulua River and eastward along the southern bank of the Sankuru River. What is problematic about all these maps is the neatness with which such ethnic boundaries are drawn, establishing 'homelands' for different groups that are in all probability extremely artificial, and codified only within colonial ethnographic mapping of Africa.

Within the polyglot ethnic communities in the vicinity of Lusambo, Luebo and Luluabourg, at least from the 1890s, people may well have adopted and adapted customs and ideas from their close neighbours, particularly as a breakdown of old political and social groupings occurred.[12] But this notion of change rests on a foundation that assumes that social, political and cultural boundaries were hermetically sealed before being thrown into the melting pot. It is not only possible, but rather probable, that such processes were old and ongoing, and accelerated as people came to towns to look for new fortunes.

Furthermore, style elements would have been disseminated by the passage of people both into and out of the town of Lusambo, and back to other centres such as Luluabourg to the south, Luebo to the west, Basongo to the north-west and Kamina to the south-east. It must also be remembered that headrests were intensely personal objects, and that men carried them with them on journeys, a practice still continuing into the 1950s.[13] Headrests may well have been passed on from senior to junior generations, and, if they were, they were often revered and kept as relics relating to the deceased.[14] In any event, it is likely that many of the headrests collected in and around Lusambo in the period between the 1880s and the 1950s were not very old, as new ones would be made with each generation. Thus, stylistic continuity and change, adoption and absorption within an area that had seen communication among various language groups continuing over a long period must be considered as a process in which an area-wide stylistic complex could have evolved, rather than one in which a number of narrow, ethnically circumscribed styles were perpetuated. This kind of model is acceptable also in light of Vansina's tracing of commonalities among the western Bantu speakers of this area who shared vocabularies around iron working and the production of wooden utensils (Vansina 1990), so common ur-styles for headrests across Bantu-speaking Africa are not totally beyond the realms of reasonable speculation. This possibility will be discussed in more depth in chapter 7.

The following discussion of headrests from the Kasai–Shaba region is intended to show how constructions of ethnically defined styles of headrests are limited, not only because of the assumptions of ethnic exclusivity, but also because, within the time frame in which collecting took place, old orders were coming under increasing pressure, crumbling and possibly disintegrating. It may be significant, therefore, that the Musée Royal de l'Afrique Central, the depository of Belgian colonial collecting in Africa, has a collection of Congolese/DRC headrests garnered largely between 1890 and 1960, the period of Belgium's direct colonial impact on the Congo/DRC region, while most of the later acquisitions of headrests have been from East and Southern Africa, areas previously neglected in the collection.

The columned headrests provenanced to this Lusambo–Luluabourg–Luebo territory seem to belong predominantly to one of two possible variant stylistic conformations. In one, sculptural complexity is achieved through the carving of the column into various combinations of cotton-reel shapes, while the bases are carved as discs with relief decoration on the vertical or sloping sides. The second variant seems almost an inversion of the first, with the greater sculptural complexity reserved for the base, while the column is quite simple. This impression is enhanced when one recognises that these bases could be regarded as compressed cotton-reel shapes, suggesting a process of inversion. However, as will become clear from the following discussion of particular examples, this inversion of forms does not indicate a correlation with ethnic interrelationships such as that proposed by Lévi-Strauss (1963). Whether it had any other significance in social terms is impossible to ascertain owing to the lack of information on the use and making of these objects. In the vast majority of both these variants, the platform is butterfly-shaped, with varying degrees of constriction at the centre, and many of them have relief panels on their ends.

Variant 1 (figures 117–134)

Examples of this variant collected in or near Lusambo are illustrated in figures 117–125. All of these have shallow circular or rectangular bases whose upper surfaces are concave and generally have engraved or relief decoration on their vertical sides, although in some (e.g. fig. 127), the base is plain, bar the addition of brass tacks. The butterfly-shaped platforms often have relief or engraved decorative panels at the short ends, and are supported by a column that tapers towards a set of multiple rings at its centre. Figures 117, 118 and 120 are attributed to the Songye; figure 119 has a less certain provenance, apart from 'Kasai', having been accessioned somewhat later than the others (1955), but clearly belongs to the same stylistic group. However, this does not mean that this example can be attributed to the Songye on stylistic grounds alone. Maes (1929, pl. V, figs. 6, 7) illustrates two examples that are almost identical to these, one attributed to the 'Batempa' (i.e. Tempa: Songye speakers) in the region of Lusambo and the other to the Lulua (Luba speakers) in the region of Luebo. It must be noted further that examples with both circular and rectangular bases are attributed to the Songye, but other similar examples are attributed to the Lulua (fig. 121) and Kete (fig. 122), collected in the district of Luluabourg.[15]

It seems that the examples collected late in the history of the Belgian Congo are even more difficult to place, because of a general lack of collection data. Thus, while it would be tempting to attribute an example such as figure 123 to the Songye, because an apparent majority of collected examples of this form are attributed to this ethnic group, this would be highly problematic. Another example (fig. 124), with double platforms, one superimposed above the other, which otherwise conforms to the elements of this variant, is, however, provenanced to 'Shaba, Kinda Kamina', which would suggest a Luba user at least, while a very similar example accessioned five years earlier (Musée Royal de l'Afrique Central, no. 56.33.15), which has no surface decoration, is provenanced very generally to 'Kasai', a sign not only of curatorial caution, but of classificatory uncertainty. The object could have originated in a Luba community within Kasai, but could equally possibly have been made in another community within this area. A further variant on this type has a support with a square section (fig. 125) and with a spiral at its centre, accessioned in 1957 and provenanced to 'Kinda Kamina' in 'Shaba'. It has a stylistically similar partner collected much earlier, in 1919 (Musée Royal de l'Afrique Central, no. 22723), whose provenance is probably Lusambo.[16]

The occurrence of this type eastward into the Katanga–Upemba region is further confirmed by an example, collected in Luba territory near Mwanza by William Burton in the late 1920s (fig. 126), where the square base with its engraved decoration echoes the examples attributed to 'Songye' and 'Bena Lulua' (i.e. Lulua), but the support is square and not round. Burton collected material from the Luba in and around the mission station at Mwanza and from Songye groups to the north, and it is possible that the examples he sent back to Johannesburg could have been made by a Songye carver. However, Burton refers to five headrest designs used by the Luba[17] at Mwanza, each having its own name, of which this appears to have been an illustrative example, which probably had not been used. Many headrests of this variant provenanced to Katanga (Shaba) do show a more fully sculptural approach to the column. This can be seen even in a simple example such as figure 127, where the column has two sharp-ridged swellings forming a simple, but three-dimensional hour-glass shape.

A number of headrests of the same style as figure 128 in the Musée Royal de l'Afrique Central[18] are provenanced to Milundila in Shaba Province, which is also Luba territory. They conform to the same stylistic principles as the 'Lusambo' examples, using the tapered column, with a series of rather more bulbous rings at the centre as a support for a butterfly platform. However, the circular base is more idiosyncratic, having four engraved grooves at the 'cardinal' points of the base, which slopes inwards to the centre on the base around the column. Similar grooves are present on the edges of the bowls of a number of the *mboko*, or bowl-bearing figures attributed, but not firmly provenanced, to the Luba.[19] While the presence of this feature on these headrests may thus be regarded as diagnostic of a Luba origin, it may equally be linked to a particular function, possibly that of containing some form of powerful substance.[20] The *mboko* was typically used to contain white clay used in a number of ceremonies or rituals, and these headrests with their grooves may have been similarly used as containers.[21] Two closely related headrests are illustrated in Maes (1929, pl. V, figs. 4, 7), one being attributed to the Songye of Lusambo district and the other to the Lulua of Luebo district, but these have decorated bases without the distinctive grooves.

Other examples of this variant, also attributed to the Luba, are stylistically distinct from the examples from the Lusambo–Luebo–Luluabourg complex outlined here only in their treatment of the column. One of the earliest documented examples,[22] attributed to the Guha (fig. 129), was collected by Edward Coode Hoare, who was in the Congo Free State with Stanley in 1889. Like the examples provenanced to Lusambo and Luebo, it has a column that is constricted and articulated to form a cotton-reel shape at the centre, with ridges above and below. The platform is butterfly-shaped with herringbone relief panels on its ends, and the circular base is domical. The fact that it shows very little sign of wear and has its original staining still visible raises the possibility that items such as headrests had, by the 1880s, become desirable among Europeans as mementoes of their journeys to exotic lands, and that indigenous Congolese were making them for sale, although there is no reason to assume that they were made in a style any different from that current in a particular district at that time.

A variety of forms of elaboration of the column is seen in examples provenanced to Kinda Kamina in Shaba province, nominally Luba territory, and, although they were accessioned over a period between the 1930s and 1950s, they suggest that there was room not only for idiosyncrasy, but also for continuity. The three illustrated here (figs. 130–132) use combinations of cotton-reel shapes and rings in the composition of the column, but they vary in the shape and decoration of their bases and platforms. The division of the vertical faces of the bases of such headrests (figs. 131 & 132) into panels might be taken as a feature diagnostic of a particular style, as it is present on a number of headrests in the Musée Royal de l'Afrique Central that follow this same pattern, sometimes with plain columns. Yet others have cotton-reel columns and plain bases. Two examples that use the same kind of columns as supports and circular bases with geometric decoration, but combine these with figurative carvings, not as supports, are also attributed to the Luba.

One, in the Museum für Völkerkunde in Berlin, was bought from Frobenius (although not collected by him) in 1904, and was provenanced to 'Urua', i.e. Luba territory (Krieger 1978, fig. 270). The other, in the Musée Royal de l'Afrique Central (no. 34588), was accessioned in 1932. The styles of the figurative carving of these two are, however, significantly different, suggesting that their attribution to an over-arching Luba ethnic category is highly problematic, something discussed at greater length below.

Final confirmation of the area across which this headrest type was used and customised is provided by another example collected by William Burton (fig. 133) in the district of Mwanza, which lies in the east of Luba territory, bordering on Hemba and Songye areas, in the late 1920s. It has a cotton-reel-shaped column with a ridged relief on its projections, while the base and the platform ends are elaborated with relief decoration. Among the objects excavated by Burton at Sanga on the north side of Lake Kisale was a ceramic headrest of the Kisalian period (fig. 134), possibly made for use as a burial object.[23] Being made of ceramic, it is of necessity very much less articulated than the wooden examples, with a single columnar support on a circular domical base, from which it is visually clearly separated by three moulded rings. It suggests that the use of this kind of headrest had a very long history in the region, as the Kisalian culture in Sanga can be dated to between the ninth and fourteenth centuries (Huffman 1992:70).[24] If this dating in reliable, it situates this headrest in a period contemporary with the headrests of the 'Tellem', and leaves us with the conclusion that a search for the origins of this particular headrest form within one specific ethnic community must be considered a well-nigh futile quest, something that can be reinforced by a return to Lusambo and the second variant of this headrest type.

Variant 2 (figures 135–144)

The headrests in figures 135 and 136, acquired by the museum from the same collector, show striking similarities, but figure 135 is attributed to the Kete of Luebo and figure 136 is attributed to the Songye of Lusambo. They both use a simple column supporting the platform and mounted on a base that is almost the same height as the column. The bases are carved as variations on a squat cotton-reel theme, topped by a disc with a slightly concave upper surface. The proportion of the column to the base is not generally even, with columns often being much taller than the base, as in figures 137 and 138, which are attributed to the Songye of Lusambo and the Lulua of Luebo, respectively. But the range of attributions stretches further, to include the Lele of Basongo (collected by Maes himself), the Kete of Luebo and the 'Zappo Zapp' of Luluabourg and d'Ibanche (Maes 1929, pl. V, figs. 15, 17, 24, 25). The headrests attributed to the last group have beads tightly encasing their columns, and one has a fringed skirt: both these features are found on other examples, but from Lusambo, attributed to the Songye (Maes 1929, pl. V, figs. 21, 29). A further example, collected by Torday in 1908 among the Tetela at Mokunji, near Lusambo (British Museum, no. 1908 6-22.143) also has beads around both column and base, but differs slightly from the others in that its base has a conical lower section separated from the upper convex disc by a vertical ring.

The convex upper surfaces of the bases on all of these headrests are similar to those in variant ones of this type, but the curve is often more marked. In figure 139, provenanced to Lusambo, but attributed to the Tempa, a Songye-speaking group, the upper part of the base forms a hollow bowl in which the column stands, suggesting that it could have been used to contain something. The base as a container is more fully realised in an unprovenanced example from the Wellcome Collection in the British Museum (fig. 140), but here the vessel is a plain cylinder inside which traces of a black viscous substance have coagulated around the base of the column, perhaps paralleling the possible use of the base in headrests attributed to the Luba discussed earlier (fig. 128). Despite these small variations, the extraordinary homogeneity of style among these headrests defies any attempt to make exclusive ethnic attributions, something that appears true of even the most distinctive group of headrests within this regional group.

Torday, in his visit to Lusambo in 1908, collected a headrest of this type that is distinct from those just discussed in its particular manipulation of the elements of the base (fig. 141). Here the central moulding of the cotton-reel shape is interrupted at three points on its circumference by a diamond-shaped notch, creating the effect of three legs, and there is no articulation of upper or lower discs. But the upper surface of the base remains convex. There are two projections at the ends of the platforms, hollowed through their vertical axes to form two loops. This example is attributed to the Isambo of Lusambo, but it is very similar to another example, attributed to the Kete of Luebo, collected by Maes in 1914, but which has only one platform projection (fig. 142).[25] The Isambo are an offshoot of the Kuba (Vansina 1978:165), although the relationship between these groups may not be very strong (Mack 1990:59). Following this provenancing, two later acquisitions to the Musée Royal de l'Afrique

Central might be attributed to the 'Kuba' Isambo. One of these (fig. 143) has a column that tapers to its centre and a cotton-reel base without any notches, but it has interlace designs on the vertical surface of its lower section. The other (fig. 144) has a column carved as a spiral, reminiscent of forms associated with Luba headrests, a cotton-reel base with a stepped upper section like the 'Lulua' example in figure 138, a central section that is completely hollowed through to form four bent legs, and two panels of interlace on the vertical sides of its lower section. The interlace on these two bases is of the same general type as those recorded among the Kuba by Cornet (1982), and is very closely associated with Kuba art in all its manifestations. Both these possibly Isambo examples and the Kete one (fig. 142) have panels in relief on the ends of the platform, although their relief designs all differ.

It seems that this group of headrests bears witness to exactly the kind of cultural and stylistic interchange of which Torday was so disparaging in his search for what he thought would be the 'true' ethnic identity of these Congolese peoples, but such interchange was inevitable, given the increasing instability of political and social relations in the area around Lusambo and beyond in the late nineteenth and early twentieth centuries. Given that the vast majority of these headrests of this variant are provenanced to the Kasai–Katanga region, which excludes the Kuba, and that many of them are nevertheless embellished with designs that have been, probably mistakenly, predominantly associated with Kuba art, it seems that the search for ethnic underpinnings of particular styles is necessarily doomed. If, as Vansina suggests, the main distinction among ethnic groups in this region is one of social structure on a political level, rather than one of language or kinship structures, then one must question the bases on which these stylistic divisions are drawn. The main distinction that Vansina draws among the groups to whom this form of headrest has been attributed is based on the state formations of Luba and Luba-related peoples, as opposed to the arrangement of the Songye into large villages under powerful chiefs (Vansina 1966:164). The linguistic marking of difference is not great, and all these groups are patrilineal, suggesting some cultural coherence on a general level.[26] Olbrechts (1946), in his pioneering study of the art of the Congo/DRC, included Luba and Songye in a single stylistic complex. While these two larger complexes have, with some justification, been separated in subsequent literature, on the grounds of both the formal style and the usage of objects, the overall homogeneity that underlies the stylistic variations of this particular columned headrest style from this region suggests that such separations are too simple. This can be further explored through an examination of figurative headrests attributed to particularly the Luba, Songye and Lulua.[27]

It seems, then, that the distribution of stylistic characteristics within the single-columned headrests from this region cannot be linked in any fixed way to particular ethnicities. The picture is, of course, further complicated by the fact that headrests of entirely different forms have been provenanced, or attributed, to many of the groups living in this region. This suggests that headrests designs in this region, as in others discussed in this study, may have been differentiated according to use, but the evidence for this is scanty. As mentioned above, Burton recorded the existence of five headrest designs in current use in Luba territory around Mwanza in the 1920s, and records the names of two, although he states that each of the five had its own name. He, however, does not appear to have noted any differentiation according to the gender, age, status or occupation of the users of the headrests that might be adduced to explain the variety, suggesting rather that differences resulted from the personal preference of the individual.

And that, really, is the crux of the matter: the headrest, of all forms of African art, was one of the most personal, and therefore must have been subject to a number of possible variations at an individual level. In the area of Lusambo in the period between 1880 and 1920, it is possible that headrests were copied, modified, traded and transported over large distances. Methodologies of categorisation that are fixed in ethnic paradigms of the 'typical' style cannot accommodate the larger stylistic homogeneity within patterns of ethnic diversity. Ultimately, affixing an ethnic name to an object confers on it the notion of seamless unity inherent in the entire baggage of ethnic identity: abstracted notions of unified culture and practices divorced from both the object and its specificity of use that allow the object to become one of an ethnically defined species.

Variant 3: Yansi/Teke/Mfinu: A conundrum for regional classification (figures 145–150)

A separable group of columned headrests, distinguished from those discussed above by the shape of the platform and, sometimes, the base; by the use of metal strips or wire around the columns and bases, and/or finely drawn linear decoration on the surfaces of their bases and platforms; and by the number of examples that have multiple-columned supports, defy not only strict ethnic divisions, but call into question the usefulness of regional divisions such as those proposed by Vansina (1966) or revised by Biebuyck (1985:60–61) for the classification of material culture styles in the Congo basin.

The single-columned headrests in question (figs. 145–149) have relatively deep platforms with crescent-shaped upward curvature; in some cases their columns are wound with wire or flat metal strips, and their bases are circular, rectangular or pyramidal. At its simplest, the type is represented by an example attributed to the Ngombe (fig. 145), which has no surface decoration, bar the metal strips wound around the column. Another, more complex example (fig. 147), which has no secure attribution, has both the base and the surfaces of the platform covered by finely carved linear geometric decoration, while in figure 148, attributed to the 'Banfumu' (i.e. Fumu), the base and column are covered by strips of metal wound around the surfaces, and the platform is covered with linear engraved decoration, presenting the most complex example in the range. Another example, figure 149, which has a column wound with wire and finely engraved linear decoration on the base and platform, is attributed to the Mongo, while the only firmly provenanced Yansi example (fig. 140) has a wire-wound column and no linear surface decoration. Maes (1929, pl. I, figs. 1–16) illustrates a number of these single-columned forms,[28] but his grouping ignores differences in platforms and bases. The examples with the features outlined above (Maes 1929, pl. I, figs. 2, 4, 5, 6, 8, 9; pl. II, fig. 2) are attributed to a number of different ethnic groups: the Yansi (only one: fig. 150), Teke, Mfinu[29] Bokala, Bunianga, Loei and Ngombe. All but the latter two Maes grouped under the regional category called 'Middle Congo', a category that is problematic, but which is based on documented examples. He also noted that it was not known whether the peoples between the Ngombe in the north and the Yansi, Teke and others of the southern reaches of the area in which this style type appears made or used headrests, and does not offer an explanation for its widely separated occurrence (Maes 1929:9–10). Biebuyck (1985:23) mentions Yansi use of such headrests as well, but cites documentation that suggests that they were made by the Mbala for Yansi clients, thus further weakening the case for limited ethnic attribution on the basis of styles.

In contrast to Maes's ethnic grouping of headrests, which appears to have been driven by the need to keep similarly styled objects together, both Vansina (1966) and Biebuyck (1985:60–61) separate the Yansi, as belonging *culturally* in the lower Kasai region, from the Teke, Fumu (a western Teke sub-group), Mfinu and Tsong, who are placed under 'People of the Makoko kingdom and related peoples'. This lack of regional unity in cultural and linguistic terms across the producers of a single headrest type is further evident in the fact that the Ngombe (Maes 1929, pl. II, figs. 1–4, 6–11) inhabit the area of Ubangi, in the north of the DRC, while the 'BaLoei' (i.e. Loei) (Maes 1929, pl. I, fig. 31) live in the region of the lower Ubangi, near the equator. Vansina (1966:28) mentions the Ngombe only in passing as Bantu speakers largely assimilated by non-Bantu-speaking 'Sudanese' peoples who moved into the area from the north,[30] and makes no mention of the Loei.

Yet, for my purposes, it is the very distance, approximately 900 kilometres (as the crow flies) across the rainforest, and even further along the Congo River, that separates these different peoples that is important, because among the headrests they produce are variations of a narrowly defined single type, a phenomenon that confounds the notion of a regional style, such as that used by Maes, and that crosses linguistic boundaries, albeit only within a circumscribed geographical area. It may also be important that many of these ethnic groups appear to have been located next to major navigable waterways, allowing for a degree of contact and thus an interchange of objects and ideas, something Dewey (1993:53) suggests in his discussion of headrests of this type from the Joss Collection, but without taking the northern producers into account.

In attributing unprovenanced examples to particular ethnicities, Maes's catalogue has been used as a source by a number of different authors, but its structure has led to a number of problems. Maes illustrated only one example of a single-columned, wire-wound headrest, attributed to the Yansi (Maes 1929, pl. I, fig. 2, fig. 50). Another very similar example that also does not use studs on the base (fig. 149) is attributed to the Mongo. Of the three single-support examples attributed to the Teke by Maes (1929, pl. I, figs. 1, 3, 7), only one has a circular column, and none has metal wound round it. Dewey, drawing on Maes, nevertheless gives two similar examples in the Joss Collection a 'Yansi/Bokala?' and 'Teke?/Mfinu?' attribution (Dewey 1993:52–53). It is tempting to take a similar path with another example of a very similar type in the British Museum, collected by H. H. Johnston (fig. 146), accessioned in 1893, and attributed to the Ngoni of Malawi. It has a conical base like those in the first sub-set of columned headrests, and a column with entasis that is carved with rings from the base to the crescent-shaped platform, which has ends carved with notches into a 'W' shape, reminiscent of some Somali examples. All of these features, except the platform ends, correspond to features found in the 'Yansi' examples discussed above, but this is the only one with this particular combination. As Johnston collected other headrests in the Kasai region (see below), it is possible that this one presents us with another variation of a type common in the region.

## Variant 4: Multiple-columned headrests (figures 151–168)

It is almost only within the parameters of the headrest type with column and base developed as distinctly separated elements that one finds a significant number of headrests with multiple columns as supports. Since, in virtually all these examples, the columns are arranged in a straight line, they must depend upon the possibility of an elongation of the base, something that occurs largely in those headrests where the base is articulated as a distinct unit of the structure, although there are some Southern African examples where this principle is contradicted (see below). The majority of the examples discussed, however, exhibit the independent base and column structure, and while they have been treated as a separate category, their structural relationship to the headrests of the preceding sets of single-columned headrests should be clear.

The distribution of multiple-columned headrests is not, however, completely coterminous with the distribution of single-columned headrests, there being many instances where, within ethnic categories, single-columned headrests were made, but no multiple-columned examples, and vice versa. The vast majority of the multiple-columned examples are provenanced to the same region as the single-columned headrests of the second variant, from the south-western regions of the DRC, through Kasai and Katanga, although a significant number have also been provenanced to south-east Africa, including Zimbabwe, Mozambique, Botswana and the northern provinces of South Africa.

*Southern DRC: Ubangi, Kasai and lower Congo (figures 151–161)*

Multiple-columned headrests attributed to peoples in the Kasai and Ubangi regions raise problems of attribution similar to those encountered with the single-columned variety. Maes illustrates ten examples (Maes 1929, pl. I, figs. 29–32; pl. II, figs. 3–5, 10–12), of which three are double headrests. They are attributed to the same range of ethnic groups as the single-columned variety in the Ubangi, Kasai and lower Congo regions. They also deploy many of the same stylistic and structural features as these others, from the engraved linear decoration of bases and/or platforms (figs. 151–155, 160 & 161), to the use of metal strip-binding of the columns (figs. 152, 157 & 158).

Figure 154 is one of a number illustrated by Maes (1929, pl. II, figs. 10–12), all of which appear to be precisely provenanced to the Ngombe of Ubangi. The structure of these headrests with two single columns each supporting a separate platform, with a third in between the two platforms, does not appear to be repeated elsewhere in the region, the closest similarity being with some examples provenanced to the Kuba (see fig. 167 and Maes 1929, pl. IV, figs. 11–14).[31] An example (Maes 1929, pl. II, fig. 12) very similar to that illustrated in figure 154 is clearly provenanced to the Ngombe of Bongandari in the Maringa district. In this instance, a strong case appears to exist for a narrowly attributable ethnic style, but the small number of clearly provenanced examples still reduces certainty — it could have been a very narrowly defined village style.

Another variation on this type in Ubangi is attributed to the 'Banfumu' (i.e Fumu) by Maes (1929, pl. I, fig. 28), (fig. 155). One companion piece in the Musée Royal de l'Afrique Central, accessioned post-Maes (fig. 156), has the same basic structure of a small platform supported by two columns with segmental profiles on a domical base, while a third example has three supports, the two outer ones being segmental and the inner one circular (Musée Royal de l'Afrique Central, no. 36933). All three use engraved geometrical decoration on the supports, similar to that seen on others from the region (although the execution is somewhat rougher), but they are distinguished through their extremely attenuated vertical proportions. As only the example published by Maes (fig. 155) has a provenance, and only three have been identified in museum collections, a definitive attribution of these headrests to the Fumu becomes problematic. While the three might appear to represent a close-knit *stylistic* unit, it is a style that would, given the time gap between their dates of accessioning into the museum collections, have extended over a period of 50 years. Part of the problem here is that we have little information about the makers and users of these headrests, so it is impossible to know if these three objects could be the work of a single carver, or if they were made by individuals for their own use, but according to the template common in their geographical locale.

The attribution of other headrests with multiple columns is equally problematic. Some are unequivocally attributed by Maes to peoples of the Kasai, including three very different examples, which he provenances to the Teke in the Stanley Pool district (Maes 1929, pl. I, figs. 17, 18, 30),[32] one of which has wire-bound outer columns. Two headrests from the British Museum, similar to one of Maes's 'Teke' examples (1929, pl. I, fig. 30), have, however, been attributed to the Yansi by William Fagg. One (fig. 157) was collected in 1866 in the lower Congo/DRC by W. Dundas, who was 'with Stanley in the Congo', and the other (fig. 158) was collected by H. H. Johnston, who collected it on the 'Upper Zaire river' at Bóló bó in 1885. These examples, all of which use four columns, metal strips, studs and platforms that do not extend far beyond the outer columns, suggest the difficulties of attributing this apparently idiosyncratic headrest type to any one ethnic group, as there do not appear to be any clearly distinguishable markers exclusive to any one of them. Furthermore, the extensive use of metal cladding in the form of flat strips rather than wire on these objects does not offer a means of separating them on the basis of the form of metal used. Examples using flat strips have been attributed or provenanced to a great variety of different ethnicities, from Ngombe to Teke and Mfinu, as have those using wire strips. Similarly, the use of metal studs is found on examples attributed to a number of different ethnic groups. One unprovenanced example from the Wellcome Collection in the British Museum (fig. 159), which has eight columns on an oval base, has metal studs on a similarly shaped platform, but no metal cladding. Yet its overall appearance suggests a similar provenance.

But the problem does not end within this western region of the DRC. As Dewey (1993:53) suggests, many of the decorative features found in this region are shared across a number of different ethnic divisions. Even an analysis of the structural and decorative combinations of each headrest within stylistically related parameters does not reveal any cohesion among particular headrest forms and single ethnicities.

*Extensions of the style region*

Maes (1929, pl. II, fig. 5) illustrates a headrest, provenanced to Sanga, with three columns wound with metal strips, a chamfered rectangular base decorated with closely engraved lines and a platform with moderate upward curvature, a formation with strong affinities to some Ngombe examples, such as figure 151, but also finding echoes in two examples in the British Museum. Accessioned in 1890, these two (figs. 160 & 161) were donated by the Baptist Missionary Society and were attributed to 'Congo, Eastern Tribes', to which was added an insecure attribution of 'Basongye?' (i.e. Songye). In these examples, the crescent curve and linear surface decoration of the platforms are very similar to those noted for the stylistic complex identified in the discussion of figures 146–158, above. One (fig. 160) has a chamfered rectangular base with engraved linear decoration, but the columns are plain. The other (fig. 161) has an oval base with engraved decoration very similar to that noted on some Songye and Lulua headrests discussed above (e.g. figs. 117, 118 & 123). Here the three columns are fluted with engraved vertical lines not seen on many other examples. The upper surface curvature on the platform is very marked, rather like the Ngombe example (fig. 154) or the Loei example (fig. 151) discussed above. A third example illustrated in Maes (1929, pl. V, fig. 28) attributed to the 'Tempa (Songye)' also has a rectangular base, two downward-tapering columns, and a platform that has a very pronounced butterfly shape, similar to those seen in single-columned examples attributed to the Songye (figs. 136 & 137).[33] Given this mixture of elements, it would be tempting to suggest a hybrid style, but, seen on a wider scale, this combining of elements is common to a large proportion of the headrests provenanced from the lower Congo and Kasai regions. Thus, to find any purportedly pure styles that were 'mingled' to produce a bewildering variety within set formal parameters appropriate to columned headrests is thus not only rather pointless, but it points to a problematic need to trace an origin for every variant. Yet there are some examples whose cohesion to a particular template suggests that particular styles did form under specific circumstances.

*Kuba variants: The possible 'ethnic' style (figures 162–167)*

Similar multiple-columned examples are provenanced to the Kuba kingdom, a polity in which ethnic identity was formed in relation to a federation of a number of different, fragmented ethnic groups under a single leader (Vansina 1978). Not only was there some degree of political centralisation and a concomitant codification of visual language (Cornet 1982), there was an apparent acceptance of the terms of this identity formation among most of the groups involved. The Kuba examples have either rectangular (Maes 1929, pl. IV, figs. 11–14) or shield-shaped bases, columns that tend to be carved with a faceted, polygonal profile and rectangular to butterfly-shaped platforms. They are almost all undecorated, except on the upper surface of the platform, where designs of a type generally associated with the 'Kuba' (Cornet 1982) are executed (in varying degrees of fineness) as panels on either side of the central strip. There tends to be a marked contrast between the relatively rough carving of the base and supports, displaying the adze marks and thus the process of carving, on the one hand, and the smooth intricate finish and patina of the upper surface (fig. 165), on the other.

The examples of this type that Maes published in 1929 were all double headrests, with the two platforms supported on two columns each, and no intervening central support, although one five-columned piece (fig. 167) suggests some affinity to Ngombe examples (cf. fig. 154). They all have a distinct horizontality, partly because they are double headrests, and partly because the proportions of their columns to their platforms and bases emphasise their lateral extension. But a similar horizontality is equally evident in the single headrests of this kind, such as the examples illustrated here (figs. 162–166), but of which there are many more in the Musée Royal de l'Afrique Central, all of which were accessioned in the period 1950–53, as was the example in figure 167. On the basis of this pattern of acquisition, it appears that the single headrest using a multiple-columned support was possibly a later form than the equivalent double headrest among the 'Kuba',[34] although single headrests with bent legs (see figs. 351 & 352) have earlier dates. But there are problems with this hypothesis.

Vansina (1978) and Cornet (1982) have both established that there is no monolithic Kuba entity; that the Kuba kingdom was made up of groups of different origin. Vansina (1966:4–5) lists five groups among the 'Central Kuba' and many others as 'peripheral' Kuba, a category to which the Isambo have been assigned, and to which the Shoowa, according to Vansina, also belong, not only because their language is so different from that of the central Kuba, but also because their fabric designs are so different (Meurant 1986; Adams 1978). It is possible that different headrest designs, including not only these columned examples, but also the bent-legged headrests attributed by Maes to the 'Kuba' (Maes 1929, pl. III), were linked to the various sub-groups among the Kuba and related peoples, although the paucity of accurate provenancing makes this impossible to establish. The fact that there is also a clear stylistic link between the bent-legged examples (figs. 351 & 352) and the multiple-columned headrests in figures 162–167 via the arrangement and decoration of platform and base suggests that these are variants of a single style. Further, because it is reasonable to assume that the headrests accessioned in the 1950s were made some time prior to that date, we can conclude that the basic structural elements must have persisted within changes effected over a long time and across a number of different producing groups.

Common to many of the multiple-columned examples, belonging to both the Kuba and other groups, is the degree of decoration applied to the upper surfaces of the platforms. The design's physical relief would have imprinted itself on the sleeper's lower jaw area, but it would have been clearly visible when the headrest was not in use, suggesting that these objects were aesthetically embellished for reasons other than pure utility.

## Back to the melting pot ...

There are also examples of multiple-columned headrests attributed by Maes to the Tetela (Maes 1929, pl. V, figs. 31, 31 [sic]),[35] Nkutu (Songo Meno) and Tempa (Maes 1929, pl. V, figs. 27, 28), all of which have a strong stylistic affinity to the Kuba examples, both in the shapes of the columns and the platforms. The provenance given for two examples is Lubefu and one is from Lusambo, both areas that fall within the Lusambo melting-pot region discussed above, and, for this reason, cannot be convincingly linked to particular or pure 'ethnic' styles.

Another two examples in the Musée Royal de l'Afrique Central provenanced to the Lualaba region (fig. 168 and Maes 1929, pl. V, fig. [32])[36] are quite distinct from the Kuba forms, having domical bases, thin circular columns and propeller-shaped platforms. They are distinct too from two others also attributed to the Luba (fig. 116), (Maes 1929, pl. V, fig. 36) which both have butterfly-shaped platforms and columns articulated by raised rings around their circumference, but have different bases.[37] The variety of forms in headrests attributed to the Luba cannot necessarily be explained through an appeal to sub-divisions among the Luba speakers either, where like characteristics would be concentrated in a single sub-group or region. Examples with articulated columns have been provenanced to both Lake Mweru and the Lualaba region, and their different bases do not suffice to suggest that they were parts of defined sub-styles.

The lobed base of the example published by Maes (1929, pl. V, fig. 36) is particularly unusual for this region — he illustrates only one other, attributed to the Yaka of the Popokabaka region (Maes 1929, pl. V, fig. 26). Another extremely similar example (fig. 168), a double headrest with two platforms, appears to bear this attribution out, having on one of the supports a face carved in relief, in a style that recalls those on other headrests attributed to the Yaka (cf. figs. 83 & 87). While the structure of the supports and bases of these examples could be argued to be common to the southern DRC region, the lobed base is unusual in the context of the DRC. In this example, the two lobes, although they are joined by a rectangular bar, nevertheless form distinct bases for each of the two square-profile supports. This appears, from what is known of DRC headrests, to be an aberrant construction, seen in very few other examples, it being a feature most closely linked to headrests from south-east Africa. As we have seen, however, the lobed base was used in examples found in Tellem caves, on examples with either single or multiple supports (cf. figs. 4 & 10–12), and may have had a wider distribution across Africa in the past, but it is prominent in the headrests made in the south-east African region.

## The south-east African region: Impossible boundaries

Multiple-columned headrests within the south-east African region appear to have been made and used by a number of different ethnic groups, and exhibit a bewildering variety of combinations of columns with other forms in the structure of the support. For the purpose of clarity, only those that use columns as the major support element will be discussed here, and I will deal with the variations on this theme in the chapter on south-east African headrest types. An example (fig. 170) that can be used to stand as a transition between Luba examples and the Southern African examples that follow has a domed oval base similar to that in figure 169, and a rectangular platform with a deep profile similar to Ngombe examples (figs. 145 & 154). It is unusual, however, in that one of its columns is deeply fluted, and both columns originally had a breast shape projecting outwards parallel with the short ends of the platform. The museum records suggest this was collected among the Kalanga, a part of the larger Shona group,[38] and the presence of such breast shapes accords with similar breasts on other examples from the same ethnic complex (Nettleton 1985).

The earliest published examples of multiple-columned headrests from this region are to be found in Müller and Snelleman's *L'Industrie des Cafres du Sud-Est de l'Afrique* (Müller & Snelleman c. 1892, pl. XIV, nos. 13, 14). The drawings include three examples, of which two are simple, and one has three columns in a triangular formation, flaring outwards to join at the base. The three are all provenanced to regions in present-day Mozambique — Inhambane, Chiloane and Gaza — and may thus be placed under the generic ethnic label of the Tsonga. But this kind of multiple-columned headrest appears to have been fairly widespread among a variety of other peoples in Southern Africa, including the Shona, Tsonga, Ndau and possibly Tswana. While certain stylistic features of the headrests of this type may be used as a guide to establishing their ethnic origins, these cannot be regarded as being either definitive or exclusive markers.

The simpler examples illustrated by Müller and Snelleman (c. 1892, pl. XIV, nos. 13, 14) both have chamfered bases, one with two columns on a circular, flaring base, and the second with three columns on a flatter oval base, and both have pendants with engraved designs at the under sides of the short ends of their platforms. These features are found on many headrests firmly attributed to the Tsonga speakers of South Africa and Mozambique (Becker & Nettleton 1989; Becker 1999), but there are other examples with similar features provenanced to Zimbabwe, and thus possibly attributed to Shona

CHAPTER 5 Authenticity and History | 157

speakers. One of these (fig. 171), provenanced to the Kalanga (a sub-group of the Shona), has four columns on a chamfered circular base very similar to one illustrated in Müller and Snelleman and provenanced to 'Zambèze' (pl. XIV, no. 13).

Among the examples that have a clear provenance and an early date is one in the British Museum, collected by Bent in Mashonaland ('Chibi's country') in 1891 (fig. 172), which has a horizontally placed, rectangular, box-like structure bridging the middle of the two columns of the support and a raised chamfered base with a decorative band around the centre of its sloping side. This base is lobed, however, so that each column stands on its own lobe. The chamfered lobed base appears more consistently on headrests attributed to the Shona than it does on Tsonga examples, but this is not a hard and fast rule; one such example (fig. 173) has three columns bridged by a rectangular box, the outer columns having a slight inward curve, all of which stand on a tall chamfered oval base. In another example, three columns stand on a raised chamfered oval base with a triangular projection at the centre of each of its longer sides (fig. 174). The latter two headrests were collected by H. Jaques[39] in the 1920s and 1930s in Tsonga territory in what is now Mpumalanga, and their provenance is thus secure, as is their ethnic attribution. Another two examples, however, both with bi-lobed and chamfered bases, were collected by Leo Frobenius (fig. 175) prior to 1928, possibly in present-day Mozambique, and J. T. Bent (fig. 176) in 1892, in present-day Zimbabwe. Frobenius attributed his to 'kaffern', probably meaning the Shangane[40] or Tsonga, while Bent's is recorded as 'Bechuana' (i.e. Tswana). There is little difference between them, except that the example collected by Bent (fig. 176) has a triangular projection between the lobes and decorative carvings on the upper edge of the short ends of the platform, both features that appear most commonly on headrests provenanced to the Shona.[41] Its attribution to the Tswana, therefore, seems somewhat puzzling, although this might simply demonstrate that Shona-style objects were used by Tswana speakers, or even more likely, that it was collected among the Kalanga, who live in north-eastern Tswana territory. All five of the Southern African headrests included in this category (figs. 172–176) share the same structural features and formal assumptions, yet they are accompanied by records of three different ethnic origins.

Other examples of shared features in Tsonga and Shona headrests are a legion, as can be illustrated by other examples in which the columns are bridged by a central horizontal element. Two with firm Shona provenances have horizontal links with fluted vertical surfaces between the columns: one (fig. 177) has two columns on a lobed base with a rounded projection between the lobes, and the resultant tri-lobed shape is repeated in the horizontal bridge between the columns; the other (fig. 178) has three columns on a bi-lobed base with a central triangular projection. Both have pendants set back from the under sides of the short ends of their platforms, and engraved decoration on these pendants and on the upper end of the platform's short ends, but the headrest in figure 178 has, in addition, engraved decoration in the form of nested triangles on the upper surface of the platform in a pattern, something that does appear to be an exclusively Shona feature (Nettleton 1985; Dewey 1993). In 1892 William Distant published drawings of figures and headrests (among other items of local manufacture) made by the 'MaGwamba' (i.e. Gwamba), a Tsonga-speaking enclave in the Spelonken area of the then Transvaal Republic (Distant 1892:102). One of these drawn headrests has a lobed base with a triangular projection at the centre, although this one appears to have been flat, and it has a two-tier columned support (fig. 179) with a tri-lobed flat central element forming a transition between the four paired columns of the lower section and the two single columns of the upper section. Distant's drawing does not indicate whether there was any engraved surface decoration on the headrest.

Columned headrests in south-east Africa, then, also elude closed ethnic classification in terms of stylistic features, because there are too many elements that are common to all these headrests to allow for closed ethnic definitions, and there are examples that appear totally idiosyncratic and thus defy any ethnic categorisation. The similarities between Shona and Tsonga headrests, on the other hand, does point to real historical situations of contact and exchange, and this has led both Dewey (1993) and Becker (1999) to suggest that a more useful way of classifying such headrests might rest on regional rather than ethnic criteria, an issue to which we will return in other sections of this study.

What this survey of the columned headrests produced in African societies has shown is that stylistic elements have to be very carefully delineated to be used as classificatory tools, and that ethnic stylistic boundaries possibly cannot be fixed. As a result, the idea that there is a single form of headrest that can be considered as an 'authentic' template belonging to a single ethnic group has to be rejected. As each headrest is in some way unique, differentiated from all others by small idiosyncratic elements, they may be grouped, but the grouping has to allow for change, for borrowing, for collaboration and for pure [re]invention. The subsequent sections of this study of headrests will be dealing with other headrest types that are delineated on the basis of their formal structures in the first instance, and subsequently discussed in terms of ethnic and individual variations. Wherever links and similarities seem to exist that make some kind of geographical, cultural historical and chronological sense, these have been marked. But I have resisted any kind of African diffusionist model to explain similarities among objects from far-flung locales, relying rather on the idea that because humans have the same corporeal structures and similar needs for aesthetic embellishment, they will arrive at similar solutions. At the same time, a need for individuation, for marking objects as particular and personal, is an extension of the recognition of people as unique. In the analysis of headrests from various regions that follows, we will return to issues of attribution, but will also look at histories of understanding their ethnic difference and they way they have been used to signal difference and similarity.

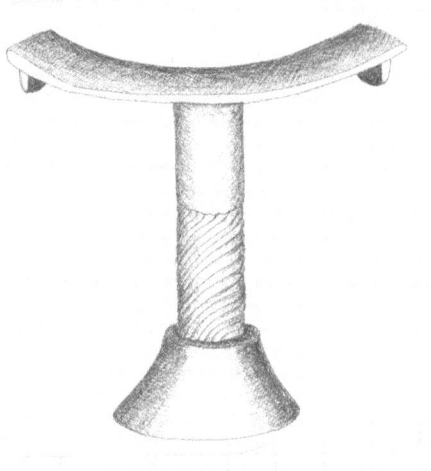

109 Tshwane (Pretoria), National Culture History Museum, collected by H. P. Junod, 1940, South Africa, *Transvaal, Shangaan* (Shangane), Tsonga', wood, 13 cm h.

110 Müller and Snelleman (c. 1892, pl. XV, no. 2), *Zoutpansberg, Transvaal*, probably Tsonga, wood, 17 cm h.

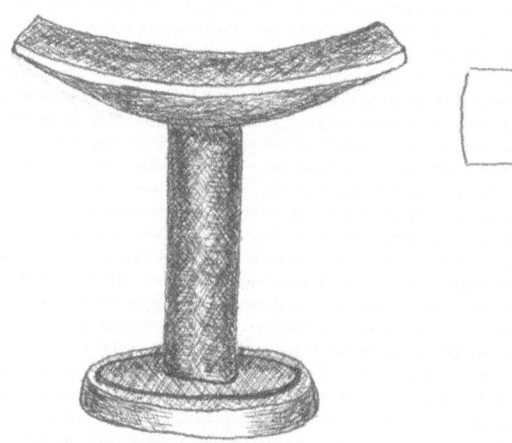

111 Musée Royal de l'Afrique Central (no. 672), (Maes 1929, pl. II, fig. 1), Democratic Republic of the Congo, *Bangoi (Giri)region, Bangala district, BaLoei* (Loei), wood, metal wire, 12 cm h.

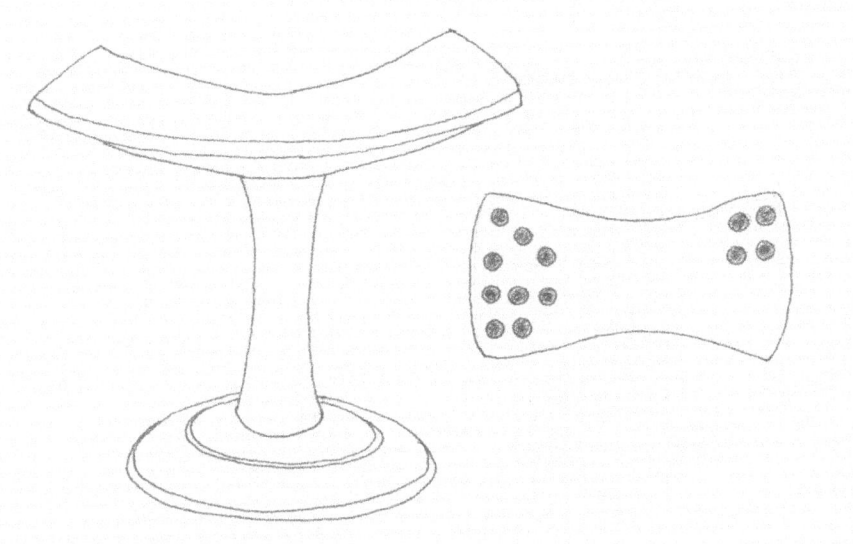

112 Musée Royal de l'Afrique Central (no. 36720), Democratic Republic of the Congo, 'Kasai' (region), '*Sapo Kanwamba*', wood.

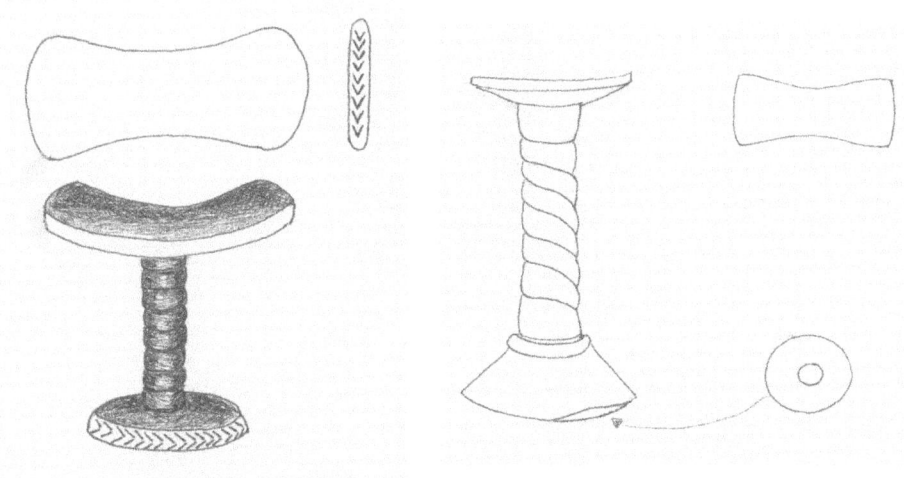

113 British Museum (no. 1954 N23), (Wellcome Collection, no. 232216, 'Mashona?'), Democratic Republic of the Congo, 'Luba', wood, 14 cm h.

114 British Museum (no. 1954 N23), (Wellcome Collection, no. 9256), Democratic Republic of the Congo, *Bankusu Nkuta? Lualaba Nyangwe*, 'Luba?', bone, 8 cm h.

**162** | AFRICAN DREAM MACHINES

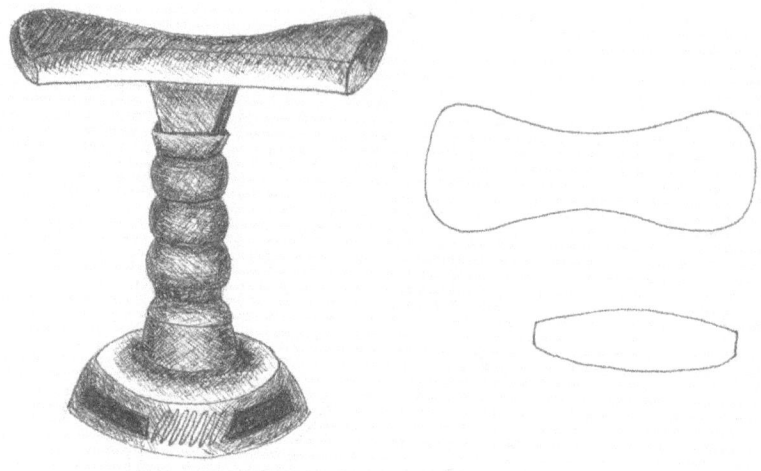

115   British Museum (no. 1904 6-11.5), collected by Emil Torday, 1904, Democratic Republic of the Congo, *Lake Mweru* (region), *BaLuba* (Luba), wood, 12 cm h.

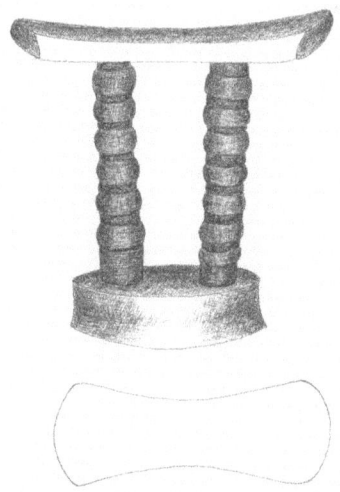

116   British Museum (no. 1904 6-11.6), collected by Emil Torday, 1904, Democratic Republic of the Congo, *Lake Mweru* (region), *BaLuba* (Luba), wood, 13.6 cm h.

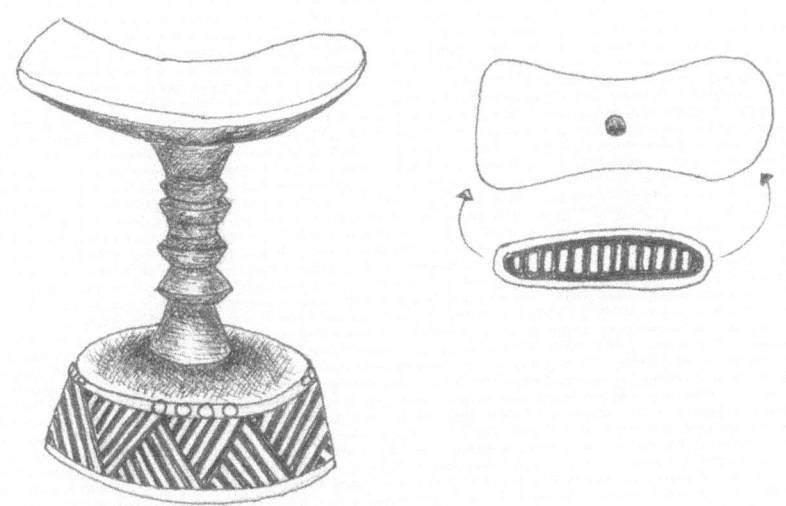

117   Musée Royal de l'Afrique Central (no. 22718), (Maes 1929, pl. V, fig. 5), Democratic Republic of the Congo, *Sankuru* (region), *Lusambo* (district), *BaSongye* (Songye), wood.

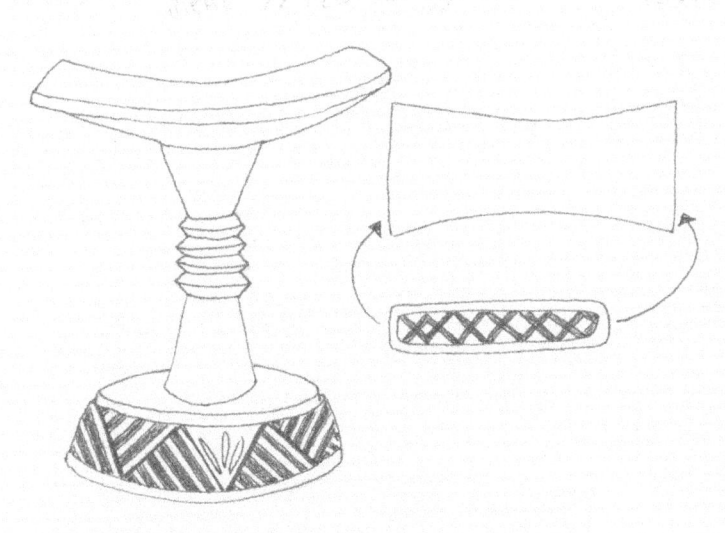

118   Musée Royal de l'Afrique Central (no. 22724), (Maes 1929, pl. V, fig. 4), Democratic Republic of the Congo, *Sankuru* (region), *Lusambo* (district), *[Ba]Songye* (Songye), wood, 11.5 cm h.

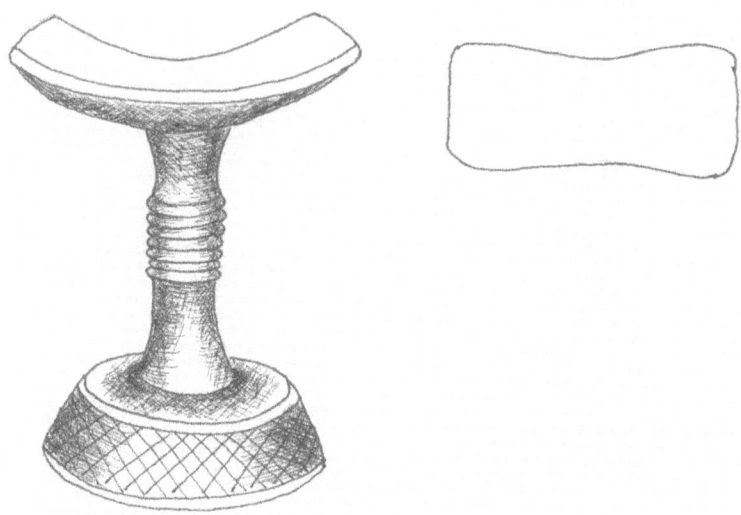

119   Musée Royal de l'Afrique Central (no. 55.80.6), Democratic Republic of the Congo, 'Kasai' (province), wood.

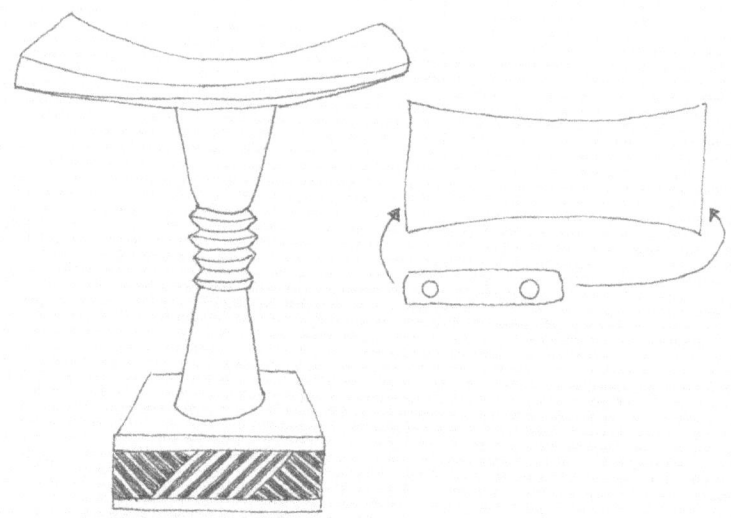

120   Musée Royal de l'Afrique Central (no. 22720), (Maes 1929, pl. IV, fig. 19), Democratic Republic of the Congo, *Lusambo* (district), *BaSongye* (Songye), wood, 13.5 cm h.

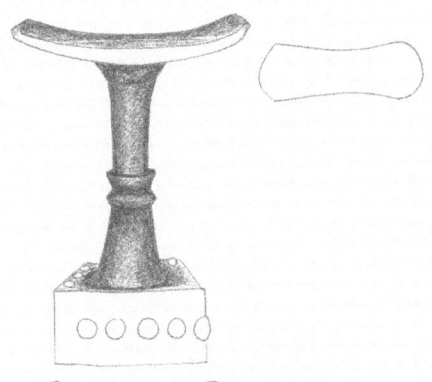

121 Musée Royal de l'Afrique Central
(no. 22711), (Maes 1929, pl. IV, fig. 16),
Democratic Republic of the Congo,
*Luluabourg* (district), *Bena Lulua* (Lulua),
wood, 14 cm h.

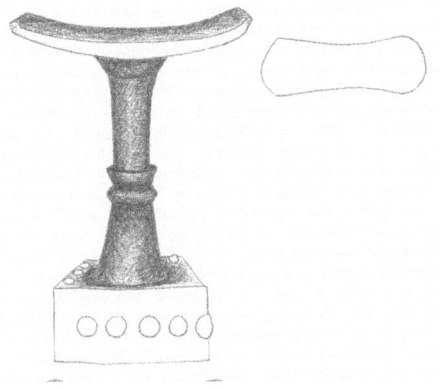

122 Musée Royal de l'Afrique Central
(no. 22722), (Maes 1929, pl. IV, fig. 17),
Democratic Republic of the Congo, *Luluabourg*
(district), *Bakete* (Kete), wood, 10.5 cm h.

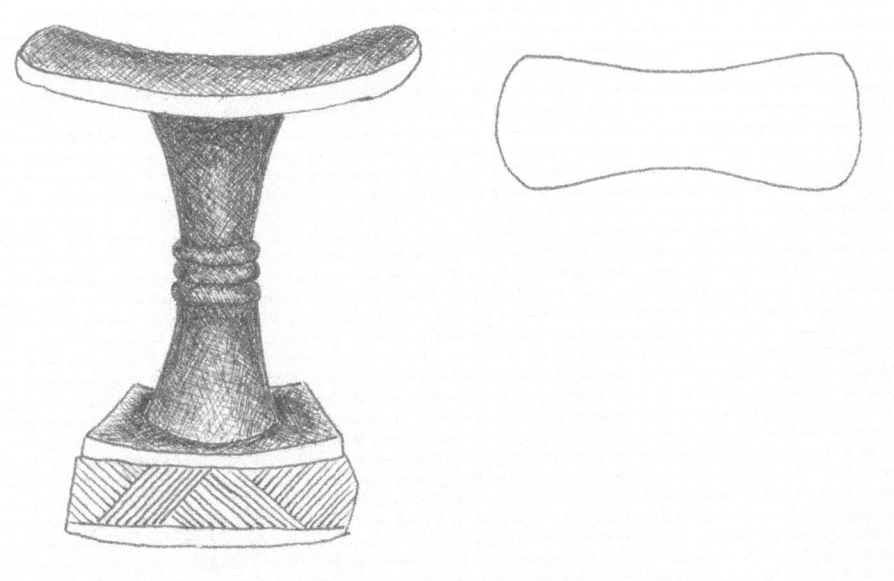

123 Musée Royal de l'Afrique Central (no. 53.4.14), Democratic Republic of the Congo, *Kasai?* (province), wood.

**166** | AFRICAN DREAM MACHINES

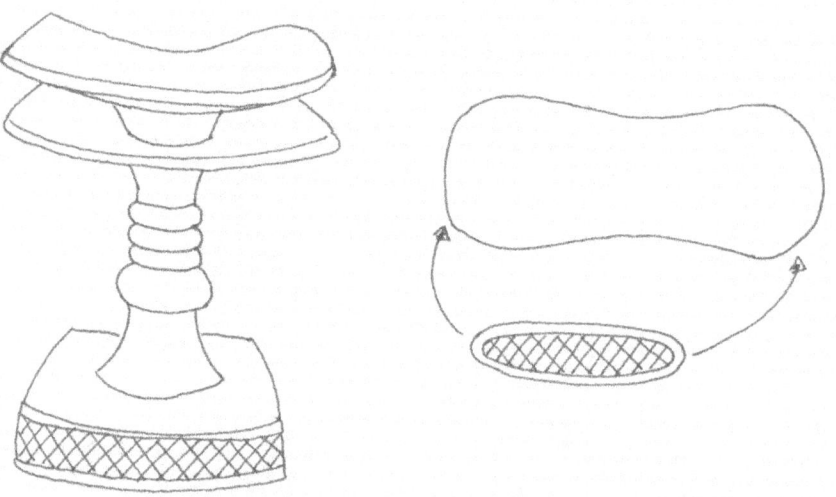

124  Musée Royal de l'Afrique Central (no. 62.34.1), Democratic Republic of the Congo, *Shaba* (province), *Kinda Kamina* (region), *Luba?*, wood.

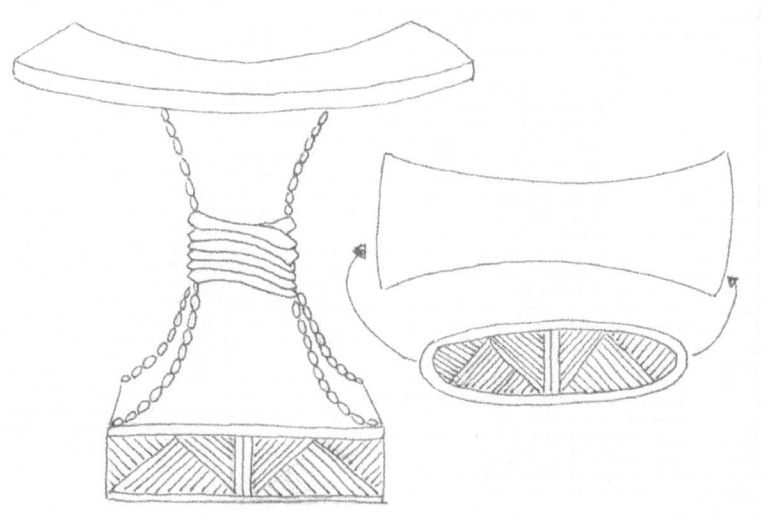

125  Musée Royal de l'Afrique Central (no. 57.32.35), Democratic Republic of the Congo, *Shaba* (province), *Kinda Kamina* (region), wood.

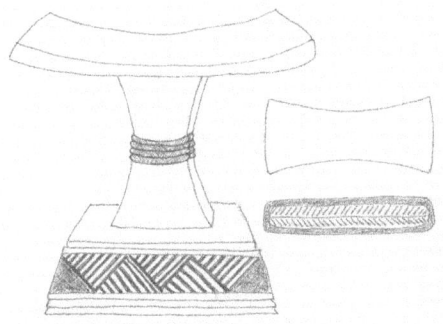

126  University of the Witwatersrand Art Galleries, Museum of Ethnology (no. WME 083), collected by William F. P. Burton, late 1920s/1930s, Democratic Republic of the Congo, *Shaba* (province), *Mwanza district*, wood, 15.5 cm h.

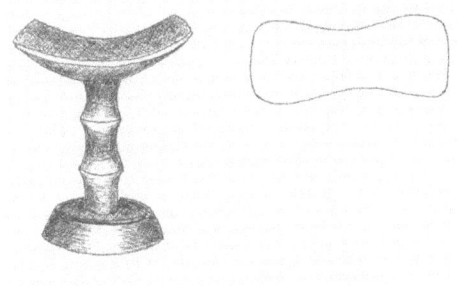

127  Musée Royal de l'Afrique Central (no. 57.53.20), Democratic Republic of the Congo, *Shaba?* (province), *Kinda Kamina?* (region), wood.

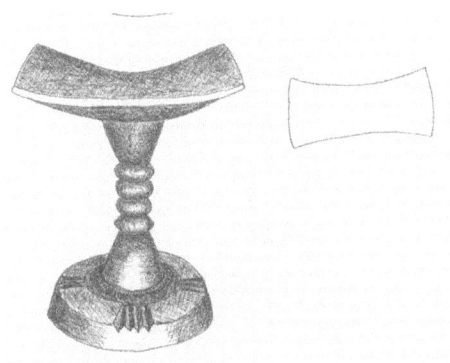

128  Musée Royal de l'Afrique Central (no. 35646), Democratic Republic of the Congo, *Shaba* (province), *Location Milundila*, wood.

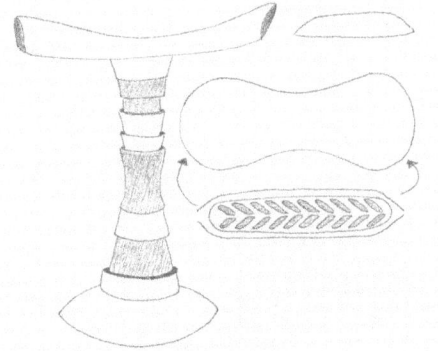

129  British Museum (no. 1889 2.12.3), collected by Edward Coode Hoare, 1889, Democratic Republic of the Congo, *Congo Free State*, *Guha*, wood, 14 cm h.

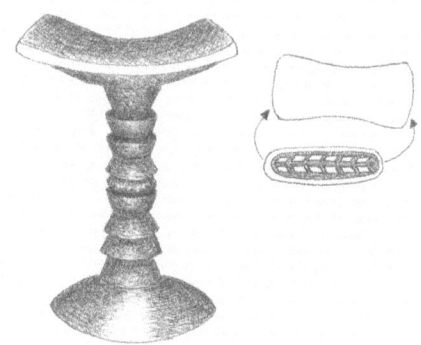

130  Musée Royal de l'Afrique Central (no. 31652), Democratic Republic of the Congo, wood.

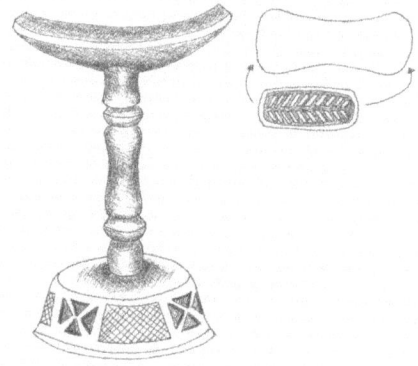

131  Musée Royal de l'Afrique Central (no. 55.35.18), Democratic Republic of the Congo, *Shaba* (province), *Kinda Kamina* (region), wood.

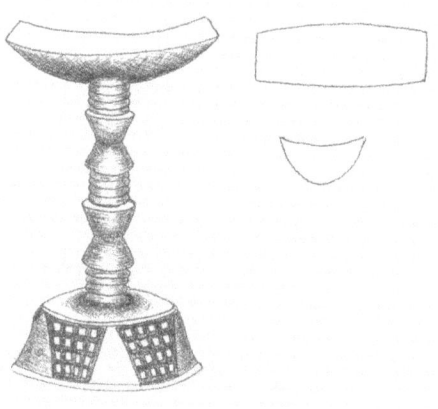

132  Musée Royal de l'Afrique Central (no. 54.74.22), Democratic Republic of the Congo, wood.

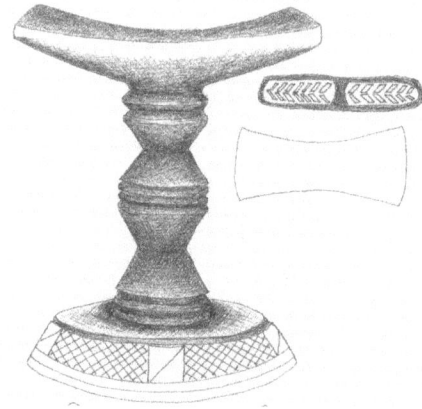

133  University of the Witwatersrand Art Galleries, Museum of Ethnology (no. WME 026), collected by William F. P. Burton, late 1920s/1930s, Democratic Republic of the Congo, *Shaba* (province), *Mwanza district*, wood, 13.2 cm h, design called *Mapingo a Muswayo*.

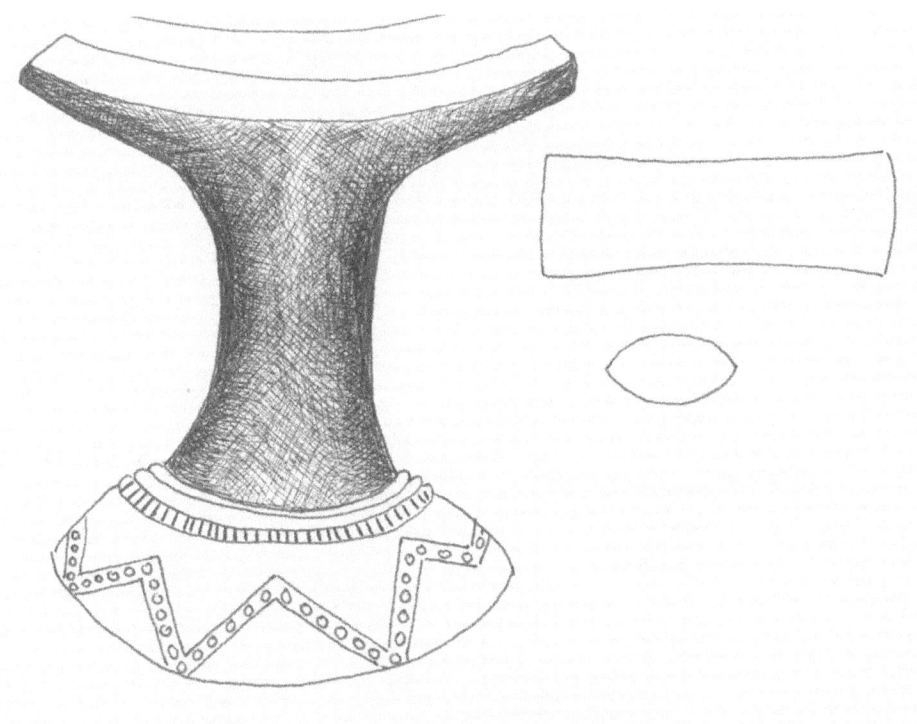

134  University of the Witwatersrand Art Galleries, Museum of Ethnology (no. WME081), collected by William F. P. Burton, late 1920s/1930s, Democratic Republic of the Congo, Shaba (province), Sanga (region), *Luba/Kisalian period*, fired clay, 8.2 cm h.

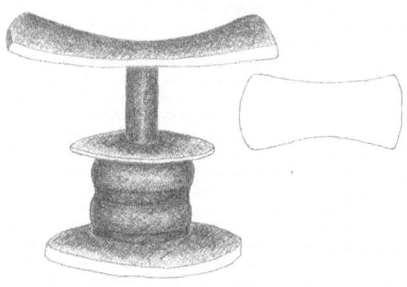
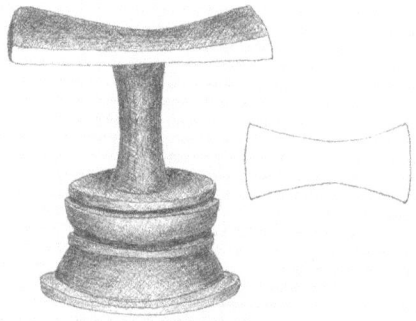

135 Musée Royal de l'Afrique Central (no. 7341), (Maes 1929, pl. V, fig. 18), acquired from M. Castelain, Democratic Republic of the Congo, *Luebo* (district), *Bakete* (Kete), wood, 13 cm h.

136 Musée Royal de l'Afrique Central (no. 7341), (Maes 1929, pl. V, fig. 20), acquired from M. Castelain, Democratic Republic of the Congo, *Lusambo* (district), *BaSongye* (Songye), wood, 14.5 cm h.

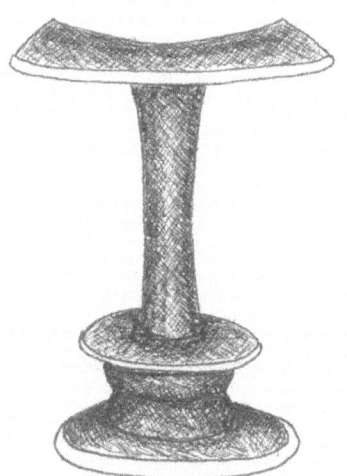
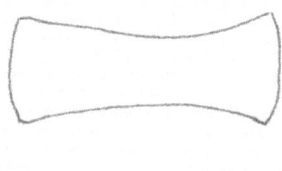

137 Musée Royal de l'Afrique Central (no. 26074), (Maes pl. V, fig. 16), Democratic Republic of the Congo, *Lusambo* (district), *BaSongye* (Songye), wood, 14 cm h.

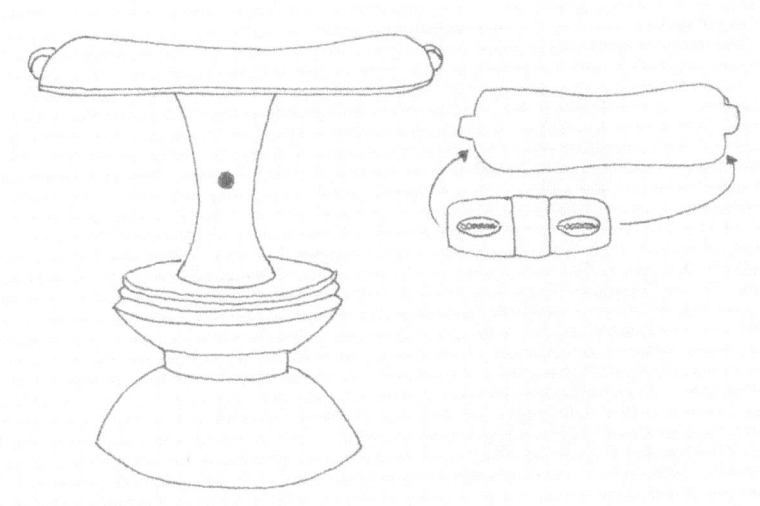

138   Musée Royal de l'Afrique Central (no. 30534), (Maes 1929, pl. V, fig. 23), Democratic Republic of the Congo, *Luebo* (district), *Bena Lulua* (Lulua), wood, 11.5 cm h.

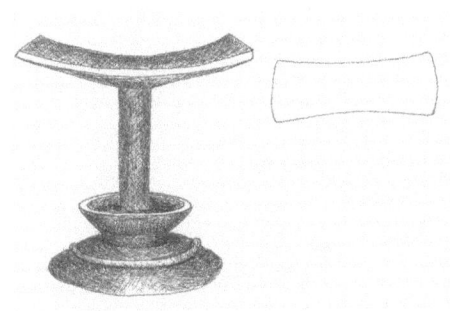

139   Musée Royal de l'Afrique Central (no. 30533), (Maes 1929, pl. V, fig. 16), Democratic Republic of the Congo, *Lusambo* (district), *Batempa* (Tempa), wood, 13 cm h.

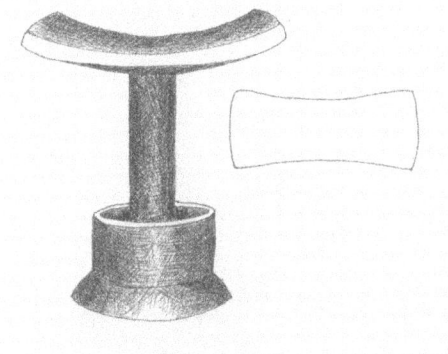

140   British Museum (no. 1954 N23), (Wellcome Collection, no. 22635 [52010]), Democratic Republic of the Congo, no provenance, wood, 13.5 cm h.

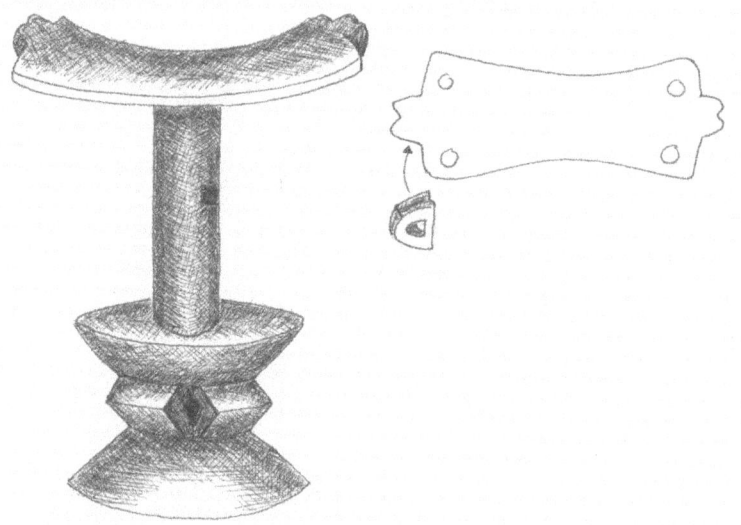

141  British Museum (no. 1908 Ty133), collected by Emil Torday, Democratic Republic of the Congo, *Lusambo* (district), *Kuba, Isango* (Isambo), wood, 12.7 cm h.

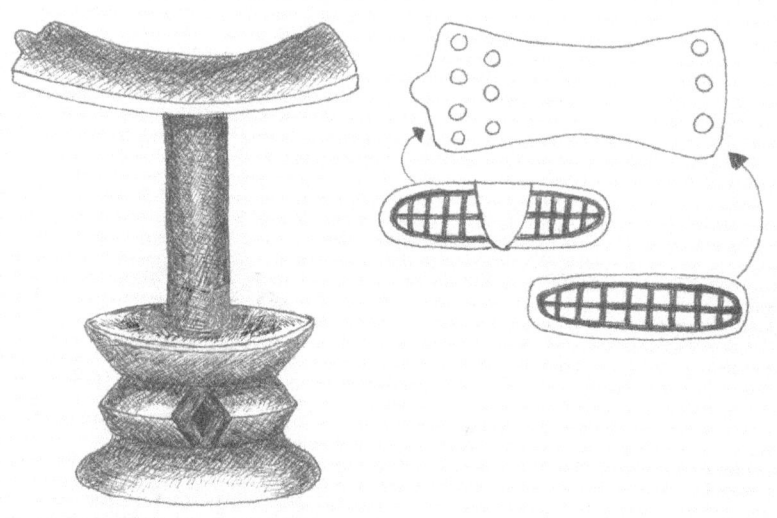

142  Musée Royal de l'Afrique Central (no. 19361), (Maes 1929, pl. IV, fig. 15), collected by M. Maes, Democratic Republic of the Congo, *Luebo* (district), *BaKete* (Kete), wood, 11.5 cm h.

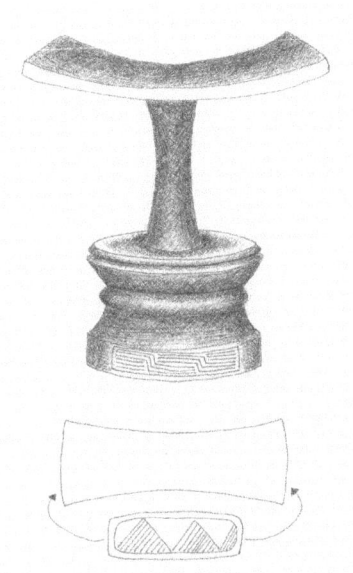

143  Musée Royal de l'Afrique Central (no. 59.48.73), Democratic Republic of the Congo, no provenance, wood.

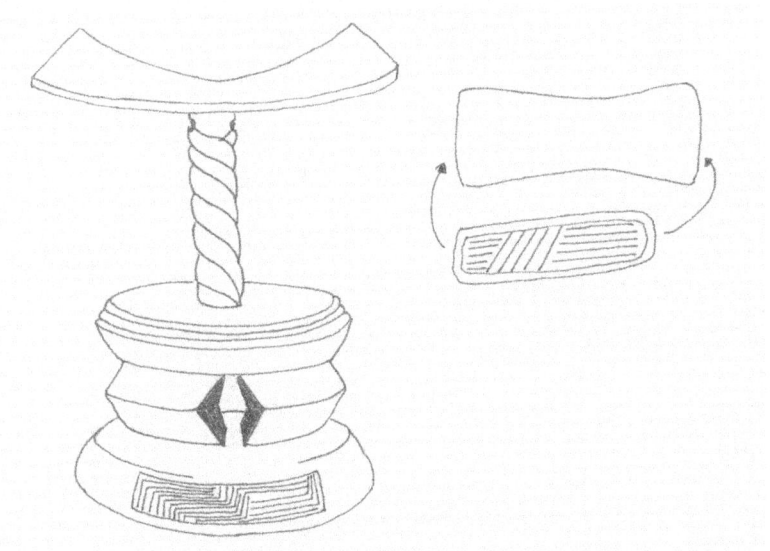

144  Musée Royal de l'Afrique Central (no. 59.48.74), Democratic Republic of the Congo, no provenance, wood.

## 174 | AFRICAN DREAM MACHINES

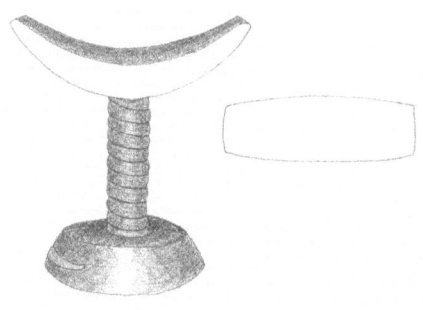

145 Musée Royal de l'Afrique Central (no. 8091), (Maes 1929, pl. II, fig. 2), Democratic Republic of the Congo, *1912*, *Mongala* (region), *Bangala* (district), *Ngombe*, wood.

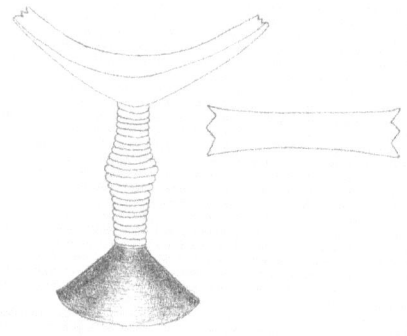

146 British Museum (no. 93.8.4.79), collected by H. H. Johnston, 1892, *SE Africa? Nyasaland? Angoni?*, Democratic Republic of the the Congo?, wood, 17.5 cm h.

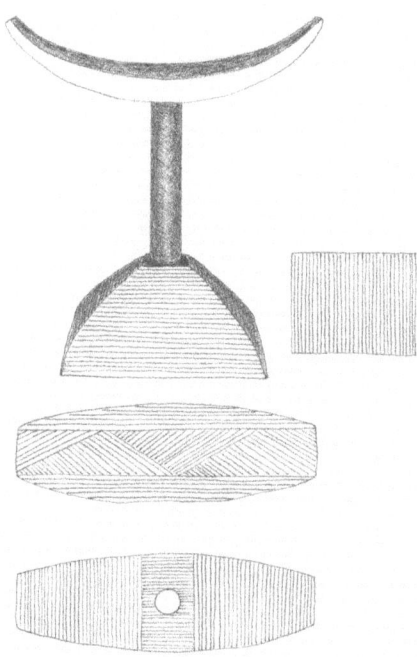

147 British Museum (no. 1949 Af46.580), Oldman Collection, *Belgian Congo?* (Democratic Republic of the Congo), *BaLuba* (Luba), wood, 14 cm h.

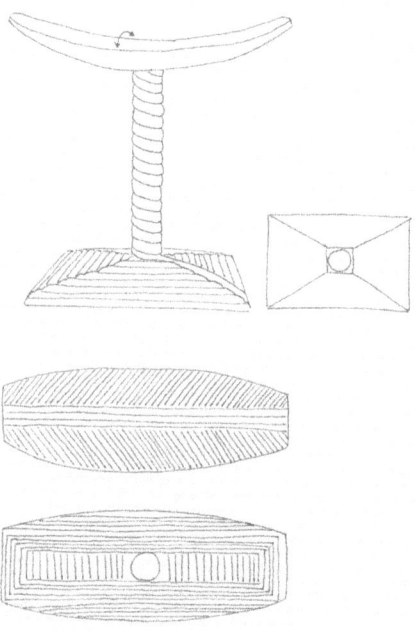

148 Musée Royal de l'Afrique Central (no. 17245), (Maes 1929, pl. I, fig. 5), Democratic Republic of the Congo, *1914*, *Stanley Pool* (district), *Banfumu* (Fumu), wood, metal strips, 16 cm h.

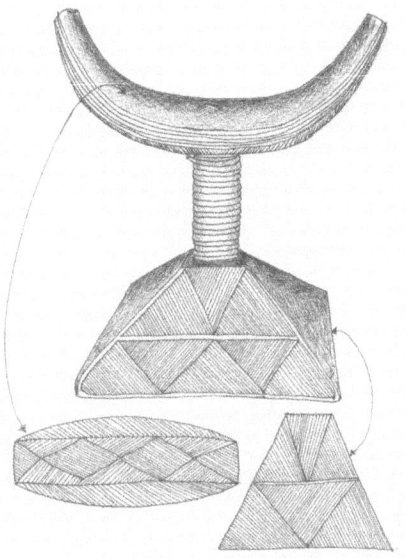

149 Musée Royal de l'Afrique Central (no. 59.34.4), Democratic Republic of the Congo, 'Mongo', wood, metal wire, 16 cm h.

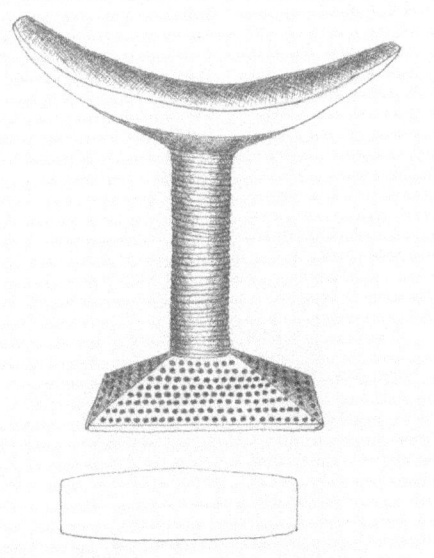

150 Musée Royal de l'Afrique Central (no. 12350), (Maes 1929, pl. I, fig. 2), Democratic Republic of the Congo, *Busende* (region), *Bayanzi* (Yansi), wood, metal studs, wire, 13 cm h.

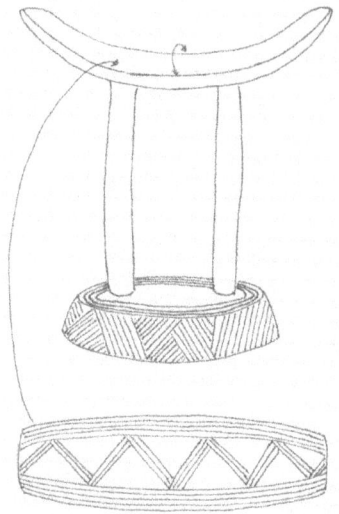 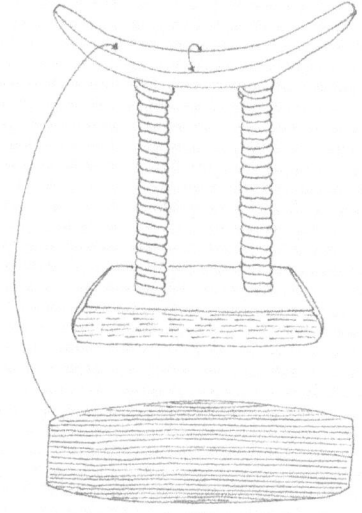

151  Musée Royal de l'Afrique Central (no. 26173), (Maes 1929, pl. I, fig. 31), Democratic Republic of the Congo, *Lower Ubangi* (region), *Equateur* (province), *Baloei* (Loei), wood, 12 cm h.

152  Musée Royal de l'Afrique Central (no. 17200), (Maes 1929, pl. I, fig. 32), Democratic Republic of the Congo, *Ubangi* (district), *Ngombe*, wood, metal strips, 13 cm h.

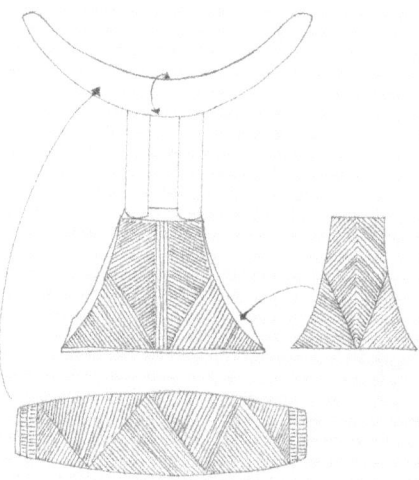 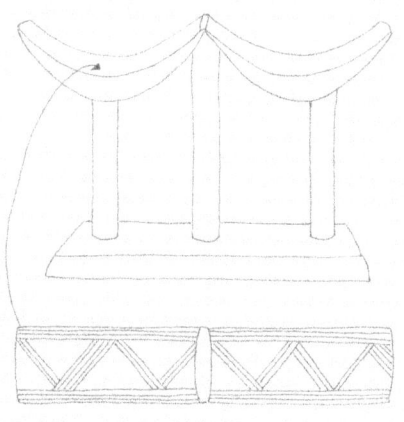

153  Musée Royal de l'Afrique Central (no. 20157), (Maes 1929, pl. I, fig. 29), Democratic Republic of the Congo, 1917, *Ubangi* (district), *Sango*.

154  Musée Royal de l'Afrique Central (no. 8310202), (no collection data available, but cf. Maes 1929, pl. II, fig. 12), Democratic Republic of the Congo, "Ngombe", wood.

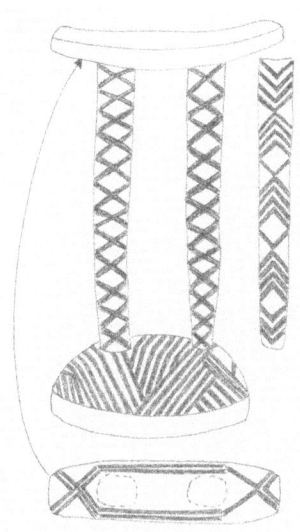 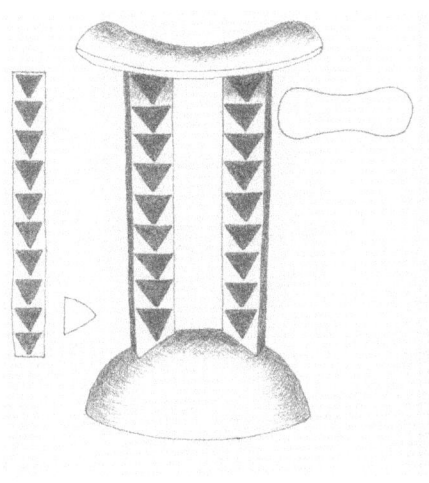

155 Musée Royal de l'Afrique Central (no. 17203), (Maes 1929, pl. I, fig. 28), Democratic Republic of the Congo, 1917, *Kasai* (province), *Banfumu* (Fumu), wood, 19.5 cm h.

156 Musée Royal de l'Afrique Central (no. 51.60.3), Democratic Republic of the Congo, *Kasai?* (province), *Banfunu* (Mfinu), wood, 19 cm h.

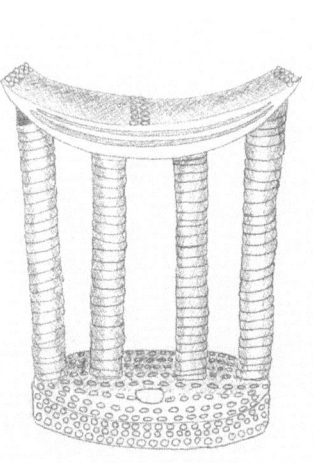 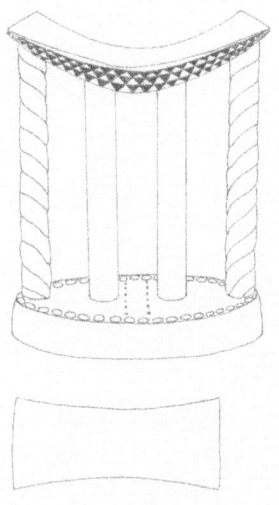

157 British Museum (no. 1923.11.16.19), *From W. Dundas, Bathhurst. Collector was with Stanley in the Congo*, Democratic Republic of the Congo, 1866. Lower Congo Yansi? (attributed by W. B. Fagg), wood, metal strips, studs, 16 cm h.

158 British Museum (Af+2364), collected by H. H. Johnston, Democratic Republic of the Congo, *1885, Bólóbó, Upper Zaire River, Yansi*, wood, metal strips, studs, 15 cm h.

**178** | AFRICAN DREAM MACHINES

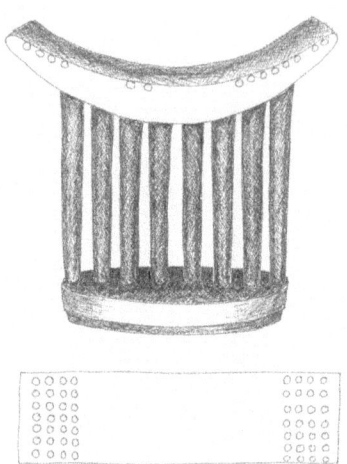

159 British Museum (no number), (Wellcome Box, no. 80/no. 43693), Democratic Republic of the Congo, wood, metal strips, studs, 15.5 cm h.

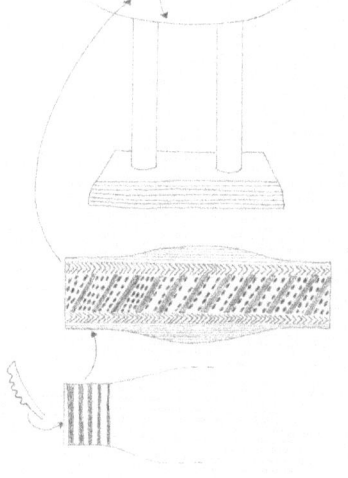

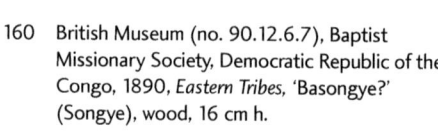

160 British Museum (no. 90.12.6.7), Baptist Missionary Society, Democratic Republic of the Congo, 1890, *Eastern Tribes*, 'Basongye?' (Songye), wood, 16 cm h.

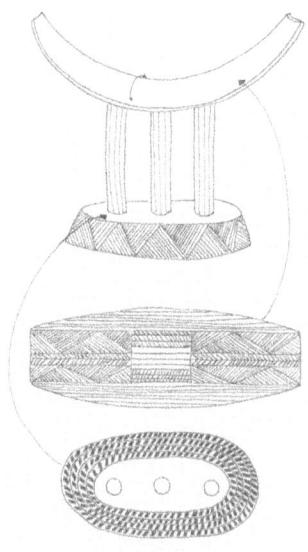

161 British Museum (no. 90.12.6.6), Baptist Missionary Society, Democratic Republic of the Congo, 1890, *Eastern Tribes*, 'Basongye?' (Songye), wood, 17.3 cm h.

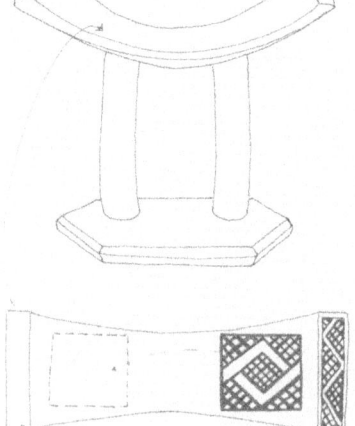

162 Musée Royal de l'Afrique Central (no. 50.9.1), Democratic Republic of the Congo, *Kasai* (region), *Kuba*, wood.

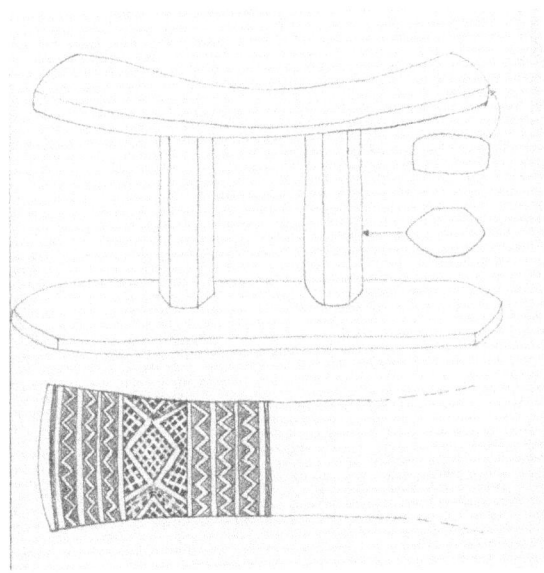

163   Musée Royal de l'Afrique Central (no. 53.74.6958), Democratic Republic of the Congo, *Kasai* (region), *Masoka* (district), *Location Matumba, Ngong/Kuba*, wood.

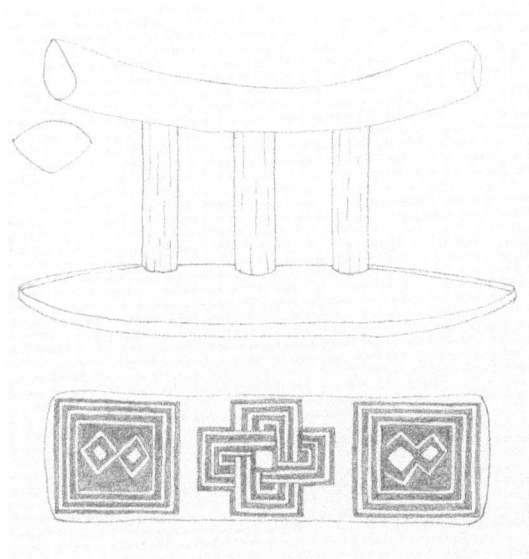

164   Musée Royal de l'Afrique Central (no. 52.48.101), Democratic Republic of the Congo, 'Kasai' (region), 'Kuba', wood.

180 | AFRICAN DREAM MACHINES

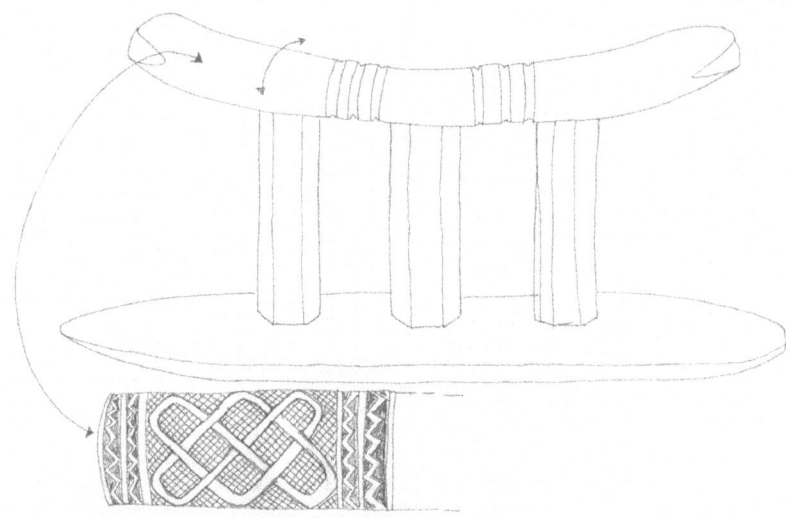

165  Musée Royal de l'Afrique Central (no. 53.74.6732), Democratic Republic of the Congo, *Kasai* (region), *Ibend Missumba* (district), *Ngong/Kuba*, wood, 14.6 cm h.

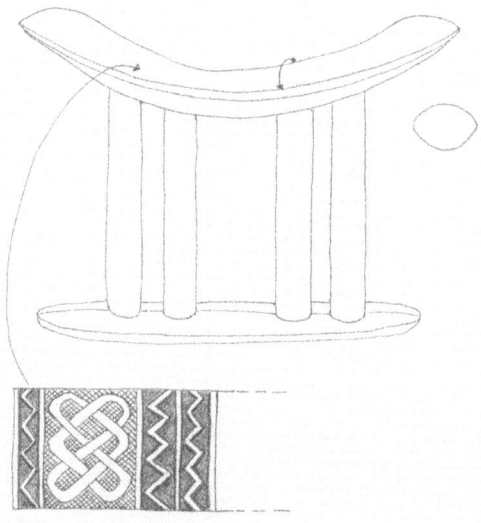

166  Musée Royal de l'Afrique Central (no. 50.9.2), Democratic Republic of the Congo, 'Kasai' (region), 'Kuba', wood.

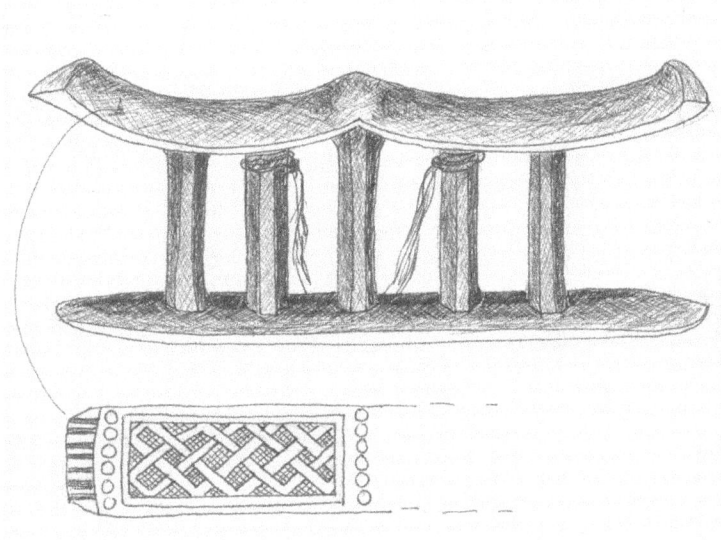

167   Musée Royal de l'Afrique Central (no. 53.26.1), Democratic Republic of the Congo, 'Kasai' (region), 'Kuba', wood, 16.9 cm h.

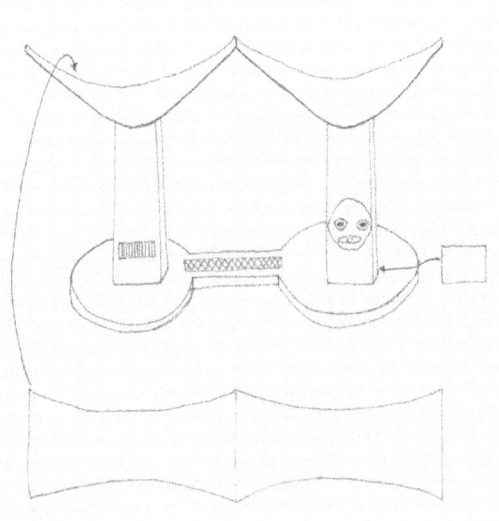

168   Musée Royal de l'Afrique Central (no. 43176), Democratic Republic of the Congo, Luba? (cf. Maes 1929, pl. V, fig. 32, *Lualaba region, BaLuba* [Luba], and Musée Royal de l'Afrique Central, no. 36718), wood, 15.3 cm h.

**182** | AFRICAN DREAM MACHINES

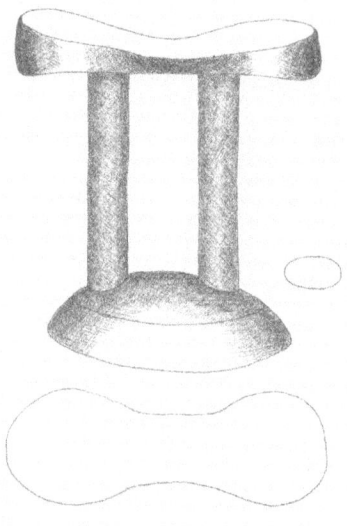

169 Musée Royal de l'Afrique Central (no. 32846), Democratic Republic of the Congo, no provenance, wood, 13 cm h.

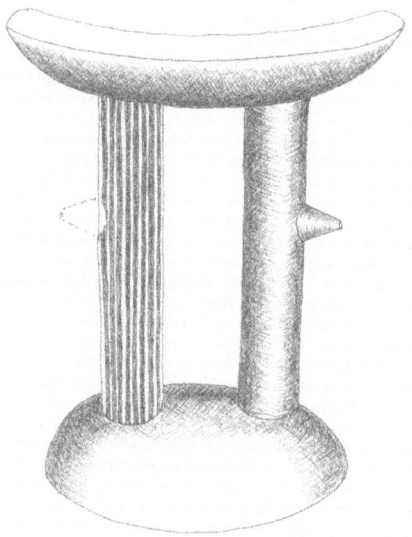

170 British Museum (no. 1947 Af18.101), collected by Phillip Smith, *Southern Rhodesia* (Zimbabwe), *Shona*, wood, 12 cm h.

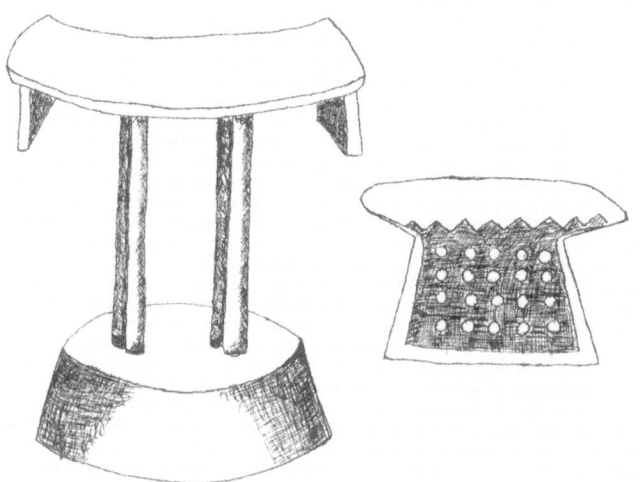

171 British Museum (no. 1949 Af26.1), donated by A. P. Rae, *Southern Rhodesia* (Zimbabwe), *Shona, Makalanga*, wood, 14.5 cm h.

CHAPTER 5  *Illustrations: figures 109-179* | **183**

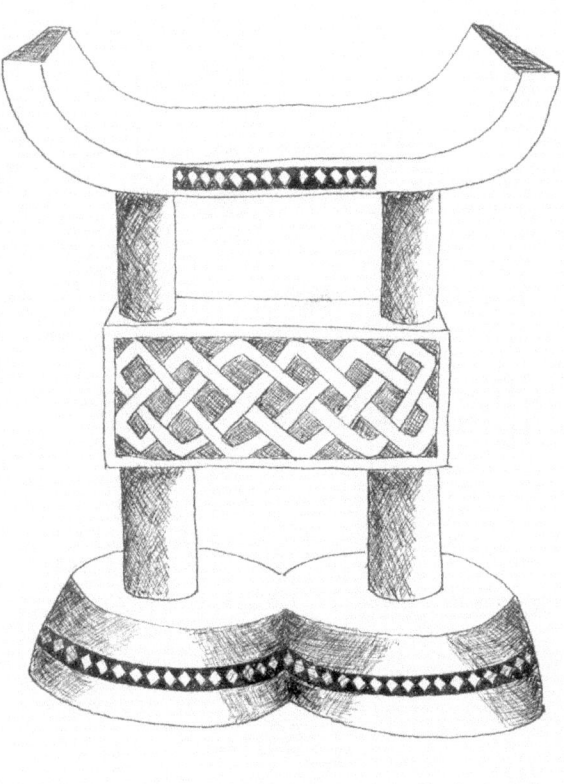

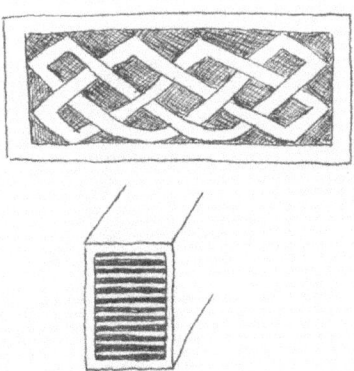

172  British Museum (no. 1892 7-14 1 55), collected by J. T. Bent *in Chibi's country, Southern Rhodesia (Zimbabwe), Shona,* wood, 14 cm h.

**184** | AFRICAN DREAM MACHINES

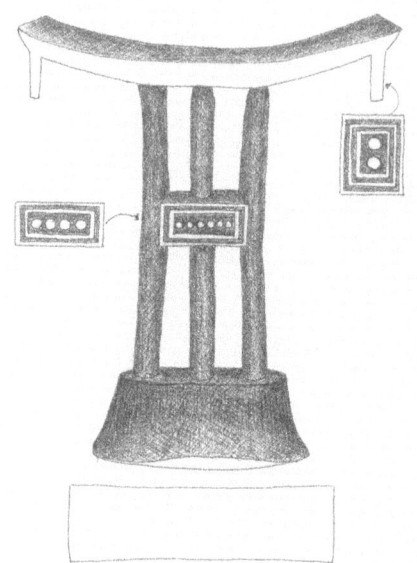

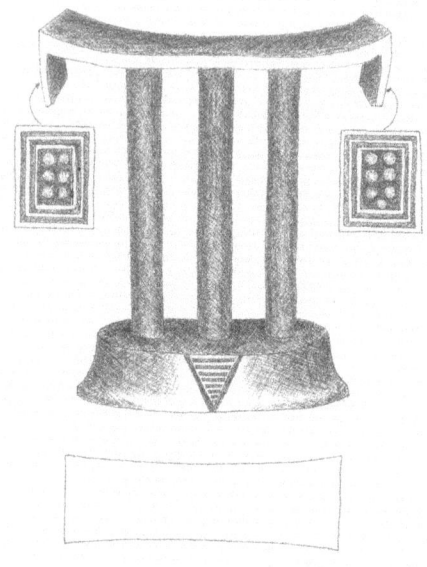

173   Johannesburg Art Gallery (Jaques Collection, no. 50/937), (Wanless 1987, no. 109), collected by A. A. Jaques, pre-1929, South Africa, Limpopo Province, *Elim, Shangaan* (Shangane), wood, 13.5 cm h.

174   Johannesburg Art Gallery (no. 1987.3.61), collected by A. A. Jaques, pre-1929, *Transvaal* (Limpopo Province), *Elim, Shangaan* (Shangane), wood, 14.5 cm h.

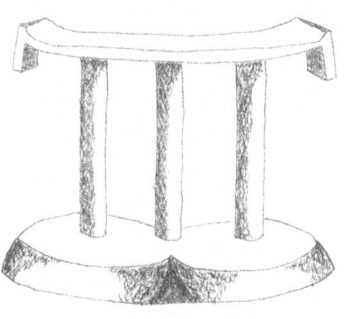

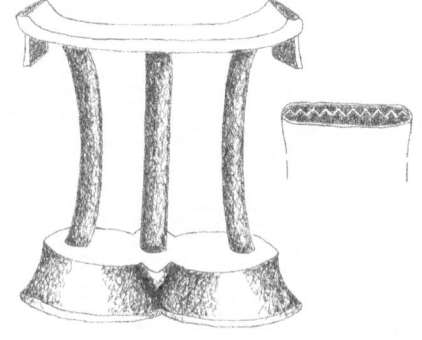

175   Frankfurt, Museum für Völkerkunde (no. 26676), collected by Leo Frobenius, South Africa, 1928, *"Kaffern"*, wood, 12.5 cm h.

176   British Museum (no. 1892 7-14 153), collected by J. T. Bent, Botswana? Zimbabwe?, *"Bechuana"*, wood, 12 cm h.

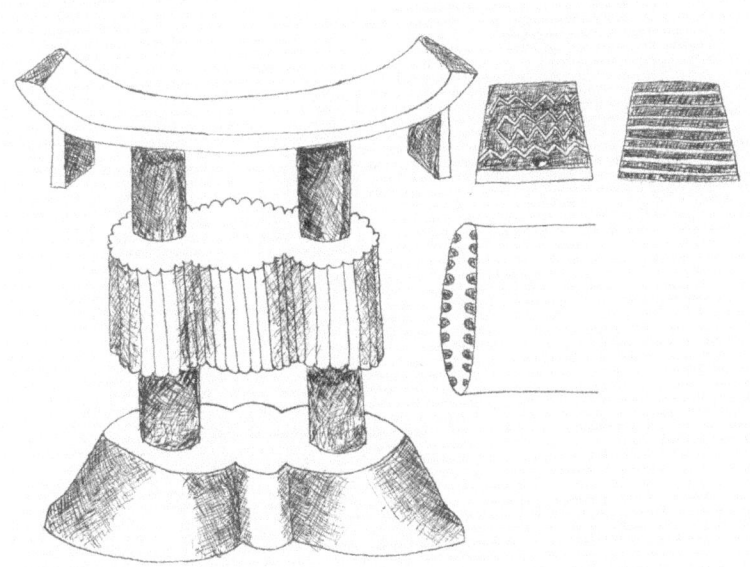

177 British Museum (no. 1931 11-1859), acquired from Alban Head, *Southern Rhodesia* (Zimbabwe), *Mashona* (Shona), wood, 10 cm h.

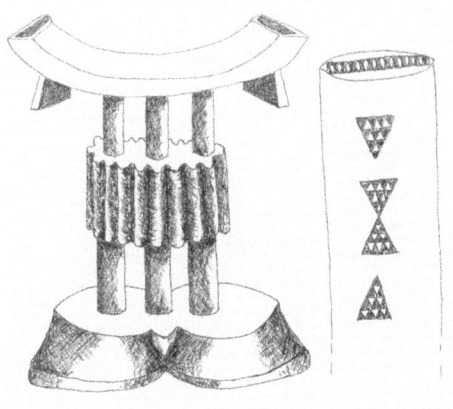
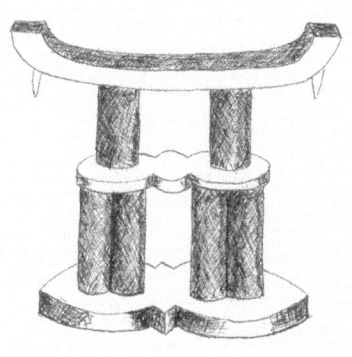

178 British Museum (no. 1935 2-2 21), donated by J. Leveson, Zimbabwe, *Mashonaland*, Shona, wood, 14 cm h.

179 Drawing after Distant (1892:102), [Ma]*Gwamba* (Gwamba), *Spelonken*, *Transvaal* (Limpopo Province).

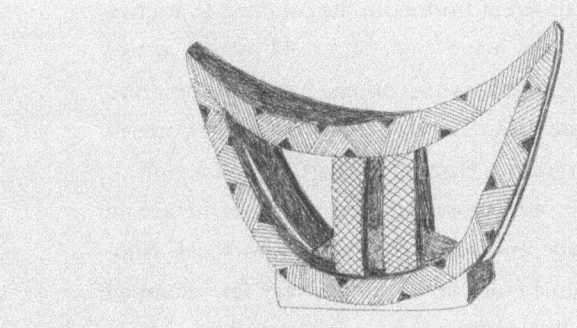

# 6 | East African Headrests: Identity, Form and Aesthetics

ALTHOUGH WE HAVE examined the single-columned headrest in many of its manifestations across the African continent, many other headrest types remain, some of which are constructed on design principles completely different from both the columned varieties. Many of these are very restricted in distribution, being made and used by one or two ethnic groups within particular linguistic clusters, while others have a widespread distribution across ethnic and linguistic boundaries. This chapter examines the patterns of distribution and collection of a variety of headrest types in the East African region.

The headrests from this region that have been most collected and documented in European museums are those that were made and used by peoples who speak Nilo-Saharan and Afro-Asiatic languages.[1] The same collections contain very few examples from peoples who speak Niger-Congo languages, more particularly Bantu languages, in the East African region, encompassing the Sudan, Ethiopia, Somalia, Kenya, Uganda and Tanzania. This lack is somewhat peculiar, given that, although neither East nor Southern Africa is renowned for its figurative sculpture, headrests of various shapes and sizes made by Bantu language speakers in Central and Southern Africa were avidly collected, yet headrests made and used by East African speakers of Bantu languages are singularly sparse in European collections. This is probably not because these peoples had no tradition of hairstyling: Routledge and Routledge (1910), for example, give a careful and detailed description of the construction of hairstyles using bark, ochre and mud among the Kikuyu of Kenya, but make no mention of headrests or of woodcarving.

One mention of headrests made by Bantu speakers in Tanzania, made by Hore in his 1883 account of the territory's 'twelve tribes', speaks of the necessity for small wooden pillows to protect the elaborate hairstyles of the 'Waguha'. But, while Hore does stop to give a description of Goma canoes, and proclaims them 'triumphs of native African art' (which, it must be noted, are not now preserved in museums, probably having been too large to transport easily to the colonial centre), he does not spend any further time on headrests (Hore 1883:14–15). A number of Ngoni headrests from Tanzania in Berlin are reproduced by Krieger (1990), but no others by Bantu speakers with a longer history of settlement there. These Ngoni headrests will, for historical and typological reasons, be treated with those of the Bantu speakers of Southern Africa.

However, that there are a number of headrest types securely provenanced to the East African region, which are, in some cases, widely distributed across the region,[2] gives the lie to the notion that particular types are necessarily bound to particular groups, because there are always too many exceptions to this rule. Some cases of such breadth in distribution can be traced back to at least the beginnings of the colonial era, but others appear to be more recent. This conclusion is based on my reliance on examples accessioned in European museums early in the twentieth century, particularly those in the United Kingdom, to set some kind of benchmark for the ethnic identities claimed for, and the history of, the objects illustrated and types adumbrated from these. The absence of headrests from Bantu-speaking groups may be an accident of collecting, but it is curiously echoed in the (rather eccentric) book on the peoples of Kenya by Adamson (1967), in which she dwells extensively on people's hair, dress and some peoples' headrests, especially those of the Suk, Turkana, Rendille and Borana, but apparently found Bantu speakers less notable in their exotic capital. In this she follows earlier explorer-hunter Major Powell-Cotton, whose account of his early travels in Africa includes photographs of the same peoples' hairstyles and again is somewhat silent on the heads and headrests of Bantu-speaking peoples (Powell-Cotton 1904). Similarly, Johnston's more 'scientific' book on Uganda records extraordinary Nilotic-speaking men's hairstyles, but has much more neutral images of Bantu speakers, such as the Ganda (Johnston 1902).[3]

The headrests in this chapter are discussed according to a similar framework as that used in the previous chapters, partly in an attempt to trace the variety of forms within single ethno-linguistic groups, in order to explore their identities, and partly to establish links among them on a wider scale. It is possible to outline a number of structural genres here, from the block-like forms of Ethiopian examples, through those with a single support with clearly demarcated bases and/or platforms, to others that involve tied legs and ubiquitous, minimally altered, branch forms. I have been tempted to deal with these in a kind of 'national' format, but this raises too many problems. So I have opted once again for a formal typology, because through it I can overcome preconceived notions of identity and begin to look to possible ways of linking forms of these objects to their functions and meanings. It also allows me to overcome the monumental problem of the colonial division of Africa into states that divorced ethnic nationality from state formation. Thus, for example, Somali-style headrests generally, but not exclusively, belonged to persons speaking the Somali variant of Cushitic languages, regardless of the nation state of their present domicile. The order of the discussion is arbitrary and does not suppose any chronological origins for any group of headrests. It begins with an examination of Somali forms, partly because there is one set of Somali headrests that is particularly, and sometimes exclusively, associated with this ethnic group, but which nevertheless poses a problem, and partly because it simultaneously gives the lie to the notion of a simple ethnic style.

## 'SOMALI' HEADRESTS (FIGURES 63–69 AND 180–197)

The distribution of headrests among the Somali peoples is not clearly delineated in the literature. Lewis (1955:83) speaks of the practice of 'the nomads' (i.e. northern Somali) of taking their headrests to the fields, but cites Puccioni's view that in Somalia (i.e. in the south), headrests are used only by the Hawiya and Digil. He mentions headrests in relation to Somali hairdressing practices, again citing Puccioni to explain the apparently limited distribution of headrests among the southern Somali peoples. Lewis (1955:136) further cites Cerulli's (1956) account of the use of headrests by men and women among the Mijertein section of the Darod,[4] but this introduces some ambiguity into the discussion, because it implies that the Somali had a specifically female form of headrest. Arnoldi's (1984) summary of Somali arts also does not deal with specific lineage-based clans, or those clusters clans that are often cited as 'ethnic' groups, e.g. Darod or Issa, but that may be more properly classified as sub-groups within the Somali families (see Lewis 1955:14ff.). Further, she seems to suggest that headrests are used by pastoralists in the northern region of Somalia (Arnoldi 1984:27–28), but she does not mention their use among other Somali groups. Dewey (1993:40), however, suggests that headrests are used both in the Shabeelle River area, as well as among the nomadic southern Somali, citing Loughran and Puccioni, but there is no description or classification of the forms these headrests take.

Headrests from the area of the Horn of Africa, including Somalia, Djibouti and a large number from its neighbouring north-east African territories, especially Ethiopia and Kenya, have been given a blanket ethnic classification of 'Somali'. There are, however, a number of headrest styles from this region, which suggests that this blanketing is somewhat problematic. The Somali as a whole speak a single Afro-Asiatic, Cushitic language, and are therefore related to other, neighbouring Cushitic speakers, such as the Afar. Given that the Somali have a complex, segmentary lineage structure in which significant distinctions are made between Somali and their vassals, the Sab, the differentiation of particular headrests among particular 'Somali' groups is as important to note as is the difference between Afar and Somali headrest styles. Lewis (1955:31) points out that the 'Somali' themselves draw a distinction between the Somali proper and the Sab: the former regard themselves as superior to the Sab, although both trace their descent to a single eponymous ancestor. Thus *Somali* is a term used to distinguish supposedly 'noble' Somali from others, and a racial differentiation is adduced to suggest that the Sab have a greater admixture of 'Negro' characteristics than the true Somali (Lewis 1955:31). Lewis (1955:15) traces the genealogy of these two main sections into large 'families', of whom the Dir family, especially the Issa and Darod[5] sub-groups of the 'Somali' and the Rehanwin[6] sub-group of the Sab are most important here, for it is to these groups that most of the headrests under discussion have been attributed. However, one specific type of headrest has been attributed to the Boni, a group name that does not appear anywhere in Lewis' account of the Somali.

The Boni, according to Prins (1965:189), inhabit 'the savannah hinterland of Lamu and the Bajun Island between the lower Tanu and Juba Rivers' and are hunter gatherers who have a symbiotic relationship with the Swahili townsmen and the wandering Somali herdsmen. Prins recounts that the Boni headrests are made from one particular type of tree that branches into two limbs of equal diameter, about 20–25 cm, and it is in this use of branches that these headrests may find their affinity with those carved by Nilotic and Nilo-Saharan speakers of the East African region. He maintains that they are different from those in the Vienna Museum für Völkerkunde[7] attributed to the 'Daret [i.e. Darod] Somali' and collected in Afmadu, and suggests that they and the ones in the British Museum were most likely made by the Boni and sold to the Somali (Prins 1965:191).

Although the headrests with conical bases and single-columned supports discussed in chapter 4 (figs. 63–69) are firmly provenanced to Somali territory, they are not of the type particularly attributed to the Somali. The two headrest types most commonly associated with the Somali peoples are to be found in a number of publications, most recently Falgayrettes (1989) and Dewey (1993) — who follows Arnoldi's (1984) account — and in Van der Stappen's (1996a) *Aethiopie* catalogue. These include headrests that have a single round or rectangular columnar support[8] (fig. 180), sometimes carved to represent a three-dimensional interlace (fig. 181),[9] and those attributed to the Boni and Darod that have two supports with triangular sections that curve inwards (fig. 182).[10] Both types have platforms that curve sharply upwards at their ends, and bases that are circular and taper inwards to the bottom. The examples published by Dewey and Arnoldi do not appear to have exact provenancing, whereas Van der Stappen's examples do.

Prins (1965), whose single example is very closely documented, claims that the headrests of the second type are properly attributable only to the Cushitic Boni (of southern Somalia and eastern Kenya) and, although Dewey (1993:40) suggests that the Boni examples are squatter, with different patterns from the Somali examples, these differences are not visible in the published examples. Van der Stappen's (1996a:204) examples of this type, collected among the Issa Somali in the Ali Addé region of Djibouti, would, according to this analysis, appear to be 'typical' of the Somali, but the distinction may be misleading, for another, unpublished example in the Musée Royal de l'Afrique Central,[11] which appears to be very similar to Prins's Boni example, has the notation 'Hawiya-Digil, Darod, Ogaden Somalie', linking it firmly to 'Somali' as an ethnic category.[12]

Prins (1965) spends considerable time in a rather esoteric analysis of the meaning of these headrests and their decoration.[13] That these headrests lend themselves to such interpretive endeavours is probably a result of the degree of aesthetic elaboration that is expended on them, at least in the case of the examples published by Prins, Falgayrettes, Dewey and Arnoldi, and the example in the Musée Royal de l'Afrique Central. All show a masterful handling of relief interlace motifs, which appear to be a hallmark of the most technically skilled 'Somali' craftsmanship.[14] This kind of decoration, although not always of the same excellence, is found on other examples attributed to the Somali, but these show some variation on the basic structure, and there are examples with the same structure, but no decoration, attributed to both the Somali and the Boni.

The British Museum, the Pitt Rivers Museum and the Powell-Cotton Museum[15] collections contain a number of headrests of both these types, and many of them have detailed documentation that allows us to reach some firmer conclusions about their makers and their distribution, and to challenge the encompassing 'Somali' classification. Examples such as one (fig. 183) collected at Moti in Italian Somaliland by Major Powell-Cotton was accessioned in 1934 with the notation, 'Ogaden, Somali, Darod'. It has a plain square pillar support, the sides of which angle inwards, to form a star-shaped section, a circular base that tapers downwards and a platform with ends that curve upwards. The last two features are shared by another four examples: two in the Powell-Cotton Museum and deriving from Jubaland in northern Kenya, both attributed to Somali, with one being noted as Rehanwin and for male use.[16] This clearly establishes a Somali identity for such headrests. Occasionally, the star-shaped or square pillar is replaced by a three-dimensional single interlace form such as one (fig. 181) accessioned in 1957, collected in

Tanganyika (now Tanzania) by Admiral Sir George Leclerc Egerton, and classified as 'Swahili (Somali style)'. While no date of collection is available, the accompanying documentation suggests that it dates to the late nineteenth century, and thus establishes a widespread use of the same pattern of headrests outside core Somali territory.[17] The second example (fig. 184), accessioned in 1904, was acquired from one E. A. Hollis, and has the following attribution: 'East Africa, Djibouti, Somali'. It is unusual in that it has a base whose sides are embellished with engraved relief lines, as are the undersides of the platform. This degree of decorative relief carving seen here is common on Somali headrests with V-shaped supports, but not on single-pillar examples, and the very dark, almost black patina of this example is also unusual.

Two examples from the Powell-Cotton Museum have the same column structure, but have engraved decoration only on the undersides of their platforms, and one has a leather strap identical to that on a purportedly 'Wanyika, Giriama'[18] example (fig. 186). Both have clear provenance to Somali peoples.[19] But, two examples with circular columns have decoration similar to this (figs. 63 & 65), as does another, from the Wellcome Collection, also attributed to the Somali. It has a pillar of which two sides are indented, a circular base with relief triangular decoration, and a platform that is basically rectangular with two small projections from the sides of its short ends, the same arrangement of the platform as in Somali columned headrests (figs. 66 & 67), and relief decoration at its ends. A final example (fig. 185),[20] which follows the same pattern, but which has no decorative embellishment, is attributed to the 'Esa' (i.e. Issa), as are many of the others that have the same platform arrangement.

Another example of this headrest type (fig. 186), with a nineteenth century accession number, was donated to the British Museum by A. W. Franks, but was collected in Tanganyika (i.e. Tanzania) by Colonel Hugh Lane and is attributed to the 'Wanyika, Giriama'. I have not encountered any other headrests attributed to these groups in European museum collections, so the attribution must remain suspect. Nevertheless, the provenancing of the headrest appears secure, meaning that it was used by, and possibly made by, or at least bought from someone in that ethnic cluster, and it has two idiosyncratic features that differentiate it from the more common Somali examples. One is the two small lugs that project from the underside of the platform on either side of the support, and the other is the profile of the platform. If the provenancing of this headrest, and those in figures 180–185, to the Somali of Ethiopia and Djibouti is correct, it suggests that not only did this headrest type have a fairly widespread distribution on the east coast, but also that it was subject to an infinite variety of subtle differentiations. It appears, therefore, that looking to distinguish ethnic sub-styles among Somali examples via the structure of the headrest as a whole is less likely to yield results than an examination of details such as the proportions of supports to platforms, notching of ends, placing of relief decoration and use of colour.

Both the headrests in figures 181 and 183 still have leather thongs attached to them,[21] thongs that were used by their owners to carry their headrests around with them, thus clearly indicating the latters' mobility. Other Somali types may also have travelled with their owners, for example, those of the second type (discussed below) were slipped over the hand and 'worn' around the forearms of their owners. As they and their owners crossed ethnic borders, so the styles in which these headrests were carved would change, and variants would result. One such is an extraordinary example in the British Museum (fig. 187), which has a support composed of two round columns forming a V shape between a shallow conical base and an extended rectangular platform. This example, attributed to the Issa, does not show much sign of use, but has extensive relief decoration on almost every available surface, including interlace on the 'branches' of the support, this being a common feature on headrests of the second type. This example is very similar in its decorative detail to one with a single-column support (fig. 63), suggesting that both single-columned headrests and those with V-shaped supports could have been made by individual carvers. It is possible to see the structure of the example in figure 187 as transitional between Somali headrests of these two types, both being provenanced to the Issa. This hybridity might have arisen as a response to a new market for headrests among British colonial personnel, as is probably the case with these two examples, as neither shows signs of use.

A large number of the headrests of the second type (those with V-shaped supports) housed in the British Museum, the Pitt Rivers Museum and the Powell-Cotton Museum were collected by Major Powell-Cotton and his daughters, with detailed collection data, including exact longitudinal and latitudinal co-ordinates of the place of collection, which may enable a clearer distinction between types. These headrests (figs. 188–194) all have two curved supports, forming a V, but, unlike the rather flat and minimally curved cross-sections of the supports in the Boni examples published by Falgayrettes, Prins, Dewey and Arnoldi (cf. fig. 182), the sections of these supports are either deep triangles with curved sides or shallower crescent shapes. Some have interlace patterns on their broader (figs. 188–191) and outer faces, like the Boni ones, while on others these surfaces are plain, and some have designs in relief on the undersides and ends of their platforms and/or on their bases (figs. 188 & 189). They can be arranged into three groups, based on formal distinctions in their structures.

The first encompasses those headrests that are relatively slender in their proportions and have a triangular indentation on both sides of the underside of the platform, each with its apex pointing towards the short end. The platform ends are finished with an indented oval, often with relief decoration. The platform itself is realised in three-dimensional form, with the oval cross-sections of the ends flattening out towards the centre of the headrest. Many of these examples have a base that peaks at its centre in a marked point, and uninterrupted relief interlace patterns that run down the length of the outer sides of the supports (figs. 188–191).[22] Two examples (fig. 188)[23] are definitively attributed to the 'Kotiche (Cotice)'[24], and another three to 'Italian Somaliland', with closer identification of the sub-groups of 'Ogaden, Somali, Darod, Banguei(?), Bambilia' (fig. 189), 'Ogaden, Somali, Darod, Gelib' (fig. 190) and 'Tunne huts, Somali, Darod, Elai Rehanaren' (i.e. Rehanwin), (fig. 191). Of two examples in the Pitt Rivers Museum, one is provenanced to Zanzibar,[25] while the other is attributed to the Somali and provenanced to 'Jubaland near Kismayu'.[26] A large number of this type are held by the Powell-Cotton Museum, some from Italian Somaliland and some from Jubaland; most of them are said to have belonged to men.[27]

The second group (figs. 192 & 193) shares with the first the slender proportions of the supports, as seen from the short ends of the headrest, but, in these examples, the spread of the supports is so broad that their upper ends encompass the ends of the platform, i.e. the platform does not project beyond the edges of the supports. The platforms are thus less three-dimensional at their ends than those in the first group. Some have relief decoration on the outer thin edges of the supports (fig. 193), while others are left plain. Two examples have clear provenancing to Italian Somaliland, and the example in figure 192 has further notations that it was 'made in Rehanwin' with the ethnic attribution to 'Darod, Elai'; a similar example in the Pitt Rivers Museum is provenanced to 'Gobuen Village'.[28] The third (fig. 193) has a generic provenance to 'Somali'.

In the third group are headrests whose supports are broad and deep, but flatter in profile, so that there is a marked, and thus surprising, contrast between the linear appearance of their front views and the heavy width of their side views. These examples (figs. 194 & 195) still a have pronounced point at the centres of their bases and reliefs in interlace form on the outer sides of their supports, sometimes divided into separate sections, all features that are shared with others of this type. The example in figure 194 is provenanced as being 'made in Rehanwin', as being 'Darod' and as 'bought from Ogaden, Kotiche [i.e. Cotice] Afmadu', while another very similar example from the same source[29] is provenanced to 'Haval village, Tuni, Somaliland', with the 'ethnic' notations 'Rehanwin or Hania, Elai'. These notations are somewhat puzzling, given Lewis's (1955:14ff.) emphatic separation of Sab (Rehanwin) from Somali (Darod), but might be explained in terms of his assertion that, when the Darod moved into Rehanwin territory around the Juba River, they took positions first as vassals to and then as units independent from their hosts. Under these circumstances, it is possible that the Darod and Rehanwin shared similar headrest styles, or even that headrests were made by one group for another. Two examples in the Powell-Cotton Museum bear out this provenancing, one being unambiguously attributed to Jubaland, and the other to 'Darod and Ogaden peoples, Yonte Dir'.[30]

The three distinct sub-styles that are apparent across these examples may simply be the result of three different workshops, but cannot necessarily be ascribed to different 'ethnic' styles. Because almost all of the British Museum, many of the Pitt Rivers Museum and all of the Powell-Cotton Museum examples were collected by the same individual across the same time period,[31] they clearly would represent only a limited historical time depth, but, together with other examples, they do allow a spatial distribution of the same headrest type to be suggested for the period 1900–38. If the single example (fig. 193) that was accessioned much later (1962) was also collected later than the others discussed here, it may be seen as representing the tail end of a tradition that has largely disappeared.

While it would be dangerous to base a conclusive outline of ethnic styles on the evidence provided by these headrests, they nevertheless suggest that we should reconsider the Somali–Boni divide, not only because the differences between the headrests collected by Powell-Cotton and the examples published by Arnoldi and Dewey as 'Somali', and by Prins as 'Cushitic Boni' are a matter of proportion, but also because they are very subtle. Not only do the examples provenanced to the Cotice and Darod/Rehanwin have supports that are more slender from the side view, but they are all more emphatically three-dimensional than the examples published by Arnoldi and Dewey that have only implied ridges on the inner sides of their thicker and flatter plank-like supports. That the decoration of most of the British Museum and Pitt Rivers Museum examples, but not of all the Powell-Cotton Museum ones, is apparently less intricate and possibly less technically accomplished than the published 'Boni' examples, may or may not be a significant factor, but the specific structural treatment of the supports probably is.

A final example may help to flatten the distinction by drawing it more firmly. An example of this type, also with curved, thin supports whose profile is markedly planar, but which has little decoration on the two arms (fig. 195) was acquired from Dr Eva Ptak by the Staatlisches Museum für Völkerkunde in Munich in 1977, and, along with two other examples, is definitively attributed to the Boni of Tanzania.[32] The difference between so-called Boni and Somali (Somali as in Ogaden, Darod and Cotice/Rehanwin) headrests outlined above is thus marked via this example as inhering not in the decoration, but in the sculptural quality of the arms. So, because the general style of the examples definitively attributed to the Somali is similar to that which Prins suggested to properly belong to the 'Cushitic Boni', it does not make sense to separate the two styles.

However, Somali headrest typology does not begin and end with these two major formal types. Besides a single example in the Powell-Cotton Museum, clearly based on the type with branching triangular shaped supports, but here with four round supports,[33] some highly individual forms with early dates expand the limens of Somali headrest style. Three headrests in the British Museum, which are provenanced to the Somali, do not conform to any of the types absolutely peculiar to the Somali/Boni discussed above, but their platforms and decoration are clearly related to the round-columned examples discussed earlier (figs. 65, 66 & 67) in their deployment and choice of decorative elements. One (fig. 196) has an unusual or even unique support, which is cross-shaped, with its upper arms separated by a semi-circle and extending laterally to support the platform, while the lower arms are separated by a square space and planted firmly on the base, giving the whole a vaguely anthropomorphic quality. The decorated underside and notched ends of the platform are similar to those of Somali columned headrests (figs. 65 & 66), but the base takes the form of a peaked dome with relief decoration coloured in yellow, blue and red, colours that are repeated on the triangles under the platform. The decoration continues from the base onto the triangular section at the bottom of the support that projects upwards between the legs, largely consisting of dots, but also with flat coloured sections. This example, like two of the columned examples (figs. 64 & 65) was collected by Lt. Col. P. E. Alden in British Somaliland, and, on the basis of its similarity to others of this columned variety, may possibly be attributed to the Issa.

While the use of colour on Somali headrests was found only on these examples, all of which have notched ends on their platforms, colour appears to be quite a common feature on Ethiopian examples. These particular Somali headrests may thus represent forms in which Oromo or Gurage or even Afar influence is strongly marked, especially those that are variants of the columned, conical-based Oromo and Gurage forms. Such influence or correspondence is to be expected in Somali forms, as not only did the Somali settlement push the Oromo out of present Somali territory, but there has been significant contact among the Somali, the Oromo and the Afar in western Somalia and eastern Ethiopia (see Lewis 1955:46). Two other examples, collected by Brig. Gen. Sir Eric Swayne, commander-in-chief in British Somaliland in the period 1884–97, are both on the large side, with rather heavy and squat forms that are not related to other Somali types except, vaguely, to that collected by Alden (fig. 196). Neither shows much sign of wear or use, and their decoration is largely engraved or burnt onto their surfaces. One (fig. 197) has a support of very thick rectangular pillars with rectangular lugs projecting from the top and bottom of their outer sides, and very large shield-shaped 'flaps' descending from the ends of the plateau, but not separated from it. The conical base is similar to the bases of the Somali columned headrests. The same composition is repeated on only one other example, in the Powell-Cotton collection, which in the display is marked as a woman's headrest. The second of Swayne's headrests (fig. 207) is discussed with the block forms below, because, although it is probably Somali in origin, it is of a very different type.

These latter, apparently idiosyncratic, forms demonstrate that, not only was there no single nor pair of canonical Somali headrest types as suggested by Arnoldi (1984), but there was a large variety of headrest forms in this ethnic group, which is presented in the literature as having a closely knit cultural unity. The distribution of their provenancing among British and Italian Somaliland, Ethiopia and northern Kenya also belies the idea that 'Somali' headrests were mainly found in northern Somaliland. Furthermore, the Somali headrests with a V-shaped support belong to a structural type with a much wider distribution, also manifested in the bifurcated branch headrests used by Nilotic speakers from Kenya and the Sudan (see figs. 245–251).

## BLOCK-FORM HEADRESTS

In her catalogue *Support des Rêves*, Falgayrettes (1989:41) suggests that block-shaped headrests are to be seen as exploiting the qualities of pure form, a completely modernist notion. In their wooden manifestations, block-shaped headrests might be classed with branch headrests, or possibly with some logs-as-headrests, as the simplest forms made by

African peoples.[34] It is tempting to suggest that such headrests could be used to establish some kind of hierarchy among headrest forms, in terms of their use by persons of particular status, age or gender, but there is little evidence to support this. It is also tempting to see the block forms as relics of earlier forms, as kind of ur-headrest forms, but this, too, is problematic, not only because they are still made and used alongside other forms, but because this suggestion takes us back to a search for 'origins' within an evolutionary schema. As this discussion proceeds, we will return to these issues.

Headrests used by the peoples of central Ethiopia, including the Oromo, Gurage, Sidama and Arsi, encompass a number of different forms. Not only are there a number of variants on the single-column type discussed in the section on columned headrests, but there are a number of variants of two further types, whose orientation is horizontal rather vertical, and neither of which bears much formal structural relation to the columned types. In these second and third types, there is a much greater integration of the platform and base, where they exist as distinguishable elements. I did not see any of these headrests in the museums I visited, and, although one is illustrated by Falgayrettes (1989), they really only came into widespread public view after the publication of Van der Stappen's (1996a) catalogue. Almost simultaneously, a flood of headrests from Ethiopia, including both the columned headrests and those with integrated base and platform, appeared on the flea markets of South Africa and possibly elsewhere. However, within two years they were no longer widely available from this source, suggesting that, in the wake of Van der Stappen's collecting expedition, people had sold their headrests *en masse*, as it were.[35] Although the examples illustrated by Van der Stappen do not appear to have been recently made, and are unlikely to be very recent products,[36] he made no attempt to give an historical perspective, as there is simply not enough hard historical information available. It is probable, however, that these headrests form part of a long-standing tradition in which different headrest types may have been used by different gender or age segments of particular Ethiopian ethnic groups. The Oromo[37], Gurage[38] and Arsi, to whom most 'Ethiopian' headrests are attributed, inhabit the central highlands of Ethiopia, although, because their migrations can be traced back through present-day Somalia, it is tempting to seek the origins of these practices there.

The fact that these headrests are displayed and sold as 'Ethiopian' requires some comment. The single-columned headrest type from Ethiopia has been shown to encompass a large degree of variation, especially in the arrangement of the conical bases, either smooth or in tiers, and these have been definitively attributed to ethnic groups such as the Oromo, Gurage, Arsi and Afar (figs. 43–59). While these headrests are structurally homogeneous, and this to some extent justifies their being called 'Ethiopian', the same structural principles are evident in other headrests from the same ethnicities outside Ethiopia, for example, the Oromo in Kenya.[39] There are, in addition, other ethnic groups, such as the various sub-groups of the Somali and the Afar in Ethiopia, whose headrests are also represented in Van der Stappen's (1996a) catalogue, and which are stylistically closer to types better known from Somalia, Kenya and Uganda (figs. 180–195). Because these ethnic groups cross the colonially drawn national boundaries, the association of headrests with the nationality 'Ethiopian' is highly suspect. A similar situation can be claimed for the horizontal headrests discussed below.

The most basic headrest forms documented from Ethiopian ethnic groups are basically shaped blocks of wood, oriented horizontally so that many of them are wider than they are tall. Most do not have bases, nor are their platforms clearly delineated, appearing merely as a curved top of the block. Some, attributed to the Oromo by Van der Stappen (1996a:108), (fig. 198), have sides that taper towards the bottom of the headrest, while others that he collected among the Sidama in the region of Sidamo are distinguished by their straight sides. The latter also differ from the Oromo examples in that they have a greater degree of decorative relief on their surfaces (figs. 199 & 200).[40] A surprising visual correspondence can be drawn between these and examples of Tellem headrests (see figs. 23 & 24), but without our being able to make any other correlations, not least because of the distances of time and space between the Ethiopian and Tellem examples.

Of examples tentatively, but exclusively, attributed by Van der Stappen to the Oromo[41] (fig. 201), some have more exaggeratedly tapering sides, with elliptical bases of different depths, while others have rectangular or conical bases.[42] The way in which these headrests are arranged in the catalogue suggests that Van der Stappen is attempting to set up a progression from the simple block-like forms to more complex forms of the columned headrest variety discussed in chapter 3, as though they represent different stages in an evolution of form. But they were all collected at the same time, and must be regarded as synchronic variations on probably different themes, with some hybrid forms between. A similar arrangement occurs with his treatment of other examples that could also be seen as variations on a theme, but that appear to be considered as a development. Such a developmental schema can also be read in Falgayrettes' arrangement of illustrations of Ethiopian headrests in conjunction with Egyptian examples. Falgayrettes (1989: 42–43)

CHAPTER 6 *East African Headrests: Identity, Form and Aesthetics* | 201

juxtaposes four headrests, starting at top left with an Egyptian headrest in which the long sides of the basic rhomboid block are carved back to reveal a projecting platform and base separated by a 'support' with curved sides, a formation very similar to an example that Van der Stappen (1996a:63) provenanced to 'Ethiopia' (fig. 202). Facing this example in Falgayrettes is an Ethiopian headrest (again without ethnic attribution) of the type attributed to the Sidama by Van der Stappen (1996a:199–201), (figs. 199 & 200), and the visual juxtaposition suggests some notion of correspondence at least. The text in Falgayrettes' catalogue is, in this section, almost entirely formalist, driven by an imperative to examine the qualities of form, and, while no direct claims are made for evolution, the formal affinities are used to suggest a pan-human similarity, largely through the inclusion here of a Japanese (?) example made of stone.

Van der Stappen's arrangement, however, is even more suggestive of an evolutionary schema. One moves from a headrest (fig. 202) on the top left of one page (Van der Stappen 1996a:42, no. 62), where the long sides of the rectangular support have been carved back to allow both the platform and elliptical base to project, to further examples[43] where the plane of the support has been penetrated to create a support divided into three sections, the outer two supports being more slender than the central one, which is in turn penetrated by smaller rectangular spaces (fig. 203). The surfaces of the central supports and the sloping upper surfaces of the bases are covered by fine engraved decoration of herringbone and parallel lines. The second of these examples is attributed by Van der Stappen to either the Gurage or Arsi, but another three examples of the same type,[44] attributed definitively to the Arsi (fig. 204), show some possibly significant differences. One of these[45] has a support similar to that in figure 203, but it is much simpler than the Gurage/Arsi examples, and has an apparently more three-dimensional arrangement of the side planes. This difference in volume is even more evident in the example in figure 205, where the side elements of the support appear to have a triangular section, while the central section follows an inverted cone shape extending into an inverted V, formed by two more or less cylindrical legs. In all of these examples, the platform is contained by the sides of the support, projecting only on the long sides of the headrest. Yet, in the Arsi examples, the base and the platform are realised as more clearly independent forms, and they are reminiscent of some Somali examples with V-shaped supports (figs. 188–190). Once again, there does not appear to be a progressive change in these forms over time. Their differences may be ascribable to different ethnic affiliations, but, even though there appear to be echoes among some Arsi and Somali examples, these headrests do not find close parallels in other East African societies. Instead, their closest cousins appear in forms made and used by the Barwe Tonga of Zimbabwe (fig. 266), the Himba of Namibia and Botswana (fig. 267), and the Ntwane of South Africa, but even these and the more clearly rectangular, block forms of some Cokwe and other Angolan groups' headrests (figs. 268–272), start from a different design premise, one in which the platform is separated from the support and the base.

The block-like forms of many of these Ethiopian headrests form such a distinct contrast to the examples with conical bases and columns for supports that it would be difficult to imagine that the choice of one of these particular patterns could be a matter of purely personal whim or fancy. These differentiations are much more likely to mark significant classificatory divisions within these societies. Thus, one might argue that the different forms may have functioned not only to distinguish ethnic groups, but also to make other social distinctions within ethnic boundaries. So, while a regional differentiation is suggested by the fact that columned Arsi examples seem to have been collected by Van der Stappen largely in the Lakes region of Ethiopia, whereas the more planar Arsi examples were collected in the Shoa region, neither area yielded one type exclusively.[46] There remains, therefore, the possibility that the different types of headrest were used by different genders, particularly as the columned Arsi examples bear the annotation that they were used by women. While it is impossible to push this discussion further without firmer empirical data, it is important to note that gender differentiations in headrest forms have also been recorded in the context of Somali headrests with columnar supports, and that both gender, and age and status are marked in headrest styles among other East African groups, such as the Pokot and Turkana.

That there is stylistic cross-over from one group to another is evident from four headrests identified by unimpeachable records as 'Somali', but which are quite unlike other headrests more generally associated with Somali speakers, because they have completely idiosyncratic features. One (fig. 206) is crescent-shaped, with the frame of the crescent opened up in a bow-like fretwork resting on a square base, and with all vertical surfaces covered with engraved decoration. In its shape and horizontal orientation it most closely resembles some of the Ethiopian transformations of a simple block form discussed above, although its yellow wood and surface decoration are much more similar to Somali examples. And it comes with very detailed documentation of provenance. Its unique structure suggests a level of experimentation that once again must be put down to a changing form of patronage for carvers' works.

The second, collected by Brig. Gen. Swayne (fig. 207), shows no distinction between base and support, nor between support and platform. The base flares outwards and three black projecting flutes run vertically up the centre of the face, with two black lines placed horizontally, one to mark the edge of the base, the other half-way up the height of the support. The platform is differentiated from the support only decoratively, by hatched triangles rising to sharp ridges at its ends and curving down the sides of the support and scrolling upwards at the bottom. An example very similar to this in the Brenthurst Collection (Davison 1991b:198)[47] was probably attributed to the Somali on the basis of its similarity to the example in the British Museum, which appeared to have exemplary and incontestable provenance. The collector, Swayne, spent years in Somaliland, but his brother donated the objects to the British Museum, introducing possible margins of doubt. The provenance is borne out, however, by a well-nigh identical example from the Powell-Cotton Museum, collected in Port Mogadiscio (Somaliland) from the 'Hauia People'. But this headrest and Swayne's do not appear to have been used to pillow anybody's head: the wood is still as clean as it was when it left the carver's workshop. Yet it is unlikely that they were made specifically for external consumption, given that most indigenous buyers would have expected to buy their headrests in similarly pristine condition.

The presence of painted relief decoration is known from other Somali examples (see figs. 66 & 67), but its use on these two headrests appears to be closer to that on a 'Suk' example collected by J. Ainsworth[48] before 1921, and some others in the Pitt Rivers Museum in Oxford, collected by Jean Brown in the 1970s. This again brings us to the question of hybrid styles. The Pokot inhabit areas of northern Kenya that are quite far removed from the northern parts of Somalia that formed the British colony. That the colonial boundaries were clearly not impermeable is evident from the Somali migration into Jubaland, and contact between people in the northern part of Kenya was clearly quite developed, as is reflected in accounts such as Powell-Cotton's in 1904 and Adamson's (1967) some 63 years later.

## HEADRESTS WITH ARTICULATED SUPPORTS, BASES AND PLATFORMS

Headrests in which a single column or multiple columns support the platform and stand on a base have been shown to be common to a number of different ethnic groups in the East African region. But there are other types that use vertical supports that are not columnar, as in the case of the Somali examples discussed above, which appear to have a fairly wide distribution through the Sudan, Uganda and northern Kenya. Headrests with the same basic structure are dealt with here, although there is not a great deal of correspondence among them in terms of their proportions and decorative elements.

### Polygonal supports and angular bases (figures 208–212)

The first type is constituted by a set of headrests in which the base is angular — sometimes wider than the platform, which is supported by a polygonal support. Platform shapes vary, but in the small sample of headrests available for inspection, the majority appear to have a butterfly shape in plan and an exaggerated upward curve in elevation. Three examples that are very close in appearance are all provenanced to the Sudan: one (fig. 208) was collected by E. E. Evans Pritchard before 1928 and is provenanced to the 'Gaam (Ingassana) on the West Bank of the Nile';[49] the second, from the Wellcome Collection, now in the British Museum,[50] has no attached information; and the third, almost identical one was collected by S. F. Nadel in the Sudan, in the Nuba Hills of the Kordofan Province, and is attributed to either the Kadero or the Nuba.[51] The supports of these examples taper upwards in a manner that recalls quite closely the tapering central supports of some examples of Ancient Egyptian wooden headrests (fig. 29), and the curvature of the platforms is similar across all these examples.

Two further examples of this type are firmly provenanced to the Sudan. One (fig. 209) was inherited by the British Museum from the Royal Artillery, and has an old label firmly stuck to the upper surface of its base identifying it as 'Dervish Muslim', and 'Tami' from south-eastern Sudan. Its support is hexagonal and is bound spirally with rope, something commonly found among the tied headrests from Kenya and Uganda (figs. 237 & 238). The second (fig. 210), collected by Major Powell-Cotton among the 'Beni Amir' of 'Tokar' in the 'Andal Valley' of the 'Red Sea Province', has a flatter base and support, but nevertheless demonstrates that the type was used among Nilotic- and Cushitic-speaking peoples across a widespread area. Finally, there are two examples of this type of headrest that use multiple supports, one (fig. 211) with a single platform, two supports and a slightly domical base, but which is otherwise very similar to the Sudanese examples discussed above. It has a later acquisition number, but has a provenance to south-eastern Sudan. The second (fig. 212) is from the Musée Royal de l'Afrique Central and has three supports, the two outer ones being fatter and supporting larger platforms than the central one, but the profiles of the supports and the plane and cross-sections of the base are very similar to the Sudanese examples. It is attributed to the Zande or Ngbandi of the lower Uele, and was acquired relatively early in the museum's history. The Ngbandi, however, are considered to have been originally a group of Bantu speakers who have adopted a Sudanic language relatively recently (Peek 2000), and therefore the headrest type may have passed in the same direction as the language.

Pinning an ethnic identity to this kind of headrest thus becomes highly problematic. Jedrej (1995:1) positions the Gaam (who are part of the southern Funj and Nilotic speakers) in a 'geographical borderland between the Ethiopian Highlands and the grassland plains in the Nile in north-west', and suggests that they are also part of a cultural borderland, being surrounded by the Amhara and Oromo in the east and the Dinka and Nuer to the south. The headrest type, also provenanced to other groups in the area, however, suggests that everywhere is a borderland in relation to the distribution of material culture forms. It is possible to suggest that these headrests may constitute the remnants of a widespread form from the Red Sea Province to south-eastern Sudan and into the north-eastern DRC. This form is distinct from other forms of the columned types discussed above and from examples to be discussed below. Its stylistic proximity to Ancient Egyptian examples, while tantalising, is, however, impossible to account for without re-entering the nineteenth century tropes of comparative study or the black consciousness tropes of reclaiming Egypt for an Africa defined as negroid and 'black'.

## Planar supports and domical bases (figures 213–225)

A second type with an even wider distribution in East Africa has in common a domical base, generally hollowed out underneath to form a container, a planar support with sides that curve inwards and a conspicuous platform. In this group, the platforms vary widely in shape, and it may be argued that it is only the details of the shape of the platform, the base and the surface decoration that could allow ethnic style differentiations to be made. These headrests are most commonly associated with the Turkana peoples of Kenya (fig. 213),[52] but the examples found in museums and in well-documented sources in the literature suggest that the plain type is very widely distributed. Trowell and Wachsmann (1953:157) suggest that this is a Karamojong type, but given that the Turkana are an offshoot of the Karamojong,[53] this distinction does not concern us here.

Most examples have been securely provenanced to Nilotic speakers, including the Longarum of the Sudan (fig. 214),[54] the Mursi (fig. 215) and the Nyangatom in Ethiopia,[55] and the Tiati Pokot of Kenya (figs. 216 & 217). All these groups speak Nilo-Saharan languages and apparently share a number of cultural institutions,[56] and only the most subtle of differences is visible in this group of headrests, found most in the curvature of the platforms, the shapes of the curves in the supports and the height of the domical base. Examples have also been collected in Nuer territory, one in 1917 (fig. 218), and at least one other by Evans Pritchard.[57] A single example in the British Museum is attributed to the Kamba of Mombasa in Kenya (fig. 219), a very unlikely attribution, because while the Kamba are renowned carvers, they are Bantu speakers, and there are no other securely provenanced examples in any of the sources I have used of headrests from Kenyan Bantu-speaking peoples. The museum's acquisitions record, however, suggests that it was collected from a person or place in Uganda, before or in 1910, and that would make it more likely an example from a Nilotic-speaking group such as the Karamojong.

An example of this type published by Dewey (1993:46, fig. 26) as 'Turkana?' (fig. 220)[58] has a platform with a strong convex curvature from one lateral side to the other. Such curvature is most commonly found on two-legged branch headrests, and some headrests of this type (figs. 216 & 217) provenanced to the Pokot and, somewhat fewer, to the Turkana. The base of this example is also different in its angular projection,[59] and we begin to perceive in looking closely that each headrest has its own identity, even within a single type attributed to a single ethnic group. Figure 221 is provenanced to the Turkana by Best, and it appears very different from Best's securely provenanced example (fig. 213) in terms of its exaggerated curves in the support, its squatter proportions, the division of its platform into lobes, and the complete lack of curvature in the platform.[60] An example attributed by Wolfe to the Kenyan Karamojong (fig. 222) has an almost identically shaped platform to that in figure 221: it is bi-lobed and flat, but this one has, quite unusually, engraved and blackened decorative elements on its upper surface. Van der Stappen publishes a number of examples from Ethiopia, three of which are shown here (figs. 223–225), with platforms whose narrow centres widen out in fan shapes at their ends. One, from the Mursi (fig. 223), has a flat platform, but the other two, from the Kara (fig. 224) and Bashada (fig. 225), have very strong, convex (side-to-side) and concave (end-to-end) curvatures. There are elaborate engraved linear designs on their bases and platforms, and on the support of the Kara example. Turton (1977) has described the relative isolation of the Mursi in Ethiopia, yet it is clear that they share a number of cultural traits with other pastoralists in the Sudan–Ethiopia–Kenya borderland, including headrest forms. It may be significant, though, that such elaborate forms are all relatively recently recorded, and may well have resulted from contact among groups such as the Oromo and Gurage, where elaborate relief decoration is recorded in older headrest forms, and the Mursi and Bashada, where it is not. Most of the securely provenanced older examples of this type originate from Nilo-Saharan-speaking communities, and it is probable that they spread from these communities to their Cushitic- or Bantu-speaking neighbours. It is also possible that some of these headrests were made by craftsmen from outside the user communities.

## Variations on the theme or individual solutions (figures 226–229)

That craftsmen in this East African area were likely to produce objects that used, but altered, basic themes of utilitarian types commonly seen in their environs is evident from the three headrests in figures 226–228. In the first two, which are securely provenanced to the Pokot (figs. 226 & 227), two round feet flow directly into the central support, which, in both instances, has a central section set back from the outer surface. Their platforms are both propeller-shaped, but that in figure 227 is more convex. The latter also has decoration in the form of aluminium and copper pointille inlay, and each of the lateral leather handles has beads sewn to its surface. These two examples, both collected in the field, are not matched by any in other collections, nor in the literature consulted for this study, and it could be argued that they represent entirely individualistic solutions to headrest design, but within the bounds set by 'traditional' forms.

A third variation on this relatively unusual form is exemplified by three headrests, one published by Wolfe as Turkana, Kenya (fig. 228); another published by Falgayrettes (1989:50) as Karamojong, Uganda; and one in the Pitt Rivers Museum provenanced to the Pokot. All three have two angular feet rising up into the central support, with a fine central channel on the vertical line. Wolfe's example (fig. 228) has a rope of intertwined beads looped through the convex platform and running down this central channel. It in some ways presages the forked or tied headrests dealt with below. Similarly, another example (fig. 229), collected by Jean Brown in the 1970s, has two feet and partly separated legs, again suggesting a relationship with the fork-legged examples most commonly associated with the Pokot and Turkana/Karamojong (see figs. 245–251). None of these examples fits neatly into an ethnic stylistic category; and even though Brown's notations[61] suggest that they were easily assimilated into Pokot classificatory systems and used by members of the younger generations in the age-grade sets of the Pokot, they were not widely used. The significance of age grades for different kinds of headrest forms surfaces with these examples, and will be looked at in more detail below.

## Headrests with leather-encased supports (figures 230–238)

A very early headrest, provenanced to Omdurman in the Sudan (fig. 230), was probably collected in the late 1800s, was donated to the Halifax Museum before 1900, and was transferred to the Manchester University Museum in 1921. Clearly, its provenance is insecure, and it is an example of a type most often attributed to the Bari of the Sudan and Uganda. It has a domical base with two projections framing a central V-shaped projection, front and back. The support is heavy and square-shaped with a metal ring passed through its lower section and another set into the upper end, allowing access to a small interior chamber and providing an anchor for a leather thong. The platform has a distinct butterfly shape, and is flat and very thin in profile. An almost identical example in one of the diorama display cases at the Powell-Cotton Museum is attributed to the Latuka (Sudan), and is said to be a stool.[62] Its closest relatives are a headrest in the British Museum (fig. 231), donated by the Church Missionary Society and securely provenanced to the Bari of the Sudan, along with a second example (fig. 232) that, although it comes from the same source, has a less-secure provenance. The first of these shows the headrest in its naked form: it also has a base with a V-shaped central projection between its feet, but its support is formed by two columns with flat struts between them, both with holes for threading thongs.[63] The second (fig. 232) shows the headrest clothed in a woven encasement of, unusually, reptile skin, with a plug on one side allowing access to the container so formed. This example has, more typically, two block-like projecting feet, without the V-shaped projection. The platform shapes are also quite different, although both have inlaid metal decoration on them. Similar examples are also securely provenanced (fig. 233) to the Bari on the west bank of the Nile, an example collected by Evans Pritchard, and (fig. 234) to the Bari of Sudan's Mongalla Province. These show the stylistic range of this type quite clearly, although the encasement of the latter is made a single piece of leather rather than woven thongs of strips of skin. Another example, in the

Powell-Cotton Museum,[64] collected by the Major and his wife on one of their early expeditions, has the following annotation: 'Sudan, owner Abdulah Hamet, lizard skin, "schedette" Mongalla huts, coll Maj & Mrs', thus confirming the use of a particular material, a use that appears peculiar to these forms. Two further examples of this type in the Liverpool World Museum collection[65] have for one a secure attribution to the Shilluk, and for the other a secure provenance to the Dinka. This probably does not mean that they were made by other ethnic craftsmen, but rather that objects made by Bari craftsmen might have been used by others in the same region, and that a number of neighbouring groups used objects made by Bari craftsmen.[66]

These examples all have a somewhat square appearance, but the proportions, in fact, vary quite considerably from one example to another. One example in the Pitt Rivers Museum (fig. 235), collected between 1882 and 1890 by a British missionary and registered as 'Somali', has, by comparison with the previous five examples, slight proportions, both in the 'feet' and the thinness of the platform. But this does not necessarily point to a shift in ethnic manufacture: an almost identical example from the British Museum's portion of the Wellcome Collection (fig. 236) is provenanced to the Bari, as is an older example in the British Museum (fig. 237), which was acquired in the late nineteenth century from the Petherick Collection, establishing an early date for the tradition. A final confirmation of the association of this type with the Bari comes from an example (fig. 238) with a much thinner and thus more elegant body, but with block-like feet like the first ones in the group presented here. This one was collected by Evans Pritchard, is dated to 1936 and provenanced to the Bari, 'Teaba Kaka' on the upper Nile. Thus the issue raised around the ethnic identity of this headrest type by Dewey (1993:33–34) is largely answered by the archive. While this particular headrest form is relatively limited in its spread, with only a few recorded from ethnic groups other than the Bari, and a similar particularity in style is found also in Bari columned headrests,[67] both nevertheless share a number of structural features with the headrests of other groups. One of these, the encasement of the supports into a single form — a clothed body, as it were — distinctly articulated from both the feet and from the platform, is quite similar to the practice of binding or encasing the supports in headrests with two legs by groups of Nilotic speakers in the region comprised by southern Sudan, northern Kenya and Uganda. The use of reptile skin, however, tends to set the Bari examples apart from those of other groups on another level, in that reptile skin must surely have carried connotations of prestige or ritual significance. Accessing reptile skin is quite different from obtaining skins from domestic animals, or even from game that is hunted for meat. Some of these aspects are dealt with in the last chapter, but it is important to note that headrests are often dressed in a variety of ways, this being one of the more elaborate and least domesticated. Most bound headrests in the East African region employ leather from domestic beasts for their clothing.

### Two-legged, tied headrests (figures 239–261)

These headrests form another, almost completely distinct type that is largely associated with one particular linguistic grouping in the area of Uganda, Kenya and the Sudan; i.e. the Kalenjin, Nilotic speakers, who include the Karamojong–Turkana, the Suk–Pokot–Tiati Pokot and the Lango–Acoli,[68] all of whom have social organisations based on age grades and transhumant cattle herding mixed with agriculture. Bender (2000:49) suggests that the commonalities of basically egalitarian political structures, with shamans or charismatic hunters providing leadership, but with little power, and an economy based on herding and raiding, led to the development of similar forms of kinship structures, clans, lineages and age grading among all these groups. Furthermore, Murray (1998:84) suggests that the Cushitic speakers occupying the highlands of Kenya were there prior to the Nilotes and Bantu who adopted the Cushitic traits of cyclic age sets. Interestingly, all the Nilotic-speaking groups in question here make or use at least two or more headrest types, but they all share one type that has particular structural principles.

The salient feature of this headrest type is its use of two supports for a platform that always has a convex curve from side to side. The supports take the form of thin, splayed legs that are tied together, either by a twisted cord of fibre or hide (figs. 239, 243 & 254–261), by a wooden cross-bar (figs. 240–242) or by a woven leather encasement (figs. 245–252). Some of the oldest examples of these headrests in the British Museum and in the Pitt Rivers Museum are variously attributed to the Karamojong, Pokot and Soga (e.g. figs. 246–251), but a somewhat later example from the Musée Royal de l'Afrique Central (fig. 250) is attributed to the 'Turkana (Karamoja)', (i.e. Karamojong).[69] Some almost identical examples of this type in the British Museum are securely provenanced to the Suk in the Kamasia Reserve of Kenya, having been exhibited on the Empire Exhibition of 1925.[70] Only one of the early Turkana examples (fig. 251) has extensive beadwork of the

CHAPTER 6 *East African Headrests: Identity, Form and Aesthetics* | 211

type common on the Pokot examples collected in the field in the 1970s (figs. 245 & 246).[71] In almost all cases, there is a leather thong (or an iron ring) attached to the headrest to enable its portability, but in the encased examples, two thongs are attached to the thin sides of the headrests in such a way that, when the headrest stands upright, it takes on the appearance of a figure (fig. 251). This is even the case with an example in the Musée Royal de l'Afrique Central[72] (fig. 252), which is provenanced to the Karamojong, but has quite unusual decorative relief carvings on the exposed sections of the legs.

The tying or encasement of the legs with leather thongs appears to have a structural purpose. Headrests of this type are carved from a branch, chosen because it has two smaller branches growing perpendicular to its length in a symmetrical V shape. The platform of the headrest is carved from the larger branch and the two legs are carved from the smaller branches. This can be seen clearly in fig. 253, where the branch that forms the support bifurcates only half-way along its length. There would be a tendency for the V-shaped legs to splay and break while the headrest was in use; tying them together braces the legs and prevents this from happening. In cases where there is a gap between the tie and the platform, this form provided a convenient way of securing the headrest over the wrist of the wearer. Fuller encasement often provided a hollow container for the owner to keep small objects in, this being clearest in the encasements of Bari headrests where the tying is not structural. But in Pokot and Turkana headrests (e.g. figs. 245 & 251), the tying of the headrest often becomes so elaborate as to suggest a human being, particularly a human body. The beaded sections of the Pokot examples are very reminiscent of beaded waistcoats worn by some Sudanese youths photographed by Fisher (1984).

In all of these examples, the platform is carved as a structurally and visibly independent element that projects far over the supports, standing out like shoulders above a torso or like a flattened head. Other examples of tied headrests, however, do not have this distinction between their constituent parts. These forms are those most commonly associated with the Karamojong and Turkana in particular, being featured in many of the photographs of these peoples that apparently record their 'interesting' customs.[73] The difference between these and the other tied types can be clearly seen in a comparison between a Karamojong example already discussed (fig. 244), where the legs fork at the centre of the underside of the platform, and another Karamojong example (fig. 254), where the platform flows directly into the legs to form a truncated A shape. These two both have silver-colour aluminium pointille inlay into the surface of the legs, a practice that appears to be relatively recent. The second structural arrangement, where the legs are relatively narrow and the platform curves both concavely along its length and convexly from side to side, is found in other examples,[74] one of which is provenanced to the Sudan–Uganda border (fig. 255), and has, in addition, a ridge along the length of the underside of the platform. The museum records suggest that both were collected in the first quarter of the twentieth century, and it is possible that both were made and used by Karamojong.

Examples provenanced to the Turkana, on the other hand, generally have legs that are much wider from the lateral aspect, so that they appear more as bent planes, meeting the platform, which also curves, at a very acute angle. Examples are to be found in a number of published sources, including Donovan (1988:47, 488) and Best (1993:157, 158); one of the latter is illustrated here (fig. 256), largely because there is a dearth of examples with early acquisition numbers in the museum collections I have studied. Two other examples were published by Wolfe (1979:17, nos. A5, A4), both attributed to the Turkana. For the most part, these seem to be completely plain, although there are examples with carved and inlaid decoration,[75] something they share with the next set of headrests.

In their accounts of the Turkana and Karamojong, Gulliver and Gulliver (1953: 36, 57) suggest that this type of headrest was the original form used by these groups, but that it had been superseded by the type with a single support (what they call a 'bar'), which I take to be of the type seen in figures 213 and 221, above. They claim that the tied, two-legged type was in use only among older men, and suggested that this was a result of fashion. However, it is as likely to have been a result of differences of use among age sets, as was demonstrated by Best (1993) and is paralleled by Pokot practice. One example of this type in the Pitt Rivers Museum was collected by Jean Brown among the Pokot (fig. 257): she notes this one as having been made and used by a sandal diviner, whereas another of this type, she implies, was commonly used by the middle grades in the age-grade system (Brown 1978, Pitt Rivers Museum, no. 1978.20.259).

Another group of tied headrests (figs. 258–261) all have a horizontal emphasis, quite distinct from the vertical emphasis of the Pokot or Karamojong examples (figs. 244–252). These were carved from a single piece of wood that appears to have been bent into a bow-shape and tied by means of a thong threaded between the legs and to lugs underneath the platform, probably in an attempt to provide a brace (figs. 258 & 259). It is possible that these ties were what gave the headrests their distinctive shape in the first instance, but they would also have prevented splaying of the 'legs' when heads, heavy with ancestral hair, were placed on them. One example from the Musée Royal de l'Afrique Central (fig. 260) has no lugs beneath the rest section, and its line flows more smoothly from legs into curved platform than the other examples, being therefore more like the Karamojong examples discussed above (figs. 254 & 255).

Trowell and Wachsman's (1953:157) rather bald scheme of attributions suggests that these are Acoli. The ethnic attribution of these headrests is, however, very problematic. Four examples[76] were accessioned into the British Museum, collected by a Col. Lupton Bay Hearne, and donated to the museum by A. W. Franks in the late nineteenth century — one record gives a date of 1882. At that time, they were provenanced to the Lango in Uganda. In the 1930s, J. H. Driberg went through the museum's collection and wrote on these records 'not Lango'. But an example accessioned in 1934, collected by a Dr L. Corbett, is still attributed to the Lango. This, of course, raises a number of conundrums. Do we assume that those who collected these objects were ignorant of ethnic niceties in Uganda? Can we assume that Driberg did not observe headrests in use among the Lango, which were, nevertheless in their repertoire in the late nineteenth century? Do we assume that the Lango used headrests made by other groups? According to Trowell and Wachsmann (1953:157), this type is Acoli, and, according to Curley (1973), the Lango acknowledge a kind of superfraternity with the Acoli. Further, according to Faye (1999:1119), the Lango broke away from the Luo in the sixteenth century and migrated southwards, adopting customs from different groups along the way, including, in the eighteenth century, the Acoli language. Given this, it is quite possible that the original attribution of these headrests should stand, and that the Acoli/Lango confusion is something that comes from placing too much store on political ethnic divisions.

The two examples in figures 261 and 259 also demonstrate another interesting phenomenon. Figure 261 has two V-shaped lugs that appear to be completely gratuitous, because the leather thong that 'ties' the legs does not attach to the lugs, in which there are no holes. In the other headrest (fig. 259), the function of the lugs can clearly be seen. The latter headrest shows signs of considerable use, while the former does not. This would suggest that figure 261 was not made for use, and was, indeed, not used, but sold to the person who collected it in its pristine state, another curiosity to add to the cabinet, but made even more curious by the now inexplicable projections under the platform. On the other hand, it is possible that these projections have other, rather signifying than structural, functions, possibly referring to cattle.

### An envoi: The question of the aesthetic

Dewey (1993:24–28), in his discussion of the aesthetics of the headrests, makes extensive use of Schneider's (1956) article on Pokot visual art. This he embeds within a discussion of African judgements of the relative attractiveness of objects such as headrests, as opposed to the Euro-centric project of understanding these objects as beautiful or as works of art. But both Schneider and Dewey seem to be linking the notion of the 'aesthetic' to the notion of beauty in its purely visual sense.[77] Schneider suggests that the Pokot distinguish between the notion of 'good' ('*karam*') and that of 'pretty/beautiful/good to look at/unusual' ('*pachigh*') (Schneider 1956:102). The notion of good was here linked to the aptness of an object for its function, whereas pretty/beautiful tended to be associated especially with decoration and the unusual. From this, Schneider draws the conclusion that we can see Pokot 'art' as consisting of objects with 'purely aesthetic functions' (Schneider 1956:105), and, rather ambivalently, that

> the headrest was deductively classified as an object of art because, although it has non-aesthetic functions, it is carried about by its owner like a decorative cane and is polished and decorated. To the Pakot [i.e. Pokot] only the gloss and incised or inlaid designs are beautiful. A headrest without these is not beautiful in any way (Schneider 1956:106).

However, that objects with utilitarian functions can have a particular aesthetic of *aptness*, where appearance and function are appropriately dovetailed, has been explored throughout the history of making, and is clearly a part of many cultures' understandings of aesthetics, as is evident from Danto's (1988) very eloquent essay on the design history, aesthetics and iconography of chairs. The ways in which proportions are worked out, matching platforms to legs; the ways in which beaded decoration and weaving are elaborated; the burnished patina; and the strength-to-delicacy ratio of many of these headrests are not just a matter of function: they are testaments to the extraordinary aesthetic 'eyes' and 'hands' of the makers and users of these objects. This is a point made strongly by Abbink (1999: 42) in his discussion of Me'en attitudes to utensils, where he points out that the Me'en do not prize artefacts as beautiful objects ('*an-de-she'i*'), but do value those where there is an 'equal presence or overlap of functional efficiency and aptness of form [to function]', which is denoted by the term '*shektin*'.

That we can consider these as aesthetic objects does not therefore seem out of alignment with Pokot attitudes — their headrests may not, in their functionality, have been considered beautiful, but they could be beautiful objects. However, what is a little confusing in all of this is that, in the headrests classed as Pokot that have been discussed above, there is a great deal of attention paid to patina, to woven encasements, to added beads and occasionally to inlaid decoration, but seldom to engraved designs. So, it would have been useful to know which kinds of headrests Schneider was actually referring to, because there is also a clear difference in the appearance and therefore in the modes of dovetailing functional and aesthetic considerations in different types of Pokot headrests. If we compare the following:

1) figures 216 and 217, which are of a type most commonly associated with the Karamojong, and have little decorative elaboration, although there is a suggestion that the shape of the base may be significant; with
2) figures 226, 227 and 229, a type possibly common to the Pokot and Turkana, but where one (fig. 227) has silver pointille inlay and another (fig. 229) has metal studs and glass beads added; and with
3) figures 240, 241 and 243, a type common to the Pokot and Karamojong, often without any decoration; and finally with
4) figures 245–247, also common to the Pokot and Karamojong, many with added beads, but all with woven encasements.

We then have to ask whether it makes sense to separate them out according to their degrees of embellishment, because that is what the Pokot would have done had they followed their own rules of classification (as laid out by Schneider in 1956). Jean Brown's collection and documentation[78] of Pokot headrests offers a rich resource for understanding some of the variations within Pokot headrest manufacture and use, and from this it would appear that the most heavily embellished headrests, the ones in category 4, above, with a multitude of beads (e.g. fig. 245) were given to young men by their best friends at the time of their initiation, and were used by young men of the junior generation within Pokot age grades. Those in categories 1 and 2 Brown records as having been made and used by older men, figure 227 having been made by a man of some standing, and those in category 3 as used by women, but made by their husbands — the diagnostic feature here being the presence of a groove in one foot, and an association with a goat — or by persons of special standing, such as an entrails diviner.[79]

That different aesthetic standards apply at different levels of the social hierarchy should alert us to the possibility that Schneider's categories of good and beautiful are too limited, and are framed within a Western understanding of 'art' as necessarily 'aesthetic', by which we must understand 'beautiful'. Further, the fact that Brown records that many of these headrests were made by their owners with a spear and that it is spears that link men to status and to ancestors (besides their elaborate hairstyles, of which more later) raises the issue of the life history of objects, and should therefore alert us to the dimensions of function of a headrest that reach way beyond a simple view of it as a pillow. Among the Me'en, one can only acquire artefacts of daily use that have the property of shektin by exchanging something for it with a person with whom one has a non-commercial relationship (Abbink 1999: 43), something that can be contrasted directly with the vassal relationship between specialist Fuga craftsmen and Gurage clients discussed by Pankhurst and Nida (1999). Such differentiations in social relationships between patrons and makers will also have impacted on the degrees and kinds of investment in labour and resources for aesthetic elaboration. The numerous terms for describing cattle prized for their appearance among Nilotes such as the Dinka and Nuer (Coote & Shelton 1992), and the ways in which the aesthetics of cattle infiltrate other aspects of the visual experience and values of these peoples add an expanded dimension to our understanding of the notion of aesthetics. They also, however, reinforce the notion that objects are made 'beautiful' on purpose, and that understanding what constitutes 'beauty' is part of an art historical enquiry.

This chapter has documented the degree of variation of headrest types in East Africa, and has also demonstrated that there is no easily defined stylistic cohesion of headrest forms among different ethnic groups. The aesthetic dimensions of these headrests are undoubtedly part of their attraction for collectors and their admirers: they are what make the headrests more than ethnological specimens of other people's practices, and my choice of particular examples is also clearly influenced by these factors. The next chapter will discuss formal aspects of headrests made by Bantu speakers, and there the choices are also guided by an appreciation of objects not just for their explicatory value in relation to hypotheses of identity, but also for their formal, technical and material 'shine'.

CHAPTER 6 *Illustrations: figures 180-261* | **217**

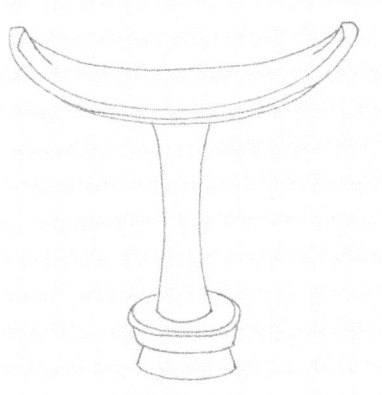

180  Van der Stappen (1996:83, no. 205), *Collected 1995 in region of Ali Adde, Republic of Djibouti, Somali (Issa)*, wood, 19 cm h.

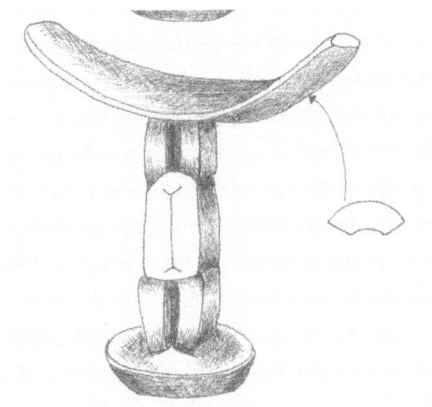

181  British Museum (no. 1957 Af14.21), collected by Admiral Sir George Egerton, *East Africa, Tanganyika Coast, Swahili*, wood, 18.8 cm h.

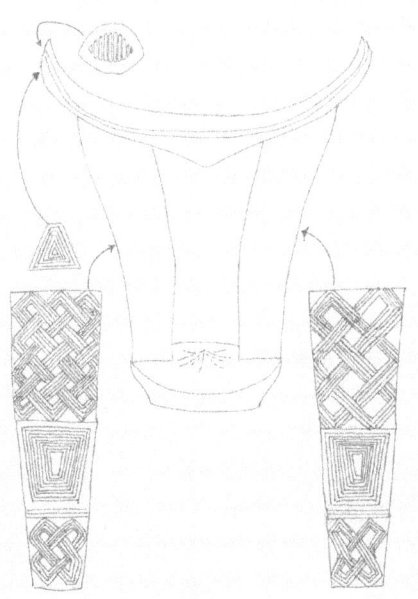

182  British Museum (no. 1935 11 08 13), collected by Major P. H. G. Powell-Cotton, *Italian Somaliland, Tunne Huts, Somali, Darod, Elai Rehaneren* (Rehanwin), wood, 18.9 cm h.

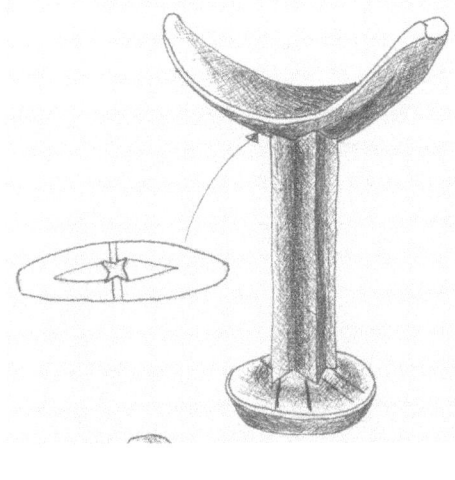

183  British Museum (no. 1933.11.08.7), collected by Major P. H. G. Powell-Cotton, *Italian Somaliland, Ogaden, Somali, Darod*, wood, 16.2 cm h.

## 218 | AFRICAN DREAM MACHINES

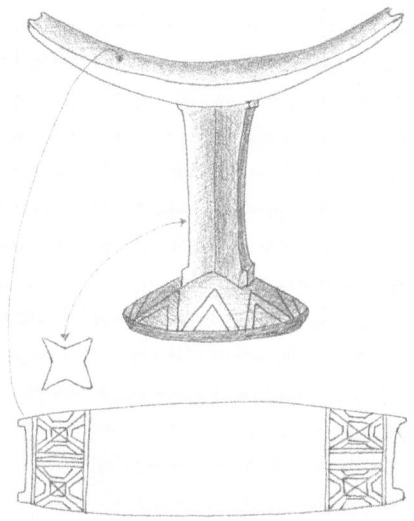

184  British Museum (no. 1904.240), collected by E. A. Hollis, *East Africa, Djibouti, Somali*, wood, pigment, 16.1 cm h.

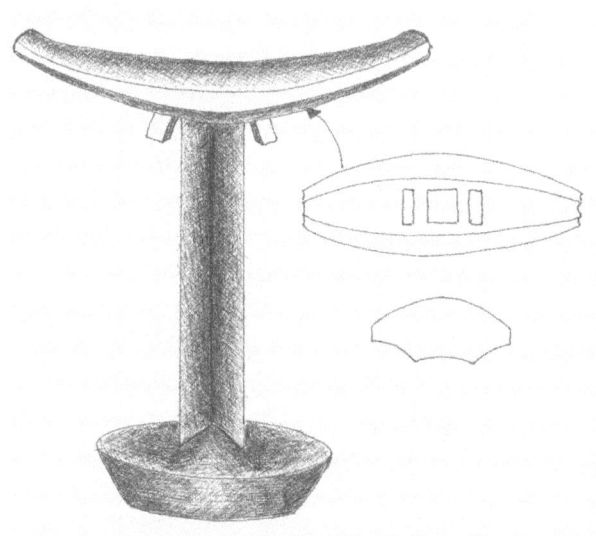

185  British Museum (no. 1954 Af23), (Wellcome Collection, no. 191331), *Somali, Esa* (Issa), wood, 16.95 cm h.

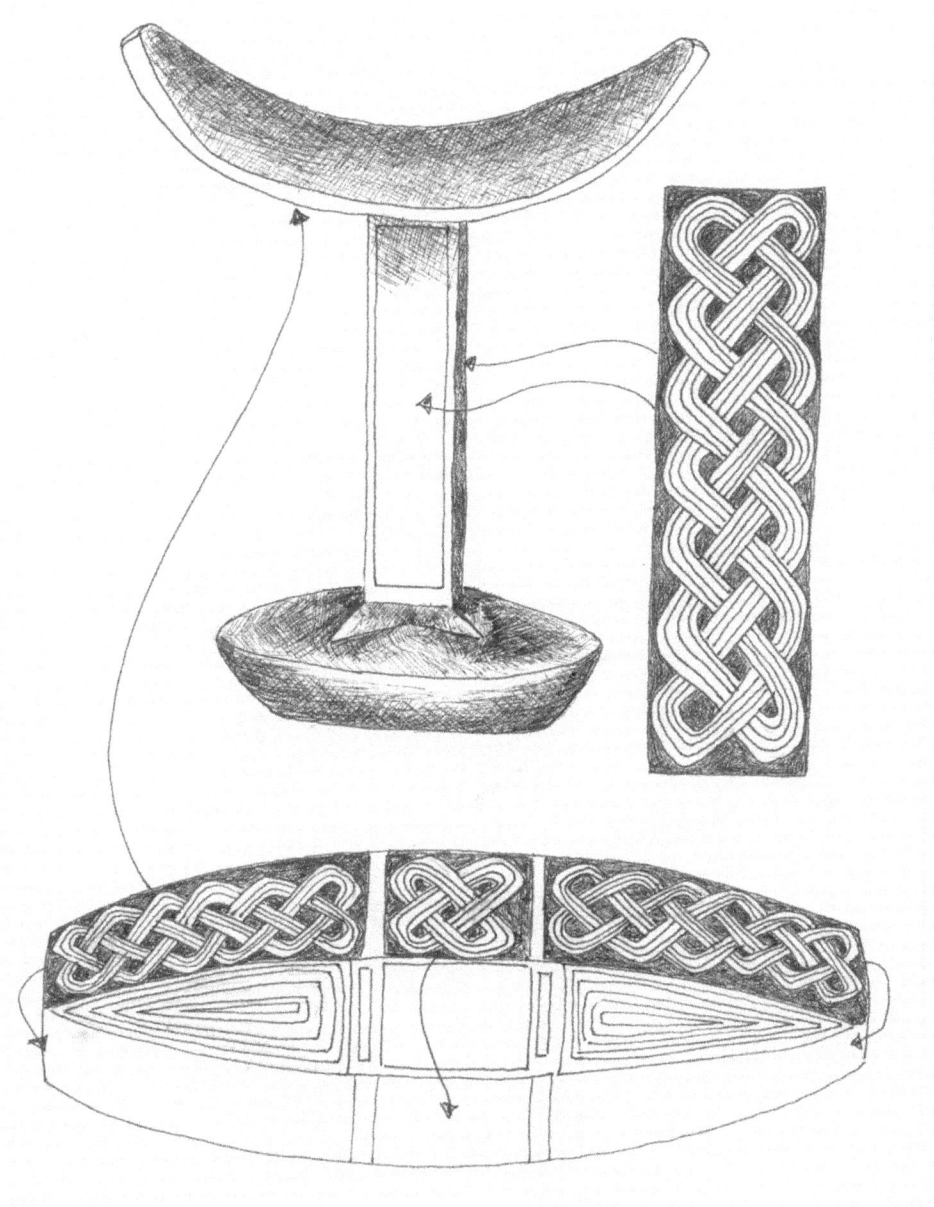

186  British Museum (no. +2227), collected by Colonel H. W. Lane, *Donated by A. W. Franks (xii 84)*, *Tanganyika, Wanyika, Giriama*, wood, 15.9 cm h.

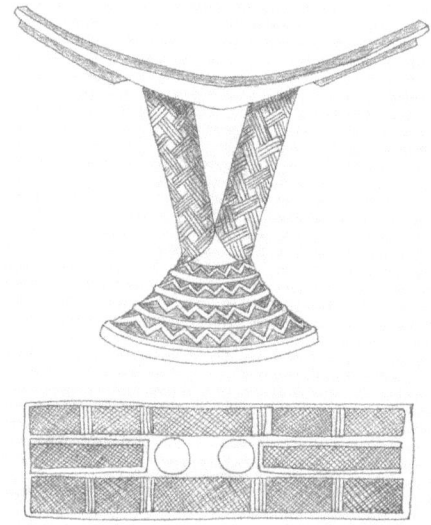

187 British Museum (no. 1954 Af23), (Wellcome Collection, no. 161615), *Somali, Esa* (Issa), wood, 19.4 cm h.

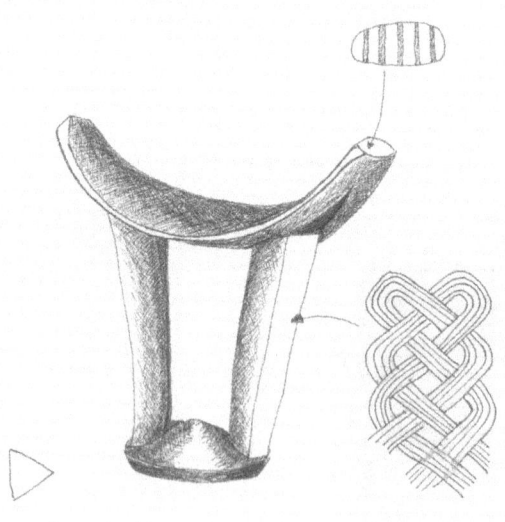

188 British Museum (no. 1935.11.08.5), collected by Major P. H. G. Powell-Cotton, *N.E. Africa, Italian Somaliland, Somali, Kotiche* (Cotice), wood, 16.7 cm h.

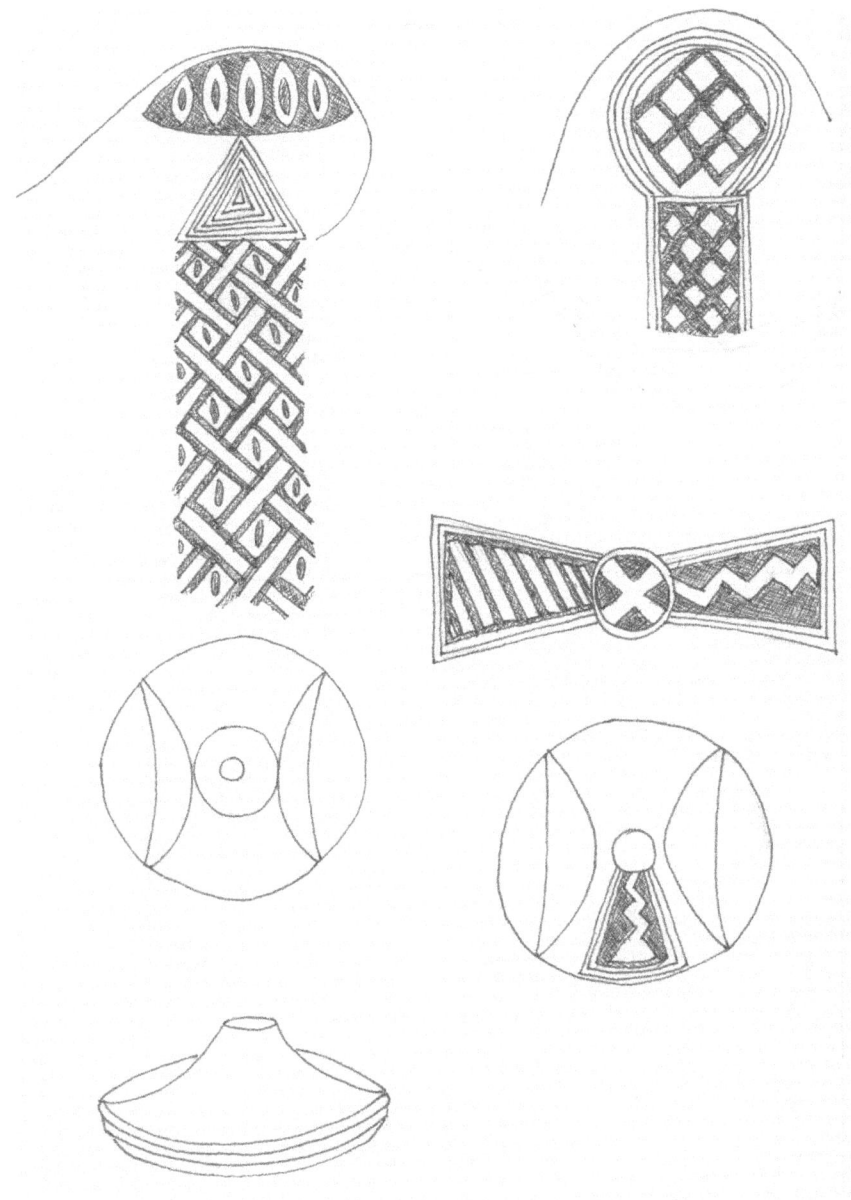

189 British Museum (no. 1935.11.08.8), collected by Major P. H. G. Powell-Cotton, *Italian Somaliland, Ogaden, Somali, Darod, Banguei(?), Bambilia*, wood, 16.6 cm h.
190 British Museum (no. 1935.11.08.9), collected by Major P. H. G. Powell-Cotton, *Italian Somaliland, Ogaden, Somali, Darod, Gelib*, wood, 16.8 cm h.

## 222 | AFRICAN DREAM MACHINES

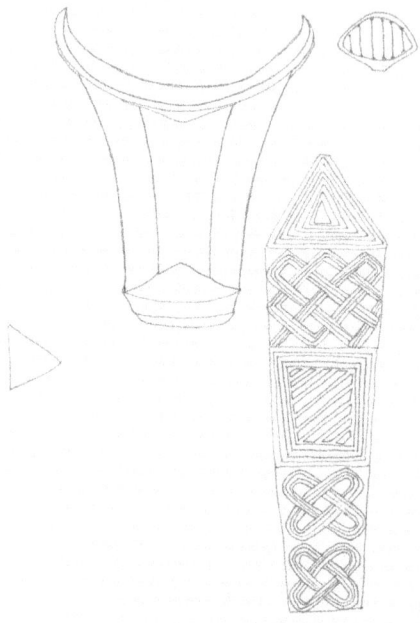

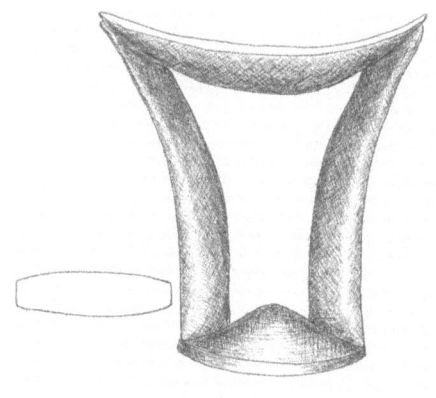

192 British Museum (no. 1935.11.08.12), collected by Major P. H. G. Powell-Cotton, *Italian Somaliland, Somali, Darod, made in Rehanwin, Elai subtribe*, wood, 17.4 cm h.

191 British Museum (no. 1935.11.08.13), collected by Major P. H. G. Powell-Cotton, *Italian Somaliland, Tunne huts, Somali, Darod, Elai Rehanaren* (Rehanwin), wood, 18.9 cm h.

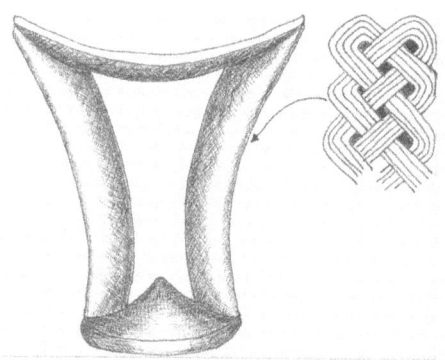

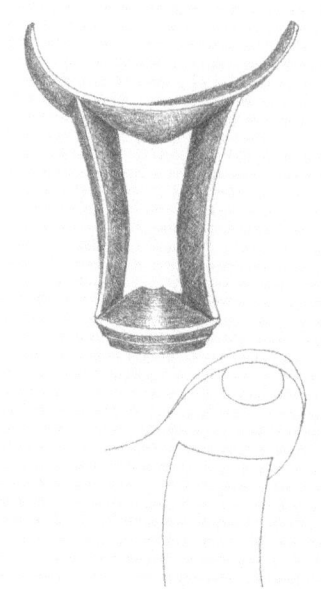

193 British Museum (no. 1962 Af17.79), Church Missionary Society, *North East Africa, Somali Republic, Somali? Boni?*, wood, 16.8 cm h.

194 British Museum (no. 1935.11.08.12), collected by Major P. H. G. Powell-Cotton, *Italian Somaliland, made in Rehanwin, bought from Ogaden, Somali, Darod, Kotiche* (Cotice), *Afmadu*, wood, 17.5 cm h.

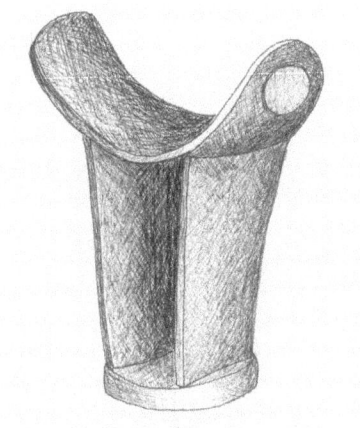

195   Munich, Staatlisches Museum füür Vöölkerkunde (no. 84.302.919), acquired from Dr Eva Ptak, 1977, *Tanganyika, Boni*, wood, 16 cm h.

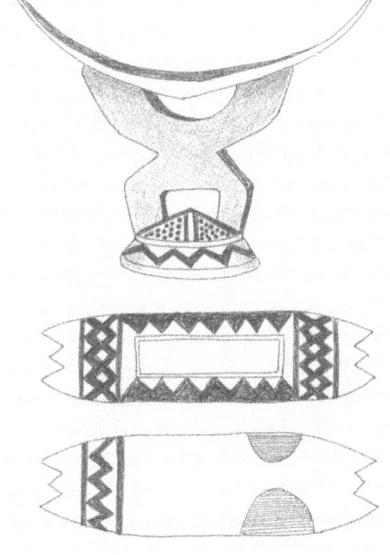

196   British Museum (no. 1928. 5.9.2), collected by Lieutenant Colonel P. E. Alden, *British Somaliland, Somali*, wood, 17.4 cm h.

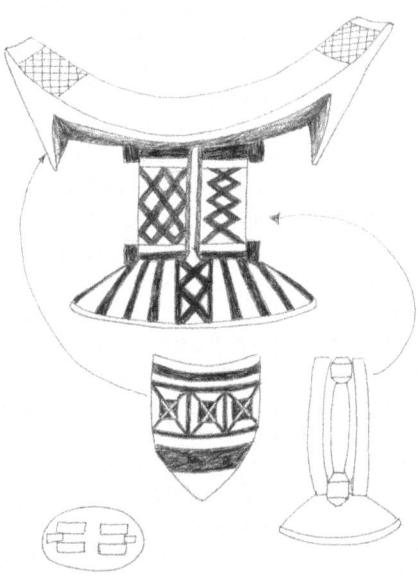

197   British Museum (no. 1933 11-14-15), collected by Brigadier General Sir Eric Swayne, donated by H. G. C. Swayne, *NE Africa, Somaliland, 1884-1897*, 'Somali', wood, 16.97 cm h.

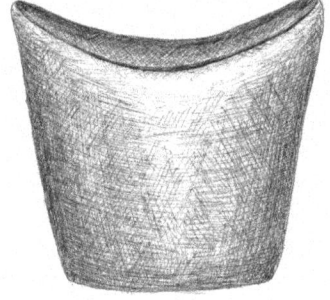

197   British Museum (no. 1933 11-14-15), collected by Brigadier General Sir Eric Swayne, donated by H. G. C. Swayne, *NE Africa, Somaliland, 1884-1897*, 'Somali', wood, 16.97 cm h.

**224** | AFRICAN DREAM MACHINES

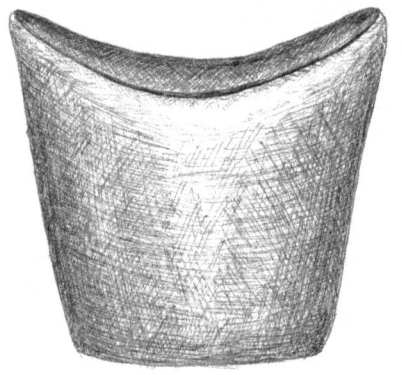

198  Van der Stappen (1996:56, no. 109), *Collected 1995*, Ethiopia, 'Oromo(?)', wood, 19 cm h.

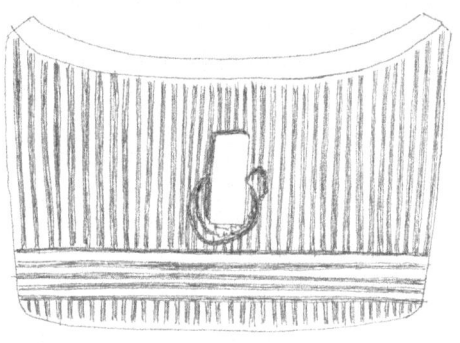

199  Van der Stappen (1996:80, no. 200), *Collected 1991*, Ethiopia, *Sidamo region, Sidama*, wood, 18 cm h.

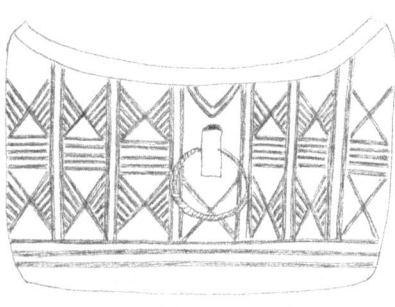

200  Van der Stappen (1996:81, no. 201), *Collected 1991*, Ethiopia, *Sidamo region, Sidama*, wood, 17 cm h.

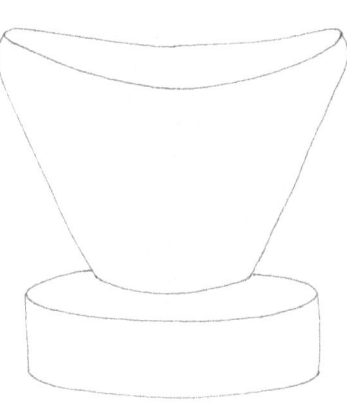

201  Van der Stappen (1996:57, no. 111), *Collected 1998*, Ethiopia, 'Oromo(?)', wood, 19 cm h.

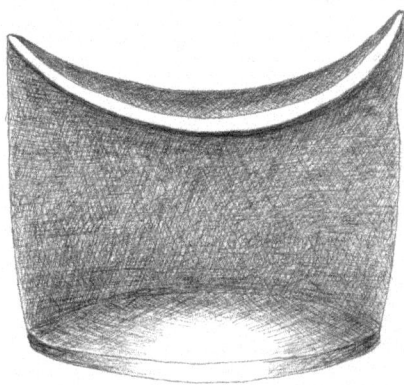

202  Van der Stappen (1996:42, no. 63), *Collected 1995*, Ethiopia, wood, 14 cm h.

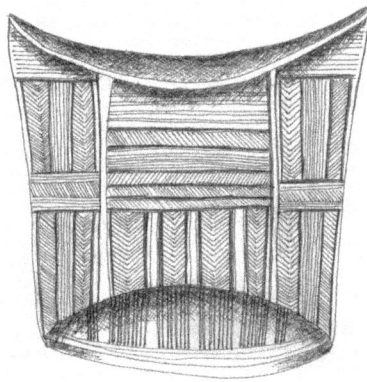

203  Van der Stappen (1996:43, no. 67), *Collected 1993*, Ethiopia, *Guraguéé* (Gurage) *or Arsi*, wood, 20 cm h.

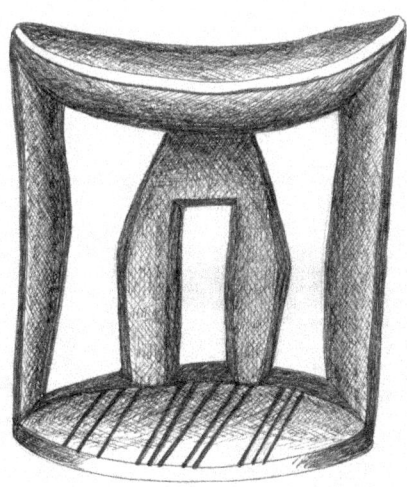

204  Van der Stappen (1996:73, no. 171), *Collected 1995*, Ethiopia, *Central region of Shoa, Arsi*, wood, 19 cm h.

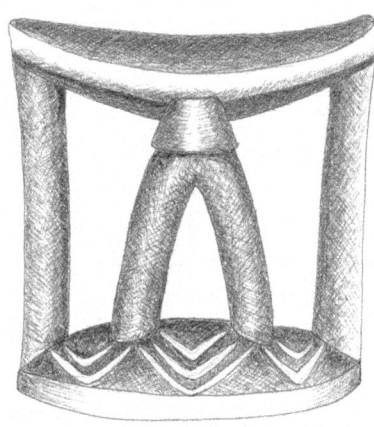

205  Van der Stappen (1996:73, no. 170), *Collected 1995*, Ethiopia, *Central region of Shoa, Arsi*, wood, 17 cm h.

226 | AFRICAN DREAM MACHINES

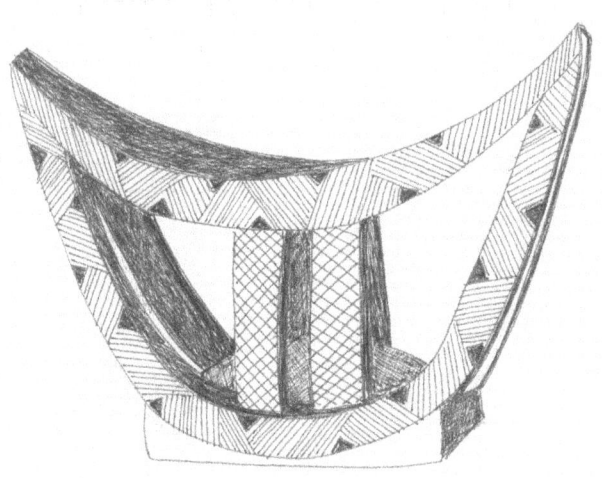

206  British Museum (no. 1928.5-94), collected by Lieutenant Colonel P. E. Alden, *Somaliland, Yehaleh, Somali of Dolbahouta tribes, Doba hunca*, wood, 16 cm h.

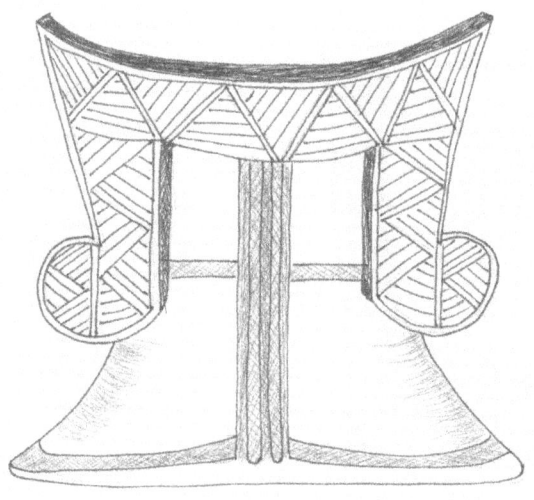

207  British Museum (no. 1933.11-16-18), collected by Brigadier Sir Eric Swayne, *Commander-in-chief, British Somaliland 1884-1897*, donated by H. G. C. Swayne, *Somali*, wood, 17 cm h.

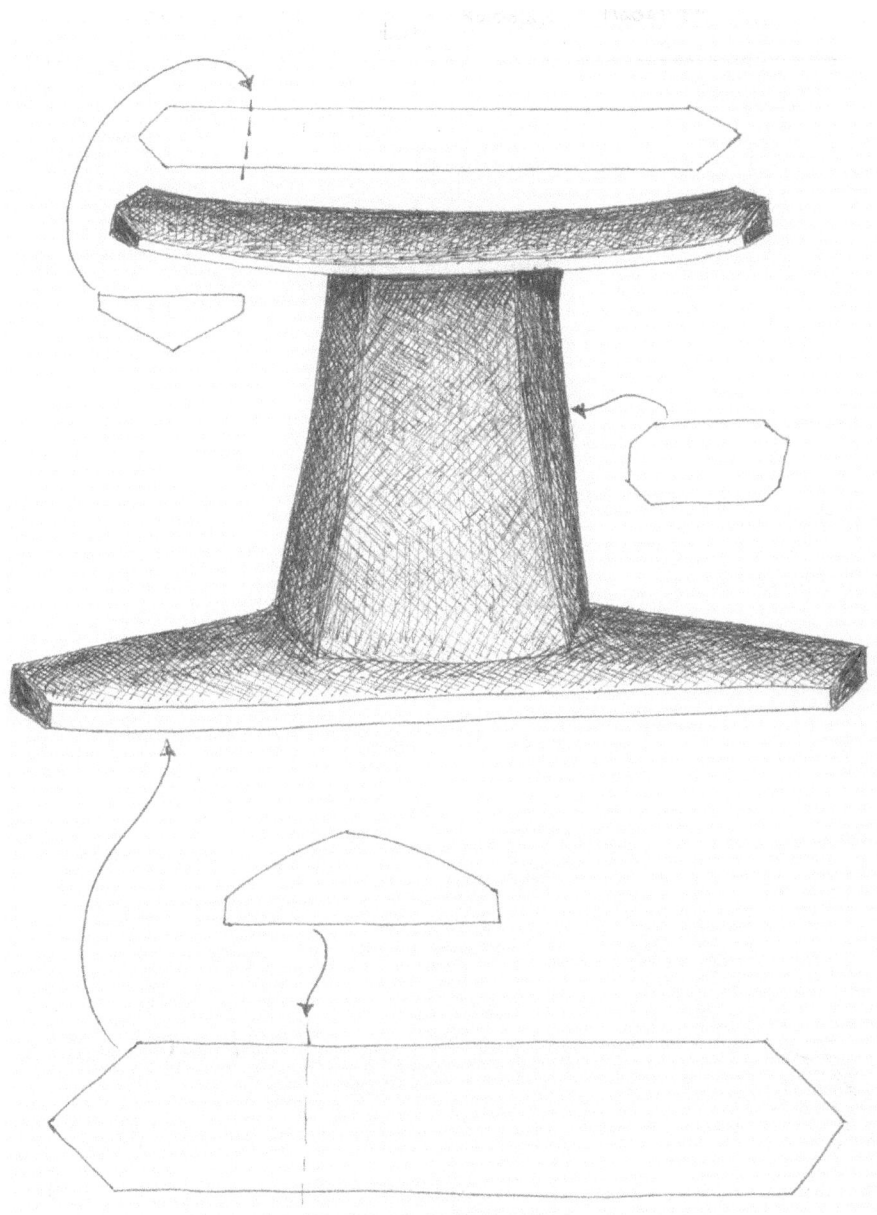

208 British Museum (no. 1929 6209.07), collected by E. E. Evans Pritchard, *West Bank of the Nile, Sudan, Ingassana* (Ingessana), wood, 10 cm h.

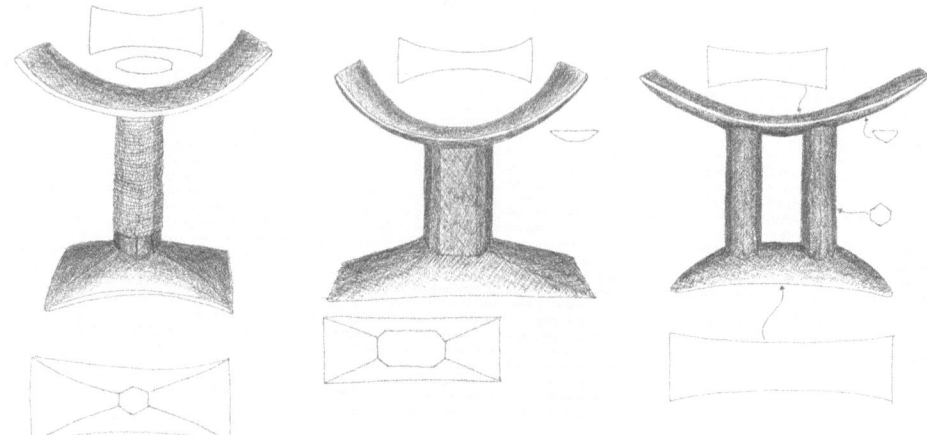

209  British Museum (no. 1933 11-10.29), *Anglo-Egyptian Sudan, Tami (Dervish Muslim)*, wood and fibre, 20 cm h.

210  British Museum (no. 1935 3-7.21), collected by Major and Misses Powell-Cotton, *Anglo-Egyptian Sudan, Andal Valley, Red Sea Province, Tokar, Beni Amir*, wood, 14.4 cm h.

211  British Museum (no. 1956 Af23-4), donated by Satti Awad H. E. Sayed, *Eastern Sudan*, wood, 16.7 cm h.

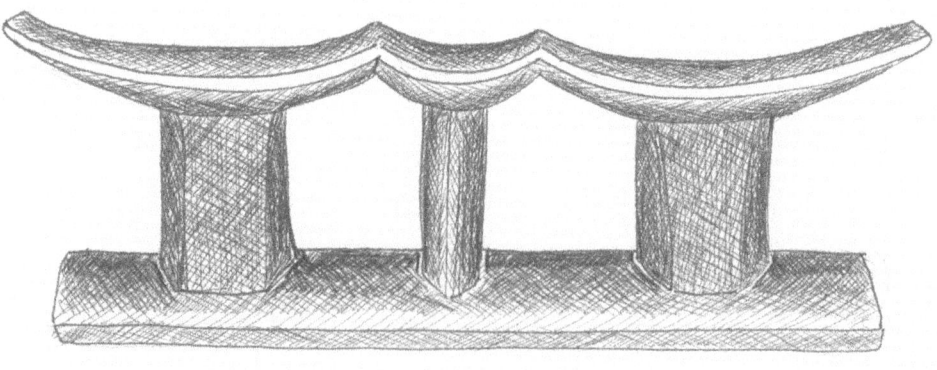

212  Muséée Royal de l'Afrique Central (no. RG 28228), Democratic Republic of the Congo, *Lower Uele, Zande or Ngbandi*, wood, 14.8 cm h.

CHAPTER 6 *Illustrations: figures 180-261* | **229**

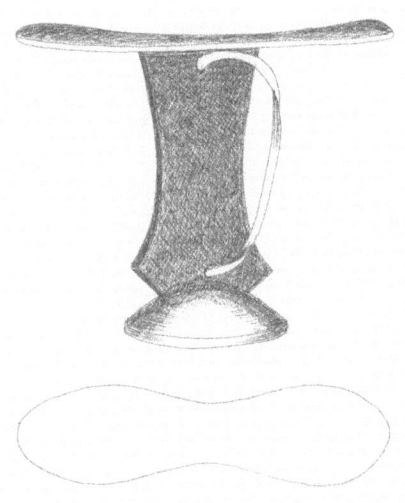

213   Best (1993:152, 146), Kenya, Turkana, *echico long/ngichikolong*, wood and leather, 15 cm h.

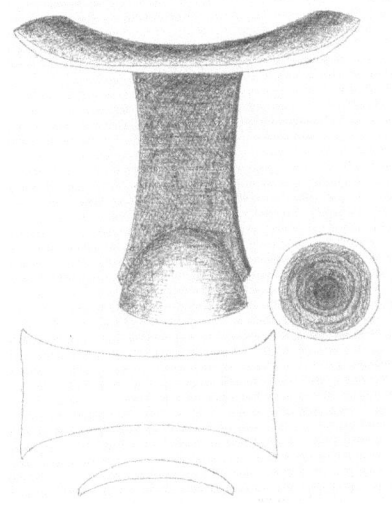

214   British Museum (no. 1979 Af6.149), collected by John Mack, *Sudan, Longarum*, wood, leather, 16.5 cm h.

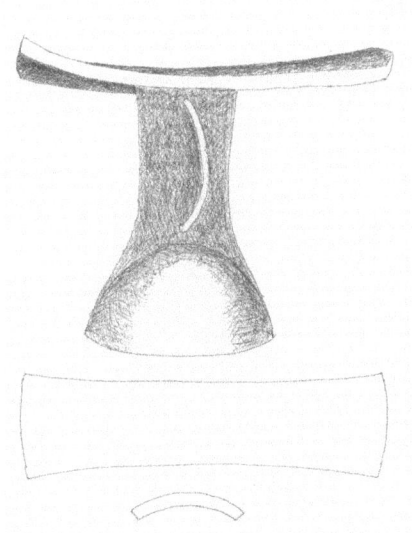

215   Manchester University Museum (no. 09763/46), collected by David Turton, Ethiopia, Mursi, *ali/ale, Made and used only by adult men*, wood, leather, 11.75 cm h.

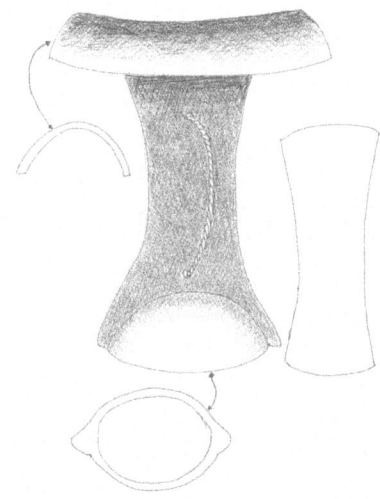

216   Oxford, Pitt Rivers Museum (no. 1978 20.261), collected by Jean Brown, *Kenya, Mt Elgon, Pokot (Tiati Pokot), ngachar/ndege. The mark left by the base in the soil is said to be like a donkey's hoof-print*, wood, leather, 17.8 cm h.

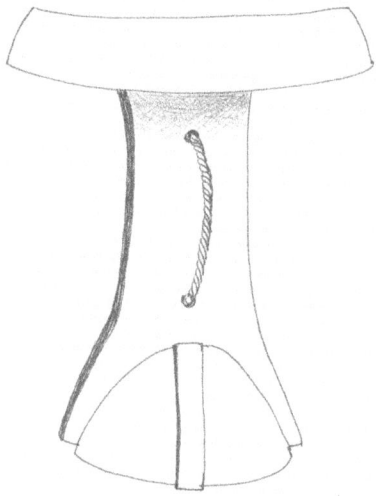

217  Oxford, Pitt Rivers Museum (no. 1978 20.44), collected by Jean Brown, *Kenya, Mt Elgon, Pokot (Tiati Pokot), ngachar/ndege. The mark left by the base in the soil is said to be like a donkey's hoof-print*, wood, leather, 17.8 cm h.

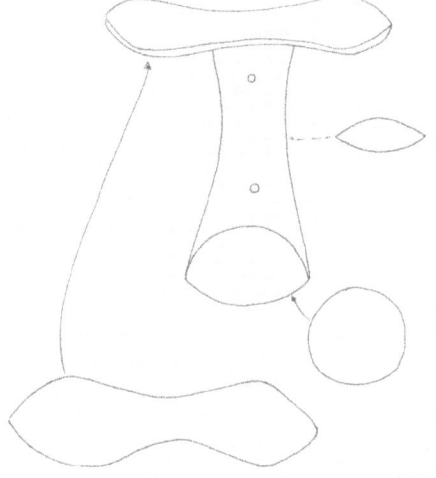

218  Oxford, Pitt Rivers Museum (no. VI.55), *Collected by Major Gayer Anderson on the Sudan-Abyssinia frontier, Sudan, pre 1917, Nuer*, wood, 16.3 cm h.

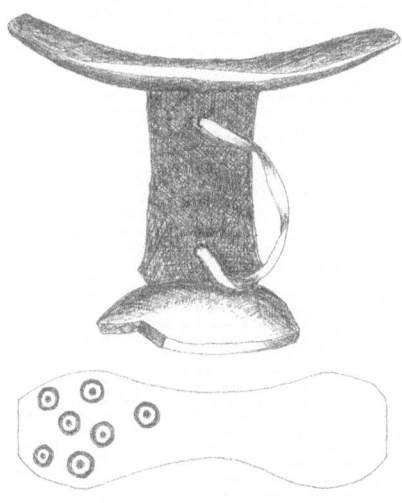

219  British Museum (no. 1910.9229.22), collected by F. Spire *(Juja Busoga, Uganda Protectorate, 1910). Kenya: Mombasa, Kamba*, wood, leather, 13.4 cm h.

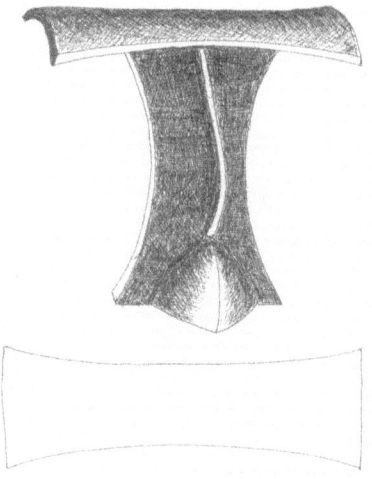

220  Dewey (1993:46, fig. 26), *Kenya, Turkana*, wood, metal, 15 cm h.

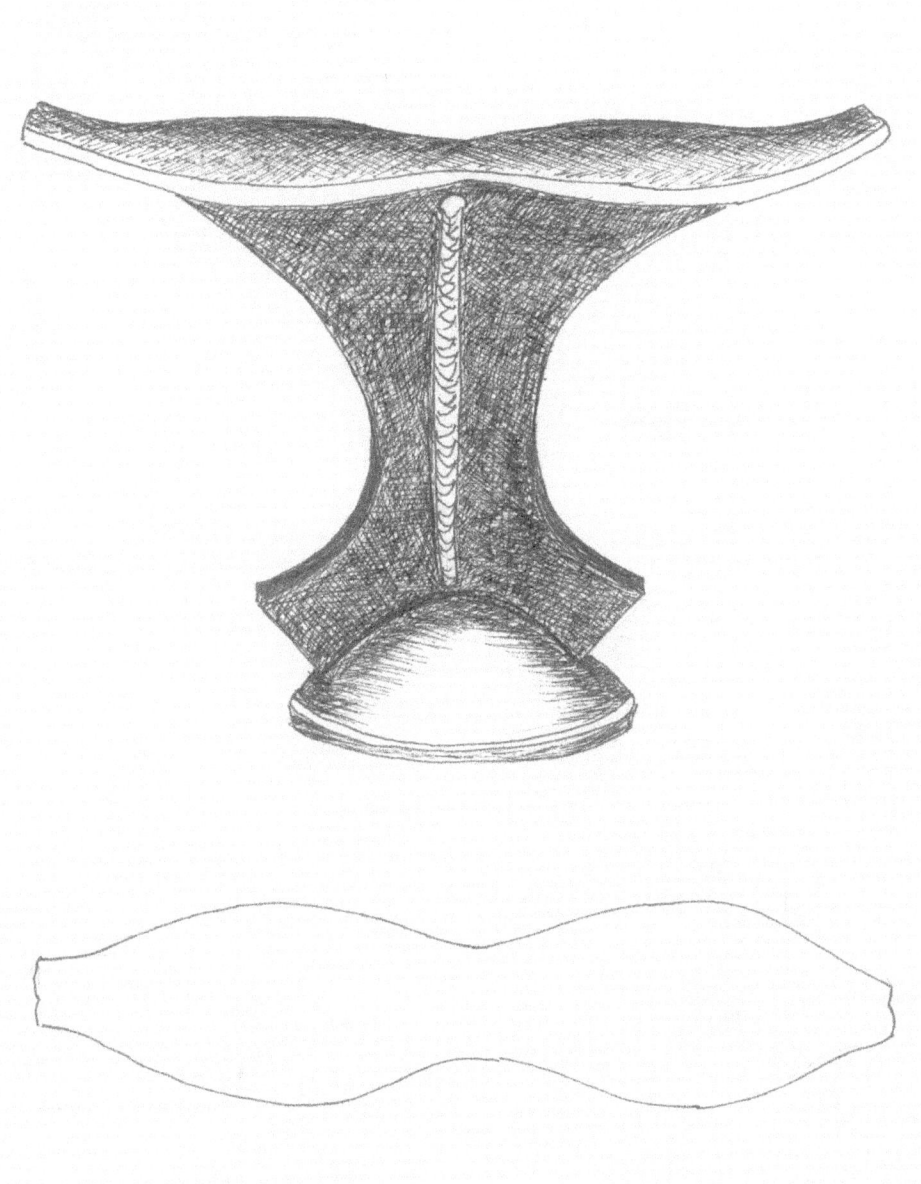

221　Best (1993:155, no. 149), Kenya, Turkana, *echikolong/ngichikolong*. Made and used only by adult men, wood, leather, 17 cm h.

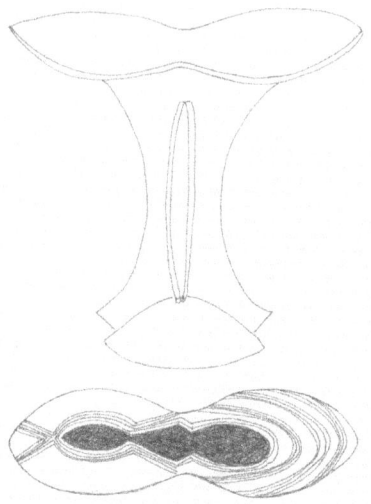

222   Wolfe (1979:17, fig. A3), *Kenya, Karamojong*, wood, leather, metal 15 cm h.

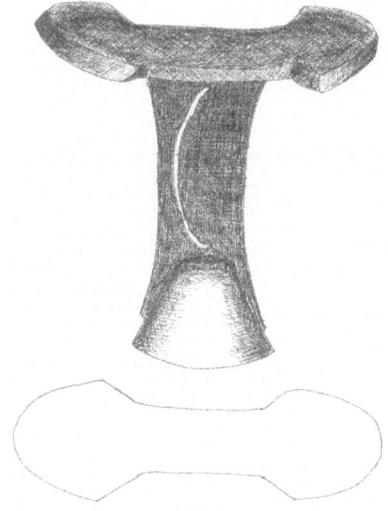

223   Van der Stappen (1996:100, no. 266), *Collected 1994*, Ethiopia, *'Mursi'*, wood, fibre, 19 cm h.

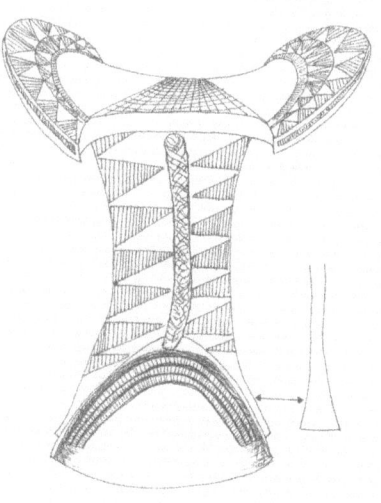

224   Van der Stappen (1996:130, no. 376), *Collected in 1995, in the village of Dus, Ethiopia, Kara, Used by adult men*, wood, leather, 14 cm h.

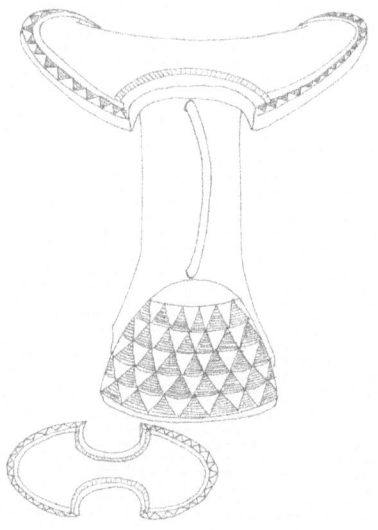

225   Van der Stappen (1996:106, no. 288), *Collected in 1994 in the village of Argudéé. Bashada, Ethiopia, borokoto*, wood, leather, 13 cm h.

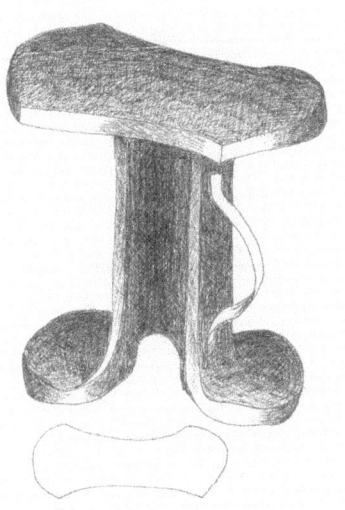

226 Musée Royal de l'Afrique Central (no. 83.13.1), *Kenya, Baringo District, Pokot, chebarsiat,* wood, leather, 17.3 cm h.

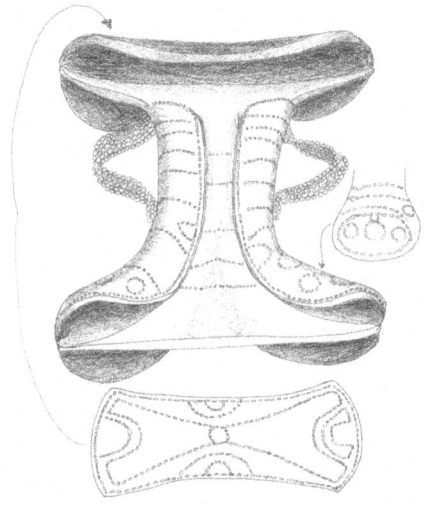

227 Oxford, Pitt Rivers Museum (no. 1973.20.35), collected by Jean Brown, *Kenya, E of Mt Elgon, Pokot (Tiati Pokot) ngachar, Made by its owner, Chunel, a herd-owner and member of the senior set of the junior generation in the age-set system,* wood, leather, metal, beads, 17 cm h.

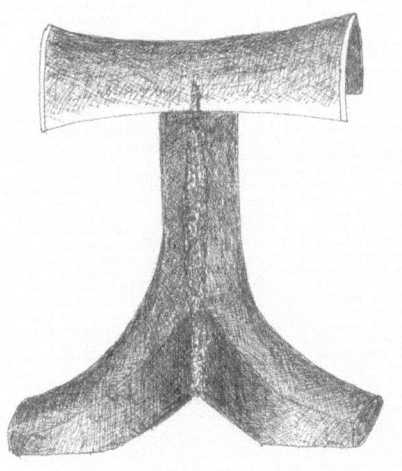

228 Wolfe (1979:18, fig. A6), *Kenya, Turkana,* wood, beads, fibre, 16 cm h.

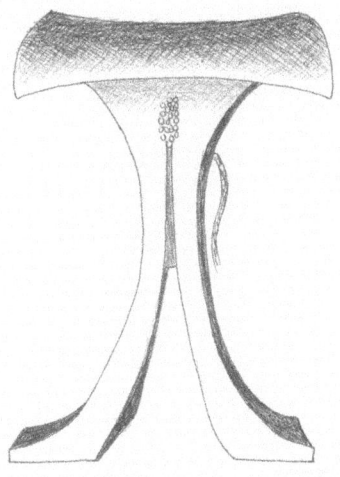

229 Pitt Rivers Museum, Oxford (no. 1978.20.263), collected by Jean Brown, *Kenya, E of Mt Elgon, Pokot (Tiati Pokot), ngachar,* wood, bead, metal, 14 cm h.

**234** | AFRICAN DREAM MACHINES

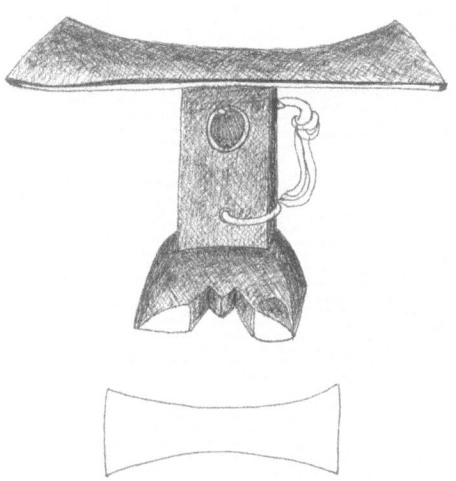

230 Manchester University Museum (no. CA 37), donated by Cecil Barber, September 1921 (from the Central African register), *Halifax Museum. Sudan, Omdurman,* wood, leather, metal, 12 cm h.

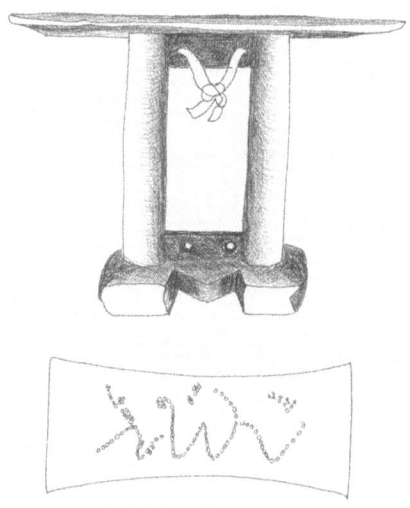

231 British Museum (no. 1953 Af24.17), donated by the Church Missionary Society, *Anglo-Egyptian Sudan, Bari,* wood, leather, metal, 13.2 cm h.

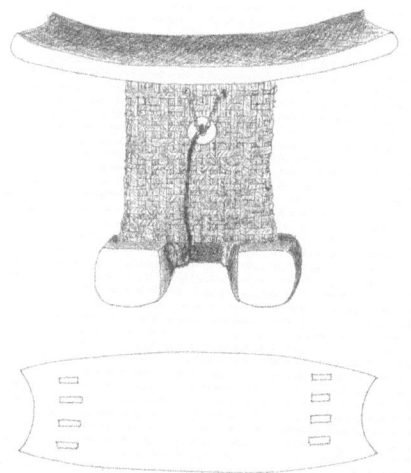

232 British Museum (no. 1953 Af24.18), donated by Church Missionary Society, *East Africa, Uganda or Anglo Egyptian Sudan, Bari(?),* wood, reptile skin leather, fibre, metal, 17.3 cm h.

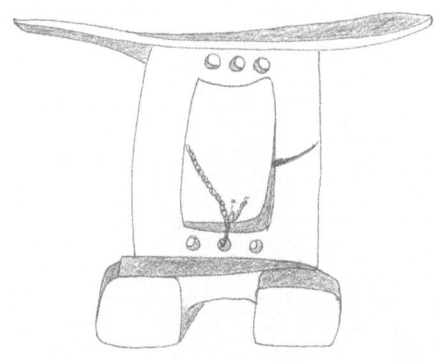

233 British Museum (no. 1928.4.9.72), collected by E. E. Evans Pritchard, *Anglo-Egyptian Sudan, Western Bank of Nile, Bari,* wood, leather, fibre, 14 cm h.

CHAPTER 6 *Illustrations: figures 180-261* | **235**

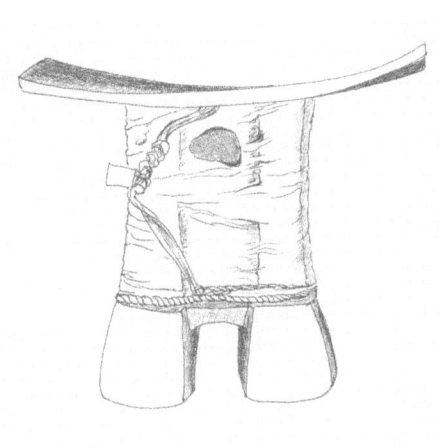

234 British Museum (no. 1924 3.8.131), collected by E. E. Evans Pritchard, *Anglo-Egyptian Sudan, Mongalla Province, Bari*, wood, leather, fibre, 20.5 cm h.

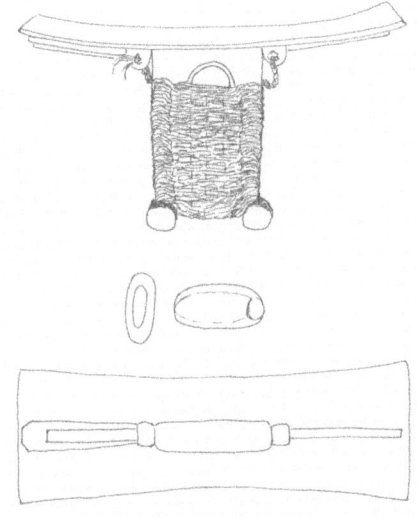

235 Oxford, Pitt Rivers Museum (no. B IV), *Collected by Rev WE Taylor between 1882-1890. Donated by Mrs Taylor in 1927. East Africa, 'Somali'*, wood, leather, fibre, 16 cm h.

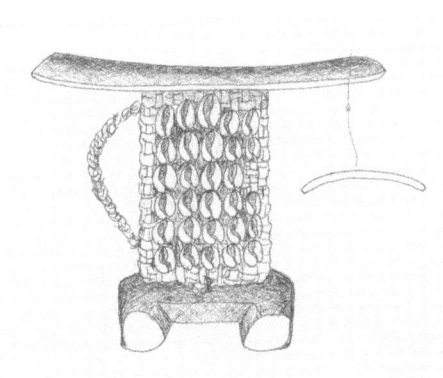

236 British Museum (no. 1954 Af23), (Wellcome Collection, no. 242 588), *Anglo-Egyptian Sudan, Bari*, wood, leather, fibre, cowrie shells, 14.9 cm h.

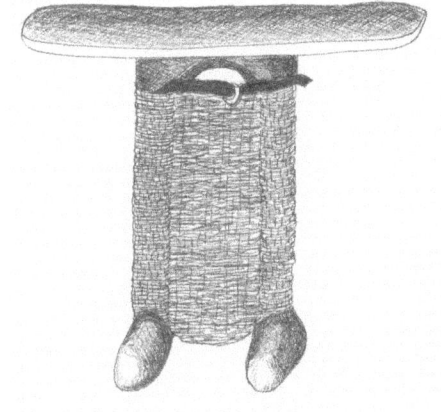

237 British Museum (no. 2718), collected by Petherick, donated by Henry Christy, *NE Africa, Uganda/Anglo-Egyptian Sudan, Bari(?)*, wood, leather, 17.5 cm h.

236 | AFRICAN DREAM MACHINES

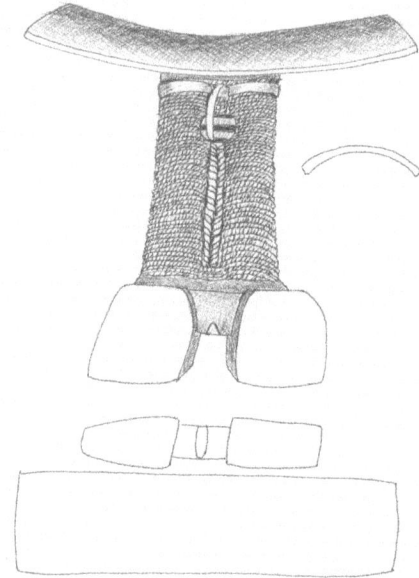

238 Oxford, Pitt Rivers Museum (no. XII 264 B), collected by E. E. Evans Pritchard, 1936, *Upper Nile, Sudan, Bari, Teaba Keka*, wood, leather, fibre, 19 cm h.

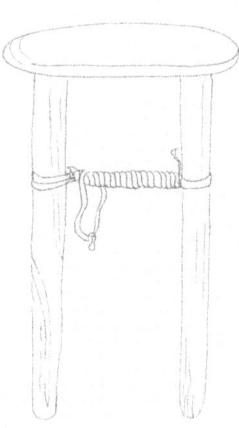

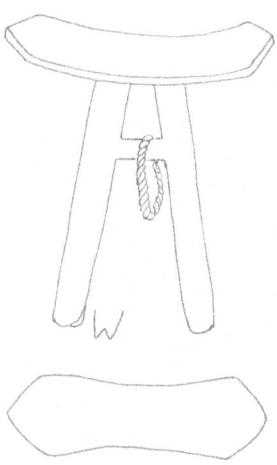

239 British Museum (no. 1934.4.10.32), donated by Rev. H. Paget-Wilkes, *Uganda, Southern Karamojo (Karamojong)*, wood, leather, fibre, 20.1 cm h.

240 Oxford, Pitt-Rivers Museum (no. 1978.20.45), collected by Jean Brown, Kenya, *East of Mount Elgon, Pokot (Tiati Pokot). This is a woman's headrest, made by a husband for his wife. It has a groove in one foot signifying a) the vagina and b) the split in a goat's hoof*, wood, fibre, 15 cm h.

CHAPTER 6 *Illustrations: figures 180-261* | **237**

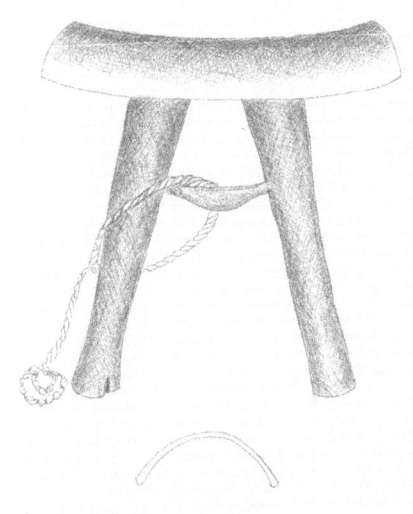

241 British Museum (no. 1954 Af34.1), donated by A. M. Champion (National Bank of India), *collected ca 1932, Kenya, Western Suk (Pokot), Ajarr*, wood, fibre, 16 cm h.

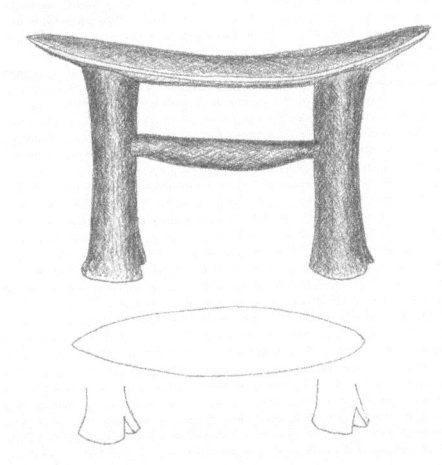

242 British Museum (no. 1954 Af23), (Wellcome Collection, no. 158 615), Uganda, 'Soga(?)', wood, 14.7 cm h.

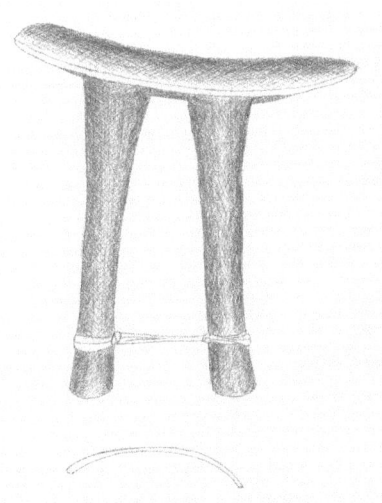

243 British Museum (no. 1925 11-23-2), Kenya Empire Exhibition Committee, *Kenya, Suk(?) Pokot(?)*, wood, leather, 17 cm h.

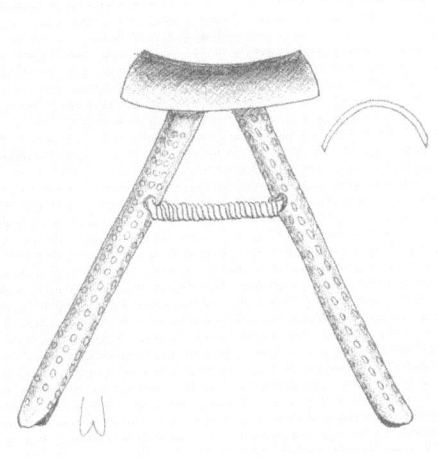

244 Oxford, Pitt Rivers Museum (no. 1978.9.3), Donated by DE Weatherhead, CMG MBE, in East Africa 1900-1935, *Uganda?, Karamojong?*, wood, leather, metal, 24 cm h.

## 238 | AFRICAN DREAM MACHINES

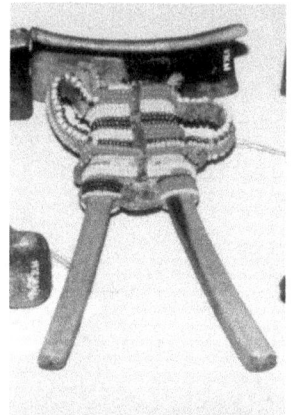

a

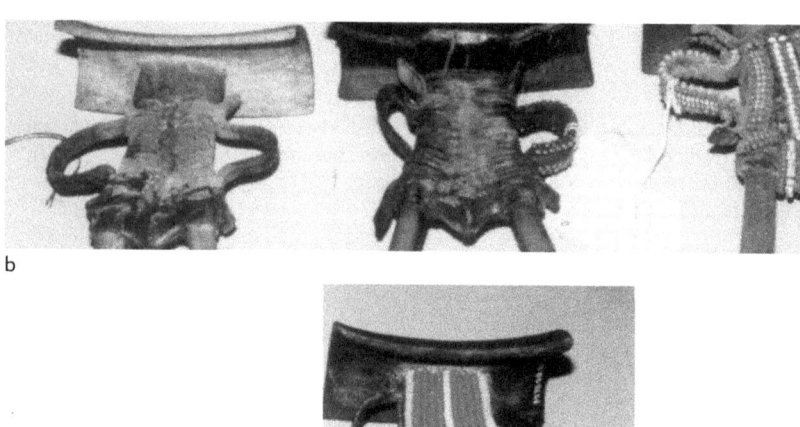

b

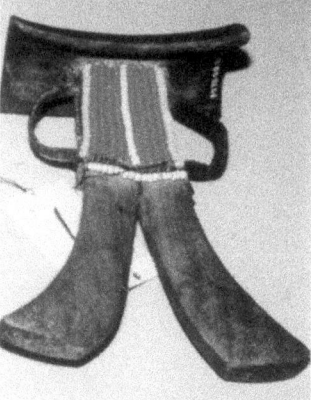

c

245   Oxford, Pitt Rivers Museum (left: no. 1978.20.264), collected by Jean Brown, *Western Kenya, East of Mount Elgon, Pokot (Tiati Pokot)*. *Ngachar/champerit, type given to a young man on his initiation, by his best friend*, wood, beads, fibre, hide, 22.5 cm h; (right: no. 1978.20.265), collected by Jean Brown, *Western Kenya, East of Mount Elgon, Pokot (Tiati Pokot)*. *Ngachar, made and used by men of the youngest age-set*, wood, beads, fibre, hide, 20.5 cm h; centre: details of Pitt Rivers Museum, nos. 1978.20.262 (l), .43 (c), .33 (r).

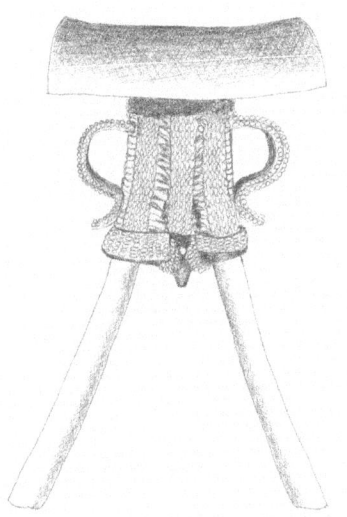

246 Musée Royal de l'Afrique Central (no. RG 78.79.2), *Uganda, Karamojong*, wood, leather, beads, wire, 20.8 cm h.

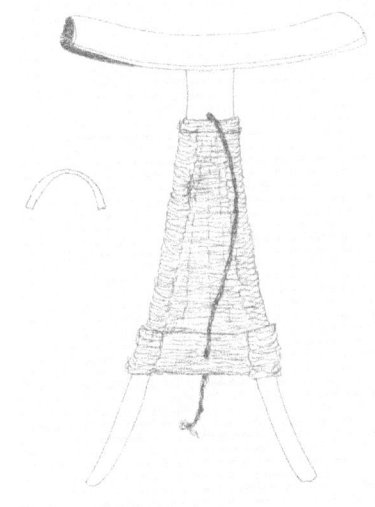

247 British Museum (no. 1925 11.23.1), Kenya Empire Exhibition Committee, *Kenya, Kamasia Reserve, Suk*, wood, fibre, leather, 24 cm h.

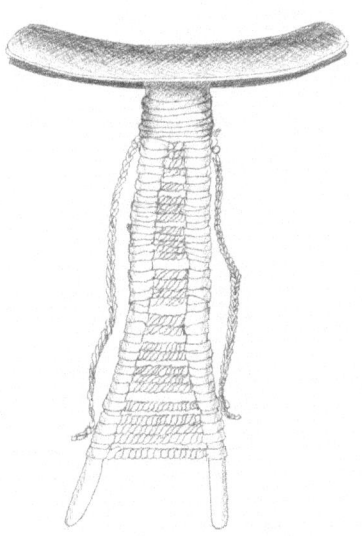

248 British Museum (no. 1912 12.30.1), collected by Major R. G. Bright, *Kenya, Turkana (cf Junker "Travels in Africa"?)*, wood, fibre, leather, 27 cm h.

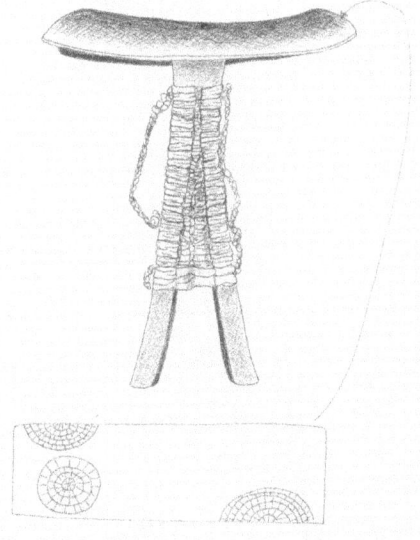

249 British Museum (no. 1947 34.2), collected by A. M. Champion, *Kenya, Turkana*, wood, fibre, leather, 20 cm h.

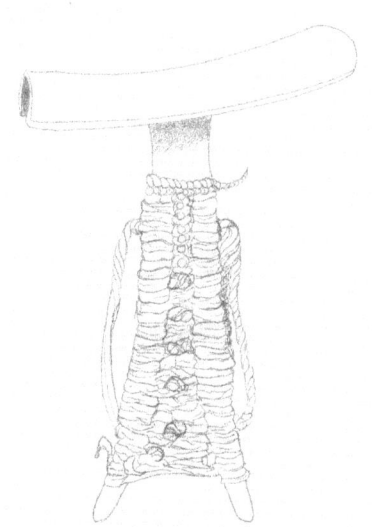

250   Musée Royal de l'Afrique Central (no. 67.63.1153), *Uganda, Turkana (Karamoja)* (Karamojong), wood, leather, metal, 27.5 cm h.

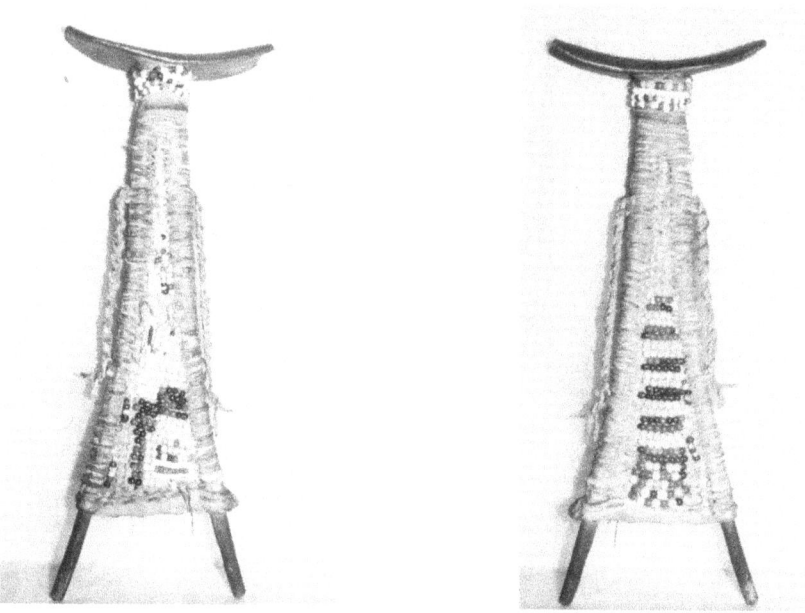

251   British Museum (no. 1947 Af16.37), collected by C. W. Hobley *(Kenya 1890-1910)*, donated by Miss F. Hobley, *Kenya, Turkana*, wood, leather, glass beads, 30 cm h.

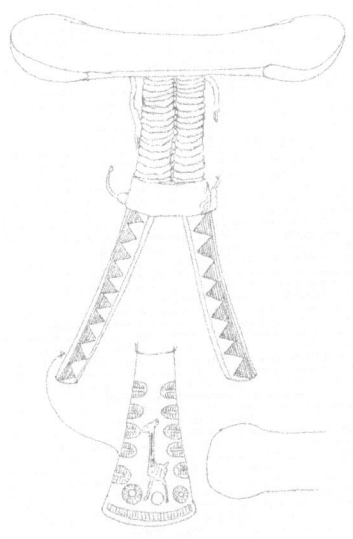

252 Musée Royal de l'Afrique Central (no. RG 79 15.5), *Kenya, Karamojong*, wood, leather, pigment, 18.6 cm h.

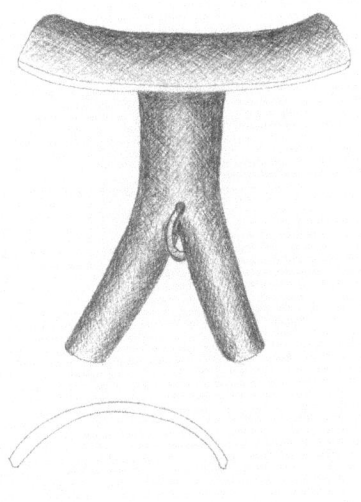

253 British Museum (no. 1934 4-10.30), collected by Rev. H. Paget-Wilkes, *Uganda, Southern Karamojong*, wood, *Cowhide, greased with animal fat*, 18.7 cm h.

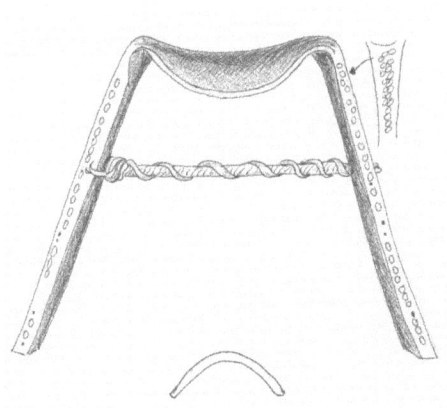

254 British Museum (no. 1934 4.10.33), collected by Rev. H. Paget-Wilkes, *Uganda, Southern Karamojong*, wood, metal, leather, 19.5 cm h.

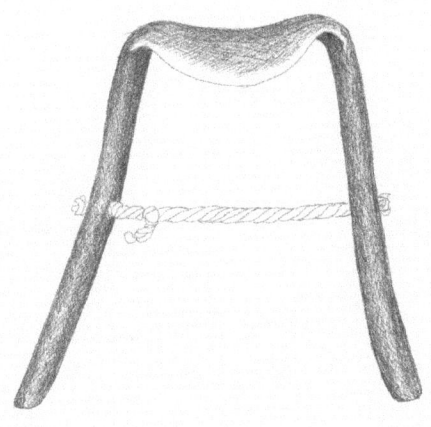

255 British Museum (no. 1947 Af34.31), collected by A. M. Champion, 1933, *Sudan/Uganda Border, Karamojong?*, wood, leather, 17.3 cm h.

**242** | AFRICAN DREAM MACHINES

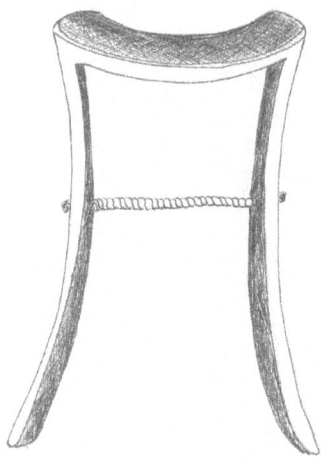

256 Best (1993:157, no. 150), *Kenya, Turkana*, wood and leather, 14 cm h.

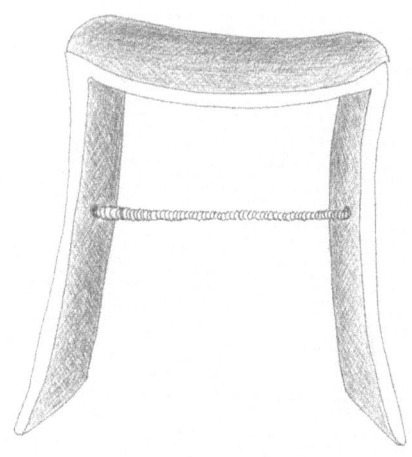

257 Oxford, Pitt Rivers Museum (no. 1978.20.258), collected by Jean Brown, *Kenya, East of Mt Elgon, Pokot (Tiati Pokot). Made and used by a Sandal-diviner. This type is made and used mainly by the junior set of the senior generation and the senior set of the junior generation*, wood, leather, 15.5 cm h.

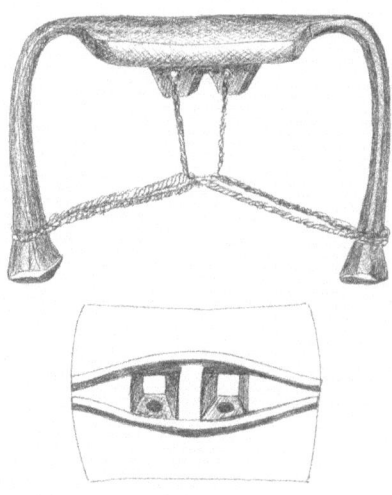

258 British Museum (no. 1934-6-5-23), collected by Captain Blaine, *Uganda, Lango(?), Acoli(?)*, wood, leather, 11.9 cm h.

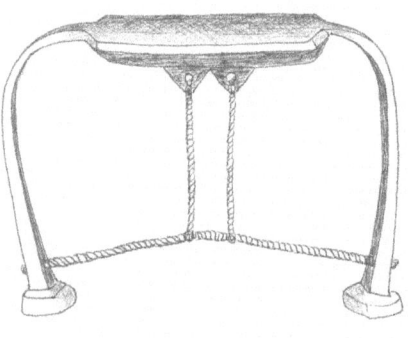

259 British Museum (no. CC + 8305), *Collected by Hearne (Lupton Bey collection no 32), donated by A. W. Franks, 1882, Uganda, Lango/not Lango (attributed by J. H. Driberg)*, wood, leather, 10.6 cm h.

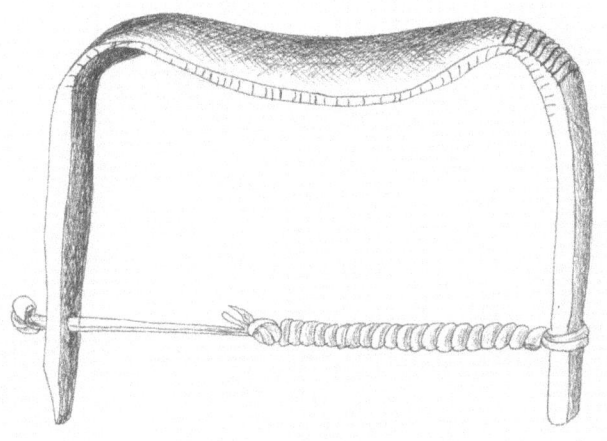

260   Musée Royal de l'Afrique Central (no. RG 79.37.1), *East Africa*, wood, leather, 19 cm h.

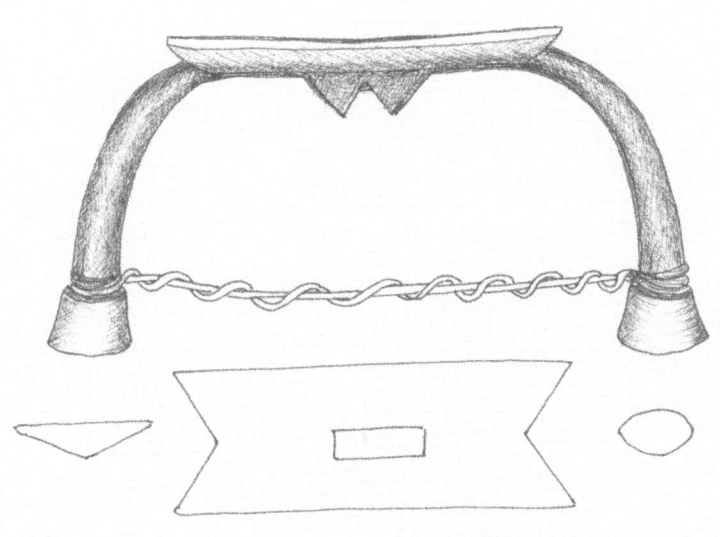

261   British Museum (no. 1947 Af15.1), from Newberry Borough Museum, *East Africa, Uganda*, wood, leather, 11.1 cm h.

# 7 | Tracing Histories: Central and Southern African Connections

## HISTORY AND THE NOTION OF THE 'BANTU EXPANSION'

THE MAJORITY OF headrests from Central Africa, especially from the Congo basin and the neighbouring savannah regions to its east, are made with columns, whereas columned headrests are in the minority in south-Central and Southern Africa. Yet both headrests with columns and those with other supports are made and used by speakers of Bantu languages that are related to one other. The idea that Bantu languages spread across Africa from the Niger–Benue area approximately 2,000 years ago seems to be accepted among most historians, anthropologists, linguists and archaeologists, and, although the details of this history are debated endlessly, it appears that shared languages point to some kind of shared origins. The politics of these origins, however, leads into quagmires when applied to cultural studies, and any attempt to link particular headrest types to particular branches of Bantu languages is doomed to failure, partly because the making of headrests is neither universal nor even ubiquitous among Bantu speakers, and because specific headrest types are often not peculiarly made by speakers of one branch of the language. The idea that specific cultural forms belong to speakers of one particular language, or group of languages, or branch of an ur-language (in this case, Bantu) is possibly appropriate to archaeological domains, but it does not have much relevance in more recent history, where types and styles of headrests have surfaced in widely spaced locations, as evidenced in the case of the headrests with columns. Yet the possibility of the existence of an African commonality in cultural forms, which we might hope to derive from such a study of African objects, or indeed from African systems of thought such as that evidenced by divination (Peek 2000), is seriously diluted by a realisation that some Zulu headrests appear to be formally much closer to headrests from the peoples of Tonga in the Pacific Ocean than they are to those of the Tsonga of Mozambique.

I have established a limited number of structural types among the headrests examined in this chapter, but within these structural types there is even more variation than was found in the columned types, or in the East African forms already discussed. The two main divisions are:

1) those headrests that articulate the support as separate from both the base and the platform, showing a similar concern for a visual syntax of support as the columned examples; and

2) headrests that have a horizontal orientation, often with no base, and either fat legs of various shapes (suggesting animal imagery) or a more complex geometric structure

(suggesting architectural referents) supporting a platform that is semi-circular or triangular in profile, contained between the legs and with minimal curvature lengthwise. There are, of course, numerous examples that fall between these, but there are not enough to disrupt the general scheme.[1] Within these outlined types, many sub-divisions and attributions can be made according to ethnic categories, some of which have been the subject of in-depth examination and debate by Dewey (1991; 1993), Becker (1999; 1992) and Nettleton (1985), and others by Klopper (1989; 1992). I do not wish to enter into detailed debates about these issues here, because I aim to develop a sense of the patterns of commonality among these headrests in order to get beyond the intricacies of ethnic styles. Yet, once again, there are inevitably instances where particular headrest styles are confined to one particular language/ethnic group, and these will be noted. I have established design principles that often appear to be based on some form of geometry and correspondence of parts or planar symmetries, which are common to particular types of headrests and therefore transcend ethnic boundaries. This is, of course, also related to another aspect of style that I pursue in chapter 8: that which relates to content, to what is signified by the headrest — the issue of iconography.

The images referred to in this chapter are predominantly of Southern African examples, i.e. from south of the Zambezi. There are two main reasons for this. Firstly, as noted above, the vast majority of non-figurative headrests, i.e. those without figure sculptures as supports, from Bantu-speaking peoples in Central Africa, take the form of columned supports dealt with above. Further, the vast majority of headrests with figure sculptures as supports for the platforms are from Central Africa, and will be discussed in the chapter on iconography and meaning (chapter 8). The second reason is that more headrests appear to have been collected among Southern African Bantu-speaking peoples than among most other African groups, with the possible exception of some particular East African groups such as the Pokot and the Somali.[2] The circumstantial causes for these accidents of collecting have been addressed to some extent in chapter 1 — with headrests from Southern Africa, in particular, substituting for independent figurative sculpture of the type apparently so abundant from the Cameroons, east to the Rift Valley and Great Lakes and south to the plains of northern Zambia and Angola, which also produced countless headrests.

The closely knit stylistic formations of the two headrest types outlined in this chapter are completely different from many of the forms in use among Nilotic and Cushitic speakers outlined in chapter 6, although there are some significant exceptions. The stylistic commonalities extend to the patterns common on both the abstract and figurative headrests within the Southern and Central African headrest corpus. Any significance these similarities and differences may have for the debates around the notion of Bantu migration and expansion[3] is not pursued here, largely because there are so few old examples with which to work, and because there has been so much movement of people with their objects, and thus object types and styles, across and within this vast region in the past two and a half centuries (Kriger 1999).

However, if it is assumed that style is like a language with structural principles and vocabularies that can be traced back in time, then it might be possible to use stylistic analysis as a pointer to historical developments, in the same way as Ehret (2000) proposes for vocabularies in language. In *Paths in the Rainforests*, Vansina (1990:49) reiterates the theory (as a fact) that the Bantu languages originated in Nigeria around the Benue River, expanding southwards and eastwards, and splitting into two branches, Eastern and Western Bantu, whose separation, according to glottochronological evidence, dates back to *c.* 3000 BCE. While the linguistic evidence of such developments appears to stand (Williamson & Blench 2000), despite a wide-ranging debate, the problems appear to be much more severe when one tries to match linguistic histories with archaeological accounts of pottery and iron working as means of recounting history (De Maret & Nsuka 1977; Vansina 1995; Kriger 1999), and so the evidence supplied by wooden artefacts with life spans of approximately 50 to 150 years, whose mobility is also ubiquitous, has limited plausibility as evidence documenting historical movement of people in deep time. Nevertheless, the survival of very old examples in Dogon territory of headrest types only encountered in recent times in Central and Southern Africa suggests tantalising connections in the perhaps not so distant past. The fragmentary nature of this evidence, however, does not allow anything more than a nod in the direction of noting such correspondences. It certainly does not allow for an analysis of the stylistic elements as pointers to origins of, or affiliations or affinities among different ethnic groups.

## VERTICAL COMPOSITIONS

This larger category can be sub-divided into a number of smaller sub-divisions, and in many respects these correspond to elements outlined for columned headrests in chapter

3. I have included in this section two columned headrests (figs. 343 & 357) from the south-east (Zimbabwe–Mozambique), both as a reminder of the similarity of structural principles of the larger type and as a referent for other structural types that use combinations of columns with other elements. I have here concentrated on the forms of supports as the primary defining characteristic in grouping these headrests into types, but shapes of platforms and bases, the motifs used in relief carving on surfaces and the addition of flaps to platforms may distinguish different area, ethnic or individual styles from one another.

Because the complexities of stylistic attributions have been debated in the existing literature, I am going to use the terms *Shona* and *Tsonga* as loosely constituting the two main stylistic groupings in the area south of the Zambezi and north of the Limpopo rivers and stretching from Botswana, eastwards to the coast of Mozambique, with a small projection south into northern South Africa. Both Dewey (1991) and Becker (1999) have unpacked these ethnic divisions and have shown how inaccurate they are, except possibly as overarching names for cultural complexes, as is the notion of the Luba. I have therefore not used the ethnic sub-divisions as a category here,[4] and will argue that some of the regional specificities of style argued for by Dewey (1993) do not hold up to the scrutiny of visual analysis. I have similarly simply worked with the attributions given to headrests from the south-western Democratic Republic of the Congo (DRC) and Angola as Yaka, Teke, Cokwe and Lunda, taking into account the similarities among their cultural institutions (Biebuyck 1985; Bourgeois 1984).

## Panel/pillar supports

It is tempting to propose this as the first and most immediately obvious relative of the columnar support, except that here the support takes the form of a rectangular panel or plank, distinguishable from the rectangular pillar by its breadth and relatively shallow depth. But all is not so simple, for the panels can vary in breadth and relative height, and in some instances may be combined with other forms, such as columns. Headrests using panels (mostly rectangular, but sometimes shaped in other ways) as supports are found among a number of different peoples from Central and into Southern Africa, although in some, significantly specific styles or genres emerge as belonging to narrowly defined ethnic clusters. Furthermore, while the panel is always thin and is often kept intact, with its planar sides disrupted only by shallow relief sculpture, in other instances the panel is penetrated completely, at times forming a fretwork of geometric lines. Quite often the kind of support panel used seems to dictate the kind of base, but the platform shapes are more likely to be related to ethnic preferences, as borne out by parallels between these forms and columned headrest types. Figures 262–267 offer a cross-section of headrests using a single panel as a support for an articulated platform. The bases of these examples and their overall conformations differ quite extensively, and in two, the panel has been penetrated so that it appears like fretwork, but they form a group that follows a single structural principle. They are provenanced to six different ethnic groups, many of whom created headrests with a number of variations on the basic theme of the two-dimensional panel support, and all of whom use very similar decorative geometries.

Central African variants

Variations on the simple panel can take a number of different forms, and are found largely among peoples in Angola and the south-western DRC, particularly the Lunda, Cokwe and Yaka, of which examples are illustrated in figures 268–272. In these, there are effectively two panels with long sides parallel to each other and to the length of the platform, and each panel has geometric relief carving on its outer surface, which has been turned into fretwork in the example in figure 272. This generally abstract pattern turns a figurative corner in other examples, also attributed to the Yaka and Cokwe, in which the base is rendered as a box with a roof, thus representing a house (figs. 273–275). The sides of some of these are also penetrated to form fretwork geometries (fig. 275), and one (fig. 277), attributed to the Pende, takes on an extraordinary form in which the roof is no longer supported by a set of panels, but by a set of three-dimensional, curved, bracket-shaped legs set at right angles to the long sides. In all of these examples, the platform is separated from the roof of the house support, sometimes by a short column, and all have rectangular bases and butterfly platforms. They form a clearly defined sub-genre within this larger group of headrests.

The penetration of the panel support is found in other examples, where the panel is shaped so that the sides form a sharp point and the panel reads as a diamond without its top and bottom apices. In some examples (e.g. fig. 278),[5] this diamond is penetrated at its centre by a square hole; in others, it is formed of two panels parallel to each other (fig.

279), but in all cases the design imperative appears to be the parallelism of panel to base and platform as a goal. This formal solution has, however, not moved away from the premise of supports being necessarily rectangular, something found also in Shona examples, where the bases are often composed of circles or arcs in plan.

## A Southern–Central African cross-border style (but mostly Tsonga)

Numerous Southern African headrests originate from an area running through Zimbabwe from Botswana and into eastern Mozambique, which Becker (1999) and Dewey (1993) agree, although in different terms, is one in which style cannot be fixed to ethnicity. The spread of this style also demonstrates the ways in which the basic premise of the planar panel can be maintained with infinite variation, although at times it may beg the question of design premise. For example, the support of the headrest in figure 280 could be seen as a ribbed panel, similar to that in figure 262, but cut in two and provided with two joined bases. The support in figure 281, on the other hand, which has the same structure as figure 280, except that one side is without ribs, could be read more clearly as two rectangular pillar supports.[6] In examples such as those in figures 282 and 283, the reading of the supports as independent pillars rather than the remnants of the panel from which they were carved is emphasised by the size of the spatial interval between them. The single bar linking the supports in the headrest in figure 282 emphasises this space, traversing it in parallel to the platform above. In figure 284, however, the multiplication of parallel horizontal bars between the two pillars reinforces the reading of the support as a pierced rectangular panel, as each of the transverse bars corresponds with the curved relief ribs on the surfaces of the pillars.

In all of these examples where there are such divided panels/square pillar supports, the base is divided into two lobes, as opposed to the single lobe on the single-panel support. But this logic is by no means absolute, as is demonstrated by the next example, figure 285, where the single ribbed panel, albeit penetrated by a large circular hole, has a bi-lobed base, in this case with a triangular projection at the juncture of the two lobes (also seen in fig. 282). All of these examples have lugs under the platforms, but some are parallel to the long sides of the platform and pierced (figs. 280, 283 & 285), while the rest are parallel to the short ends of the platform and solid semi-circles. Some have relief decoration in rectangular panels on the upper ends of the platforms parallel to the short ends. All were collected among Tsonga speakers in what was then the Transvaal Province (now Gauteng, Limpopo and Mpumalanga Provinces, and parts of North West Province) of South Africa and in Mozambique by Swiss missionaries, and can — and have been — taken to be one of a number of such headrest types typical of this linguistic group.[7] But there are examples that suggest that this style is not so clearly confined to a single ethnic group in a single part of the wider region.

Figure 286 appears at first glance to conform to the same principles, but its two square-profile pillars frame a slightly recessed, plain rectangular panel. The base is again bi-lobed, and there are decorative panels on the upper surfaces of, and pendant lugs parallel to, the short ends of the platform. This example has explicit record of provenance in Swaziland, yet it has been called 'Tsonga' by both Wanless (1989) and Becker (1999) on the basis of style, although it differs in its sculptural spirit from others that are securely provenanced to Tsonga speakers. This is in spite of the present of arched handles projecting from the sides of the support, something also seen in figures 285 and 284, and, on a smaller scale, figure 203. If anything, this example should awaken us to another aspect of the aesthetics of such designs, i.e. that the identity of aesthetic difference may reside in things other than simple structural elements, and rather more in subtle renderings of decorative surfaces and in attitudes to symmetry and regularity.

Figures 287–292 illustrate this quite clearly. These headrests have a main panel as support, poised at a 45-degree angle to the base and the platform, either as a simple ribbed panel (fig. 287), a double ribbed panel (fig. 288), or fluted panels in combination with loops (figs. 289 & 290) or with columns (figs. 291 & 292). One (fig. 288) has a base in the form of a human foot, an iconographic detail repeated on a number of forms of Tsonga carving, including other headrests. But the rest of these examples have bi-lobed bases, of which the last (fig. 292) is different in that it is not planar: its sides flare out towards its base, and the central projection between the lobes contracts towards the base so that it forms a wedge shape. This treatment of the base may be sufficient to suggest a different 'hand', but is more likely to indicate its origin in a different style area, something attested by the provenance recorded in respect of these examples. All of those with the flat bases are from the collection made in Mozambique in the late 1920s during a period of drought when the locals sold their headrests to the Swiss missionaries at Inhambane and Manjacaze in exchange for maize meal (Wanless 1989; Becker 1999). The last example (fig. 292), however, is provenanced to a Tswana origin in its museum records, and the more three-dimensional base may be more commonly associated with headrests made by Shona speakers and those in close contact with them. Another example (fig. 293), where the supports are clearly conceived as pillars rather than as a split panel, and where the base has flared sides, is from the same source, and is also attributed to the Tswana, although it must be noted that there is a large Shona-speaking community in what is now Botswana.

A group of headrests closely related to those examples, where the support appears like a divided panel, was collected by Frobenius on his expedition to Southern Africa (figs. 294–298), and Dewey (1993) has identified these as having been collected either on the border between Zimbabwe and Mozambique, or in Mozambique itself among the Barwe Tonga.[8] These have the same pillar/panel structure as the Tsonga examples, with two or three panel supports whose surfaces are decorated with chevrons, diamonds and triangles in shallow relief, but in different combinations on the two faces. In two of these (figs. 294 & 295), the panels are linked by a simple cylindrical bar; one has no link (fig. 296), another (fig. 297) has a fretwork of two vertically superimposed cross shapes between the panels, and the last (fig. 298) has three panels. All have deep, flaring bi-lobed bases, the last three with a central triangular projection, and all have similar platforms that are slightly butterfly-shaped. Dewey suggests that these properly constitute a particular style, but in the larger scheme of the south-east African headrest production, they appear to be clear exemplars of a kind of stylistic continuum spreading across a large region, in which they present elements associated both with clearly Shona forms and distinctively Tsonga ones. Both Dewey (1993) and Becker (1999) have demonstrated the overly constructed and overly inclusive nature of these identity terms, and the probable relatedness of the headrest forms produced in this area. But there are some headrests that do appear to be more clearly defined as specifically Shona, which were, however, not necessarily made and used by all Shona groups.[9]

The 'Shona' style nexus

All of the headrests that are discussed in this sub-section use a combination of circle and triangle elements, sometimes carved as fretwork, but almost always arranged within a two-dimensional plane as the remnants of a central panel. Their distinctive designs sets them apart from all other headrests from this region, although there are some other designs in the region that clearly derive from, quote, or develop out of or alongside these distinctive forms. Some examples were published among the headrests collected in 'Zambèze' Province of Portuguese East Africa in Müller and Snelleman's illustrated catalogue of c. 1892 (fig. 299). Four of the illustrated headrests have the combinations of circles and triangles that are outlined below, and because they have all been given the same provenance, whereas others of the same type collected by Müller and Snelleman have other provenances, it would appear that style regions cannot be determined easily within this particular headrest form. Dewey has attempted to deliver such a set of criteria for positing differences among northern, central, eastern, south-western and western areas styles of headrests, but I have found that his analysis is not convincing on a formal level and against evidence such as that recoverable from the early literature.[10] Because his taxonomy is reliant on provenance, without a real explanation of the formal parameters of the style, my analysis here is based on formal properties and follows the same pattern I have used before (Nettleton 1985, 1990).

In Müller and Snelleman's drawing (fig. 299) there are four examples of headrests with circle and triangle supports. Of these, nos. 3 and 5 use a combination of triangles placed above and below circles, on either side of a central horizontal panel that links the circles; no. 2 has similar triangle and circle supports flanking a central vertical column or rod; and no. 4 has a further set of two triangles in the centre above and below the linking central horizontal panel. These headrests, which Müller and Snelleman (c. 1892, pl. XIV, notes to no. 3) remark are the commonest form in 'Zambèze', are clearly part of a single stylistic group, mostly associated with the Shona and Zimbabwe. The term *Zambèze* is meant by Müller and Snelleman (c. 1892:4) to include that part of the Zambezi River basin that extends (inland) from the river mouth to Tête, and they state that the majority of objects represented in their book are from Mozambique. They also note that the area they encompass in the book includes many different ethnic groups, listing most of the better-known Southern African language groups, but also noting that the people did not refer to themselves by these names (Müller and Snelleman c. 1892:5). This might be an important thought to hang on to when considering issues of identity as expressed through the forms of objects used and made by different groups in this area, as it will allow us to deal better with the apparent overlapping of ethnic stylistic boundaries.

The headrests in figures 301–303 represent a single type that corresponds to Müller and Snelleman's nos. 3 and 5 in figure 299 and to a headrest collected by Bent (1892) and illustrated in his account of his travels in Mashonaland (fig. 300), but in these there is an increasing penetration of the triangle elements to form an open fretwork above and below the central panel and the circles.[11] A similar pattern follows in figures 304[12] and 305, where the two circles are subsumed into the central panel, as well as in figure 306, where two breast forms occupy the centre of the two circles, which are joined by a bar above and below, but where the centre of the horizontal element is also hollowed out.[13] A further variation on this theme in figure 307 has paired circles punctuating each end of each side of the central panel, but subsumed into it. The reverse side of the circle-central panel of figure 301 also reads as a continuous horizontal panel element. All of these headrests have secure general provenance to the Shona-speaking peoples, and one in the South African Museum in Cape Town is recoded as 'Manyika',[14] and they all share formal characteristics beyond the arrangements of their supports. All have flaring bases, all are bi-lobed, and most have central triangular projections. All have carved geometric designs in relief on their support surfaces, and none has pendants or lugs from the underside of the platform. The platforms are somewhat narrower at their centres than their ends, four have relief decoration on the upper ends of their platforms, and three (including the South African Museum example) have an opposed triangle low-relief decoration on the upper surface of the platform. The latter feature is seen only on two of Müller and Snelleman's examples, but it is suggested by Dewey (1993:107) to be a significant feature of the eastern Shona style.[15]

It is, however, found on some examples of headrests of the following group in which the central panel between the circles and triangles is vertical,[16] including no. 2 in Müller and Snelleman's group of Shona headrests (fig. 299). Figures 308–313 show further variants among the supports in this headrest type, from those with deep bases and solid proportions, as in figures 308 and 309, to others with shallower, and in two cases (figs. 311 & 312), flat bases, but taller and more elegant proportions. The width of the central panel varies enormously, from pillar proportions in figure 310, to the wide panels of figures 312 and 313, and figure 310 is the only example with a single oval base, with diamond relief patterns on its upright sides. Figure 311, collected by Frobenius and attributed/provenanced to the Zezeru (a Shona sub-group), is the only one in this group with pendants from the platform.

The issue of provenance of these headrests impacts on the definition of style areas, and is complicated by the probable regional extensions of usage of this kind of headrest: even if they were all made by Shona-speaking craftsmen, they were used by members of many other groups. So while the slightly aberrant example in figure 312 is recorded by Frobenius as having been collected in the Charter district of present-day Zimbabwe, and the also slightly unusual (in the choice of relief decoration on the panels) example in figure 309 is recorded as coming from Mashonaland, both are clearly related to the headrest in figure 314, which has, however, a very clear — and early — provenance to the Batoka (also called the Toka, a sub-group of the Tonga from northern Zimbabwe–Zambia). The latter headrest is distinguished only by different proportions of the triangles and circles, by the upward curve of the platform and by the way it joins to the support. Two examples with vertical panels between the circle and triangle elements, collected by a Dr H. Stannus in Nyasaland among the Ngoni prior to 1950, constitute another instance of this spread, and another with a horizontal panel, also provenanced to Malawi, but from a different collector, appears to confirm this.[17]

Headrests whose supports comprise a panel interposed between a pair of triangle and circle forms are in the vast majority among those unequivocally provenanced to Shona speakers. But there are other patterns used in the supports that nevertheless belong within the same group. These include one that omits the central panel entirely (fig. 315), an example collected somewhere between Salisbury (now Harare) and Tête before 1902, and others that simply multiply the number of triangle and circle forms, of which examples can be seen in figures 316 and 317, both of which have a sure provenance to Shona territory. That this type is of equal antiquity to other Shona forms is evident from another collected by Bent prior to 1892.[18] Yet others multiply the number of circles to six (fig. 318),[19] so that the triangles are reduced accordingly. Most have bi-lobed bases, although the kind of design logic involved in these headrests, where each element of the support rests on its own lobe of the base, might suggest that a tri-lobed base — found on a few examples — would be more appropriate. Most examples have the kind of relief geometry on their planar surfaces that is associated with other triangle and circle headrest forms so peculiar to the Shona. It is possibly this geometry that, together with the base and platform shapes common in these headrests, distinguishes the variations on these themes as belonging to the same design nexus.

Some of these variations can be seen in figures 319–327. My reason for grouping these together is that they all follow the same design logic as the circle and triangle examples, but some omit some circles (figs. 319 & 320), others eliminate all reference to the circle motif (figs. 321–323) and still others redeploy these elements in quite idiosyncratic ways (figs. 324–326). The five examples (figs. 319–323) in which the triangles form the main part of the support, all with horizontal linking panels, also have flaring bases, three of which are lobed. The fourth (fig. 320) shares with one of the most idiosyncratic examples (fig. 324) a flared oval base. All these examples have a relatively secure provenance to Shona speakers, but cannot be tied to a single district, nor to a single ethnic sub-group. This then raises the possibility that such design freedom was not unusual in Shona headrest making, and that the use of other forms in headrest supports, often having no reference to triangles or circles, yet recorded as coming from Shona territories, would not necessarily indicate an origin outside of the central Shona 'heartland' in Zimbabwe, as suggested by Dewey (1999), such as the most contracted of all the triangle and circle examples I encountered in my museum peregrinations (fig. 327). Many variants correspond in form to headrests both from the south-eastern seaboard and from the larger Central African Congo basin region, at points returning us to a pan-Bantu design consciousness, but at others reinforcing a smaller regional distribution.

### The cross-shape support

This section analyses headrests whose supports form a cross shape, or a variant of this basic form seen in the use of bent legs, although again, boundaries are difficult to draw between these. In most of these examples, the distinctions among base, support and platform noted in all the Southern and Central African examples of panel and pillar forms are visible, but not in those that most clearly exemplify the cross-shaped legs. While regional differences in the use of basic forms do emerge here, there is sufficient coherence across the designs to justify not sub-dividing this discussion by region.

The most striking and possibly the clearest examples of cross-shaped support headrests are attributed to the Yaka and/or Teke, most of them collected early in the twentieth century in the south-western DRC.[20] The simplest form of cross is seen in figures 328–330, where the support merges with both the platform and base (although the platform is somewhat wider and deeper than the base), to form two opposed triangles, with a more or less prominent figurative element at the centre. There are also several examples that do not have any figurative elements.[21] In all of these headrests, however, the planar integrity of the face of the panel from which the support is carved is maintained parallel to the long sides of the platform and base. In this they relate to headrests from other groups where the base and the platform are more clearly distinguished from the cross-shaped support.

The cross shape can, however, also be constituted by examples in which the panel is more obviously evident, as in figures 331 and 332, both with clear provenance to Popokabaka in the Kwango region of the DRC. Here the cross is implied by the horizontal triangular sections cut out of the upright sides of the panels, a design that reads as a complete opposite of the split diamond panel in figure 279, almost as though they had been designed as reversals of each other. However, the latter is from Kinda Kamina in Katanga, far enough away to make any relationship improbable. In figure 332 there are two such cross shapes framing a central column, an arrangement particularly similar to the Shona forms in figures 309 and 310. A further similarity between these outlines to those of the supports on headrests that consist of bent or curved, square-sectioned pillars or narrow panels can be seen in the examples in figures 333–340. In all of these examples, the supports curve inwards, towards the centre of the platform on its lateral plane. In some instances they are joined by a horizontal bar (figs. 334, 335 & 337), in some there is a circular or semi-circular element nested into the centre of the curve of the support parallel to the long sides (figs. 335 & 337–340) and in some there is a central vertical slab (fig. 338) or column (fig. 339). In all of them, the platform is treated as separate, but the DRC examples have a more steeply curved platform and often rectangular bases (figs. 336[22] & 337), as opposed to the lobed or oval bases of the Southern African examples (figs. 333–335). The planar parallelism of the support to the sides of the plateau, so clear in the panel supports, is maintained, although it is disrupted by the three-dimensionality of the bases. The difference between this and a more three-dimensional understanding of the cross motif is seen in relation to the following group of headrests (figs. 341–348), all of which are from Southern Africa, and probably belong to the stylistic group that Dewey (1993) denotes south-eastern Shona, or Becker (1999) as 'Tsonga', but with the reservation that these are invented terms.

The headrest in figure 341 follows a Tsonga pattern in its arrangement of bi-lobed base, minimally curved platform with decorated ends and pendants, and its planar, complete, cross-shaped support with semi-circular loops projecting from the lateral angles. At the centre of this cross is a horizontal panel with parallel engraved lines. The absolute planar parallelism of this form is disrupted only by the bi-lobed base. Figures 344 and 345, whose provenance is less secure, but which are from the region of Shona linguistic dominance, both have platform pendants and an element across the centre of the cross support, again recalling the Shona cross and circle type. The base of figure 345 is unusual in that it is rectangular, tall and hollowed out with an aperture at one of the short ends, the probability being that this was a built-in snuff-box.[23] In both of these, the planar integrity of the panel-style headrest in fully adhered to — the base of figure 344 is lobed, but polygonal rather than circular. The headrest in figure 342 follows the same pattern, but the introduction of a central, cog motif, which appears to hold the cross's centre together, is a clearly more three-dimensional element. This is even more evident in figure 343, where the cylindrical columns of the support curve inwards and are also visually 'gathered' together by a cog. In figures 346–348, however, there is a consistent and almost total disruption or ignoring of such planar imperatives as the platform might suggest, with supports that mix the planar with the circular and bases that are almost completely three-dimensional. In figure 348, the base becomes a flaring cone from which two planar branches form a V supporting the platform, so that the cross is now only implicit.

### The Kuba and other Kasai peoples' bent-legged headrests

A quite distinctive set of headrests where the bent-legged supports form a cross shape, many of which were published by Maes (1929, pl. III, figs. 1–22; pl. IV, figs. 1–10), appear to belong to a specific region of the DRC, the Kasai–Sankuru region, with many of his examples attributed to the Kuba, Nkutu and Kete, and a few to the Songye from, once again, the melting pot of Lusambo. These are all characterised by a support with two to three rounded legs bent inwards so that the apices of the triangular shapes thus formed point to the centre of the headrest.

Only one example (fig. 349) of this type from Southern Africa is represented here,[24] one that has a long pedigree, but also demonstrates quite clearly the similarities and differences with the DRC examples. It is essentially vertical in its orientation, the legs being closely spaced, the base deep and the proportions of platform length to the height of the whole roughly equal. The legs also have a surprising delicacy of scale that is in stark contrast to the other examples illustrated here. The first (fig. 350) has a much more horizontal orientation, with widely spaced legs and a rectangular base that is decorated with a form of herringbone/interlace pattern, as well as studs on its platform end, but maintains the parallelism of the planar surfaces. This example is recorded as Songye. The two that follow (figs. 351 & 352), however, have more fully rounded legs, more deeply curved platforms, rectangular bases, and generally squat and horizontal proportions. Figure 352 has a set of bent legs that appear to have been prevented from meeting in the centre, severed by a very clear vertical cut, although examples with a join and a thus bent H/cross shape were published by Maes (1929, pl. II, figs. 13–15). Two examples provenanced to the Ngombe (figs. 353 & 354) offer an almost complete inversion of this Kuba-centred style with legs planar and bent outwards framing a diamond shape, deep platforms, and oval and half-log-shaped bases. Their relationship to the cross and the interlace is in their framing of a particular space or gap, and is thus different from the previous examples, yet akin to them and to the next one in terms of their geometry.

The final example included in this section on bent legs (fig. 354) is a somewhat idiosyncratic, but not unique, headrest in which the legs cross in front of/behind each other parallel to the plane of the platform length, almost as though two parts of a three-dimensional interlace had been used to form them. Both end in feet parallel to the base and the platform. The interlace motif is ubiquitous as the relief decoration on Kuba carving,[25] including these headrests, and is found on those of many other peoples, including the Shona, but less often the Tsonga. Yet it is clear that the geometric elements of the supports of many Kuba, Shona and Tsonga headrests (among others) use similar geometrical principles of fractals and repetitive or sliding symmetry, most often on a planar rather than a fully three-dimensional scheme, as is the case here.[26]

## Arcs, columns and three-dimensional interlacing

A number of headrests in which arcs are combined with one another, with columns, or with both, are commonly provenanced to sites across the region that runs from Botswana in the west, through southern Zimbabwe, and then sweeps through central and southern Mozambique, encompassing a number of different ethnic groups. Figures 356–362 offer a small sample of such forms, their subtle variations and their component elements. Each of these has a lobed base, sometimes with triangular projections between the lobes; all have pendants from the undersides of the plateau, some with carved decoration, and three have carved decoration on the upper ends of the platforms. There is thus no way of distinguishing these from one another on stylistic grounds, and their ethnic identity rests entirely on their having a reliable provenance. It is also notable that in all of these examples, the forms are arranged in parallel, with the long sides of the platform, as in figure 363, where two semi-circular arcs are superimposed, back to back and separated by a short, fat cylinder, but parallel to the platform.

Contrasted to this is the use of two half-loop shapes, superimposed at right angles to each other so that they appear like links in a chain, interlacing in three dimensions, as a support in a number of Congolese headrests, of which figure 364 is an example. This form of support appears on a number of examples in the Musée Royal de l'Afrique Central, all with different attributions and provenances, from Kioko, to the Luba and Butaan Gili in Kwango.[27] A similar form, but one that takes virtuosity to a new height, was collected by Ella Winter in c. 1945 (fig. 365), apparently in Mozambique. Here the two loops are separated and the top loop rests on the lower, so that the two loops embrace the same space, but at right angles to one another, and the platform balances on the lower loop. Because they are so delicately poised, this would have made the act of sleeping on such a headrest an art in itself.[28] The virtuosity of the carving in these examples and the full realisation of the three-dimensionality of their interlacing forms recalls Somali examples (fig. 181), but in the latter, the interlace was never fully three-dimensional. That such *tours de force* were not a development of Tsonga carving only in the twentieth century is confirmed by one illustrated by Müller and Snelleman (c. 1892), (fig. 366), in which the cylindrical supports twist, without touching one another, and connect the platform to the base around a column of air. Similar examples are known from the Jaques Collection (cf. Becker 1991; 1999; Wanless 1985–87).

Some inklings of history

It is almost impossible to give a complete overview of Tsonga and Shona headrest support shapes, but there is one other significant grouping that warrants attention, as it may be used to present a particular sub-style of headrests among these peoples, or to argue for a very widespread connection among headrests of peoples through Malawi, Zimbabwe, north-western Botswana, central and southern Mozambique, and the north-western parts of South Africa. This group relates in form to the arc and column type (figs. 358–362) and to the clustered-column form (fig. 179) discussed earlier. These headrests (figs. 367–372) have a base or flaring columnar legs, a cross bar with either further columns, or a set of planar pillars arranged above this, supporting the platform. Many have been conclusively provenanced to the Limpopo Province of South Africa,[29] where Tsonga speakers settled after the wars between Gungunyane and the Portuguese in Mozambique in the nineteenth century (Becker 1999; Harries 1989). Only one of this type (and it is much slighter and more 'Tsonga' in its proportions) is found in Müller and Snelleman's (*c.* 1892, pl. XV.5) illustrations (fig. 367), and it is of uncertain provenance, 'probably BaSotho', while another, collected by the Rev. Philippe Jeannerat before 1894 (Neuchâtel, no. IIIC 3027)[30] is recorded as having belonged to the 'chief of the Ba Hlengwe' (i.e. Hlengwe, a sub-group of the Tsonga), but it had not been extensively used prior to its arrival in Jeannerat's possession and its subsequent transfer into the museum stores. Some further examples are shown in figures 368–371, to indicate the possible spread of this style and the complex permutations it presents to any attempt to pose clear-cut ethnic or regional division of styles. Figure 368 is a drawing after Distant's (1892) illustration of 'MaGwamba' (i.e. Gwamba)[31] headrests from the Spelonken area of the Limpopo Province, and it corresponds to others in the Johannesburg Art Gallery, as well as one in Geneva. The example in figure 369, however, where the splayed legs stand on a Shona-style lobed base, is provenanced to Mutali in eastern Zimbabwe, where Ndau, Shona and possibly even Tsonga elements meet. Figure 370, which has similar splayed legs, but without the base, is provenanced merely and generally to 'Mashonaland', while figure 371, where the base is lobed but polygonal, and the legs are planar was collected by Theodore Bent (1892) in 'Chibi's country', probably south-western Zimbabwe.

The final nail in the coffin of any attempt to define a particular overarching ethnic identity for this style of headrest construction must be the headrest in figure 372, definitively provenanced to Malawi. It is documented in the museum records as 'Shona style', but looks much closer to Barwe Tonga examples, both in its dumpy proportions and in the treatment of the reliefs on the planar surfaces. If this is a hybrid example, it is also testament to the degree of contact among and movement of peoples in the southern part of Africa over the past 200 years.

From the examples presented here, it is possible to conclude that most of the almost infinite variations within these headrest types had been current in Central and Southern African Bantu-speaking societies for some time. The interchange of stylistic elements among different ethnic groups certainly pre-dates the arrival of the curious Europeans who were to collect these objects as indices of strange practices. Yet, once it was known that Europeans were prepared to pay for such objects, it seems to have been common practice among the 'natives' to produce such objects for sale to outsiders. This is particularly clear from some of the examples of headrests in European museum collections, for example the Swiss collections from Mozambique,[32] where pristine, unused headrests with their pokerwork colouration still in strong contrast with the light colour of the wood, something disguised by, but often still discernible under, the warm and glowing patina of examples that had in fact pillowed somebody's head, among other things. The new examples were collected as samples of local native workmanship, or as specimens that attested to their customs, and their sharp edges and bright contrasts do not appear to have concerned those who collected them. But the Jaques Collection does not contain any of these; Jaques appears to have understood that if his collection were to count as more than mere 'ethnographic wood', as one private collector opines of the new pieces, he would have to seek out those that were 'authentic' as defined by the art market. Early examples of such unused headrests, such as two figurative examples using bovine figures as supports, one donated to Neuchâtel by N. Jaques in 1903, and the other by Jeannerat in 1894, show that this was already an established practice long before Kaltenrieder, another Swiss missionary, started to exchange maize meal for headrests in the famine season of winter 1938 (Becker 1999).

This is significant because there is a growing trade in objects made in Southern Africa in the nineteenth century, many of which are being repatriated from Europe to South Africa, or are finding their ways into European museums under the general rubric of the 'authentic' and even the 'masterpiece'. It is from a stance in which one can unpick such a history that I wish to approach the final group of headrests in this chapter.

## HORIZONTAL COMPOSITIONS

Ehret (2000) suggests that there has been a widespread dispersal, over two millennia, of similar cultural traits down the east coast of Africa, something that appears to be confirmed by the forms of headrests found among, especially, the coastal Nguni of Southern Africa and their Ngoni offshoot in Malawi and Tanzania, with only a few isolated parallels in Cameroon. These headrests always have a horizontal orientation, being much longer than they are tall, and also often have legs resting directly on the ground. In this they are related to a form of headrest that appears to have been ubiquitous among pastoralists in East Africa from the Sudan, through Uganda, Kenya and Tanzania, and evident also among Nguni speakers in both 'Zulu' and 'Xhosa' territory, the tripod (sometimes quadruped) branch-style headrest of which a selection is included in figures 373–382, and whose provenance, without unambiguous records, would be impossible to determine on stylistic grounds.

## Branch headrests: A short digression

Geographically speaking, the headrests in figures 373–382 belonged in the section on East African headrests (chapter 6), and they do, indeed, share important characteristics with many of the Pokot and Karamojong headrests discussed there, especially the ways in which they exploit the form of the branches from which they are made (see p. 210, figs. 239ff., above). In these examples, however, the headrest follows a longitudinal, horizontal imperative rather than a vertical one. Many of these headrests, which all have three or four legs, are made by the same ethnic groups as those who made the more vertically oriented, two-legged variety discussed above, but there is some logic to regarding the horizontal variety as more basic than the vertical one. The headrests are arranged here in a way that leads from those where there has been little interference with the natural shapes of the branches, except in the shaping of the joining branch to form a platform (figs. 373–375). In figure 376, only one of the legs still has its 'natural' shape, and the whole headrest has been polished and patinated. Figure 377 represents one of a number of this type of headrest collected by Evans-Pritchard among the Nuer of Sudan, and it has very little by way of patination. A Dinka headrest of this type (fig. 378), however, is constructed with legs from a single branch forming the legs of one side of the headrest, while two further legs have been joined on by a tenon on the other, and the whole has a more defined platform. Figure 381 falls somewhere between this horizontal branch-style headrest and the two-legged variety. And, finally, figures 379, 380 and 382 show examples in which various refinements of the form come to have almost figurative allusions, such as the phallic form of one leg in figure 379 and the animal-like stance in figures 380 and 382. The underside of the platform in figure 380 has a deliberately marked median ridge along its length, making the analogy with a male animal more explicit.

## Back to the Zulu — and Swazi, and North Sotho

Figure 383 presents a photograph of a number of young Zulu-speaking men engaged in a leisurely session of personal grooming, with one of these branch headrests placed in the left foreground as though indicating the ways in which the groomed hair was to be preserved. This image I shall return to at a later stage, but the headrest can be contrasted to that which appears in Angas's (1849) portrait of King Mpande (fig. 384). The example in Angas's image is fully carved out of a block of wood, unlike the tripod headrests, which, even if parts are worked over, depend initially on serendipity in the choice of a particular branch. Mpande's headrest, as invented by Angas (in the sense that he placed it in the picture), has a horizontal platform section supported by fat, bulbous legs, and is decorated with black pokerwork triangles. Mpande's headrest thus corresponds almost exactly to examples in the British Museum, one of which was transferred from Kew Gardens to the British Museum in 1866, indicating that it had been collected prior to that date. A number of such headrests with these dumpy legs or others that more closely approach a horn shape are residents of the British Museum storerooms. Many of them are exquisitely carved with finely engraved relief interlace lines, some with parts darkened (e.g. figs. 385 & 386), and others left light (fig. 387).[33] The darkened relief decoration of very fine engraved fluting corresponds very closely to the designs on large blackened vessels, ascribed to the Zulu in most museum stores, but more generally to North Nguni in some collections (Davison 1991b), (fig. 388).[34] These vessels have been avidly collected and reproduced in the literature as masterpieces of 'Nguni', while others with wider spaced ridges in their fluting have, more problematically, been assigned to 'Swazi'[35] carvers. They are indisputably 'masterpieces' of indigenous carving, but these examples were not used in Zulu society, and have thus been promoted as prestige items from this source only by twisting our understanding of the processes of patronage involved and by misunderstanding aspects of history. Their decoration replicates on a large scale the kind of decorative carving applied to small snuff containers among many peoples in the region, including Nguni speakers. It was, however, only under Mswati II (1840–65) that the peoples who made up the 'Swazi' nation (including Nguni, Sotho and Tsonga speakers) came to be called 'Swazi' and were thus clearly differentiated from other state formations in the region (Bonner 1983). Their material culture could, by the later nineteenth century, be clearly distinguished from that of the Zulu, but it is doubtful whether this separation could have happened as early as 1860. The early museum records are unambiguous in provenancing these objects to Natal (now KwaZulu-Natal Province)[36] and attributing them to the Zulu. One of these was subsequently reattributed to the 'Swazi' at a more recent date, but without any reason. The only example that mentions the Swazi is one elaborate example from the Wellcome Collection that has the following notation: 'Milk vessel, Swazi King's principal wife's, Swaziland, South Africa' and with the date, September 1953. From this point, it seems, 'Swazi' is the ethnic name that superseded 'Zulu' for the makers of the vessels, without any real evidence to support the shift.

From the dates at which these large vessels and associated headrests entered European collections, it may be concluded that they were envisaged by their Zulu makers as extensions of those smaller objects, made for new and demanding patrons. For none of the headrests that displays this type of fluting and none of the large fluted bowls that I have examined appears to have been used, except as items of display. Their patinas are dull, and what oil there is has been applied evenly to preserve the black pigment of their surfaces; it is not a patina that arises from handling. The acquisition records for another two of these bowls in the British Museum[37] are enlightening: both refer directly to the catalogue for the 'Natal' section of the 1862 International Exhibition in London (Mann 1862), on which a number of such bowls and headrests were displayed. The acquisition record for one (British Museum, no. 1559) suggests that it was made for holding sour milk, the vernacular name '*umgenge*' is quoted, and the object is said to have been made by 'a renowned Kafir artisan named Unobadula', as is the second, very much more complex double-bodied vessel (British Museum, no. 1560). The fact that these bowls have elaborate stands encircling them also sets them apart from ordinary, or even moderately elaborate milk pails known to have been in use in KwaZulu-Natal. These stands, moreover, are reminiscent of the (much discussed) chair on which Angas represented Mpande sitting, which was itself a copy of European prototypes.[38] In neither example is there any evidence of sour milk residue, nor of its ever having been cleaned, as the patina is pristine, and it is probable that these objects were originally made for sale to the 'Natal' commissioners, specifically for display in London. One of the commissioners, Dr Robert Mann, wrote the catalogue that is quoted in the British Museum acquisitions register. These particular specimens were subsequently bought on auction by Henry Christy. That the whole process of commissioning, displaying and then auctioning these artefacts then created a market for such objects is borne out by the evidence recently published by Stevenson (2005) demonstrating that there was already a roaring trade in curios from Southern Africa very early in its colonial history.

Exactly how early this started is difficult to gauge, but Henry Frances Fynn, who opened trade with Dingiswayo around 1785 at Delagoa Bay, suggested that Dingiswayo was an accomplished carver who had introduced the art to his people, and recounts a number of the kinds of things they produced (Fynn, cited in Wilson 1969:115). The fact that this account repeats a common trope for kings and leaders of African states in the nineteenth century does not discount it as a useful record of the availability of curious objects to European traders. And what could be more curious to the European mind than headrests? One of the type illustrated in Gardiner's (1836) account of Zulu country, an extraordinary invention with 16 horn-shaped legs linked by bars at their bases and the platform at the top, and including two pots with lids, both covered with finely engraved lines, one at each end of the platform's upper surface, has resided in the British Museum stores since the 1860s.[39] A similar example, but with only 12 legs, was drawn by Leila Hawkins as plate 14 of her album of images and texts of objects on the 1862 exhibition (Hawkins & Christy 1862). Yet there is little evidence that headrests of this type continued to be made into the twentieth century, almost all examples in European museums having nineteenth or early twentieth century accession dates.

What these examples also suggest is that there was a preference for particular types of Zulu headrests among dealers and souvenir hunters, and even the collectors in the colonial metropoles — something supported by the correspondence between the kinds of 'Zulu' headrests in the Brenthurst Collection, put together in London by Jonathan Lowen from the early 1970s onwards from objects bought on auction, apparently originating from nineteenth century sources. The majority of examples in the Brenthurst Collection correspond to the types seen in figures 389 and 390, whose multiple splayed legs have a mixture of flutes and raised pyramidal squares as relief decoration, the latter of which constitute the famous *amasumpa*,[40] seen on a variant of this type in figure 390. All of these headrests have impeccable pedigrees and can be surmised or proven to have been made in the nineteenth century. The first (fig. 389) was sold on a London auction in 1902, and accessioned into the Wellcome register in 1933; the second (fig. 390) was accessioned by the Norwich Castle Museum prior to 1915, and is possibly by the same carver as figure 389; while the third (fig. 391) was collected by Viscount F. M. Wolsely and donated to the British Museum by Dowager Viscount Wolsely in 1917. That this one may have been made prior to 1879 and the fall of the Zulu kingdom is possible, because Wolsely was a British officer in the Zulu wars, and the others before 1900 is probable, but there are so many of this type and variations of it, many from relatively early dates, that one must surmise a fairly long-standing tradition.[41]

There is, however, a second type of headrest also often associated with the Zulu where the legs are formed by heavy, rectangular (occasionally polygonal), upward-tapering legs with *amasumpa* or flutes (vertical and horizontal) as relief decoration on them (figs. 392–395). They also share with the flared-leg variety decoration carved on the ends of their platforms, but those with two or four legs are more likely to have a central lug that projects, umbilicus-like, from the underside of the platform and suggests animal allusions in the iconography of such headrests (figs. 394 & 395). Examples with fluted legs are often attributed to the Swazi (fig. 394 & 395), and many have been provenanced to this source, but it would be a mistake to attribute all fluted examples thus, as is demonstrated by the examples in figures 389 and 390.[42] Another example from Munich (fig. 396), obtained from one Mr Meyer, with a clear provenance to KwaZulu-Natal 'Zulu Kaffern', has been changed to 'Swazi?, Zulu?' in the register, and this in spite of the heavy proportions, which would support a Zulu origin. The tendency to make such attributions seems to rest on the notion — one that is simply not tenable — that the finely engraved black bowls so admired by collectors (fig. 388) emanated from the Swazi court, and that all such fluting then corresponds to this supposed stylistic centre.[43] Examples that are indisputably provenanced to the Swazi include two relatively recent acquisitions to the Tshwane (Pretoria) National Culture History Museum (figs. 397 & 398), which are comparable to, presumably older, examples in the Brenthurst Collection.[44] All share a slighter proportions in the legs and cross-bar than more 'Zulu' types, although the apparently older and possibly Swazi examples[45] and the provenanced Zulu example from Munich (fig. 396) all also have tails between the legs at one or both ends of the platform. But these examples have their legs joined into a single fan shape at either end of the platform, as opposed to the Zulu examples, which have either four flaring or two or more heavy rectangular legs, and do not have lugs at the centres of their platforms. All these headrests, however, appear to be firmly embedded within a single overriding Northern Nguni type, and it is probable that the Swazi examples were adaptations of a form common among leaders within Nguni society, specifically made for princes of Nguni lineage within the Swazi political structure, which post-dates the formation of the Zulu kingdom.[46]

Headrests of the Mpande portrait type are numerous in the nineteenth century record, but they range in form from the four fat-legged type seen in figure 399[47] to eight-legged examples such as that in figure 400, which was transferred from Kew Gardens to the British Museum in 1866, and is almost identical to another of the same type collected by Frederick Clayton in the Tugela River region of KwaZulu-Natal in the later nineteenth century.[48] Related, too, are examples in which the thorn/horn-shaped legs are more elongated (fig. 401),[49] and another from Manchester University Museum (fig. 402), accessioned in 1937, which has a set of three blade-like crescents linking the horn legs on either side parallel to the length of the platform. There is an unusual amount of surface relief decoration on this example, but there are others where the horn legs are linked by bars (fig. 403), and some where there are smaller thorn-like projections between the legs.[50] These examples all demonstrate, through a digression from the headrest type of the Mpande portrait, how varied Zulu headrests were in the nineteenth century, yet it is possible to demonstrate that even more kinds of headrests were made by Zulu speakers in the nineteenth century, which were, however, only collected in the twentieth century. The case for this argument is strengthened by the fact that a fairly bewildering number of horizontal headrests styles securely provenanced to Zulu makers and users (of which a few are outlined here) are held in European and South African museums.

Some extraordinary examples in the Wellcome Collection and other historical material in various museums across the United Kingdom provide evidence for this greater variety of headrest forms among Nguni speakers in KwaZulu-Natal and beyond. The representation of Zulu headrests as being limited in formal design variation may have resulted from what I see as a misreading of an argument put forward by Klopper (1989; 1992) in which she proposed that finely carved Zulu headrests *within the Zulu kingdom* may have been reserved for members of the royal court, because of the ways in which Zulu monarchs were able to monopolise the work of skilled craftsmen until the destruction of their kingdom in 1879. But that this was not the case in those parts of Zulu-speaking KwaZulu-Natal not under the sway of the Zulu kings is evident from the objects taken to the international exhibitions that were recurrent events in Europe from the 1860s onwards, and from more recent field-based collections. Of course, many less carefully carved objects were taken to Europe — some of the older headrests like Mpande's in Angas's portrait are of this type[51] — but most, such as the one from the Manchester University Museum (fig. 399), were more beautifully executed. Many had never been used (fig. 404), and their burned decoration still appears as fresh today as it was when they were first made. Extraordinary examples from the British Museum's stock of Wellcome material include figure 405, which has fluted legs and a distended belly form between them, probably a snuff-box, and figure 406, with a distended belly between two columns, all mounted on a large bi-lobed base, undoubtedly an influence from the Shona/Tsonga carving styles to the north. However, the label stuck to this headrest gives us another possible avenue of investigation, for it claims the headrest to have originated in Mashonaland, although the engraved chequerboard pattern is common in other Zulu-provenanced headrests. The fluted legs of figure 405 belong within the Zulu/Swazi ambit, as does its combination of dark surface and engraved triangular chequerboard patterning.

The headrests in figures 405 and 406 are two from a large number in museums in the United Kingdom (and some from elsewhere) classed as 'Zulu'. Some of the related examples, often attributed to the 'Matabele', are stylistically liminal, displaying both Zulu and Shona/Tsonga traits, but with very strange proportions and with varying degrees of competence in their carving. These are illustrated in figures 407–416, and they demonstrate a range of formal compositions that defy simple classification. Klopper (1991) argues that, because headrests often came into homesteads as parts of the dowries of wives within Zulu exogamous marriages, there would be a number of different headrests within a single homestead. This mixing of styles within single districts is demonstrated by collections made by independent private collectors[52] and by headrests obtained by South African institutions in recent years. These include headrests with block-like *amasumpa*-embellished legs (fig. 417) from Mtunzini, others with supports that appear like shelves (figs. 418 & 419), still others with arches (fig. 420), and some that are simple blocks (fig. 421) of similar height and width to the legged examples, and embellished on their vertical faces with very low reliefs, typically using the same chequerboard motifs as those on the more exuberant nineteenth century examples outlined above. Many appear to have a strong similarity to Tsonga forms (figs. 409–412), while figures 415 and 416, both provenanced to KwaZulu-Natal, have been attributed to the Zulu and, like many others of this kind of hybridity, show very few signs of use.

The relative paucity of horn-shaped legs among the supports of these headrests is striking, given their common presence in the nineteenth century examples, and there appear to be many more recent headrests with a kind of architectural reference (arches, shelves, boxes, and one rather like a bottle rack[53]) than are visible in the historical records as preserved in museums. A distinction between the rather animal-like references of the legged/horned headrests and the more planar architectural examples remains, but the shapes of the legs tends relate to the *amasumpa*-embellished splayed type rather than the bulbous forms of Mpande's portrait headrest.

Other headrests with related forms have been recorded from both peoples who live in polities ruled by leaders who fled the upheavals of the origins of the Zulu kingdom, especially the Swazi, the Shangane in Limpopo Province of South Africa and the Malawian and Tanzanian Ngoni. The Swazi form has been examined above, and the best-known

Tsonga–Shangane examples are two collected by A. A. Jaques in the 1920s in the Bushbuck Ridge area,[54] but they are clearly hybrid, hovering somewhere between Tsonga elaborations and Swazi–Zulu fluting. Other hybrid Zulu–Swazi–Tsonga examples involving the use of circles, overall patterning and or blackening by burning, have been provenanced and attributed to the Tsonga, although they are very similar to the examples in figures 416 and 417,[55] not only in form, but also in an absolute lack of use.

Six Ngoni examples published by Krieger (1990:514–19) from the Berlin Museum für Völkerkunde (figs. 422–425) appear to represent a more robust tradition from Malawi–Tanzania, which maintains the horn-shaped legs of the early Zulu examples outlined above, but includes protuberances, usually symmetrical, from the ends of the platform, suggestive of head and tail, or two heads. Two (figs. 422 & 425) have an umbilical lug under the platform, and another (fig. 424) a shallow triangular form to the underside of the platform. Some (e.g. fig. 423) retain the Zulu-style form of blackened chevron decoration on the sides of the platform, but Ngoni forms tend to have a more elegant set of proportions with elongated legs and thinner bodies than most Zulu examples. Krieger's examples' accessions are all dated to between 1898 and 1916, and thus present early, and, probably, pre-tourist forms.[56] These early Ngoni forms do not allow, however, the postulate that originally Zulu headrests followed a similar pattern, in the fashion of some root form, an ur-Nguni horn-shaped-leg headrest,[57] especially as some figurative Ngoni headrests in Stuttgart, also collected relatively early, do not follow the same pattern, but have flat, splayed legs, thin platforms and animal heads.

Given the Ngoni's postulated origin from the northern Swaziland–Mpumalanga Province border region, it is not surprising to find that some of the headrest forms published by Krieger (1990) in fact correspond as strongly to North Sotho headrest types known from the eastern Limpopo and Mpumalanga lowveld and from Sekhukhuneland on the Limpopo highveld. These headrests are at times very simple, as in the case of Tau examples (figs. 426 & 427), but some, mostly from Sekhukhuneland, are more complex (figs. 428–430). All of these share the use of an inverted triangle to form the central section, with thick legs at either end and dumpy proportions. Some have heavy round legs, others have splayed rectangular legs like the Stuttgart Ngoni examples, and many have elaborate engraved interlace decoration (fig. 429), and occasionally an overtly animal head is carved at one end of the platform and a tail at the other (figs. 426 & 430). The North Sotho forms are little known outside South Africa, and there are very few examples available in museums, so it is difficult to make any conclusive statements about them, but they all share the pointed belly shape, and often the same form of animal reference in the heads and tails as is found in Ngoni examples. Assuming that the Ngoni examples are survivals from an originary source, that source was nevertheless one in which hybridity was already present in a mix between Zulu and Sotho forms, something also evident in the Swazi example discussed above (fig. 395) with its dumpy fluted legs. It is remarkable that Ngoni should have remained so stylistically intact, their forms repeated over the course of a century in a new location, whereas Mzilikaze's Ndebele and Matshangana/Manukosi's 'Shangaans' (i.e. Shangane) seem not to have retained the Zulu style. Perhaps Zwgendaba (Ngoni) and his followers removed themselves so far from their origins that they found their identity threatened by the distance and they held onto its indices in forms of material culture, while Mswati, Matshangana and Mzilikaze were all sufficiently close to the parent 'Zulu' group to require their separation via an abandonment of some indices of identity.

Yet all the offshoot groups prided themselves on their 'Zulu' origins, a pride that may, however, have been reinforced through European attitudes that privileged 'Zulu' peoples as superior to their neighbours (Nettleton 1989). This pride is most notably expressed in the retention of the distinctive men's headring, documented in photographs from Malawi, Mozambique, Zimbabwe, Swaziland and South Africa[58] (fig. 431), and, in some cases, in the continued use of a particular form of support for the heads that wore such crowns. Among the Tsonga–Shangane, where the headring was retained, but was rested on a pillow of the Tsonga type, spoken Zulu was considered important for male members of the ruling elites, especially those who migrated to the Transvaal after the wars between Gungunyane and the Portuguese in Mozambique.[59] Yet the form of the headrest is only one form through which identity might be expressed, and slight or large variations within the treatment of the same structures could turn headrests into almost completely different animals from those that formed the 'original'. A famous example of such hybridity, collected by Jaques in the Tsonga region of Limpopo Province (fig. 432), is of the horizontal headrest type (considered Nguni), with fluted legs (considered Swazi), with an open chequerboard design between the legs (apparently unique, but related to chequerboard designs on other Zulu headrests), and with a serrated tail at one end balanced by a carved head with headring (of the same type as the heads found on Tsonga staffs), below which a curved swelling could be read as either a bovine dewlap or a human belly.

But tracing such origins proves to be almost impossible, unless one could propose an 'evolution' of this headrest type from the branch headrests with which this section began. For this is the only kind of headrest to have been collected from that other 'half' of the Nguni-speaking complex, the peoples of the Eastern Cape who are referred to here as 'Xhosa',[60] and one explanation for this lack of horizontal headrest types among the Southern Nguni groups might be that they were, unlike the KwaZulu-Natal peoples, outside the range of obligatory adoption of Zulu prestige symbols. That Zulu speakers commonly made and used such headrests and Xhosa speakers did not puts the idea that language and forms of material culture are linked into serious doubt, even though the whole complex of Nguni speakers shared the use of the branch headrests with pastoralists and pastoralist/agriculturalists of East Africa.

The development of a wide variety of deeply embellished headrest forms was probably, in all cases, dependent on the development of some degree of craft specialisation in both iron smithing and wood carving, occupations that may have been linked in Central and Southern African Bantu-speaking societies, if only in the provision of metal implements by metal smiths to carvers. Some of the headrests from this region show a great deal of technical and aesthetic refinement, something not often achieved by amateurs making their own objects. It will not do to try to account for variation in terms of an everyone-for-himself explanation: not only are there some records of the fame of particular carvers, there is also the evidence supplied by the headrests themselves, where one can trace the hands of master carvers and the one-off ineptitudes of individuals. And some headrests are given extraordinary status through the use of figurative imagery in their supports, or more explicitly, supports in the form of recognisable three-dimensional sculptures of humans and animals, dealt with in the next chapter. These were undoubtedly often made by master carvers working for discerning patrons, as were many of the non-figurative examples.

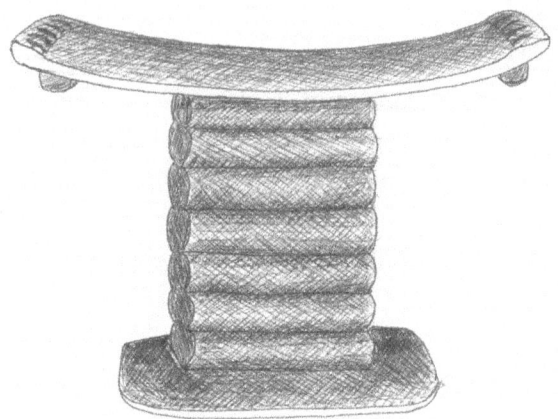

262  Geneva, Musée d'Ethnographie (no. 16052), *Collected by Kaltenrieder, donated 1940, Mozambique,* 'Tsonga', wood, 12 cm h.

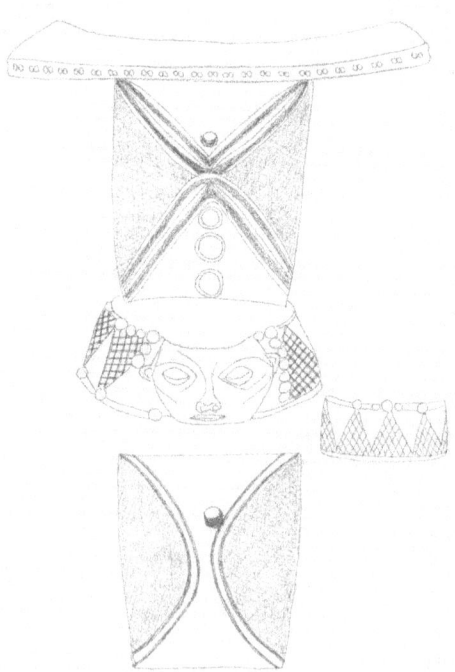

263  Musée Royal de l'Afrique Central (no. 60.39.1), Democratic Republic of the Congo, *Kwango* (region), *Suku(?)*, wood, 14.3 cm h.

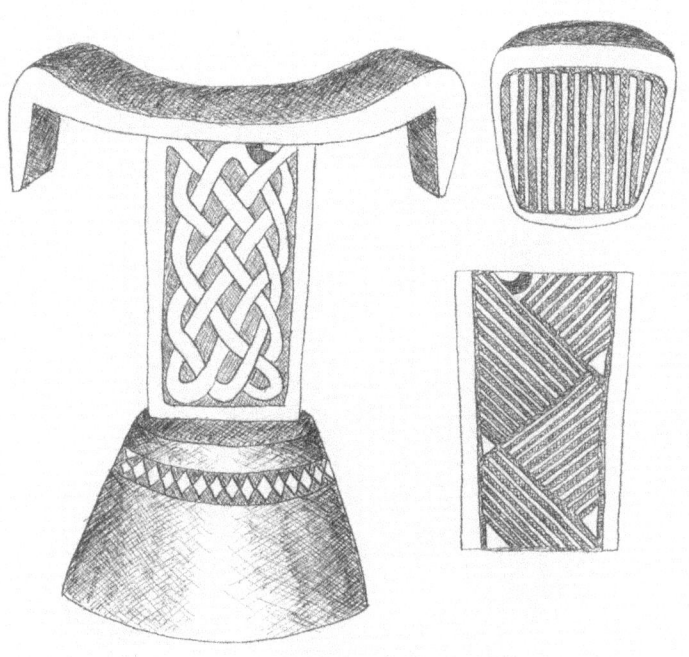

264  British Museum (no. 1949 Af46.807), Oldman Collection, *Rhodesia* (Zimbabwe), *Shona, Kalanga*, wood, 17.5 cm h.

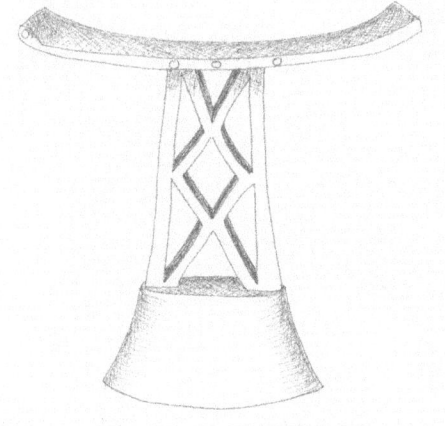

265  Musée Royal de l'Afrique Central (no. 23475), Democratic Republic of the Congo, *Upper Kasai* (region), *Koko*, wood.

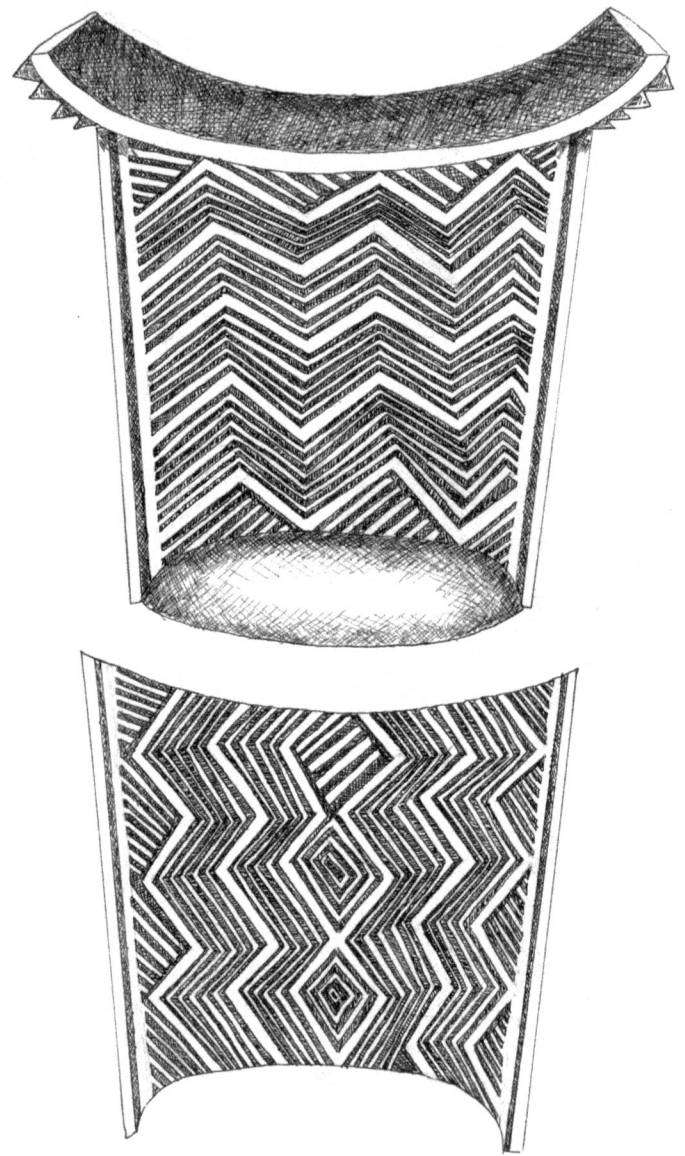

266  British Museum (no. 1921.616.41), donated by Miss Hurst, *Rhodesia* (Zimbabwe), Tonga, wood, 17.5 cm h.

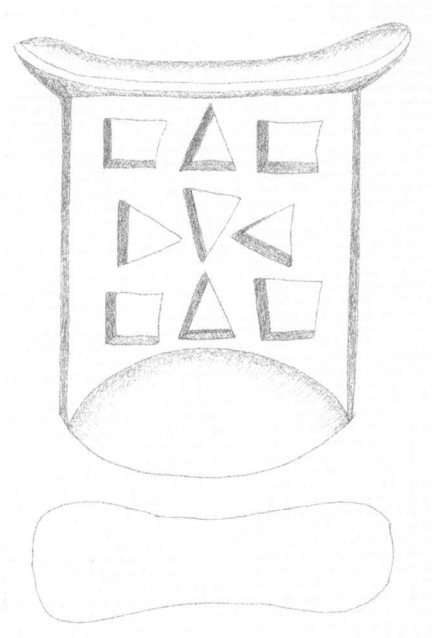

267  Johannesburg, private collection, Namibia/Angola, *Himba*, wood, 17 cm h.

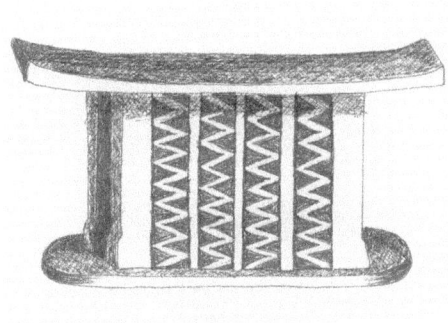
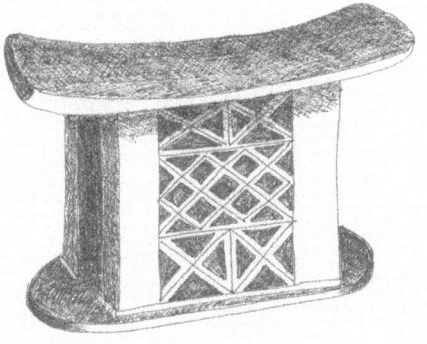

268  British Museum (no. 1954 Af23), (Wellcome Collection, no number), *Angola, Chokwe* (Cokwe), wood, 14 cm h.

269  Lisbon Museu Dundo (no. A1061), (Bastin 1961, fig. 146,1), Angola, *Chokwe* (Cokwe), *Shambwanda Chieftaincy*, wood, 11.2 cm h.

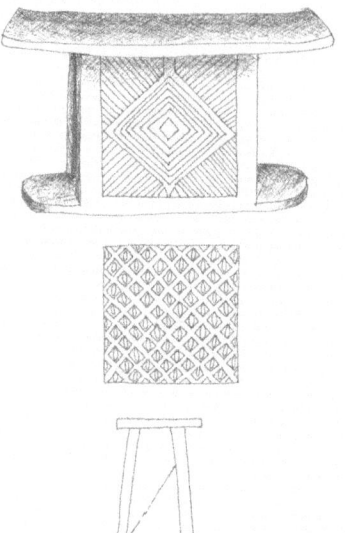

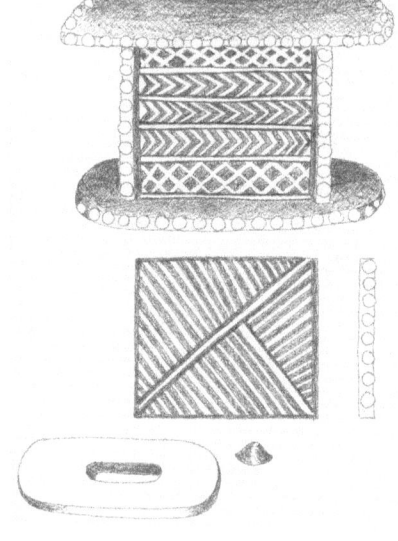

270  Musée Royal de l'Afrique Central (no. RG34934), Democratic Republic of the Congo, 1933, *Kasai* (province), *Kapanga* (district), *[Lunda]*, wood, 13 cm h.

271  Musée Royal de l'Afrique Central (no. RG 35738), Democratic Republic of the Congo, *Kasai?* (province), *Lunda?*, wood, metal, 12 cm h.

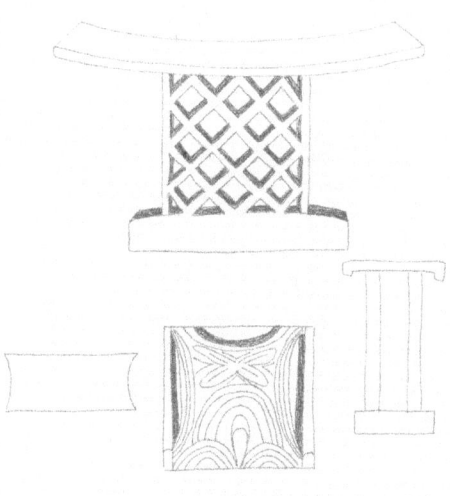

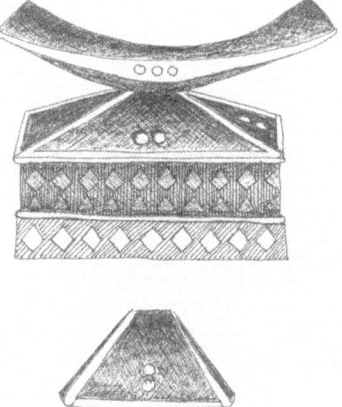

272  Musée Royal de l'Afrique Central (no. RG 2790), (Maes 1929, pl. VI, fig. 12), collected by Daelman, Democratic Republic of the Congo, *1911*, *Dilolo* (region), *Lunda*, wood, 11 cm h.

273  British Museum (no. 1954 Af23), (Wellcome Collection, no number), Democratic Republic of the Congo, 'Yaka', wood, 12.8 cm h.

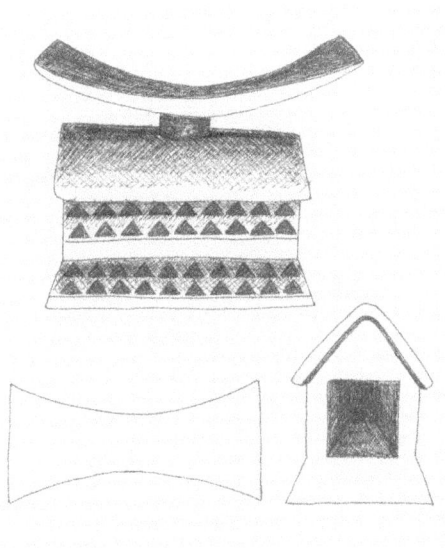

274 British Museum (no. 1954 Af23), (Wellcome Collection, no. 43700), Democratic Republic of the Congo, 'Yaka', wood, 13.8 cm h.

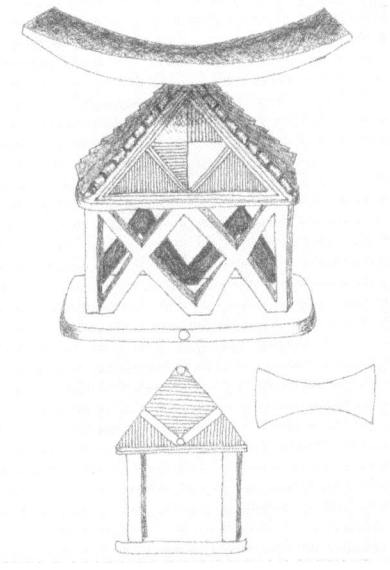

275 Musée Royal de l'Afrique Central (no. RG 52.48.107), Democratic Republic of the Congo, 'Chokwe' (Cokwe), wood, metal, 13.8 cm h.

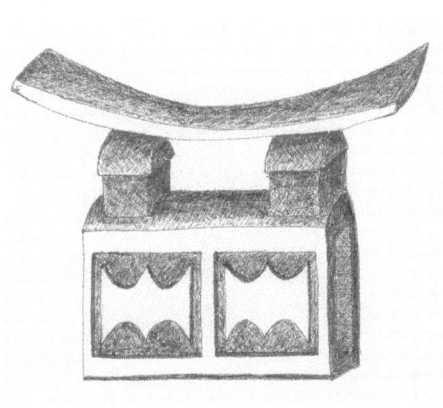

276 Musée Royal de l'Afrique Central (no. RG 51.41.10), Democratic Republic of the Congo, *Yaka?*, wood, metal, 14 cm h.

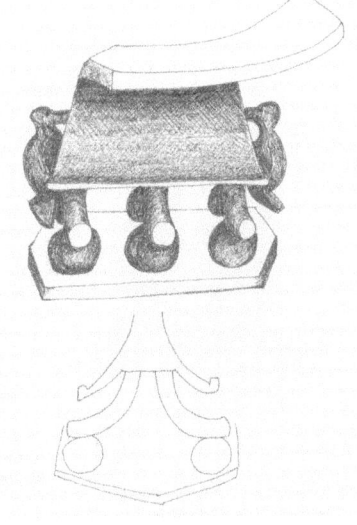

277 Musée Royal de l'Afrique Central (no. RG 32870), Democratic Republic of the Congo, *Kasai* (province), *Pende*, wood, 14 cm h.

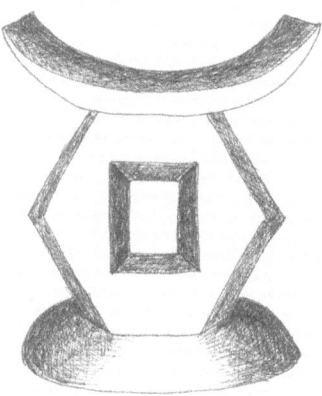
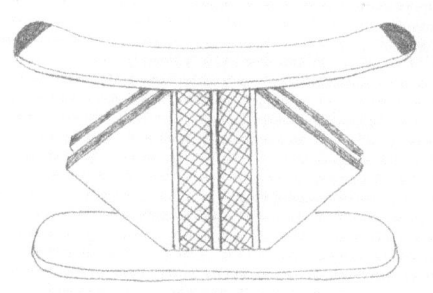

278   British Museum (no. 1908.6.22.142), *Collected by Norman Hardy, Torday expedition,* Democratic Republic of the Congo, 'Songye', wood, 16.3 cm h.

279   Musée Royal de l'Afrique Central (no. 60.39.201), Democratic Republic of the Congo, *Shaba* (province), *Kinda Kamina* (district), *Songye?*, wood.

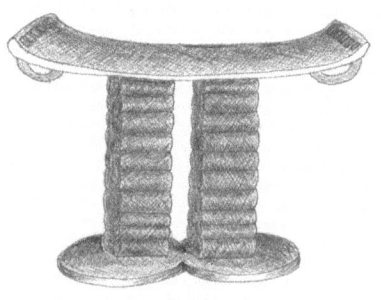
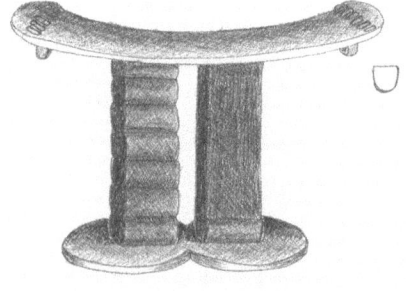

280   Geneva, Musée d'Ethnographie (no. 16067), collected by Kaltenrieder, *Mozambique, Lourenco Marques* (Maputo), *Manjacase* (Tsonga), *mukhamelo,* wood, 13.7 cm h.

281   Johannesburg Art Gallery (no. 1987 3.61), collected by A. A. Jaques, pre-1929, South Africa, *Transvaal* (Limpopo Province), *Elim, Shangaan* (Shangane), wood, 13 cm h.

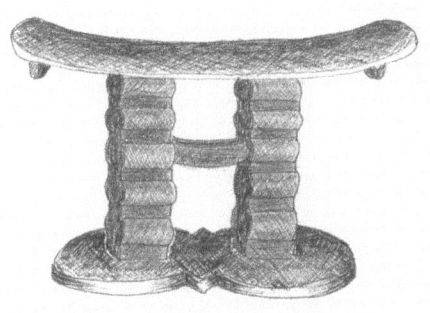

282 Geneva, Musée d'Ethnographie (no. 16065), collected by Kaltenrieder, *Mozambique, Tsonga*, wood, 14 cm h.

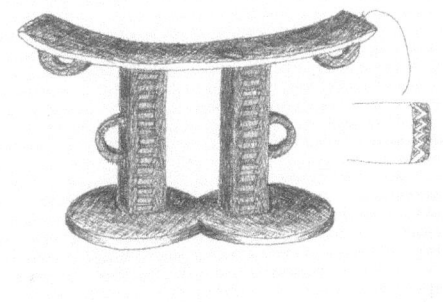

283 Johannesburg Art Gallery (no. 1987.3.55), collected by A. A Jaques, pre-1929, South Africa, *Transvaal* (Limpopo Province), *Elim, Shangaan* (Shangane), wood, 13 cm h.

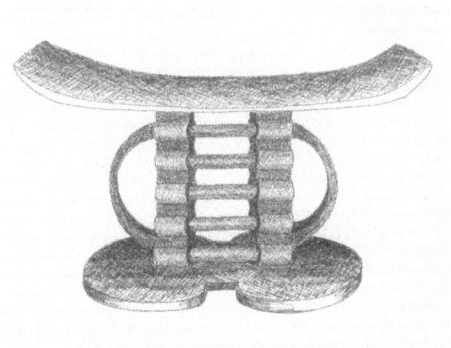

284 Johannesburg Art Gallery (no. 1987.3.), collected by A. A. Jaques, pre-1929, South Africa, *Transvaal* (Limpopo Province), *Elim, Shangaan* (Shangane), wood, 14 cm h.

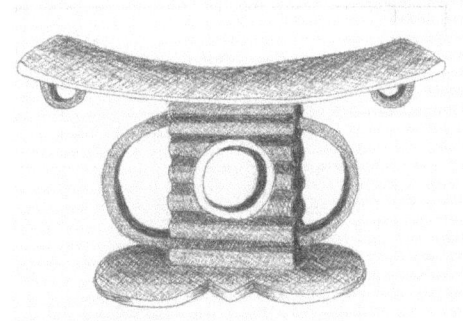

285 Johannesburg, MuseumAfrika (Wanless 1987:63, no. 211), Mission Collection, *Collected in Mozambique, Tsonga*, wood, 13.5 cm h.

**282** | AFRICAN DREAM MACHINES

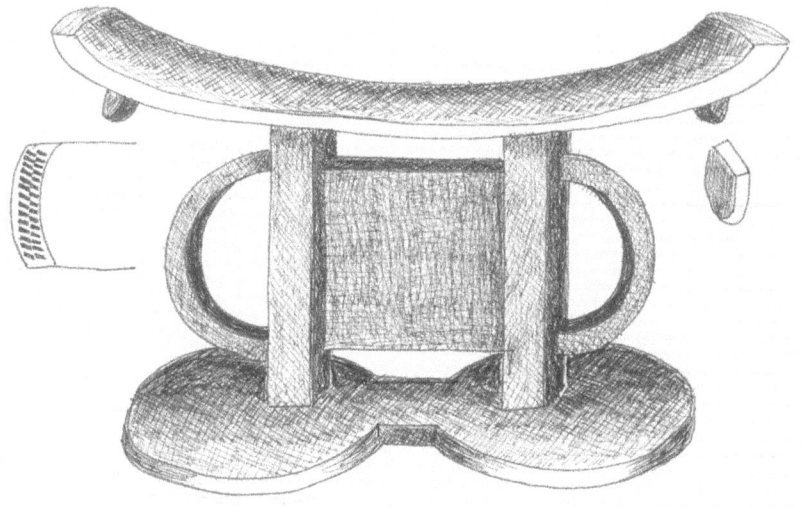

286  Johannesburg, MuseumAfrika (no. 74/2611), *Collected by brother of the donor, Dr G Theiler (Pretoria [Tshwane])* in Swaziland in 1900, wood, 14 cm h.

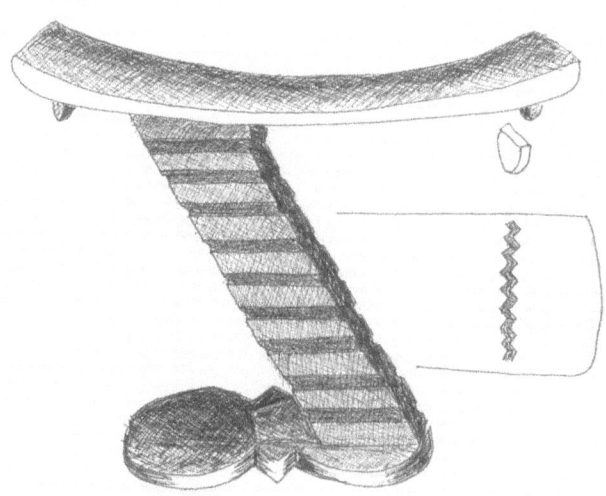

287  Johannesburg Art Gallery (no. 1987.3:33), collected by A. A. Jaques, pre-1929, South Africa, *Transvaal* (Limpopo Province), *Elim, Shangaan* (Shangane), wood, 13 cm h.

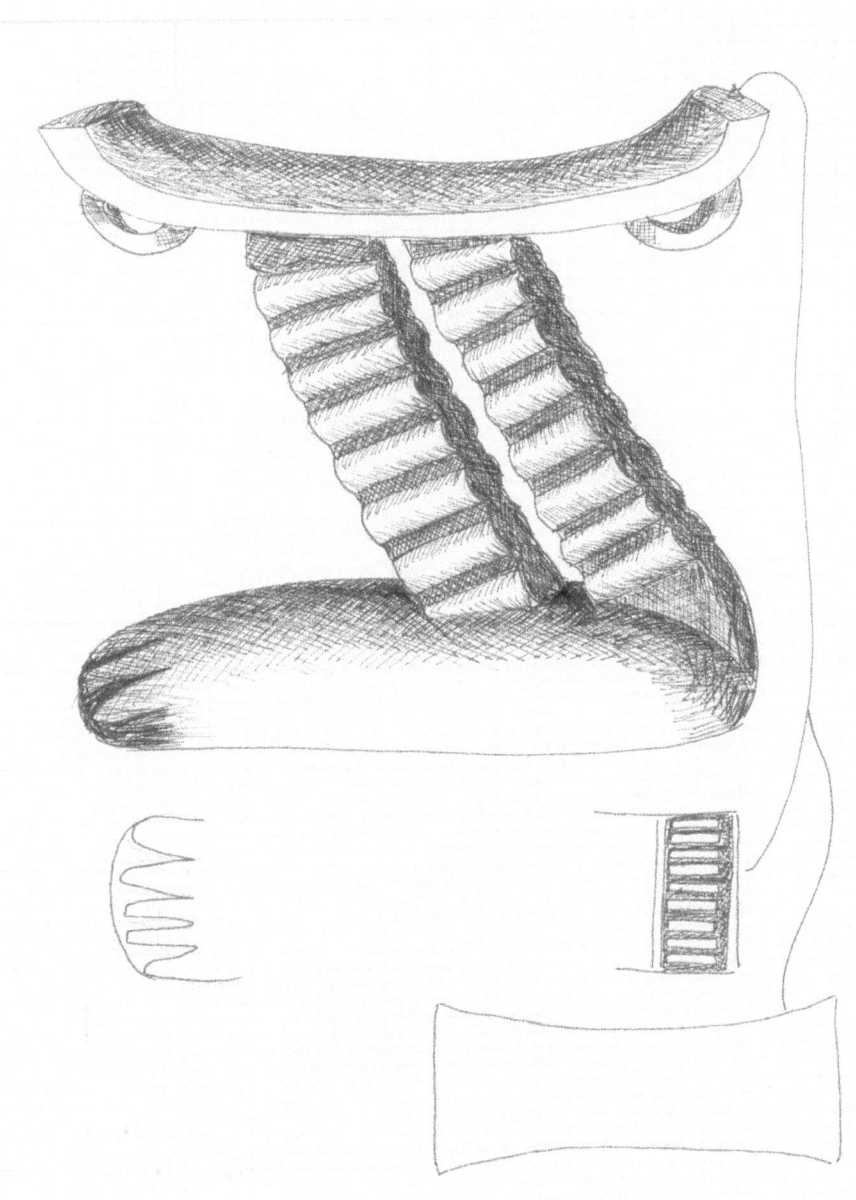

288  British Museum (no. 1947 Af152), from Newbury Borough Museum, *Southern Rhodesia* (Zimbabwe), wood, 13 cm h.

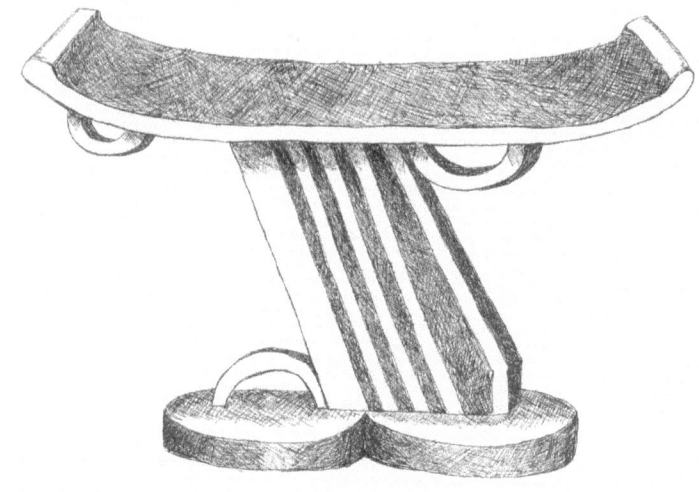

289   Johannesburg Art Gallery (no. 1987.3 35), (Wanless 1985:59), collected by A. A. Jaques, pre-1929, South Africa, *Transvaal* (Limpopo Province), *Elim*, *Shangaan* (Shangane), wood, 12 cm h.

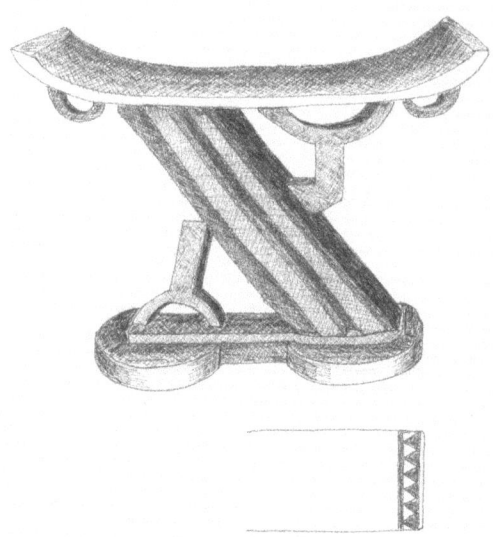

290   Johannesburg Art Gallery (Jaques Collection, no. 50/970), (Wanless 1985:106), collected by
     A. A. Jaques, pre-1929, South Africa, *Transvaal* (Limpopo Province), *Elim*, *Shangaan* (Shangane), wood, 13 cm h.

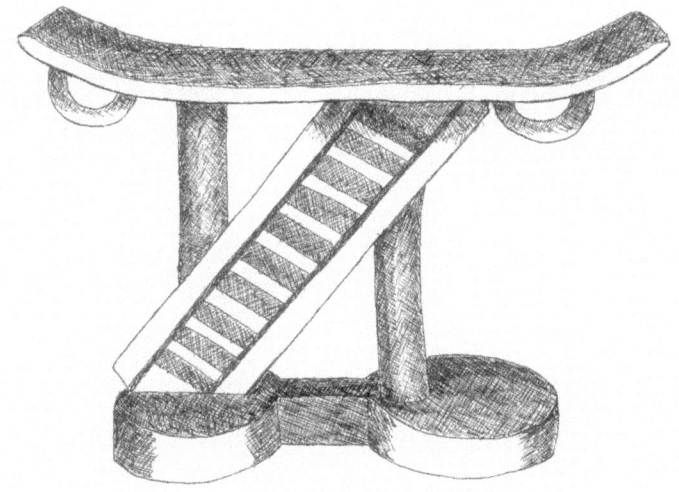

291  Johannesburg Art Gallery (Jaques Collection, no. 50/958), (Wanless 1985:95), collected by A. A. Jaques, pre-1929, South Africa, *Transvaal* (Limpopo Province), *Elim*, *Shangaan* (Shangane), wood, 14.5 cm h.

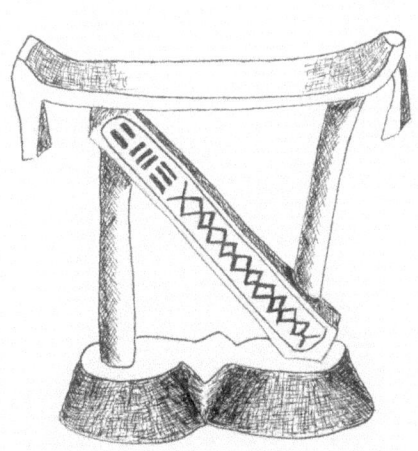 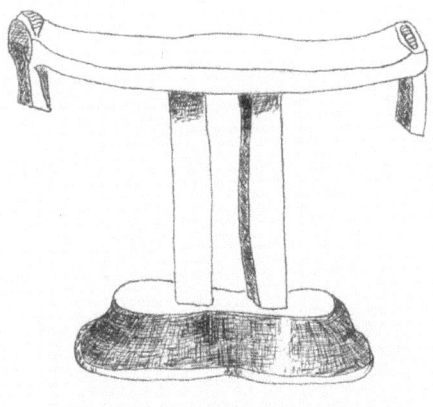

292  Hamburg, Museum für Völkerkunde (no. 13:173:144), bought from *"Kowietzko"*, late nineteenth century, *Destroyed in World War II*, Botswana?, *Betchuaan* (Tswana), wood, 15.7 cm h.

293  Hamburg, Museum für Völkerkunde (no. 13:174:29), bought from *"Kowietzko"*, late nineteenth century, *Destroyed in World War II*, Botswana?, *(Betchuan)* (Tswana), wood, 16 cm h.

286 | AFRICAN DREAM MACHINES

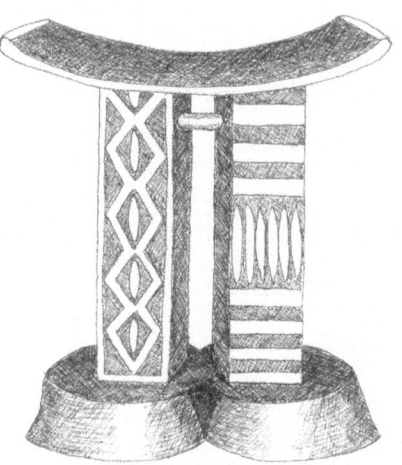

294  Frankfurt, Museum für Völkerkunde
(no. 2646), collected by Frobenius expedition,
1928, *Southern Rhodesia* (Zimbabwe)/*Mozambique*,
*Maduma* (Barwe Tonga), wood, 15 cm h.

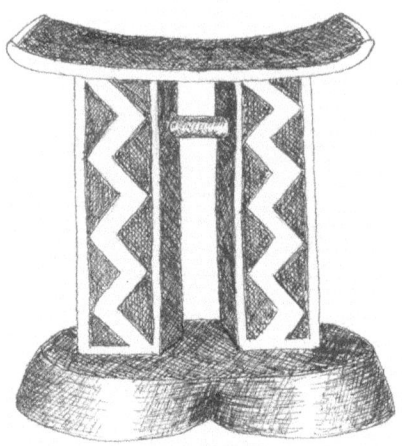

295  Frankfurt, Museum für Völkerkunde
(no. 2472), collected by Frobenius expedition,
1928, *Southern Rhodesia* (Zimbabwe)/*Mozambique*,
*Maduma* (Barwe Tonga), wood, 15 cm h.

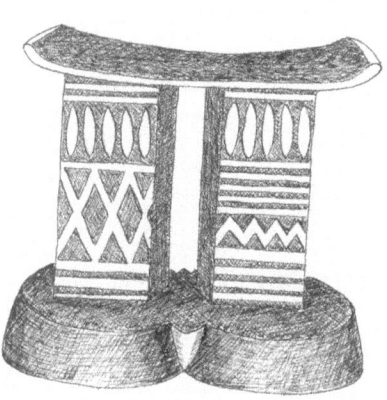

296  Frankfurt, Museum für Völkerkunde
(no. 2473), collected by Frobenius expedition,
1928, *Southern Rhodesia* (Zimbabwe)/*Mozambique*,
*Maduma* (Barwe Tonga), wood, 14 cm h.

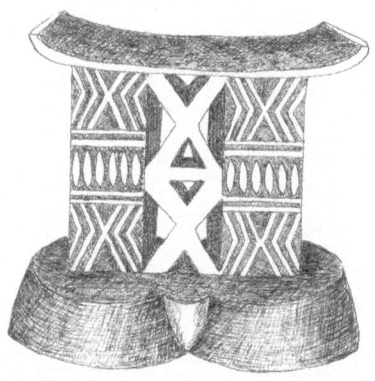

297  Frankfurt, Museum für Völkerkunde
(no. 2437), collected by Frobenius expedition,
1928, *Southern Rhodesia* (Zimbabwe)/*Mozambique*,
*Maduma* (Barwe Tonga), wood, 14 cm h.

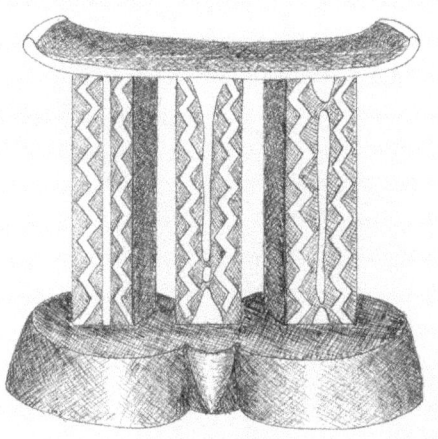

298 Frankfurt, Museum für Völkerkunde (no. 2450), collected by Frobenius expedition, 1928, *Southern Rhodesia* (Zimbabwe)/*Mozambique (Tonga?)*, wood, 15 cm h.

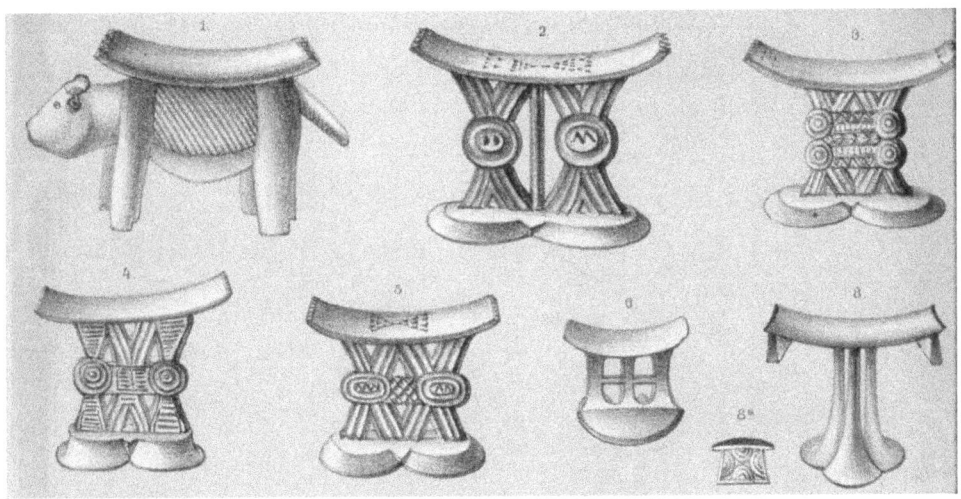

299 Müller and Snelleman (c. 1892, pl. XIV detail), 1) Zambèze , 2) Zambèze , 3) Zambèze , 4) Zambèze , 5) Zambèze , *The Headrests in nos 2 to 5 represent the most common forms in the Zambezi (region) ... these headrests are found in all dwellings, and, when taken on a voyage, are suspended from a cord at the waist* (notes to pl. XIV).

**288** | AFRICAN DREAM MACHINES

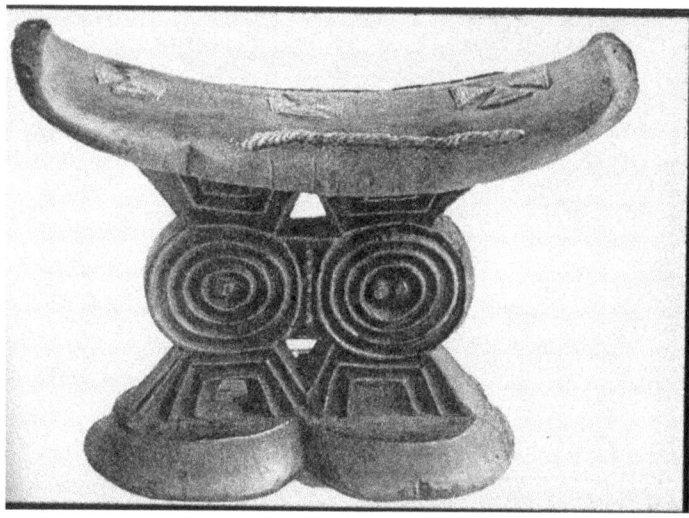

300  Bent (1892:35), *Wooden Pillow*, Mashonaland.

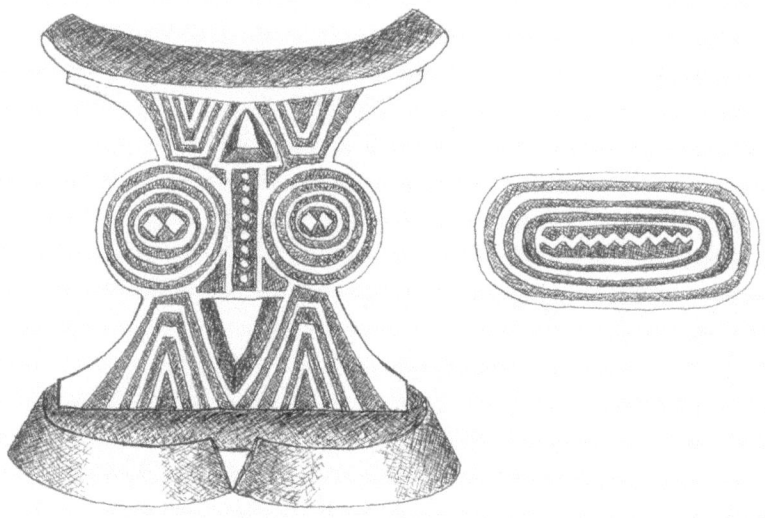

301  British Museum (no. 1935.7-15, 3), Carson Collection, pre-1900, *Southern Rhodesia* (Zimbabwe), *Shona*, wood, 11 cm h.

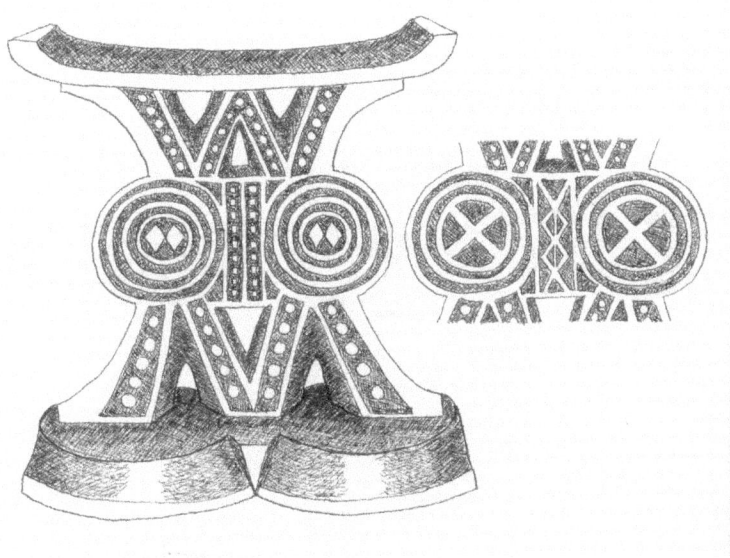

302  British Museum (no. 1935.7-15, 5), Carson Collection, pre-1900, *Southern Rhodesia* (Zimbabwe), *Shona*, wood, 11 cm h.

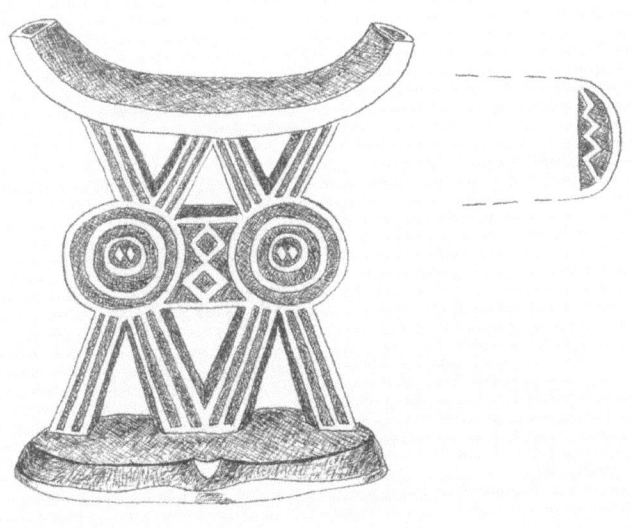

303  British Museum (no. 1921.6-16, 43), Hirst Collection, *MaShonaland, Southern Rhodesia* (Zimbabwe), *Shona*, wood, 12 cm h.

**290** | AFRICAN DREAM MACHINES

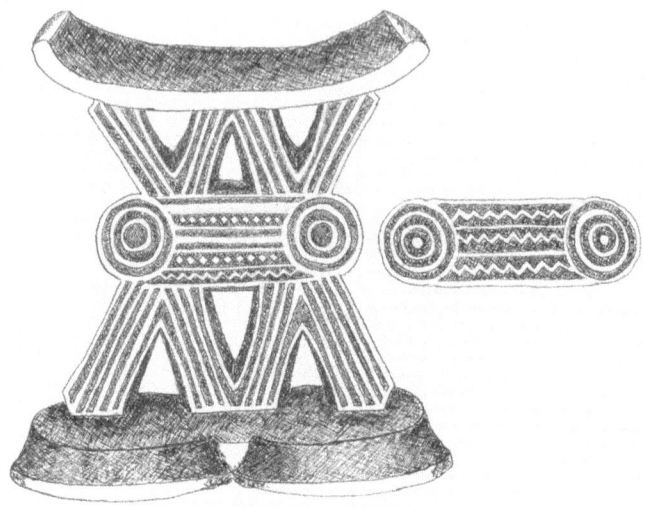

304 British Museum (no. 1949 Af46 811), Oldman Collection, *Southern Rhodesia* (Zimbabwe), *Shona*, wood, 12 cm h.

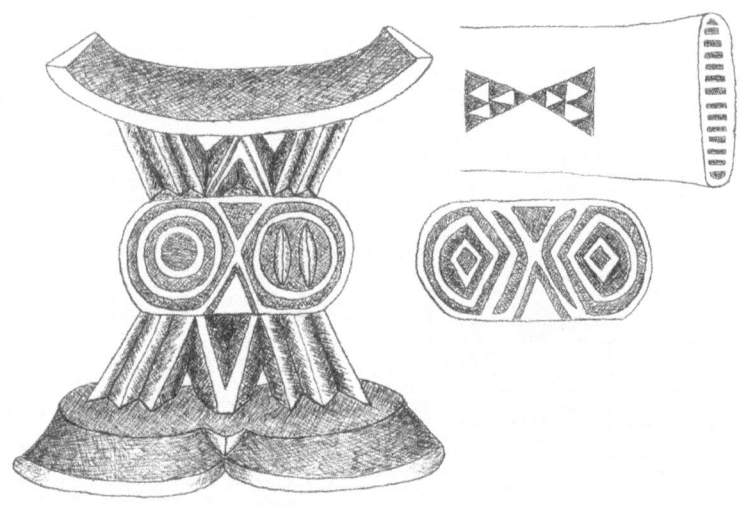

305 British Museum (no. 1892 7-14,26), collected J. H. T. Bent, pre-1890, Zimbabwe, *Mashonaland*, wood, 13.1 cm h.

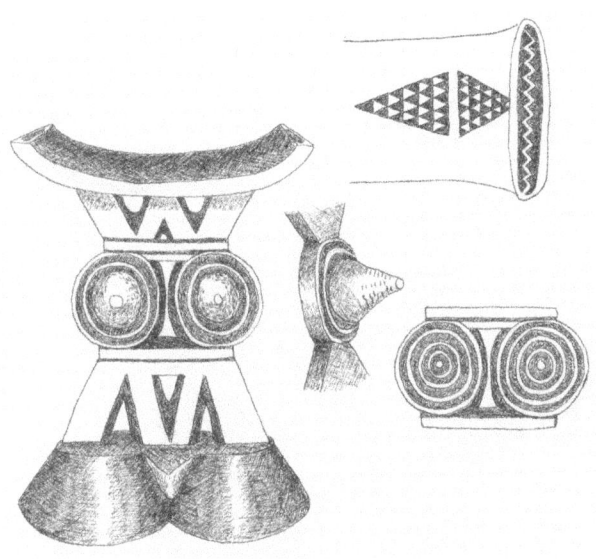

306  British Museum (no. 1949 Af46 810), Oldman Collection, *Southern Rhodesia*, (Zimbabwe), *Shona*, wood, 11.5 cm h.

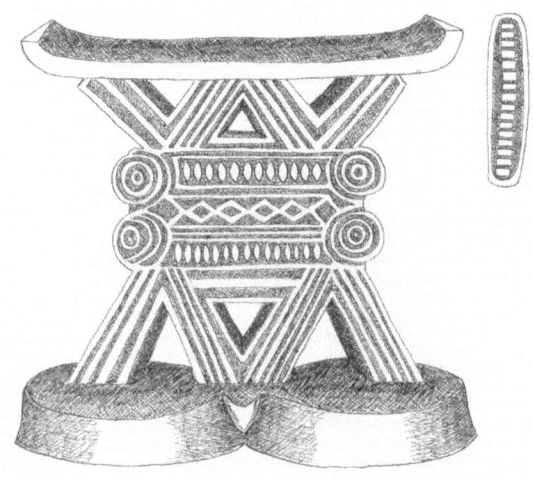

307  British Museum (no. 1949 Af46 814), Oldman Collection, *Southern Rhodesia*, (Zimbabwe), *MaShona/MaKalanga* (Shona/Kalanga), wood, 14 cm h.

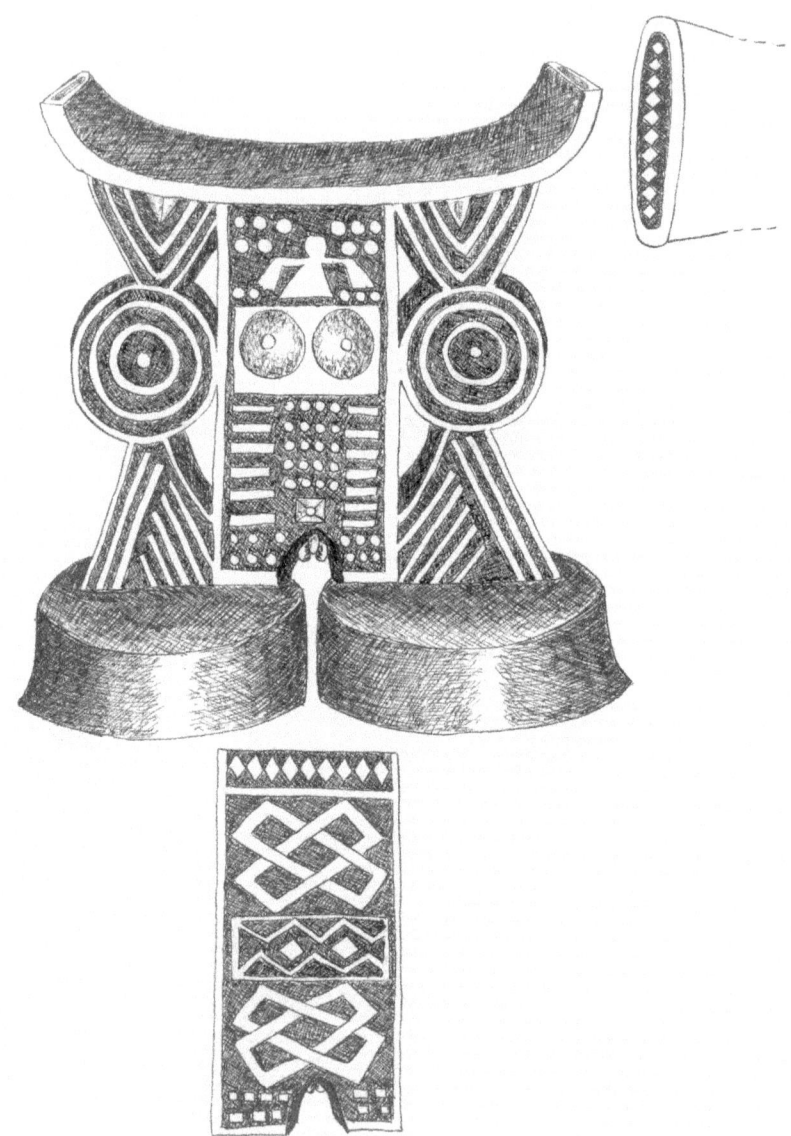

308 British Museum (no. 9763), acquisition date 1876, collection of Dr W. G. Atherstone, *Southern Rhodesia (Zimbabwe)*, *Mashonaland*, wood, 14.5 cm h.

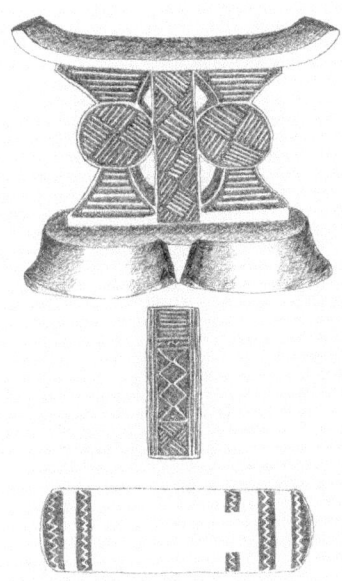

309  British Museum (no. 1935.7-15.1), Carson Collection, pre-1900, *Southern Rhodesia* (Zimbabwe), *Mashonaland*, wood, 12 cm h.

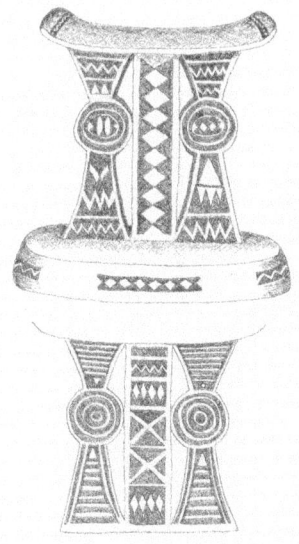

310  British Museum (no. 1954 Af23), (Wellcome Collection, no. 52014), *Southern Rhodesia* (Zimbabwe), *Shona*, wood, 13 cm h.

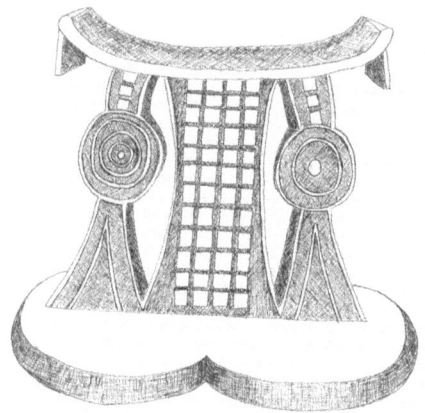

311 Frankfurt, Museum für Völkerkunde (no. 2500), collected by Frobenius expedition, 1928, *Southern Rhodesia* (Zimbabwe), *Zezuru*, *mutsago*, wood, 14.5 cm h.

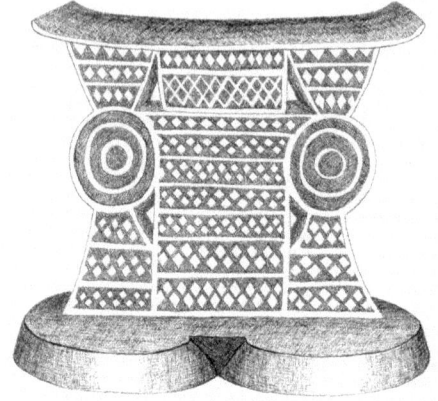

312 Frankfurt, Museum für Völkerkunde (no. 2515), collected by Frobenius expedition, 1928, *Southern Rhodesia* (Zimbabwe), Charter district, wood, 14.5 cm h.

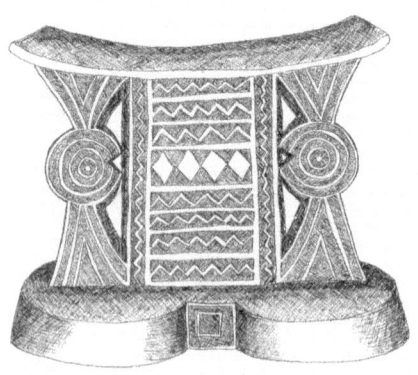

313 Antwerp, Museum voor Volkenkunde (no. AE 3537), *Southern Rhodesia* (Zimbabwe), *Shona*, wood, 16 cm h.

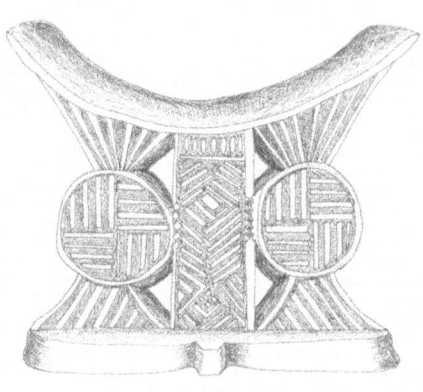

314 British Museum (no. 1906.12.11.28), collected by W. Eatherley, *Rhodesia* (Zambia), *Buni District, Batoka* (Toka), *Tonga*, wood, 15.2 cm h.

CHAPTER 7 *Illustrations: figures 262-432* | **295**

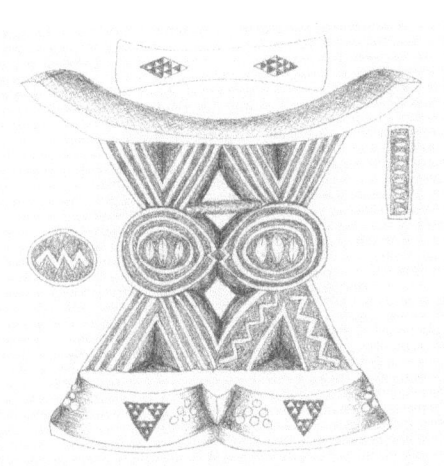

315   British Museum (no. 1902 16.9), collected by Tomalin, *Southern Rhodesia* (Zimbabwe), *between Salisbury* (Harare) *and Tête on the Zambesi*, Shona?, wood, 16.5 cm h.

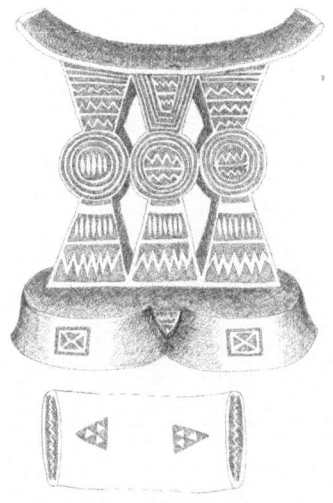

316   British Museum (no. 1902 .16.8), collected by Tomalin, *Southern Rhodesia* (Zimbabwe), *between Salisbury* (Harare) *and Tête on the Zambesi*, Shona?, wood, 15.1 cm h.

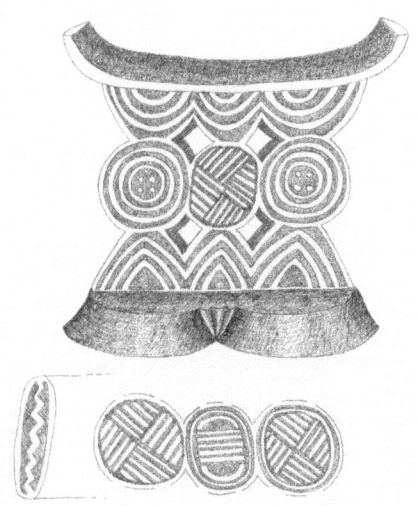

317   British Museum (no. 1949 Af46.812), Oldman Collection, *Southern Rhodesia* (Zimbabwe), *MaShona/Makalanga* (Shona/Kalanga), wood, 13 cm h.

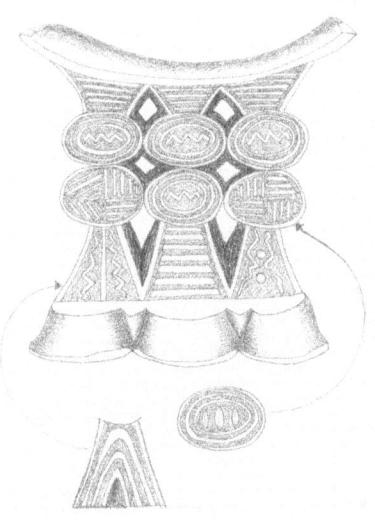

318   British Museum (no. 1949 Af46.813), Oldman Collection, *Southern Rhodesia* (Zimbabwe), Shona, wood, 16.3 cm h.

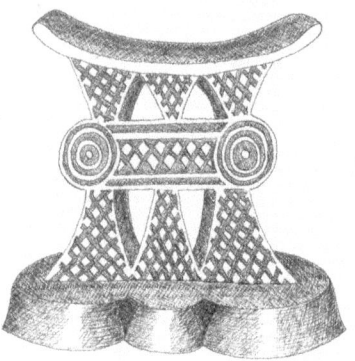

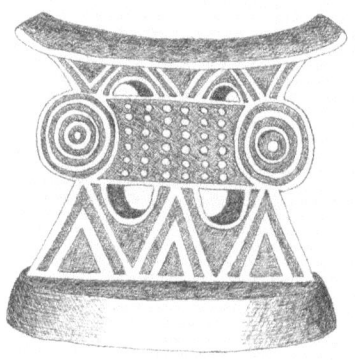

319 Brighton Museum, The Green Centre (no. R1437/2), collected by Rev. Polly, 1913, *Southern Rhodesia* (Zimbabwe), *Shona*, wood, 12.5 cm h.

320 Frankfurt, Museum für Völkerkunde (no. 2516), collected by Frobenius expedition, 1928, *Southern Rhodesia* (Zimbabwe), *Charter District*, *Shona*, *mutsago*, wood, 17 cm h.

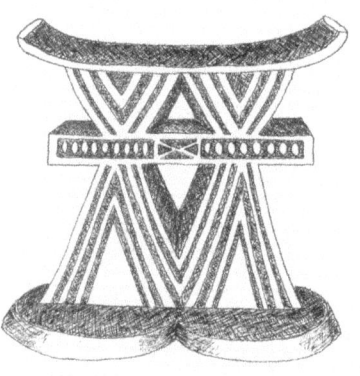

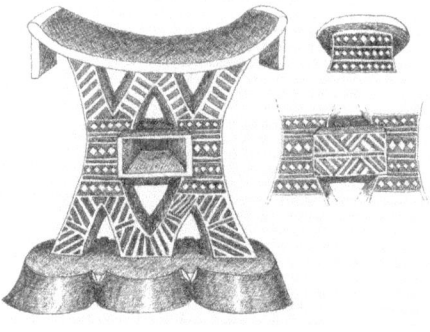

321 Frankfurt, Museum für Völkerkunde (no. 2504), collected by Frobenius expedition, 1928, *Southern Rhodesia* (Zimbabwe), *Charter District*, *Shona*, *mutsago*, wood, 15 cm h.

322 British Museum (no. 1954 Af23), (Wellcome Collection, no. 232563), *Rhodesia* (Zimbabwe), *Mashonaland*, wood, 15.2 cm h.

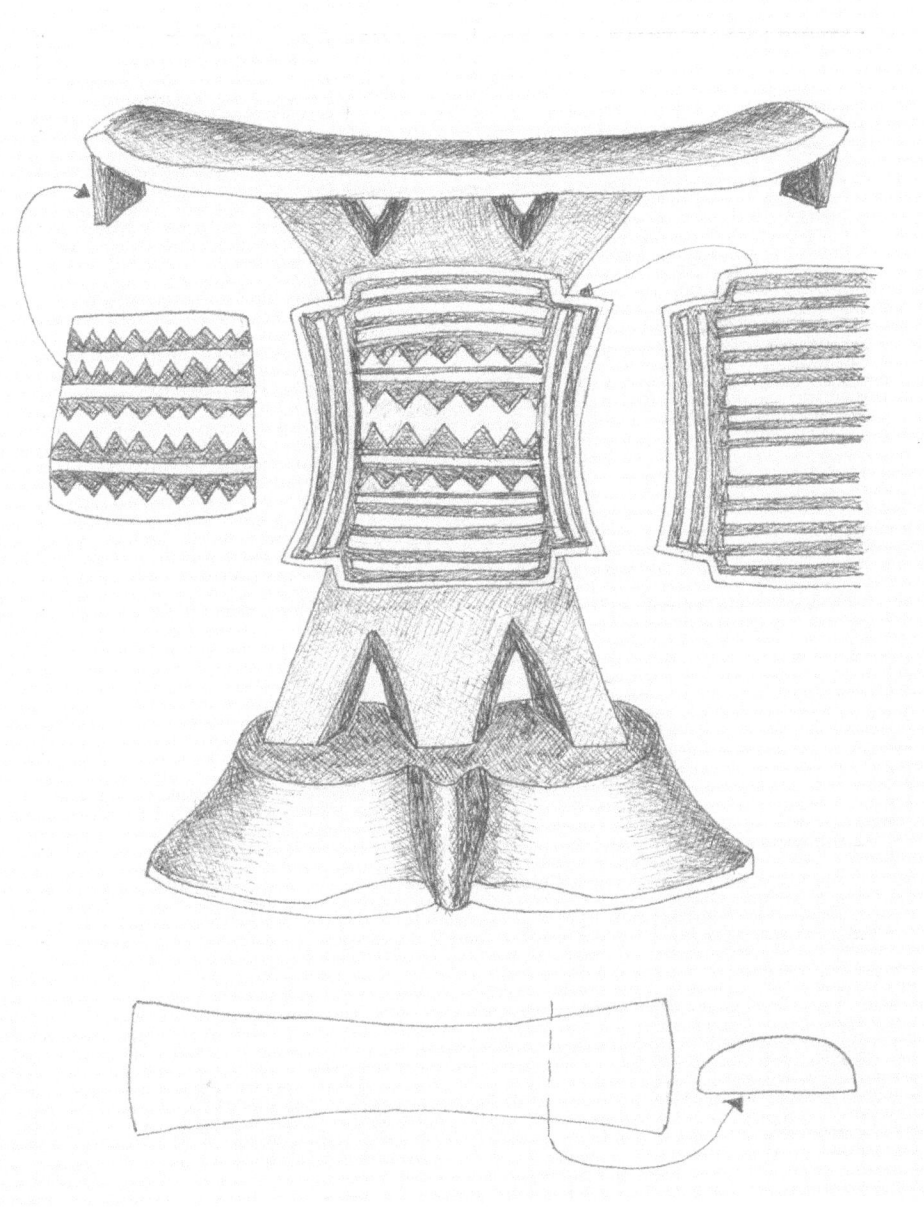

323 Liverpool, World Museum (no. 1992.05.29), *Ex collection, Hoylake United Reformed Church Museum 1911*. Natal (KwaZulu-Natal), *Shona/Tsonga?*, wood, 5 cm h.

## 298 | AFRICAN DREAM MACHINES

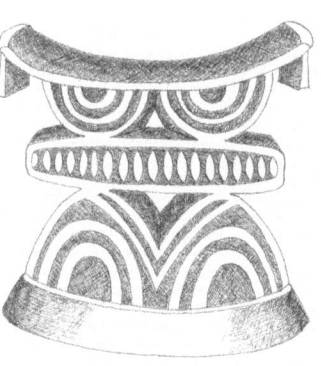

324  Frankfurt, Museum für Völkerkunde (no. 2512), collected by Frobenius expedition, 1928, *Rhodesia* (Zimbabwe), *Shona/Zezuru, mutsago*, wood, 14 cm h.

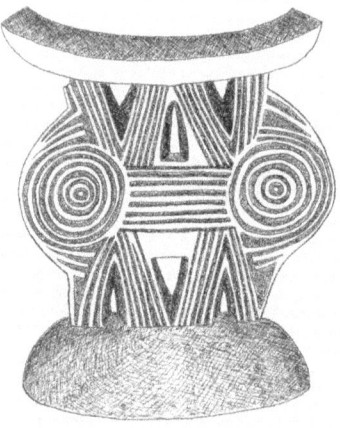

325  British Museum (no. 92.7.14.22), collected by J. T. H Bent, pre-1892, *Southern Rhodesia* (Zimbabwe), *Mashonaland*, 'Shona', wood, 15 cm h.

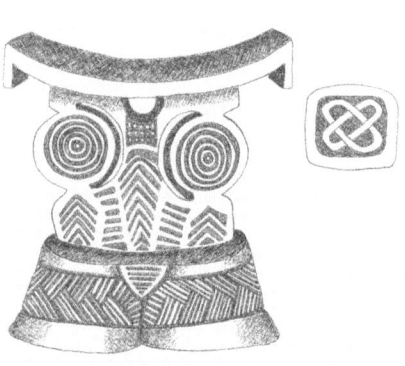

326  British Museum (no. 1949 Af46 815), Oldman Collection, *Southern Rhodesia* (Zimbabwe), 'Shona', wood, 14.5 cm h.

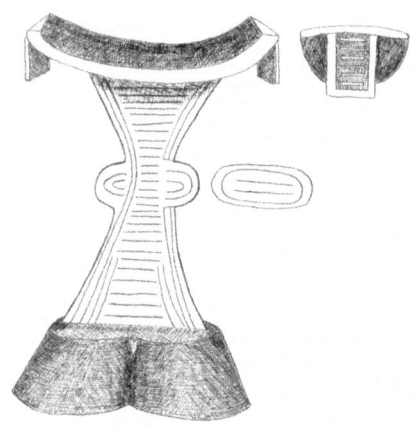

327  British Museum (no. 1949 Af46.808), Oldman Collection, *Southern Rhodesia* (Zimbabwe), *MaShona/MaKalanga* (Shona/Kalanga), wood, 14.2 cm h.

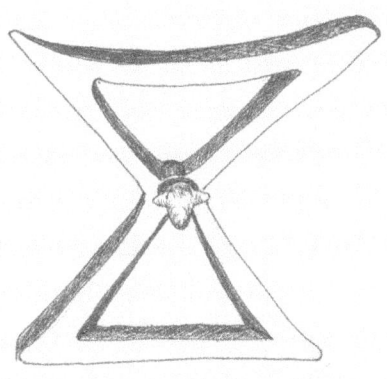

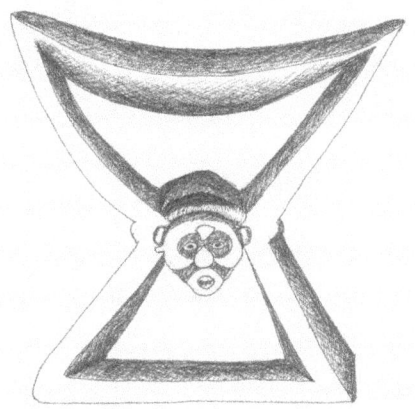

328  British Museum (no. 1954 Af23), (Wellcome Collection, no. 92074 [43692]), Democratic Republic of the Congo, 'Yaka?', wood, 13.5 cm h.

329  British Museum (no. 1949 Af46.353), Oldman Collection, Democratic Republic of the Congo, 'Yaka', wood, 14.7 cm h.

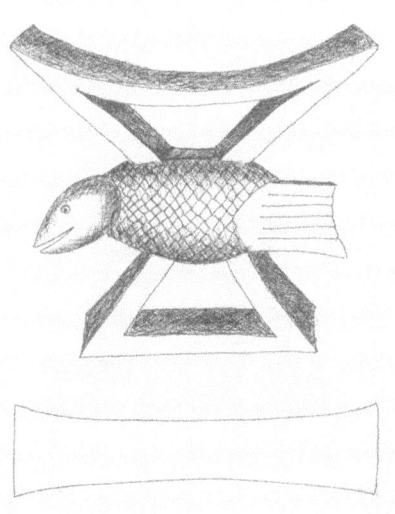

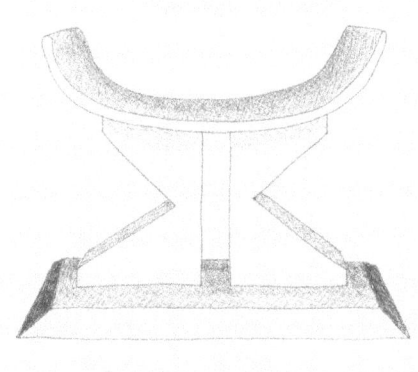

330  Musée Royal de l'Afrique Central (no. 32835), pre-1931, Democratic Republic of the Congo, 'Yaka?', wood.

331  Musée Royal de l'Afrique Central (no. 33046), pre-1931, Democratic Republic of the Congo, Kwango, Popokabaka, 'Yaka?', wood.

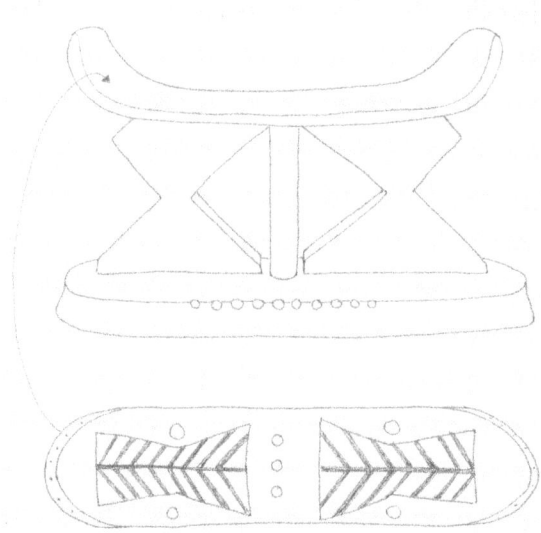

332 Musée Royal de l'Afrique Central (no. 33048), pre-1931, Democratic Republic of the Congo, Kwango, Popokabaka, 'Yaka?', wood.

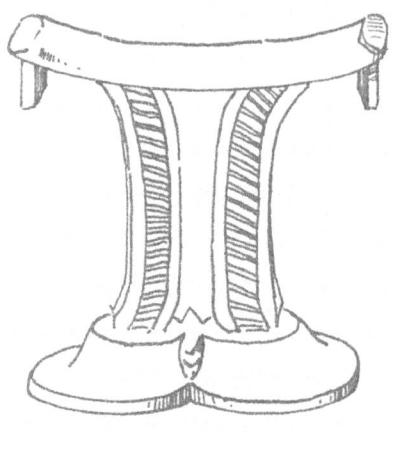

333 Hamburg, Museum für Völkerunde (no. 15.53), donated by Frau M. Mendelsohn, destroyed in Second World War, *Southern Africa, Betschuanen* (Tswana), wood, 14.2 cm h.

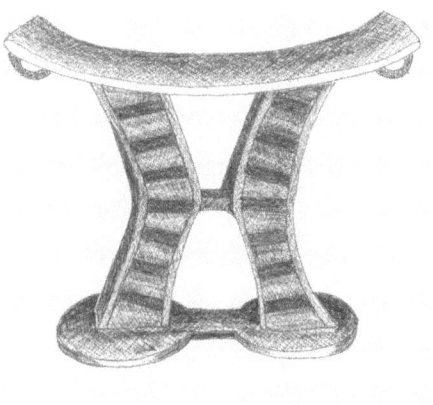

334 Johannesburg Art Gallery (no. 1983.37.9), collected by A. A. Jaques, pre-1929, South Africa, *Transvaal* (Limpopo Province), *Elim, Shangaan* (Shangane), 'Tsonga', wood, 12.5 cm h.

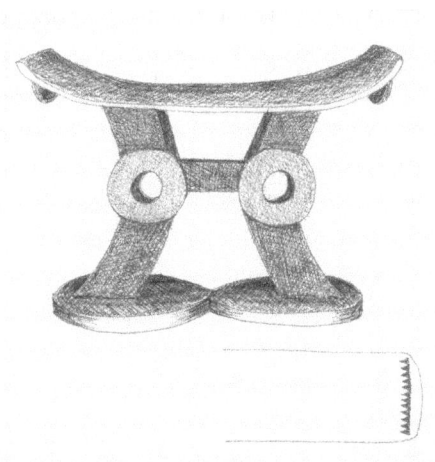

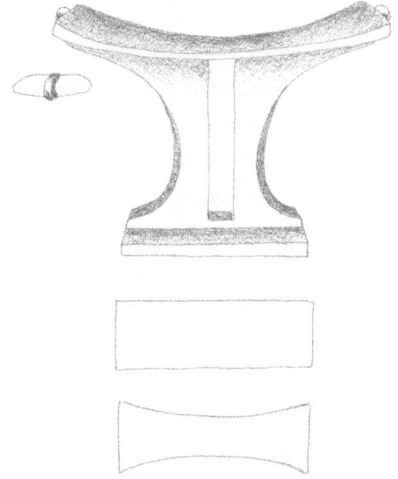

335  Johannesburg Art Gallery (Jaques Collection, no. 50/971), (Wanless 1987:107), collected by A. A. Jaques, 1928, South Africa, *Transvaal* (Limpopo Province), *Elim*, *Shangaan* (Shangane), 'Tsonga', wood, 13.5 cm h.

336  Musée Royal de l'Afrique Central (no. 19234), (Maes 1929, pl. VI, fig. 2), Democratic Republic of the Congo, *Mushenge*, *Kuba*, wood, 11 cm h.

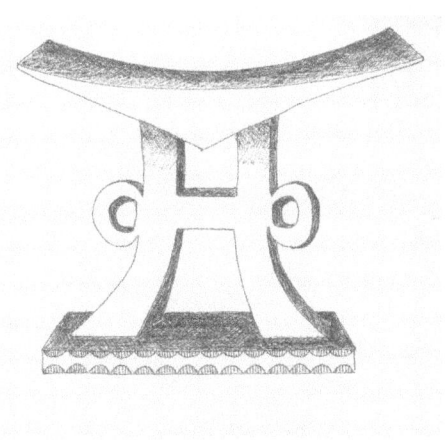

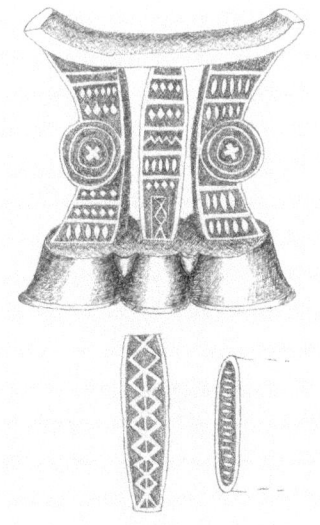

337  Musée Royal de l'Afrique Central (no. 32822), Democratic Republic of the Congo (no information given), pre-1931, Teke/Yaka?, wood.

338  British Museum (no. 1899.4.22.1), Dimley Olden Collection, *Southern Rhodesia* (Zimbabwe), *Mashonaland*, 'Shona', wood, 14.7 cm h.

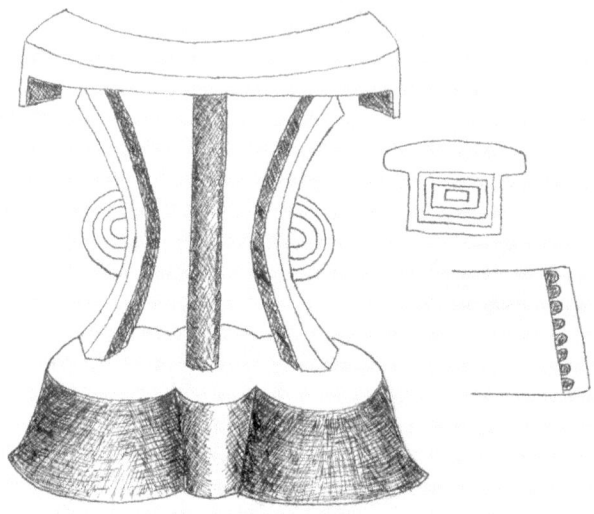

339  British Museum (no. 1954 Af23), (Wellcome Collection, no. 140183), *Southern Rhodesia* (Zimbabwe), Mashonaland, *mutsago*, wood, 13.8 cm h.

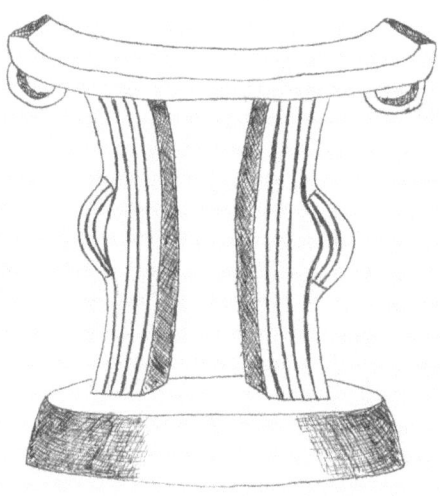

340  Frankfurt, Museum für Völkerunde (no. 2677), collected by Frobenius expedition, 1928, *Rhodesia* (Zimbabwe), *Shona/Zezuru*, *mutsago*, wood, 13 cm h.

CHAPTER 7  *Illustrations: figures 262-432* | **303**

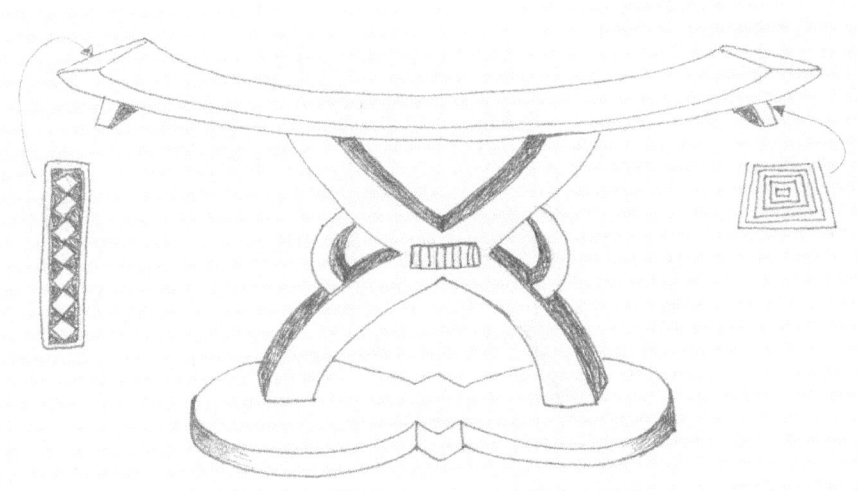

341 Johannesburg Art Gallery (Jaques Collection, no. 50/909), (Wanless 1985:47), collected by A. A. Jaques, pre-1929, South Africa, *Transvaal* (Limpopo Province), *Elim*, *Shangaan* (Shangane), 'Tsonga', wood, 14 cm h.

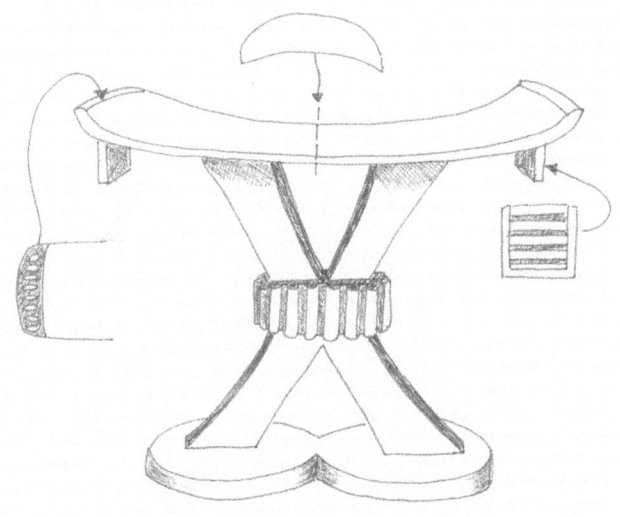

342 Neuchâtel, Musée de Ville (no. IIIC 3026), *Bought from Philippe Jeannerat, 1894, Mozambique*, 'Tsonga', wood, 11 cm h.

304 | AFRICAN DREAM MACHINES

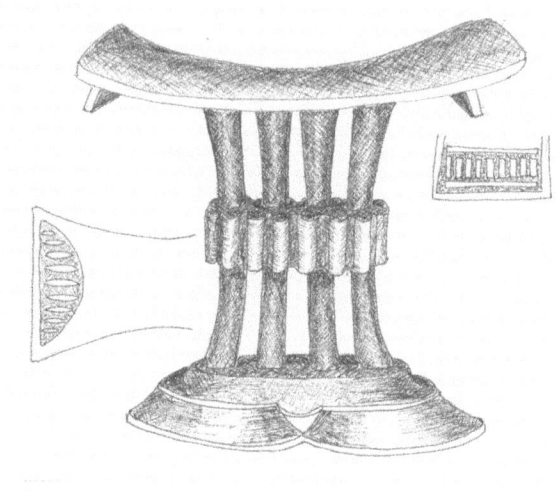

343   British Museum (no. 1954 Af23), (Wellcome Collection, no. 75384), *Southern Rhodesia* (Zimbabwe), Shona/Tsonga?, wood, 14.5 cm h.

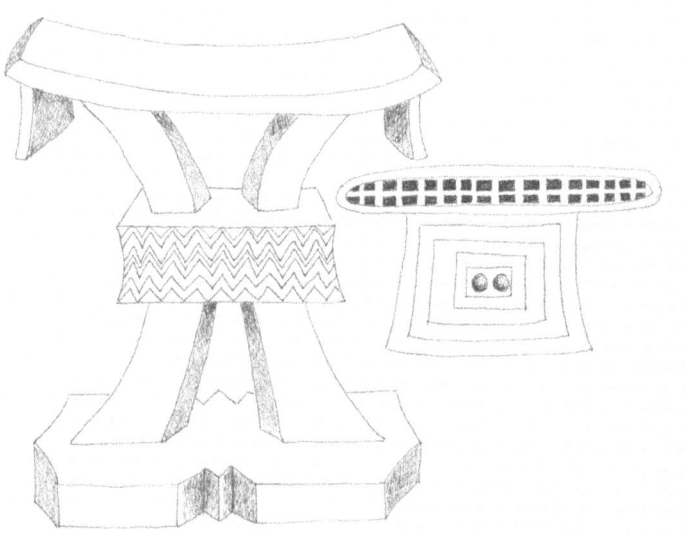

344   British Museum (no. 1954 Af23), (Wellcome Collection, no. 127303), *1930, Southern Rhodesia* (Zimbabwe), Shona/Tsonga?, wood, 15 cm h.

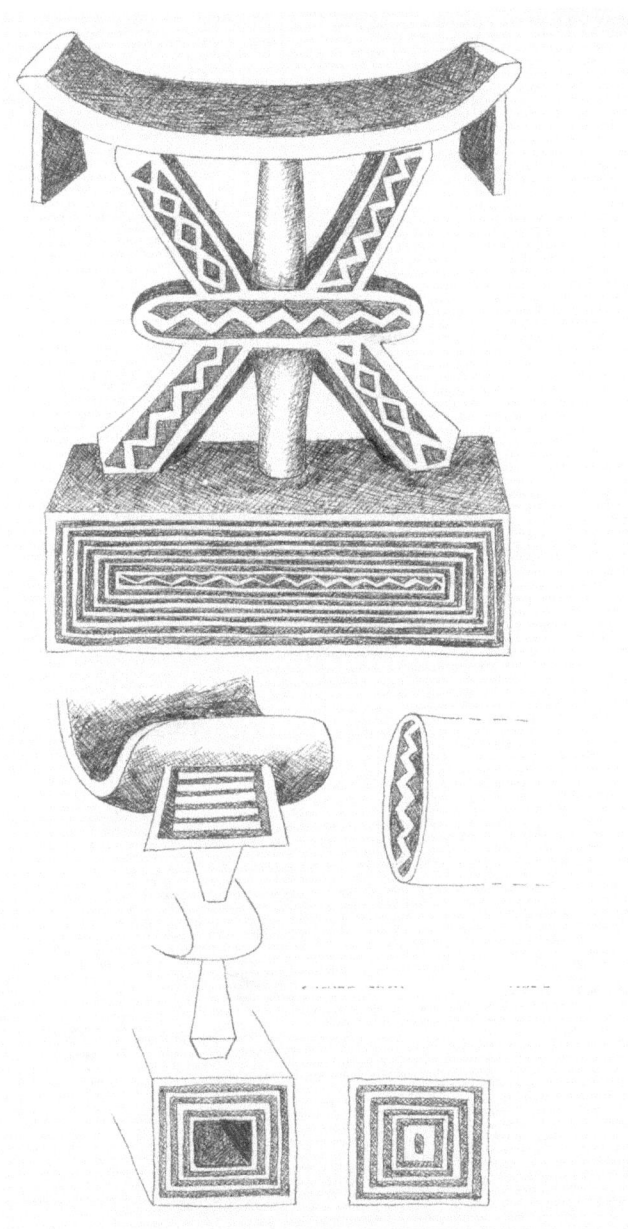

345 British Museum (no. 1954 Af23), (Wellcome Collection, no. 7504), *Southern Rhodesia* (Zimbabwe), Shona/Tsonga?, wood, 14.4 cm h.

306 | AFRICAN DREAM MACHINES

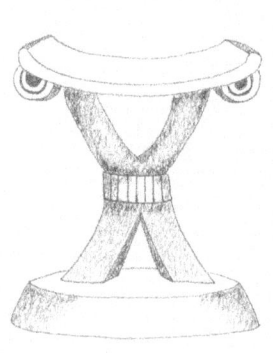

346 Brighton Museum, The Green Centre (no. R834/1), donated Mr Bolt, 1908, *Southern Rhodesia* (Zimbabwe), Shona/Tsonga?, wood, 14 cm h.

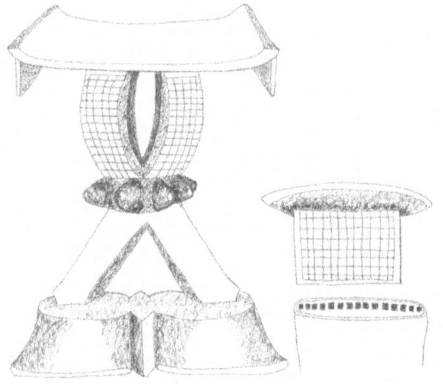

347 British Museum (no. 1949 Af46 807), Oldman Collection, *Southern Rhodesia* (Zimbabwe), *Shona*, wood, 13.4 cm h.

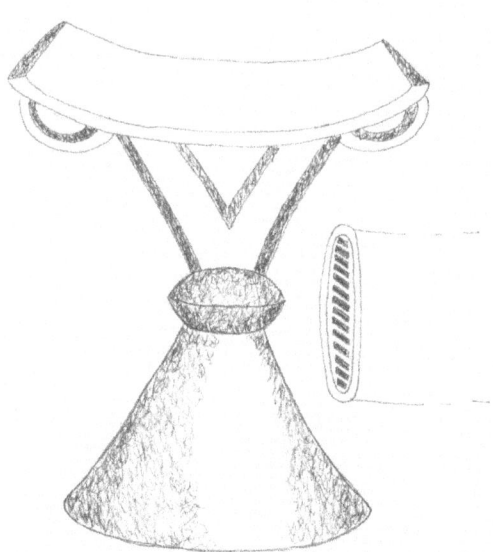

348 British Museum (no. 1926 10-16.8), acquired from Mary Cust, *Southern Rhodesia* (Zimbabwe), Shona/Tsonga?, wood, 16 cm h.

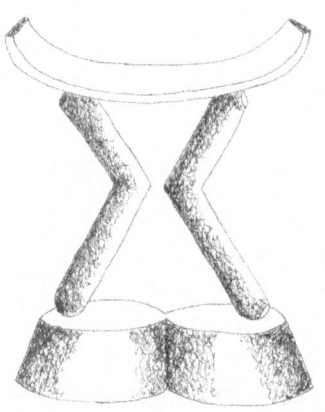

349 British Museum (no. 1892 7-14.152), collected by J. T. H. Bent, pre-1892, *Southern Rhodesia* (Zimbabwe), Shona/Tsonga?, wood, 14 cm h.

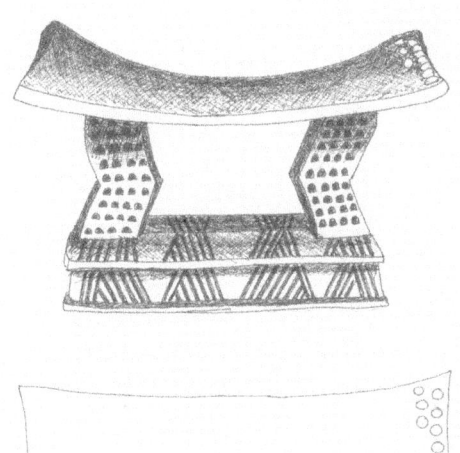

350 Musée Royal de l'Afrique Central (no. 55.117.65), Democratic Republic of the Congo, *Kasai* (province), *'Songye'*, wood, 13 cm h.

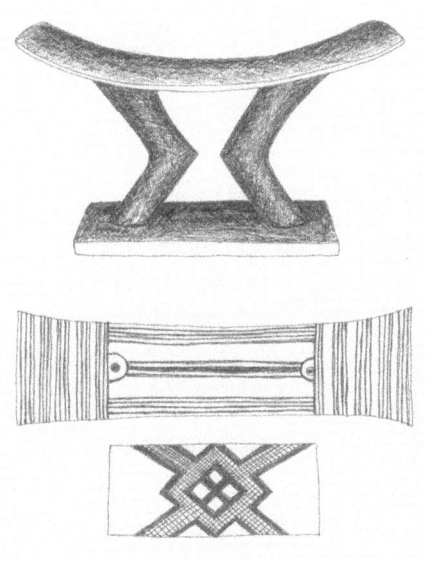

351 Musée Royal de l'Afrique Central (no. 52.48.112), Democratic Republic of the Congo, *Kasai* (province), *Kuba*, wood, 18 cm h. (Design at bottom is that of the plateau centre of Musée Royal de l'Afrique Central, no. 14306.)

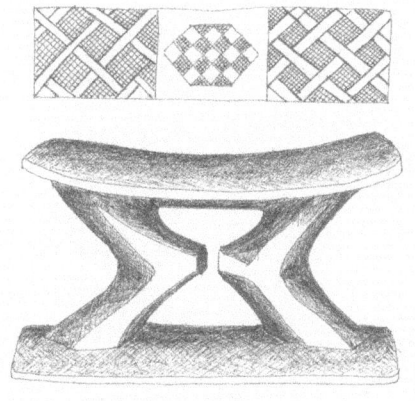

352 Musée Royal de l'Afrique Central (no. 51.71.48), Democratic Republic of the Congo, *Kasai* (province), *Kuba*, wood, 10.6 cm h.

308 | AFRICAN DREAM MACHINES

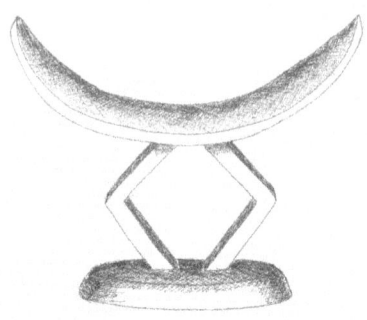

353  Musée Royal de l'Afrique Central (no. 12323), (Maes 1929, pl. II, fig. 6), Democratic Republic of the Congo, *Equateur* (province), *Basankusu* (region), *Ngombe*, wood, 11 cm h.

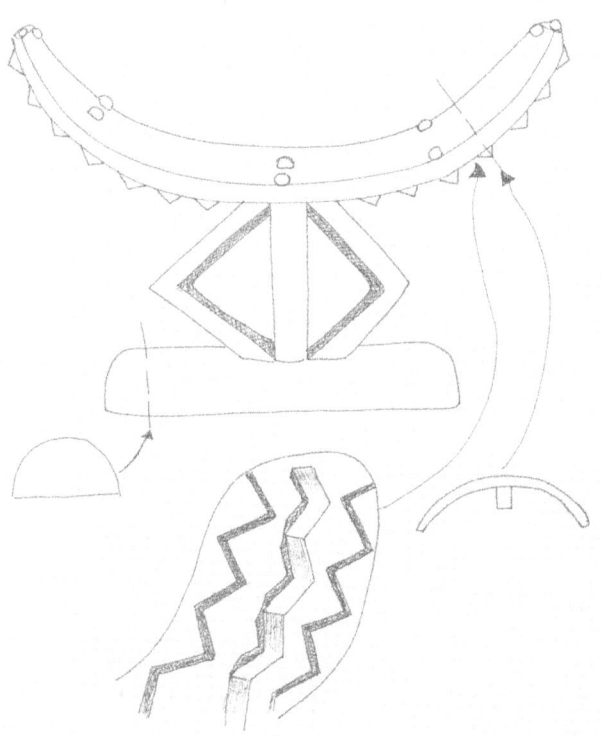

354  Musée Royal de l'Afrique Central (no. 8918), Democratic Republic of the Congo, *Equateur* (province), *Basankusu* (region), *Ngombe*, wood, 11 cm h.

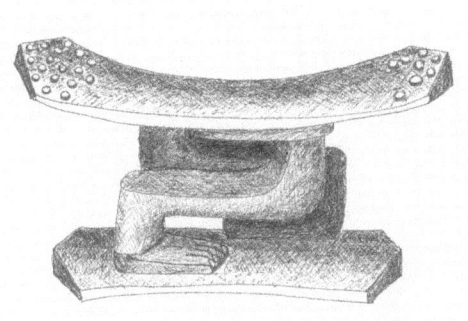

355 Musée Royal de l'Afrique Central (no. 43171), Democratic Republic of the Congo, *Kasai* (province), *Kuba*, wood, 14 cm h.

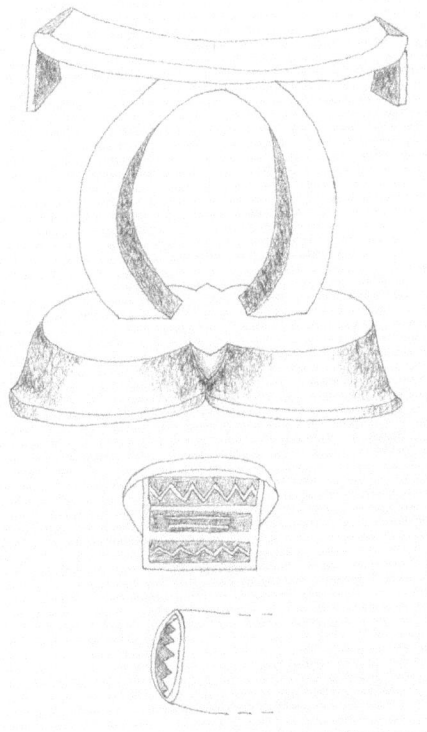

356 British Museum (no. 1935.7-15.5), Carson Collection, pre-1900, *Rhodesia* (Zimbabwe), *Mashonaland*, *mutsago*, wood, 14.7 cm h.

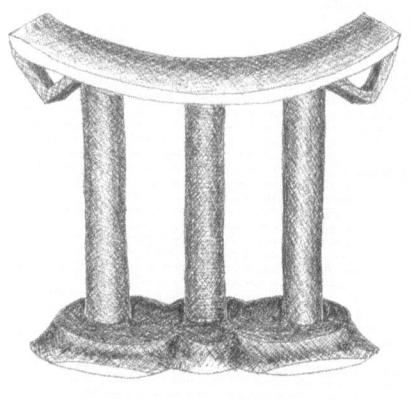

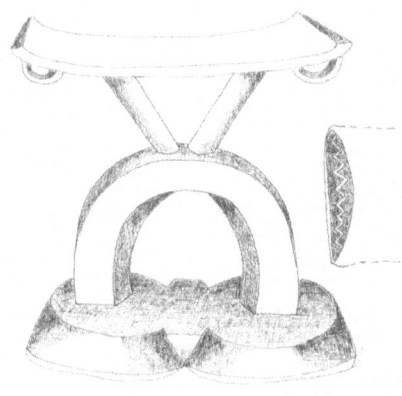

357  Johannesburg Art Gallery (Jaques Collection, no. 50/944), (Wanless 1985:81), collected by A. A. Jaques, pre-1929, South Africa, *Transvaal* (Limpopo Province), *Elim, Shangaan* (Shangane), 'Tsonga', wood, 16 cm h.

358  British Museum (no. 1954 Af23), (Wellcome Collection, no. 232215), *Southern Rhodesia* (Zimbabwe), *Mashonaland*, wood, 12.5 cm h.

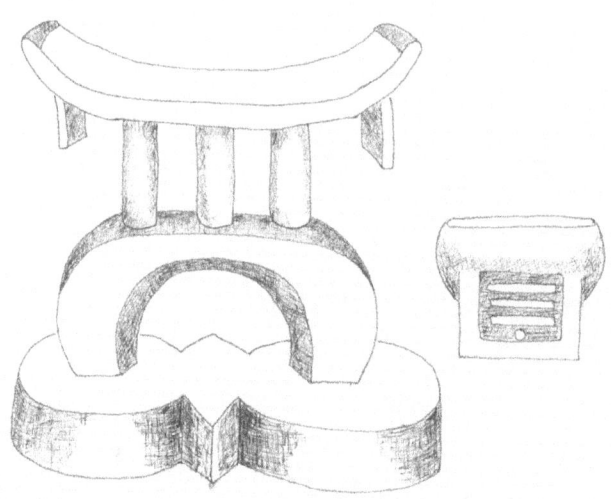

359  British Museum (no. 1931 11-18 58), collected by Alban Mead, *Southern Rhodesia* (Zimbabwe), 'Mashona? Tsonga?', wood, 11.4 cm h.

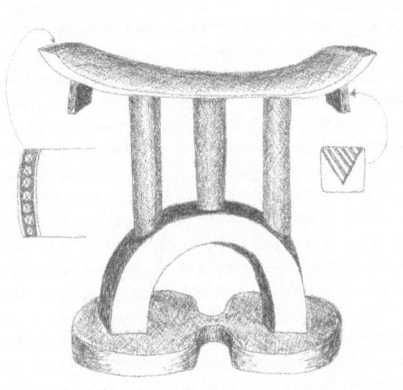
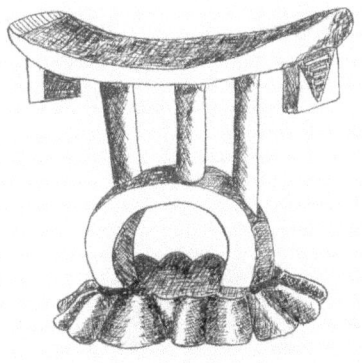

360 Neuchâtel, Musée du Ville (no. III C 3032), collected by H. P. Junod, *South Africa, Transvaal* (Limpopo Province), *pre 1892, 'Ronga', sicamelo*, wood, animal hair, beads, claws, 15 cm h.

361 Hamburg, Museum für Völkerkunde (no. 13.173:31), bought from *"Kowietzko", Destroyed in World War II, Southern Africa, Betschuanen* (Tswana), wood, 15 cm h.

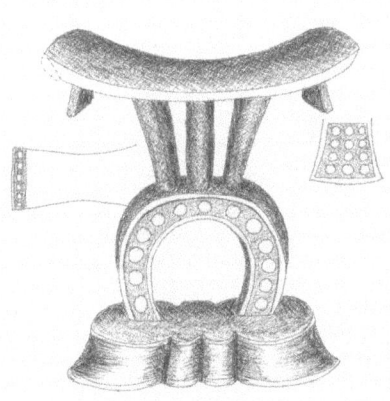
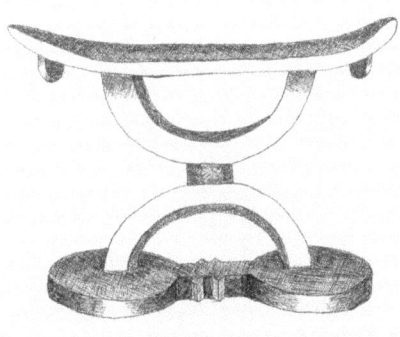

362 British Museum (no. 1954 Af23), (Wellcome Collection, no. 203788), *Mozambique, ' Tsonga'*, wood, 12.2 cm h.

363 Johannesburg Art Gallery (Jaques Collection, no. 50/940), (Wanless 1985:77), collected by A. A. Jaques, pre-1929, South Africa, *Transvaal* (Limpopo Province), *Elim, Shangaan* (Shangane), 'Tsonga', wood, 15 cm h.

## 312 | AFRICAN DREAM MACHINES

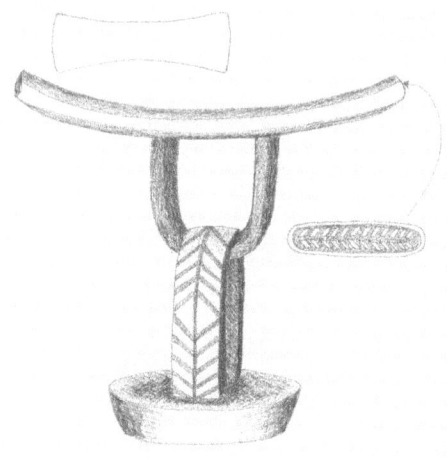

364 Musée Royal de l'Afrique Central (no. 51.12.10), *Upper Kasai* (province), '*Kioko? Luba?*' (cf. Maes 1929, pl. VI, fig. 8), wood, 14 cm h.

365 Present location unknown, Southeby, Parke Bernet[AC2][RTF annotation: }Bibliographic entry Southeby, Parke Bernet, 2004 *African, Oceanic and Pre-Columbian Art*. New York: Southeby, Parke Bernet

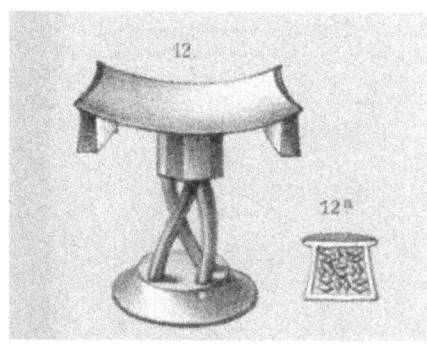

366 Müller & Snelleman (c. 1892, pl. XIV, no. 12), *Collected in Mozambique, Gaza*, 'Tsonga', wood, 12 cm h.

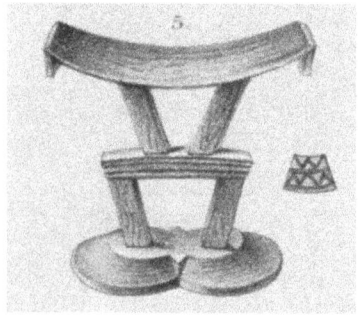

367 Müller & Snelleman (c. 1892, pl. V, no. 5), South Africa, *Probably Basotho* (Sotho), wood, 14.5 cm h.

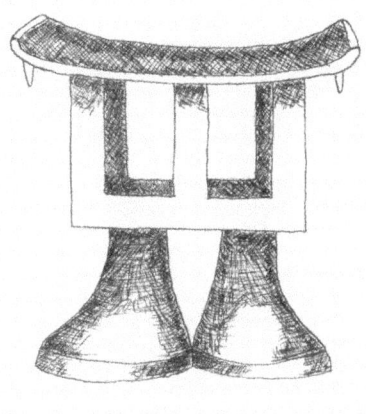
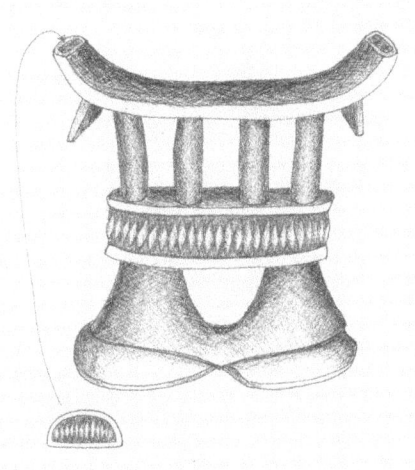

368  Drawing after Distant (1892:102), South Africa, *Transvaal* (Limpopo Province), *Spelonken, MaGwamba* (Gwamba), wood.

369  Cape Town, Iziko South African Museum (no. 75/231), *Rhodesia* (Zimbabwe), *Mutali, Shona? Ndau? Tsonga?*, wood, beads, 15 cm h.

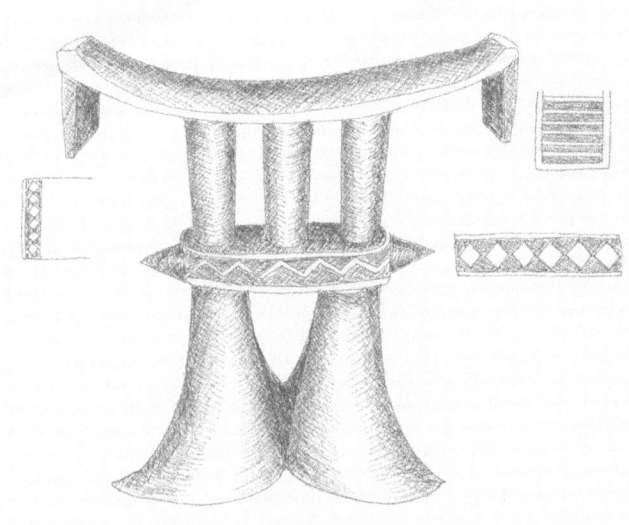

370  British Museum (no. 1954 Af23), (Wellcome Collection, no. 140090), *Southern Rhodesia* (Zimbabwe), *Mashonaland*, wood, 14.3 cm h.

**314** | AFRICAN DREAM MACHINES

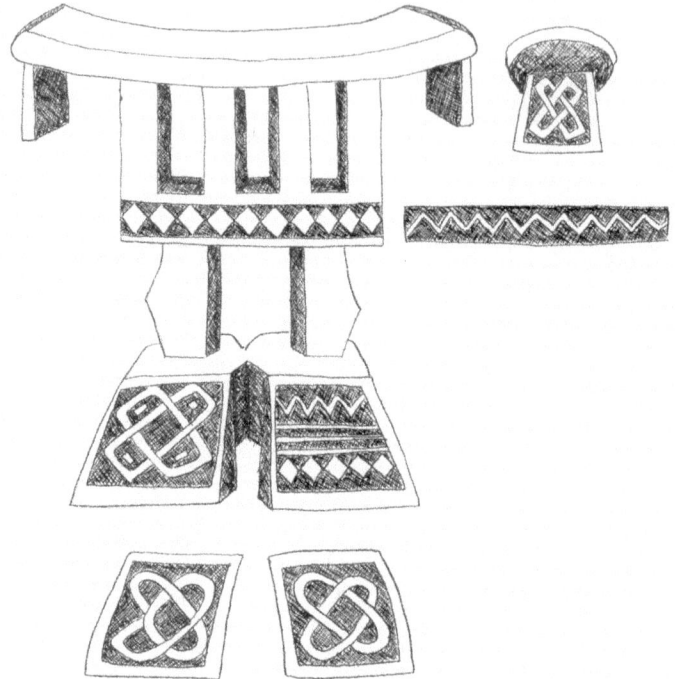

371  British Museum (no. 1892.7-14.155), collected by J. T. H. Bent, pre-1892, *Southern Rhodesia* (Zimbabwe), *Chibi's Country*, 'Shona', wood, 16.4 cm h.

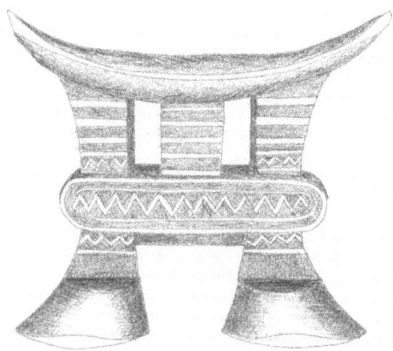

372  British Museum (no. 1954 Af1.49), on loan from John Moir (Maitland-Moir Museum), *Nyasaland* (Malawi), *"Mashona style pillow used for travelling"*, wood, 14.6 cm h.

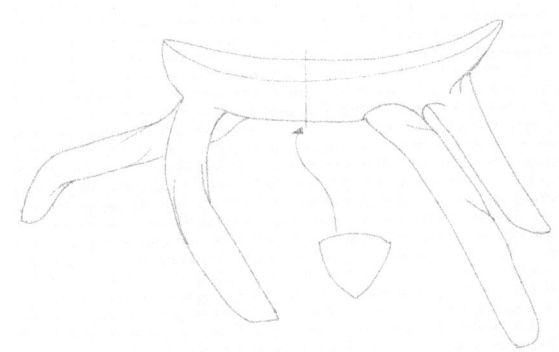

373 British Museum (no. 1934.6.5.24), *Northern Uganda*, wood, 17.6 cm h.

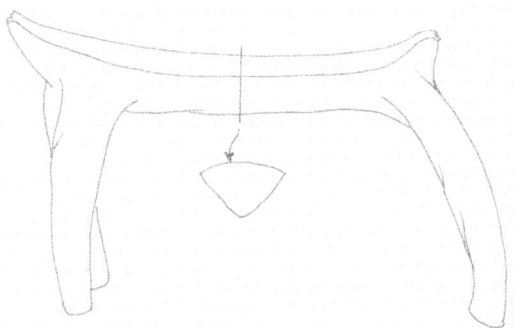

374 British Museum (no. 1947 Af16.92), collected by Rev. C. W. Hobley, 1889–1910, *Uganda/Kenya, Karamojong*, wood, 17.5 cm h.

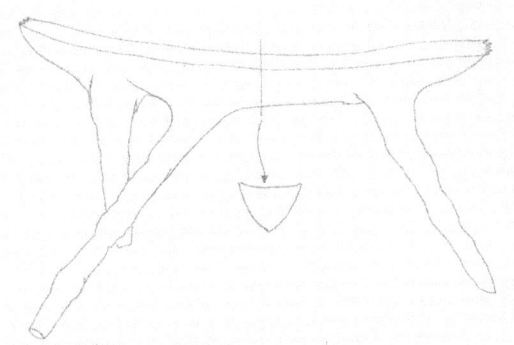

375 British Museum (no. 1947 Af16.91), collected by Rev. C. W. Hobley, 1889–1910, *East Africa, Uganda/Kenya, Karamojong*, wood, 25 cm h.

**316** | AFRICAN DREAM MACHINES

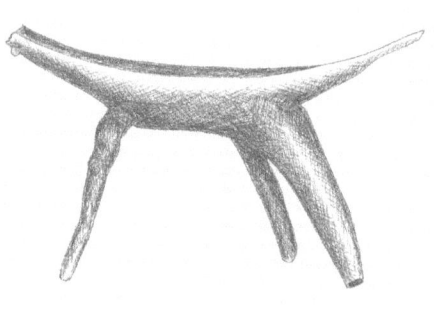

376 British Museum (no. 1972 Af11.6), collected by Brigadier General Matthews, donated by Mrs Collins, *Sudan*, wood, 21 cm h.

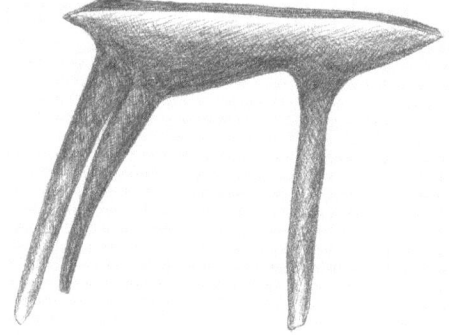

377 British Museum (no. 1931.3.21.6), collected by E. E. Evans Pritchard, *Sudan, Nuer*, wood, 18.5 cm h.

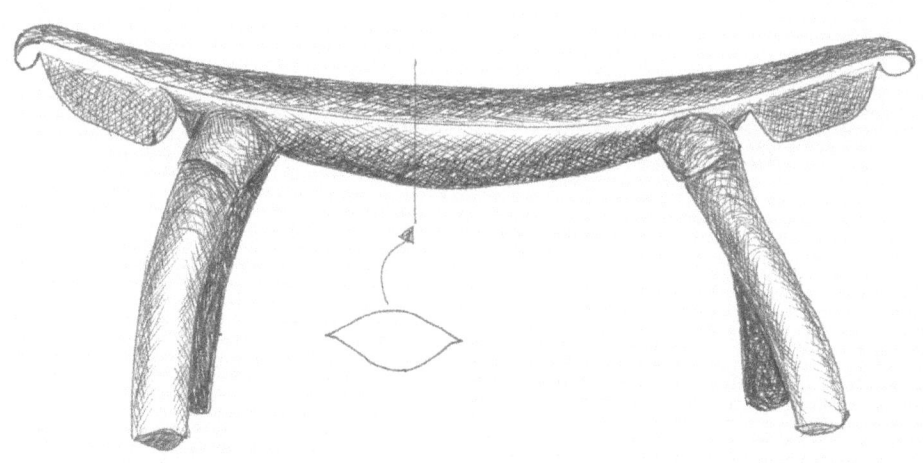

378 British Museum (no. 1934.3.8.104), *Sudan, Dinka*, wood, 21.5 cm h.

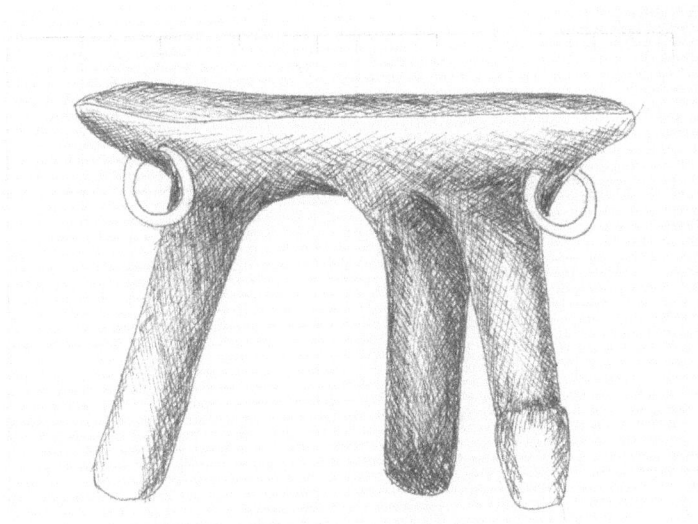

379 British Museum (no. 2727), donated by Henry Christy, 1860–69, *Northern Uganda, Bari*, wood, metal, 15 cm h.

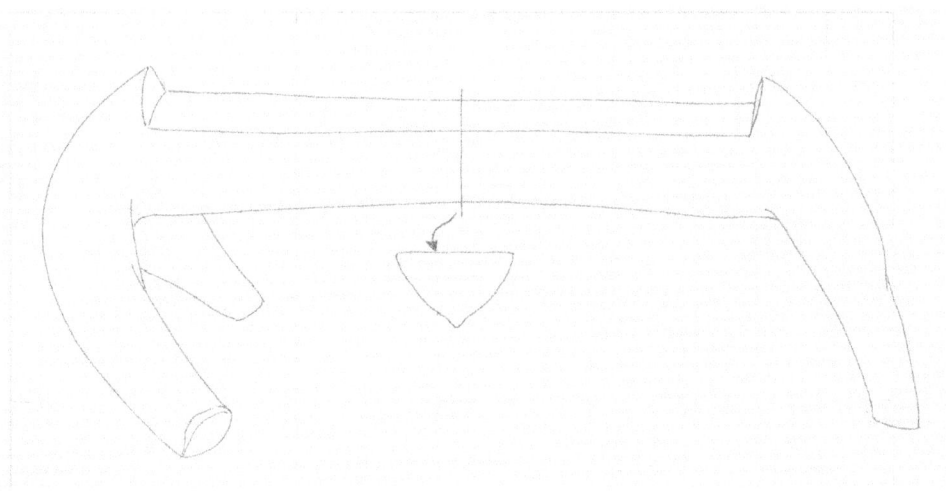

380 Manchester University Museum (no. 09763/1), collected by D. Turton, *Ethiopia, Mursi, ali*, wood, 29 cm l.

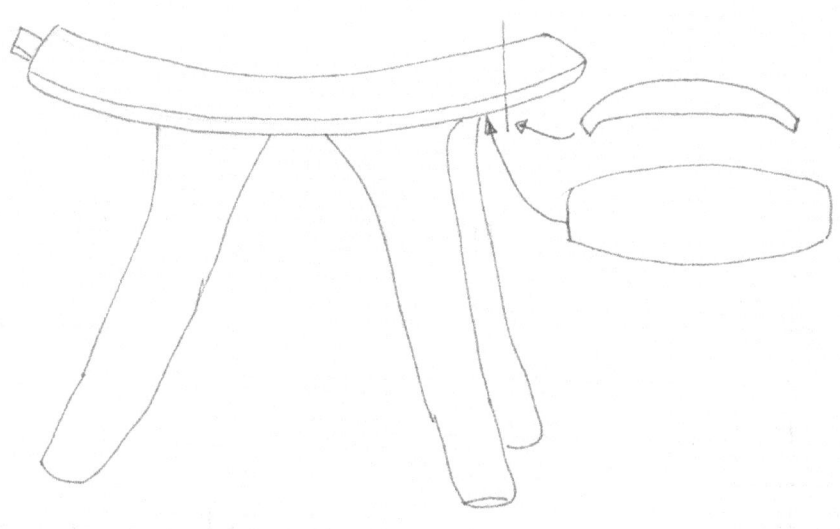

381  British Museum (no. 1947 Af16.93), *Uganda, Karamojong*, wood, 16.5 cm h.

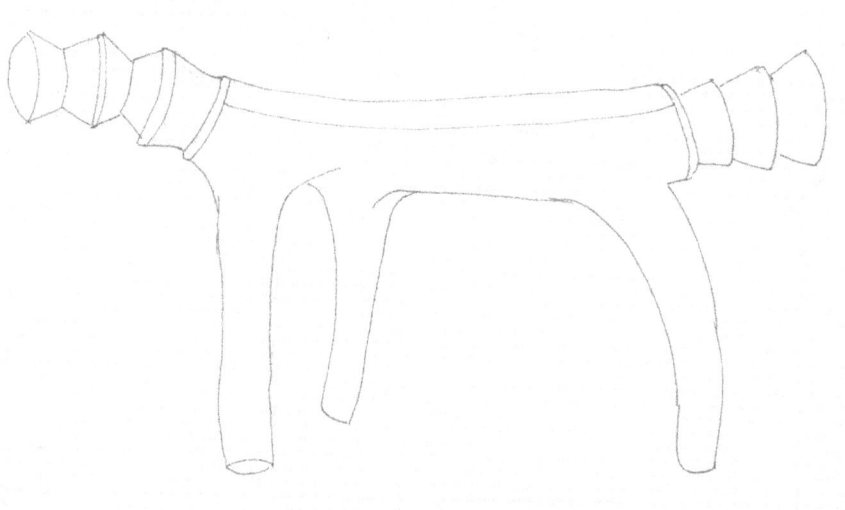

382  Oxford, Pitt Rivers Museum (no. 1979.20.86), collected by Miss Patti Langton, 1979, *Sudan, Dinka*, wood, 22 cm h.

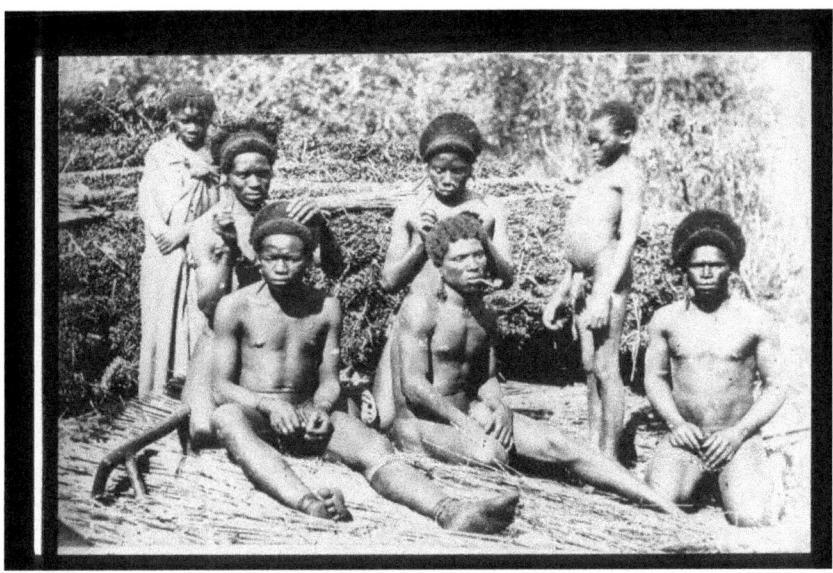

383  Cape Town, South African Archives, young Zulu men doing their coiffures, 1890s, photographer unknown.

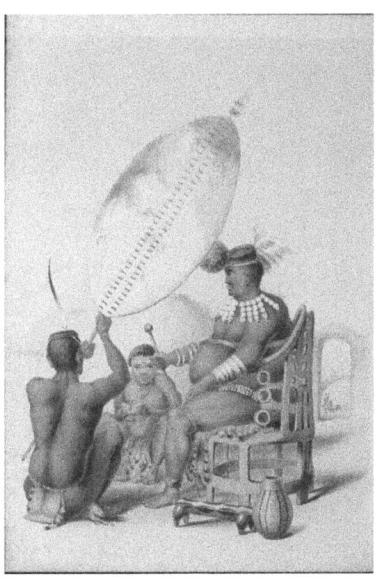

384  Angas (1849), *Umpanda: King of the Amazulus*, colour lithograph.

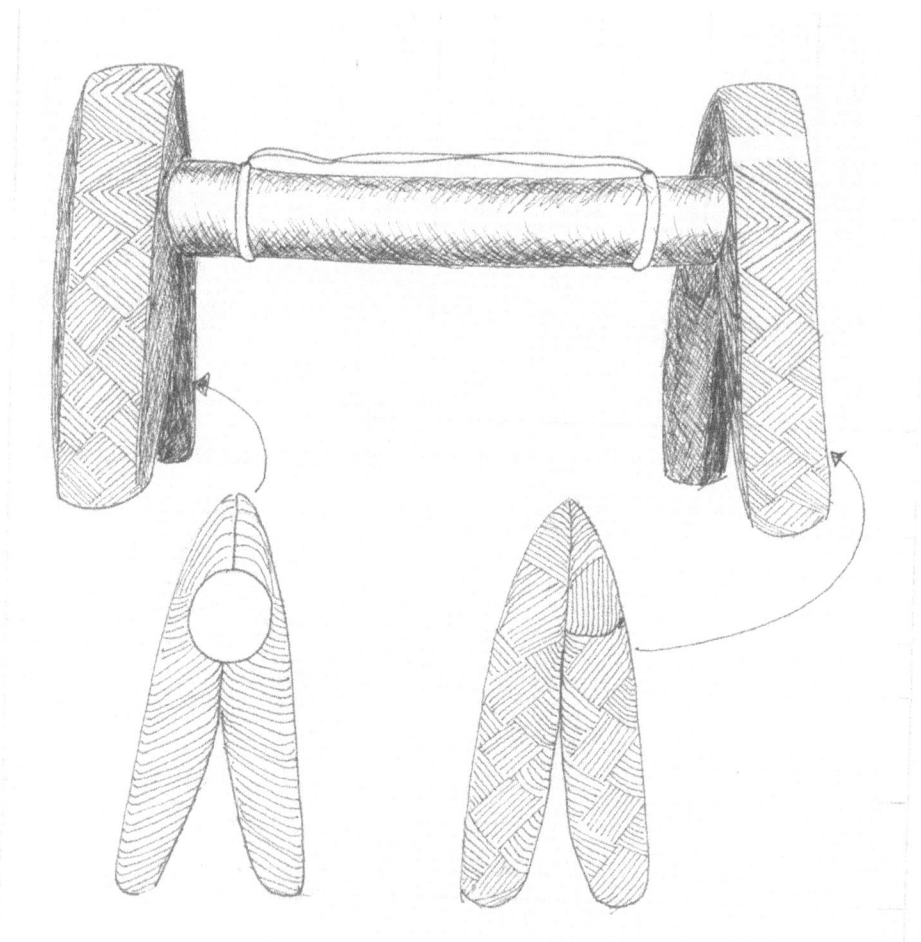

385 British Museum (no. 2183), Christy Collection, 1860–69, *South Africa, Natal, "Kafir", isicamelo or wooden pillow*, wood, leather, 16.5 cm h.

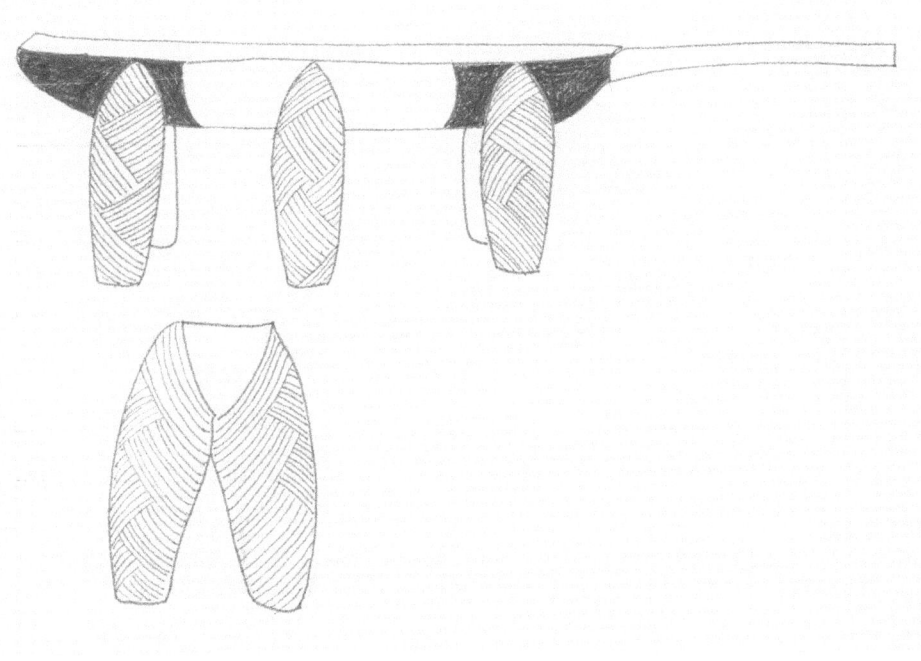

386  British Museum (no. +6046), donated by Davies Rusher, 1893, ex-Southeby, *South Africa, Natal* (KwaZulu-Natal), *"Kafir, isicamelo or wooden pillow"*, wood, leather, 10.5 cm h.

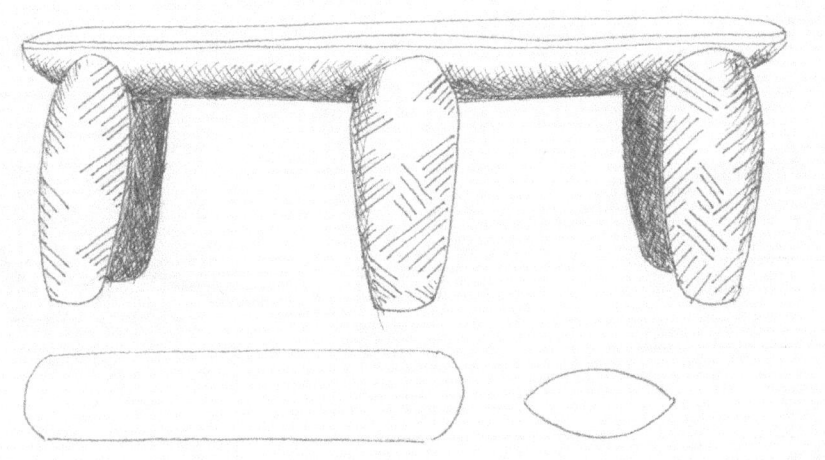

387  British Museum (no. Af23.10), *South Africa, Natal* (KwaZulu-Natal), *"Kafir"*, wood, 16.5 cm h.

**322** | AFRICAN DREAM MACHINES

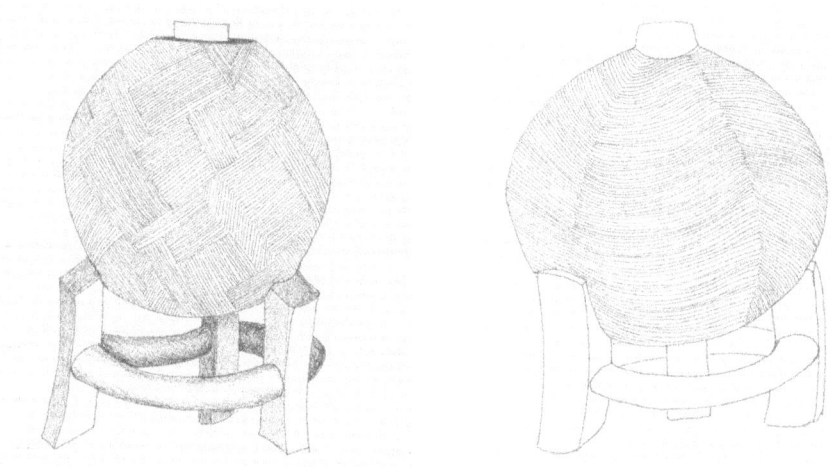

388   British Museum (no. 4876 [l], 4875 [r]), donated by Henry Christy, 1860–69, London International Exhibiton, 1862, *South Africa, Natal* (KwaZulu-Natal), *Zulu "milk pail/s"*, wood, 27 cm h (l), 30 cm h (r).

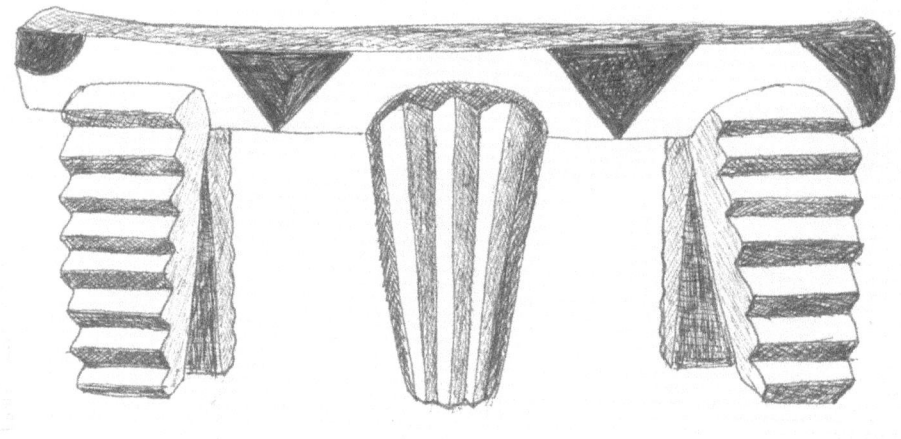

389   British Museum (no. 1954 Af23), (Wellcome Collection, no. 131119), *(Auction Car Str 14/9/1902 8/6-)*, *South Africa, Zulu,* <u>Umcamelo</u> (on adhesive label), wood, 13.9 cm h.

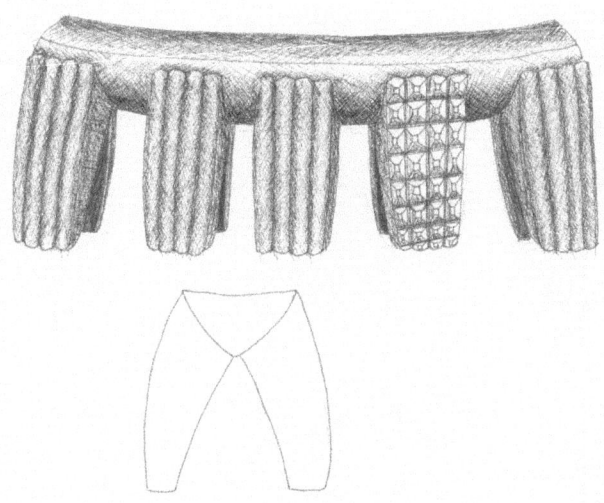

390  Liverpool World Museum (no. 56.25.136), (ex-Norwich Castle Museum, no. 117.15, before 1915), *South Africa, Zulu*, wood, 14 cm h.

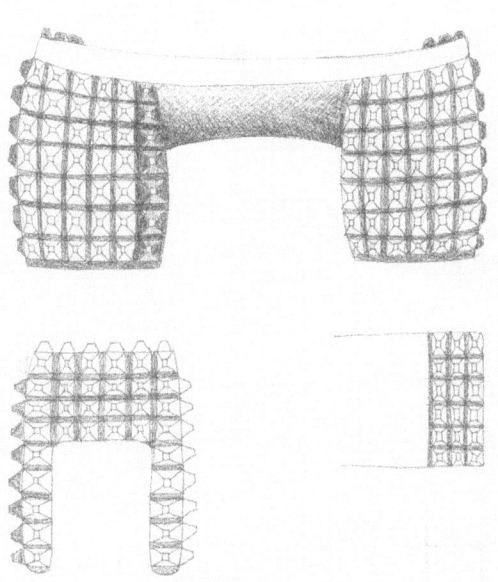

391  British Museum (no. 1917.11.3.1), collected by *(brought from Africa by)* F. M. Viscount Wolsely, donated by Dowager Viscount Wolsely, *South Africa, Zulu*, wood, 14.7 cm h.

**324** | AFRICAN DREAM MACHINES

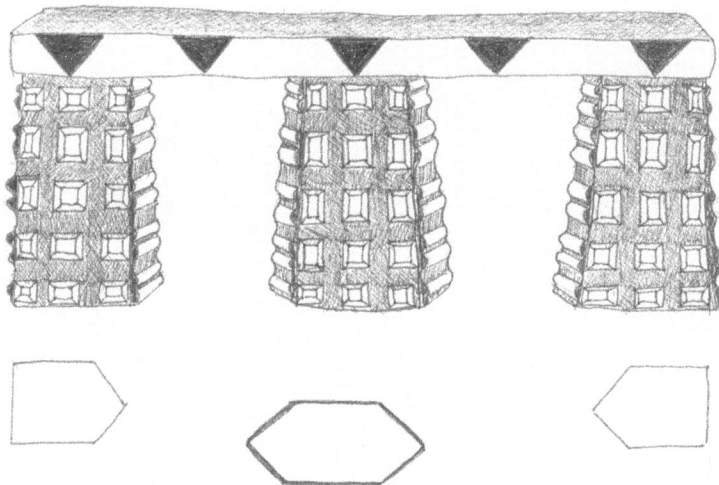

392   British Museum (no. 1921.6-16,4), *Collector Hirst, South Africa, Zulu*, wood, 13.8 cm h.

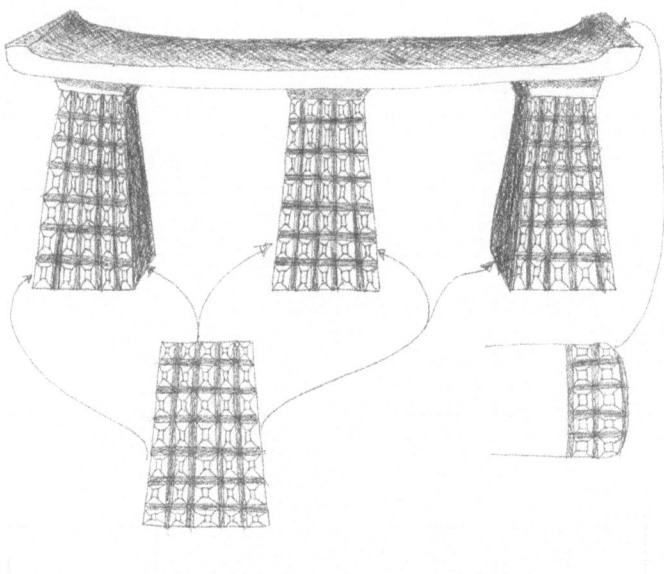

393   British Museum (no. 1947 Af19A; computer no. 1949 Af39.1), *Source Miss B Swaine, South Africa, Zulu*, wood, 14 cm h.

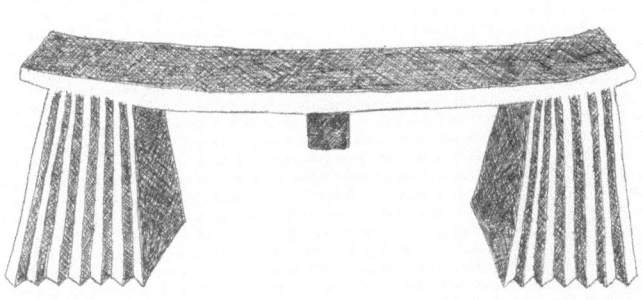

394  Johannesburg, private collection, collected pre-1929 in Eshowe, South Africa, KwaZulu-Natal, Swazi?, wood, 15 cm h.

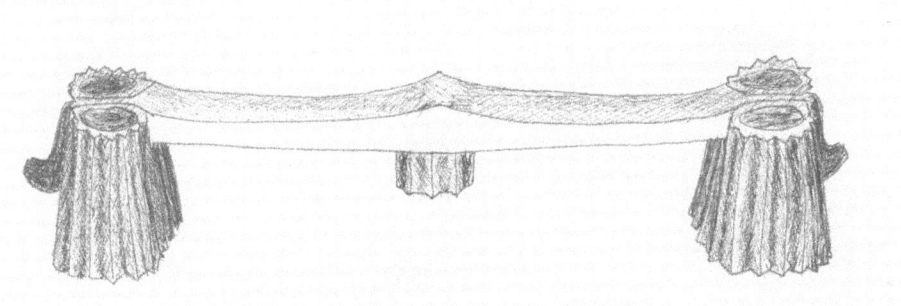

395  University of the Witwatersrand Art Galleries, Museum of Ethnology Collection, (no. WME/18), South Africa, *Transvaal* (Limpopo Province), *Swazi(?)*, wood, 14 cm h.

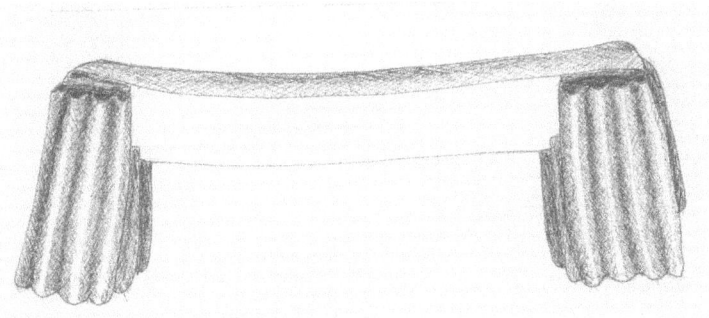

396  Munich, Staatlisches Museum füür Vöölkerkunde (no. 88-188), acquired from Meyer, *South Africa, Natal* (KwaZulu-Natal), *Zulu "Kaffern", Swazi? Zulu?, Isigqiki* (added later), wood, 13 cm h.

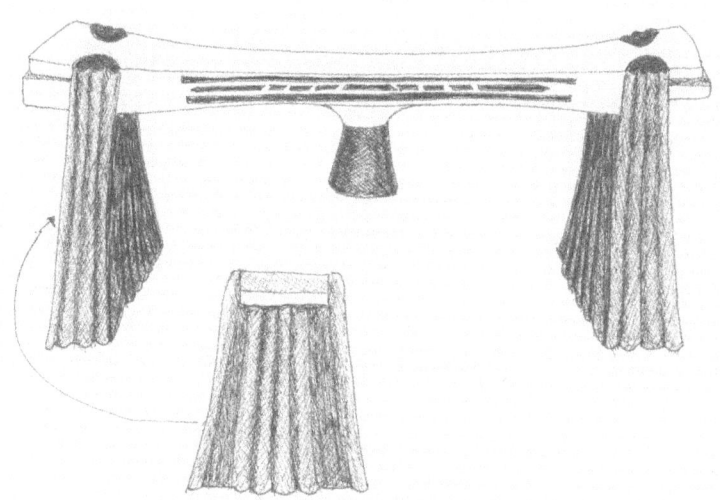

397   Tshwane (Pretoria), National Culture History Museum (no. 59.11.2), *South Africa?, Swazi*, wood, 15 cm h.

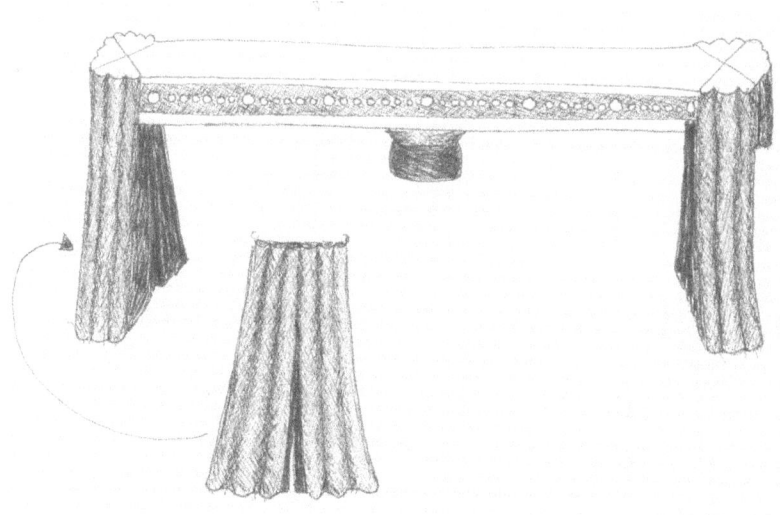

398   Tshwane (Pretoria), National Culture History Museum (no. 1971.9), *South Africa, Transvaal* (Limpopo Province), *Embuzini, Swazi*, wood, 15.5 cm h.

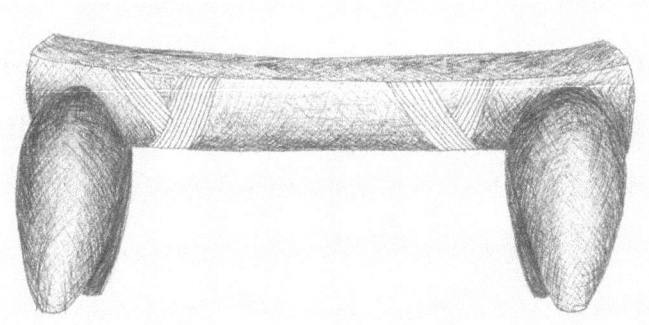

399  Manchester University Museum (no. SA 9), Clayton Collection, pre-1901, ex-Halifax Museum, *South Africa, Natal* (KwaZulu-Natal) *("Kaffir")*, 'Zulu', wood, 14 cm h.

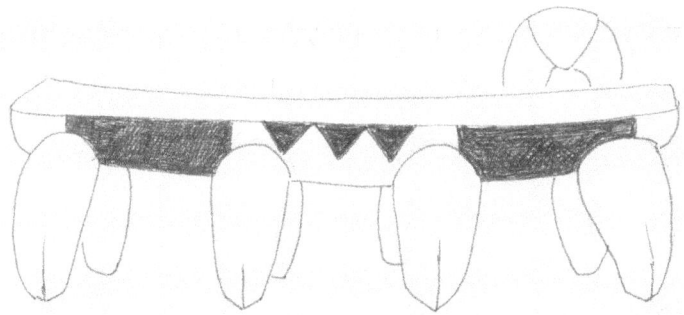

400  British Museum (no. 2182), *From Kew Botanical Gardens in 1866, South Africa ("Kafirs")*, 'Zulu', wood, 15.2 cm h.

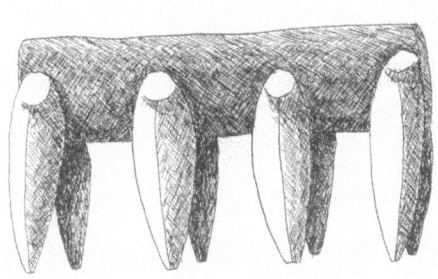

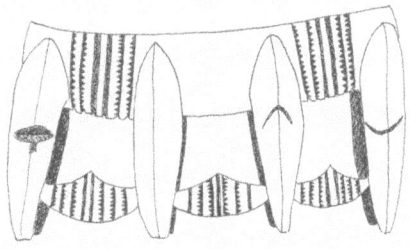

401  British Museum (no. 1934 7-12.6), collected by Major General Sir Reginald Thynne during the Anglo-Zulu War, donated by Lady Baddely (née Thynne), *South Africa, Zulu*, wood, 14 cm h.

402  Manchester University Museum (no. 05156), donated G. S. Thomas, *South Africa, Zulu*, wood, 11.4 cm h.

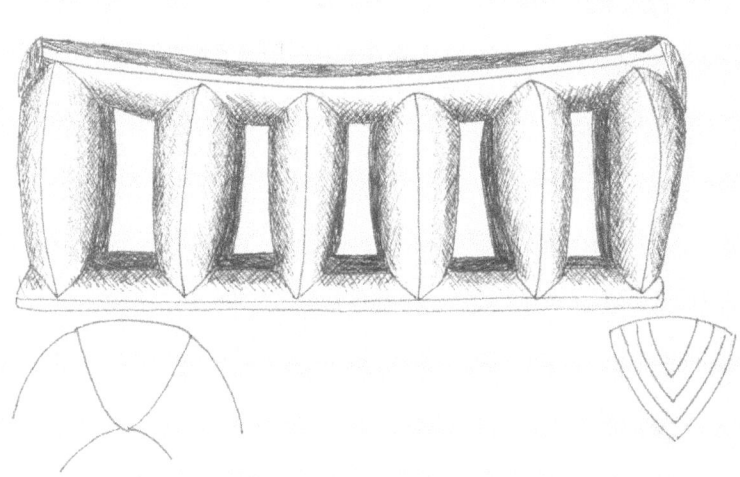

403  British Museum (no. 1917 11.3.3), *Collected by F. M. Viscount Wolsely in the Anglo Zulu War, Donated by Dowager Viscount Wolsely*, South Africa, Zulu, wood, 15 cm h.

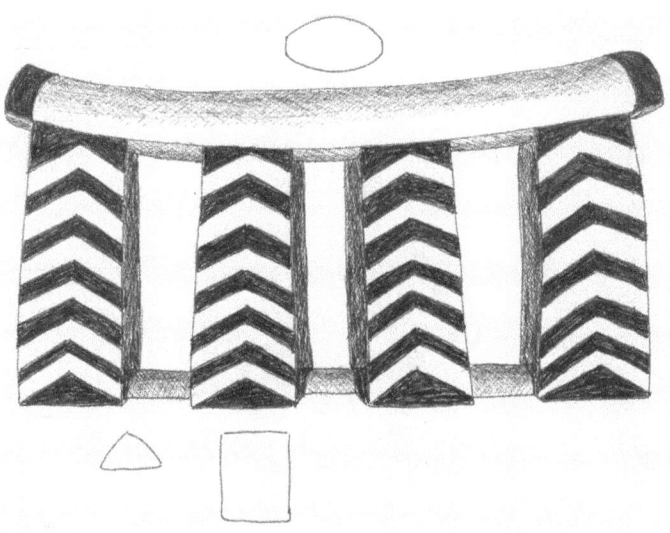

404  British Museum (no. 1898.10-12.6), *acquired from F. E. Foxon (underside of label reads: FE Foxon Esq Headrest. S.Africa, Natal,* stamped *Res Magistrate 11 March 87, Umgeni Division)*, South Africa, Zulu, wood, 19.3 cm h.

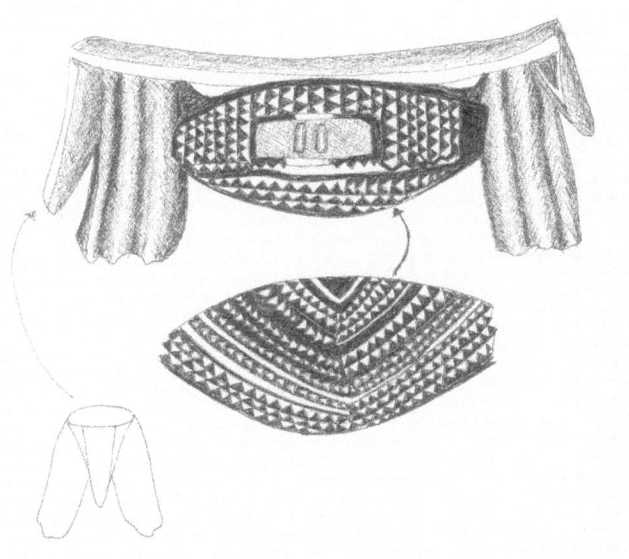

405   British Museum (no. 1954 Af23), (Wellcome Collection, no. 76224), *South East Africa, [Zulu]*, wood, 12 cm h.

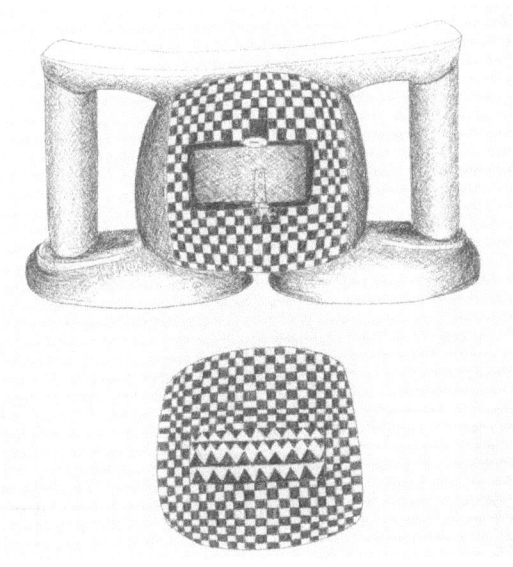

406   British Museum (no. 1954 Af23), (Wellcome Collection, no. 233043), (on the label appears: *headrest and box, Mashonaland, S. Africa*), *South East Africa, [Zulu]*, wood, 12 cm h.

330 | AFRICAN DREAM MACHINES

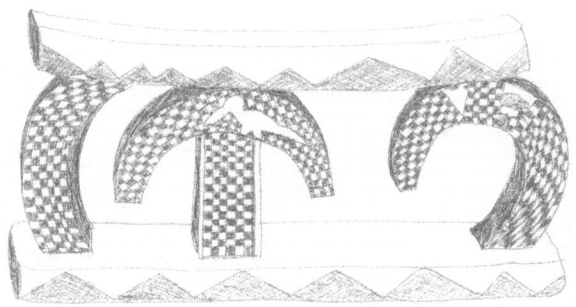

407  British Museum (no. 1954 Af23), (Wellcome Collection, no. 231238), *South Africa [Zulu]*, wood, 20.1 cm h.

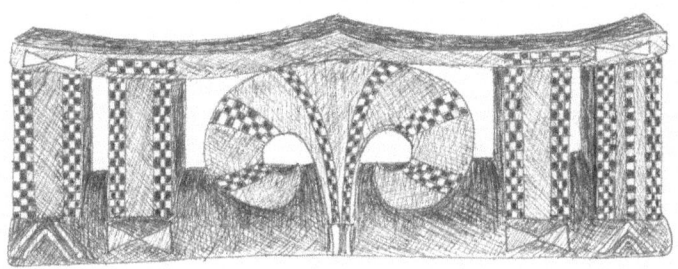

408  British Museum (no. 1954 Af23), (Wellcome Collection, no. 171768), *South Africa [Zulu]*, wood, 12.3 cm h.

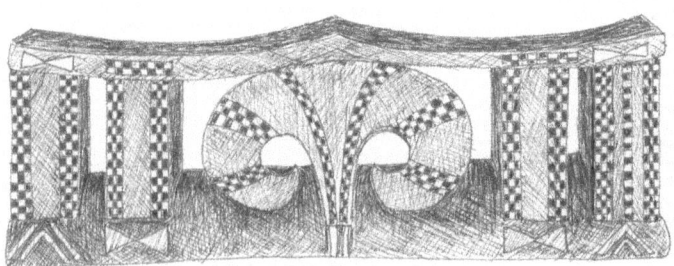

409  British Museum (no. 1921.6-16.47), donated by Miss Hirst, *Southern Africa, Matabele?*, wood, 16.4 cm h.

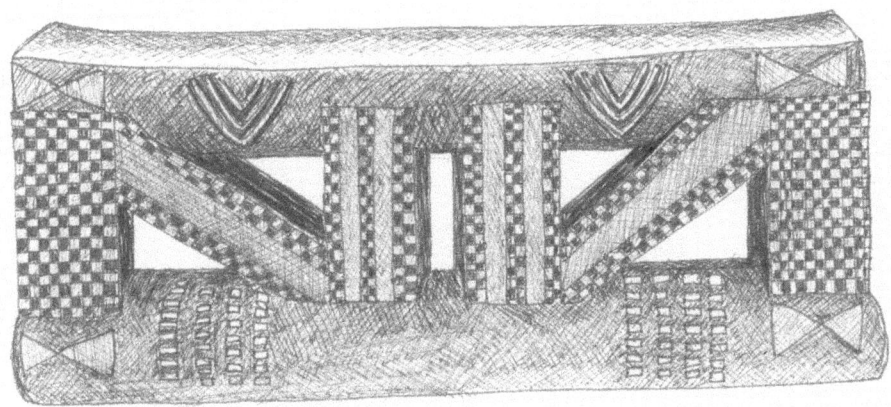

410   British Museum (no. 1954 Af23), (Wellcome Collection, no. 19767), *Southern Rhodesia, Zimbabwe/South Africa?* (sticker on headrests reads *pillow from Zululand*), wood, 12.3 cm h.

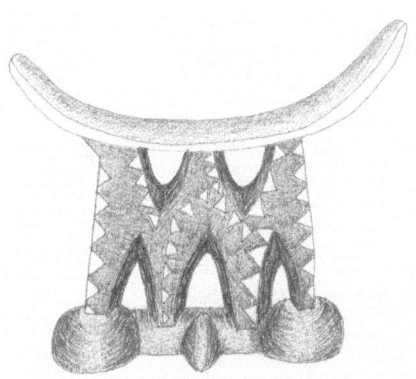

411   Tshwane (Pretoria), National Culture History Museum (no. 8342), *South Africa, KwaZulu-Natal Zulu, Hlabisa*, wood, 13 cm h.

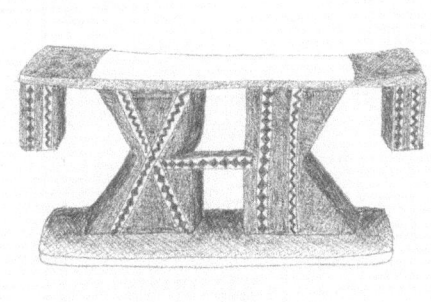

412   British Museum (no. 1944 Af4.254), *Collector Mrs A. G. Beasley, South Africa, Natal* (KwaZulu-Natal), *"Bantu"*, wood, 15 cm h.

**332** | AFRICAN DREAM MACHINES

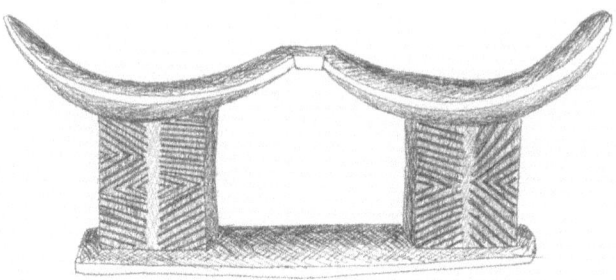

412   British Museum (no. 1944 Af4.254), *Collector Mrs A. G. Beasley, South Africa, Natal* (KwaZulu-Natal), *"Bantu"*, wood, 15 cm h.

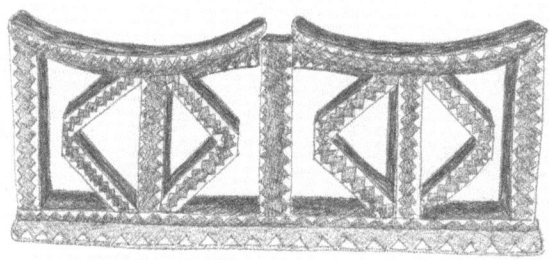

413   Manchester University Museum (no. 1928.243), *South Africa, Zulu*, wood, 20.2 cm h.

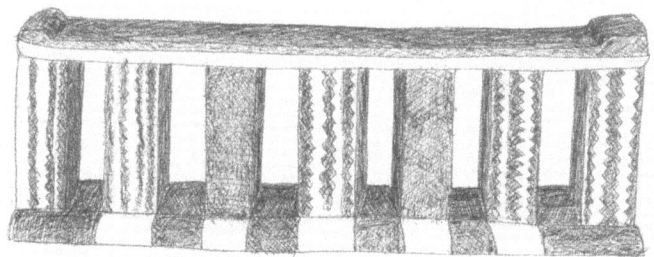

414   Manchester University Museum (no. 1932.301), *Speake Collection, 1882–84, South Africa, Zulu*, wood, 16.4 cm h.

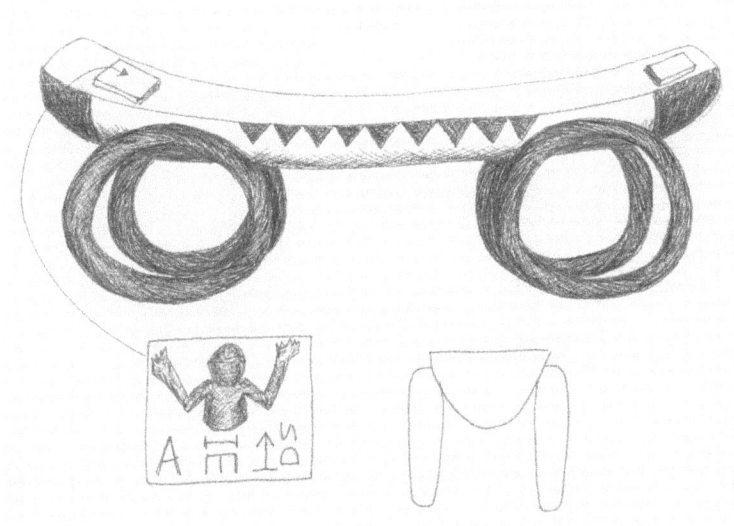

415   Munich, Staatlisches Museum für Völkerkunde (no. 88.530), collected by Wilhelm Joest, *South Africa, Natal* (KwaZulu-Natal), *"Zulu Kaffern"*, wood, pokerwork, 13.6 cm h.

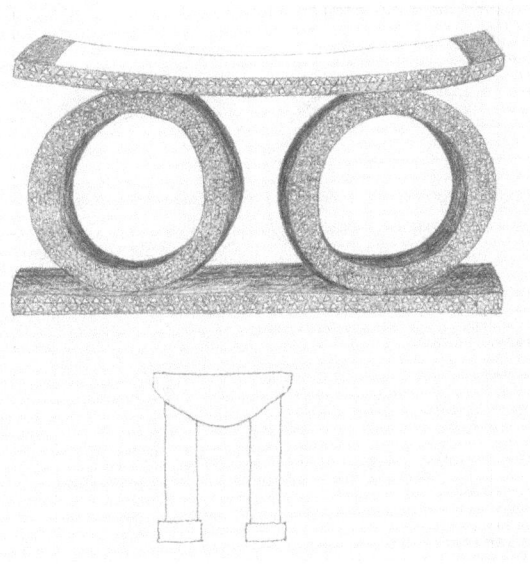

416   Edinburgh, Royal Scottish Museum (no. 1891.2), *South Africa, Natal* (KwaZulu-Natal), *Zulu*, wood, 15 cm h.

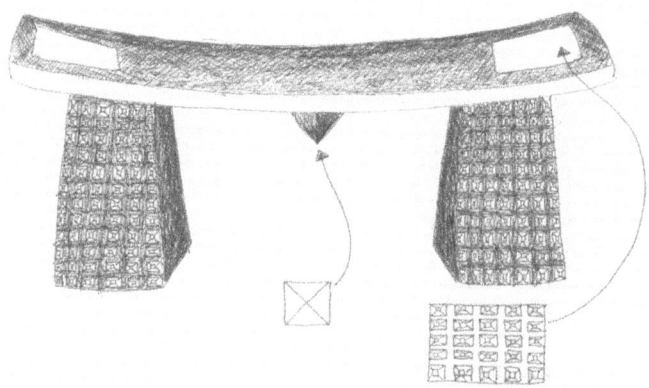

417  Tshwane (Pretoria), National Culture History Museum (no. 68.2), *South Africa, KwaZulu-Natal, Mtunzini, Zulu*, wood, 13 cm h.

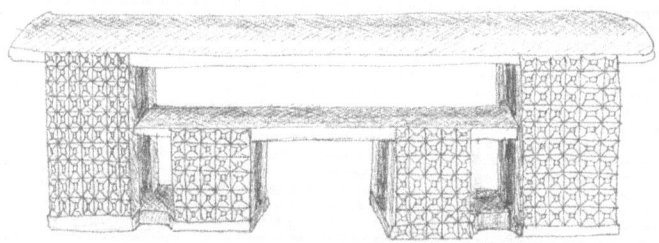

418  University of the Witwatersrand Art Galleries, Standard Bank African Art Collection (no. SBF 83.31.1), *South Africa, KwaZulu-Natal, Zulu (Attributed to Nominwe Dladla, Msinga)*, wood, 12 cm h.

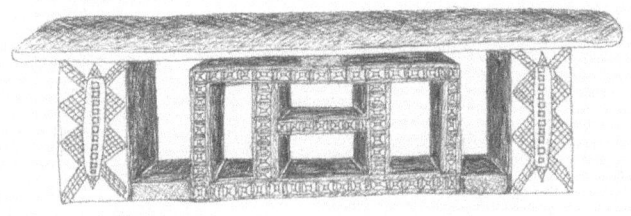

419  University of the Witwatersrand Art Galleries, Standard Bank African Art Collection (no. SBF 92.49.01), *South Africa, KwaZulu-Natal, Zulu*, wood, 13.6 cm h.

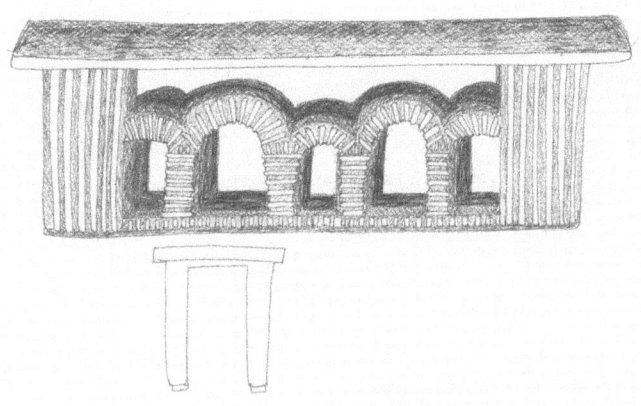

420 University of the Witwatersrand Art Galleries, Standard Bank African Art Collection (no. SBF 83.26.2), South Africa, KwaZulu-Natal, Zulu, wood, 12 cm h.

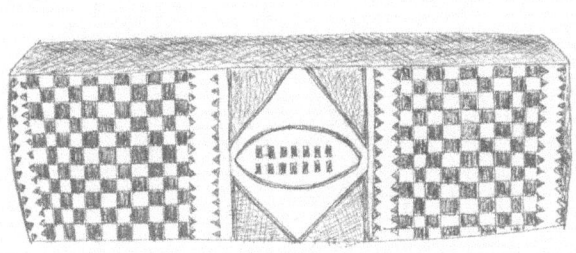

421 Port Elizabeth, private collection of Clive Newmann, King George VI Art Gallery (1999, cat. no. 26), South Africa, KwaZulu-Natal, Msinga (made by Bhajwa Gcwensa of Emgeni, Msinga, but possibly by Mbhekeni Mzolo c 1935. Owned by Makhashe Hadebe of kwNgubukazi, Msinga Top), wood, 14.7 cm h.

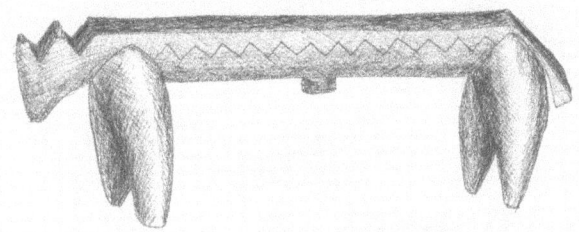

422 Berlin, Museum für Völkerkunde (no. III E 7064), collected by Füüllerborn, 1898, Tanzania, Ngoni, Seat of wood in form of animal. <u>mlongosi ya muischo</u>, wood, 54.3 cm l.

### 336 | AFRICAN DREAM MACHINES

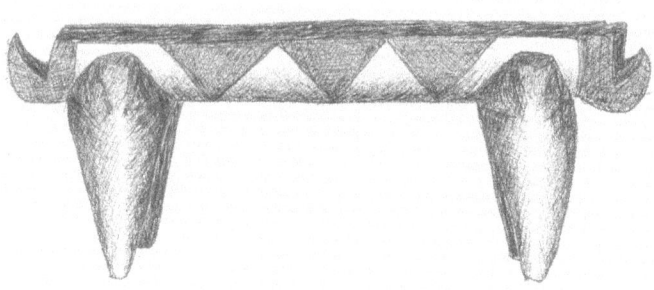

423  Berlin, Museum für Völkerkunde (no. III E 7124), collected by Füllerborn, 1898, *Ganderas Town, Tanzania, Ngoni, Seat of wood*, wood, 43 cm l.

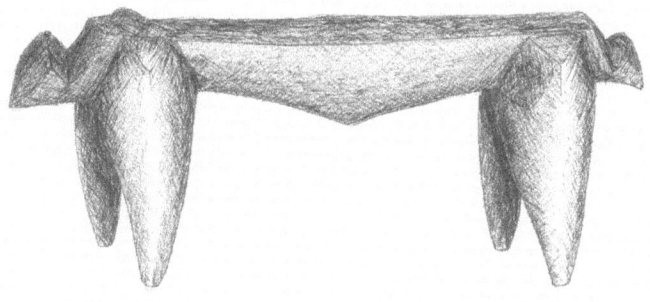

424  Berlin, Museum für Völkerkunde (no. III E 16458), collected by Landemann, 1916, *Tanzania, Ngoni, Headrest of wood laterally stretched with stylised animal heads on the ends*, wood, 54 cm l.

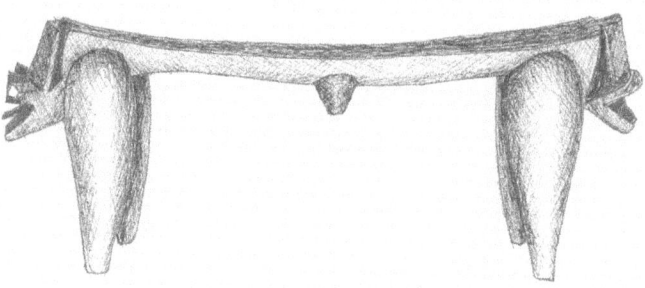

425  Berlin, Museum für Völkerkunde (no. III E 12358), collected by Perrot, 1907, *Tanzania, Ngoni, Headrest from Nyassa*, wood, 55 cm l.

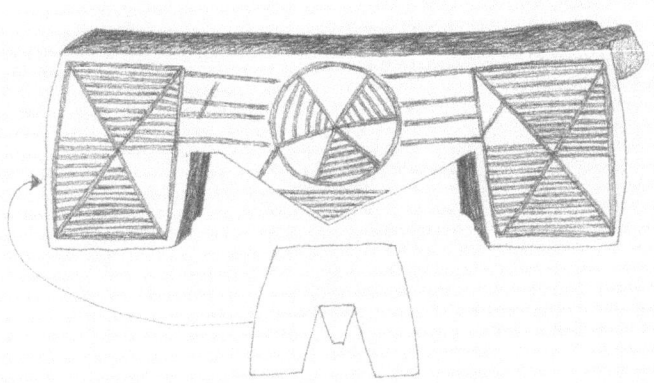

426 Tshwane (Pretoria), National Culture History Museum (no. 37.129), *Transvaal* (Limpopo Province), *Sekhukhuneland, Tau*, wood, 14 cm h.

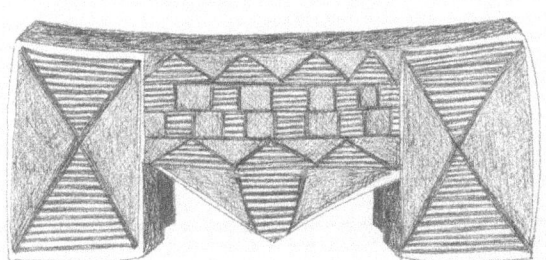

427 Tshwane (Pretoria), National Culture History Museum (no. 37.129), *Transvaal* (Limpopo Province), *North Sotho, Tau*, wood, 15.5 cm h.

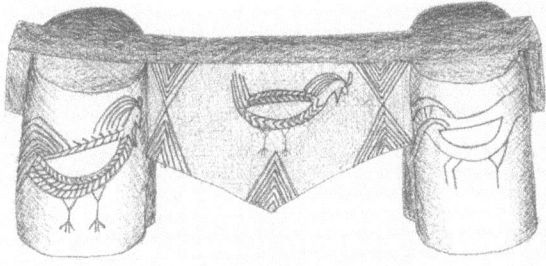

428 University of the Witwatersrand Art Galleries, Museum of Ethnology Collection, South Africa, *Transvaal* (Limpopo Province), *Pedi*, wood, 14 cm h.

## 338 | AFRICAN DREAM MACHINES

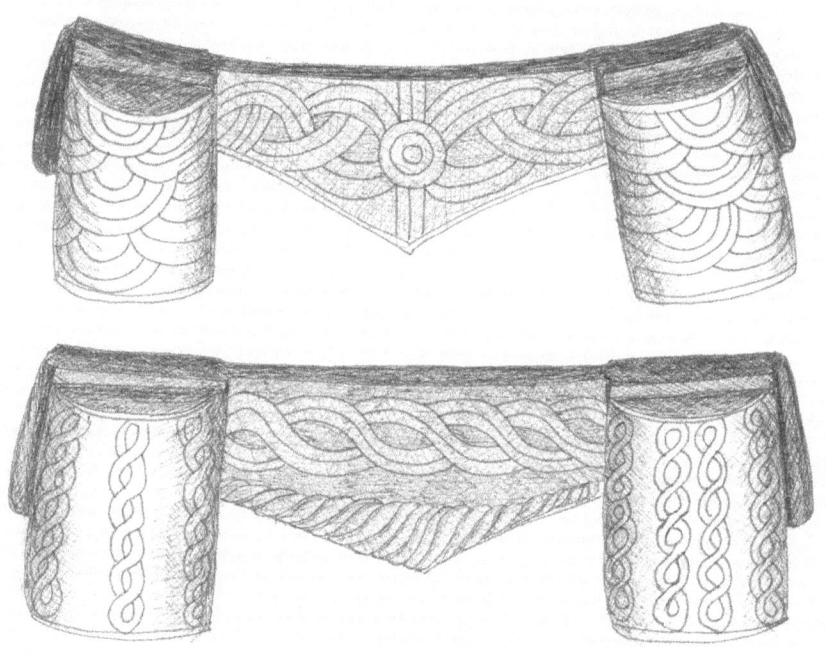

429 Tshwane (Pretoria), National Culture History Museum (no. 8057), *South Africa, Transvaal* (Limpopo Province), *Sekhukhuneland, Pedi*, wood, 38 cm l.

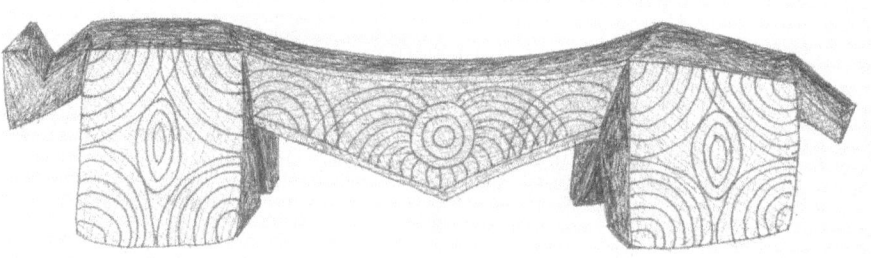

430 Munich, Staatlisches Museum für Völkerkunde (no. 50.11.19), *South Africa, Transvaal* (Limpopo Province), *Sekhukhuneland, Nkoane's Kraal, Pedi*, wood, 13 cm h.

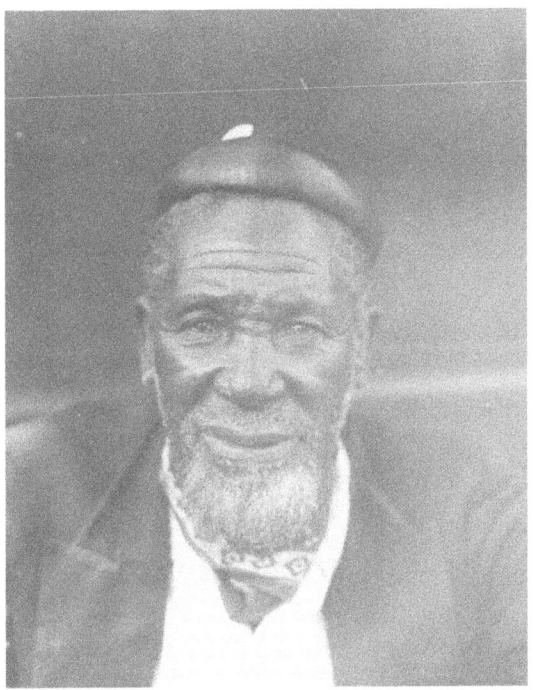

431   University of the Witwatersrand Art Galleries, Museum of Ethnology postcard collection, collected and donated by N. J. van Warmelo, late 1920s/1930s, *Grandson of Gungunyane*, South Africa.

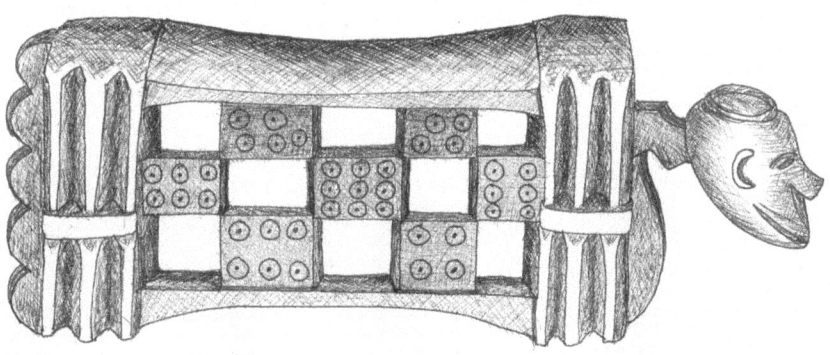

432   Johannesburg Art Gallery (no. 1987.3.8), collected by A. A. Jaques, pre-1929, *South Africa, Transvaal (Limpopo Province), Elim, Swazi*, wood, 13 cm h.

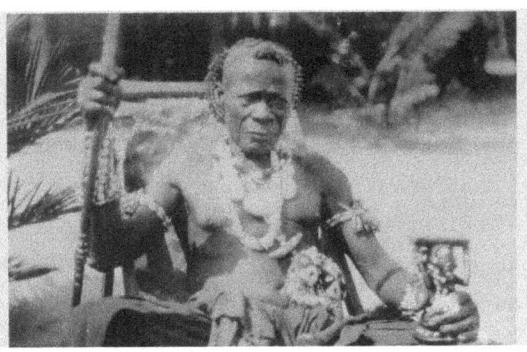

# 8 | Not Just a Curious Beauty: The Anatomy of Meaning in Useful Objects

## FETISHISING HAIR

A PHOTOGRAPH OF Chief Twito Kilukwe[1] (fig. 433) seated in a Western-style chair, dressed in 'traditional' finery, holding a staff in his right hand and a very small, but nevertheless probably functional, headrest in his left hand is an appropriate place to start an examination of discourses about function and meaning in relation to African headrests in particular, and the African or other material culture (including 'art') in general. The photographic portrait was 'taken' by William F. P. Burton, a missionary with the Preston Assemblies of God Church, at Mwanza, in Shaba (now Katanga) Province of what was then the Belgian Congo (now the Democratic Republic of the Congo or DRC) some time in the 1920s, as part of a project to record the customs of the local peoples. Burton's contribution was one among a number of others in which ethnic identities were created around the idea of a number of super-tribes, one of which was the Luba.[2] Many of his photographs are part of what he saw as an effort to record the ways of life of the Luba (Becker 1991), some being formally posed and others apparently less so, allowing the possibility of reading them differently.[3] That this image of Chief Kilukwe was staged in a particularly sympathetic way can therefore be seen as resulting from a negotiation in its construction between the sitter and the photographer.[4] The chief's Western-style chair, his elaborate shell and bead necklaces, beaded hairstyle and beaded tortoise-carapace vessel (balanced on his knee) are all objects that are documented as signs of status within Luba society of the time. But the headrest is not. While stools with female caryatid supports and staffs are fully documented as having been major status insignia within Luba history,[5] there is no record of an equivalent status for headrests, even though they are recorded as having a place in important ritual contexts.[6] Yet Chief Kilukwe had agreed to present himself, at missionary request, to the missionary camera with his beaded tortoise-shell container on his knee and his tiny headrest in his left hand balancing the staff in his right. The head of the sitter is framed by the bun hairstyle, by the white shells around his neck and by the upper reaches of the staff. This composition fits closely with Western notions of how portraits function — they record the idiosyncrasies of individual faces. While, from the Western view, the beads and shells encode both status and ancestral connection, in Luba cosmology it is probable that they reference a named spirit, who stands for a chief or king of the same name.[7] But the inclusion on the periphery of the image, distributed around the person of the sitter, of objects that denote power, status and spiritual presence to an African audience, and exotic otherness to any other audience, destabilises the importance given to the individual, Chief Kilukwe, as subject at its centre.

The headrest in this image is given prominence, yet it is also kept out of reach of the viewer (and by implication, of the grasping colonial power), held firmly, yet almost caressingly, in the resting hand of the man who owns it. In this it can be contrasted with another of William F. P. Burton's photographs of Congolese 'traditional' leaders, Chief Kajingu with his stool (fig. 434). Here, the chief stands with long fold-over voluminous skirt and bare torso, white shell necklace and a beaded cap on his head,[8] fly whisk and spear in his right hand, left hand poised on his hip. His left foot stands on a woven Luba grass mat, rolled out, it seems, specifically for his caryatid stool to stand on. The kneeling man in the background, whose — notably Western-style — clothing provides a light background shade against which to read the dark wood of the stool, does not touch the mat. Neither he nor Chief Kajingu touches the stool. Thus the stool assumes equal status to the standing chief, and both are, by virtue of being simultaneously at front and centre stage, afforded greater importance than the kneeling man in Western clothes. He, despite his evident lesser status, nevertheless holds a rifle decorated with metal tacks of the type so ubiquitously used in decorating headrests. The tacks enhance the prestige of the rifle and, as part of a long-standing trade in metals in the area, denote the status and wealth of its owner (Herbert 1984:160ff.; Kriger 1999). Both Chief Kajingu[9] and Chief Kilukwe have had themselves and their own cultural images of power foregrounded in these photographs, even though the trappings of Western intrusion hover in the props and clothing, and in the very presence of the photographer. Chief Kajingu's stool is an official object; it is framed and untouched by any of the protagonists; it is the proof of his entitlement to office, yet Kajingu does not sit on it, despite the fact that there is evidence that figurative stools were used as seats by Luba kings. Its presence in the photograph indicates the degree to which the historical prohibitions, which kept Luba royal stools hidden away, wrapped in white cloth, in special huts in unnamed villages, had broken down by Burton's time, as he had access to a number of these objects.[10] Yet, while Chief Kilukwe's headrest is his own, his object of desire, his personal and beautiful belonging, and possibly a link to his ancestors, like Chief Kajingu's stool, it is offered to the view of those whom Burton represented, those whose chair has been appropriated for the king to sit on — for the photograph at least — (rather than his stool) as a sign of power.

The headrest in the portrait of Chief Kilukwe, then, is clearly regarded as something special, a belonging, an object of longing, or it probably would not have been placed there. While such figural caryatid headrests were, like the stools with figure caryatids, not the absolute preserve of Luba chiefs and kings, they were also not ordinary. This one is apparently (unfortunately, we can only access it through the portrait photograph) carved with great finesse: the kneeling caryatid, who bends her arms to hold up the platform in the effortless and thus power-laden manner common to most Luba female caryatid figures, is decorated with beads, and has a surface patinated from careful and fond handling, indicating her elevated value. In this context, a third photograph by Burton of Chief Kilukwe takes on some importance (fig. 435). For here, Kilukwe is in a quite different *habitus*, one in which his power is recognised by his dress and being, not by trappings and European portrait conventions. Seated cross-legged on a grass mat locally woven from indigenous fibres, against a background of palm leaves and an entourage of young boys, the chief is engaged in carving a headrest with a female caryatid. While it is possible that Burton asked Chief Kilukwe to let him photograph the process of carving a stool, it is clear that this photograph is differently choreographed from the more formal picture of the king on a Western-style chair with his regalia. Here the chief looks almost as though he had been caught 'unawares', in an unstaged moment, and his facial expression speaks volumes about this invasion of his space, as does his entire pose about his sense of dignity. Burton (1961) reports on the high regard in which carvers were held among the Luba, and that kings were sometimes carvers. But, while headrests made by chiefs would, presumably, have also had seriously enhanced value, it is significant that, in the formal, posed portrait, where he had the power to decide what to include (fig. 433), Kilukwe chose to have himself portrayed as the owner, rather than as the maker of a headrest.

While it is probable that the headrest in this image was used to pillow Kilukwe's head, his hairstyle would have required some such support, it remains difficult to imagine. The difficulty arises in this particular case from the delicateness of the headrest in the image, but more generally it may be ascribed to the lack of match between the standards of comfort set by the Western notion of a pillow, on the one hand, and the difficulty Westerners have in imagining wooden (or ceramic) headrests being put to use at all, and the resulting disbelief led to many different photographs being taken of African people sleeping on headrests as though to prove the point.

Maes (1929) opens his discussion of the headrests of the Belgian Congo (now the DRC) with a photograph of a person 'sleeping' (eyes open) on a headrest, and, on page 9, an image of a Ngombe corpse, supine, with its head supported by a headrest. His is the first instance in the history of writing on African headrests to use photographs as images that would explain *how* such objects were used, a tradition still followed by Dewey in 1993, and premised on Western lack of familiarity with such usage. This search to familiarise the unfamiliar is evident in much of the literature on African cultures published in the twentieth century, and particularly in popular literature.

Joy Adamson, a white English colonial in Kenya, who made her name with the book *Born Free: A Lioness of Two Worlds* (1961), published in 1967 a very ambitious, but also rather strange book, *The Peoples of Kenya*. The premise of this book is entirely presaged in the earlier one, which opposed 'two worlds' in Kenya — the wild and free versus the controlled and modern. Adamson sought to record the customs of the various different ethnic groups in Kenya, and like many other Westerners before and after her, she was fascinated by people's hairstyles and therefore by their provisions for maintaining these hairstyles through the use of wooden pillows. Her photograph of a Pokot man using his headrest is instructive in the difference of attitude it betrays towards the headrest from that manifested by Chief Kilukwe and Burton in constructing the portrait of Kilukwe. In this photograph (Adamson 1967:87), the man, who is the object being photographed, and thus the subject of the image, lies supine on the ground, his head balanced at about a 20 degree angle to his body, looking strangely similar to Maes's Ngombe corpse. The headrest is barely visible, as it is tucked away under the head of the user and hidden by his elaborate mud-pack hairstyle, and the man is also barely visible, because the profile view of a person lying supine on the ground does not allow the body much volume, and his physical presence is thus completely diminished. So the slightly raised head takes on a renewed importance, as it defines the person as living, and as it defines him as completely 'other' from the European behind the lens and outside the frame. In recording customary usages, it disregards the unpromising nature of the subject's almost complete lack of physical presence within a flat, expansive African landscape. Yet it parallels the exotic intent of images made/taken by curious Westerners of fully three-dimensionally and vertically present Africans with extraordinary hairstyles, especially from East and Central Africa, and, in perhaps less-well-known examples, from Southern Africa (Bryant 1929) that proliferated in the mid-to-late nineteenth and early twentieth centuries.

These include images of Kenyans and Ugandans taken by Sir Harry Johnston and Major Powell-Cotton in the late nineteenth and early twentieth centuries. One of Johnston's (1902, fig. 469) photographs has been used in a recent display (2005) in the Sainsbury Galleries of the British Museum to accompany a Suk headdress of mud and hair, which floated like some alien object in a vast glass display case above and in front of the image. That such objects were cut off the heads of their owners under some form of powerful persuasion is not often mentioned, however. Powell-Cotton describes the stratagems he had to use to get a Karamojong man to part with his hairstyle, an object that is also on display, but in the Powell-Cotton Museum in Birchington on Sea:

> It was from one of these men that I managed to buy a big chignon. From the time of my arrival at Anamuget, I had been constantly approaching one or the other of the elders ... [finally he] found an old fellow who was less disinclined ... [eventually] the promise of one of our oldest sheep and a long bit of iron chain won me the day (Powell-Cotton 1904:320).

That the major pursued this quest in the face of his knowledge that such hairstyles were built up by the addition of hair from deceased grandfathers and fathers among both Pokot (fig. 436) and Karamojong, where men end up carrying the physical relics of ancestors' bodies around with them like antennae, an idea similar to the Rastafarian belief that their dreadlocks 'communicate' with Yah (Jah), is an index of the degree to which his fascination became an obsession. Further, that this fascination remains today is evident from the incongruity of displaying people's hairstyles in museums, and this is increased in the small sea-side town of Birchington on Sea,[11] where the Powell-Cotton Museum, stuffed with taxidermied animals, small dioramas and display cabinets brimming with other peoples' goods, and cupboards below these with even more, has on prominent display items made of people's hair, or to cover people's hair, or to prevent people's hair from becoming disarranged.

To suggest that Western fascination with hairstyles in African colonies reached the level of a kind of fetishism is, from the evidence in the historical record, not to overstate the case. Leach (1958) discusses the ways in which hair becomes magical and sacred in human societies, including those of Europe and the supposed 'civilised' world. By the end of the nineteenth century in Europe, polite society required that men's hair be kept short, their beards trimmed and their moustaches neat and tidy. Their hair was to be parted, usually in the centre (Corson 1965:420), and where it was allowed to grow long, or if it were too curly or unruly, it was licked into place with Macassar oil. Forgotten were the long locks of the eighteenth century, the pomaded and powdered wigs (Corson 1965, pls. 67–77), and the artifice of wilder, but jaw-length styles of the early nineteenth century (Corson

1965, pls. 93–98), often accompanied by hirsute chins and upper lips. Nineteenth century European women's hair was also expected to be kept tidy: while it was allowed, or even required, to be long, it had to be tied back, or among the upper classes, piled up in curls or elaborate chignons and decorated with flowers for important social occasions. Only young unmarried women and girls were allowed the freedom of loose hair (Corson 1965, pls. 136–139). Dishevelled hair was only acceptable where it was artfully induced, otherwise the image of the woman with dishevelled hair was associated with wildness, and probably with loose morals as well.[12] Once again the seventeenth to eighteenth century history of women's enormous chignons, built over wire frames or later over woollen wadding, with additions of real hair from other heads, which were a serious health risk (Corson 1965:337–38), was also assigned to a forgotten past.

But the fetishisation of hair as a sign of civilisation and good health is still common: it is most visible in the armed forces of most nations and in conventional Christian-dominated state schools, where any deviation from the accepted norms has to be defended in terms of ethnic tradition, or where allowances are made for women, but not for men. In fundamentalist Christian, Muslim and Jewish communities,[13] hair on women's heads is hidden, partially or completely, from public view and visible long hair is confined to male followers of the mystic traditions, and to ultra-orthodoxies. It is therefore not difficult to imagine the fascination that people brought up in regimes in which control of hair through regular grooming, washing, cutting and shaving was equated with godliness and moral fortitude would have felt when they saw hairstyles that were no less, but, in fact, many times more constructed and controlled. But these coiffures expanded the head and sculpted its volume in a semi-permanent form, and were therefore measured against the control of the short or long and tied back, as an image of complete otherness. The fascination is mild in Bent's account of the Shona, referred to in chapter 1; it grows by leaps and bounds over the next decade, especially as photography offers an increasingly swift and convenient means of recording this phenomenon. The fetishisation of African hairstyles could thus be seen to fulfil a lack in the Western imagination of how bodies can be differentiated; and so hair became racialised, not only because of a supposed difference in physical structure between 'black' and 'white' hair, but also because to a Western Victorian and early twentieth century mindset according to which these creations of sculptural forms, using a material that itself was considered suspect, were unhygienic.[14] In some senses, these hairstyles were likely, as much as body modifications, to render Africans liable to be labelled as 'freaks', the most extreme form of othering next to the monstrous. As Garland-Thomson (1996:1) says of the 'unexpected body': '[it] fires rich, if anxious narratives and practices that probe the contours and boundaries of what we take to be human.' The fetishisation of difference through hair was to inspire one of the more bizarre of all attempts to 'civilise' the natives' bodies according to Western Christian norms, and in the face of the fact of blackness — Fanon's 'epidermal schema'[15] — as the bodily inscription of difference, from which it is impossible to escape.

Photographs of Africans by explorers and missionaries in the late nineteenth and early twentieth centuries, all of which concentrate on representations of otherness and hybridity, tend to fall into two fairly neat categories. In one group are those images of Africans classed as heathen natives, pagans in varying stages of dress/undress and with varying elaboration of hairstyling, scarification or body painting, evident after 1900 in images scattered throughout the magazines produced by mission societies for their publics back 'home'. For example, in the April 1909 issue of *The Herald of the Primitive Missionary Society*, a profile photograph of a (very beautiful) 'Girl of the Nsit Country', showing a woman fully clothed in a Western-style dress, but with a comb-like hairstyle from forehead to the nape of the neck, is accompanied by this short text: 'Heathenism in its most repulsive forms .... It is on the womanhood of Africa that heathenism presses most heavily' (*Herald of the Primitive Missionary Society* 1909:61).[16]

This kind of photograph, concentrating on 'primitive customs', with people in both indigenous and Western-style dress, is more common in archives of explorers such as Torday, who, in one notable image made a Dumba[17] woman bend her head forward so that the arrangement of the hair across the crown is displayed to view.[18]

In the other group there are the more common missionaries' images of Africans who have been brought to supposed 'civilisation', in the guise of Christian-mission converts, their bodies clothed in their Western-style, white Sunday best. The latter images are those that dominate the pages of the missionary societies' magazines from the late 1890s onwards, as photographic illustrations become more common. In these, men and women are not inevitably in Western dress, but they are almost all transformed through their hair, on which a brave attempt had been made, with varying degrees of success, through cutting and styling, and possibly some pomading, to impose a parting or path. One of the more extraordinary of these, an image of a convert to Christianity called only Dado, who moved from East Africa to Oxford (where he died), the subject is shown dressed in a suit, starched white shirt and with his hair cut and parted, and thus tightly controlled. His photograph appeared in a regular column of *The Missionary Echo* by Rev. Robert Brewin (1910), called 'The boys of East Africa', which was apparently aimed at the youth in England. It is one of many images intended to show 'progress' in religious colonisation through the ways in which African bodies were brought into the ambit of Western Christian norms.

Interestingly, however, as the twentieth century progressed and Western colonialists became aware of how their impositions of norms for the body were transforming the human landscapes of Africa, many missionaries, including William Burton, Carlos Esterman, Herman Tönjes, Alexandre Jaques[19] and others, became, like contemporary ethnographers, recorders of those supposedly 'vanishing' pure and authentic — although nevertheless heathen and uncivilised — practices, and this trope still informed the ethnographic photography of Leni Riefenstahl (1976a; 1976b), Gert Chesi (1980) and Angela Fisher (1984). The missionaries, the ethnographers and the colonial civilisers, including the great corporations that moved into the continent in search of money and resources while claiming to be bringing 'progress', used their images as the 'before' part in their 'before-and-after' publicity for the claimed advantages of Western cultural norms (Geary 1991), and they all follow the same fascination with the taboos of hair and other bodily matter that informs all responses to questions of grooming and hygiene. The success of their endeavour is reflected in the fact that in the earlier part of the liberation struggle, members of the African intelligentsia and political avant-garde such as Kwame Nkrumah and Nelson Mandela not only wore Western-style suits; they also parted their hair in the Western style. In the only photograph of Mandela after his arrest and prior to his sentencing in the infamous treason trial of 1962, taken by Eli Weinberg, where he wore a cloth around his body in a rejection of the Western suit, his hair is nevertheless neatly parted (Bedford 1993:56). That dress and hair have become so intricately woven into identity politics is in part a result of the 'civilising' mission, yet it seems that African dress is more likely to be promoted in establishment circles than are African coiffures.

As one can see from indigenous forms of coiffure, many styles have been possible in African hairstyling, but the parting, with hair neatly arranged to either side, has a particularly demure and non-African flavour. It is the correct, the neat, the appropriate companion to the forms of clothing favoured by the colonisers of the faith, customs and bodies of African peoples. It contrasts completely with, for example, hairstyles in Bryant's (1929) images of Zulu men of the nineteenth century, in Torday's (Mack 1990) images of

Congolese peoples, in Johnston's (1902) images of Suk men in Uganda and in Powell-Cotton's (1904) images of various different Kenyan peoples. The continuation of such hairdressing practices into the twentieth century is evident from photographs taken by numerous photographers from Torday (Mack 1990) and Lang (Schildkrout & Keim 1990) to art historians such as Herbert Cole[20] and those attached to publications such as *Libertas* (1944a:41, 32; 1944b:28, 29), and studio photographers such as Gatti (1939: 154), whose images appear to be aimed particularly at the tourist market. In all of these images, the African hairstyles represented are constructed so that they are controlled, but not flat, sometimes symmetrical, but always sculptural, enhancing stature and reinforcing in-group status and identity. They are also made to be neat, for, as a number of commentators have pointed out, in African societies as much as in others, unkempt, untidy hair is a sign of mental or moral disorder, of a position on the periphery of ordered society.[21]

The sculptures of human figures such as those of the Hemba, Boyo, Bembe, Luba, Tabwa, Pende, Yaka and Suku, for example, are generally endowed with elaborate coiffures to indicate their beauty and status.[22] But they present idealised images, or visualised ideals, which are involved in a never-ending circle of information and invention, where sculptures suggest possibilities as much as they record practices.[23] Elaborate African hairstyles represented a considerable investment of time and resources on the part of the wearer of the coiffure and its maker. It is unlikely that the complex African coiffures captured on film were made by the wearers themselves. This is certainly the case with many of the hairstyles discussed in Sieber and Herremann's (2000) edited volume on African hairstyling, and is evident from Burton's notes on, and photographs of, Luba hairstyling processes in the region of Mwanza mission in the 1920s and 1930s (figs. 437 & 438), where he remarks on the length of time involved in making such forms.[24] Burton records the hairstyles of different people with some detail, allowing for an analysis not only of ethnic styles, but also of styles associated with people of different age groups. Luba women are on record as having travelled inordinately long distances to view the hairstyles on chiefs' stools (Burton 1961:24), but there are also clear indications that inventiveness was valued in creating new styles. That both the photographs and the sculptures skew the record is, however, probable, for, from both the Burton and the Torday image archives, it appears that elaborate hairstyles were, at least by the early twentieth century, largely a pursuit of the younger adults and required an investment of time and resources possibly not available to all.

Esterman (1970) claims that, among the Wila of Angola, hairstyling is considered an art, and that one becomes a hair artist by divine calling. Many of these hairstyles involve the extension of the natural hair through the addition of other materials and the weaving or braiding of hair over basketry frames, and require elaborate designing around multiple partings and built-up crests, or the building of volumes of hair through the addition of mud. Torday's photographs of Pende, Dumba and Mbala men and women, and some Kuba men, especially of the Bushong aristocracy, record a wide cross-section of such hair sculptures within the south-western DRC,[25] all made by hair sculpture specialists. Powell-Cotton (1904:393) photographed men of the Dodinga hills in Kenya (fig. 440) to illustrate their hairstyles, which he describes as being constituted of

> hair daubed with clay into a matted mass and brought down all round like a pudding bowl and only attached by the crown ... the chief men had the whole surface covered with discs of leather — 1–2 inches in diameter — on which were sewn white and red beads in a spiral pattern (Powell-Cotton 1904:397–98).

It appears that Pokot, Karamojong and Turkana men also had help in putting together their ancestral hairstyles, although these all appear to have followed exactly the same templates: young men with small mud-packs; older men with added ancestral hair. This suggests that they represent a greater degree of both prescriptive normalcy and proscriptive avoidance than those of other groups, and they therefore raise notions of the sacred and questions of pollution more fully than those hairstyles that are less ancestrally linked.[26]

Hair has been discussed by many anthropologists since Leach's famous essay (Leach 1958), which looked at the ways in which hair has been treated as an extraordinary substance in human cultures. One of the more useful ways of understanding the significance of hair is through Douglas' notion of the body as a bounded system, which acts as a metaphor for other bounded systems, including social ones (Douglas 1966). As a bounded system, the body contains matter, so exuviae from the body come to be regarded as 'matter out of place', forms of pollution, both physical and metaphorical, as Douglas demonstrates in her analysis of menstruation taboos. Hair has a particular place in this bounded system, one that it shares with nails: both grow from under the skin, and both continue to grow throughout a person's lifetime, and so, like the horns of antelope or cattle, the tusks of elephant or warthogs, the claws of feline predators or the talons of birds of prey, they are considered, in many African societies (and elsewhere), to be particularly potent. In Akan society, the hair and nails of deceased members of the lineage are collected and stored in a special jar, and hair and nails of persons may be collected by sorcerers intent on doing harm to their victims (Cole & Ross 1977:120). But hair and nails still attached to the body are part of the living body: they are the ultimate forms of ambivalent physical presence, marking the boundary and yet transgressing it, and in virtually all human societies have become substances that act as a means of demonstrating control of the body. So hair and nails can be sculpted, coloured, grown long or cut short; but, because hair can be shaved off and plucked out without doing grievous bodily harm, it is more useful for thinking about pollution and control than nails, or even teeth, which are sometimes filed or chipped in particular ways. Hair also marks the head, framing the face, which is the prime marker of individual identity, and covering the crown of the head, which is associated with the ancestral soul of the individual in many African societies.[27] The continuation of sculptural hairstyling well into the twentieth century in rural Africa also signalled the continued need for forms of support for the heads to which the hairstyles were attached, and thus the production of headrests survived in many parts of Africa until very recent times.[28]

The fascination with forms of African hairstyling on the part of Western missionaries, explorers and ethnographers outlined above extended to the headrest itself, and the collected headrests in Western museums dealt with in this study are a result of this synecdochic transferral. The headrest in this discourse becomes a trope for all the other aspects of heads and hair within Western collections: because the headrest is itself not self-explanatory of its function beyond its African context, it is always explained in terms of its physical function as a support for the head, as a piece of furniture or, possibly, as an adornment of the body. But the headrest in many African societies goes far beyond such utilitarian understandings of function and significance.

## FIGURES SUPPORTING HEADRESTS

In the simplest terms, headrests perform as substitute bodies, raising heads of sleeping persons above the ground or floor or sleeping mat, and anything from a simple log, to a branch headrest, to a headrest with an elaborately carved figure as its support could fulfil this function. It is certainly the case that many of the headrests used in Africa were of the simplest variety with little or no transformation of the material, found form. But as the examples illustrated in this volume attest, many headrests were visually and conceptually complex, encompassing notions of support and thus references to the body in more or less overt ways. Headrests with human figures carved on the support are the most literal and obvious examples, and the majority of these are from the Central African region. To understand their significance at more than the most superficial level, one would have to understand them in the context of figure carving within each ethnic group, and, as this is clearly beyond the scope of this study, I have taken only selected examples as significant within my examination of headrests as performative objects.

It is useful here to return the headrest in Chief Kilukwe's portrait (fig. 433) in particular. The figure here follows the prescribed pattern for single caryatids in Luba stools and headrests: arms raised to hold the platform and legs bent to either side of the body as it kneel-sits on the base, although paired figures assume both standing and seated positions.[29] The hairstyle, not entirely visible from the photograph, nevertheless appears to be very elaborate, with a significant extension of the bun at the back of the head. This emphasis on the hairstyle in Luba carvings of human forms is comparable to the sculpted hairstyles actually created on the heads of younger members of Luba society and recorded by W. F. P. Burton in the Mwanza region in the 1930s (figs. 439, 441 & 442). The correspondence is most clearly visible in the so-called Shankadi-style headrests (fig. 443) published by numerous authors, and attributed to either workshops or individual sculptors,[30] but it is also visible in more naturalistically carved examples such as those illustrated by Krieger (1978) and one photographed by Burton in Mwanza (fig. 444).[31]

The Luba[32] caryatid headrests, however, represent only one, albeit the most numerous, the most varied, the most commonly illustrated, and therefore the only well known, of many variants on this structural theme, made by carvers of headrests in the Sankuru basin.[33] On a very particular scale, the styles of carving of human caryatid figures may be constructed as distinctive elements that allow for an attribution of authorship to smaller groups within larger ethnic boundaries, simply because they enable a close comparison with free-standing figural sculpture from the same groups, although examples of such free-standing sculptures from Luba areas are not as numerous as those from other groups (cf. Neyt 1994; Roberts & Roberts 1996). But these searches only ever take place within a narrow range of 'masterworks' that have found homes in European museums and private collections, and whose pedigrees are often founded on the names of their 'original' *European* owners such as Charles Ratton and Helena Rubenstein.[34] Examples from a number of different sources, and well represented, although in a scattered fashion, in the literature on African art, indicate the range of sculptural styles and iconographic variations possible in these headrest with human caryatid sculptures across the southern DRC, from the Yaka[35] and Pende in the west, through the Mbala, Kuba and Lulua to the Songye, Luba, Tabwa, Hemba and related peoples in the east. The kneeling female caryatid is most predominant in headrests provenanced to Luba origins, and is found relatively frequently on Kanyok and Yaka examples, but is rare among headrests from peoples such as the Lulua,[36] whom Vansina suggests were a nineteenth century offshoot of the Luba within Kasai (Vansina 1966:161–62) and the Songye, northern neighbours of the Luba.

The same configuration of base and platform as that of columned headrests (discussed in chapter 3) is, however, found in most of these caryatid headrests, regardless of their ethnic origin, with the figures taking the place of the column. Lulua caryatids are often distinguished by the extreme complexity of their scarification patterns,[37] but, like those of the Songye, Mbala and Kanyok, they stand with their hands on their stomachs, their bodies being the vertical substitutes for the column. In many of these carved figure supports,[38] the feet are enlarged so as to cover almost the whole of the upper surface of the base, and the platform is supported directly on the head (in some there is an intervening column). In some, the figure's hands rest on the stomach; in others, the arms are bent so that the hands grasp the ends of the platform.[39] Yet the figure carvings are distinguishable in terms of ethnic styles. Most Songye caryatid headrests display a very particular, and somewhat softened version of the Songye angular figural style (figs. 445 & 446). The provenancing of two examples (Maes 1929, pl. VII, figs. 10, 11) within the Lusambo district might suggest that they, and thus the style, represent a particular regional interpretation of a common form, one apparently shared by Nsapo[40] groups (Dewey 1993: 65), around Luebo. While most Luba caryatids are gendered as female, most of the other ethnic groups' headrests include both male and female figures. Yet gendered identity is not always clear. All the Songye examples discussed have reduced physical gender markers, so that it is the absence of breasts rather than male genitals in some examples that suggests a male rather than a female identity.

By contrast to the human caryatid forms, examples of headrests with animal caryatids are more difficult to assign to ethnic groups on the basis of the figural carving style alone, or on the basis of the animal species used as caryatids. Most are attributable to Central and Southern African peoples. Some omit the base and have a column above the back supporting a platform with decorated ends (figs. 447–450). In these examples, the style of carving of the figures is so ubiquitously similar that the shape of the column and the platform, and the base where there is one, is more likely to point to an identifiable provenance on a general level.[41] For example, Maes (1929, pl. VI, fig. 11) published an animal headrest of this type, attributing it to the Kioko of upper Kasai, an attribution given also to a similar headrest in the same plate (Maes 1929, pl. VI, fig. 15). Superficially, the carving of these animal caryatids may appear similar, partly because most appear to represent bovines or antelopes, but the differences in the columns and platforms separate them clearly, one (Maes 1929, pl. VI, fig. 11) being of the type made in the Kasai–Sankuru–Shaba region, and the other (Maes 1929, pl. VI, fig. 15) belonging in the Shona–Tsonga complex of south-east Africa.

The example in figure 447, acquired by the Berlin Museum für Völkerkunde from Leo Frobenius in 1916 and firmly provenanced to Katanga, follows the same figural carving style for the horned quadruped, but has a cotton-reel-shaped column and butterfly platform, both of which correspond closely to non-figurative headrests collected in the same region, but not exclusively among Luba speakers. Another example, in the Museum Rietberg in Zurich, has a round base supporting a buffalo figure with a column very similar to the abstract examples attributed to the Luba, Songye and Lulua peoples.[42] Stolid and straight-legged bovines also grace examples from the Southern African region, provenanced or attributed to the Shona and Tsonga peoples, with few elements allowing for definitive separation of these two ethnic styles (figs. 448–450), although most carry the platform on multiple columns, as opposed to the single columns of most DRC examples. Once again, a significant number of these Southern African examples appear to have been made for sale directly to Western patrons in the late nineteenth and early twentieth centuries.[43] These animals contrast strongly with the bent-legged and thus more animated animals of a greater variety of species that support, often without an intervening column, the platforms of headrests attributed to Cokwe, Lunda, Yaka and Teke carvers (figs. 450–452), but which are seldom represented in the literature on these peoples. The animal species represented in the Luba, Shona and Tsonga examples are mostly bovine (i.e. buffalo, for the Luba, who live in a tsetse-fly area, and whose cultural hero, Mbidi Kiluwe, is 'very handsome with a skin as black as the majestic buffalo' [M. N.

Roberts 2000:66]) or antelope, which stand as metaphorical signs for diviners (M. N. Roberts 2000). For the southern groups, they are more likely cattle, goats or antelope (figs. 447–449). The Cokwe, Pende and Yaka examples include canines (figs. 450 & 451) and pigs (fig. 452), as well as birds.[44]

A few examples of headrests with unambiguously carved animal figures as supports have been attributed to the Zulu,[45] and some also to the Ngoni, but these are all examples that appear to have been made for colonial patrons, and the Zulu ones are all from collections that were put together in Europe and North America from objects taken there by missionaries, or for the great exhibitions of the nineteenth century.[46] They all appear to be associated with materials and the styles prominent in goods exported from what was then Natal to the international exhibitions discussed in the previous chapter. There are, however, many examples of Zulu, North Sotho, Swazi and Ngoni headrests where animal imagery is present, but not overtly, as in a direct representation of a bovine.

And it is here that a discussion of meanings and functions of headrests, embedded in forms and in iconographic details, becomes interesting. In all instances, the figures appear to add something to the headrest: in Western terms, headrests with such figures are more likely to make their way into art exhibitions, or into the pages of the glossy catalogues that accompany such exhibitions; and in African terms, it is probable that such headrests acquired a greater prestige and value within certain groups, and thus demonstrated the prestige of their owners, as appears to be the case with the headrest belonging to Chief Kilukwe (fig. 433), discussed above. But it is also possible that figuratively carved supports on headrests are extensions of an iconography of bodies already embedded within the headrests, both in their functions — whether physically supporting the head, or being used as symbols of status or indices of identity — and in their decorative and structural elements. It is this aspect of headrest iconography that I wish to pursue further.

## HEADRESTS AS PERFORMANCE PIECES

Because headrests are objects ostensibly made primarily for use as a support for the head, it could be suggested that their aesthetic dimensions are additions that happen over and above their utilitarian function, a view apparently shared by the Pokot.[47] But that headrests did not function only as supports for the heads of their sleeping owners is attested in numerous documents recording other uses to which they were put. From simply lying around the homestead; to being carried over long distances, attached to their owners in one or other manner, most often by the wrist, sometimes from the waist, attached to, or carved with staffs, or on top of bundles on the head; being placed as a signal outside the house of the wife chosen for a night's cohabitation; being used in various divination procedures or ancestral veneration; or being presented to the colonial gaze as signs of power, headrests carried with them sets of messages easily read by members of the community from which they came, but which are lost in their transformation into art objects via the conduit of the West's fascination with and fetishisation of the 'other'. Far from being merely synecdochic of peoples' hairdressing practices and sleeping routines, these objects are performance pieces whose actors have left the scene and their incarceration in museums has turned them into the atrophied props of ethnological display. The ways in which these objects were used ensured that they derived more than metaphorical potency from the bodies of their users, and it is therefore important to develop an understanding of their performative and aesthetic significance.

In its use as a pillow, the headrest was placed under the head of the reclining person at the base of his/her head, where it joins the neck at the back if lying supine, or behind the jaw if lying on his/her side. It raised the head off the ground, but was in many cases thus rendered virtually invisible to a spectator, even though it distinguished the sleeping living body from a dead body. The headrest supported the live body for the duration of a person's sleep, and absorbed sweat, hair and bits of skin from the person's body, becoming a physical extension of that body even when not in use. Gell has proposed that all art objects will be understood better if they are understood as possessing forms of agency and, further, that this understanding arises from the same 'fund of sympathy which allows us to understand the non-human, non artefactual "other" as a copresent being' (Gell 1998:96). Once the being-ness of the object is established (via Taussig's (1993) argument that the magic of similarity and the magic of contact are related, because both premise access to bodies, either by images or by exuviae), Gell suggests that objects can be argued to be parts of distributed bodies — bodies that are themselves fractal. While Gell (1998:131ff.) uses this argument to understand the proliferation of image idols, I think it can be turned to understand aspects of the headrest as an extension of the individual: a detached and thus distributable part of a body — a body that is fractal because it extends its essence to those things with which it makes contact. Gell (1998:104) argues that exuviae are not merely metonymical signs for the body of a person, but are parts of a body distributed across spaces and — I would suggest — time. The headrest, like the seat of an adult Akan person, is an object that is literally impregnated with the exuviae of its owner, with sweat, hair grease and skin fragments. Some are used as carriers for grease that can be applied to the skin, in a circle of embrocation from one body to another.[48] And, like the Akan seat, in many instances a headrest may come to stand for its owner's body, being buried in the place of the body that is absent, or being passed down from one generation to another as an ancestral relic, something recorded among African peoples such as the Swazi (Marwick 1940), the Shona (Dewey 1993) and the Tsonga (Becker 1992). The Dogon/Tellem headrests found in burial caves in the Bandiagara cliffs (figs. 4–26), and the ceramic headrests (fig. 134) recovered from an archaeological site of the Kisalian period and a burial site in the Sanga region of Katanga, in the Luba heartland, speak to a long-standing use of the headrest as a substitute body after death. Headrests were present in the burials of Ancient Egypt, and according to Maes (1929), the headrest of the deceased was specifically used by the Ngombe of Ubangi when they laid out the corpse of the deceased for burial. The headrest thus ensures both the containment and control of that — potentially pollutant — distributed body of its first owner/user, on the one hand, and its — still controlled — distribution across time and space in the hands of the person's descendants, on the other.

Distribution across time and space of such potentially powerful extensions of the body, however, is not confined to the headrest: it is physically manifest in the practice of including ancestors' hair in the coiffures of the living among the Pokot and some related East African peoples. This can be seen as a physical manifestation of what Gell, citing Wagner, argues to be a form of genealogical enchainment:

> Any individual person is a 'multiple' in sense of being the precipitate of a multitude of genealogical relationships, each of which is instantiated in his person; and conversely, an aggregate of persons such as a lineage or tribe is one person in consequence of being one genealogy — the original ancestor is now instantiated, not as one body, but as many bodies into which his one body has transformed (Gell 1998:140).

The huge chignons acquired by some Pokot men meant that they were carrying the weight of several generations of genealogical relations on their heads, and that their headrests were used to support this very genealogical chain. Even those men who were too young to have attained the position of bearers of the chain of relations in their hair nevertheless carried in their own mud-pack hairstyles the potential for further extensions of the genealogical chain, and they used headrests to allow them to achieve the greatest extension they could. The physicality of this enchainment in the Pokot case throws into clearer relief the extraordinary impact that the giving over of an entire hairstyle by one Pokot individual to Major Powell-Cotton could have had on social and genealogical relations within the group. But one could argue that the removal of headrests from their original settings would have been equally disruptive — Jean Brown appears to have acquired an inordinately large number of headrests among the Tiati Pokot in the mid 1970s, possibly in a period in which forms of genealogical enchainment had altered significantly within the Kenyan cultural landscape of the time.

But physical embrocation of the individual onto his/her headrest is not necessarily linked to the presence of an elaborate coiffure, for the headrest keeps the entire head off the ground, and in a mundane sense kept it clean. The headrest nevertheless allowed the head to maintain a direct link to the ground on which it stood. This linkage to the ground may be important in societies where ancestors are bound to the land, to the ground that the living occupy and the lands they cultivate or where their cattle graze, a linkage expressed in the Bantu languages in variations on *mipasi* (Tabwa), *pansi* (Nguni) or *pasi* (Shona). In Luba thinking, Bavidye and other ancestral spirits are placed in the ground (Roberts & Roberts 1996). In many of these societies, dreams are considered to be sent by ancestors, and because dreams are dreamt on headrests, the headrest is a kind of antenna to the ancestors, and the strength of the signal is increased if the headrest is inherited from a senior relative.[49] The act of sleeping thus endows the headrest with agency: the headrest performs its function as a body, standing to support the reclining person. In the portrait of Chief Kilukwe with which I started this discussion (fig. 433), his headrest is balanced by a staff in his other hand, suggesting an analogy that has been explored by A. F. Roberts (2000) in relation to the Tabwa Tulunga diviner's staff. Drawing from Derrida, Roberts suggests that the staff acts as an 'optical prosthesis', allowing its owner a special form of support. Similarly, that which allows the head support in the course of dreams, which may enable dreams because of its links to the ancestral realm, is a special form of support. But it also functions as a means of expressing a genealogical link to the extended world of the living in the form of the ancestors, and not necessarily only when being used to sleep on, but also while it is carried, as among the Karamojong, or simply left standing around ancestral altar sites, such as one in a rather enigmatic photograph by Eileen Krige — whose be-hatted shadow is visible on the left — of a headrest in HaModjadji (fig. 454). The link with the staff as a means of support is further enhanced in those Tsonga examples in which a headrest is carved integrally with a staff, in some instances long enough to have functioned as a physical support for the body, but in others being short and sometimes elaborately carved, in the same forms as were used on dance wands carried in various rituals.[50] Some are carved with a head with an Nguni-style headring at the top (fig. 455), others in the shape of a gun (fig. 456), both of which could be seen as offering visual clues for a link to ancestral authority.

That the headrest constitutes a link to the ancestors is heightened by analogy with those cases where actual bodily remains of deceased ancestors may be used to support the heads of their descendants. Among the Venda of South Africa, the corpse of the deceased king would be allowed to disintegrate on a raised platform in a special burial hut. Once the body had rotted away, the skull and the pebbles from the king's stomach would be recovered and the new king could be invested. Part of his investiture included sleeping on the skull of his deceased predecessor (Stayt 1931; Van Warmelo 1932), a rite very similar to the burial rites of a Tabwa chief, whose skull becomes the headrest of his successor (Roberts 1996[51]). A similar account is offered by Womersley (1984), but here the new Luba king has a specially carved headrest provided for the night in which he cohabits with his sister as part of his investiture. In all these cases, it becomes clear that the linkage with the deceased and the spirit world is of prime importance in the use of a headrest.

The role of ancestors in providing information to the living is part of the foundational premise of almost all sub-Saharan forms of divination, and it is therefore not surprising that headrests should be linked, in a variety of different ways, to the performance of divination as well. The best-known examples of this linkage are the Luba, Cokwe, Lunda and Lwena uses of headrests in divination. The particular Luba form of divination relevant here is that in which the headrest forms the base for a rubbing oracle — an object with an open square frame large enough for the diviner and the client to each grasp it with two fingers, and topped by a sculpted head with elaborate hairstyle. This is called a *kashekesheke* or *katatora*.[52] Theuws (1962:276) explicitly states that this object is rubbed up and down on top of a headrest, although both Burton's (fig. 457) and Roberts and Roberts's (1996) photographs show that this is not necessarily a prescribed part of the process, and Nooter

(1992b:325) says that it is rubbed on a mat or the ground. In Theuws's (1962:275–76) account, the diviner takes the headrest, one that has been ritually prepared for this purpose at the time of the diviner's initiation, and warms the platform over a fire, wiping it on the scar over his heart. He then warms the *kashekesheke*, and, having spat on it, together with the client, grasps its lower frame in order to begin rubbing it up and down on the prepared surface.[53] The movement of the *kashekesheke* continues while the diviner asks a whole series of questions to which the object offers responses by sticking on the surface of the headrest, refusing to move or jumping up and down to produce a tapping sound.[54] The head of the *kashekesheke* is usually made to face the client (D'Orjo de Marchovelette 1954), and acts as an extension of the person of the diviner: as the medium of the spirits (fig. 457). The head could thus be seen as replacing, or acting as — i.e. performing — the head of the person who would normally sleep (or have slept) on the headrest. According to Roberts and Roberts (1996), the form of the *kashekesheke* is communicated to the diviner by an ancestor in a dream, and it is always a female, although this is often not clear in the sculpted form itself. It is possible to suggest that where the *kashekesheke* is used with a headrest, it forms an extension of the rubbing oracle form used by Kuba and related peoples. Here the base of the rubbing oracle is often a carved animal, most likely to be a crocodile (Mack 1990), which closely resembles a headrest form.

In the Cokwe–Lunda–Lwena case, a miniature headrest, replicating the forms of the full-sized headrest, is present in the contents of some diviners' baskets.[55] According to Rodrigues de Areia (1974), they are explained as a means of interpreting dreams and thus of solving problems. They accompany other objects of a variety of origins and representing a number of different aspects of the Cokwe world view. The baskets include small figures of humans, rather sketchily carved, which are called *mahamba* (plural form; singular: *hamba*), and represent ancestral spirits, those closely linked to the living rather than the cultural heroes of the group.[56] In neither Luba nor Cokwe and Lunda divination is the headrest used simply as a pillow. It stands in both instances as a means of reaching the spirit world, where ancestors or tutelary spirits may be able to communicate with the living, in order to enlighten the living on the causes and remedies for a variety of misfortunes. Similar uses of the headrest in communicating with the spirits are recorded by Dewey among the Shona, and by myself among diviners in Tsonga territory (Nettleton 1990). The capacity of the headrest to encapsulate these functions is expanded through the forms that it takes and the designs with which it is perfected, i.e. through its iconographic complexity.

Among the Tiati Pokot headrests collected by Jean Brown and now in the Pitt Rivers Museum are a number that are linked directly to diviners and divining. Most Pokot make their own headrests, but some are made by the sandal diviner within the group for particular clients, as part of a healing process (see fig. 257). Another example, which is almost identical to that in figure 241,[57] collected some 40 years earlier, Brown notes as having been made by an entrails diviner. While she does not develop this theme, it is nevertheless clear that Brown regarded this information as important to the understanding of different headrest types among the Pokot. It seems probable that particular headrests would have had special functions in relation to who made them and who used them. Those made by a diviner might be suggested to have had extra significance and potentiality in providing the user with a link to both the ground and to the ancestors.

## ICONOGRAPHIES OF HEADRESTS AS BODIES

An extraordinary headrest in the Musée Royal de l'Afrique Central in Tervuren (fig. 458), considered Luba because of the style of the carving, brings together a number of the themes considered in relation to the headrests as performance pieces. But, because we can only apprehend it as an isolated object that has been removed from its original *habitus*, we have to be able to read its signs, or at least to identify the clues that would make the object more than just a curious beauty. The platform of this pillow is held up by a female figure who conforms to Luba models, but she is placed in a container, a skeumorphic basket that follows the forms of Luba baskets closely. The fact that baskets were used by diviners to store divination materials (Roberts & Roberts 1996), and that they featured in many instances as containers for powerful substances by Luba and related groups' healers and members of male associations,[58] allows us to postulate that this image makes visible links between spiritual power and those who divine, in the same way as Luba bowl-bearing figures, called *mboko*,[59] do (cf. Nettleton 1992; M. N. Roberts 2000). That which supports the platform here is a sculpture of a human body, also a skeumorph, this time of a human female body with breasts and an elaborate hairstyle. The torso of this figure displays none of the designs found on most Luba caryatids that reproduce, but in idealised form, the scarification patterns that were required for any mature woman in Luba society in the past. In this instance, the outer skin of the headrest support is supplied by the carved replica of a basket, with its own scarification forms. It suggests a link to the ancestors and to divination through a very particular iconographic motif, and the residue of substances in the basket suggests that it may have been used in ways not related to supporting the head in sleep. Similar links are suggested by more common headrest forms, where female figure supports are carved replete with elaborate bodily scarification in a mimetic style.

Some Luba body art forms are recorded in Burton's photographs (e.g. figs. 459–461), largely as evidence, for Burton, of apparently outlandish practices. Nooter, however, offers a different reading of such Luba female bodies:

> The words and textures, forms and fantasies that inspire eroticism in Luba art seem to be closely linked with spiritual domains, or to cosmology and systems of signification and 'writing'. Every detail of the female image is inscribed; from the swelling scarifications and pendulous labia, to the sumptuous coiffures and the gleaming black skin. These are not only considered by Luba men to be ideal features in a woman, but are also regarded as features attractive and meaningful to denizens of the spirit world (Nooter 1992a:86).

If we follow Nooter's understanding of these designs and their realisation on bodies as having spiritual links (see also M. N. Roberts 2000), whether achieved through their evocation of senior women or of ideal notions of fertility, it seems that the scarifications are more than mere tegumentary enhancements intended to arouse male desire. Such readings are backed up by Roberts's (1990) analyses of Tabwa forms of scarification, which suggest a parallel link between the designs of the scarification patterns and a Tabwa cosmology.

Most reports of scarification in African societies demonstrate that scarification is seen as a means of perfecting human appearances. Bohannan (1956) suggests that for the Tiv, scarring is one of the most important prerequisites for beauty, and describes at length the bodily scars placed on women's backs and bellies. Drewal (1988) speaks of how Yoruba *kolo* scarification is seen to enhance the bodies of the people brave enough to have them done (mostly women). Scarring among the Nuba was, according to Faris (1972; 1988) more extensive on women's bodies than on men's. Roberts (1988) points to the similarities among Hemba, Tabwa and Ndembu scarification patterns, all of which seem to have been concentrated on the bodies of women, and the Burton archives and the evidence offered by sculpture suggest the same for the Luba, while Torday's[60] photographs and Maes's (1939) article on mother figures in DRC art offer similar evidence for the Kongo, the Yombe, the Pende and related groups. Further, archival photographs of scarification among the Tsonga are all of women,[61] and historical records point to the same situation among the Shona (Dewey 1991; Berlyn 1968). While there are, of course, well-known exceptions such as the Ndengese, the Kuba and Lulua, where men were as extensively scarred as women, it appears to have been more common in many African societies for the female body to be designed and written into culture through extensive cicatrisation than for the male. The link of scarification to body aesthetics, via notions of both beauty and perfection, is clearly expressed in the following Shona praise poem:

> When I think of your beauty marks,
> Which run in a curve on your brow,
> Which are etched on your cheek,
> And are marked on your lip,
> Then my heart too has its fulfilment (Hodza & Fortune 1979:312, fn. 5).

The notion of the scarred body as a marked container, a sign of ability to endure pain, is particularly apposite to my reading of the headrests of many African groups as substitute bodies.

To understand the chains of significance of the decorated skin of the headrest, it is necessary to look at the conceptual relationship between carving designs and the making of marks on the body. In both cases, the transformation of a smooth, unmarked surface into a seductively tactile and visually complex one functions to mark the figure as civilised, as having been moved several steps away from nature, and as having some degree of status.[62] The figures have acquired skins that can be caressed with the hand and the eye, although perhaps the tactile is more important, as is noted by Barley (1994) in his discussion of African pot decoration. Skin, as Douglas (1966) demonstrates, is a boundary, keeping the contents of the body in their place and preventing pollution. The marking of the skin can be seen, therefore, as a clear demarcation of the body as a bounded system, discrete and individual, which is brought into adult society by the application of patterns that give the person a different kind of corporal identity — the identity of a group defined by gender, age, marital status, specialised knowledge and aesthetic taste. That the marks change over time does not in itself rob them of their significatory relevance, although it may obscure this. The acquisition of these marks is part of a long process, sometimes life-long, of marking the body. The skins of the headrests could thus be seen to connote a corporal ancestral presence, a body that is civilised and perfect, and that supports the head, which is the location of the personality and the link to the ancestors. It is important to understand here that the person, in Southern African Bantu-speaking peoples' ontologies, is a composite being; and the notion of 'somebody' (some body) where the body stands for the person (*muntu*) cannot be expressed in these languages, because the terms are different. The body is the corporeal, and it is marked to bring it into a community, to make it civilised and to perfect it. Scarring the headrest thus also transforms it as a body, makes it civilised and provides a link to the ancestors.

Roberts (1988) draws attention to the Tabwa use of the term '*kulemba*' to denote scarification as a practice, and the scarifications themselves, but also to its use to denote more general forms of marking, which he relates to the English term 'inscribe'. Among the Shona, the same name, *nyora*, is used for the designs on the headrests as for the designs on the skins of women, and both have been related to be a means of identification of the lineage, *rudzi* (Berlyn 1968). Dewey (1993; 1991) has argued there was not a direct correlation of one design to one lineage, yet Hodza and Fortune (1979:312, fn. 5) suggest that the designs differed among clans, and that special names attached to the scars on different parts of the body for the different genders. The designs and the skins or surfaces on which they are embellished can thus be read as links to the ancestors via the lineage. On most Kuba headrests (figs. 162–167, 351 & 352), elaborate designs are found only on the upper surfaces of the platforms, following patterns common in many other Kuba art forms, including those on women's bodies, although Vansina (1978) suggests that the marks on women's bodies, and on drinking horns and cloth, follow patterns distinct from those used on wooden objects made by men. Similar patterning is found on the platforms of some possibly Songye examples (figs. 112, 160 & 161) and on those of a number of groups in the Ubangi region (figs. 147–154). On many Shona headrests (figs. 108, 305, 306, 315 & 316), less extensive engraved relief decoration is used on the platform surface. In all of these instances, the user of the headrest might wake up with an impression of these marks on his/her skin. Nooter's (cited in Dewey 1993:69) observation that a certain scarification pattern, placed on the inner, and thus relatively hidden, part of the upper arm of a woman, where her husband habitually lays his head, is given the Luba name *musamo* (headrest), and in some sense localises the particular intimacy of some scarification and suggests a reason for its extension to the headrest as an intimate object.

In the figurative headrests of DRC groups, including the Songye, Tabwa, Hemba, Lulua, Yaka, Pende and Mbala, the figures are often male and without scars. But among the Luba and the Lulua, the scarification marks on the bodies of the sculpted support figures, like their hairstyles, appear to mimic reality directly: they represent scars on bodies. In other headrests (figs. 100, 102–108 & 113–179), the markings are not applied to supports sculpted in a manner visually mimetic of actual bodies. These markings are applied to ends of platforms, sometimes to their upper surfaces, to their pendants, to bases and to supports of varying shapes, and they use the same motifs as those that appear in so much actual tegumentary art. In some cases, they are applied to supports whose forms may suggest bodies, a suggestion that is thereby enhanced by the presence of the scars.

In a manner similar to that in which Roberts (1988:54) reads a Tabwa comb as a stylised figure, I suggest that one can read many of the supposedly 'abstract' headrest forms illustrated here as figures. This suggestion is supported to some extent by analogy with the case of Luba stools, where the older, non-figurative forms such as those photographed by Burton, and annotated by him as important titles to kinship (University of the Witwatersrand Art Galleries 1992), (fig. 462), may also refer human and spirit beings (Nooter 1992c). I have made the argument elsewhere that Shona headrests, such as those in figures 300–307, can be read as female figures,[63] an argument that depends on reading the supports as torsos, some of which have clear breasts (figs. 306 & 308), but many of which also have triangular projections at the centres of their bi-lobed bases (figs. 301–309, 315–318, 322 & 323). Dewey (1991:200–1) acknowledges that at least two of his Shona interviewees identified these as female genitals, or the female groin area, an association that becomes very clear in some Shona examples (fig. 306). The same feature in some Tsonga headrests seems to have similar connotations (figs. 282, 285, 363, 365 & 463). The entire base structure with its two lobes in these examples is visually parallel to the way in which so many Luba examples scroll the female caryatid's legs backwards so that the figure's genitals touch the base. Dewey (1991; 1993) has established that Shona see the concentric circle motifs, which are central to many Shona headrests (figs. 299–320), as referring to the spiral whorls cut from the base of conus shells, called *ndoro* among the Shona and *mpande* among the Tabwa and Luba (Roberts 1990:40), and used among all these groups and others as a prestige body ornament that links the wearer to the ancestors. Among the Tabwa, it is read as a spiral and offers a reference to the passage of generations and ancestry, and thus the course of time itself.[64] The motif also appears prominently among the scarification motifs on the back and head of a Kuba man photographed by Torday,[65] but without any interpretation. In Venda, the same form is called *mato a ngwena* (eye of the crocodile) or *mato a ndau* (eye of the lion) (Nettleton 1985), while among North Sotho groups such as the Pedi it has also been called *mato a ndau*. In Bastin's (1961) lexicon of Cokwe designs, it is also (whether concentric circles, squares or diamonds) called an 'eye'. The significance of this eye motif in relation to the ability to 'see' in a metaphysical sense is undoubtedly important in the context of the headrest as an aid to dreaming. However, in the Shona headrests, this motif becomes another scar on the surface of the body of the headrest, which is, as Dewey (1993) agrees, primarily female.[66] The concentric circle motif is given a primarily 'breast' reference in the beaded collars worn by Kenyan women represented in many of Adamson's (1967) portraits of ethnic types, and the possibility remains that this reading is not unreasonable in the Shona context.

It appears to me that a similar case can be made for the resonance with which many more of these small, valued and intensely personal objects, as figures, as supports, spoke to and of their owners in a number of other groups as well. Let me hasten to say, however, that I am not suggesting that all African headrests follow the same pattern, but there are a number in which the argument applies. Separating them out may depend on the information available on how motifs are named and understood in the different groups. The extensive scarification of Kuba headrest platforms (figs. 162–167, 351 & 352) and the dressing of various headrests from the lower DRC[67] all produce images that are evocative of figures. That many of the headrests from the Central and Southern African region that follow the same X or hour-glass shape as the Shona examples (figs. 331–340) are scarified, use circle motifs (figs. 337–339) or projecting breast shapes (figs. 344 & 347), and often have lobed bases suggests that this conformation of headrest as figure is widespread among these Bantu speakers.

It is a conformation that is quite different from the inference of figures in Nilotic peoples' headrests. Certainly, some of the headrests collected by Jean Brown among the Tiati Pokot and some earlier ones from Suk and Karamojong sources also suggest human figures on a visual level (figs. 245–252). It is not only the composition of the headrest with two legs and woven 'body', but a platform that can be read as shoulders, and two handles, one on either side of the 'body' as arms, which makes these headrests reminiscent of figures — the associative process calls to mind Paul Klee's transformation of the arches of an aqueduct in his painting *Marching Aqueduct*. The association with human figures is also enhanced by the embellishment of the headrest with beads in the Tiati Pokot examples, arranged in a fashion resembling clothing (figs. 245 & 246), and in some Oromo or Gurage examples, which likewise have full beaded regalia (fig. 44), although many are painted with red, deep green and yellow pigment (figs. 45 & 46). While there is the problem that we do not have any indigenous corroboration of a reading of the headrest as a figure, the objects remain suggestive of miniature human forms. In some Tiati Pokot headrests, one foot is given a V-shaped groove (figs. 240 & 241), a feature that Jean Brown identifies as signifying either a vagina or a goat's cloven hoof to the Pokot. She notes in the following sentence that goats are looked after by women. The identification of these headrests as female is indicative of the gender of their users — married women. A similar feature on examples from the same region, but from other collections or ethnic groups (figs. 242 & 244) probably points to a similar gendering of the headrest form, but it is one that does not involve a differentiation of the overall composition. It does not represent a female figure: it suggests a figure; and is gendered as female through the addition of a particular sign.

The embellishment of many of these examples with beads or with metal inlay also involves a process of addition or accumulation; it adds another dimension, related to scarification, to our understanding of these objects as things of value, of power and of enhanced desirability. Glass beads as imported luxury items had, in many African cultures, an exchange value that dated back to the mid-nineteenth century and a symbolic and rarity value that dated even earlier. Because beads came in brilliant colours, they could be used to express ideas linked into the values of colour — semiotic systems outlined by Turner (1967; 1969) and De Heusch (1982) for Bantu speakers, but also for the Yoruba by Drewal and Mason (1998), among many others. The colours of beads that generally dominate in most earlier Pokot beadwork schemes were red, white and black/deep blue (fig. 251), but by the mid 1970s this was no longer the case for the Pokot examples collected by Jean Brown (fig. 245). Beads that are normally used to enhance the appearance of the wearer, to increase his/her prestige, or to mark out his/her professional status[68] are here attached to part of the owner's distributed body, to the substitute body on which he/she rests. It is therefore no stretch to suggest that adorning the body of the headrest with beads acts in a similar fashion, not only making the analogy with the body more obvious, but also making it more beautiful and suggesting its high status. This once again leads back to the portrait of Chief Kilukwe (fig. 433), whose headrest is heavily invested with beads, suggesting a spiritual presence.

In some examples, the headrest is further invested with power by the addition of other objects alongside or instead of the beaded strings: animal claws, small horns and packets of powerful substances, all of which suggest the presence of extra-human sources of power (McGaffey 1993). Bourgeois (1984:70) records that Yaka headrests generally contained packets of powerful substances — 'charms' — placed inside cavities, which protected the sleeping owner against witchcraft. One example collected by Junod among the Transvaal (then the pre-Anglo-Boer War South African Republic) Tsonga in the 1890s[69] has attached bird claws; black, white and yellow beads; and animal hair, suggesting that it belonged to a diviner or healer (fig. 464). Some Shona, Zulu and Tsonga headrests had snuff or tobacco boxes (figs. 172, 173, 322, 323, 345, 405, 406 & 415) included in their designs, the snuff or tobacco being used to rub offerings to the ancestors on the headrest. Both of these practices suggest an animation of objects analogous to the empowerment of *minkisi* among the Kongo, Songye and Luba, among others. The binding of headrests in metal wire or strips from the western DRC (figs. 145, 148–150, 157 & 158) is also suggestive of the ways in which numerous African peoples bound their limbs in metal rings. It is also suggestive of forms of binding used to contain the powers of *minkisi*. The addition of metal studs, which is more widespread across the DRC region (figs. 112, 120, 123, 125, 141, 142, 150 & 157–159), or inlaid aluminium, a specifically Nilotic feature (figs. 227, 231, 244 & 254), all suggest powers associated with metal as a ritual and therefore as a prestige material.

That many headrests do not overtly represent human bodies is clear from the many illustrations of headrests supported by columns in this study. But the presence of engraved or three-dimensional designs on these headrests, and their encasement in woven materials, in beaded garments or in metal wrapping may nevertheless suggest the articulation of skins or clothing over bodies. The headrest thus comes to announce the presence of a support for the head, and a link to the powers of ancestral and other spiritual beings. Its elaborated forms are only really visible when the headrest is not in use, not supporting the head, or not acting as a seat or as a rest for a leg, as some do or did. It is under these circumstances that the headrest as figure is most apparent and most visible.

But these figures may not be entirely or exclusively human and, in these cases, the iconographic extensions, like the extensions to hair, become more complex.

Some Luba headrests represent animals such as buffalo and antelope, and antelope are common on Tsonga and Shona headrests (figs. 447 & 450). Given that headrests are a locus of dreaming, and thus a link to the ancestors, the presence of these animals as caryatids may be significant. M. N. Roberts (2000) discusses the metaphorical relationship between diviners and a particular species of antelope that is, like diviners, able to submerge itself under water and thus visit the realm of spirits. The presence of other animals in the headrests of the Yaka, Teke, Suku and Cokwe peoples (figs. 451–453) points to other significant connections to the ancestors. Bourgeois (1984:70) mentions headrests of the Yaka (*musaw)* and Suku (*mikkumu*) as including 'a carving of a leopard, antelope, male or female human, or a miniature pitch-roofed dwelling'. This iconography is similar to the animal imagery that appears not only in Yaka and Suku masks, but also in Cokwe ones, where the association of particular animals with ancestral power is made quite clear.[70] The aardvark is a case in point: it is linked to the ancestors because it digs in the ground, the place of the ancestors (Jordan 1998:73; Roberts 1995:81), whereas the dog may be important because of its ability to smell, an ability revered among the diviners of the Pende (Strother 2000) and Yaka (Bourgeois 1984).

Animal references in headrests extend from the overtly representational images discussed above to others more subtly encoded, as in the horn-shaped legs of many Zulu (figs. 399–403) and Ngoni (figs. 422–425) headrests, or the Zulu use of the warts pattern (*amsumpa*) (figs. 390–393) discussed in more detail by Klopper (1991). The reading of the apparently more abstract headrests of the Zulu, Swazi (figs. 397 & 398), Ngoni and North Sotho (figs. 426–430) as animal is significant to our understanding of their function, as in these cases a link to ancestral presence is evoked, via the importance that cattle and goats have as sacrifices to, and thus as media of communication with, deceased members of the group. But the reference to these animals may also be tied into imagery centring on wealth and status — the bull-ness of masculine identity discussed by Klopper (1991), or the wealth of a man with many cattle, or with many wives. Such masculinity can also be read in the similar indices of bull-ness in Swazi headrests — the lug under the platform being an 'umbilicus' of the animal — and in the more overtly animal versions of Ngoni and North Sotho headrests. In Venda Domba songs, the headrest is called the 'goat' of the ancestors, and goats are, significantly, more often used in ancestral veneration than cattle among both the Tsonga and Venda (Nettleton 1990). In some Tsonga headrests, human heads finish up the bodies of quadrupeds, making therianthropic forms whose enigmatic references can only be guessed at. In one example from the Koninklijke Museum voor Ethnologie at the University of Leiden (fig. 465), the head of the figure is female, with a pointed top-knot hairstyle more common among the Zulu, while the head on the famous 'Swazi' example from the Jaques Collection (fig. 432) has an Nguni male headring.[71] There is also an example of this enfiguring of the headrest in a Shona example (see Nettleton 1985, fig. Sh 20): generally Shona headrests, as female and as figures, lack heads, something that resonates with the Shona view that a man's wife's body (representing her fertility) belongs to her husband, while her head (representing her ancestral identity) belongs to her father (Hodza & Fortune 1979:324).[72] While the placing of carved heads on one end of headrests' platforms makes them quite animal-like, the relationship of human to animal forms is expressed differently in Shona examples, where the body of a quadruped is covered in triangular scarification marks like those found on the bodies of human females.[73]

The complexities of metaphorical strings that this imagery invokes can also be partially untwisted in those headrests whose bodies are in the form of architectural elements. Apart from the numerous headrests with elaborate columns, which, however, were not a feature of historical African architecture south of the Sahara, there are many headrests that invoke architectural references more or less directly, including examples from the Yaka and Cokwe and from the Zulu. Yaka headrests invoking miniature houses are illustrated by Bourgeois (1984), and some are represented in figures 273, 274 and 276, with a Cokwe example in figure 275 and a Pende one in figure 277. These all share the use of a similar decorative motif: an open-work lattice in the Cokwe example, the open structure of the Pende example and the dominant diamond motif on one Yaka example. Strother (1993: 160) observes that the lattice-work pattern, hidden under the roofs of the dwellings reserved for the high chiefs of the Pende, is linked visually and metonymically to a species of iguana/crocodile that is the chief's 'cousin'. The linkage of this pattern to crocodile imagery is also found in Shona divining instruments (*hakata, makakata*), and in Venda court arts (Nettleton 1985), with similar linkages to chiefly power and ancestral realms of pools of water. Among the Cokwe, Bastin (1961) records this motif as referring to a Gaboon viper's markings, and similar references are recorded for the same pattern among the Kuba (Cornet 1982). The presence of interlace motifs on Kuba headrests is more akin to the scarification of their skins, but also reflects the 'horror vaccui' of their architectural weaving. Such parallels suggest that metaphorical constructions in which particular patterns are linked to animals with liminal properties and thus great power are widespread among Bantu-speaking peoples from the DRC southwards. Thus, architectural elements are also metaphors for animals, for chiefs and for bodies, and, among the Zulu, for ancestral shades (Nettleton 1990). The headrests therefore constitute visual thinking strings that wind themselves round one another in a variety of imaginings.

Headrests from Africa, thus, were never mere pieces of furniture. Objects of intense desire, made with care and attention to detail, they had social and religious functions that gave them a deeply human and spiritual significance. Many broke in the course of use and were lovingly mended by their owners, who tied or sewed the broken pieces in place with wire. They are evidence of the depth of African inventiveness and artistry in developing and maintaining traditions of thought. One may postulate that the headrest forms discussed in this study allow us to understand the commonalities of persons and cultures in Africa, commonalities that start at the local village level and expand through the regional and ethnic levels, and outwards like the contours of a map to encompass similarities between, for example, Bantu-language speakers, or Nilotic-language speakers. These commonalities extend back to mediaeval times in West Africa, the DRC and Zimbabwe, echoing aspects of African history in material forms that did not become stagnant or rigidly bound by tradition. This study has attempted to undo many of the existing stereotypes around understanding African objects as products of unchanging and stagnant traditions and to introduce the possibility of using different theoretical stances to understand the significance of these objects as historical material, but also as things made — material and tactile — and as things not only thought-provoking and thus intellectual, but also linked to deeper strata of spiritual connection.

CHAPTER 8 *Illustrations: figures 433-465* | **373**

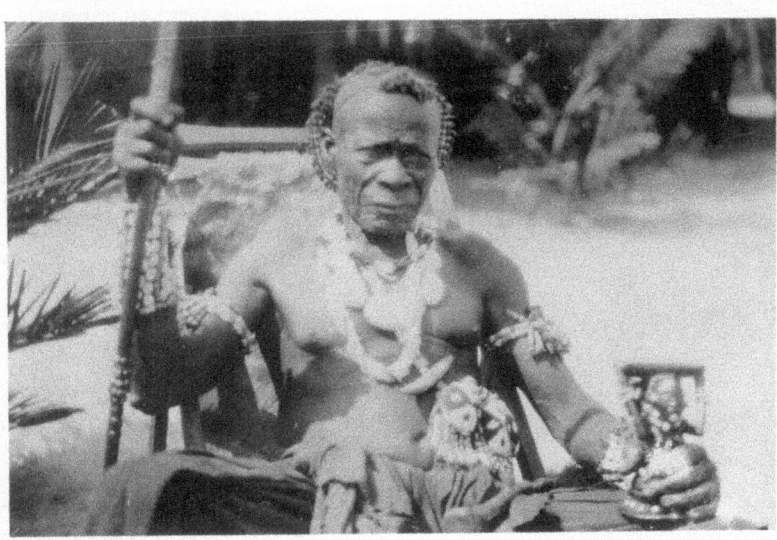

433 University of the Witwatersrand Art Galleries, Museum of Ethnology Collection (no. BPC 13.9), taken and donated by William F. P. Burton, late 1920s/1930s, Democratic Republic of the Congo, Mwanza, *Chief Twito Kilukwe*, black and white photograph.

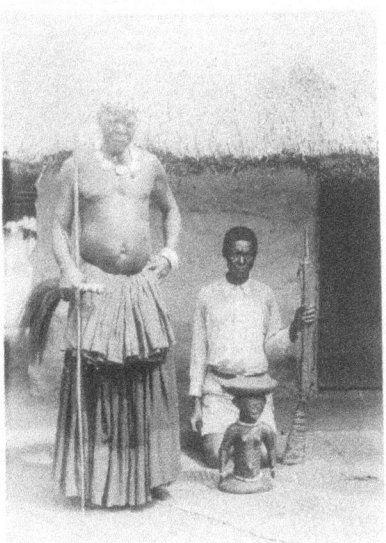

434 University of the Witwatersrand Art Galleries, Museum of Ethnology Collection (no. BPC 13.11), taken and donated by William F. P. Burton, late 1920s/1930s, Democratic Republic of the Congo, *My old Friend, Chief Kajingu with his stool*, black and white photograph.

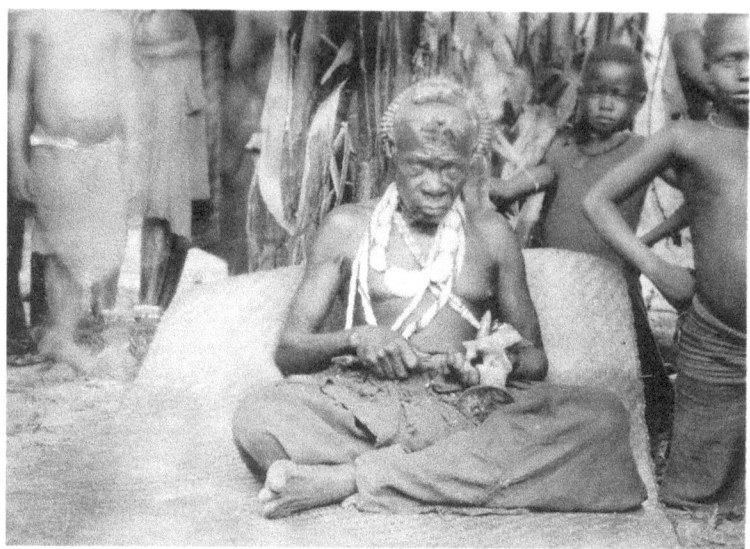

435   University of the Witwatersrand Art Galleries, Museum of Ethnology Collection (no. BPC 13.8), taken and donated by William F. P. Burton, late 1920s/1930s, Democratic Republic of the Congo, *Chief Twito Kilukwe*, black and white photograph, Mwanza.

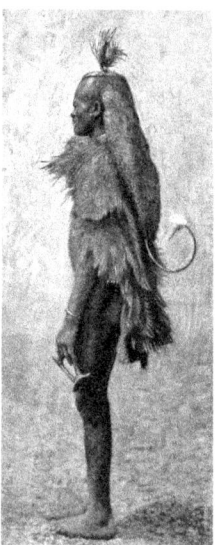
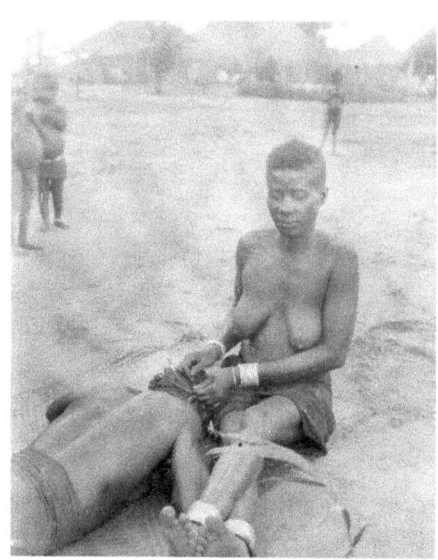

436   Johnston (1902, vol. 2, fig. 468), *A Suk from Lake Sugden, Uganda*, nineteenth century.

437   University of the Witwatersrand Art Galleries, Museum of Ethnology Collection (no. WME BPC 12G.27), taken and donated by William F. P. Burton, late 1920s/1930s, Democratic Republic of the Congo, *Hairdresser at Lake Samba*, black and white photograph.

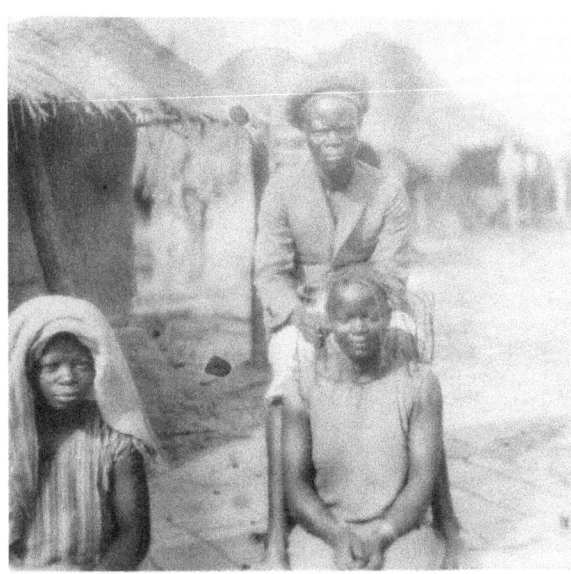

438  University of the Witwatersrand Art Galleries, Museum of Ethnology Collection (no. WME BPC 12G.25), taken and donated by William F. P. Burton, late 1920s/1930s, Democratic Republic of the Congo, *Making a Kilukwe Coiffure*, black and white photograph.

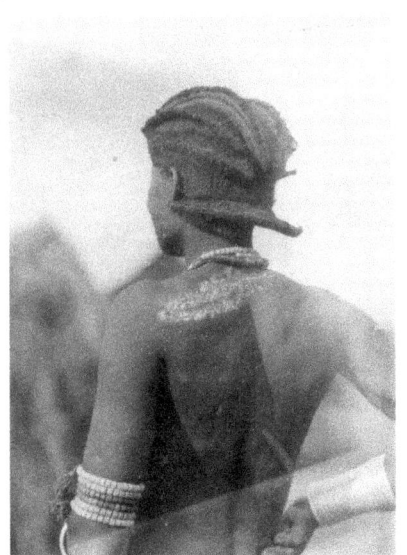 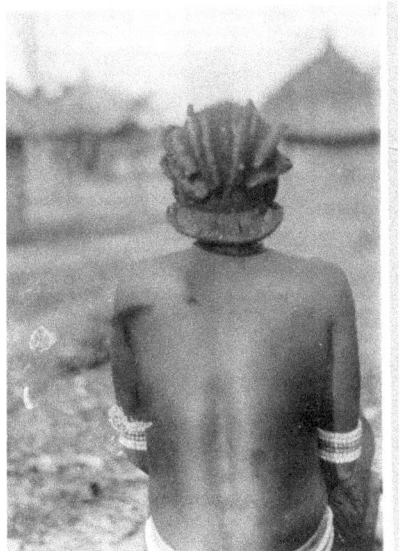

439  University of the Witwatersrand Art Galleries, Museum of Ethnology Collection (no. WME BPC 12G.28, left; 12G.30, right), taken and donated by William F. P. Burton, late 1920s/1930s, Democratic Republic of the Congo, *Bene Munonga hairstyle*, black and white photograph.

376 | AFRICAN DREAM MACHINES

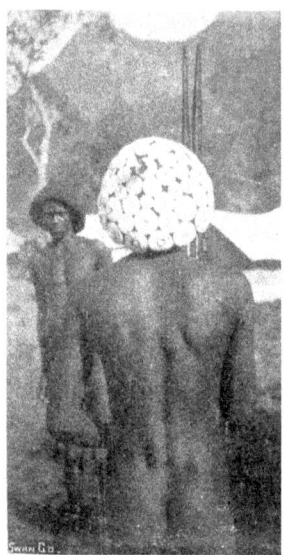

440  Powell-Cotton (1904:439), *Man of the Dodinga Hills*, Kenya.

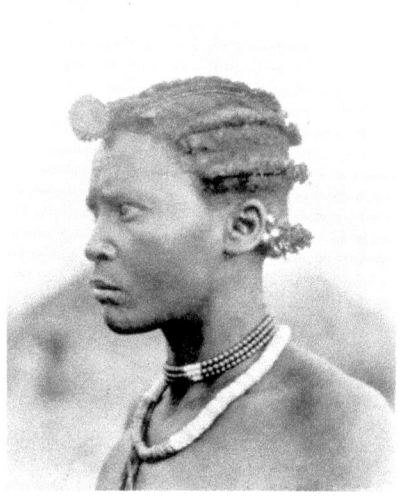

441  University of the Witwatersrand Art Galleries, Museum of Ethnology Collection (no. WME BPC 12G.30), taken and donated by William F. P. Burton, late 1920s/1930s, Democratic Republic of the Congo, *Bulunga hairstyle*, black and white photograph.

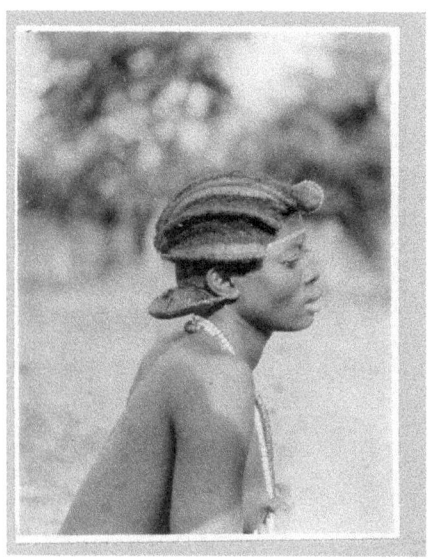

442  University of the Witwatersrand Art Galleries, Museum of Ethnology Collection (no. WME BPC 12G.39), taken and donated by William F. P. Burton, late 1920s/1930s, Democratic Republic of the Congo, *Bene Munonga hairstyle*, black and white photograph.

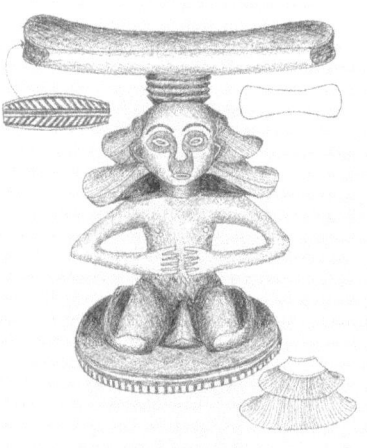

443  Berlin, Museum für Völkerkunde (no. IIIC 19987), purchased from Leo Frobenius, 1904, Democratic Republic of the Congo, *Luba (Shankadi)*, wood, pigment, 18.4 cm h.

CHAPTER 8 *Illustrations: figures 433-465* | **377**

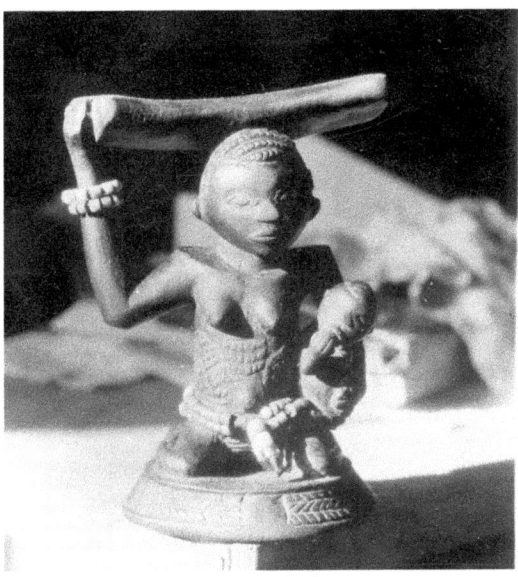

444   University of the Witwatersrand Art Galleries, Museum of Ethnology Collection (no. WME BPC 07B.1), taken and donated by William F. P. Burton, late 1920s/1930s, Democratic Republic of the Congo, *A Luban Pillow*, black and white photograph.

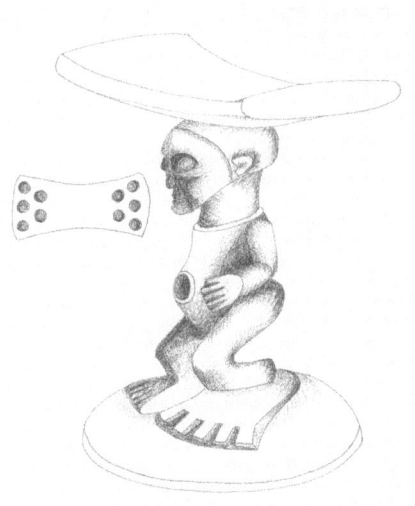 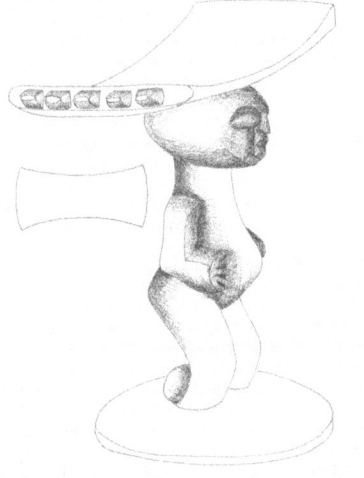

445   British Museum (no. Af1954 N23), (Wellcome Collection, no number), Democratic Republic of the Congo, 'Songye', wood, 13.8 cm h.

446   British Museum (no. Af1954 N23), (Wellcome Collection, no. 96827), Democratic Republic of the Congo, 'Songye', wood, 13.8 cm h.

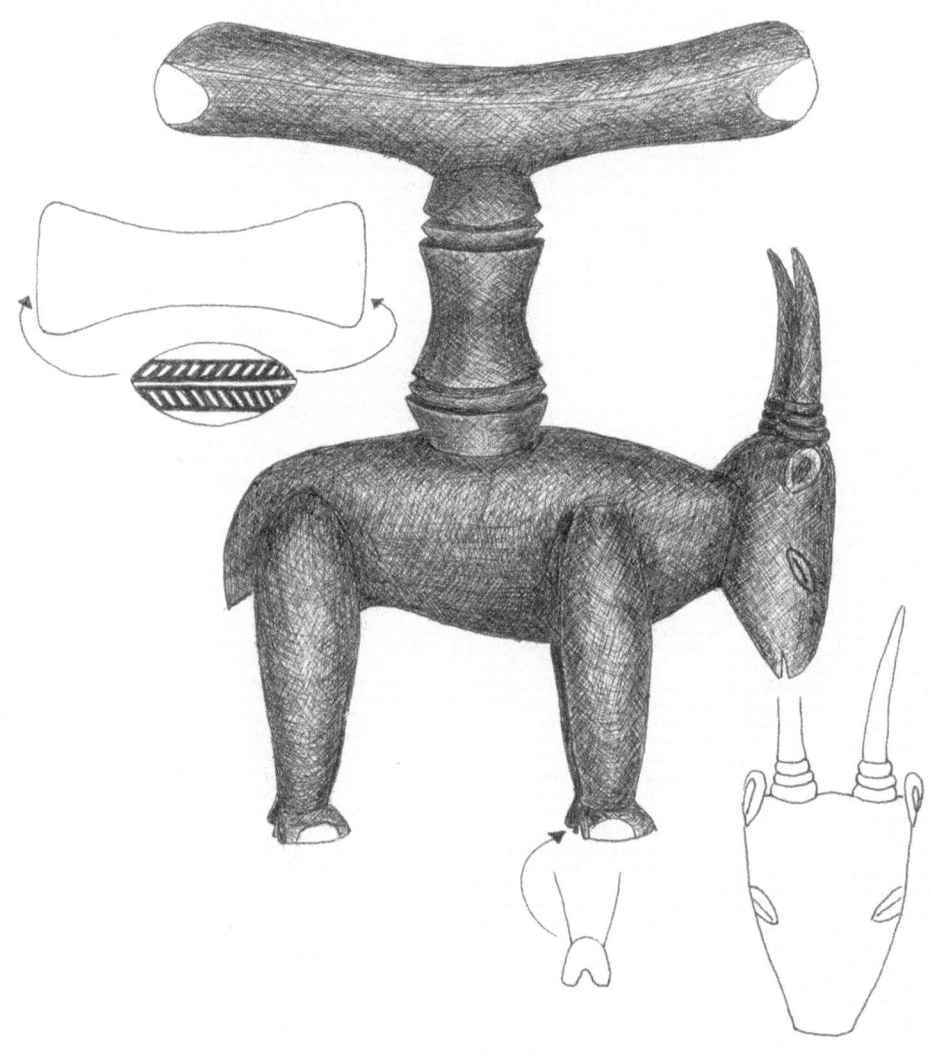

447  Munich, Staatlisches Museum für Völkerkunde (no. 16.16.2), Dietzel, Frobenius, May 1916, Democratic Republic of the Congo *(Kongo Warsch) Kalenga, Katanga*, wood, 15 cm h.

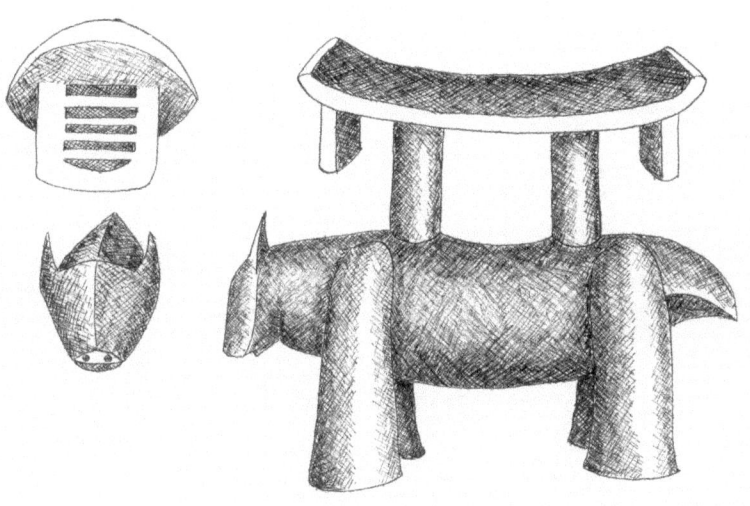

448　British Museum (no. 1949 Af46), Oldman Collection, *Southern Rhodesia*, (Zimbabwe), Shona/Tsonga, wood, 15 cm h.

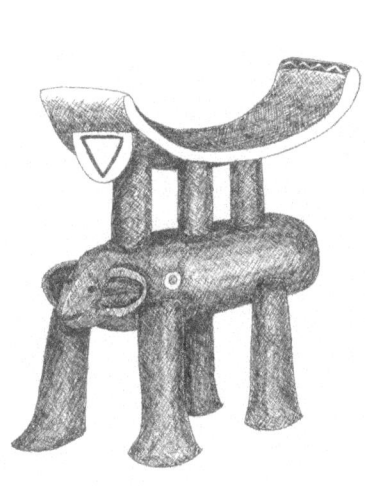

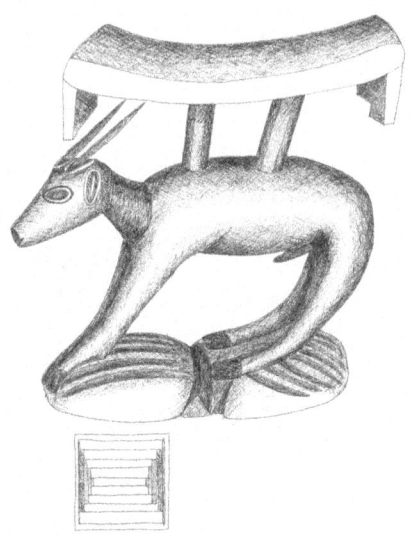

449　Tshwane (Pretoria), National Culture History Museum (no. 4654), South Africa, *Transvaal* (Limpopo Province), *Pilgrim's Rest*, Tsonga, wood, 15 cm h.

450　Paris, Musée de l'Homme (no. N4 90.65.11), *Southern Africa/Mozambique,* 'Tsonga', wood, 16 cm h.

**380** | AFRICAN DREAM MACHINES

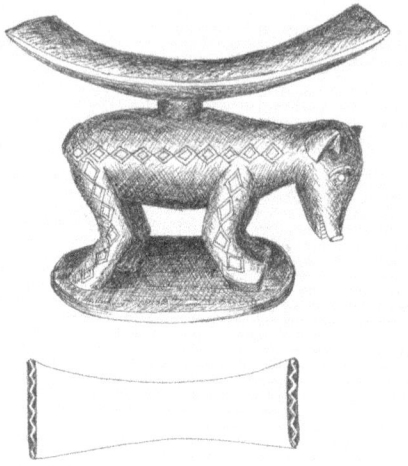

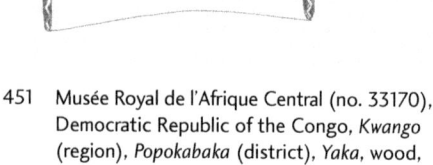

451   Musée Royal de l'Afrique Central (no. 33170), Democratic Republic of the Congo, *Kwango* (region), *Popokabaka* (district), *Yaka*, wood, 12.2 cm h.

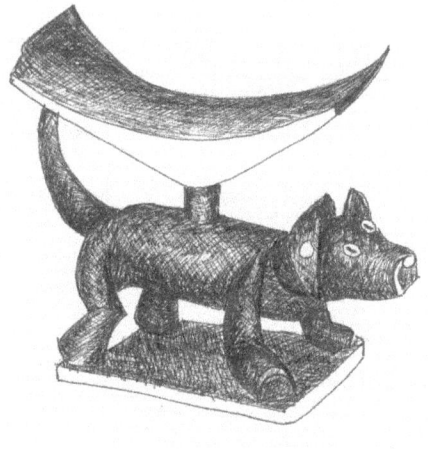

452   British Museum (no. 1949 Af46.351), Oldman Collection, Democratic Republic of the Congo, 'Yaka', wood, 13 cm h.

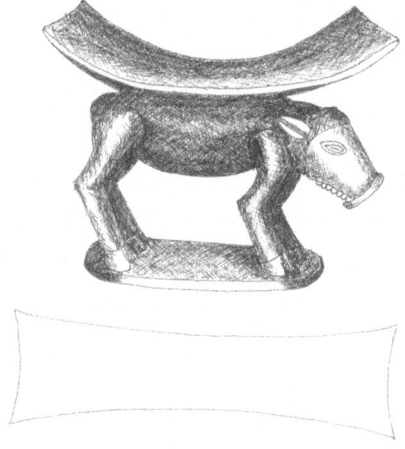

453   Musée Royal de l'Afrique Central (no. 32833), Democratic Republic of the Congo, *Kwango* (region), *Yaka*, wood, 15.9 cm h.

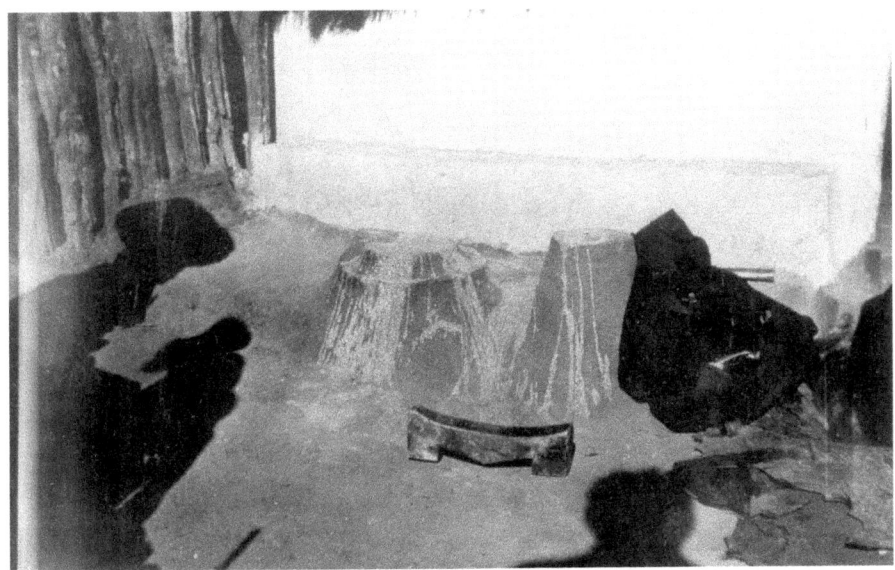

454  University of the Witwatersrand Art Galleries, Museum of Ethnology Collection, taken by Eileen Krige, 1930s, South Africa, Transvaal (Limpopo Province), *Lobedu Ancestral Shrine and headrest, HaModjadji*, black and white photograph.

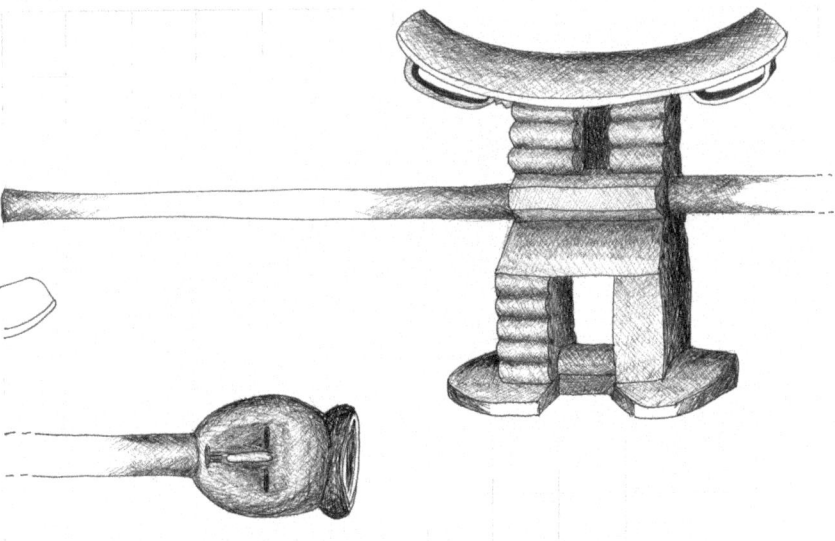

455  British Museum (no. 1954 Af23), (Wellcome Collection, no number), *South East Africa*, 'Tsonga', wood, 12 cm h (headrest), c. 50 cm l (stick).

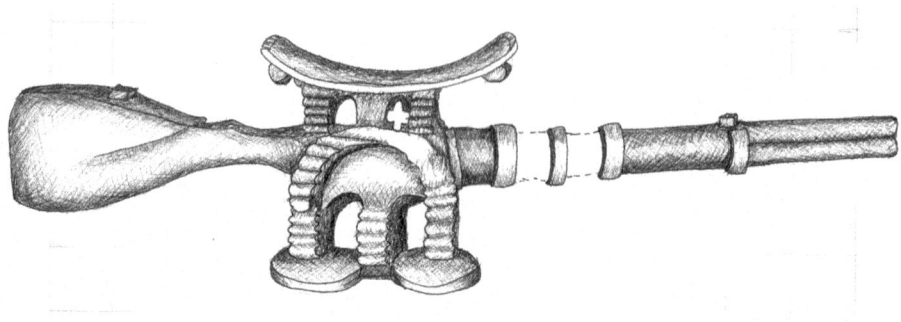

456 British Museum (no. 1954 Af23), (Wellcome Collection, no number), *South East Africa*, 'Tsonga', wood, 12 cm h (headrest), 73.5 cm l (gun).

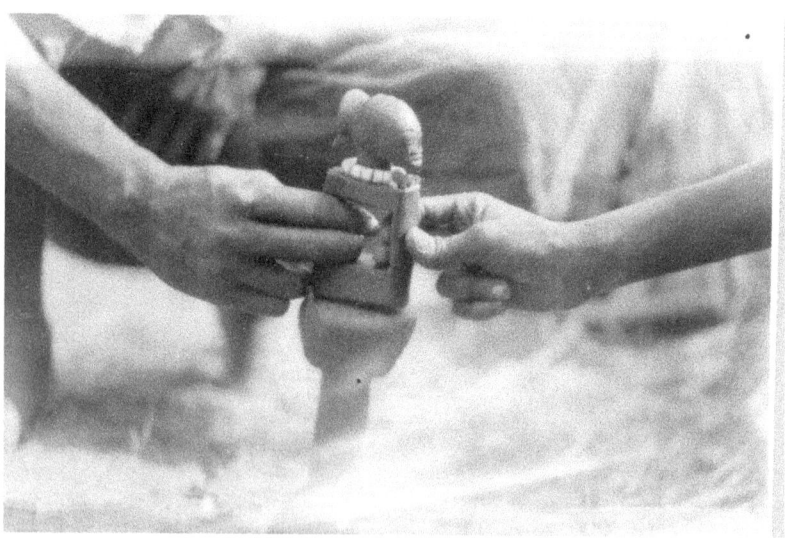

457 University of the Witwatersrand Art Galleries, Museum of Ethnology Collection (no. BPC 05.3), taken and donated by William F. P. Burton, late 1920s/1930s, Democratic Republic of the Congo, *Luba Divination with <u>Kashekesheke</u>*, black and white photograph.

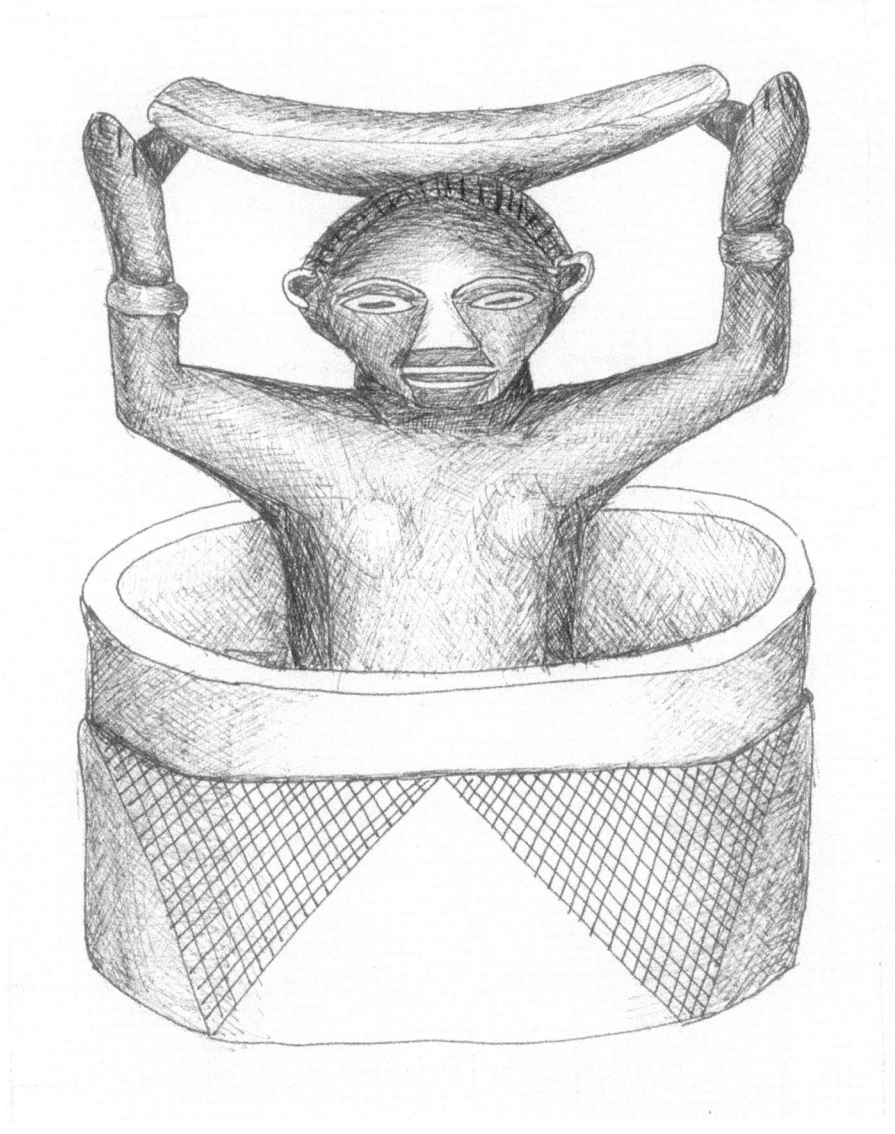

458   Musée Royal de l'Afrique Central (no. 50.13.1), Democratic Republic of the Congo, 'Luba', wood, 18 cm h.

**384** | AFRICAN DREAM MACHINES

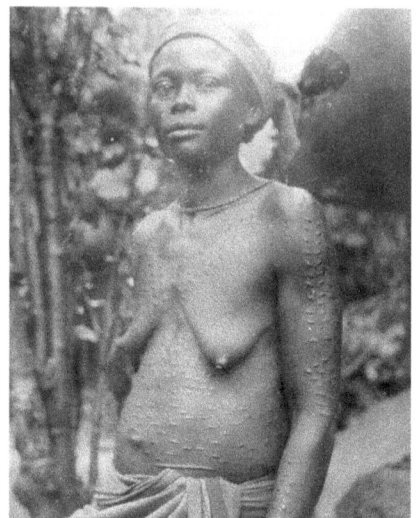

459  University of the Witwatersrand Art Galleries, Museum of Ethnology Collection (no. BPC 21.5), taken and donated by William F. P. Burton, late 1920s/1930s, Democratic Republic of the Congo, *Budya Scarification*, black and white photograph.

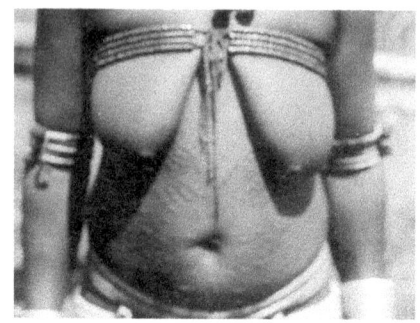

460  University of the Witwatersrand Art Galleries, Museum of Ethnology Collection, (no. BPC 12.G. 36), taken and donated by William F. P. Burton, late 1920s/1930s, Democratic Republic of the Congo, *Busanga Woman*, black and white photograph (detail).

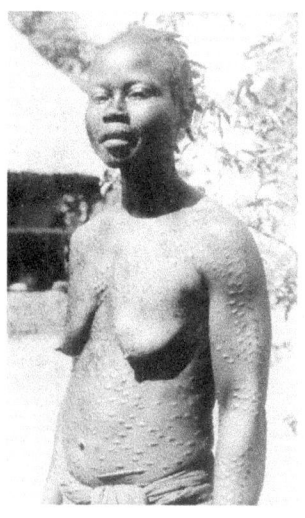

461  University of the Witwatersrand Art Galleries, Museum of Ethnology Collection (no. BPC 21.8), taken and donated by William F. P. Burton, late 1920s/1930s, Democratic Republic of the Congo, *Mwanza Scarification*, black and white photograph.

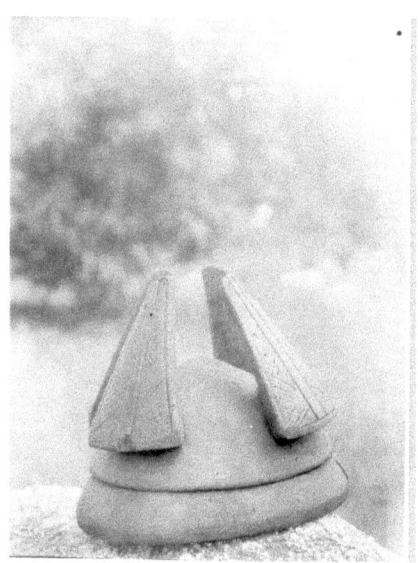

462  University of the Witwatersrand Art Galleries, Museum of Ethnology Collection (no. BPC07A.8), taken and donated by William F. P. Burton, late 1920s/1930s, Democratic Republic of the Congo, *Jealously guarded remains of a stool, which is the sole title deed to Mwanza chieftainship*, black and white photograph.

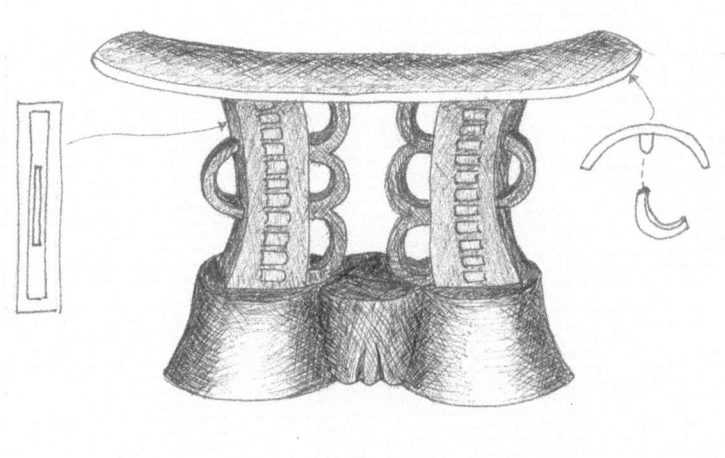

463   Johannesburg Art Gallery (no. 1987.3.109), collected by A. A. Jaques, pre-1929, *South Africa, Transvaal* (Limpopo Province), *Elim, Tsonga*, wood, 13 cm h.

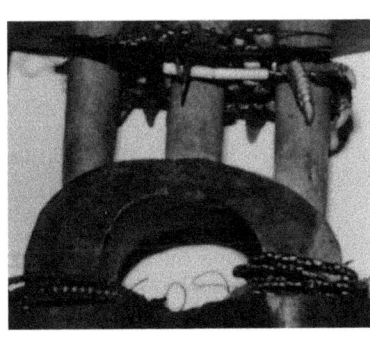

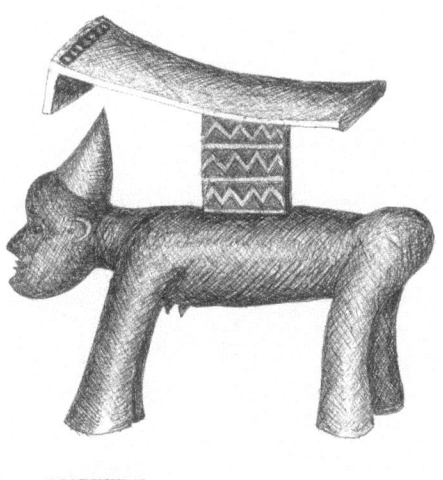

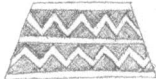

464   Neuchâtel, Musée de Ville (no. III C 3032), collected by H. P. Junod, 1894, South Africa, *Transvaal* (Limpopo Province), wood, 15 cm h.

465   Leiden, Koninklijke Museum voor Volkerkunde (Müüller & Snelleman *c.* 1892, pl. XV, no. 3), South Africa, *Transvaal* (Limpopo Province), wood, 16 cm h.

# Notes to Chapters

## CHAPTER 1

1 Malraux's *Voices of Silence* was first published in English in 1954; the version referred to here is a later (1974) edition.
2 Elkins (2002a; 2006), Onians (2001; 2006) and Summers are some proponents of such global studies, although they approach the question from very different angles. We will return to their arguments later.
3 This discomfort is reflected in the debate, or perhaps stand-off, between art history and anthropology about the disciplinary domain in which objects made by people outside the West are best studied; see the essays in Coote and Shelton (1992) and Westermann (2005).
4 Coombes (1994:141–42) traces the early recognition in England of ethnographic objects as 'art' and the increasing emphasis on their formal properties through an examination of writings on the Mayer Collection in the *Liverpool Museums Bulletin*, 1901–06. But there was no systematic study of these objects as 'art' in this period.
5 See, for example, the outline of the history of writing on native North American art given by Berlo and Phillips (1998), as compared to Trowell and Neverman's (1967) formalist appreciation of African and Oceanic art, and Thomas's (1999) analysis of the history of Maori and Aboriginal forms in contemporary Australasia.
6 Recently, the subject of a re-examination was discussed in a set of essays edited by Biebuyck and Petridis (2001) on the work of Frans M. Olbrechts, whose contribution is enormously important.
7 The four essays in the Phaidon collection of Berenson's writings published in 1952 were originally published between 1894 and 1907, and were devoted to identifying characteristic area styles and individual artists; see Kleinbauer (1971:1–105) for a general discussion of the historiography of Western art history.
8 One important exception to this was Mead, Bird and Himmelheber (1963), in which Himmelheber's article dealt with individual African sculptors. Attempts to isolate particular artists' hands have occurred most often in studies of Benin (Dark 1975; Fagg 1963, figs. 22, 23),

but also in Yoruba art studies (e.g. Bascom 1969; Carrol 1961; 1967; Fagg & Pemberton 1982; Abiodun, Drewal & Pemberton 1989; 1994; Picton 1994a; 1994b), as well as in some Democratic Republic of the Congo contexts (Olbrechts 1946; Felix 1990; Neyt 1977; 1994).

9   This is evident in both Vansina's (1984) approach to art history in Africa, where historical dimensions are adumbrated along linguistic lines, but ignore inter-linguistic possibilities, and Elkins's (2006) analysis of the possibility of writing art histories for modernism outside the West.

10  For example, even those studies that challenged many of the shortcomings of the art historical processes outlined above, such as *Tradition and Creativity in Tribal Art* (Biebuyck 1969), *The Traditional Artist in African Society* (D'Azevedo 1973a) and *Art and Aesthetics in Primitive Societies* (Jopling 1971), all have contributions on artists and broader contexts, but all are framed in the tense of the fixed present. None of them is overtly or intentionally historical in orientation. Picton's recent publications on Yoruba carvers are perhaps those that most closely approximate an historical account (Picton 1994a; 1994b). Coote and Shelton (1992:4–6, 9) suggest that anthropology should be involved with social aspects of art rather than with the individual, and thus run against recent attempts to identify individual artists and their works as significant features of explanation of art in Third World societies.

11  Once again, one could cite exceptions such as Raphael's (1968) studies of Cezanne, Schapiro's (1980) studies of mediaeval art, Honour's (1961; 1968) studies of Chinoiserie and neo-classicism, Antal's (1966) work on classicism and romanticism, Nochlin's study (1971) of realism, and, of course, at a more populist level, Berger's *Ways of Seeing* (1972). But the real turning point came later and was perhaps best characterised by such works as Clark's (1973) on Courbet, and Baxandall's (1972) on fifteenth century Italian painting.

12  The idiosyncrasies of Crowther's aesthetic judgements are commented on by Elkins (2006).

13  I have no intention of entering a debate about the essential nature of 'art' or whether 'art' is tied to an aesthetic essence. Crowther, in outlining a critique of what he names 'hard relativist' and 'soft relativist' positions, however, lays bare the soft underbelly of what he calls a 'logical' approach to defining art cross-culturally. The basis of this logic, that art is necessarily mimetic and a series of representations, is, however, very problematic.

14  In neither of these is there an acknowledgement of forms that are not figurative, with the exception of material from Islamic parts of the world, where iconoclasts are in charge. The aesthetic values of Chinese and Japanese calligraphy are not foregrounded, nor are their ceramic traditions, both of which are accorded high aesthetic status in their respective societies.

15  Dutton suggests that 'there is no "current Western sense" of art, but various, radically different and rival senses of the concept, each partially implicated in competing social practices and theories of "art"' (Dutton 1995:35). However, there is sufficient consensus in most circles that historically in Europe and North America 'art' has been defined in narrow parameters (earth-works, installations and performance pieces notwithstanding), and in most contemporary contexts where such definitions matter, these parameters remain valid (see Steiner 1996).

16 Duncan suggests that in high modernism , 'the work becomes high art when the critic treats it as such in the press or in some other public forum' (Duncan 1993:172). The mediation of the critic is considered to be 'good' by Duncan when the critic assigns aesthetic value to the work in the form of 'transcendent meanings' (Duncan 1993:173). That this view of the power of the critic in assigning value may be oversimplified does not obscure the fact that artists and art historians have mediated the transformation of African carvings into high art by much the same process as that outlined by Duncan.

17 One has to go no further than the collected essays in Rubin and Varnedoe's *Primitivism in Twentieth Century Art* (1985), or, most quintessentially, Rubin's own introduction to this catalogue (Rubin 1985), to find this kind of view expressed a number of times.

18 This master narrative was reproduced in the first exhibition of Picasso's work to reach South Africa, at the Standard Bank Gallery in Johannesburg in early 2006, where all the African objects on show were masks and figures from West and Central Africa.

19 See Leighten (1990) for a critique of, particularly, Picasso's position *vis-à-vis* the 'primitive' African art that he used as a source in his break with the Western tradition. See also Bois's elegant semiological deconstruction of Picasso's use of African images in the creation of cubist imagery (Bois 1987). Perry, Frascina and Harrison (1993) also discuss the question of the exotic in relation to the early modernists: Cubism and German Expressionism, especially the German art movement know as Die Brucke.

20 The assumption that 'art' necessarily encompasses 'representation' in a 'naturalistic' mode underpins much of Western art historical research and writing, both before and after the advent of abstract painting, the apotheosis of modernism. It is allied with the notion of art as non-functional and as therefore separate from other forms of material culture. These issues will be addressed again in different contexts below.

21 Following Crowther's (2004) argument, the value of non-Western arts lies in their contribution to the global understanding of aesthetic renewal as innovations in ways of presenting the world. Elkins's (2006) analysis of the avant-garde and modernism also stresses the centrality of the notion of innovation in the valuation of works within a global, or world, art history.

22 This argument is in direct contrast to that offered by Manning (1985:169, 172), who equates representational forms with African court arts, and abstract forms with so-called egalitarian societies in Africa. There are a number of problems with his argument and his exemplification, but the major one here is that he does not cite any of the 'abstract' forms from egalitarian societies: even Kota reliquary figures are figurative. The abstract forms that might have been relevant to modernist artists from 1906 to 1915, such as Kuba cloth, Yoruba appliqué, and Igbo house and body painting, are not mentioned in this article, which attempts to redeem Rubin's notion of 'affinities'.

23 This position is, however, debatable, as the political and specifically colonial contexts in which they were working raised a number of issues centring on excesses committed by the colonial powers in Africa (cf. Leighten 1990; Firth 1992:24).

24 Berlo and Phillips (1998) discuss the problems of authenticity as they affect our understanding of native North American art and its development across regions and time.
25 See Price (1989) and Torgovnick (1990) for detailed analyses of 'primitivism' as a modernist phenomenon, and Dutton's (1995) critique of aspects of their work.
26 In the light of recent critiques of Bhabha, particularly his omission of the senses in which difference might be manipulated by the colonised subject as a form of resistance (see Dirlik [1994] and Parry [1994] for such critiques), I must emphasise that we are here dealing with difference as constructed by the coloniser, and not manipulated to any degree by African producers of art objects.
27 Steiner (1994:110) discusses this dichotomy between the functional object and the functionless object, and the ways in which functional objects have been allowed to transgress the boundaries in terms that seem to suggest that figures are in some way less functional than other objects. But what many commentators seem to elide is the fact that 99 per cent of the objects from Africa that we now define as 'art' were originally made to fulfil a function, and divorcing a Kongo *nkisi* from its functions is as violent as divorcing a headrest from its functions.
28 See Read (1967:24–43) for a simplified example of this kind of approach.
29 This phrase was first used by Clifford (1988:190), but I use it here for its reverberations with notions of evolution and connections with natural history.
30 This lack of differentiation of tasks according to a hierarchy is widely known in African art/material culture studies, and is used as one of the arguments to attack notions of 'authenticity' in 'primitive' art that are grounded in Western preconceptions about the status of the artist; see Shiner (1994: 227) and Kasfir (1992:45) for discussion of this issue.
31 Gell's subsequent suggestion that art objects are art objects because of their agency in social relations will be discussed later, as it bears directly on the ways in which objects come to have significance within particular societies (Gell 1998).
32 Of course, exactly what is meant by 'aesthetic' here is not clearly defined, but it seems to be dependent on mastery of carving skills, on degrees of 'elaboration' and on the range of innovation that takes place within circumscribed boundaries of style.
33 Shiner does not appear to be able to accommodate the inclusion of 'primitive' artefacts in the art category, partly because he sticks to a very tight definition of what he understands by the term *art*. One might suggest that, as this definition (Shiner 1994:225) excludes objects made by historically oppressed groups of people — women, the colonised others, mere workers, etc. — we need to redefine art and its relation to craft so that we will not be forced into the dilemma that Shiner outlines whereby students must either 'force the arts of other societies into an alien mould of high Art or appear to denigrate them as mere crafts' (Shiner 1994:226). Steiner (1996), on the other hand, suggests that the entire canon of art functions in a quasi-mystical fashion in which inclusion has to function in relation to exclusion, and that the only way to address these problems is to entirely debunk the canons of art.

34 See, for example, Delange (1974, fig. 181), Willett (1971, fig. 11) and Leuzinger (1972:360, fig. z18). It is significant that of these three authors, Delange is the only one to include some of the figurative art that was known to have come from Southern Africa (Delange 1974, figs. 183, 184), although she does not discuss them. Information on these figures was available in an earlier German language survey of African sculpture, Von Sydow's *Afrikanischen Plastiek*, published in 1954. Holy's survey *Masks and Figures from Southern Africa* was published in 1967 and was thus also available to those who were writing the canonical surveys, but who chose to ignore Southern Africa.

35 See Sieber (1980). Further explorations of the headrest and other personal objects from Africa were made in the exhibition and booklet *The Art of the Personal Object* at the National Museum of African Art, Washington, DC (Ravenhill 1991) in which Southern and East African objects were prominent, and in the Fowler Museum of Cultural History exhibition *Sleeping Beauties* (Dewey 1993), thus reinforcing the notion that both these regions are largely without figurative forms.

36 See, for example, Hodder (1977) and Brown (1978), where the headrests are studied largely as indices within a system of signs that point to identity differentiation.

37 As yet, no single volume dealing with these objects has been produced, and apart from the discussion of examples in Dewey (1993:32–51), Wolfe (1979) and Van der Stappen (1996a), most information is scattered in ethnological accounts and more recent studies of the distribution of material culture in the East African region.

38 However, there are problems with this view: in some cases, the plainest objects are the most significant in ritual. Such is the case presented by Chappell (1977:23–30) on the gourds made by Fulani groups in northern Nigeria, where the most meaningful 'ritual' object was a plain, white gourd that involved none of the aesthetic elaboration such as that used on gourds for dowries. Chappell was unable to discover any 'meaning' for the highly decorated objects in the metaphoric mode suggested by this definition of Firth's. Similar conclusions can be drawn from Cole's account of Mbari houses among the Igbo, where the most important objects were iron rods and white porcelain plates (Cole 1982).

39 This can be seen from such exhibition catalogues as Fondation Dapper (1989) and Jordán (1998), in which no headrests with abstract designs appeared, despite the fact that both Baumann (1935) and Bastin (1961) have made comparative studies of headrests and their designs from this region. Similarly, Roberts and Roberts (1996) and Neyt (1994) include only a few examples of headrests, all of which have figurative supports.

40 The relationship between function and meaning will be discussed later in this book, but there can be little argument that style and form, as well as function and iconographic content, are likely to affect our understanding of the meaning of the object as an art object.

41 See Southeby, Parke Bernet (1973; 1974a, no. 126; 1974b, no. 480; 1975, no. 151).

42 Accompanying the text are illustrations of apparently 'good' examples, available from various dealers, with prices attached. The prices indicate the escalation of value of the objects once they move out of the African context.

43 This is clear from collections held by museums in Southern Africa: the Iziko South African Museum in Cape Town houses ethnographic artefacts, while the Iziko National Gallery in Cape Town houses art. Similar divisions hold good in the National Museum and Gallery of Zimbabwe in Harare.

44 Headrests could, of course, function in many contexts within a person's life, but this was not necessarily apparent to the person who collected the object either in the field or in the auction or gallery. The multiplicity of functions of headrests and their resultant meanings or readings will be discussed elsewhere.

45 For examples (mostly Southern African), see figs. 301, 302, 305, 387, 421 and 422.

46 See British Museum, nos. 2182 and 2183. Another, earlier example, was accessioned in 1855 (British Museum, no. 1855.12.20.89) and documented as having been collected by the Baptist Missionary Society and donated from the Haslar Hospital by the Lords of the Admiralty. But it is clearly of Ancient Egyptian origin and seems to have found its way into the collection through a series of accidents and misattributions, as the only other Ancient Egyptian examples in the collections have been kept there for comparative purposes (John Mack, personal communication, 1991).

47 The date at which the British Museum established an 'Ethnological Gallery' — a display of artefacts as opposed to collections of specimens — was 1845, but the transfer of objects from Kew only followed after the Great Exhibitions of the early 1860s. These connections will be followed up further below.

48 See Brantlinger (1985), Coombes (1985), Stocking (1987), and also Davison (1991a), who gives an overview of the changes that occurred in collecting practices in museums in the later nineteenth century and places them within a wider historical context.

49 The idea that objects can stand in a synecdochic relationship to a society, culture or style has been discussed by many authors; see, for example, Pearce (1995) and Gell (1998).

50 A good example of this is the case of the so-called Afro-Portuguese ivories, produced in West Africa specifically for trade with Europeans, which were included in various royal repositories and in curiosity cabinets (see Curnow 1983; Bassani & Fagg 1988). These appear to have been imported into Europe in comparatively large numbers in comparison with the far more isolated acquisition of so-called 'traditional' pieces, such as the Yoruba divination board in the Wieckmann Collection (see Jones 1994; Fagg & Pemberton 1982:31–32; Abiodun, Drewal & Pemberton 1989:17, 21).

51 Although the 1716 catalogue of the collection includes wooden spoons joined by chains, thought to have come from Southern Africa, Jones does not discuss these, as there seems to be some doubt as to whether they were part of Wieckmann's original collection (see Jones 1994:30).

52 See, for example, the articles in Impey and McGregor (1985), particularly Laurencich-Minelli (1985), Seelig (1985), Scheurleer (1985), and Bassani and Fagg (1985).

53 Headrests are known from West Africa, for example, headrests from the Ivory Coast, possibly Baulé (see Musée Royal de l'Afrique Central, nos. 70.29.2, 75.24.5; Dewey 1993:83, 84, 85). Vogel

(1997:204) records the use of 'old-fashioned' neckrests in the shrines made by Baulé for the ancestors, but she does not illustrate any of these. Numerous examples are known from the Bandiagara cliffs in Mali, classified as 'Tellem': see Falgayrettes (1989:26, 27, 43) and Dewey (1993:93, 94, 95, 96, 97). Dewey also published examples from the Joss Collection, including the following classifications: Senufo, Fulani, Lobi, Dagari, Nuna and Bobo (Dewey 1993:86–92). However, so very few of these are documented or illustrated and so few are represented in museum collections that it is almost impossible to make a meaningful study of them, or to form a base on which to compare them with other peoples' headrests.

54 Of course, here I do not include headrests from Ancient Egypt that were being collected from the time that Europe first became interested in Egyptian archaeology and that are well represented in European museum collections in Paris, Brussels, Berlin, Munich and London.

55 Examples of such 'headrests' — or are they miniature stools? — are included in the collections of the Musée Royal de l'Afrique Central in Tervuren: see nos. 70.29.2 and 75.24.5. Both are (relatively) recent acquisitions.

56 The manual was produced by the Royal Society to provide guidelines for amateurs gathering information on the peoples encountered and subjugated in the British exercise of imperialism.

57 Later the Cape Province of a post-1910 united South Africa, and the area now made up of the Western, Eastern and Northern Cape Provinces.

58 Now KwaZulu-Natal Province of South Africa, but referred to as 'Natal' in the discussion that follows, since it is nineteenth century perceptions that are the issue.

59 It is possible that the commissioners for the exhibition acquired many of the objects that were displayed from mission stations in the region of Natal, rather than from the depths of the Zulu kingdom. The mission station at Umvoti may have been one of these. I am indebted to Dr Sandra Klopper for this insight. It raises a number of questions in relation to the ways in which 'Zulu' as an art historical category has been constructed.

60 This fascination was shared by numerous others. Bishop Clayton made an extensive collection of snuff paraphernalia, which he donated to the British Museum.

61 The ways in which African material culture came to be recognised as 'art' have been discussed at some length by both Nettleton (1973) and, more recently, by Coombes (1994) in her discussion of Victorian and Edwardian encounters with African objects.

62 See British Museum, nos. 1892 7-14.176, 1892 7-14.156, 1892 7-14.26, 1892 7-14.154, 1892 7-14.22, 1892 7-14.155 and 1892 7.14.151. In fact, Bent's collection represents a wide cross-section of headrest types associated with Shona speakers, as well as an Ethiopian example.

63 See Mann (1862:17–20) and Schweinfurth (1875).

64 This connection between patterns on Shona headrests and the motifs used in female scarification has been noted by Berlyn (1968), and debated by Dewey (1993:122–25) in response to Nettleton (1990:147–54; 1985:124ff.). It seems that such references may be generically recognisable as referencing female scarification, among other things (see Hodza & Fortune 1979:312).

65 In Southern African studies, especially among the Venda and Shona, there has been a consistent search for Semitic/Hamitic elements in these cultures, culminating in the identification of the Lemba, a Venda sub-group, as Hamitic. This identification has persisted to this day and is one of the abiding myths of Southern African popular ethnography, but it also functions to allow the origins of cultural practices to be shifted from the indigenous people on to the mythic Hamites, including the Queen of Sheba; see Garlake (1973, figs. 47–49).

66 These were for about 40 years separated from the main British Museum stores, while the Ethnographic Department of the museum occupied separate premises and was called the Museum of Mankind.

## CHAPTER 2

1 Schapiro's definition of style has been used because it has been so influential in the discipline of art history and in the field of anthropology, having made a significant appearance in an anthology on style as a category of cultural analysis edited by Kroeber (1957), one of the fathers of American anthropology.

2 Here the term *affinity* is used in the sense that it was used in the catalogue *Primitivism and Twentieth Century Art* (Rubin & Varnedoe 1985). The affinities that Falgayrettes (1989) sets up are similarly based entirely on formalist criteria without any demonstrable connections between the time and place of manufacture of the juxtaposed forms.

3 The question relevant to differentiated explanations for aspects of styles of material objects is outlined by Carr and Neitzel as follows: 'If an artifact's style is perceived and can be analysed, then which attributes reflect, for example, technological constraints, the identity of social units of various spatial scales, personal identity, or motor habits?' (Carr & Neitzel 1995:4).

4 Onians (2001) has suggested that if we are to make sense of the world's art as a whole, we should be looking at what is common to all humans, and clearly the basic structure of the body is one of these. But the degree to which emotional and intellectual aspects of human behaviour intervene in the creation of forms and in the delineation of the aesthetic is far more interesting than basal structures could ever be.

5 This can be demonstrated through an examination of both so-called Dogon headrests discussed below (in this chapter) and those of peoples of northern and western Kenya, such as the Pokot, Karamojong, Turkana and their neighbours, including the Acoli (chap. 4) or the stylistic complex of Tsonga and Shona headrests of south-east Africa (chap. 4). These instances will be discussed in detail below.

6 See, for example, Roe's claim of style's 'recognizability as a unique product of a given people, the denizens of a certain place and time' (Roe 1995:30).

7 See Kasfir (1984) for an in-depth analysis of the shortcomings of the tribal model and of the attempts that have been made to replace it with other models.

8  See Preziosi's discussion of the reification of objects into types and the relations that are set up between the objects as types/texts and their contexts (Preziosi 1989:36).
9  See Belting (1987) for a brief discussion of the place of Hegel's theory in art history, something that he suggests is no longer applicable: 'Precisely that which Hegel defines as the universal essence of art — its symbolization in objective form of a historical Weltanschauung — must ultimately, and paradoxically, be a phenomenon of the past' (Belting 1987:10).
10 In the recent collection of essays on style from archaeological and ethnological perspectives edited by Carr and Neitzel (1995), almost all the authors work with the assumption of close-knit social units as the units of stylistic practice. Voss and Young's chapter deals with the notion of the individual, defined as 'self', but only within the context of the group, as a factor in the delineation of stylistic practice (Voss & Young 1995). These issues will be addressed below in greater detail.
11 Something of this process is reflected in Elkins's (1997) discussion of the processes of styles analysis of Ancient Chinese bronzes, in which he sees a continuing atomisation of styles and successive periods, which also does not allow for contestation.
12 Silverman, for example, offers the following critique of Geertz's methodology: 'Geertz's cultural texts express multiple idioms, but these expressions mainly reference dominant ideologies and their construction of public reality.' So Geertz's interpretations are seen as silencing 'oppositional and alternative voices' (Silverman 1990:135). But in this, Geertz is not that different from 'traditional' anthropology, which also searched for essential cultural traits and belief systems in the societies, which it transformed into texts.
13 This is a rather reductive rendition of Alpers's (1983) differentiation between the northern and southern Renaissance, but nevertheless demonstrates the ways in which collective culture is seen to have characteristics that manifest themselves across the products made by individual minds. It can also be paralleled to the differentiation of French from Italian or English Gothic architecture, in which differences in form are ascribed to some aspect of national character.
14 Shennan (1978) argues that in archaeology there are three basic misconceptions commonly applied to the notion of cultures: that they are regarded as 'things' to which the attributed characteristics of living organisms can be applied; that they are constituted of formal regions rather than functional ones; and that they are always constructed as having 'core areas'. These misconceptions are not much different from the problems of 'styles' in art historical practice discussed here.
15 Roe proposes that '[s]tyle provides a frame, a voluntarily imposed obstacle, within which play can occur. So, too, *all of culture is a megastyle ...*' (Roe 1995:45; emphasis added).
16 Syson and Thornton (2001) argue that the appreciation of design as an intellectual factor vs. skill in making as manual was developed through the emergence of a particular form of art patronage in the Renaissance period in Europe.
17 Wolheim's position is critiqued by Elkins (1997) as not allowing for the sometimes less than targeted thinking that may happen in an artist's head while he/she is working.

18 This is discussed further below, but it is important to remember that large African ethnolinguistic groups may have little political and social cohesion across their breadth, because many of them are colonial inventions rather than historical entities (see Klopper 1992:11–25; Jewsiewieki 1989; Roberts & Roberts 1996; Vail 1989).

19 This is argued from two very different viewpoints by both Crowther (2004) and Elkins (2006), with the latter laying this formation at the door of Western modernist art history.

20 Here the cases of particularly the Yoruba, Edo and Akan courts come to mind (see Abiodun, Drewal & Pemberton 1989; Ben Amos 1980; MacLeod 1981). Dogon sculpture with its apparent links to so-called Tellem sculpture is another example where attempts have been made to reconstruct an homogeneous history (see Leloup 1988; 1994; Ezra 1988; Laudé 1973; Bedaux 1988).

21 See, for example, Maurer and Roberts's (1985) discussion of Tabwa, Neyt's (1977) discussion of Hemba, and Neyt's (1994) and Roberts and Roberts's (1996) discussion of Luba sculptural styles.

22 This argument is made by Elkins in the context of a review of David Summers' *Real Spaces: World Art History and the Rise of Western Modernism.* However, in *Stories of Art*, Elkins (2002b) encourages his readers to understand that there is a multiplicity of ways of dealing with the writing of history, and this, presumably, would not exclude constructs arrived at through formal analysis of visual phenomena.

23 See, for example, Leuzinger (1972, pls. T10, W8, Z19), Trowell (1967, pls. 136–140) and Willett (1971, pls. 219, 220, 222).

24 This collection includes African, Oceanic and Asian headrests, as well as figurative sculpture from Africa. Ross (1994) published a catalogue of the 'art' from this collection, in which only five headrests feature; of these, two are clearly figurative, two are abstract, but suggestive of figures, and only one is purely abstract. Dewey's (1993) publication, however, includes both figurative and abstract examples.

25 Appiah (1992) puts this insistence on differentiation down to the need to 'clear a space' for a particular person's/people's art *in the market place* as part of a modernist and postmodernist cultural process. A similar point is made by Elkins (2006) in discussing modernism and its extension outside the West.

26 That is, from the present Democratic Republic of the Congo (DRC).

27 For example, the notes for Maes's (1929) figures 31 and 32 in plate I are included in the section containing the notes for plate II (Maes 1929:10), so as to keep the notations for 'Ngombe' headrests together, and thus preserve the notion of ethnic stylistic integrity, even though this is belied by the forms of the headrests themselves.

28 Apart from offering a critique of Maes (1929), Biebuyck (1985), in his overview of Zairean/DRC art production, indicates which groups within the south-western DRC made and used headrests. Because of the context, there is no analysis of visual types and very little detail of use and production.

29 Also known as Tshokwe or BaTshokwe, and Chokwe or BaChokwe; standardised to Cokwe throughout.

30 The question of the non-figurative headrest among the Luba is discussed at greater length in chapters 5 and 6, below.
31 Some of this material appeared recently on the Internet version of the exhibition at <http://www.h-net.msu.edu/-etoc/profiles/menjiye bio.html>, where newer headrests were attributed to individual carvers, and ethnic attributions were given passing attention; see also Silverman (1999).
32 Dewey's (1993) catalogue includes a number of East African headrests, but each example is dealt with individually, and no attempt is made to establish a broader picture of the distribution of styles and types across ethnic boundaries.
33 That part of the Zambezi River basin that extends (inland) from the river mouth to Tête.
34 In her PhD thesis, Becker (1999) provides a thorough-going critique of the processes whereby these headrests have come to be classified as 'Tsonga', an issue that will be dealt with below in the section on Southern African regional styles.
35 There is some disagreement of views between Dewey and myself on both the stylistic attributions and iconographic interpretations of Shona headrests, but these will be addressed in more detail elsewhere in this study.
36 Dewey's discussion of Southern African headrests in the *Sleeping Beauties* catalogue is heavily dependent on these publications (Dewey 1993).
37 See the catalogue by the KwaZulu-Natal Local History Museums (1996).
38 The ethnic classification 'Dogon' itself might be seen as problematic. Leloup (1994) outlines six different dialects for Dogon, suggesting that the inhabitants of the Bandiagara plateau 'the native Tombo of the northern plateau, the Djennenke in the west, the Dogon migrants from the Mande area who mixed with the inhabitants of the Southern cliff face and with Voltaic peoples' achieved 'cultural unity ... in the seventeenth and eighteenth centuries'. However, such cultural unity remains undemonstrated, as most work among 'the Dogon' has been done in the area of Sanga. See Van Beek (1991) for the most recent critique of Griaule's studies of Dogon as a unified culture.
39 See Bedaux (1977:74). Caves at Sanga, Nokara and Hombori were investigated by a Dutch team from the Institute for Anthropobiology of the Rijksuniversiteit, Utrecht, yielding a number of headrests of both iron and wood (Bedaux 1977:82–84).
40 The existence of a Tellem group no longer seems to be in question, but whether there was any cultural or political coherence among the pre-Dogon inhabitants of the Bandiagara cliffs area is debatable (see Bedaux 1977:74; Ezra 1988:27–28; Laudé 1973:25; Leloup 1994:135–43; 1988:45–46). Leloup (1988:47–48) suggests that a group called Niongon may have been neighbours of the Tellem proper prior to the arrival of the Dogon. But, while she associates some sculptures with this group, there is no evidence that they made and used headrests.
41 Bedaux distinguishes 'Tellem' from their predecessors, named 'Toloy' (Bedaux 1977:74), and suggests a thousand-year gap between the two, and he distinguishes 'Tellem' as a genetic group distinct from Dogon, on the basis of skeletal comparisons (1977:78).

42 Exactly this appeal is exploited for such works in books such as Sannes's *African 'Primitives'* (1970), where a number of so-called 'Tellem' statues are reproduced, one of which has a date attached and an explanation for its longevity.

43 Leloup (1988:46), citing Glanville, suggests that the 'Tellem' were of a physical type common in Central Africa rather than West Africa. The inference thus is that they would have migrated northwards into the Dogon region, but the questions remain, from where and when? Their headrests show such a range of different styles that these could not really be used to suggest an origin.

44 Such headrests are illustrated in Dewey (1993:93, 94, 95) and Falgayrettes (1989:26, 27, 29), and further examples are in the Musée Royal de l'Afrique Central (nos. 66.14.1, 78.17.6, 73.30.1, 78.17.7, 78.16.9, 89.15.1).

45 This example was donated by Desplanges to the Musée de l'Homme in Paris (Falgayrettes 1989:47), and is one of the earliest recorded examples of Tellem/Dogon headrests.

46 This is a process that seems to be parallel to ones evident from an examination of some north-east African headrests discussed in chapter 6, below.

47 Dewey (1993:96, 97) illustrates two of these, one of which might have been a stool. He cites three in the Metropolitan Museum of Art in New York, and there are two with head-like projections in the Musée Royal de l'Afrique Central (nos. 63.15.1, 63.15.2).

48 See Musée Royal de l'Afrique Central, nos. 78.73.2 and 79.20.8.

49 Bedaux (1977; 1988) does not illustrate any of this type, and I have not found any others in the museum collections consulted.

50 See Bedaux (1977:52) and Musée Royal de l'Afrique Central, nos. 78.73.3, 79.20.9 and 65.67.1.

51 Dewey (1993:95) discusses this briefly, associating the 'low' headrests mentioned by Bedaux with the flat rectangular boards such as that illustrated by Bedaux (1977:52), although this is not obvious from his discussion of the headrests in this catalogue.

52 Bedaux (1977:74, 77) seems to share Fagg's scepticism of the label 'Tellem' as it was used by Laudé (1973) and others to distinguish Tellem as 'old' from Dogon as relatively 'new' sculpture. But he notes that there is a certain degree of stylistic variation in Tellem sculpture, decided on the basis of particular items' relative abstraction/naturalism and their anthropomorphic or zoomorphic form. The use of 'the Dogon' as a stylistic category is itself somewhat problematic (Bedaux 1977:76). Leloup (1988; 1994) has suggested that both regional styles and individual hands are discernible among the Dogon sculptures (1988:49), but she here appears to be flattening out time, suggesting stylistic continuity from the terracotta workshops of Djenne of the fourteenth and fifteenth centuries to the Djenneke sculptures of the present. Once again, the historical dimension is eliminated.

53 Bedaux (1977:77) gives a list of caves investigated by the Dutch expedition using a C14 (carbon-dating) method.

54 Bedaux uses the term *votive* only for the iron headrests (Bedaux 1977:83), but this distinction may be misleading.

55 Evans Pritchard offers two alternative views of the social significance of material culture: 'Technology from one point of view is an oecological process: an adaptation of human behaviour to natural circumstances. From another point of view material culture may be regarded as part of social relations, for material objects are the chains along which social relationships run, and the more simple is a material culture the more numerous are the relationships expressed through it' (1969:89). It is interesting to note here that although he collected headrests among the Nuer and deposited them in both the Pitt Rivers Museum in Oxford and the British Museum in London, he does not mention them in his section on the ecology of the Nuer in this book.

56 See Vail (1989) and Harries (1989) for an historical discussion of ethnicity, and Picton (1991) for an application of this in relation to Yoruba art.

57 The colonial construction of larger ethnicities has been discussed at length; see in particular Vail (1989). But, in these larger colonial groupings, there were differences of political and religious orientation that would have been reflected in the fragmentation in art production. Such fragmentation has been further complicated by religious conversion (Christian, Muslim or indigenous faiths), by uneven distribution of Westernised education opportunities, by urbanisation, etc. All these factors have led to a further erosion of what was essentially an imposed unity. See, for example, Bravman's study of Islam's impact on the historical arts of West Africa (Bravman 1974).

58 Interest in the identification of individual African artists in the field of sculpture has grown extraordinarily over the past 20 years, and there are a large number of publications that discuss various instances (see, for example, Abiodun, Drewal & Pemberton [1994] and Leloup [1994], and the two special issues of *African Arts* edited by La Gamma [1998; 1999], which were devoted to this question). But there is very little material on artists, carvers or otherwise, who do not produce figurative sculpture. Dewey identifies the 'hand' of a Songye headrest carver (1993:65), but this is done on the basis of caryatids, i.e. figures. This emphasis on sculpture once again reflects the Western bias in the delimitation of what constitutes 'art' and its 'artists'.

59 It is not being suggested that colonial officials, such as G. I. Jones, or Kenneth Murray in Nigeria, or William Fagg in many places, were deliberately working towards this end, but they were enmeshed within a wider system of colonial rule in which such endeavours were not seriously questioned, and were reproduced at all levels of study of the 'other'.

60 These include Bascom (1969), Carroll (1967), Johnson (1986), D'Azevedo (1973a), McNaughton (1988) and Silver (1983), and in many of these cases the issue of 'tradition' is not the main focus of the discussion, and in many instances there were both a body of works and a body of practices, handed down over a number of generations, to which artists in African societies could — and can still — refer. This is not to suggest that either the body of works or practices were uniform or unchanging, but that they constituted living traditions within which producers worked and users used their products.

61  Carr and Pryor (1995:259–96) give a good example of such a system of apprenticeship among North Carolina native American basket weavers, looking at the transmission of styles from individual, to family, to artisan groups, and the play between 'enculturation' and individual choices. With the exception of McNaughton's (1988) study of Bamana blacksmiths, few equivalent studies of African artisanal groups have been carried out.

## CHAPTER 3

1  I attempted a broader correlation of Southern African headrest types with larger linguistic groupings within the Southern African region, analysing some of the iconographical content of the headrests (Nettleton 1990).
2  These included the collections of the Museum of Mankind, London; the Manchester University Museum; the Pitt Rivers Museum, Oxford; the Royal Scottish Museum, Edinburgh; the Musée Royal de l'Afrique Central, Tervuren; the Museum Rietberg, Zurich; the Staatlisches Museum für Völkerkunde, Munich; the Musée d'Ethnologie, Geneva; the Musée d'Ethnologie, Neuchâtel; and the Musée de l'Homme, Paris.
3  These include the Iziko South African Museum, Cape Town; the Museum, Harare; the Africana Museum (now MuseumAfrika), Johannesburg; the Johannesburg Art Galleries; the National Open Air and Culture History Museum, Tshwane (Pretoria); and the Killie Campbell Museum, Durban.
4  This distribution may be a result of collection practices, and a result of the institutions researched, as an exhaustive study of German museum collections was not possible. Given German control of Tanganyika/Tanzania prior to the First World War, this may be a significant gap.
5  Ravenhill (1991) discusses some headrests used by the Baulé peoples of the Ivory Coast, and Vogel (1997:204) comments on their use in Baulé ancestral treasuries. Some examples are attributed to West African pastoralists (Dewey 1993), and one example in the Museum of Mankind, collected by W. Jeffreys, is provenanced to the Igbo of Nigeria.
6  Where possible, photographs were taken of the headrests in museum collections, while sketches or photocopies of existing photographs of headrests were made in other instances. All headrests were measured and their decorative motifs were recorded, as were their constituent materials, state of preservation and signs of usage.

In addition, museum records were consulted for 1) date of acquisition; 2) provenance; 3) identity of collectors; 4) attribution to 'ethnic' groups; and 5) any supporting documentation in museum archives. Where headrests formed part of particular collections made by missionaries, anthropologists or others, the objects that constituted the rest of these collections were recorded. Where records had been kept of publication of photographs of headrests, these were noted. Museum numbers of all examples were recorded.

A particular problem was encountered at the Musée Royal de l'Afrique Central in Tervuren, as neither taking photographs of objects nor consulting museum acquisition records or archival material was permitted. Information requested for headrests that was provided was extremely sketchy; few examples were provenanced, and the majority do not appear to have been attributed to any ethnic groups.

7   I am aware that 'appropriating' the material culture of other peoples is in itself somewhat akin to cultural theft (see Root 1996), but I do this in an attempt to make sense of a phenomenological problem that confronts me as an academic living in the margins; as a white African whose roots have been transplanted.

## CHAPTER 4

1   Charles G. Seligman was a professor of ethnology at the University of London in the 1920s and 1930s, whose anthropological work centred on anthropometry (see Seligman & Seligman 1932).
2   No information is available about this collector, but he was, presumably, in the British colonial forces in north-east Africa. The person from whom the headrest was acquired, a Mrs Collins, was possibly his daughter.
3   Liverpool World Museum, no. 21.12.15.49, collected by Captain C. R. Breading, 'Abyssinian specimen'.
4   Elizabeth Dell of the Brighton Museum, personal communication, 1997.
5   It is the earliest example of the type that I have traced in European museums. Bent donated/sold other headrests to the British Museum, most of them from 'Mashonaland'.
6   The acquisition records of the Wellcome material in the British Museum give only a date (1954) before which these examples were collected, but which may extend a good deal further back in time. Unfortunately, the Wellcome archives are not accessible.
7   Huntingford (1955:21) provides the following brief description of Oromo headrests: 'concave headrests with one leg, sometimes ornamented with beads'; but spends much more space describing the hairstyles of women (1955:69–71).
8   This exhibition was traced in its cyber form at <http://www.h-net.msu.edu/-etoc/profiles>.
9   The French spelling of Gurage (which is the American form) is Guarague. Gurage is used consistently in this study, unless a different spelling is quoted.
10  Huntingford explains the name 'Oromo' as follows: 'The people known to the Ethiopians as Galla call themselves Oromo, pl Oromata, and their language *afan oromo;* or Ilma Orma (*ilm orma*), "sons of men" (*afan orma*, "language of men")' (Huntingford 1955:11).
11  In another publication linked to this same exhibition, edited by Van der Stappen, Van Praet (1996:237) notes that there are 22 million Oromo speakers in Ethiopia, and that they encompass a rich cultural milieu, marked by internal divisions according to religion, political organisation, economic activity, ethnic affinities and geographical dispersion.
12  None of the headrests attributed simply to the Oromo (Van der Stappen 1996a:56–62) has any differentiation noted as to gender specificity. Of the four examples attributed to the Arsi, two are

said to have been used by women, but the others have no gender attribution (Van der Stappen 1996a:70–71), nor is any such attribution given to other headrest types collected in Arsi country. Most of the headrests of this type attributed to the Afar (Van der Stappen 1996a:91–94) are said to have been used by men.

13 Headrests by two contemporary Fuga carvers, Menjiye Tabeta and Gebre Wolde Tsadik, were featured on the Ethiopia exhibition website run by H-Net; see <http://www.h-net.msu.edu/~etoc/profiles/menjiye_a5.html>, accessed 14 June 1999. Similar headrests are featured in Phillips (1995).

14 I am here tempted to say 'less aesthetically refined', but these headrests have an appeal of a kind related to modernist sensibilities, a kind of art 'brut'.

15 Lewis (1955:180) remarks that there is very little arable land available within Afar territory that would enable them to settle and establish tribal boundaries. However, artisanal skill is not necessarily linked to sedentary lifestyles, and the difference between the finely carved and polished Somali headrests and the art brut appearance of Afar ones demonstrates this quite clearly.

16 Also known as the Esa; standardised to Issa throughout.

17 Hassen (1990:170) shows how complex this specialisation was in some Oromo kingdoms. Within the *massera* of Garuqqe were 'workshops for the various artisans .... The carpenters made beds, doors, windows, and above all else, stools, for which the Gibé region is still famous.'

18 Huntingford (1955:19) suggests that the Oromo originated in the area of Somalia, migrating into Ethiopia around the twelfth century. However, Hassen, following Haberland (Hassen 1990:4), claims that the 'ancestral home of the Oromo was in the cool highlands of the Bale region' (Bale borders on Somalia), and that they migrated to their present territory before the fourteenth century (Hassen 1990:xii).

19 See pp. 198ff. & figs. 197–205, below.

20 Major P. H. G. Powell-Cotton was a prodigious collector of Somali material, some of which he sold to the British Museum and the Pitt Rivers Museum, but much of which went to the Powell-Cotton Museum in Kent (discussed in greater detail in chap. 8). He, his wife and his two daughters all travelled extensively in Africa and made careful collection notes for most of their acquisitions. I am indebted to Julie Hudson of the British Museum for help in tracing information on the Powell-Cotton family and to the staff at the Powell-Cotton Museum for their generous help.

21 This is further complicated by another example that is probably Somali by virtue of the distinctive carved patterns on the underside of its platform, but follows the same pattern as the Ethiopian examples in other respects (Liverpool World Museum, no. 21.12.15.48, 'Abyssinian Headrest', collected by Captain D. R. Breading).

22 The terminology used for the geographical locus of Somali speakers is somewhat confusing. It seems that the term *Somaliland* was generally used in British anthropological circles to refer to the part of Somalia under British control, i.e. British Somaliland. The area of Eritrea was called

French Somaliland or Eritrea, and the Italian Protectorate Somalia (cf. the map in Lewis [1955]). I am therefore assuming that the example collected by Powell-Cotton was indeed collected in Somaliland.

23 A very similar example published by Dewey (1993, fig. 8) is tentatively provenanced to Ethiopia, on the basis of similarity to one published by Haberland as 'Borana' (Dewey 1993:36).

24 See pp. 132–43, below. Another example of a very different structural type collected by Alden has the same type of platform, relief and painted decoration, demonstrating the possible variation of types in a single style area (British Museum, no. 1928 5.9.2).

25 Its similarity to an example attributed, but without any comment, to the Fulani by Dewey (1993:89, pl. 87) seems to complicate the issue unnecessarily.

26 The third example in the British Museum follows exactly the same pattern: British Museum, no. 1954 Af23 (1785–1789)B (Wellcome Collection, no. 1666686 [TB 188]).

27 Figure 70 shows a headrest given by a Dr Crispin to the British Museum in 1923 and is firmly attributed to the Dinka. Figure 71 is from the Wellcome Collection and is provenanced to Gondokoro.

28 Also known as the Hungaan or Huangana; standardised to Hungana throughout.

29 Also known as the BaHolo; standardised to Holo throughout.

30 Also known as the Mwila or MWila; standardised to Wila throughout.

31 Also known as the Ovahimba; standardised to Himba throughout.

32 The name Bambala is standardised to the form Mbala throughout.

33 Maes (1929, pl. I, figs. 15, 16), which are attributed to the Boma and Mangbetu, respectively.

34 Another example from the Musée Royal de l'Afrique Central (no. 53.74.3306) is extremely worn on the upper surface and is also attributed to the Teke. However, in William F. P. Burton's photo of a Luba divination ceremony (fig. 457), it is exactly this kind of headrest that is being used to support the Katatora.

35 A very similar example to this was illustrated by Maes (1929, pl. I, fig. 13), also using a marked entasis in the column, although Maes's example has a taller base and is attributed to the 'BaTeke' (i.e. Teke) of 'Léopoldville/Stanleyville'. Of two more examples of this type with the same attribution in the Musée Royal de l'Afrique Central (nos. 3653 & 43197), one has a clearly butterfly-shaped platform.

36 This example was published by Bourgeois (1984:73, fig. 54). Of the 11 examples of headrests he illustrated, it is the only one of this type, although they appear to have been quite commonly associated with the Yaka. One example illustrated by Bourgeois has a figure balanced on the conical base in place of the column (Bourgeois 1984:71, fig. 50), but the structural elements of base and platform are the same as the others of this type. This type of headrest is not mentioned by Biebuyck in his discussion of the Yaka (Biebuyck 1985:196).

37 Exactly how problematic the issue of attribution can be is attested by the case of one example of this type that has no surface decoration, a butterfly-shaped platform and platform flaps.

404 | AFRICAN DREAM MACHINES

Originating from the Oldman Collection in the British Museum (no. 1949 Af46 688), it is recorded as 'Somali' and has an annotation 'school/style of Ancient Egypt' in the register. This categorisation clearly demonstrates both the difficulties of attribution caused by the similarities of styles across regions and a pervasive need among collectors to align these headrests with ancient civilisations.

38 The attributions to the Hungana and Northern Mbala derive from Emil Torday, whose annotations generally appear to be accepted; see Mack (1990). The Teke attributions derive from Maes (1929) on the basis of ethnographic documentation in the Musée Royal de l'Afrique Central, and from Maesen. However, the attributions of headrests of this type to the Yaka and Holo do not appear to be based on the same degree of documentation, and often rely on the analysis and classification of the carving style of figurative features on these headrests rather than on any structural or formal differences in the headrests as functional sculptures.

39 See Bastin (1961, figs. 144–153) for Cokwe headrests using this shallower rectangular platform.

40 These headrests are in the British Museum (two) and Pitt Rivers Museum (two), and they give different dates for collection, the British Museum recording 1936 and Pitt Rivers 1937.

41 Figure 94a and 94b show the hollow undersides of the bases of the headrests in figures 90 and 93; this is discussed below in relation to another example, which is attributed to the Luba (see fig. 97).

42 British Museum, no. 1938.3-19.2 and Pitt Rivers Museum, no. X178.

43 There is a great variety of structure and style in the headrests collected among the Himba in the 1980s. Gender differentiation may lie in the differences between structural types as well. This is discussed elsewhere.

44 This headrest had not been given a museum number in 1990/91. Its Wellcome number is 232216, and the information cited here is on the label attached to the headrest itself.

45 Cf. Musée Royal de l'Afrique Central, nos. 52.48.96 and 52.48.107, both of which have different supports on conical bases and herringbone patterns on the ends of the platforms.

46 A very similar example, with a sloping conical base and a column bisected by a horizontal rectangular cross-bar hollowed out in the centre, is attributed by Dewey (1993:66, fig. 61) to the Tabwa, and he notes that this possibly sets the eastern limits of the distribution of this type of headrest.

47 That part of the Zambezi River basin that extends (inland) from the river mouth to Tête.

48 The complexities of Shona and Tsonga headrest classification will be discussed in a later chapter.

49 See Nettleton (1996) for a discussion of this tendency to attribute Southern African objects in German collections to the Tswana in relation to leather dolls from South Africa, and Nettleton (1989).

## CHAPTER 5

1 I did not have access to the records of the museum, and my request for information on headrests collected after 1929, the date of Maes's catalogue of the museum collection, drew an almost

complete blank for examples collected from 1950 onwards. I have therefore assumed that I was supplied with little information because the information was lacking.

2   These two, in both their platform shapes and their plain columns, are clearly related to Teke examples with conical bases and columned headrests discussed in chapter 4. Clearly, this demonstrates that the divisions I have drawn between different headrest types is arbitrary, but it must be emphasised that I do not see them as watertight. These examples are also very similar to headrests with rectangular bases and single columns illustrated by Maes on the same page (Maes 1929, pl. I, figs. 2, 6, 8, 9) and attributed to the Yansi, Funu (Mfinu), Bokala and Bunianga, but these I am going to examine separately below as a particular instance in which ethnic identity may be considered as evident in both the form and decoration of the headrest.

3   The second example (Musée Royal de l'Afrique Central, no. 43914) does not have any brass tacks, but is in all other respects identical to the one in figure 112. It was accessioned in 1946 and is provenanced to Kasai, Kapanga.

4   This is provided from information on the label attached to the object: see the caption for the illustration. However, it is impossible to confirm this by cross-reference to Wellcome Collection records.

5   The second is almost identical: see British Museum, no. 1904 6-11.4.

6   Lobed bases are not common in the columned Congolese headrests, and, although there is an example of a lobed base from the Tellem corpus (fig. 14), this form is very much associated with Shona and Tsonga headrests from south-east Africa.

7   Biebuyck (1985:7–8) appears to share Mack's (1990:49–51) assessment of Frobenius's methods as being less appropriate than Torday's in conducting field work. In spite of the shortcomings of both, however, they provide us with some of the more reliable sources of documentation of actual objects.

8   Also called the Isango; standardised to Isambo throughout.

9   Vansina gives only the briefest of mentions of this (Vansina 1966:241; 1978:77–78), but more information is available from the Tourist Bureau for the Belgian Congo and Ruanda-Urundi (1956:11–13, 305).

10  According to this last source referred to, the whole Congo from the coast to the falls, from the Bangala to Luluabourg, was occupied by colonial forces, and the 1890–92 actions against Ngongo Luteta were part of four successive expeditions east of the Kasai and into Katanga under the leadership of Le Marinel, Stairs and Delcommune.

11  Gille (c. 1950) gives figures for the towns for 1938 and 1944, but Luluabourg does not have entries for these years.

12  Biebuyck (1985:11–13) gives a useful synopsis of the breakdown of traditional ways of life under colonial administration in the Belgian Congo: the extent of outside intervention and manipulation varied widely, thus accounting for different levels of continuities and discontinuities in the autochthonous ways of living. Faced by the ethnic and political

fragmentation of the native population, the colonial government issued *arrêtés* and decrees aimed at administrative centralisation (Biebuyck 1985:11).

13 See Maesen et al.'s photograph (1959) of a Teke traveller with his headrest (Van Wassenhove 1996:65, pl. 47), one that now resides in the Musée Royal de l'Afrique Central.

14 Ironically, in an area in which the use and meaning of art objects has been extensively documented, especially among the Luba, Kuba and Songye, little or no information on the manufacture, use or final destiny of headrests is available from the literature on the art of the DRC region. But the possibility exists that headrests went to the grave with their owners, or in place of their owners' bodies (Dewey 1993), if they were not first sold to colonial agents and anthropologist collectors.

15 Dewey (1993, no. 60) illustrates an example of this type. He attributed it tentatively to the Songye.

16 I do not have an exact provenance for this example, but, by analogy with others with contiguous accession numbers (cf. figs. 118 and 120), it seems likely that it was collected in the vicinity of Lusambo, and that it might have been made/used by a Songye speaker. However, another example with a number in the same range (fig. 122), (Musée Royal de l'Afrique Central, no. 22722) is listed as 'BaKete' (i.e. Kete).

17 Burton's annotations appeared on the backs of photographs he sent to the Anthropology Department of the University of the Witwatersrand. See University of the Witwatersrand Art Galleries (1992, cat. no. 30). These divisions are discussed further below.

18 See, for example, Musée Royal de l'Afrique Central, nos. 35641 and 3565. Although I was not able to check this, it would appear that all three came to the museum in a single batch in 1934.

19 For example, see Maes (1929), Nettleton (1992), Neyt (1994), Petit (1996) and Roberts (1998).

20 It may equally be constructed as the traces of some idiosyncratic practices of the user of the object. The assumption that practices in the use of objects such as headrests within any particular group are necessarily homogeneous and thus guided by principles of conformity also rests on anthropological abstractions of actions on the ground.

21 An extraordinary example of a figurative headrest in the Musée Royal de l'Afrique Central seems to bear out the suggestion that headrests might have been used in ways other than for mere pillowing of the head. In this example (Musée Royal de l'Afrique Central, no. 50.13.1), a figure of indeterminate gender with an elaborate hairstyle that, together with the upward bent arms, supports a plain platform is placed in a carved basket form. The use of the basket here may be significant, as it suggests a link to divination and dreams. This will be further discussed in chapter 8.

22 There may be earlier examples in the Musée Royal de l'Afrique Central, but I have not been able to examine their records, and I have not examined American collections that may have examples dating back to Stanley's expeditions in the Congo/DRC, although none of these have surfaced in recent literature on early collections of African art in the United States.

23 See Huffman (1992:72) and University of the Witwatersrand Art Galleries (1992, cat. 33) for details of the Burton archaeological material.

24 De Maret (1982:94) suggests that, while it is possible to make distinctions among different traditions, each of which may cover several phases, the continuities in Upemba history over the past 1500 years are more striking than the differences — so Kisalian, Kabambian and recent Luba pottery styles flow into one another, suggesting that a similar continuity may have been present in wood-carving traditions.
25 Another very similar example (Musée Royal de l'Afrique Central, no. 43190) is given a very general attribution to Kasai Kapanga.
26 Homogeneity and difference in this larger region are not much discussed in the literature. Theuws's *Balubas et Balubaises* was based on an assumption of the spread of Luba culture beyond 'pure' Luba boundaries, but has largely been discredited in later literature. However, the 'confusions' that arose in the past among Luba, Hemba and Tabwa styles of carving, on the east of Luba territory (see Roberts 1996; Neyt 1994) are an index of the extreme limitations of ethnic stylistic attribution within this area.
27 See, for example, British Museum, no. 1954 Af23 (Wellcome Collection, no. 96827), another with no number (both the latter Wellcome Collection, box 80), and no. 1927.12.7.1; and Musée Royal de l'Afrique Central, nos. 54.134.54, 40.554 (Maes 1929, pl. VII, fig. 11) and 16967 (Maes 1929, pl. VII, fig. 10). These are discussed further in chapter 7.
28 Other examples of these forms, not listed by Maes, in the Musée Royal de l'Afrique Central, e.g. nos. 55.85.9, 53.37.71 and 3027, follow the same pattern, but have less-secure provenances.
29 The Mfinu are also known as the BaNfunu or Nfunu; standardised to Mfinu throughout.
30 See McGaffey (2000) for a discussion of these issues in relation to the spread of forms of initiation across different African societies.
31 However, these Kuba examples are differently structured, each platform being supported by its own paired columns so that at the point at the centre where the platforms meet, no support is used. The example in fig. 167 is thus an exception. They also appear to have consistently more robust proportions with a greater horizontal emphasis than the Ngombe ones. See below for a further discussion of the Kuba types.
32 Maes's (1929, pl. I, figs. 17, 18, 23, 30) 'Teke' examples of multiple-columned headrests are problematic because of the stylistic range they exhibit. Pl. I, fig. 17 and fig. 30 are structurally similar, one with two, the other with four columns, an oval base and platforms that do not extend far beyond the outer edge of the base or columns. But figure 17 has very different proportions to figure 18, being extremely tall in relation to its width, something that appears to tie it more closely to the 'BanFumu' (i.e. Fumu) example in plate I, figure 23. The third example (pl. I, fig. 18) has an extraordinary base, oval in plan with the vertical faces flaring outwards in convex curves to a median ridge, and with a ring-like projection on the upper flat surface between the two columns. Similar examples attributable to the Teke have not been found in other museum collections, and while this example may well be of Teke origin, it certainly serves to illustrate how idiosyncratic forms may have become in the making of personal objects.

33 This example is annotated by Maes as having been used only by women 'to conserve their coiffures', suggesting that there was some kind of gender specificity to particular headrest structures (Maes 1929:28, pl. V, fig. 28).

34 This suggestion might be reinforced by a single example of the same form in the British Museum (no. 1954 Af23 2007), provenanced to 'Lualaba' and accessioned in 1954.

35 See fn. 36.

36 The example illustrated in Maes (1929, pl. V, fig. 32) is problematic, as in the notations to plate V (Maes 1929: 28, 29), figure 31 appears twice, and there is no figure 32. However, the notes group like ethnicities together, which the images do not, and figures 31 and 36, which have some stylistic relation to each other, are both listed as Luba.

37 See above for a more detailed discussion of these examples.

38 I use the terms *Tsonga* and *Shona* here, although they are now contested. Both Tsonga and Shona appear to have been linguistic labels attached to disparate groups of peoples, and subsequently to their arts. Both can be divided into dialectic sub-groups, and their political histories show fragmented rather than homogeneous arrangements. See Becker (1999) and Harries (1989) on the Tsonga, and Bourdillon (1982), Beach (1980) and Ranger (1989) on the Shona.

39 Jaques was a Swiss missionary whose collection of Tsonga headrests remains unique in its depth of examples gleaned from a small geographical area; see Becker (1991; 1999) for an analysis of the importance of Jaques's collection.

40 A Tsonga sub-group; also known as the Shangaan or Shangana; standardised to Shangane throughout.

41 This assertion is based on a very large survey of headrests attributed to and provenanced to both groups, a survey that it would be impossible to repeat here, but of which aspects will be taken up in subsequent chapters.

## CHAPTER 6

1 I am following the outline of African language classification given by the various authors in Heine and Nurse (2000), Williamson and Blench (2000) and Bender (2000). That there is some confusion still in linguistic classification in Africa is visible in the differences in language classifications by two fairly recent encyclopaedias on Africa, i.e. Appiah and Gates (1999) and Murray (1998).

2 Which I have taken to include modern Sudan, Ethiopia, Eritrea, Somalia, Kenya, Uganda, Rwanda, Burundi, Tanzania and possibly Malawi.

3 It is interesting to note that in the British Museum displays of African material (Sainsbury Galleries, June 2005) a large Suk hairstyle — disembodied — hangs in a display case next to one

of Johnston's photographs of a Suk-speaking man, and much the same practice is followed in the Powell-Cotton Museum's mini dioramas, of which more later. This is discussed in greater detail in chapter 7.

4   This reference is also found in Arnoldi (1984).
5   Also known as the Daret; standardised to Darod throughout.
6   Also known as the Rehanwein; standardised to Rehanwin throughout.
7   I have not been able to visit Vienna to confirm this.
8   See Arnoldi (1984:30) and Van der Stappen (1996a:205).
9   Cf. Arnoldi (1984:30).
10  Cf. Falgayrettes (1989:57), Dewey (1993, pl. 19), Arnoldi (1984:28) and Van der Stappen (1996a:204).
11  Musée Royal de l'Afrique Central, no. 75.69.78.
12  As with many of the other attributions cited in this work from the Tervuren records, this may be a problematic one, as I was not allowed to check the records and do not know who made the attribution. However, given the fact that I was given such a paucity of information on most examples, one might assume that this one is fairly reliable.
13  Prins sees the frontal view as presenting an image of a cow's head with horns and the side view as an image of a circumcised penis. He struggles with the issues of repetition, mirroring and reverse imaging discussed more coherently in recent literature on mathematical systems; see Washburn (1983) and Gerdes (1997).
14  The illustration in Van der Stappen (1996a:204) only shows a 'front' view of the headrest, and it is thus impossible to make any deductions about the decorations that appear to be present on the sides of the supports.
15  The Powell-Cotton Museum is a private, family museum run under a board of trustees for the family on their land in Birchington on Sea, on the Kent coast in the United Kingdom. I visited the museum in June 2005.
16  These are Powell-Cotton Museum, nos. 1400 l (provenanced to 'Hindi Gosha cut') and 1182 (provenanced to 'Buracaba (town) Somali, Rehanwin, Elai male').
17  There is a second example of this type in the British Museum (no. 1979 Af12.2.2), accessioned in 1979, but which has an older acquisition number (Q75 Af392), which is attributed to the 'Somali (?)', a tentativeness that is probably warranted because of the spread of this style among other groups. A very beautiful example of this type was collected by Powell-Cotton in Jubaland and is on display at the Powell-Cotton Museum, and two examples, one with a circular column and another with a square pillar whose angles are tangential to the sides of the platform, and which thus appears as a diamond in plan (Powell-Cotton Museum, nos. 1033 & 1079), are respectively provenanced as follows: 'Jubaland 1935, Port Chisimao Somali, Darod Ogaden' and 'Somalia, Havia Tunne Hills, Elai made? Male'.
18  Also know as the Giryama; standardised to Giriama throughout.

19 The museum attributions are as follows: no. 1367, 'Margherita Yunne male's, unknown maker' and no. 1652, 'Bangamoyo Mahawi or Gosha Maghava', both from Jubaland in 1935.
20 British Museum, no. 1954 Af23 (Wellcome Collection, no. 191331). This example formed part of the Wellcome Collection and had not been fully accessioned in 1990–91 when I conducted this research, so the number may have changed in the interim.
21 As does the example from the Wellcome Collection, no. 1979 Af12.2.2 and many of the examples in the Powell-Cotton Museum, one of which, no. 1367, is almost identical to the purportedly Giriama example's strap.
22 Two further examples of this type in the Pitt Rivers Museum (nos. III.6 & VIII.204) are attributed to the Somali.
23 The second is British Museum, no. 1935.11.8.5.
24 Alternate spellings; standardised to Cotice throughout.
25 No. III.6. Donated to the museum in 1900 by H. Martyn Gibb, it is one of the earliest recorded examples of the type that I found in the museums visited.
26 Donated by Juxon Barton in August 1928.
27 Powell-Cotton Museum, nos. 392, 391, 1591, 365, 419, 1386, 1560, 330, 1596 and 331.
28 This example (Pitt Rivers Museum, no. IX.440) was donated by Miss D. Powell-Cotton.
29 British Museum, no. 1935.11.8.11.
30 Powell-Cotton Museum, nos. 1629 and 1416, respectively, while the notation to a third, in a showcase, says that this is used by men.
31 Fig. 193 is the only exception, having been collected in the Somali Republic, and given to the British Museum by the Church Missionary Society in 1962.
32 This headrest has a number of photographs associated with it showing the process of manufacture, and the museum records give the vernacular name for the headrest as '*barleh*'. Another headrest from the same source (Munich, no. SMFV 83-302-204), which appears much older, follows the same pattern, but with the decorative fields broken into horizontal registers, and a third example (Munich, no. SMFV 41.4.656) of a somewhat earlier date, together suggest a continuous tradition.
33 Powell-Cotton Museum, no. 1398, collected in Jubaland in 1935.
34 Of course, Falgayrettes (1989) also includes Japanese block forms in this discussion, but these are ceramic and could be argued to be constructed in an additive mode, as are other modelled forms, as opposed to wooden examples where the amount of wood removed in the subtractive process of carving diminishes the closer one gets to the cylindrical shape of the wood from which the object is carved.
35 The headrests on sale in Johannesburg were sold from a central clearing house in Johannesburg by Ethiopian middlemen, and came with very little documentation as to geographic or ethnic provenance.
36 In an article on Ethiopian carver Menjiye Tabeta and the Fuga of Gurageland, on the H-Net website in 1999, it is explained that most new objects among the Gurage are carved from light-

coloured wood and painted in magenta, purple, green and yellow. An example in the British Museum still has some traces of colour visible through its patina. See <http://www.h-net.msu.edu/-etoc/profiles/menjiye_info.html>, accessed 14 June 1999.

37 Van Praet (1996) noted that there are 22 million Oromo, forming a major political and ethnic force in Ethiopia, but that there is a marked degree of cultural and religious diversity among them. He also points to a large number of Oromo in Kenya. Rikitu (2001) gives a figure of 30 million Oromo living in the Baale Arsi and Boorana regions of Ethiopia, of whom 85 per cent are rural and 15 per cent urban dwellers.

38 It has been argued on the H-Net Ethiopia website that Gurage headrests are made largely by a sub-ethnicity, the Fuga, and traded by them to the Gurage; (<http://www.h-net.msu.edu/-etoc/profiles/menjiye_info.html>, accessed 14 June 1999); cf. also Pankhurst and Nida (1999), who discuss Gurage and Fuga wood objects (but not headrests). Whether or not the Fuga are a separate ethnicity is somewhat irrelevant, given the fact that the columned headrests of the Gurage are so similar to those of the Oromo and Arsi. This rather demonstrates the similarities of form among these Afro-Asiatic speakers.

39 Van Praet (1996) and Todd (1896), who noted that the missionary Ormerod and his wife had been making good progress in the conversion of Galla (Oromo) and Pokomo (Pokot) at Golbanti.

40 Van der Stappen (1996a:198–201). Guarage examples in the Michigan State University collection are illustrated on the H-Net Ethiopia web site: <http://www.h-net.msu.edu/-etoc/profiles/menjiye_a5.html>, accessed 14 June 1999.

41 Van der Stappen (1996a:110, 111).

42 Van der Stappen (1996a:113, 114).

43 Van der Stappen (1996a); cf. p. 42, no. 62 to p. 43, nos. 69 and 70.

44 Van der Stappen (1996a:73, nos. 169–171).

45 Van der Stappen (1996a:73, no. 169).

46 See Van der Stappen (1996a:164–66). A group of headrests carved by one carver, Gebre Wolde Tsadik, published in Silverman (1999:111) includes examples of a number of these types, bearing out the suggestion that the differences are not to do with ethnic divisions, at least not at the point of production.

47 Jonathan Lowen, who put this collection together, commissioned Margaret Carey to work on the attributions of items in the collection to different ethnicities, a task she had previously undertaken at the British Museum. These attributions are not always defensible.

48 Manchester University Museum, no. G3234.

49 Gaam is the standardised name used throughout; Ingassana (alternate spelling Ingessana) is an alternate name for this group. According to Launer (1981), 'Ingassana' is a derogatory Arabic term applied to these people, who are divisible into four sections: *jok kulek, jok tau, jok buek* and *jok gor*, each with distinctive dialect, music and dance. Cerulli (1956) mentions that the Gaam/Ingassana grease their hair, that men wear a circle of curls around the head

and that women have curls only at the back, but she does not mention headrests or other woodwork by these people, whereas she does mention that the south-west Sidama make headrests caled *sugana* or *zala*. Cf. also Jedrej (1995) for a discussion of Gaam/Ingassana religious institutions.
50 British Museum, no. 1954 Af23 (TB 186), (Wellcome Collection, no. 2036/9).
51 Another, almost identical headrest in the museum in Glasgow (no. 9'70 4c) is provenanced to South Africa, but is very unlikely to be from that geographic region.
52 See Donovan (1998), Dewey (1993:45–46) and Best (1993:152–56). A very similar example in the Liverpool World Museum (no. 1987.10.5) has a secure and detailed provenance to Karamojong of the 'Moroto area, Namagunga, Uganda'.
53 For detail on the Karamojong/Jie and Turkana, see Gulliver and Gulliver (1953:29–39, 55–81), Faye (1999:1898–99) and Best (1993).
54 Mack gives a more detailed account of the distribution of these headrests in the Sudan among the Toposa, who closely are related to the Turkana, Didinga and Larim. He also points to their distribution among Cushitic speakers such as the Hamar (Mack 1982:117). Turton (1977) suggests that the Hamar and Mursi are 'enemies' and share no traits.
55 See Van der Stappen (1996a:133–34).
56 Hodder (1977) gives a synopsis of some of the complexities within the Baringo district of Kenya, tracing the ways in which influence passes, particularly among the Njemps, Tugen and Pokot.
57 Pitt Rivers Museum, no. 1941.4.67 is provenanced to the Nuer or Anuak, but both provenances are queried. I am opting for the first, but the uncertainty may have been Evans Pritchard's.
58 His attribution is based on one published example in Wolfe (1979:17); other similar examples are to be found in Donovan (1988:47, fig. 8) and the University of the Witwatersrand Art Galleries, Standard Bank Collection of African Art.
59 An example with a similar base, but with a bi-lobed platform, is in the Musée Royal de l'Afrique Central (no. 78.30.2). This one is simply attributed to north-west Kenya.
60 There is a similar example in the Musée Royal de l'Afrique Central (no. 81.48), which is attributed to north-eastern Uganda.
61 Jean Brown, Pitt Rivers Museum, nos. 1978.20.263 and 1973.20.35.
62 No number is visible in the display, but the object is documented as coming from the east bank of the Nile in southern Sudan. An example in the Brenthurst Collection (no. JL-E 9), (Davison 1991b:194) has an almost identical base, but a flat support and propeller-shaped curved platform. It is attributed to the Karamojong.
63 There is an almost identical example in the Liverpool World Museum (no. 7.6.20.58), presented by W. L. L. Loat esq., and provenanced to 'Bari, Gondokoro, Uganda'. A similar example in the Powell-Cotton Museum is attributed to the 'Moru tribe', but its legs are closer together and it only has one hole in the top and bottom cross-sections between them.
64 Powell-Cotton Museum, no. 22 1 33b.
65 No. 1936.148.8, Shilluk, southern Sudan, collected by Major J. J. Bramble (Sudan Political

Service) and no. 56,24.371, Dinka/Bari, southern Sudan, collected by Captain R. Stacy (Norwich Castle Museum) before 1913.

66  Westermann (1970) records that younger men among the Shilluk had very elaborate hairstyles and used 'neckrests'. However, he says their headrests took the form of animals — hippopotamus, giraffe, camel, ostrich or ibis. While he says that most men can make headrests, there are also Shilluk specialists called *bote tani* (Westermann 1970:106). I came across none of these in European collections.

67  Bari columned headrests have a quite different arrangement of their bases from those of other groups in the same region (see above, p. 85, figs. 70 & 71).

68  I have attached these groups in this way because various ethnographies suggest that the relationships among the linked groups are strong. This is to some extent reflected in the similarities of form in the headrests provenanced to these groups. Acoli is the standardised spelling of this name; also spelt Acholi.

69  The Gullivers claim that this headrest type was adopted by the Turkana and Karamojong from the Toposa, who are one of the sub-groups of the Jie, as are the Turkana (Gulliver & Gulliver 1953:2, 36, 57).

70  See British Museum, nos. 1924 12-10 and 1925 11-23-1.

71  Variants of this type were extensively documented in the collection made by Jean Brown in the1970s and bought by the Pitt Rivers Museum in 1979.

72  No. 79.15.5.

73  Such photographs are to be found in various museum collections, including some in the Manchester University Museum, in the F. H. Rogers Collection and in the Musée Royal de l'Afrique Central, and are published in Falgayrettes (1989:54).

74  The Pitt Rivers Museum has three of these from the same source (no. 1978 9.3-4), and the one illustrated here. One in the British Museum (no. 1947 Af16.90) is provenanced to the Karamojong and was collected early — between 1890 and 1910, as was another (no. 1934 4-10.32) also provenanced to the southern Karamojong.

75  See Musée Royal de l'Afrique Central, nos. 70.84.1 and 81.42.8; Munich Staatlisches Museum für Völkerkunde, no. 83.202-22; and Wolfe (1979:17, no. A4).

76  British Museum, nos. cc+8305, cc+8304, cc+8306 (NN) and 1979 Af1 2493.

77  That a deeper reading of aesthetic theory would yield other arguments has not been tested by these authors, but see Danto (1989).

78  Pitt Rivers Museum, no. 1978.20.1ff

79  Pitt Rivers Museum, no. 1978.20.32

## CHAPTER 7

1  See Nettleton (1990) for a discussion of this division in Southern Africa.

2  See particularly Jean Brown's detailed collection of Tiati Pokot headrests at the Pitt Rivers

Museum in Oxford, and Major and the Misses Powell-Cotton's collection of Somali headrests in the Powell-Cotton Museum in Birchington on Sea, both discussed in chapter 4.

3   That this debate can rouse emotions and shake up the Africanist scholarly community is evident in the way it manifested itself in 1997 on one of the internet H-Net listserve debates, with contributions from Colleen Kriger, David Schoenbrun, Eloi Tollo, Roland Oliver, David Killick, Dax Driver and Norman Etherington, among others (*Bantu Dispersal*, H-Safrica, <h-safrica@h-net.msu>, 6–19 March 1997).

4   See Bourdillon (1982) for a classic account of the Shona sub-divisions, and Junod (1927) for the Tsonga.

5   This is one of a number of similar examples in the Musée Royal de l'Afrique Central.

6   In fact, Becker uses the two-pillar structure as one of her categories of division of headrest types, along with a number of others that I have found to be quite sound, but which are too detailed to recount here.

7   See Becker (1999) for a discussion of the ways in which 'Tsonga' has been made and used as an art historical category.

8   Dewey publishes a few examples of the same type, which are in the Jos Collection (1993: 108–9, 150).

9   *Shona* is a term used in colonial parlance for people speaking related languages in the Zimbabwe, north-east Botswana and western Mozambique areas, including the Manyika, Korokore, Zezuru, Karanga and Kalnaga, as well as, sometimes, the Ndau (see Ranger 1989; Bourdillon 1982; Dewey 1993).

10  Dewey (1991; 1993) has suggested that with the greater detail of information available to him than was available to me (Nettleton 1985), he could develop a clear picture of regional styles among Shona. However, his eastern, central and northern styles do not appear to me to have anything separating them: see, for example, Dewey (1993), figs. 12 & 20 — central style — vs. fig. 15 — eastern style — where all the elements are laid out in exactly the same way. It is, however fairly clear that southern Shona headrests generally do approach more closely to Tsonga styles — or perhaps it is vice versa.

11  All of these are in the British Museum. They are all from collections made before 1930, and have secure provenance in Zimbabwe.

12  Another example of this type, collected by a Miss A. Henderson, in the British Museum (no. 1971 Af13.4), has unusual geometric decoration down the edges of the support as well. It has the generic attribution of Shona.

13  Hans Himmelheber collected an almost identical example in the Inyanga region among the 'Wawesa' (Munich, Museum für Völkerkunde, no. 33-2-2). It also has no pendants and no platform decoration, except at its ends.

14  See Nettleton (1985, fig. Sh 28; South African Museum, no. 1724). This example has opposed nested triangle motifs on its platform's upper surface.

15 In fact it appears to be the *only* feature that distinguishes his eastern style, exemplified in his figure 15, and his central style, exemplified in his figure 20 (Dewey 1993).
16 See Nettleton (1985, fig. Sh 38) where one of these, from the National Culture History Museum in Tshwane (Pretoria), is illustrated. It was collected in what Dewey would call the central area, but does not have pendants or lugs, which are seen on its companion in the latter illustration, whose exact provenance is not secure, but which was collected much earlier. An example in the British Museum (no. 1940 Af21.6), which is unusually wide, but follows the same pattern as these examples, but without any decoration on the platform, is provenanced to the 'Unwini tribe'.
17 British Museum, nos. 1950 Af4,3 and 1950 Af4,4. The only difference between these and the 'Shona' examples seems to lie in the use of irregular patterns on the upper surface of the platform. The third example (British Museum no. 1957 Af1.49) is notated as coming from Nyasaland and as being used for 'travelling'.
18 British Museum, no. 1892 7.14.154. A rather strange variant on this theme is one from the Wellcome Collection now in the British Museum (1954 Af23 [Wellcome Collection, no. 166 434]), where there are four triangle and circle elements, but the centre circles are squashed into vertical ovals and the decoration consists of zig-zags contoured to the outlines of the support. The lack of specific provenance makes it difficult to place such examples.
19 Cf. also Nettleton (1985) fig. Sh 52b, an example from the British Museum pre-dating 1900.
20 These examples include a number from the Musée Royal de l'Afrique Central for which I was not allowed access to any records. Attributions have been based on educated guesswork.
21 Cf. Musée Royal de l'Afrique Central, nos. 2387 (four pyramid knobs both sides of centre) and 32824 (divided diamonds in rows 3x3, and nested triangles and cross hatchings, making a cross).
22 A number of examples of this types were published by Maes (1929, pl. VI, fig. 3, Kuba Lusambo; pl. VI, fig. 5, Kuba beads; pl. VI, fig. 4, Lulua; pl. VI, figs. 20, 21, Luebo). Some of these were dressed with beads wound around the panels in the way women would wrap their bodies.
23 This arrangement of built-in snuff-boxes is to be found on many examples of Southern African headrests of very different types. The link between snuff and ancestors, and among ancestors, dreams and sleeping, and therefore the link to headrests, is explored elsewhere in this study.
24 My sampling of Southern African examples has been wide-ranging, but cannot claim to be exhaustive, given the propensity to variation of single types across the region.
25 Cornet's (1982) extensive analysis of geometric motifs and their names among the Kuba bears this out, and Meurant's (1986) analysis of Shoowa cloth motifs also develops this.
26 A similar three-dimensional scheme of crossed legs is evident on a double headrest said to have belonged (with some justification) to the Zulu king, Dinizulu (KwaZulu-Natal Local History Museums 1996:68, fig. K32). The formal elements of this headrest are different from those normally associated with Zulu headrests (see below, nos. 382ff.), and appear to be hybrid between Zulu and Tsonga.

27 Cf. Musèe Royal de l'Afrique Central, nos. 54.25.15 and 70.17.2, both of which have the same two-tiered base; no. 675 (Maes 1929, pl. VI, fig. 8); and no. 53.74.408 from Butaan Gili; while one was collected by William F. P. Burton in the Mwanza region (University of the Witwatersrand Art Galleries 1992:29–30).
28 A similar example, but without provenance, is published by Dewey (1993, fig. 71).
29 See Wanless (1985, nos. 31 &32); also Distant (1892).
30 Becker (1999) discusses the roles of the different Swiss missionaries in the construction of the category 'Tsonga' in its ethnic inclusiveness as an art historical entity. Jeannerat was one of these missionaries.
31 Gwamba are a sub-group of the Tsonga, and were early migrants to the area known as Spelonken in present-day Limpopo Province, South Africa. They were named *knobneusen* by the early Voortrekkers from the Cape in the 1830s.
32 These include examples in Geneva (Musèe d'Ethnologie), Neuchâtel (Musée de Ville) and Munich (Staatlisches Museum für Völkerkunde), as well as some from the Wellcome Collection now in the British Museum.
33 These are perhaps the finest surviving examples of the type; there are others, including British Museum nos. 2184 and 1910.10.5.83 (collected by Sir Bartle Frere in what was then Natal, now KwaZulu-Natal Province, in the nineteenth century), that are less distinguished. An almost identical example to this is found in the Brenthurst Collection, but with more detailed carving, which shows very little sign of wear; (see Davison 1991b:160, no. 215), and an example with a more delicate platform and round legs in the Musèe Royal de l'Afrique Central (no. RG57.32.31) extends the possibilities of the type further. This example has the rather unusual feature of a handle carved as a loop at one end of the platform, suggesting its mobility.
34 Another, slightly smaller, but more intricate example of this kind in the British Museum, also listed as deriving from the London International Exhibition of 1862, and referred to in the catalogue for Natal (i.e. KwaZulu-Natal), p. 18, is said to be a 'milk or beer pot'. Its two mouths would make it almost completely non-functional. Other complex examples in the Brenthurst Collection are to be found in Davison (1991b), but none has a clear provenance, and attributions are made to 'North Nguni' and Swazi.
35 One of this type of bowl in the Brenthurst Collection (Davison 1991b, pl. 32) was identified as 'Swazi/North Nguni', and this seems to have been accepted as a blanket ethnic identity for all similar examples, including one from the Museum of Natural History and Ethnography in Lille (Joubert & Martin 2002:152, pl. 55), in spite of there being no clear provenance for most of them.
36 British Museum, nos. 1561, 2175, 2176, 3256, 4875, 4876, 1559, 1560 and 1569.
37 British Museum, nos. 1559 and 1560, of which 1559 is very similar to one in the Brenthurst Collection.
38 Cf. Klopper (1989; 1992) and Berning (1996), who relies almost entirely on Klopper's argument.
39 British Museum, no. 1181a, 'Kaffir headrest with bowl at each end', Henry Christy, 1860–69.

40 See Klopper (1992; 1991) for a discussion of the *amasumpa* motif.

41 A fourth example, in the Liverpool World Museum (no. 49-41-57), also from the Wellcome Collection and without much information attached, has fluted legs and carved zig-zags on the platform ends, but again appears to be relatively unused, although beautifully patinated.

42 Another example in the Liverpool World Museum (no. 56 24 180; ex-Norwich Castle Museum, no. 186.928, from Miss Long and accessioned before 1928) has its central leg fluted vertically, and the two outer ones fluted horizontally, but in all other respects corresponds to the examples with *amasumpa* reliefs. It is attributed to the Zulu, as opposed to a headrest from the Conru Collection (Klopper & Nel 2002, fig. 7), where the tendency to label anything with fluting as 'Swazi' is demonstrably problematic.

43 This idea has been perpetuated in the labelling of all such objects as Northern Nguni/Swazi throughout the catalogue of the Brenthurst Collection (Davison 1991b) without any regard for its historical accuracy. See above.

44 See Davison (1991b, figs. 74 & 77, and cat. no. 219, p. 160); see also Glasgow Museum (no. 70.4 d), an earlier acquisition, but with no accurate provenance, and one in the National Culture History Museum in Tshwane (Pretoria), (no. 8076), which has ear-shaped projections facing upwards at the ends of the platform and is provenanced as Swazi.

45 One in the Johannesburg Art Gallery, Brenthurst Collection (no. JL E 57), which has no provenance, and another collected by Rev. Buchler in the Bushbuck Ridge area called Tsonga (MuseumAfrika, no. 41/1047d), but similar to another from the same source (MuseumAfrika, no. 41/5) attributed to the 'Swazi'.

46 See Bonner (1983) for a detailed history of the Swazi state and its relationship to other North Nguni and Sotho entities.

47 Less finely finished examples are British Museum, nos. SA56, whose label reads 'Kaffir Pillow, Natal, Captain Garden', and on which there is a sticker that reads 'Duplicate Kew 10.11.76', and 577, which is from the Christy Collection (no. 1860-69).

48 British Museum, no. 1936-10-15-23.

49 A very similar example to this, collected by Frederick Clayton, now in the Manchester University Museum (no. SA8), via the Halifax Museum, where it was accessioned pre-1901, suggests that the records for the headrests in figures 399 and 400 may have become confused in the museum itself — the headrest in figure 400 is reproduced in the Brenthurst Collection catalogue (Davison 1991b:87–88) with the provenance given here. The Manchester example, however, has one column at each end of the platform and two loose to the centre on the sides, but slightly staggered.

50 See British Museum, no. 1944 Af4.257, ex-Blackmore Museum, and pre-1931.

51 British Museum, no. 577 is one of this type, also from the Henry Christy Collection of 1860–66. It is made of a soft, pale wood with black staining, and does not begin to measure up to the craftsmanship of others.

52 See King George VI Art Gallery 1999 — a collection of headrests from the Msinga district in KwaZulu-Natal, part of the old Zulu kingdom. Frank Jolles (University of KwaZulu-Natal) has also put together research on district-specific headrests, also with a wide range of types evident in his collection now in the Natal Museum, Pietermaritzburg.
53 Some of these are illustrated in Davison (1991b).
54 Davison (1991b, pl. 16, cat. nos. L17–L20) and Joubert and Valentin (2002, figs. 85, 86).
55 See Joubert and Valentin (2002, figs. 89, 90), the latter having entered the Koninklijke Museum voor Volkenkunde in Leiden in 1890, while the former was acquired by the Musée de l'Homme in 1931.
56 Although Malawi was a British colony (Nyasaland) and Tanganyika (Tanzania) passed from German to British control in 1918, there are very few Ngoni headrests, or in fact any other ethnically distinct Malawian groups, such as the Cewa, in British museums. But there are a number of Ngoni headrests in German museums, presumably from Tanzania, which was first a German colony. Why there is such a difference between these two Ngoni headrest types has been addressed by Michael Conner (cited in Dewey 1993), who suggests that it has to do with the multiplicity of origins claimed by people who were brought together under the Ngoni 'banner'. It is more difficult to account for the lack of such headrests in British museums.
57 This position is implicit in Dewey's (1993) argument and in Conner's (1991, cited in Dewey 1993) account of the Malawian Ngoni headrests. The Ngoni, having fled the area in the vicinity of northern Swaziland under Zwagendaba, settled in Malawi and Tanzania. Conner found that some Malawian Ngoni claimed to be able to relate headrest styles to where their ancestors came from *before* the Ngoni arrived.
58 Examples abound in Duggan Cronin's published photographs, and in others; the two reproduced here are from other sources.
59 I was told by a number of Tsonga–Shangane chiefs in what is now the Limpopo Province in 1978 that those descended from Zulu forefathers, especially the *isinduna* in the Bushbuck Ridge area, learned to speak Zulu to distinguish themselves from commoners. Conner (1991, cited in Dewey 1993) has noted a similar Zulu pride among Ngoni speakers in Malawi.
60 See Nettleton, Ndabambi and Hammond-Tooke (1989) for clarification on the use of this name for the Nguni speakers of the Eastern Cape as a whole.

## CHAPTER 8

1 This photograph and others in the Burton archive are in the University of the Witwatersrand Art Galleries' archive; cf. University of the Witwatersrand Art Galleries (1992).
2 See Colle (1913) for one of these early attempts, and Verhulpen (1936) for an attempt at sorting out the 'true' Luba from those influenced by the Luba.
3 That such possibilities are evident in many aspects of mission photography is evident from a growing literature on the subject, including Geary (1991; 2002).

4  Geary (2002), among others, has argued that the sitter in a photograph is not necessarily a passive participant in the process of making the image, even in colonial situations, where the 'native' subjects were relatively powerless.

5  See Roberts and Roberts (1996:155), where they suggest that 'stool' elicits discourse relating to the underpinnings of authority in a given locale, while staffs are used to explain how power arrived at a certain place.

6  Womersley (1984:70) describes how, during the investiture of a new ruler (king), the wooden headrest on which he was to lie during his seclusion was surrounded by the skulls of all the deceased kings. Theuws's (1962) account of the headrest in divination is discussed in further detail below.

7  This interpretation was suggested by Allen Roberts in a personal communication, 21 April 2006.

8  The crowns visible in both these photos and in at least one other by Burton were important pieces of chiefly regalia in Luba kingdoms, being passed down from father to son 'as an heirloom' (University of the Witwatersrand Art Galleries 1992, cat. 247).

9  Another portrait of Chief Kajingu by Burton also has him sitting, this time in three-quarter view, and three-quarter length close-up with his regalia and a comment that his wearing his cap for the photograph was unusual as he, Kajingu, was 'afraid of having it taken from him' (cited in University of the Witwatersrand Art Galleries 1992, cat. 247).

10 See Nooter (1992a:81) for a discussion of the ways in which royal insignia were made secret and thus rendered more powerful. Burton's photographs included a number of these stools (University of the Witwatersrand Art Galleries 1992, figs. 50–52).

11 The incongruity is felt very strongly here. Birchington on Sea is a tiny sea-side town on the Kent coast, close to the holiday resorts of Margate and Ramsgate, with a single high street, and is about as far from rural Africa as it is possible to imagine. The museum is part of a large house ten minutes' walk from the station, situated in a fenced park and surrounded by neat English farmland, although the park has its obligatory wooded area. Inside is this huge curiosity cabinet, a reliquary containing the fetishes of colonial exploration.

12 See Contini (1965) and Corson (1965) for various insights into the development of hair fashions in Europe, and Craik (1995) for a discussion of the management of the body through a variety of regimes, including hairstyling.

13 I am aware that all societies have particular regimes of the body, but it is the Judaeo-Christian tradition that appears to have a problem with hair among all its adherents. In Buddhist practice, only monks deal with hair as a problem, by shaving it off. In Rastafarian practice, one has the opposite of this form of control of hair, but the acceptance or promotion of dreadlocks as mandatory for all believers is as much a mechanism of control as shaving the head.

14 Mercer (1994) discusses the significance of revivalist hairstyling among Africans in the diaspora, suggesting that there are three strands to the phenomenon in which straightening represents a third way between white and black forms. This view is challenged by Kennell (2000), who

suggests that in African-American culture, at least the black–white opposition is crumbling. See Erasmus (2000) for an analysis of this problem in apartheid South Africa.

15 Fanon suggests that the individual undergoes 'a slow composition of [my] *self* as a body in the middle of a spatial and temporal world — such seems to be the schema' (Fanon 1967:111). Noting that the schema is not imposed, but is instead 'a definitive structuring of self and the world', he suggests that 'in the face of racism, corporeal schema crumble — its [*sic*] place taken by a racial epidermal schema' (Fanon 1967:112).

16 A search of missionary journals, including *The Missionary Echo of the United Methodist Free Churches*, 1894–98, yielded very few photographs of Africans, but plenty of missionaries and their Chinese converts. There are more Africans after 1900. *The Herald of the Primitive Methodist Missionary Society* has many more images of Africans, but converts outnumber those who remained with indigenous belief systems. *The Kingdom Overseas*, in its first volume (1933:7, 157, 273), produced a large number of images of Ila persons with elaborate hairstyles, all taken by Rev. E. W. Smith. *The Missionary Herald,* published by the American Board of Commissioners for Foreign Missions, has, from 1900 onwards, a number of photographs of indigenes, especially those from KwaZulu-Natal in South Africa.

17 Also known as the Babunda or BaBunda; standardised to Dumba throughout.

18 British Museum, no. Af/CA134/66. See also images in Mack (1990).

19 See University of the Witwatersrand Art Galleries (1992), Esterman (1970), Tönjes (1996) and Davison (1991b).

20 Dewey (1993, fig. 1) reproduces one of Cole's photographs of a Pokot initiated man with mud-pack hairstyle and headrest.

21 See Lawal (2000), Jordán (2000) and Boone (1986) for a discussion of this in different groups. It could be argued that Rastafarians' dreadlocks are no less a display of control over the peripheries of the body, especially as the dreadlocks are so often hidden from view.

22 Allen Roberts (personal communication, 2006) suggests that there was an entire range of hairstyles among the Tabwa, although these are not as clearly reflected in the sculpture as hairstyles are among the Luba.

23 Roberts (1998:51) recalls Laudé's (1973:26) notion that the relationship between the visual and the oral is a dialectical one: that 'oral myth arises from sculptured works'.

24 Other photographs of hairstylists at work include one by Mrs Jaques among the Tsonga at Pilgrim's Rest in the then eastern Transvaal Province in the 1920s and the image of Zulu dandies discussed above in the section on tripod forms (fig. 382).

25 Of the examples in the Torday archive at the British Museum, the hairstyles of the Dumba appear to be most elaborate (e.g. nos. Af/CA131/44 & Af/CA136/55) and the most elaborate Kuba hairstyles appear to be those of Bushong women (e.g. no. Af/CA143/14). Mbala hairstyling in these photos involved hair in braids from the forehead back, with extensions from the nape down the back (nos. Af/CA134/22 & Af/CA132/3). Pende hairstyles for men were mop-like, with extensions (nos. AfCA132/96 & Af/CA/136/4).

26 A number of images that, although intended to capture 'ethnic' types, also capture different hairstyles can be found in a number of issues of *Libertas* magazine (1944a; 1944b). These include some Tutsi hairstyles, in which younger men wear their hair in three large cone-shaped projections, while older men have multiple mud-pack sausage-like crests running from the forehead to the nape of the neck.

27 Drewal (1977) and Lawal (2000) have both looked at this aspect of hair and its styling in Yoruba society, and it is dealt with by other authors in the volume edited by Sieber and Herremann (2000). See also Arnoldi and Kreamer (1995) for a discussion of the significance of the head in African societies.

28 That there has been a revival of sculptural hairstyling in the past ten years does not appear, however, to have signalled the return of the headrest, and Western women wearing 'beehive' hairstyles in the 1960s had to make do with a bone-shaped pillow equivalent that went better with a bedstead and mattress. Small canvas folding headrests were sold for use on the beach in California in the past, but they do not appear to have been developed for everyday use (Allen Roberts, personal communication, 21 April 2006).

29 Luba examples are numerous, but see, for examples, Maes (1929, pl. VII, figs. 1, 2, 4, 5, 6, 21, 22); Beumers (1996, nos. 45, 46, 47); and Neyt (1994:174, 175, 177, 180, 181, 185, 186, 187, 188, 189, 190, 191).

30 These attempts started with Olbrechts' (1946:71–74) identification of the Buli style, and was followed by others, including De Maret, Dery and Murdoch (1973). Dewey seems to accept the notion of regional sub-styles, suggesting possible ascription of headrest styles to different regions of Luba territory (Dewey 1993:69). Neyt (1994: 174–90), who divides the Luba headrests that he illustrates according to specific workshops, seems to be the only scholar who has attempted to move away from a pan-ethnic framework, but his attributions have been challenged by Petit (1996:89) and Roberts (1998). Many more Luba caryatid headrests were published in Krieger (1978, vol. III, pls. 262–275).

31 This example is almost identical to one in the Museum Rietberg in Zurich (no. RAC 131), the only difference being in the scarification of the stomach.

32 Headrests configured similarly to that in the portrait of Kilukwe discussed above, with kneeling female or (occasionally) male caryatids, whose legs scroll behind the buttocks, covering the top of the base, as they do in many stools from the same region, are almost exclusively attributed to the Luba, in spite of an enormous range of different figural styles. The range of style from naturalism to extreme stylisation in these headrests and other figurative and non-figurative objects, of course, calls into question the validity of looking for a Luba style as an homogeneous category. Luba style has been defined in relation to only well-known figurative sculptures and disregards the differences offered by specific instances of individual headrests.

33 Luba, Bena Lulua (i.e. Lulua), Songye, BaKete (i.e. Kete) and Kanyok headrests with figures as supports are illustrated by Maes (1929, pls. V, VI). Examples from the Joss Collection have been attributed by Dewey (1993, pls. 54, 57, 58, 62–68) to the Binji, Songye, Luba and Hemba, but they have no secure provenance.

34 One only has to look at the repeated use of particular examples from Falgayrettes (198 plates) to Neyt (19 plates) to see the paucity of variation in the examples used in setting up the notion of the type of figurative caryatid headrest ascribed to the Luba.
35 Bourgeois (1984: figs. 50, 53, 55, 56) illustrates a number of these, but many of them are attributions rather than having unambiguous provenances.
36 British Museum, nos. Af54 N23 1751 and Af54 N23 1752; Maes (1929, pl. VII, figs. 9, 12, 14, 15, 18).
37 See Maes (1929, pl. VII, figs. 9, 12, 14, 15, 18), Musée Royal de l'Afrique Central, no. 36762 and British Museum, nos. Af54 N23 1751 and Af54 N23 1752.
38 Songye examples include British Museum, nos. 1954 N23 (no Wellcome Collection number), 1954 Nf23 (Wellcome Collection, no. 96827), 1927-12.7.1 and 1979 Af1.1815; and Musée Royal de l'Afrique Central, no. 40555, where the feet become the base, and no. 57.7.17. These headrests correspond to a style illustrated by Dewey (1993:65, fig. 57), and attributed to the master of Beneki, and to two illustrated by Maes (1929, pl. VII, figs. 10, 11). One extraordinary example from the Musée Royal de l'Afrique Central (no. 48.15.3) has bent legs, large feet and no body, but a head supported directly by the feet. Kanyok examples include Musée Royal de l'Afrique Central, nos. 56.46.2 and 20148. Mbala examples tend to exclude the lower torso, so that the legs join the chest and arms, which bend upwards to support the platform; see British Museum, no. 1907.5-28.14, and Maes (1929, pl. I, figs. 26, 27), who, however, attributes them to the 'Banfumu' (i.e. Fumu).
39 Another example in the British Museum (no. 1927-2.7.1) was donated by one J. P. Armstrong and is likewise attributed to the Songye. It appears to be in a very similar style to the example from the Wellcome Collection and may indicate the hand of a single artist.
40 A Songye sub-group.
41 Thus the headrests of the so-called Master of the Cascade hairstyle generally display a coherence of form not only in the idiosyncratic figurative elements, but also in the more conventional bases and platforms.
42 The records here are scanty. The Museum Rietberg has attributed this to 'Luba/Tabwa' and 'Zaire/Tanzania', but there is no documentation to back up a Tabwa attribution at all.
43 See Musée de Ville, Neuchâtel, nos. IIIc 3033 and IIIc 3024, and Geneva Musée d'Ethnographie, no. 7039, which has, unusually, a leopard for a caryatid.
44 Other animals appear on other headrest styles, some discussed above — see figures 88 and 330 — from Yaka and Suku sources. For birds, see Bastin (1961) and Baumann (1935); also Musée Royal de l'Afrique Central, nos. 44728, 51.13.15, 43174, 35791 and 20153. Two with distinctly ape-like heads and feet are also in the Musée Royal de l'Afrique Central (nos. 32842, 32845, 51.31.191).
45 See, for example, Davison (1991b, pl. 17) and Sieber (1980:122), both of which have unambiguously Zulu characteristics.
46 An example in the Brenthurst Collection, put together by Jonathan Lowen in London, is attributed to Zulu authorship (Davison 1991b), and Balandier and Maquet (1974:350) illustrate another under

their entry on the 'Zulu'. This seems to be the example from the Peabody Museum in Harvard illustrated by Sieber (1980: 122). A recent visit to the Peabody website offered no further information.

47 See the discussion of Schneider's reading of Pokot ideas about aesthetics and art in chapter 7.

48 See figures 61, 62, 90, 91, 92, 93, 96 and 213–225, representing examples from Angola in the south-west to Ethiopia in the north-east.

49 Examples illustrating these ideas have been more fully explored in relation to specific cases for which detailed information exists, but may be extrapolated beyond them as well. See Roberts and Roberts (1996) for a discussion of the Luba case, Roberts (1986) for the Tabwa, Nettleton (1990) for Southern African groups, Dewey (1993) for the Shona and Becker (1999) for the Tsonga.

50 A number of these headrests were published in Davison (1991b), and there are examples in the Manchester University Museum (no. SA95), the British Museum (nos. 1947 Af15.3, 1945 Af4.12, 1954 Af23) and the Staatlisches Museum für Völkerkunde, Munich (no. 50.11.18), among others.

51 And personal communication, 21 April 2006.

52 Nooter (1992b:325) notes that the name *katatora* is common in north-western Luba territory 'near the Songye'. Burton, whose mission at Mwanza was in the north-east of Luba territory, entitled his photos of this process as 'divination by lubuko' (cf. University of the Witwatersrand Art Galleries 1992, figs. 31, 32), and Theuws (1962) gives the same name for this instrument in his account of its use.

53 Every *kashekesheke* I have seen follows the same pattern, with a single face and hairstyle (though these hairstyles vary), although there are a few with 'Janus' faces, i.e. two heads joined at the backs with faces pointing in opposite directions.

54 See D'Orjo de Marchovelette (1954) and Roberts and Roberts (1996) for a discussion of Luba divination forms. The Burton photographic archive (University of the Witwatersrand Art Galleries) has a number of postcards with notations on the different forms of Luba divination.

55 Baumann (1935) mentions the use of these diviners' baskets in Lunda territory, and Lwena–Luvale examples are discussed by Wastiau (1998) and Silva (1998). Rodrigues de Areia (1974) discussed these fully, but neither Lima (1971) nor Hauenstein (1974) mentions miniature headrests among the baskets' contents.

56 Bastin (1988:68) draws this distinction between the *mahamba* and the figures of Tshibinda Ilunga and some female figures who have been associated with the Lweji.

57 Pitt Rivers Museum, no. 1973.20.32.

58 A photograph by Burton of 'A Bakasandji Dancing' (University of the Witwatersrand Art Galleries 1992, no. BPC 12G.8, fig. 22) shows one of these in the background, and Roberts (1993:68–69, figs. 2a, 2b, 2c) illustrates a number of Tabwa baskets used by members of the Bulumbu possession cult for containing white clay.

59 An *mboko* is, strictly speaking, a calabash that contains white clay. Such calabashes, or just white clay, are placed inside the carved bowls held by carved female figures, which are then, by extension, also called *mboko*.

60 British Museum, Torday photograph files, nos. Af/CA152/32 (MM005278), Af/CA153/2 (MM005346) and AF/CA153/10 (MM005345) are examples; there are also paintings of this by Norman Hardy (Mack 1990, pl. 3).
61 Of these, one by Lucy Jaques is in the Museum of Ethnology Collection in the University of the Witwatersrand Art Galleries, and one is published in Dicke (1936:172).
62 This argument is developed by a number of authors in the volume edited by Rubin (1988), and by Brain (1979).
63 Cf. Nettleton (1985; 1990), and Dewey's (1991; 1993) responses, in which I think there is some degree of misreading of my argument. Also see Becker (1999) for an assessment of both arguments.
64 Allen Roberts, personal communication, 21 April 2006.
65 British Museum, no. Af/CA/153/10 (MM005354).
66 Dewey was able to trace a number of photographs of Shona women's scarification, in none of which the concentric circle motif was visible. But its presence on the headrest, itself not a mimetic form, cannot be read literally.
67 See, for example, Maes (1929, pl. V, figs. 21, 24, 25, 29; pl. VI, figs. 5, 7).
68 This is dealt with by Drewal and Mason (1998) for the Yoruba and by Roberts (1990) for the Tabwa and related people, and is discussed by Nettleton and Hammond Tooke (1991) for the Xhosa, among others.
69 An almost identical example in the British Museum (no. 1931.11.18) with blue beads and leather attachments is recorded as 'Southern Rhodesia, Mashona' (i.e. Zimbabwe, Shona). It was acquired from Alban Head, from whom a number of other Shona examples were accessioned. As both have good records of provenance, the only conclusion that can be drawn about their style is that it was common on objects used in Mashonaland and in the former Transvaal.
70 See Jordàn's (1998) notes to figures 81–86 and 99.
71 An example that has recently come onto the market (Stevenson 2005, no. 1) demonstrates a particularly hybrid form, with splayed, tube-like legs of the Tsonga examples, but with fluting on the shoulders and one of the supports above the back referencing Swazi examples.
72 An almost identical idea is recorded by Dedering (2007) among the Tsonga, in relation to the beaded figures used by women as surrogate children before their own are born.
73 But it is more probable that figurative headrests in this style were made by Tsonga carvers for Shona clients.

# Bibliography

Abbink, Jon. 1999. 'Artifacts as "daily art" in Me'en culture.' In Raymond A. Silverman (ed.), *Ethiopia: Traditions of Creativity*, pp. 27–45. East Lancing: Michigan State University Press & Seattle: University of Washington Press.

Abiodun, Rowland, Henry J. Drewal & John Pemberton III. 1989. *Yoruba: Nine Centuries of Art and Thought*. New York: Abrams & Centre for African Art.

——. 1994. *The Yoruba Artist: New Theoretical Perspectives on African Art*. Washington, DC: Smithsonian Institution Press.

Adams, Monni. 1978. 'Kuba embroidered cloth.' *African Arts*, 12(1):24–39.

Adamson, Joy. 1967. *The Peoples of Kenya*. London: Collins & Harville.

Alpers, Svetlana. 1983. *The Art of Describing: Dutch Art in the Seventeenth Century*. London: John Murray.

Angas, George Ffrench. 1849. *The Kaffirs Illustrated*. London: Hogarth.

Antal, Frederick. 1966. *Classicism and Romanticism: With Other Studies in Art History*. New York: Icon Editions, Harper Row.

Appiah, Kwame Anthony. 1992. *In My Father's House: Africa in the Philosophy of Culture*. London: Methuen.

—— & Henry Louis Gates Jr (eds). 1999. *Africana: The Encyclopaedia of Africa and the African-American Experience*. New York: Basic Civitas Books.

Arnoldi, Mary Jo. 1984. 'The artistic heritage of Somalia.' *African Arts*, 7(4):24–33.

—— & Christine Mullen Kreamer. 1995. 'Crowning achievements: African arts of dressing the head.' *African Arts*, 28(1): 22–35.

Balandier, George & Jacques Maquet. 1974. *Dictionary of Black African Civilizations*. Trans. Lady Mariska Caroline Peck, Bettina Wadia & Peninah Neimark. New York: Leon Amiel.

Barley, Nigel. 1994. *Smashing Pots: Feats of Clay from Africa*. London: Trustees of the British Museum, British Museum Press.

Bascom, William. 1969. 'Creativity and style in African art.' In Daniel Biebuyck (ed.), *Tradition and Creativity in Tribal Art*, pp. 98–119. Los Angeles: University of California Press.

———. 1973. 'A Yoruba master carver: Duga of Meko.' In Warren L. d'Azevedo (ed.), *The Traditional Artist in African Society*, pp. 62–78. Bloomington: Indiana University Press.

Bassani, Ezio & William Fagg. 1988. *Africa and the Renaissance: Art in Ivory*. New York: Centre for African Art & Prestel.

Bassani, Ezio & Malcolm McLeod. 1985. 'African material in early collections.' In Oliver Impey & Arthur MacGregor (eds), *The Origins of Museums: The Cabinet of Curiosities in Sixteenth- and Seventeenth-Century Europe*, pp. 245–50. Oxford: Clarendon Press.

Bastin, Marie Louise. 1961. *Arts Décoratifs Tshokwe*, 2 vols. Lisbon: Museu do Dundo.

———. 1988. 'Les Tshokwe du pays d'origine.' In Christine Falgayrettes (ed.), *Art et Mythologie: Figurines Tshokwe*, pp. 49–94. Paris: Fondation Dapper.

Battiss, Walter, Henri A. Junod & Jack Grossert. 1958. *The Art of Africa*. Pietermaritzburg: Shuter & Shooter.

Baumann, Hermann. 1935. *Bei Bauern und Jägern in Inner-Angola*. Berlin: Wurfel Verlag.

Baxandall, Michael. 1972. *Painting and Experience in Fifteenth-century Italy: A Primer in the Social History of Style*. London: Oxford University Press.

Beach, David N. 1980. *The Shona and Zimbabwe, 900–1850*. London: Heinemann.

Becker, Rayda. 1991. 'Headrests: Tsonga types and variations.' In Patricia Davison (ed.), *Art and Ambiguity: Perspectives on the Brenthurst Collection of Southern African Art*, pp. 58–76. Johannesburg: Johannesburg Art Gallery.

———. 1992. 'The photographs of W. F. P. Burton.' In University of the Witwatersrand Art Galleries, *The Collection of W. F. P. Burton: 'Of Course You would Not Want a Canoe ...'*, pp. 27–37. Johannesburg: University of the Witwatersrand Art Galleries.

———. 1999. *Tsonga Headrests: The Making of an Art History Category*. PhD thesis, University of the Witwatersrand.

——— & Anitra Nettleton. 1989. 'Tsonga–Shangaan beadwork and figures.' In David Hammond-Tooke & Anitra Nettleton (eds), *Catalogue: Ten Years of Collecting (1979–1989)*, pp. 9–15. Johannesburg: University of the Witwatersrand Art Galleries.

Bedaux, Roger M. A. 1977. *Tellem*. Berg en Dal: Afrika Museum.

———. 1988. 'Tellem and Dogon material culture.' *African Arts*, 21(4):38–45, 91.

Bedford, Emma (ed.). 1993. *Ezakwantu: Beadwork from the Eastern Cape*. Cape Town: South African National Gallery.

Belting, Hans. 1987. *The End of the History of Art?* Chicago: Chicago University Press.

Ben Amos, Paula. 1980. *The Art of Benin*. London: Thames & Hudson.

Bender, M. Lionel. 2000. 'Nilo-Saharan.' In Bernd Heine & Derek Nurse (eds), *African Languages: An Introduction*, pp. 43–59. Cambridge: Cambridge University Press.

Bent, John Theodore. 1892. *Ruined Cities of Mashonaland*. London: Longmans, Green.

Berenson, Bernard. 1952. *The Italian Painters of the Renaissance*. London: Phaidon.

Berger, John. 1972. *Ways of Seeing*. London: British Broadcasting Corporation.

Berlo, Janet & Ruth Phillips. 1998. *Native North American Art.* Oxford: Oxford University Press.

Berlyn, Phillipa. 1968. 'Some aspects of the material culture of the Shona people.' *Native Affairs Department Annual*, 9(5):68–73.

Berning, Gillian. 1996. '*Indaba yamakosi ayibanjelwa mlando*? The matter of kings is not kept.' In KwaZulu-Natal Local History Museums, *Zulu Treasures: Of Kings and Commoners: A Celebration of the Material Culture of the Zulu People*, pp. 43–55. Ulundi: KwaZulu Cultural Museum and the Local History Museums.

Best, Gunther. 1993. *Marakwet and Turkana: New Perspectives on the Material Culture of East African Societies.* Frankfurt am Main: Museum für Völkerkunde.

Beumers, Erna (ed.). 1996. *Africa Meets Africa: The African Collection of the Museum of Ethnology, Rotterdam.* Rotterdam: Museum of Ethnology.

—— & Hans-Joachim Koloss (eds). 1992. *Kings of Africa: Art and Authority in Central Africa*, pp. 71–78. Maastricht: Foundation Kings of Africa.

Bhabha, Homi. 1984. 'Of mimicry and man: The ambivalence of colonial discourse.' *October*, 28:190–98.

Biebuyck, Daniel (ed.). 1969. *Tradition and Creativity in Tribal Art.* Los Angeles: University of California Press.

——. 1977. *Symbolism of the Lega Stool.* Philadelphia: ISHI Publications.

——. 1985. *The Arts of Zaire, Vol. 1: Southwestern Zaire.* Los Angeles: University of California Press.

—— & Constantijn Petridis (eds). 2001. *Frans M. Olbrechts, 1899–1958: In Search of Africa.* Antwerp: Etnografisch Museum.

Boas, Frans. 1955 (1927). *Primitive Art.* New York: Dover.

Bohannan, Paul. 1956. 'Beauty and scarification among the Tiv.' *Man*, 129:117–21.

Bois, Yves-Alain. 1987. 'Kahnweiler's lesson.' *Representations*, 18:33–68.

Bonner, Philip. 1983. *Kings, Commoners and Commisionaires: The Evolution and Dissolution of the Nineteenth Century Swazi State.* Cambridge: Cambridge University Press.

Boone, Sylvia A. 1986. *Radiance from the Waters: Ideals of Feminine Beauty in Mende Art.* New Haven: Yale University Press.

Boston, John. 1977. *Ikenga Figures among the North-West Igbo and the Igala.* Lagos & London: Ethnographica & Federal Department of Antiquities, Nigeria.

Bourdieu, Pierre. 1980. *Distinction: A Social Critique of the Judgement of Taste.* Trans. Richard Nice. Cambridge, Mass.: Harvard University Press.

Bourdillon, Michael F. C. 1982. *The Shona Peoples: An Ethnography of the Contemporary Shona, with Special Reference to Their Religion.* Gweru: Mambo Press.

Bourgeois, Arthur Paul. 1984. *The Art of the Yaka and Suku.* Meudon: Alain & Francois Chaffin.

Brain, Robert. 1979. *The Decorated Body.* London: Hutchinson.

Brantlinger, Phillip. 1985. 'Victorians and Africans: The genealogy of the myth of the Dark Continent.' *Critical Inquiry*, 12(1):166–203.

Braunholtz, H. J. 1970. *Sir Hans Sloane and Ethnography.* London: Trustees of the British Museum.

Bravmann, René A. 1974. *Islam and Tribal Art in West Africa.* Cambridge: Cambridge University Press.

Brewin, Robert. 1910. 'The boys of East Africa.' *Missionary Echo of the United Methodist Church,* 17(1):35.

Brown, Jean. 1978. 'Collection notes.' Oxford: Pitt Rivers Museum.

Bryant, Arthur. 1929. *Olden Times in Zululand and Natal.* London: Longmans, Green.

Bunzel, Ruth. 1972 (1929). *The Pueblo Potter.* New York: Dover.

Burton, William F. P. 1961. *Luba Religion and Magic in Custom and Belief.* Annales du Musée Royal de l'Afrique Central, series 8, no. 35. Tervuren.

Carr, Christopher & Jill E. Neitzel (eds). 1995. *Style, Society and Person: Archaeological and Ethnological Perspectives.* London: Plenum Press.

Carr, Christopher & J. Pryor. 1995. 'Basketry of North Carolina Indians.' In Christopher Carr & Jill E. Neitzel (eds), *Style, Society and Person: Archaeological and Ethnological Perspectives,* pp. 259–96. London: Plenum Press.

Carroll, Kevin. 1961. 'Three generations of Yoruba carvers.' *Ibadan,* 12:21–24.

——. 1967. *Yoruba Religious Carving: Pagan and Christian Sculpture in Nigeria and Dahomey.* London: Geoffrey Chapman.

Cerulli, Ernesta. 1956. *Peoples of South-West Ethiopia and Its Borderland.* London: International African Institute.

Chaffin, Alain & Francoise Chaffin. n.d. *L'Art Kota: Les Figures de Reliquaire.* Meudon: Alain & Francoise Chaffin.

Chappell, T. J. H. 1977. *Decorated Gourds in Northern Nigeria.* London: Ethnographica.

Chesi, Gert. 1980. *The Last Africans.* Johannesburg: Struik.

Clarke, T. J. 1973. *The Image of the People: Gustave Courbet and the 1848 Revolution.* London: Thames & Hudson.

Clifford, James. 1988. *The Predicament of Culture.* Cambridge, Mass.: Harvard University Press.

Cole, Herbert M. 1982. *Mbari: Art and Life among the Owerri Igbo.* Bloomington: Indiana University Press.

—— & Doran Ross. 1977. *The Arts of Ghana.* Los Angeles: Fowler Museum of Cultural History, University of California.

Colle, R. P. 1913. *Les Baluba: Collection de Monographies Ethnographiques,* 2 vols. Brussels: Institut International de Bibliographie.

Conner, Michael & Diane Pelrine. 1983. *The Geometric Vision: Arts of the Zulu.* West Lafayette: Perdue University Galleries.

Contini, Mila. 1965. *Fashion: From Ancient Egypt to the Present Day.* London: Paul Hamlyn.

Coombes, Annie. 1985. 'For God and for England: Contributions to an image of Africa in the first decade of the twentieth century.' *Art History,* 8(4):453–65.

———. 1994. *Reinventing Africa: Museums, Material Culture and Popular Imagination in Late Victorian England*. New Haven: Yale University Press.
Coote, Jeremy & Anthony Shelton (eds). 1992. *Anthropology, Art and Aesthetics*. Oxford: Clarendon Press.
Cornet, Joseph. 1971. *Art of Africa: Treasures from the Congo*. London: Phaidon.
———. 1982. *L'Art Royal Kuba*. Milan: Edizioni Sipiel.
Corson, Richard. 1965. *Fashions in Hair: The First Five Thousand Years*. London: Peter Owen.
Craik, Jennifer. 1995. *The Face of Fashion: Cultural Studies in Fashion*. London: Routledge.
Crowther, Paul. 2004. 'Defining art, defending the canon, contesting culture.' *British Journal of Aesthetics*, 44(4):361–77.
Curley, Richard. 1973. *Elders, Shades, and Women: Ceremonial Changes in Uganda*. Berkeley: University of California Press.
Curnow, Kathy. 1983. *The Afro-Portuguese Ivories: Classification and Stylistic Analysis of a Hybrid Art Form*. PhD thesis, Indiana University.
Danto, Arthur. 1981. *The Transfiguration of the Commonplace: A Philosophy of Art*. Cambridge, Mass.: Harvard University Press.
———. 1988. *397 Chairs*. New York: Harry N. Abrams.
———. 1989. 'Artifact and art.' In Susan Vogel (ed.), *Art/Artifact: African Art in Anthropology Collections*, pp. 18–30. New York: Centre for African Art.
Dark, Phillip. 1975. 'Benin bronze heads: Styles and chronology.' In Daniel F. McCall & Edna G. Bay (eds), *African Images: Essays in African Iconology*. New York: Africana Publishing Company.
Davison, Patricia. 1991a. *Material Culture, Context and Meaning: A Critical Investigation of Museum Practice, with Particular Reference to South Africa*. PhD thesis, University of Cape Town.
——— (ed.). 1991b. *Art and Ambiguity: Perspectives on the Brenthurst Collection of Southern African Art*. Johannesburg: Johannesburg Art Gallery.
D'Azevedo, Warren L. 1973a. *The Traditional Artist in African Society*. Bloomington: Indiana University Press.
———. 1973b. 'Mask makers and myth in western Liberia.' In Anthony Forge (ed.), *Primitive Art and Society*, pp. 126–250. London: Oxford University Press.
Dechamps, Paul. 1970. 'L'identification anatomiques des bois utilisés pour des sculptures en Afrique. 1, Kuba.' *Africa Tervuren*, 16(3):77–82.
———. 1971. 'L'identification anatomiques des bois utilisés pour des sculptures en Afrique. 2, Lulua.' *Africa Tervuren*, 16(4):79–85.
———. 1974a. 'L'identification anatomiques des bois utilisés pour des sculptures en Afrique. 3, Bembe.' *Africa Tervuren*, 20(1):15–24.
———. 1974b. 'L'identification anatomiques des bois utilisés pour des sculptures en Afrique. 4, Luba.' *Africa Tervuren*, 20(2):15–25.
———. 1975. 'L'identification anatomiques des bois utilisés pour des sculptures en Afrique. 5, Songye.' *Africa Tervuren*, 21(1):27–33.

———. 1976. 'L'identification anatomiques des bois utilisés pour des sculptures en Afrique. 7, Cokwe.' *Africa Tervuren*, 22(2):9–16.

———. 1982. 'L'identification anatomiques des bois utilisés pour des sculptures en Afrique. 10, Tabwa.' *Africa Tervuren*, 28(1):5–17.

Dedering, Godfrey. 2007. 'Tsonga *nwana*.' In Nessa Leibhammer & Natalie Knight (eds), *Dunga Manzi*. Johannesburg: Johannesburg Art Gallery & Wits University Press.

De Heusch, Luc. 1982. *The Drunken King, or, the Origin of the State*. Bloomington: Indiana University Press.

Delange, Jaqueline. 1974. *The Arts and Peoples of Black Africa*. New York: Dutton.

De Maret, Pierre. 1982. 'The Iron Age in the west and south.' In Francis van Noten (ed.), *The Archaeology of Central Africa*, pp. 77–100. Graz: Akademische Druck u Verlangstalt.

———, Nicola Dery & Cathy Murdoch. 1973. 'The Luba Shankadi style.' *African Arts*, 7(1):8–15, 88.

——— & F. Nsuka. 1977. 'History of Bantu metallurgy: Some linguistic aspects.' *History in Africa*, 4:1.

Dewey, William. 1991. *Pleasing the Ancestors: The Traditional Art of the Shona People of Zimbabwe*. PhD thesis, Indiana University. Ann Arbor: University Microfiche International.

———. 1993. *Sleeping Beauties: The Jerome L Joss Collection of African Headrests at UCLA*. Los Angeles: Fowler Museum of Cultural History, University of California.

Dicke, B. H. 1936. *The Bush Speaks: Border Life in the Old Transvaal*. Pietermaritzburg: Shuter & Shooter.

Dirlik, Arif. 1994. 'The postcolonial aura: Third world criticism in the age of global capitalism.' *Critical Inquiry*, 20:328–56.

Distant, William. 1892. *A Naturalist in the Transvaal*. London: Porter.

Donne, J. B. 1980. 'African art or African craft?' *Antique Collector*, 7:2.

Donovan, Alan. 1988. 'Turkana functional art.' *African Arts*, 21(1):45–50.

D'Orjo de Marchovelette, E. 1954. 'La divination chez les BaLuba au moyen du "Lubuko" ou "Katatola".' *Zaire*, 4:487–505.

Douglas, Mary. 1966. *Purity and Danger*. London: Routledge.

Drewal, Henry John. 1988, 'Beauty and being: Aesthetics and ontology in Yoruba body art.' In Arnold Rubin (ed.), *Marks of Civilization*, pp. 83–96. Los Angeles: Fowler Museum of Cultural History.

——— & John Mason. 1998. *Beads, Body and Soul: Art and Light in the Yoruba Universe*. Los Angeles: Fowler Museum of Cultural History, University of California.

Drewal, Margaret T. 1977. 'Projections from the top in Yoruba art.' *African Arts*, 11(1): 43–49, 98–99.

Duggan-Cronin, Alfred. 1928–49. *The Bantu Tribes of South Africa, Vols. 1–4*. Cambridge & Kimberley: Deighton Bell.

Duncan, Carole. 1993. *The Aesthetics of Power: Essays in Critical Art History*. Cambridge: Cambridge University Press.

Dutton, Denis. 1995. 'Mythologies of tribal art.' *African Arts*, 28(3):32–43.

Ehret, Christopher. 2000. 'Language and history.' In Bernd Heine & Derek Nurse (eds), *African Languages: An Introduction*, pp. 272–97. Cambridge: Cambridge University Press.

Eitner, L. 1970. *Neoclassicism and Romanticism.* Engelwood Cliffs: Prentice-Hall.
Eldridge, R. 1993. 'Althusser and ideological criticism of the arts.' In S. Kemal & I. Gaskell (eds), *Explanation and Value in the Arts*, pp. 190–214. Cambridge: Cambridge University Press.
Elkins, James. 1997. *Our Beautiful, Dry, and Distant Texts: Art History as Writing.* University Park: Pennsylvania State University Press.
——. 2002a. 'Review of Summers, J., *Real Spaces: World Art History and the Rise of Modernism*.' *Art Bulletin*, 86(2):378–81.
——. 2002b. *Stories of Art.* New York: Routledge.
——. 2006. 'Writing about modernist painting outside western Europe and North America.' In John Onians (ed.), *Compression vs Expression: Containing and Explaining the World's Art*, pp. 188–214. Massachusetts: Stirling & Francine Clark Art Institute & New Haven: Yale University Press.
Erasmus, Zimitri. 2000. 'Hair politics.' In Sarah Nuttall & Cheryll-Anne Michael, *Senses of Culture: South African Culture Studies*, pp. 380–92. Cape Town: Oxford University Press.
Errington, Shelley. 1998. *The Death of Authentic Primitive Art and Other Tales of Progress.* Berkeley: University of California Press.
Estermann, Carlos E. S. S. 1970. *Penteados Adornes e Trabalhos das Muilas.* Lisbon: Junta de Investigações.
Evans Pritchard, E. E. 1969 (1940). *The Nuer: A Description of the Modes of Livelihood and Political Institutions of a Nilotic People.* Oxford: Oxford University Press.
Ezra, Kate. 1988. *Art of the Dogon: Selections from the Lester Wunderman Collection.* New York: Metropolitan Museum of Art.
Fabian, Johannes. 1991. *Time and the Work of Anthropology: Critical Essays 1971–1991.* Chur: Harwood Academic Publishers, GNBH.
——. 1996. *Remembering the Present: Painting and Popular History Narrative and Paintings by Kanda Matulu.* Berkeley: University of California Press.
Fagg, William. 1963. *Nigerian Images.* London: Lund Humphries.
——. 1965. *Tribes and Forms in African Art.* London: Methuen.
—— & John Pemberton III. 1982. *Yoruba Sculpture of West Africa.* New York: Alfred A. Knopf.
Falgayrettes, Christiane. 1989. *Supports des Rêves.* Paris: Fondation Dapper.
Fanon, Frantz. 1967. *Black Skins, White Masks.* Trans. Charles Lam Markmann. New York: Grove Weidenfeld.
Faris, James. 1972. *Nuba Personal Art.* London: Duckworth.
——. 1988. 'Significance of differences in male and female personal art of the southeast Nuba.' In Arnold Rubin (ed.), *Marks of Civilization: Artistic Transformations of the Human Body*, pp. 29–40. Los Angeles: University of California, Museum of Cultural History.
Faye, Robert. 1999. 'Turkana.' In Appiah Kwame & Henry Louis Gates Jr (eds), *Africana: The Encyclopaedia of Africa and the African-American Experience.* New York: Basic Civitas Books.
Felix, Mark. 1990. *Mwana Hiti: Art in the Life of the Matrilineal Bantu of Tanzania.* Munich: F. Jahn.

Fernandez, James. 1973. 'The exposition and imposition of order: Artistic expression in Fang culture.' In Warren L. d'Azevedo (ed.), *The Traditional Artist in African Society*, pp. 194–220. Bloomington: Indiana University Press.

Firth, Raymond. 1992. 'Art and anthropology.' In Jeremy Coote & Anthony Shelton (eds), *Anthropology, Art and Aesthetics*, pp. 15–39. Oxford: Clarendon Press.

Fisher, Angela. 1984. 'Africa adorned: A continent speaks through its decorative arts.' *National Geographic*, 166(5):600–33.

Fondation Dapper. 1989. *Art et Mythologie: Figures Tshokwe*. Paris: Fondation Dapper.

Foucault, Michel. 1972. *The Archaeology of Knowledge*. London: Tavistock.

Fraser, Douglas. 1927. *Through the Congo Basin*. London: Herbert Jenkins.

Frederick, J. & G. Gielen. 1950. 'Les transports au Congo Belge et Ruanda-Urundi.' *Encyclopedie du Congo Belge*, pp. 425–40. Brussels: Editions Bieleveld.

Fry, Roger. 1925 (1961). *Vision and Design*, rev. ed. London: Pelican.

Gardiner, Harold. 1836. *Narrative of a Journey to the Zoolu Country*. London: William Crofts.

Garlake, Peter. 1973. *Great Zimbabwe*. London: Thames & Hudson.

Garland-Thomson, Rosemarie (ed.). 1996. *Freakery: Cultural Spectacle of the Extraordinary Body*. New York: New York University Press.

Gatti, C. 1939. *African Types*. Cape Town.

Geary, Christraud. 1991. 'Missionary photography: Private and public readings.' *African Arts*, 24(4):48–59.

———. 2002. *In and out of Focus*. Washington, DC: Smithsonian Institution Press.

Geertz, Clifford. 1983. *Local Knowledge: Further Essays in Interpretive Anthropology*. New York: Basic Books.

Gell, Alfred. 1992. 'The technology of enchantment and the enchantment of technology.' In Jeremy Coote & Anthony Shelton (eds), *Anthropology, Art and Aesthetics*, pp. 40–63. Oxford: Clarendon Press.

———. 1998. *Art and Agency: An Anthropological Theory*. Oxford: Clarendon Press.

Gerdes, P. 1997. *Lusona: Geometrical Recreations of Africa*. Montreal: L'Harmattan.

Gille, A. c. 1950. 'La politique indigène.' *Encyclopedie du Congo Belge*, pp. 709–48. Brussels: Editions Bieleveld.

Graebner, F. 1927. 'Knopfbanke.' *Ethnologica*, 3:1–13.

Grotanelli, Vinigi L. 1968. 'Somali wood engraving.' *African Arts*, 1(3): 8–13, 72–73, 96.

Gulliver, Paul & P. H. Gulliver. 1953. *The Central Nilo-Hamites Ethnographic Survey of Africa, Part VII*. London: International African Institute.

Haddon, Arthur. 1895. *Evolution in Art*. London: W. Scott.

Hammond-Tooke, William David. 1974. *The Bantu-speaking People of South Africa*. London: Routledge & Kegan Paul.

Harries, Patrick. 1989. 'Exclusion, classification and internal colonialism: The emergence of ethnicity among the Tsonga-speakers of South Africa.' In Leroy Vail (ed.), *The Creation of Tribalism in Southern Africa*, pp. 82–117. Berkeley: University of California Press.

Hassen, Mohammed. 1990. *The Oromo of Ethiopia: A History 1570–1860*. African Studies Series No. 66. Cambridge: Cambridge University Press.

Hauenstein, A. 1974. 'La corbeille aux osselets divinatoires des Tchokwe (Angola).' *Anthropos*, 56(1–2):114–57.

Hawkins, Leila & Henry Christy. 1862. *Gleanings of Aboriginal Ornament from the International Exhibition, 1862: Drawings and Handwritten Text for Henry Christy Esq.* Unpublished manuscript. London: British Museum, Ethnography Department.

Heine, Bernd & Derek Nurse (eds). 2000. *African Languages: An Introduction*. Cambridge: Cambridge University Press.

*Herald of the Primitive Missionary Society, The.* 1909. Vol. 5(4), April.

Herbert, Eugenia. 1984. *Red Gold of Africa: Copper in Pre-colonial History and Culture*. Madison: University of Wisconsin Press.

Her Majesty's Commissioners. 1862. *Illustrated Catalogue of the International Exhibition, Vol. III: Industrial Dept.: Colonial and Foreign*. London: Jarrold & Sons.

Hillier, Susan (ed.). 1991. *The Myth of Primitivism: Perspectives on Art*. London: Routledge.

Himmelheber, Hans. 1963. 'Dan master carvers.' In Margaret Mead, J. B. Bird & H. Himmelheber (eds), *Technique and Personality*, pp. 63–75. New York: Museum of Primitive Art.

Hodder, Ian. 1977. 'The distribution of material culture items in the Baringo district, Western Kenya.' *Man*, 12:239–69.

——. 1978. 'Simple correlations between material culture and society: A review.' In Ian Hodder (ed.), *The Spatial Organization of Culture*, pp. 3–24. Pittsburgh: University of Pittsburgh Press.

——. 1982. *Symbolic and Structural Archaeology*. Cambridge: Cambridge University Press.

Hodza, Aron & George Fortune. 1979. *Shona Praise Poetry*. Oxford: Clarendon Press.

Holy, Ladislav. 1967. *The Art of Africa: Masks and Figures from Eastern and Southern Africa*. London: Hamlyn.

Holly, Michael Ann. 1996. *Past Looking: Historical Imagination and the Rhetoric of the Image*. Ithaca: Cornell University Press.

Honour, Hugh. 1961. *Chinoiserie: The Vision of Cathay*. London: John Murray.

——. 1968. *Neoclassicism*. London: Pelican.

Hore, E. C. 1883. 'On the twelve tribes of Kenya.' *Journal of the Royal Anthropological Institute*, 12:2–21.

Huffman, Thomas N. 1992. 'Burton and the ceramic prehistory of the Upemba Basin.' In University of the Witwatersrand Art Galleries, *The Collection of William F. P. Burton: 'Of Course You would Not Want a Canoe ...'*, pp. 69–74. Johannesburg: University of the Witwatersrand Art Galleries.

Huntingford, G. W. B. 1955. *The Galla of Ethiopia, The Kingdoms of Kaffa and Janjero*. London: International African Institute.

Impey, Oliver & Arthur MacGregor (eds). 1985. *The Origins of Museums: The Cabinet of Curiosities in Sixteenth- and Seventeenth-Century Europe.* Oxford: Clarendon Press.

Jackson, Kennell. 2000. 'What is *really* happening here? Black hair among African-Americans and in American culture.' In Roy Sieber & Frank Herremann (eds), *Hair in African Art and Culture*, pp. 175–85. Munich: Prestel & New York: Museum for African Art.

Jaques, Henri A. 1941. 'Tsonga pillows.' Unpublished lecture.

Jedrej, M. C. 1995. *Ingessana: Religious Institutions of a People of the Sudan–Ethiopia Borderland.* Leiden: Brill.

Jewsiewicki, Bogumil. 1989. 'The formation of the political culture in ethnicity in the Belgian Congo.' In Leroy Vail (ed.), *The Creation of Tribalism in Southern Africa.* Berkeley: University of California Press.

Johnson, Barbara. 1986. *Four Dan Sculptors: Continuity and Change.* Chicago: University of Chicago Press & Fine Arts Museums of San Francisco.

Johnston, Harry. 1902. *The Uganda Protectorate*, 2 vols. London: Hutchinson.

Jones, Adam. 1994. 'A collection of African art in seventeenth-century Germany: Christoph Weickmann's *kunst- und naturkammer.*' *African Arts*, 27(2):28–43.

Jones, Owen. 1910 (first published 1856, repr. 1928). *The Grammar of Ornament.* London: Burnard Quartich.

Jopling, Carol, F. 1971. *Art and Aesthetics in Primitive Societies.* New York: Dutton.

Jordán, Manuel. 1998. *Chokwe! Art and Initiation among Chokwe and Related People.* Munich: Prestel.

——. 2000. 'Hair matters in South Central Africa.' In Roy Sieber & Frank Herremann (eds), *Hair in African Art and Culture*, pp. 135–45. Munich: Prestel & New York: Museum for African Art.

Joubert, Hélène & Manuel Valentin (eds). 2002. *Ubuntu: Arts et Cultures d'Afrique du Sud.* Paris: la Réunion des Musées Nationaux et le Musée National des Arts d'Afrique et d'Oceanie.

Junod, Henri A. 1927. *The Life of a South African Tribe*, 2 vols. London: Macmillan.

Kasfir, Sidney L. 1984. 'One tribe, one style: Paradigms in the historiography of African art.' *History in Africa*, 11:163–69.

——. 1987. 'Apprentices and entrepreneurs: The workshop and style uniformity in SubSaharan Africa.' In Christopher Roy (ed.), *Iowa Studies in African Art: The Stanley Conferences at the University of Iowa, Vol. II: The Artist and the Workshop in Traditional Africa*, pp. 25–43. Iowa: University of Iowa, School of Art & Art History.

——. 1992. 'African art and authenticity: A text without a shadow.' *African Arts*, 25(2):41–53.

——. 1996. 'Mytho(il)logiques.' *African Arts*, 29(1):91–93.

Kauenhoven-Janzen, Reinhild. 1981. 'Cokwe thrones.' *African Arts*, 14(3):6–74, 92.

Kemal, S. & I. Gaskell (eds). 1993. *Explanation and Value in the Arts.* Cambridge: Cambridge University Press.

Kesby, John D. 1977. *The Cultural Regions of East Africa.* London: Academic Press.

*Kingdom Overseas, The.* 1933. Vol. 1.

Kjersmeier, Carl. 1935–38. *Centres de Style de la Sculpture Negre Africaine*, vols. 1–4. Paris: A. Moramce.

Kleinbauer, W. Eugene (ed.). 1971. *Modern Perspectives on Western Art History: An Anthology of 20th-century Writings on the Visual Arts*. New York: Holt, Rinehart & Winston.

Klopper, Sandra. 1989. 'Carvers, kings and thrones in nineteenth century Zululand.' In Anitra Nettleton & David Hammond-Tooke (eds), *African Art in Southern Africa: From Tradition to Township*, pp. 49–66. Johannesburg: AD Donker.

——. 1991. '"Zulu" headrests and figurative carvings: The Brenthurst Collection and the art of south east Africa.' In Patricia Davison (ed.), *Art and Ambiguity: Perspectives on the Brenthurst Collection of Southern African Art*, pp. 80–89. Johannesburg: Johannesburg Art Gallery.

——. 1992. *The Art of the Zulu-Speakers in Northern Natal–Zululand: An Investigation of the History of Beadwork, Carving and Dress from Shaka to Inkatha*. PhD thesis, University of the Witwatersrand.

—— & Karel Nel. 2002. *The Art of South-East Africa*. Milan: 5continentseditions.

Koloss, Hans-Joachim. 1990. *Art of Central Africa: Masterpieces from the Berlin Museum für Völkerkunde*. New York: Metropolitan Museum of Art & Harry N. Abrams.

Krieger, Karl. 1978. *WestAfrikanische Plastiek*, 3 vols. Berlin: Museum für Völkerkunde.

——. 1990. *OstAfrikanische Plastiek*. Berlin: Museum für Völkerkunde.

Kriger, Colleen E. 1999. *Pride of Men: Ironworking in 19th Century West Central Africa*. Cape Town: David Phillip.

Kroeber, A. (ed.). 1957. *Style and Civilization*. New York: Cornell University Press.

Kubler, George. 1985. 'Style and the representation of historical time.' In T. Reese (ed.), *Studies in Ancient American and European Art: The Collected Essays of George Kubler*, pp. 386–90. New Haven: Yale University Press.

KwaZulu-Natal Local History Museums. 1996. *Zulu Treasures: Of Kings and Commoners: A Celebration of the Material Culture of the Zulu People*. Ulundi: KwaZulu Cultural Museum and the Local History Museums.

LaGamma, Alisa (ed.). 1998. 'Authorship in African art, part 1.' *African Arts*, special issue, 21:3.

——. 1999. 'Authorship in African art, part 2.' *African Arts*, special issue, 22:1.

Laudé, Jean. 1973. *African Art of the Dogon: The Myths of the Cliff Dwellers*. New York: Brooklyn Museum & Viking Press.

Launer, Harold M. 1991. 'Ideology, kinship and cognate descent among the Gaam (Ingessana) of Eastern Sudan.' In M. Lionell Bender (ed.), *Peoples and Cultures of the Ethio–Sudan Borderlands*, pp. 61–78. East Lansing: Michigan State University, African Studies Centre.

Laurencich-Minelli, Lara. 1985. 'Museography and ethnographical collections in Bologna during the sixteenth and seventeenth centuries.' In Oliver Impey & Arthur MacGregor (eds), *The Origins of Museums: The Cabinet of Curiosities in Sixteenth- and Seventeenth-Century Europe*, pp. 17–23. Oxford: Clarendon Press.

Lawal, Babatunde. 2000. '"*Orilonise*": The hermeneutics of the head and hairstyles among the Yoruba.' In Roy Sieber & Frank Herremann (eds), *Hair in African Art and Culture*, pp. 93–109. Munich: Prestel & New York: Museum for African Art.

Leach, Edmund R. 1958. 'Magical hair.' *Journal of the Royal Anthropological Institute*, 88:147–63.

Leighten, Patricia. 1990. 'The white peril and *L'Art Nègre*: Picasso, primitivism and anticolonialism.' *Art Bulletin*, 72(4):609–30.

Leloup, Heléne. 1988. 'Dogon figure styles.' *African Arts*, 22(1):44–51, 98.

——. 1994. *Dogon Statuary*. Strasbourg: D. Amez.

Lem, F. H. 1948. *Sculptures Soudanaises*, 4th ed. Paris: Arts et Métiers Graphiques.

Leuzinger, Elsy. 1972. *The Art of Black Africa*. London: Studio Vista.

Lévi-Strauss, Claude. 1963. *Structural Anthropology*. Trans. Claire Jacobson & Brooke Grundfest Schoep. London: Allen Lane, Penguin.

Lewis, I. M. 1955. *Peoples of the Horn of Africa: Somali, Afar and Saho*. London: International African Institute.

*Libertas*. 1944a. Vol. 3.

——. 1944b. Vol. 11.

Lima, Mesquitela. 1971. *Fonctions Sociologiques de Culte 'Hamba' dans la Société et dans la Culture Tshokwé (Angola)*. Luanda: Instituto de Investigacao Cientifica de Angola.

Mack, John. 1982. 'Material culture and ethnic identity in southeastern Sudan.' In John Mack & Peter Robinson (eds), *Culture History in Southeastern Sudan: Archaeology, Linguistics and Ethnohistory*, pp. 111–30. Nairobi: British Institute in East Africa.

——. 1990. *Emil Torday and the Art of the Congo*. London: Trustees of the British Museum.

MacLeod, Malcolm. 1981. *The Asante*. London: Trustees of the British Museum.

Maes, J. 1929. *Les Appuis-têtes du Congo-Belge*. Annales de la Musée Royal du Congo Belge, series 6, vol. 2, no. 3. Tervuren.

——. 1939. *Moedereerbeelden uit Kongo*. Annales de la Musée Royal du Congo Belge, series 6, vol. 2, no. 4. Tervuren.

Maesen, Albert, et al. 1959. 'Styles et experience dans la plastique congolaise.' *Problèmes d'Afrique Central*, 44:84–96.

Malraux, André. 1974. *The Voices of Silence*. London: Paladin.

Mann, Robert. 1862. *London: The International Exhibition: A Descriptive Catalogue of the Natal Contribution to the International Exhibition*. London: Jarrold & Sons.

Manning, Patrick. 1985. 'Primitive art and modern times.' *Radical History Review*, 33:165–81.

Marwick, B. A. 1940. *The Swazi*. Cambridge: Cambridge University Press.

Maurer, Evan & Allen F. Roberts. 1985. *Tabwa: The Rising of a New Moon: A Century of Tabwa Art*. Ann Arbor: University of Michigan Museum of Art.

McGaffey, Wyatt. 1993. 'The eyes of understanding: Kongo Minkisi.' In Wyatt McGaffey & Michael

Harris (eds), *Astonishment and Power*, pp. 27–103. Washington, DC: Smithsonian Institution Press & National Museum of African Art.

———. 2000. 'The cultural tradition of the African forests.' In John Pemberton III (ed.), *Insight and Artistry in African Divination*, pp. 13–24. Washington, DC: Smithsonian Institution Press.

McNaughton, Patrick. 1988. *The Mande Blacksmith: Knowledge, Power and Art in West Africa*. Bloomington: Indiana University Press.

Mead, Margaret, J. B. Bird and H. Himmelheber (eds). 1963. *Technique and Personality*. New York: Museum of Primitive Art.

Mercer, Kobena. 1994. 'Black hair/style politics.' In Kobena Mercer, *Welcome to the Jungle*, pp. 103–36. London: Routledge.

Meurant, Georges. 1986. *Shoowa Design: African Textiles from the Kingdom of Kuba*. London: Thames & Hudson.

Miller, Daniel. 1991. 'Primitive art and the necessity of primitivism to art.' In Susan Hillier (ed.), *The Myth of Primitivism: Essays on Art*, pp. 50–71. London: Routledge.

Müller, H. P. N. & J. Snelleman. *c.* 1892. *L'Industrie des Cafres du Sud-Est de l'Afrique*. Leiden: Brill.

Murray, Jocelyn (ed.). 1998. *Cultural Atlas of Africa*. Oxford: Andromeda Books.

Nettleton, Anitra. 1973. *Implications of the Term 'Primitive' in Relation to African Sculpture*. MA dissertation, University of the Witwatersrand.

———. 1985. *The Figurative Woodcarving of the Shona and Venda*. PhD thesis, University of the Witwatersrand.

———. 1988. 'History and the myth of Zulu sculpture.' *African Arts*, 21(3):43–51.

———. 1989. '... *in what degree ... [they] are possessed of ornamental taste*: A history of the writing on black art in South Africa.' In Anitra Nettleton & David Hammond-Tooke (eds), *African Art in Southern Africa: From Tradition to Township*, pp. 22–29. Johannesburg: AD Donker.

———. 1990. 'Dream machines: Southern African headrests.' *South African Journal of Art and Architectural History*, 1(4):147–54.

———. 1992. 'Burton's Luba *mboko*: Reflections of reality.' In University of the Witwatersrand Art Galleries, *The Collection of W. F. P. Burton: 'Of Course You would Not Want a Canoe ...'*, pp. 51–67. Johannesburg: University of the Witwatersrand Art Galleries.

———. 1996. 'Souvenirs of difference: Nineteenth-century leather dolls from South Africa.' *South African Journal of Art and Architectural History*, 6(1–4):26–39.

———, Sipho Ndabambi & David Hammond-Tooke. 1989. 'The beadwork of the Cape Nguni.' In Anitra Nettleton & David Hammond-Tooke (eds), *Catalogue: Ten Years of Collecting (1979–1989)*. Johannesburg: University of the Witwatersrand Art Galleries.

Neyt, Francois. 1977. *La Grande Statuaire du Hemba*. Louvain-la-neuve: Institut Supérieur d'Archaeologie et de l'Histoire d'Art.

———. 1994. *Luba: To the Sources of the Zaire*. Paris: Musée Dapper.

Nochlin, Linda. 1971. *Realism.* London: Pelican.

Nooter, Mary H. 1992a. 'Fragments of forsaken glory: Luba culture invented and represented (1883–1992).' In Erna Beumers & Hans-Joachim Koloss (eds), *Kings of Africa: Art and Authority in Central Africa*, pp. 71–89. Maastricht: Foundation Kings of Africa.

——. 1992b. 'Divining instruments: (*kashekesheke*).' In Erna Beumers & Hans-Joachim Koloss (eds), *Kings of Africa: Art and Authority in Central Africa*, pp. 324–25. Maastricht: Foundation Kings of Africa.

——. 1992c. 'Sièges de mémoire.' In Johannot P. Benitez & J. P. Barbier-Müller (eds), *Sièges d'Afrique Noire du Musée Barbier-Müller*, pp. 59–64. Geneva: Musée Barbier-Müller.

—— (ed.) 1993. *Secrecy: African Art that Conceals and Reveals.* New York: Museum for African Art.

Olbrechts, Frans M. 1946. *Plastiek van Congo.* Antwerp: NV Standaard Boekhandel.

Onians, John (ed.). 2001. *Atlas of World Art.* London: Laurence King.

——. 2006. *Compression vs Expression: Containing and Explaining the World's Art.* Massachusetts: Stirling & Francine Clark Art Institute & New Haven: Yale University Press.

O'Riley, Michael K. 2001. *Art beyond the West.* London: Laurence King.

Ottenberg, Simon. 2004. 'Review of Biebuyck, Daniel and Constantijn Petridis (eds), *Frans M. Olbrechts, 1899–1958: In Search of Africa.* Antwerp: Etnografisch Museum. *African Arts*, 37(4): 14, 88–90.

Pankhurst, Alula & Work u Nida. 1999. 'Menjiye Tibeta — artist and actor.' In Raymond A. Silverman (ed.), *Ethiopia: Traditions of Creativity*, pp. 113–31. East Lancing: Michigan State University Press & Seattle: University of Washington Press.

Parry, Benita. 1994. 'Sign of our times: Discussion of Homi Babha's *The Location of Culture.*' *Third Text*, 28/29:5–24.

Patton, Sharon. 1979. 'The stool and Asante chieftaincy.' *African Arts*, 13(1):74–77, 98.

——. 1981. *The Asante Stool.* PhD thesis, Northwestern University. Ann Arbor: University Microfilms International.

Pearce, Susan M. 1995. *On Collecting: An Investigation into Collecting in the European Tradition.* London: Routledge.

Peek, Phillip. 2000. 'Recasting divination research.' In John Pemberton III (ed.), *Insight and Artistry in African Divination*, pp. 25–33. Washington, DC: Smithsonian Institution Press.

Pemberton, John III (ed.). 2000. *Insight and Artistry in African Divination.* Washington, DC: Smithsonian Institution Press.

Perrois, Louis. 1990. *The Art of Equatorial Guinea: The Fang Tribes.* New York: Rizzoli.

Perry, Gill, Francis Frascina & Charles Harrison. 1993. *Primitivism, Cubism, Abstraction: The Early Twentieth Century.* London: Yale University Press & Open University.

Petit, Pierre. 1996. 'Review of Neyt, Francois, *Luba: To the Sources of the Zaire.*' *African Arts*, 29(4):87–89.

Phillips, Tom. 1995. *Africa: The Art of a Continent.* Munich: Prestel.

Picton, John. 1991. 'On artifact and identity at the Niger-Benue confluence.' *African Arts*, 24(2):34–49.
——. 1994a. 'The sculptors of Opin.' *African Arts*, 27(3):46–59.
——. 1994b. 'Art, identity and identification: A commentary on Yoruba art-historical studies.' In Rowland Abiodun, Henry J. Drewal & John Pemberton III (eds), *The Yoruba Artist: New Theoretical Perspectives on African Art*, pp. 1–34. Washington, DC: Smithsonian Institution Press.
Powell-Cotton, Percy H. G. 1904. *In Unknown Africa: A Narrative of Twenty Months' Travel and Sport in Unknown Lands and among New Tribes*. London: Hurst & Blackett.
Preziosi, Donald. 1989. *Rethinking Art History: Meditations on a Coy Science*. New Haven: Yale University Press.
Price, Sally. 1989. *Primitive Art in Civilized Places*. Chicago: Chicago University Press.
Prins, A. J. H. 1965. 'A carved headrest of the Cushitic Boni: An attempted interpretation.' *Man*, 221:189–91.
Ranger, Terence. 1989. 'Missionaries, migrants and the Manyika.' In Leroy Vail (ed.), *The Creation of Tribalism in Southern Africa*, pp. 118–50. London: James Currey.
Raphael, Max. 1968. *The Demands of Art*. Princeton: Princeton University Press.
Ravenhill, Phillip L. 1991. *The Art of the Personal Object*. Washington, DC: Smithsonian Institution Press, National Museum of African Art.
Read, Herbert. 1967. *Art and Society*. London: Faber & Faber.
Riefenstahl, Leni. 1976a. *The Last of the Nuba*. London: Collins.
——. 1976b. *The People of Kau*. London: Collins.
Rikitu, Mengesha. 2001. *The Oromo of the Horn: Cultural History, Past and Present*. London: Biiftuu Diiramaa Association.
Roberts, Allen F. 1986. 'Duality in Tabwa art.' *African Arts*, 19(4):26–35, 86–87.
——. 1988. 'Tabwa tegumentary inscription.' In Arnold Rubin (ed.), *Marks of Civilization: Artistic Transformations of the Human Body*, pp. 41–56. Los Angeles: University of California, Museum of Cultural History.
——. 1990. 'Tabwa masks: An old trick of the human race.' *African Arts*, 23(2):37–47, 101–2.
——. 1993. 'Insight: Or *not* seeing is believing.' In Mary H. Nooter (ed.), *Secrecy: African Art that Conceals and Reveals*, pp. 65–79. New York: Museum for African Art.
——. 1995. *Animals in African Art: From the Familiar to the Marvellous*. New York: Museum for African Art.
——. 1996. 'Le dernier carrefour d'un chef Tabwa.' In P. Emy, A. Stamm & M. L. Witt (eds), *Mort et Vie: Hommages au Professeur Dominique Zahan*. Paris: L'Harmattan.
——. 2000. 'Producing potent histories with the Tabwa boiling-water oracle.' In John Pemberton III (ed.), *Insight and Artistry in African Divination*, pp. 83–97. Washington, DC: Smithsonian Institution Press.
Roberts, Mary N. 1998. 'The naming game: The ideologies of Luba artistic identity.' *African Arts*, 31(4):56–73, 90.

———. 2000. 'Proofs and promises: Setting meaning before the eyes.' In John Pemberton III (ed.), *Insight and Artistry in African Divination*, pp. 63–82. Washington, DC: Smithsonian Institution Press.

——— & Allen F. Roberts (eds). 1996. *Memory: Luba Art and the Making of History*. Munich: Prestel.

Rodrigues de Areia, M. L. 1974. 'Le panier divinatoire des Tshokwe.' *Arts d'Afrique Noire*, 10(1):30–44.

Roe, P. G. 1995. 'Style, society, myth and culture.' In Christopher Carr & Jill E. Neitzel (eds), *Style, Society and Person: Archaeological and Ethnological Perspectives*, pp. 27–76. London: Plenum Press.

Root, Deborah. 1996. *Cannibal Culture: Art, Appropriation and the Commodification of Difference*. Boulder: Westview Press.

Ross, Doran H. 1994. *Visions of Africa: The Jerome L Joss Collection of African Art*. Los Angeles: Fowler Museum of Cultural History, University of California.

Routledge, W. Scoresbury & Katherine Routledge. 1910. *With a Prehistoric People: The AKikuyu of British East Africa*. London: Edward Arnold.

Royal Society. 1852. *A Manual of Ethnological Enquiry: Being a Series of Questions Concerning the Human Race, Prepared by a Sub-Committee of the British Association for the Advancement of Science. Appointed 1851 and Adapted for the Use of Travellers and Others in Studying the Varieties of Man*. London: Royal Society.

Rubin, Arnold (ed.). 1988. *Marks of Civilization: Artistic Transformations of the Human Body*. Los Angeles: Fowler Museum of Cultural History, University of California.

Rubin, William. 1985. 'Introduction.' In William Rubin & Kirk Varnedoe (eds), *Primitivism in Twentieth Century Art: Affinities of the Tribal and the Modern*. New York: Museum of Modern Art.

——— & Kirk Varnedoe (eds). 1985. *Primitivism in Twentieth Century Art: Affinities of the Tribal and the Modern*. New York: Museum of Modern Art.

Sannes, George W. 1970. *African 'Primitives': Function and Form in African Masks and Figures*. Trans. Margaret King. London: Faber & Faber.

Sarpong, Peter K. 1971. *The Sacred Stools of the Akan*. Accra: Tema.

Schapiro, Meyer. 1957. 'Style.' In A. Kroeber (ed.), *Style and Civilization*. New York: Cornell University Press.

———. 1980. *Late Antique, Early Christian and Mediaeval Art: Selected Papers*. London: Chatto & Windus.

Scheurleer, T. H. Lunsingh. 1985. 'Early Dutch cabinets of curiosities.' In Oliver Impey & Arthur MacGregor (eds), *The Origins of Museums: The Cabinet of Curiosities in Sixteenth- and Seventeenth-Century Europe*, pp. 115–20. Oxford: Clarendon Press.

Schildkrout, Enid & Curtis A. Keim. 1990. *African Reflections: Art from Northeastern Zaire*. Seattle: University of Washington Press.

Schneider, Harold. 1956. 'The interpretation of Pokot visual art.' *Man*, 56(108):103–6.

Schweinfurth, Georg. 1875. *Artes Africanae: Illustrations and Descriptions of Productions of the Industrial Arts of Central African Tribes*. Leipzig: Brockhaus.

Seelig, Lorenz. 1985. 'The Munich *kunstkammer.*' In Oliver Impey & Arthur MacGregor (eds), *The Origins of Museums: The Cabinet of Curiosities in Sixteenth- and Seventeenth-Century Europe*, pp. 76–89. Oxford: Clarendon Press.

Seligman Charles G. & Brenda Z. Seligman. 1932. *Pagan Tribes of the Nilotic Sudan.* London: Routledge.

Shack, William. 1964. 'Notes on occupational castes among the Gurage of south-western Ethiopia.' *Man*, 64:41–50.

——. 1966. *The Gurage: A People of the Ensete Culture.* London: International African Institute & Oxford University Press.

Shennan, S. J. 1978. 'Archaeological "cultures": An empirical investigation.' In Ian Hodder (ed.), *The Spatial Distribution of Culture*, pp. 113–39. Pittsburgh: University of Pittsburgh Press.

Shiner, Larry. 1994. '"Primitive fakes", "tourist art" and the ideology of authenticity.' *Journal of Aesthetics and Art Criticism*, 52(2):225–33.

Sieber, Roy. 1980. *African Furniture and Household Objects.* Bloomington: Indiana University Press.

—— & Frank Herremann (eds). 2000. *Hair in African Art and Culture.* Munich: Prestel & New York: Museum for African Art.

Silva, Sonia. 1998. 'The birth of a divination basket.' In Manuel Jordán (ed.), *Chokwe! Art and Initiation among Chokwe and Related People*, pp. 141–51. Munich: Prestel.

Silver, Harry R. 1979. 'Beauty and the "I" of the beholder: Identity, aesthetics and change among the Asante.' *Journal of Anthropological Research*, 35(2):191.

——. 1983. 'Foreign art and Asante aesthetics.' *African Arts*, 16(3):64.

Silverman, Eric K. 1990. 'Geertz: Towards a more thick understanding.' In Christopher Tilley (ed.), *Reading Material Culture: Structuralism, Hermeneutics and Post-structuralism*, pp. 121–59. London: Blackwell.

Silverman, Raymond A. (ed.). 1999. *Ethiopia: Traditions of Creativity.* East Lancing: Michigan State University Press & Seattle: University of Washington Press.

Southeby, Parke Bernet. 1973. *Ethnographic and Pre-Columbian Art.* New York, 14 November.

——. 1974a. *African, Oceanic and Pre-Columbian Art.* New York, 11 October.

——. 1974b. *Ethnographic and Pre-Columbian Art.* New York, 13 & 14 December.

——. 1975. *Pre-Columbian, American Indian, African and Oceanic Art.* New York, 13 December.

——. 2004. *African, Oceanic and Pre-Columbian Art.* New York.

Stayt, Hugh. 1931. *The BaVenda.* London: Oxford University Press.

Steiner, Christopher. 1994. *African Art in Transit.* Cambridge: Cambridge University Press.

——. 1996. 'Can the canon burst?' *Art Bulletin*, 78(2):213–17.

Stevenson, Michael. 2005. *South African Art 1848–Now.* Cape Town: Michael Stevenson.

Stocking, George. 1987. *Victorian Anthropology.* New York: Free Press.

Stolpe, Hjalmar. 1927. *On Evolution in the Ornamental Art of Savage People: Essays in Ornamental Art.* Stockholm: Aftonbladets Tryckeri.

Strother, Zoe. 1993. 'Eastern Pende constructions of secrecy.' In Mary H. Nooter (ed.), *Secrecy: African Art that Conceals and Reveals*, pp. 157–78. New York: Museum for African Art.

——. 2000. 'Smells and bells: The role of skepticism in Pende divination.' In John Pemberton III (ed.), *Insight and Artistry in African Divination*, pp. 245–60. Washington, DC: Smithsonian Institution Press.

Stuhlmann, Frans. 1910. *Handwerk und Industrie in OstAfrika*. Hamburg.

Syson, Luke & Dora Thornton. 2001. *Objects of Virtue: Art in the Renaissance*. London: British Museum Press.

Taussig, Michael. 1993. *Mimesis and Alterity: A Particular History of the Senses*. New York: Routledge.

Theuws, Theodore. 1962. *De Luba Mens*. Annales du Musée Royal de l'Afrique Central, series 6, no. 38. Tervuren.

Thomas, Nicholas. 1999. *Possessions: Indigenous Art/Colonial Culture*. London: Thames & Hudson.

Tilley, Christopher (ed.). 1990. *Reading Material Culture: Structuralism, Hermeneutics and Post-structuralism*. London: Blackwell.

Todd, W. A. 1896. 'Recollections of East Africa.' *The Missionary Echo of the United Methodist Free Church*, III, August:113–18.

Tönjes, Herman. 1996. *Ovamboland: Country, People, Mission, with Particular Reference to the Largest Tribe, the Kwanyama*. Windhoek: Namibian Scientific Society.

Torday, Emile. 1910. 'Land and peoples of the Kasai Basin.' *Geographical Journal*, 36:26–57.

Torgovnick, Marianne. 1990. *Gone Primitive: Savage Instincts, Modern Lives*. Chicago: Chicago University Press.

Tourist Bureau for the Belgian Congo and Ruanda-Urundi. 1956. *Traveller's Guide to the Belgian Congo and Ruanda-Urundi*, 2nd ed. Trans. A. Freudenberg. Brussels.

Trowell, Margaret. 1967. *Classical African Sculpture*. London: Faber & Faber.

—— & Hans Nevermann. 1967. *African and Oceanic Art*. New York: Harry N. Abrams.

—— & Klaus Wachsmann. 1953. *Tribal Craft of Uganda*. Oxford: Oxford University Press.

Turner, Victor. 1967. *The Forest of Symbols*. Ithaca: Cornell University Press.

——. 1969. *The Ritual Process*. London: Routledge & Kegan Paul.

Turton, David. 1977. 'Response to drought: The Mursi of southwestern Ethiopia.' *Disasters*, 1(4):275–87.

University of the Witwatersrand Art Galleries. 1992. *The Collection of William F. P. Burton: 'Of Course You would Not Want a Canoe ...'*. Johannesburg: University of the Witwatersrand Art Galleries.

Vail, Leroy (ed.). 1989. *The Creation of Tribalism in Southern Africa*. Berkeley: University of California Press.

Van Beek, Walter. 1991. 'Dogon restudied: A field evaluation of the work of Marcel Griaule.' *Current Anthropology*, 32(2):139–65.

Van der Stappen, Xavier. 1996a. *Aethiopie: Objets d'Ethiopia*. Tervuren: Musée Royal de l'Afrique Central.

—— (ed.). 1996b. *Aethiopie: Pays, Histoire, Populations, Croyances, Art et Artisanat.* Tervuren: Cultures et Communications, Gordon Preach, Arts International.

Van Praet, Stephen. 1996. 'Les populations de langue Oromo et le systeme Gada chez les Gudji.' In Xavier van der Stappen (ed.), *Aethiopie: Pays, Histoire, Populations, Croyances, Art et Artisanat,* pp. 33–50. Tervuren: Cultures et Communications, Gordon Preach, Arts International.

Vansina, Jan. 1966. *Kingdoms of the Savannah.* Madison: University of Wisconsin Press.

——. 1978. *The Children of Woot: A History of the Kuba Peoples.* Madison: University of Wisconsin Press.

——. 1984. *Art History in Africa.* London: Longmans.

——. 1990. *Paths in the Rainforests: Towards a History of Political Tradition in Equatorial Africa.* Madison: University of Wisconsin Press.

——. 1992. 'The Kuba Kingdom (Zaire).' In Erna Beumers & Hans-Joachim Koloss (eds), *Kings of Africa: Art and Authority in Central Africa,* pp. 71–78. Maastricht: Foundation Kings of Africa.

——. 1995. 'New linguistic evidence and "the Bantu expansion".' *Journal of African History,* 36:173–95.

Van Warmelo, Nikolaas Johannes. 1932. *Contributions to Venda History, Religion and Tribal Ritual.* Pretoria: Government Ethnological Publications, No. 52.

Van Wassenhove, Donatienne. 1996. *Sieges de l'Afrique Central: Photos d'Archive du Musée de Tervuren.* Tervuren: Musée Royal de l'Afrique Central.

Varnedoe, Kirk. 1985. 'Preface.' In William Rubin & Kirk Varnedoe (eds), *Primitivism in Twentieth Century Art: Affinities of the Tribal and the Modern.* New York: Museum of Modern Art.

Verhulpen, Edmond. 1936. *Baluba et Balubaises.* Anvers: Edition de l'Avenir Belge.

Vogel, Susan (ed.). 1989. *Art/Artifact: African Art in Anthropology Collections.* New York: Centre for African Art.

——. 1997. *Baul: African Art, Western Eyes.* New Haven: Yale University Press.

Von Sydow, Erich. 1954. *Afrikanische Plastiek.* Berlin: Gebr Mann.

Voss, Jerome A. & Robert L. Young. 1995. 'Style and the self.' In Christopher Carr & Jill E. Neitzel (eds), *Style, Society and Person: Archaeological and Ethnological Perspectives,* pp. 77–97. London: Plenum Press.

Wanless, Ann. 1985–1990. 'Headrests in the Africana Museum, Parts 1–9'. *Africana Notes and News,* vols. 26–29.

Washburn, Dorothy K. (ed.). 1983. *Structure and Cognition in Art.* Cambridge: Cambridge University Press.

Wastiau, Boris. 1998. 'Art, God and spirit possession in the interpretation of illness among the Luvale and related peoples.' In Manuel Jordán (ed.), *Chokwe! Art and Initiation among Chokwe and Related People,* pp. 129–39. Munich: Prestel.

Westermann, Diedrich. 1970. *The Shilluk People, Their Folklore and Culture.* Westport: Negro Universities Press.

Westermann, Mariëtt (ed.). 2005. *Anthropologies of Art.* Williamstown: Sterling & Francine Clark Art Institute & New Haven: Yale University Press.

Willett, Frank. 1971. *African Art.* London: Thames & Hudson.

Williamson, Kay & Roger Blench. 2000. 'Niger Congo.' In Bernd Heine & Derek Nurse (eds), *African Languages: An Introduction*, pp. 15–42. Cambridge: Cambridge University Press.

Wilson, Monica. 1969. 'The Nguni people.' In Monica Wilson & Leonard Thompson (eds), *The Oxford History of South Africa, Vol. 1: South Africa to 1870*, pp. 75–130. Oxford: Clarendon Press.

—— & Leonard Thompson (eds). 1969. *The Oxford History of South Africa, Vol. 1: South Africa to 1870.* Oxford: Clarendon Press.

Winckelmann, Johann J. 1972. *Winckelmann: Writings on Art.* London: Phaidon.

Wolfe, Eric. 1979. *An Introduction to the Art of Kenya.* Washington, DC: Smithsonian Institution Press, National Museum of African Art.

Wolheim, Richard. 1987. *Painting as an Art.* Princeton: Princeton University Press.

Womersley, Herbert. 1984. *Legends and History of the Baluba.* Los Angeles: Crossroads Press.

Worringer, Wilhelm. 1957. *Form in Gothic.* Trans. Herbert Read. London: Tiranti.

Zach, Michael. 1986. 'Kopfstutzen im Sudan.' *Anthropos*, 81(1):283–86.

# List of Illustrations

**CHAPTER 1 (p. 21)**

1    Bent (1892:35), *Wooden Pillow,* Mashonaland, Mashona.
2    Bent (1892:45), *Tattooed Women from Chibi's, Gambidgi's and Kunzi's Countries,* Mashonaland, Mashona.
3    Bent (1892:46), *Egyptian Pillow,* Ancient Egypt.

**CHAPTER 2 (pp. 47–57)**

4    Musée Royal de l'Afrique Central (no. 66.14.10), *Mali, "Tellem",* wood.
5    Musée Royal de l'Afrique Central (no. 67.19.1), *Mali, "Tellem",* iron.
6    Musée Royal de l'Afrique Central (no. 78.15.1), *Mali, "Tellem",* wood.
7    Musée Royal de l'Afrique Central (no. 78.16.9), *Mali, "Tellem",* wood.
8    Musée Royal de l'Afrique Central (no. 78.17.6), *Mali, "Tellem",* wood.
9    Bedaux (1988:44, no. 20), *Mali, "Tellem",* wood.
10    Ezra (1988:102), *Mali, "Tellem",* wood.
11    Musée Royal de l'Afrique Central (no. 78.17.7), *Mali, "Tellem",* wood.
12    Dewey (1993:95), *Mali, "Tellem",* wood.
13    Falgayrettes (1989:27), *Mali, "Tellem",* wood.
14    Falgayrettes (1989:27), *Mali, "Tellem",* wood.
15    Musée Royal de l'Afrique Central (no. 73.30.1), *Mali, "Tellem",* wood.
16    Musée Royal de l'Afrique Central (no. 78.16.8), *Mali, "Tellem",* wood.
17    Musée Royal de l'Afrique Central (no. 66.16.3), *Mali, "Tellem",* wood.
18    Musée Royal de l'Afrique Central (no. 79.20.4), *Mali, "Tellem",* wood.
19    Falgayrettes (1989:27), *Mali, "Tellem",* iron.
20    Ross (1994, fig. 7), *Mali, "Tellem",* iron.
21    Falgayrettes (1989:26), *Mali, "Tellem",* wood.
22    Musée Royal de l'Afrique Central (no. 63.15.1), *Mali, "Tellem",* wood.
23    Musée Royal de l'Afrique Central (no. 78.73.2), *Mali, "Tellem",* wood.
24    Musée Royal de l'Afrique Central (no. 79.20.8), *Mali, "Tellem",* wood.
25    Musée Royal de l'Afrique Central (no. 78.73.3), *Mali, "Tellem",* "headrest"/board, wood.
26    Musée Royal de l'Afrique Central (no. 79.20.9), *Mali, "Tellem",* "headrest"/board, wood.

**CHAPTER 4 (pp. 95–129)**

27    Brussels, Musée des Arts et Histoire, Ancient Egypt, *headrest of a contemporary of Pharaoh Pepi I, Old Kingdom,* alabaster, c. 2200 BCE.
28    Brussels, Musée des Arts et Histoire, Ancient Egypt, *headrest, Old Kingdom,* wood, metal, 14 cm h.

29  British Museum (no. 1949.46.689), Oldman Collection, *Ancient Egypt, Old Kingdom*, wood, 13 cm h.
30  British Museum (no. 1893 7.15.16), collected by J. T. H. Bent, *Ethiopia*, wood, 15.5 cm h.
31  Oxford, Pitt Rivers Museum (no. 1940.12.532), collected by Charles G. Seligman, *Upper Egypt, Bisharin(?) near Assuan*, wood, 15 cm h.
32  British Museum (no. 1972 Af11.5), collected by Brigadier General Matthews, donated by Mrs Collins, *Somalia*, wood, 16.5 cm h.
33  British Museum (no. 1939 Af30-42), collected by Dr S. F. Nadel, *c.* 1938, *Anglo-Egyptian Sudan, Jebel District, Nuba Hills, Ko'aub*, wood, 13.75 cm h.
34  Van der Stappen (1996:41, no. 62), *Collected 1995,* 'Ethiopia', wood, 17 cm h.
35  Van der Stappen (1996:42, no. 66), *Collected 1994,* 'Ethiopia', wood, 14 cm h.
36  Van der Stappen (1996:58, no. 117), *Collected 1993,* 'Ethiopia', 'Oromo', wood, 14 cm h.
37  Munich, Staatliches Museum für Völkerkunde (no. K D 12), *Tanzania/Zaire, Matengo,* wood, 15 cm h.
38  Munich, Staatliches Museum für Völkerkunde (no. 14.4.36), acquired from Rattwinkel, 1914, *German East Africa, Wagowa,* wood, fibre, 13 cm h.
39  Munich, Staatliches Museum für Völkerkunde (no. 28.1.111), acquired from Küsters, *Tanganyika (Tanzania), Namalengo (1928), msamiro,* wood, 11.5 cm h.
40  British Museum (no. 1934 05076), collected by Major Hinde, 'Kenya', wood, 14 cm h.
41  Brighton Museum (no. R844/54), collected by A. G. Mumford, accessioned 1908, *Mumford travelled through the Belgian Congo and made copious notes on the objects he collected,* Democratic Republic of the Congo, *Katanga, Luba,* wood, 16 cm h.
42  Brighton Museum (no. R1437/3), collected by Rev. Dr Polly, accessioned 1913, *Zimbabwe(?) Mashonaland/Shona,* wood, 14 cm h.
43  Munich, Staatliches Museum für Völkerkunde (no. 13.68.14), 'Ethiopia', wood, 16 cm h.
44  British Museum (no. 1954 Af23 TB 182), (Wellcome Collection, no. 41391A), 'Ethiopia', wood, beads, 14 cm h.
45  British Museum (no. 1954 Af23 TB 182), (Wellcome Collection, no. 41391B), 'Ethiopia', wood, pigment, 17 cm h.
46  Musée Royal de l'Afrique Central (no. 73.65.1), 'Ethiopia', wood, 16 cm h.
47  Van der Stappen (1996:60, no. 123), *Collected 1993 in the country of the Oromo language,* Ethiopia, Oromo(?), wood, 17 cm h.
48  Van der Stappen (1996:70, no. 165), *Collected 1991 in the Lake region, used by women,* Ethiopia, 'Arsi', wood, 18 cm h.
49  Van der Stappen (1996:58, no. 116), *Collected 1994,* Ethiopia, 'Oromo', wood, 13 cm h.
50  Musée Royal de l'Afrique Central (no. 74.57.3), 'Ethiopia', wood, 17 cm h.
51  Van der Stappen (1996:44, no. 74), *Collected 1991,* 'Ethiopia', 'Guragué' (Gurage), wood, 19 cm h.
52  Van der Stappen (1996:94, no. 243), *Collected 1995 (Wassero Village), fidéna ... only used by men,* Ethiopia, 'Guragué' (Gurage), wood, 15 cm h.
53  Van der Stappen (1996:93, no. 237), *Collected 1995 (Wassero Village), fidéna ... only used by men,* Ethiopia, 'Afar', wood, 17 cm h.
54  Van der Stappen (1996:94, no. 241), *Collected 1995 (Wassero Village), used by men,* Ethiopia, 'Afar', wood, 16 cm h.
55  Van der Stappen (1996:93, no. 239), *Collected 1995 (Wassero Village),* Ethiopia, 'Afar', wood, 16 cm h.
56  Van der Stappen (1989:61, no. 127), *Collected 1993,* Ethiopia, 'Oromo(?)', wood, 16 cm h.
57  Van der Stappen (1996:61, no. 128), *Collected 1993,* Ethiopia, 'Oromo(?)', wood, 17 cm h.
58  Van der Stappen (1989:92, no. 234), *Collected 1991 in the village of Ali Bete, used by men,* Ethiopia, 'Afar', wood, 14 cm h.
59  British Museum (no. 1949 Af46.739), *Belgian Congo* (Democratic Republic of the Congo), wood, 16.2 cm h.
60  British Museum (no. 1954 Af23), (Wellcome Collection, no. 31628 [TB 181]), *Ethiopia/Somaliland,* wood, 18.2 cm h.
61  Oxford, Pitt Rivers Museum (no. Balfour I.35.III.168), *Collected by Balfour in Aden, donated 1905,* 'Somali?', wood, 13 cm h.

62 British Museum (no. 1928 3.3.17), collected by Major Powell-Cotton *in Addis Ababa on 27th January 1900, bought by the British Museum in 1928*, Ethiopia, wood, 18.6 cm h.
63 British Museum (no. 1934 7-17.45), collected by T. Culle, *French Somaliland/Ethiopia Border, Esa* (Issa) *Tribe/Rahale?*, wood, 14.5 cm h.
64 British Museum (no. 1928 5.9.1), collected by Lieutenant Colonel P. E. Alden, *Obtained 1923 from the Somali — ordinary type in general use, 'British Somalia'*, wood, pigment, 19.5 cm h.
65 British Museum (no. 1928 5.9.3), collected by Lieutenant Colonel P. E. Alden, *Obtained 1923 from the Somali — ordinary type in general use, 'British Somalia'*, wood, pigment, 15.2 cm h.
66 British Museum (no. 1934 605 145), donated by Captain Blaine, *Somali, Somali Republic (Kenya? Ethiopia?)*, wood, pigment, 21 cm h.
67 British Museum (no. 1935.11.08.14), collected by Major Powell-Cotton, *NE Africa, Somaliland*, wood, pigment, 17.9 cm h.
68 British Museum (no. 1954 Af23), (Wellcome Collection, TB 1800, no. 15154, B. Wells), 'Somali', wood, pigment, 16.1 cm h.
69 British Museum (no. +990), *Presented by Khedive of Egypt 1-12-78, Paris Exhibition 1878* (register entry), *Nile, Congo "Azande Tribe"* (label). *NE Africa, "Neam Neam"*, 'Somali' (attributed by M. A. Carey), wood, burning, 14 cm h.
70 British Museum (no. 1923.0710.22), collected by Dr Crispin, *NE Sudan, Dinka*, wood, fibre, burning, 14 cm h.
71 British Museum (no. 1954 Af23), (Wellcome Collection, no. 22497, 1902), *Uganda, Bari, Gondokoro(?)*, wood, fibre, 16 cm h.
72 Munich, Staatliches Museum für Völkerkunde (no. 26-T-1975), acquired from Theresa Prins, *Sudan, Dinka*, wood, 21 cm h.
73 British Museum (no. 1935 Af30-42), collected by E. E. Evans Pritchard, *Anglo Egyptian Sudan, Eastern Jebel District, Nuba Hills, Koalit Tribes, Koa'ub*, wood, 18 cm h.
74 British Museum (no. 1934 6.5.65), collected by Captain G. Blaine, *Anglo Egyptian Sudan*, wood, 12.5 cm h.
75 British Museum (no. 1907.5.28.15), collected by Emil Torday, Democratic Republic of the Congo, 'Huangana' (Hungana), wood, 20 cm h.
76 British Museum (no. 1907.5.28.16), collected by Emil Torday, Democratic Republic of the Congo, *Kwango-Kwilu* (region), *Northern Bambala/KotoKoto* (Northern Mbala/Kotokoto), wood, 16.4 cm h.
77 British Museum (no. 1907.5.28.158), collected by Emil Torday, Democratic Republic of the Congo, *Kwango-Kwilu* (region), *Northern Bambala* (Mbala), wood, 18.3 cm h.
78 Musée Royal de l'Afrique Central (no. 17217), (Maes 1929, pl. I, fig. 14), Democratic Republic of the Congo, *Cataract region, BaTeke* (Teke), wood, 15 cm h.
79 Musée Royal de l'Afrique Central (no. 17248), (Maes 1929: pl. I, fig. 11), Democratic Republic of the Congo, *Stanley-Pool region, Léopoldville, BaTeke* (Teke), wood, 17.5 cm h.
80 Musée Royal de l'Afrique Central (no. 30535), (cf. Maes 1929, pl. I, fig. 13), Democratic Republic of the Congo, 1929, *BaTeke* (Teke), wood, 15 cm h.
81 Musée Royal de l'Afrique Central (no. 37385), Democratic Republic of the Congo, *BaTeke* (Teke), (1890–99), wood, metal studs, 17.7 cm h.
82 Musée Royal de l'Afrique Central (no. 53.74.3301), collected by Albert Maesen, *acquisitioned 1954*, Democratic Republic of the Congo, *Kingala, village of Bandundu, Bandundu, Teke*, wood, metal studs, fibre, 13.9 cm h.
83 Musée Royal de l'Afrique Central (no. 33171), 1931, Democratic Republic of the Congo, Kwango (region), 'Yaka', wood, 12.2 cm h.
84 Musée Royal de l'Afrique Central (no. 44555), 1945, Democratic Republic of the Congo, Kwango (region), 'Yaka', wood, metal studs, 13.3 cm h.
85 Musée Royal de l'Afrique Central (no. 60.39.1030), Democratic Republic of the Congo, Kwango (region), 'Yaka', wood, 15.5 cm h.
86 Musée Royal de l'Afrique Central (no. 56.10.10), Democratic Republic of the Congo, Kwango (region), 'Yaka', wood, metal studs, 15.5 cm h.

87  British Museum (no. 1949 Af43.352), Democratic Republic of the Congo, Oldman Collection, 'Yaka' (attributed by William Fagg), wood, metal studs, 14.8 cm h.
88  British Museum (no. 1954 Af23.1832), (Wellcome Collection, no. 8584), Democratic Republic of the Congo, 'Yaka', wood, metal studs, 18 cm h.
89  Musée Royal de l'Afrique Central (no. 40544), (no museum attribution), 1945, Democratic Republic of the Congo/Angola? Cokwe/Lunda?, wood, metal studs, 11.3 cm h.
90  British Museum (no. 1979 Af1.2119), collected by Misses A. and D. Powell-Cotton, 1936, *Angola, Mwila* (Wila), *Mucanka*, wood, 15 cm h.
91  Oxford, Pitt Rivers Museum (no. 1940.7.231) (37.268), collected by Misses A. and D. Powell-Cotton, 1937, donated 1940, Angola, *Mwila* (Wila), wood, 14 cm h.
92  British Museum (no. 1979 Af1.2006), collected by Misses A. and D. Powell-Cotton, Angola, *Mwila* (Wila), 1936, wood, 17 cm h.
93  Oxford, Pitt Rivers Museum (no. 1940.7.232) (37.268), collected by Misses A. and D. Powell-Cotton, 1937, donated 1940, Angola, *Mwila* (Wila), wood, 15 cm h.
94  Bottom view of headrests in figures 90 and 91.
95  University of the Witwatersrand Art Galleries (no. 89 4505), Angola, *Ovahimba* (Himba), wood, 17 cm h.
96  University of the Witwatersrand Art Galleries (no. 89 4411), Angola, north-east Namibia, *Ovahimba* (Himba) *men's headrest, opuwo*, wood, 17 cm h.
97  British Museum (no. 1954 Af23), (Wellcome Collection, no. 232216), collected by Steans, 8 January 2007, Democratic Republic of the Congo, *BaLuba?* (Luba), *Nyangire*, wood, 16.2 cm h.
98  Musée Royal de l'Afrique Central (no. 6567), (Maes 1929:6, pl. I, fig. 16), donated by M. Janssens of the Musées Royaux du Cinquantenaire, Democratic Republic of the Congo, *Ituri district, Mangbetu*, wood, 15.5 cm h.
99  Musée Royal de l'Afrique Central (no. 35927), (cf. 6567, 1912), Democratic Republic of the Congo, 'Kasai' (region), *Sapo-Kanwamba*, wood, 17 cm h.
100  Musée Royal de l'Afrique Central (no. 40561), Democratic Republic of the Congo, 'Kwango' (region), *Popokabaka 'district'*, wood, 14 cm h.
101  Musée Royal de l'Afrique Central (no. 57.53.19), Democratic Republic of the Congo, 'Shaba' (province), *Kinda Kamina* (region), wood, 16.3 cm h.
102  Musée Royal de l'Afrique Central (no. 52.48.98), Democratic Republic of the Congo, Kasai (region), *Kapanga 'district'*, wood, 16 cm h.
103  British Museum (no. 1949 Af46.629), Oldman Collection, *Southern Rhodesia(?)* (Zimbabwe), *Mashona* (Shona), wood, 15.4 cm h.
104  British Museum (no. 1902.107), collected by H. F. Tomalin, *Southern Rhodesia* (Zimbabwe), *between Salisbury* (Harare) *and Tete on the Zambesi*, Mashona?, wood, 14.1 cm h.
105  British Museum (no. 1952 Af26.42), collection by Main and Williams, *Southern Rhodesia, Zimbabwe? Mashona?*, wood, 14.1 cm h.
106  Frankfurt, Museum für Völkerkunde (no. NS 26675), *Collected by Frobenius? South Africa*, "Kaffern", wood, 12.5 cm h.
107  Hamburg, Museum für Völkerkunde (no. 13.174:30), bought from "Kowietzko", Destroyed in World War II, "Betshuaan" (Tswana), 'Kalanga?', wood, 14.6 cm h.
108  British Museum (no. 1954 Af23), (Wellcome Collection, no. 221010), *Southern Rhodesia* (Zimbabwe), 'Shona', wood, 14.6 cm h.

## CHAPTER 5 (pp. 160–185)

109  Tshwane (Pretoria), National Culture History Museum, collected by H. P. Junod, 1940, South Africa, *Transvaal, Shangaan* (Shangane), 'Tsonga', wood, 13 cm h.
110  Müller and Snelleman (*c.* 1892, pl. XV, no. 2), *Zoutpansberg, Transvaal*, probably Tsonga, wood, 17 cm h.
111  Musée Royal de l'Afrique Central (no. 672), (Maes 1929, pl. II, fig. 1), Democratic Republic of the

Congo, *Bangoi (Giri)region, Bangala district, BaLoei* (Loei), wood, metal wire, 12 cm h.
112 Musée Royal de l'Afrique Central (no. 36720), Democratic Republic of the Congo, 'Kasai' (region), *'Sapo Kanwamba',* wood.
113 British Museum (no. 1954 N23), (Wellcome Collection, no. 232216, 'Mashona?'), Democratic Republic of the Congo, 'Luba', wood, 14 cm h.
114 British Museum (no. 1954 N23), (Wellcome Collection, no. 9256), Democratic Republic of the Congo, *Bankusu Nkuta? Lualaba Nyangwe,* 'Luba?', bone, 8 cm h.
115 British Museum (no. 1904 6-11.5), collected by Emil Torday, 1904, Democratic Republic of the Congo, *Lake Mweru* (region), *BaLuba* (Luba), wood, 12 cm h.
116 British Museum (no. 1904 6-11.6), collected by Emil Torday, 1904, Democratic Republic of the Congo, *Lake Mweru* (region), *BaLuba* (Luba), wood, 13.6 cm h.
117 Musée Royal de l'Afrique Central (no. 22718), (Maes 1929, pl. V, fig. 5), Democratic Republic of the Congo, *Sankuru* (region), *Lusambo* (district), *BaSongye* (Songye), wood.
118 Musée Royal de l'Afrique Central (no. 22724), (Maes 1929, pl. V, fig. 4), Democratic Republic of the Congo, *Sankuru* (region), *Lusambo* (district), *[Ba]Songye* (Songye), wood, 11.5 cm h.
119 Musée Royal de l'Afrique Central (no. 55.80.6), Democratic Republic of the Congo, 'Kasai' (province), wood.
120 Musée Royal de l'Afrique Central (no. 22720), (Maes 1929, pl. IV, fig. 19), Democratic Republic of the Congo, *Lusambo* (district), *BaSongye* (Songye), wood, 13.5 cm h.
121 Musée Royal de l'Afrique Central (no. 22711), (Maes 1929, pl. IV, fig. 16), Democratic Republic of the Congo, *Luluabourg* (district), *Bena Lulua* (Lulua), wood, 14 cm h.
122 Musée Royal de l'Afrique Central (no. 22722), (Maes 1929, pl. IV, fig. 17), Democratic Republic of the Congo, *Luluabourg* (district), *Bakete* (Kete), wood, 10.5 cm h.
123 Musée Royal de l'Afrique Central (no. 53.4.14), Democratic Republic of the Congo, *Kasai?* (province), wood.
124 Musée Royal de l'Afrique Central (no. 62.34.1), Democratic Republic of the Congo, *Shaba* (province), *Kinda Kamina* (region), *Luba?,* wood.
125 Musée Royal de l'Afrique Central (no. 57.32.35), Democratic Republic of the Congo, *Shaba* (province), *Kinda Kamina* (region), wood.
126 University of the Witwatersrand Art Galleries, Museum of Ethnology (no. WME 083), collected by William F. P. Burton, late 1920s/1930s, Democratic Republic of the Congo, *Shaba* (province), *Mwanza district*, wood, 15.5 cm h.
127 Musée Royal de l'Afrique Central (no. 57.53.20), Democratic Republic of the Congo, *Shaba?* (province), *Kinda Kamina?* (region), wood.
128 Musée Royal de l'Afrique Central (no. 35646), Democratic Republic of the Congo, *Shaba* (province), *Location Milundila*, wood.
129 British Museum (no. 1889 2.12.3), collected by Edward Coode Hoare, 1889, Democratic Republic of the Congo, *Congo Free State, Guha,* wood, 14 cm h.
130 Musée Royal de l'Afrique Central (no. 31652), Democratic Republic of the Congo, wood.
131 Musée Royal de l'Afrique Central (no. 55.35.18), Democratic Republic of the Congo, *Shaba* (province), *Kinda Kamina* (region), wood.
132 Musée Royal de l'Afrique Central (no. 54.74.22), Democratic Republic of the Congo, wood.
133 University of the Witwatersrand Art Galleries, Museum of Ethnology (no. WME 026), collected by William F. P. Burton, late 1920s/1930s, Democratic Republic of the Congo, *Shaba* (province), *Mwanza district*, wood, 13.2 cm h, design called *Mapingo a Muswayo*.
134 University of the Witwatersrand Art Galleries, Museum of Ethnology (no. WME081), collected by William F. P. Burton, late 1920s/1930s, Democratic Republic of the Congo, Shaba (province), Sanga (region), *Luba/Kisalian period*, fired clay, 8.2 cm h.
135 Musée Royal de l'Afrique Central (no. 7341), (Maes 1929, pl. V, fig. 18), acquired from M. Castelain, Democratic Republic of the Congo, *Luebo* (district), *Bakete* (Kete), wood, 13 cm h.
136 Musée Royal de l'Afrique Central (no. 7341), (Maes 1929, pl. V, fig. 20), acquired from M. Castelain, Democratic Republic of the Congo, *Lusambo* (district), *BaSongye* (Songye), wood, 14.5 cm h.

137 Musée Royal de l'Afrique Central (no. 26074), (Maes pl. V, fig. 16), Democratic Republic of the Congo, *Lusambo* (district), *BaSongye* (Songye), wood, 14 cm h.
138 Musée Royal de l'Afrique Central (no. 30534), (Maes 1929, pl. V, fig. 23), Democratic Republic of the Congo, *Luebo* (district), *Bena Lulua* (Lulua), wood, 11.5 cm h.
139 Musée Royal de l'Afrique Central (no. 30533), (Maes 1929, pl. V, fig. 16), Democratic Republic of the Congo, *Lusambo* (district), *Batempa* (Tempa), wood, 13 cm h.
140 British Museum (no. 1954 N23), (Wellcome Collection, no. 22635 [52010]), Democratic Republic of the Congo, no provenance, wood, 13.5 cm h.
141 British Museum (no. 1908 Ty133), collected by Emil Torday, Democratic Republic of the Congo, *Lusambo* (district), *Kuba, Isango* (Isambo), wood, 12.7 cm h.
142 Musée Royal de l'Afrique Central (no. 19361), (Maes 1929, pl. IV, fig. 15), collected by M. Maes, Democratic Republic of the Congo, *Luebo* (district), *BaKete* (Kete), wood, 11.5 cm h.
143 Musée Royal de l'Afrique Central (no. 59.48.73), Democratic Republic of the Congo, no provenance, wood.
144 Musée Royal de l'Afrique Central (no. 59.48.74), Democratic Republic of the Congo, no provenance, wood.
145 Musée Royal de l'Afrique Central (no. 8091), (Maes 1929, pl. II, fig. 2), Democratic Republic of the Congo, *1912, Mongala* (region), *Bangala* (district), *Ngombe*, wood.
146 British Museum (no. 93.8.4.79), collected by H. H. Johnston, 1892, *SE Africa? Nyasaland? Angoni?*, Democratic Republic of the the Congo?, wood, 17.5 cm h.
147 British Museum (no. 1949 Af46.580), Oldman Collection, *Belgian Congo?* (Democratic Republic of the Congo), *BaLuba* (Luba), wood, 14 cm h.
148 Musée Royal de l'Afrique Central (no. 17245), (Maes 1929, pl. I, fig. 5), Democratic Republic of the Congo, *1914, Stanley Pool* (district), *Banfumu* (Fumu), wood, metal strips, 16 cm h.
149 Musée Royal de l'Afrique Central (no. 59.34.4), Democratic Republic of the Congo, 'Mongo', wood, metal wire, 16 cm h.
150 Musée Royal de l'Afrique Central (no. 12350), (Maes 1929, pl. I, fig. 2), Democratic Republic of the Congo, *Busende* (region), *Bayanzi* (Yansi), wood, metal studs, wire, 13 cm h.
151 Musée Royal de l'Afrique Central (no. 26173), (Maes 1929, pl. I, fig. 31), Democratic Republic of the Congo, *Lower Ubangi* (region), *Equateur* (province), *Baloei* (Loei), wood, 12 cm h.
152 Musée Royal de l'Afrique Central (no. 17200), (Maes 1929, pl. I, fig. 32), Democratic Republic of the Congo, *Ubangi* (district), *Ngombe*, wood, metal strips, 13 cm h.
153 Musée Royal de l'Afrique Central (no. 20157), (Maes 1929, pl. I, fig. 29), Democratic Republic of the Congo, 1917, *Ubangi* (district), *Sango[UOTW1]*[RTF annotation: }This is a tribe name – with an o, *wood, 14 cm h.*
154 Musée Royal de l'Afrique Central (no. 8310202), (no collection data available, but cf. Maes 1929, pl. II, fig. 12), Democratic Republic of the Congo, "Ngombe", wood.
155 Musée Royal de l'Afrique Central (no. 17203), (Maes 1929, pl. I, fig. 28), Democratic Republic of the Congo, 1917, *Kasai* (province), *Banfumu* (Fumu), wood, 19.5 cm h.
156 Musée Royal de l'Afrique Central (no. 51.60.3), Democratic Republic of the Congo, *Kasai?* (province), *Banfunu* (Mfinu), wood, 19 cm h.
157 British Museum (no. 1923.11.16.19), *From W. Dundas, Bathhurst. Collector was with Stanley in the Congo*, Democratic Republic of the Congo, *1866. Lower Congo Yansi?* (attributed by W. B. Fagg), wood, metal strips, studs, 16 cm h.
158 British Museum (Af+2364), collected by H. H. Johnston, Democratic Republic of the Congo, *1885, Bólóbó, Upper Zaire River, Yansi*, wood, metal strips, studs, 15 cm h.
159 British Museum (no number), (Wellcome Box, no. 80/no. 43693), Democratic Republic of the Congo, wood, metal strips, studs, 15.5 cm h.
160 British Museum (no. 90.12.6.7), Baptist Missionary Society, Democratic Republic of the Congo, 1890, *Eastern Tribes*, 'Basongye?' (Songye), wood, 16 cm h.
161 British Museum (no. 90.12.6.6), Baptist Missionary Society, Democratic Republic of the Congo, 1890, *Eastern Tribes*, 'Basongye?' (Songye), wood, 17.3 cm h.

162  Musée Royal de l'Afrique Central (no. 50.9.1), Democratic Republic of the Congo, *Kasai* (region), *Kuba*, wood.

163  Musée Royal de l'Afrique Central (no. 53.74.6958), Democratic Republic of the Congo, *Kasai* (region), *Masoka* (district), *Location Matumba, Ngong/Kuba*, wood.

164  Musée Royal de l'Afrique Central (no. 52.48.101), Democratic Republic of the Congo, 'Kasai' (region), 'Kuba', wood.

165  Musée Royal de l'Afrique Central (no. 53.74.6732), Democratic Republic of the Congo, *Kasai* (region*)*, *Ibend Missumba* (district), *Ngong/Kuba*, wood, 14.6 cm h.

166  Musée Royal de l'Afrique Central (no. 50.9.2), Democratic Republic of the Congo, 'Kasai' (region), 'Kuba', wood.

167  Musée Royal de l'Afrique Central (no. 53.26.1), Democratic Republic of the Congo, 'Kasai' (region), 'Kuba', wood, 16.9 cm h.

168  Musée Royal de l'Afrique Central (no. 43176), Democratic Republic of the Congo, Luba? (cf. Maes 1929, pl. V, fig. 32, *Lualaba region, BaLuba* [Luba], and Musée Royal de l'Afrique Central, no. 36718), wood, 15.3 cm h.

169  Musée Royal de l'Afrique Central (no. 32846), Democratic Republic of the Congo, no provenance, wood, 13 cm h.

170  British Museum (no. 1947 Af18.101), collected by Phillip Smith, *Southern Rhodesia* (Zimbabwe), *Shona*, wood, 12 cm h.

171  British Museum (no. 1949 Af26.1), donated by A. P. Rae, *Southern Rhodesia* (Zimbabwe), *Shona*, *Makalanga*, wood, 14.5 cm h.

172  British Museum (no. 1892 7-14 1 55), collected by J. T. Bent *in Chibi's country, Southern Rhodesia* (Zimbabwe), *Shona*, wood, 14 cm h.

173  Johannesburg Art Gallery (Jaques Collection, no. 50/937), (Wanless 1987, no. 109), collected by A. A. Jaques, pre-1929, South Africa, Limpopo Province, *Elim, Shangaan* (Shangane), wood, 13.5 cm h.

174  Johannesburg Art Gallery (no. 1987.3.61), collected by A. A. Jaques, pre-1929, *Transvaal* (Limpopo Province), *Elim, Shangaan* (Shangane), wood, 14.5 cm h.

175  Frankfurt, Museum für Völkerkunde (no. 26676), collected by Leo Frobenius, South Africa, 1928, "*Kaffern*", wood, 12.5 cm h.

176  British Museum (no. 1892 7-14 153), collected by J. T. Bent, Botswana? Zimbabwe?, "*Bechuana*", wood, 12 cm h.

177  British Museum (no. 1931 11-1859), acquired from Alban Head, *Southern Rhodesia* (Zimbabwe), *Mashona* (Shona), wood, 10 cm h.

178  British Museum (no. 1935 2-2 21), donated by J. Leveson, Zimbabwe, *Mashonaland*, Shona, wood, 14 cm h.

179  Drawing after Distant (1892:102), *[Ma]Gwamba* (Gwamba), *Spelonken, Transvaal* (Limpopo Province).

## CHAPTER 6 (pp. 217–243)

180  Van der Stappen (1996:83, no. 205), *Collected 1995 in region of Ali Adde, Republic of Djibouti, Somali (Issa)*, wood, 19 cm h.

181  British Museum (no. 1957 Af14.21), collected by Admiral Sir George Egerton, *East Africa, Tanganyika Coast, Swahili*, wood, 18.8 cm h.

182  British Museum (no. 1935 11 08 13), collected by Major P. H. G. Powell-Cotton, *Italian Somaliland, Tunne Huts, Somali, Darod, Elai Rehaneren* (Rehanwin), wood, 18.9 cm h.

183  British Museum (no. 1933.11.08.7), collected by Major P. H. G. Powell-Cotton, *Italian Somaliland, Ogaden, Somali, Darod*, wood, 16.2 cm h.

184  British Museum (no. 1904.240), collected by E. A. Hollis, *East Africa, Djibouti, Somali*, wood, pigment, 16.1 cm h.

185  British Museum (no. 1954 Af23), (Wellcome Collection, no. 191331), *Somali, Esa* (Issa), wood, 16.95 cm h.

186  British Museum (no. +2227), collected by Colonel H. W. Lane, *Donated by A. W. Franks (xii 84)*, Tanganyika, Wanyika, Giriama, wood, 15.9 cm h.
187  British Museum (no. 1954 Af23), (Wellcome Collection, no. 161615), *Somali, Esa* (Issa), wood, 19.4 cm h.
188  British Museum (no. 1935.11.08.5), collected by Major P. H. G. Powell-Cotton, *N.E. Africa, Italian Somaliland, Somali, Kotiche* (Cotice), wood, 16.7 cm h.
189  British Museum (no. 1935.11.08.8), collected by Major P. H. G. Powell-Cotton, *Italian Somaliland, Ogaden, Somali, Darod, Banguei(?), Bambilia*, wood, 16.6 cm h.
190  British Museum (no. 1935.11.08.9), collected by Major P. H. G. Powell-Cotton, *Italian Somaliland, Ogaden, Somali, Darod, Gelib*, wood, 16.8 cm h.
191  British Museum (no. 1935.11.08.13), collected by Major P. H. G. Powell-Cotton, *Italian Somaliland, Tunne huts, Somali, Darod, Elai Rehanaren* (Rehanwin), wood, 18.9 cm h.
192  British Museum (no. 1935.11.08.12), collected by Major P. H. G. Powell-Cotton, *Italian Somaliland, Somali, Darod, made in Rehanwin, Elai subtribe*, wood, 17.4 cm h.
193  British Museum (no. 1962 Af17.79), Church Missionary Society, *North East Africa, Somali Republic, Somali? Boni?*, wood, 16.8 cm h.
194  British Museum (no. 1935.11.08.12), collected by Major P. H. G. Powell-Cotton, *Italian Somaliland, made in Rehanwin, bought from Ogaden, Somali, Darod, Kotiche* (Cotice), *Afmadu*, wood, 17.5 cm h.
195  Munich, Staatlisches Museum für Völkerkunde (no. 84.302.919), acquired from Dr Eva Ptak, 1977, *Tanganyika, Boni*, wood, 16 cm h.
196  British Museum (no. 1928. 5.9.2), collected by Lieutenant Colonel P. E. Alden, *British Somaliland, Somali*, wood, 17.4 cm h.
197  British Museum (no. 1933 11-14-15), collected by Brigadier General Sir Eric Swayne, donated by H. G. C. Swayne, *NE Africa, Somaliland, 1884-1897*, 'Somali', wood, 16.97 cm h.
198  Van der Stappen (1996:56, no. 109), *Collected 1995*, Ethiopia, 'Oromo(?)', wood, 19 cm h.
199  Van der Stappen (1996:80, no. 200), *Collected 1991*, Ethiopia, *Sidamo region, Sidama*, wood, 18 cm h.
200  Van der Stappen (1996:81, no. 201), *Collected 1991*, Ethiopia, *Sidamo region, Sidama*, wood, 17 cm h.
201  Van der Stappen (1996:57, no. 111), *Collected 1998*, Ethiopia, 'Oromo(?)', wood, 19 cm h.
202  Van der Stappen (1996:42, no. 63), *Collected 1995*, Ethiopia, wood, 14 cm h.
203  Van der Stappen (1996:43, no. 67), *Collected 1993*, Ethiopia, *Guragué* (Gurage) or *Arsi*, wood, 20 cm h.
204  Van der Stappen (1996:73, no. 171), *Collected 1995*, Ethiopia, *Central region of Shoa, Arsi*, wood, 19 cm h.
205  Van der Stappen (1996:73, no. 170), *Collected 1995*, Ethiopia, *Central region of Shoa, Arsi*, wood, 17 cm h.
206  British Museum (no. 1928.5-94), collected by Lieutenant Colonel P. E. Alden, *Somaliland, Yehaleh, Somali of Dolbahouta tribes, Doba hunca*, wood, 16 cm h.
207  British Museum (no. 1933.11-16-18), collected by Brigadier Sir Eric Swayne, *Commander-in-chief, British Somaliland 1884-1897*, donated by H. G. C. Swayne, *Somali*, wood, 17 cm h.
208  British Museum (no. 1929 6209.07), collected by E. E. Evans Pritchard, *West Bank of the Nile, Sudan, Ingassana* (Ingessana), wood, 10 cm h.
209  British Museum (no. 1933 11-10.29), *Anglo-Egyptian Sudan, Tami (Dervish Muslim)*, wood and fibre, 20 cm h.
210  British Museum (no. 1935 3-7.21), collected by Major and Misses Powell-Cotton, *Anglo-Egyptian Sudan, Andal Valley, Red Sea Province, Tokar, Beni Amir*, wood, 14.4 cm h.
211  British Museum (no. 1956 Af23-4), donated by Satti Awad H. E. Sayed, *Eastern Sudan*, wood, 16.7 cm h.
212  Musée Royal de l'Afrique Central (no. RG 28228), Democratic Republic of the Congo, *Lower Uele, Zande or Ngbandi*, wood, 14.8 cm h.
213  Best (1993:152, 146), Kenya, Turkana, *echicolong/ngichikolong*, wood and leather, 15 cm h.
214  British Museum (no. 1979 Af6.149), collected by John Mack, *Sudan, Longarum*, wood, leather, 16.5 cm h.
215  Manchester University Museum (no. 09763/46), collected by David Turton, Ethiopia, Mursi, *ali/ale, Made and used only by adult men*, wood, leather, 11.75 cm h.
216  Oxford, Pitt Rivers Museum (no. 1978 20.261), collected by Jean Brown, *Kenya, Mt Elgon, Pokot (Tiati Pokot), ngachar/ndege. The mark left by the base in the soil is said to be like a donkey's hoof-print*, wood, leather, 17.8 cm h.

217 Oxford, Pitt Rivers Museum (no. 1978 20.44), collected by Jean Brown, *Kenya, Mt Elgon, Pokot (Tiati Pokot), ngachar/ndege. The mark left by the base in the soil is said to be like a donkey's hoof-print*, wood, leather, 17.8 cm h.
218 Oxford, Pitt Rivers Museum (no. VI.55), *Collected by Major Gayer Anderson on the Sudan-Abyssinia frontier, Sudan, pre 1917, Nuer*, wood, 16.3 cm h.
219 British Museum (no. 1910.9229.22), collected by F. Spire *(Juja Busoga, Uganda Protectorate, 1910). Kenya: Mombasa, Kamba*, wood, leather, 13.4 cm h.
220 Dewey (1993:46, fig. 26), *Kenya, Turkana*, wood, metal, 15 cm h.
221 Best (1993:155, no. 149), Kenya, Turkana, *echikolong/ngichikolong. Made and used only by adult men*, wood, leather, 17 cm h.
222 Wolfe (1979:17, fig. A3), *Kenya, Karamojong*, wood, leather, metal 15 cm h.
223 Van der Stappen (1996:100, no. 266), *Collected 1994*, Ethiopia, *'Mursi'*, wood, fibre, 19 cm h.
224 Van der Stappen (1996:130, no. 376), *Collected in 1995, in the village of Dus, Ethiopia, Kara, Used by adult men*, wood, leather, 14 cm h.
225 Van der Stappen (1996:106, no. 288), *Collected in 1994 in the village of Argudéé. Bashada, Ethiopia, borokoto*, wood, leather, 13 cm h.
226 Musée Royal de l'Afrique Central (no. 83.13.1), *Kenya, Baringo District, Pokot, chebarsiat*, wood, leather, 17.3 cm h.
227 Oxford, Pitt Rivers Museum (no. 1973.20.35), collected by Jean Brown, *Kenya, E of Mt Elgon, Pokot (Tiati Pokot) ngachar, Made by its owner, Chunel, a herd-owner and member of the senior set of the junior generation in the age-set system*, wood, leather, metal, beads, 17 cm h.
228 Wolfe (1979:18, fig. A6), *Kenya, Turkana*, wood, beads, fibre, 16 cm h.
229 Pitt Rivers Museum, Oxford (no. 1978.20.263), collected by Jean Brown, *Kenya, E of Mt Elgon, Pokot (Tiati Pokot), ngachar,* wood, bead, metal, 14 cm h.
230 Manchester University Museum (no. CA 37), donated by Cecil Barber, September 1921 (from the Central African register), *Halifax Museum. Sudan, Omdurman*, wood, leather, metal, 12 cm h.
231 British Museum (no. 1953 Af24.17), donated by the Church Missionary Society, *Anglo-Egyptian Sudan, Bari*, wood, leather, metal, 13.2 cm h.
232 British Museum (no. 1953 Af24.18), donated by Church Missionary Society, *East Africa, Uganda or Anglo Egyptian Sudan, Bari(?)*, wood, reptile skin leather, fibre, metal, 17.3 cm h.
233 British Museum (no. 1928.4.9.72), collected by E. E. Evans Pritchard, *Anglo-Egyptian Sudan, Western Bank of Nile, Bari*, wood, leather, fibre, 14 cm h.
234 British Museum (no. 1924 3.8.131), collected by E. E. Evans Pritchard, *Anglo-Egyptian Sudan, Mongalla Province, Bari*, wood, leather, fibre, 20.5 cm h.
235 Oxford, Pitt Rivers Museum (no. B IV), *Collected by Rev WE Taylor between 1882-1890. Donated by Mrs Taylor in 1927. East Africa, 'Somali'*, wood, leather, fibre, 16 cm h.
236 British Museum (no. 1954 Af23), (Wellcome Collection, no. 242 588), *Anglo-Egyptian Sudan, Bari*, wood, leather, fibre, cowrie shells, 14.9 cm h.
237 British Museum (no. 2718), collected by Petherick, donated by Henry Christy, *NE Africa, Uganda/Anglo-Egyptian Sudan, Bari(?)*, wood, leather, 17.5 cm h.
238 Oxford, Pitt Rivers Museum (no. XII 264 B), collected by E. E. Evans Pritchard, 1936, *Upper Nile, Sudan, Bari, Teaba Keka*, wood, leather, fibre, 19 cm h.
239 British Museum (no. 1934.4.10.32), donated by Rev. H. Paget-Wilkes, *Uganda, Southern Karamojo (Karamojong)*, wood, leather, fibre, 20.1 cm h.
240 Oxford, Pitt-Rivers Museum (no. 1978.20.45), collected by Jean Brown, *Kenya, East of Mount Elgon, Pokot (Tiati Pokot). This is a woman's headrest, made by a husband for his wife. It has a groove in one foot signifying a) the vagina and b) the split in a goat's hoof*, wood, fibre, 15 cm h.
241 British Museum (no. 1954 Af34.1), donated by A. M. Champion (National Bank of India), *collected ca 1932, Kenya, Western Suk (Pokot), Ajarr*, wood, fibre, 16 cm h.
242 British Museum (no. 1954 Af23), (Wellcome Collection, no. 158 615), Uganda, 'Soga(?)', wood, 14.7 cm h.

243  British Museum (no. 1925 11-23-2), Kenya Empire Exhibition Committee, *Kenya, Suk(?) Pokot(?)*, wood, leather, 17 cm h.
244  Oxford, Pitt Rivers Museum (no. 1978.9.3), *Donated by DE Weatherhead, CMG MBE, in East Africa 1900-1935, Uganda?, Karamojong?*, wood, leather, metal, 24 cm h.
245  Oxford, Pitt Rivers Museum (left: no. 1978.20.264), collected by Jean Brown, *Western Kenya, East of Mount Elgon, Pokot (Tiati Pokot). Ngachar/champerit, type given to a young man on his initiation, by his best friend*, wood, beads, fibre, hide, 22.5 cm h; (right: no. 1978.20.265), collected by Jean Brown, *Western Kenya, East of Mount Elgon, Pokot (Tiati Pokot). Ngachar, made and used by men of the youngest age-set*, wood, beads, fibre, hide, 20.5 cm h; centre: details of Pitt Rivers Museum, nos. 1978.20.262 (l), .43 (c), .33 (r).
246  Musée Royal de l'Afrique Central (no. RG 78.79.2), *Uganda, Karamojong*, wood, leather, beads, wire, 20.8 cm h.
247  British Museum (no. 1925 11.23.1), Kenya Empire Exhibition Committee, *Kenya, Kamasia Reserve, Suk*, wood, fibre, leather, 24 cm h.
248  British Museum (no. 1912 12.30.1), collected by Major R. G. Bright, *Kenya, Turkana (cf Junker "Travels in Africa"?)*, wood, fibre, leather, 27 cm h.
249  British Museum (no. 1947 34.2), collected by A. M. Champion, *Kenya, Turkana*, wood, fibre, leather, 20 cm h.
250  Musée Royal de l'Afrique Central (no. 67.63.1153), *Uganda, Turkana (Karamoja)* (Karamojong), wood, leather, metal, 27.5 cm h.
251  British Museum (no. 1947 Af16.37), collected by C. W. Hobley *(Kenya 1890-1910)*, donated by Miss F. Hobley, *Kenya, Turkana*, wood, leather, glass beads, 30 cm h.
252  Musée Royal de l'Afrique Central (no. RG 79 15.5), *Kenya, Karamojong*, wood, leather, pigment, 18.6 cm h.
253  British Museum (no. 1934 4-10.30), collected by Rev. H. Paget-Wilkes, *Uganda, Southern Karamojong*, wood, *Cowhide, greased with animal fat*, 18.7 cm h.
254  British Museum (no. 1934 4.10.33), collected by Rev. H. Paget-Wilkes, *Uganda, Southern Karamojong*, wood, metal, leather, 19.5 cm h.
255  British Museum (no. 1947 Af34.31), collected by A. M. Champion, 1933, *Sudan/Uganda Border, Karamojong?*, wood, leather, 17.3 cm h.
256  Best (1993:157, no. 150), *Kenya, Turkana*, wood and leather, 14 cm h.
257  Oxford, Pitt Rivers Museum (no. 1978.20.258), collected by Jean Brown, *Kenya, East of Mt Elgon, Pokot (Tiati Pokot). Made and used by a Sandal-diviner. This type is made and used mainly by the junior set of the senior generation and the senior set of the junior generation*, wood, leather, 15.5 cm h.
258  British Museum (no. 1934-6-5-23), collected by Captain Blaine, *Uganda, Lango(?), Acoli(?)*, wood, leather, 11.9 cm h.
259  British Museum (no. CC + 8305), *Collected by Hearne (Lupton Bey collection no 32)*, donated by A. W. Franks, 1882, *Uganda, Lango/not Lango (attributed by J. H. Driberg)*, wood, leather, 10.6 cm h.
260  Musée Royal de l'Afrique Central (no. RG 79.37.1), *East Africa*, wood, leather, 19 cm h.
261  British Museum (no. 1947 Af15.1), from Newberry Borough Museum, *East Africa, Uganda*, wood, leather, 11.1 cm h.

## CHAPTER 7 (pp. 274–339)

262  Geneva, Musée d'Ethnographie (no. 16052), *Collected by Kaltenrieder, donated 1940, Mozambique, 'Tsonga'*, wood, 12 cm h.
263  Musée Royal de l'Afrique Central (no. 60.39.1), Democratic Republic of the Congo, *Kwango* (region), *Suku(?)*, wood, 14.3 cm h.
264  British Museum (no. 1949 Af46.807), Oldman Collection, *Rhodesia* (Zimbabwe), *Shona, Kalanga*, wood, 17.5 cm h.
265  Musée Royal de l'Afrique Central (no. 23475), Democratic Republic of the Congo, *Upper Kasai* (region), *Koko*, wood.
266  British Museum (no. 1921.616.41), donated by Miss Hurst, *Rhodesia* (Zimbabwe), Tonga, wood, 17.5 cm h.

267    Johannesburg, private collection, Namibia/Angola, *Himba*, wood, 17 cm h.
268    British Museum (no. 1954 Af23), (Wellcome Collection, no number), *Angola, Chokwe* (Cokwe), wood, 14 cm h.
269    Lisbon Museu Dundo (no. A1061), (Bastin 1961, fig. 146,1), Angola, *Chokwe* (Cokwe), *Shambwanda Chieftaincy*, wood, 11.2 cm h.
270    Musée Royal de l'Afrique Central (no. RG34934), Democratic Republic of the Congo, 1933, *Kasai* (province), *Kapanga* (district), *[Lunda]*, wood, 13 cm h.
271    Musée Royal de l'Afrique Central (no. RG 35738), Democratic Republic of the Congo, *Kasai?* (province), *Lunda?*, wood, metal, 12 cm h.
272    Musée Royal de l'Afrique Central (no. RG 2790), (Maes 1929, pl. VI, fig. 12), collected by Daelman, Democratic Republic of the Congo, *1911, Dilolo* (region), *Lunda*, wood, 11 cm h.
273    British Museum (no. 1954 Af23), (Wellcome Collection, no number), Democratic Republic of the Congo, 'Yaka', wood, 12.8 cm h.
274    British Museum (no. 1954 Af23), (Wellcome Collection, no. 43700), Democratic Republic of the Congo, 'Yaka', wood, 13.8 cm h.
275    Musée Royal de l'Afrique Central (no. RG 52.48.107), Democratic Republic of the Congo, 'Chokwe' (Cokwe), wood, metal, 13.8 cm h.
276    Musée Royal de l'Afrique Central (no. RG 51.41.10), Democratic Republic of the Congo, *Yaka?*, wood, metal, 14 cm h.
277    Musée Royal de l'Afrique Central (no. RG 32870), Democratic Republic of the Congo, *Kasai* (province), *Pende*, wood, 14 cm h.
278    British Museum (no. 1908.6.22.142), *Collected by Norman Hardy, Torday expedition*, Democratic Republic of the Congo, 'Songye', wood, 16.3 cm h.
279    Musée Royal de l'Afrique Central (no. 60.39.201), Democratic Republic of the Congo, *Shaba* (province), *Kinda Kamina* (district), *Songye?*, wood.
280    Geneva, Musée d'Ethnographie (no. 16067), collected by Kaltenrieder, *Mozambique, Lourenco Marques* (Maputo), *Manjacase* (Tsonga), *mukhamelo*, wood, 13.7 cm h.
281    Johannesburg Art Gallery (no. 1987 3.61), collected by A. A. Jaques, pre-1929, South Africa, *Transvaal* (Limpopo Province), *Elim, Shangaan* (Shangane), wood, 13 cm h.
282    Geneva, Musée d'Ethnographie (no. 16065), collected by Kaltenrieder, *Mozambique, Tsonga*, wood, 14 cm h.
283    Johannesburg Art Gallery (no. 1987.3.55), collected by A. A Jaques, pre-1929, South Africa, *Transvaal* (Limpopo Province), *Elim, Shangaan* (Shangane), wood, 13 cm h.
284    Johannesburg Art Gallery (no. 1987.3.), collected by A. A. Jaques, pre-1929, South Africa, *Transvaal* (Limpopo Province), *Elim, Shangaan* (Shangane), wood, 14 cm h.
285    Johannesburg, MuseumAfrika (Wanless 1987:63, no. 211), Mission Collection, *Collected in Mozambique, Tsonga*, wood, 13.5 cm h.
286    Johannesburg, MuseumAfrika (no. 74/2611), *Collected by brother of the donor, Dr G Theiler (Pretoria [Tshwane]) in Swaziland in 1900*, wood, 14 cm h.
287    Johannesburg Art Gallery (no. 1987.3:33), collected by A. A. Jaques, pre-1929, South Africa, *Transvaal* (Limpopo Province), *Elim, Shangaan* (Shangane), wood, 13 cm h.
288    British Museum (no. 1947 Af152), from Newbury Borough Museum, *Southern Rhodesia* (Zimbabwe), wood, 13 cm h.
289    Johannesburg Art Gallery (no. 1987.3 35), (Wanless 1985:59), collected by A. A. Jaques, pre-1929, South Africa, *Transvaal* (Limpopo Province), *Elim, Shangaan* (Shangane), wood, 12 cm h.
290    Johannesburg Art Gallery (Jaques Collection, no. 50/970), (Wanless 1985:106), collected by A. A. Jaques, pre-1929, South Africa, *Transvaal* (Limpopo Province), *Elim, Shangaan* (Shangane), wood, 13 cm h.
291    Johannesburg Art Gallery (Jaques Collection, no. 50/958), (Wanless 1985:95), collected by A. A. Jaques, pre-1929, South Africa, *Transvaal* (Limpopo Province), *Elim, Shangaan* (Shangane), wood, 14.5 cm h.
292    Hamburg, Museum für Völkerkunde (no. 13:173:144), bought from "*Kowietzko*", late nineteenth century, *Destroyed in World War II, Botswana?, Betchuaan* (Tswana), wood, 15.7 cm h.

293　Hamburg, Museum für Völkerkunde (no. 13:174:29), bought from *"Kowietzko"*, late nineteenth century, *Destroyed in World War II*, Botswana?, *(Betchuan)* (Tswana), wood, 16 cm h.
294　Frankfurt, Museum für Völkerkunde (no. 2646), collected by Frobenius expedition, 1928, *Southern Rhodesia (Zimbabwe)/Mozambique, Maduma* (Barwe Tonga), wood, 15 cm h.
295　Frankfurt, Museum für Völkerkunde (no. 2472), collected by Frobenius expedition, 1928, *Southern Rhodesia (Zimbabwe)/Mozambique, Maduma* (Barwe Tonga), wood, 15 cm h.
296　Frankfurt, Museum für Völkerkunde (no. 2473), collected by Frobenius expedition, 1928, *Southern Rhodesia (Zimbabwe)/Mozambique, Maduma* (Barwe Tonga), wood, 14 cm h.
297　Frankfurt, Museum für Völkerkunde (no. 2437), collected by Frobenius expedition, 1928, *Southern Rhodesia (Zimbabwe)/Mozambique, Maduma* (Barwe Tonga), wood, 14 cm h.
298　Frankfurt, Museum für Völkerkunde (no. 2450), collected by Frobenius expedition, 1928, *Southern Rhodesia (Zimbabwe)/Mozambique (Tonga?)*, wood, 15 cm h.
299　Müller and Snelleman (*c.* 1892, pl. XIV detail), 1) Zambèze , 2) Zambèze , 3) Zambèze , 4) Zambèze , 5) Zambèze , *The Headrests in nos 2 to 5 represent the most common forms in the Zambezi (region) ... these headrests are found in all dwellings, and, when taken on a voyage, are suspended from a cord at the waist* (notes to pl. XIV).
300　Bent (1892:35), *Wooden Pillow*, Mashonaland.
301　British Museum (no. 1935.7-15, 3), Carson Collection, pre-1900, *Southern Rhodesia (Zimbabwe), Shona*, wood, 11 cm h.
302　British Museum (no. 1935.7-15, 5), Carson Collection, pre-1900, *Southern Rhodesia (Zimbabwe), Shona*, wood, 11 cm h.
303　British Museum (no. 1921.6-16, 43), Hirst Collection, *MaShonaland, Southern Rhodesia (Zimbabwe), Shona*, wood, 12 cm h.
304　British Museum (no. 1949 Af46 811), Oldman Collection, *Southern Rhodesia (Zimbabwe), Shona*, wood, 12 cm h.
305　British Museum (no. 1892 7-14,26), collected J. H. T. Bent, pre-1890, Zimbabwe, *Mashonaland*, wood, 13.1 cm h.
306　British Museum (no. 1949 Af46 810), Oldman Collection, *Southern Rhodesia, (Zimbabwe), Shona*, wood, 11.5 cm h.
307　British Museum (no. 1949 Af46 814), Oldman Collection, *Southern Rhodesia, (Zimbabwe), MaShona/MaKalanga* (Shona/Kalanga), wood, 14 cm h.
308　British Museum (no. 9763), acquisition date 1876, collection of Dr W. G. Atherstone, *Southern Rhodesia (Zimbabwe), Mashonaland*, wood, 14.5 cm h.
309　British Museum (no. 1935.7-15.1), Carson Collection, pre-1900, *Southern Rhodesia (Zimbabwe), Mashonaland*, wood, 12 cm h.
310　British Museum (no. 1954 Af23), (Wellcome Collection, no. 52014), *Southern Rhodesia (Zimbabwe), Shona*, wood, 13 cm h.
311　Frankfurt, Museum für Völkerkunde (no. 2500), collected by Frobenius expedition, 1928, *Southern Rhodesia (Zimbabwe), Zezuru, mutsago*, wood, 14.5 cm h.
312　Frankfurt, Museum für Völkerkunde (no. 2515), collected by Frobenius expedition, 1928, *Southern Rhodesia (Zimbabwe)*, Charter district, wood, 14.5 cm h.
313　Antwerp, Museum voor Volkenkunde (no. AE 3537), *Southern Rhodesia (Zimbabwe), Shona*, wood, 16 cm h.
314　British Museum (no. 1906.12.11.28), collected by W. Eatherley, *Rhodesia (Zambia), Buni District, Batoka* (Toka), *Tonga*, wood, 15.2 cm h.
315　British Museum (no. 1902 16.9), collected by Tomalin, *Southern Rhodesia (Zimbabwe), between Salisbury* (Harare) *and Tête on the Zambesi*, Shona?, wood, 16.5 cm h.
316　British Museum (no. 1902 .16.8), collected by Tomalin, *Southern Rhodesia (Zimbabwe), between Salisbury* (Harare) *and Tête on the Zambesi*, Shona?, wood, 15.1 cm h.
317　British Museum (no. 1949 Af46.812), Oldman Collection, *Southern Rhodesia (Zimbabwe), MaShona/Makalanga* (Shona/Kalanga), wood, 13 cm h.

318   British Museum (no. 1949 Af46.813), Oldman Collection, *Southern Rhodesia* (Zimbabwe), *Shona*, wood, 16.3 cm h.
319   Brighton Museum, The Green Centre (no. R1437/2), collected by Rev. Polly, 1913, *Southern Rhodesia* (Zimbabwe), *Shona*, wood, 12.5 cm h.
320   Frankfurt, Museum für Völkerkunde (no. 2516), collected by Frobenius expedition, 1928, *Southern Rhodesia* (Zimbabwe), *Charter District, Shona, mutsago*, wood, 17 cm h.
321   Frankfurt, Museum für Völkerkunde (no. 2504), collected by Frobenius expedition, 1928, *Southern Rhodesia* (Zimbabwe), *Charter District, Shona, mutsago*, wood, 15 cm h.
322   British Museum (no. 1954 Af23), (Wellcome Collection, no. 232563), *Rhodesia* (Zimbabwe), *Mashonaland*, wood, 15.2 cm h.
323   Liverpool, World Museum (no. 1992.05.29), *Ex collection, Hoylake United Reformed Church Museum 1911. Natal* (KwaZulu-Natal), *Shona/Tsonga?*, wood, 5 cm h.
324   Frankfurt, Museum für Völkerkunde (no. 2512), collected by Frobenius expedition, 1928, *Rhodesia* (Zimbabwe), *Shona/Zezuru, mutsago*, wood, 14 cm h.
325   British Museum (no. 92.7.14.22), collected by J. T. H Bent, pre-1892, *Southern Rhodesia* (Zimbabwe), *Mashonaland*, 'Shona', wood, 15 cm h.
326   British Museum (no. 1949 Af46 815), Oldman Collection, *Southern Rhodesia* (Zimbabwe), 'Shona', wood, 14.5 cm h.
327   British Museum (no. 1949 Af46.808), Oldman Collection, *Southern Rhodesia* (Zimbabwe), *MaShona/MaKalanga* (Shona/Kalanga), wood, 14.2 cm h.
328   British Museum (no. 1954 Af23), (Wellcome Collection, no. 92074 [43692]), Democratic Republic of the Congo, 'Yaka?', wood, 13.5 cm h.
329   British Museum (no. 1949 Af46.353), Oldman Collection, Democratic Republic of the Congo, 'Yaka', wood, 14.7 cm h.
330   Musée Royal de l'Afrique Central (no. 32835), pre-1931, Democratic Republic of the Congo, 'Yaka?', wood.
331   Musée Royal de l'Afrique Central (no. 33046), pre-1931, Democratic Republic of the Congo, Kwango, Popokabaka, 'Yaka?', wood.
332   Musée Royal de l'Afrique Central (no. 33048), pre-1931, Democratic Republic of the Congo, Kwango, Popokabaka, 'Yaka?', wood.
333   Hamburg, Museum für Völkerunde (no. 15.53), donated by Frau M. Mendelsohn, destroyed in Second World War, *Southern Africa, Betschuanen* (Tswana), wood, 14.2 cm h.
334   Johannesburg Art Gallery (no. 1983.37.9), collected by A. A. Jaques, pre-1929, South Africa, *Transvaal* (Limpopo Province), *Elim, Shangaan* (Shangane), 'Tsonga', wood, 12.5 cm h.
335   Johannesburg Art Gallery (Jaques Collection, no. 50/971), (Wanless 1987:107), collected by A. A. Jaques, 1928, South Africa, *Transvaal* (Limpopo Province), *Elim, Shangaan* (Shangane), 'Tsonga', wood, 13.5 cm h.
336   Musée Royal de l'Afrique Central (no. 19234), (Maes 1929, pl. VI, fig. 2), Democratic Republic of the Congo, *Mushenge, Kuba*, wood, 11 cm h.
337   Musée Royal de l'Afrique Central (no. 32822), Democratic Republic of the Congo (no information given), pre-1931, Teke/Yaka?, wood.
338   British Museum (no. 1899.4.22.1), Dimley Olden Collection, *Southern Rhodesia* (Zimbabwe), *Mashonaland*, 'Shona', wood, 14.7 cm h.
339   British Museum (no. 1954 Af23), (Wellcome Collection, no. 140183), *Southern Rhodesia* (Zimbabwe), Mashonaland, *mutsago*, wood, 13.8 cm h.
340   Frankfurt, Museum für Vöölkerunde (no. 2677), collected by Frobenius expedition, 1928, *Rhodesia* (Zimbabwe), *Shona/Zezuru, mutsago*, wood, 13 cm h.
341   Johannesburg Art Gallery (Jaques Collection, no. 50/909), (Wanless 1985:47), collected by A. A. Jaques, pre-1929, South Africa, *Transvaal* (Limpopo Province), *Elim, Shangaan* (Shangane), 'Tsonga', wood, 14 cm h.
342   Neuchâtel, Musée de Ville (no. IIIC 3026), *Bought from Philippe Jeannerat, 1894, Mozambique*, 'Tsonga', wood, 11 cm h.

343   British Museum (no. 1954 Af23), (Wellcome Collection, no. 75384), *Southern Rhodesia* (Zimbabwe), Shona/Tsonga?, wood, 14.5 cm h.
344   British Museum (no. 1954 Af23), (Wellcome Collection, no. 127303), *1930, Southern Rhodesia* (Zimbabwe), Shona/Tsonga?, wood, 15 cm h.
345   British Museum (no. 1954 Af23), (Wellcome Collection, no. 7504), *Southern Rhodesia* (Zimbabwe), Shona/Tsonga?, wood, 14.4 cm h.
346   Brighton Museum, The Green Centre (no. R834/1), donated Mr Bolt, 1908, *Southern Rhodesia* (Zimbabwe), Shona/Tsonga?, wood, 14 cm h.
347   British Museum (no. 1949 Af46 807), Oldman Collection, *Southern Rhodesia* (Zimbabwe), *Shona*, wood, 13.4 cm h.
348   British Museum (no. 1926 10-16.8), acquired from Mary Cust, *Southern Rhodesia* (Zimbabwe), Shona/Tsonga?, wood, 16 cm h.
349   British Museum (no. 1892 7-14.152), collected by J. T. H. Bent, pre-1892, *Southern Rhodesia* (Zimbabwe), Shona/Tsonga?, wood, 14 cm h.
350   Musée Royal de l'Afrique Central (no. 55.117.65), Democratic Republic of the Congo, *Kasai* (province), 'Songye', wood, 13 cm h.
351   Musée Royal de l'Afrique Central (no. 52.48.112), Democratic Republic of the Congo, *Kasai* (province), Kuba, wood, 18 cm h. (Design at bottom is that of the plateau centre of Musée Royal de l'Afrique Central, no. 14306.)
352   Musée Royal de l'Afrique Central (no. 51.71.48), Democratic Republic of the Congo, *Kasai* (province), Kuba, wood, 10.6 cm h.
353   Musée Royal de l'Afrique Central (no. 12323), (Maes 1929, pl. II, fig. 6), Democratic Republic of the Congo, *Equateur* (province), *Basankusu* (region), *Ngombe*, wood, 11 cm h.
354   Musée Royal de l'Afrique Central (no. 8918), Democratic Republic of the Congo, *Equateur* (province), *Basankusu* (region), *Ngombe*, wood, 11 cm h.
355   Musée Royal de l'Afrique Central (no. 43171), Democratic Republic of the Congo, *Kasai* (province), Kuba, wood, 14 cm h.
356   British Museum (no. 1935.7-15.5), Carson Collection, pre-1900, *Rhodesia* (Zimbabwe), *Mashonaland, mutsago*, wood, 14.7 cm h.
357   Johannesburg Art Gallery (Jaques Collection, no. 50/944), (Wanless 1985:81), collected by A. A. Jaques, pre-1929, South Africa, *Transvaal* (Limpopo Province), *Elim, Shangaan* (Shangane), 'Tsonga', wood, 16 cm h.
358   British Museum (no. 1954 Af23), (Wellcome Collection, no. 232215), *Southern Rhodesia* (Zimbabwe), *Mashonaland*, wood, 12.5 cm h.
359   British Museum (no. 1931 11-18 58), collected by Alban Mead, *Southern Rhodesia* (Zimbabwe), 'Mashona? Tsonga?', wood, 11.4 cm h.
360   Neuchâtel, Musée du Ville (no. III C 3032), collected by H. P. Junod, *South Africa, Transvaal* (Limpopo Province), *pre 1892*, 'Ronga', *sicamelo*, wood, animal hair, beads, claws, 15 cm h.
361   Hamburg, Museum für Völkerkunde (no. 13.173:31), bought from "Kowietzko", *Destroyed in World War II, Southern Africa, Betschuanen* (Tswana), wood, 15 cm h.
362   British Museum (no. 1954 Af23), (Wellcome Collection, no. 203788), *Mozambique*, 'Tsonga', wood, 12.2 cm h.
363   Johannesburg Art Gallery (Jaques Collection, no. 50/940), (Wanless 1985:77), collected by A. A. Jaques, pre-1929, South Africa, *Transvaal* (Limpopo Province), *Elim, Shangaan* (Shangane), 'Tsonga', wood, 15 cm h.
364   Musée Royal de l'Afrique Central (no. 51.12.10), *Upper Kasai* (province), 'Kioko? Luba?' (cf. Maes 1929, pl. VI, fig. 8), wood, 14 cm h.
365   Present location unknown, Southeby, Parke Bernet[AC2][RTF annotation: }Bibliographic entry Southeby, Parke Bernet, 2004 *African, Oceanic and Pre-Columbian Art*. New York: Southeby, Parke Bernet (2004:96, lot 84), collected by Ella Winter, c. 1945, *South African, probably* 'Tsonga', wood, 15.2 cm h.
366   Müller & Snelleman (*c*. 1892, pl. XIV, no. 12), *Collected in Mozambique, Gaza*, 'Tsonga', wood, 12 cm h.
367   Müller & Snelleman (*c*. 1892, pl. V, no. 5), South Africa, *Probably Basotho* (Sotho), wood, 14.5 cm h.

368  Drawing after Distant (1892:102), South Africa, *Transvaal* (Limpopo Province), *Spelonken, MaGwamba* (Gwamba), wood.
369  Cape Town, Iziko South African Museum (no. 75/231), *Rhodesia* (Zimbabwe), *Mutali, Shona? Ndau? Tsonga?*, wood, beads, 15 cm h.
370  British Museum (no. 1954 Af23), (Wellcome Collection, no. 140090), *Southern Rhodesia* (Zimbabwe), *Mashonaland*, wood, 14.3 cm h.
371  British Museum (no. 1892.7-14.155), collected by J. T. H. Bent, pre-1892, *Southern Rhodesia* (Zimbabwe), *Chibi's Country*, 'Shona', wood, 16.4 cm h.
372  British Museum (no. 1954 Af1.49), on loan from John Moir (Maitland-Moir Museum), *Nyasaland* (Malawi), "*Mashona style pillow used for travelling*", wood, 14.6 cm h.
373  British Museum (no. 1934.6.5.24), *Northern Uganda*, wood, 17.6 cm h.
374  British Museum (no. 1947 Af16.92), collected by Rev. C. W. Hobley, 1889–1910, *Uganda/Kenya, Karamojong*, wood, 17.5 cm h.
375  British Museum (no. 1947 Af16.91), collected by Rev. C. W. Hobley, 1889–1910, *East Africa, Uganda/Kenya, Karamojong*, wood, 25 cm h.
376  British Museum (no. 1972 Af11.6), collected by Brigadier General Matthews, donated by Mrs Collins, *Sudan*, wood, 21 cm h.
377  British Museum (no. 1931.3.21.6), collected by E. E. Evans Pritchard, *Sudan, Nuer*, wood, 18.5 cm h.
378  British Museum (no. 1934.3.8.104), *Sudan, Dinka*, wood, 21.5 cm h.
379  British Museum (no. 2727), donated by Henry Christy, 1860–69, *Northern Uganda, Bari*, wood, metal, 15 cm h.
380  Manchester University Museum (no. 09763/1), collected by D. Turton, *Ethiopia, Mursi, ali*, wood, 29 cm l.
381  British Museum (no. 1947 Af16.93), *Uganda, Karamojong*, wood, 16.5 cm h.
382  Oxford, Pitt Rivers Museum (no. 1979.20.86), collected by Miss Patti Langton, 1979, *Sudan, Dinka*, wood, 22 cm h.
383  Cape Town, South African Archives, young Zulu men doing their coiffures, 1890s, photographer unknown.
384  Angas (1849), *Umpanda: King of the Amazulus*, colour lithograph.
385  British Museum (no. 2183), Christy Collection, 1860–69, *South Africa, Natal*, "Kafir", <u>isicamelo</u> *or wooden pillow*, wood, leather, 16.5 cm h.
386  British Museum (no. +6046), donated by Davies Rusher, 1893, ex-Southeby, *South Africa, Natal* (KwaZulu-Natal), "*Kafir, <u>isicamelo</u> or wooden pillow*", wood, leather, 10.5 cm h.
387  British Museum (no. Af23.10), *South Africa, Natal* (KwaZulu-Natal), "Kafir", wood, 16.5 cm h.
388  British Museum (no. 4876 [l], 4875 [r]), donated by Henry Christy, 1860–69, London International Exhibiton, 1862, *South Africa, Natal* (KwaZulu-Natal), *Zulu "milk pail/s"*, wood, 27 cm h (l), 30 cm h (r).
389  British Museum (no. 1954 Af23), (Wellcome Collection, no. 131119), *(Auction Car Str 14/9/1902 8/6-), South Africa, Zulu*, <u>Umcamelo</u> (on adhesive label), wood, 13.9 cm h.
390  Liverpool World Museum (no. 56.25.136), (ex-Norwich Castle Museum, no. 117.15, before 1915), *South Africa, Zulu*, wood, 14 cm h.
391  British Museum (no. 1917.11.3.1), collected by *(brought from Africa by)* F. M. Viscount Wolsely, donated by Dowager Viscount Wolsely, *South Africa, Zulu*, wood, 14.7 cm h.
392  British Museum (no. 1921.6-16,4), *Collector Hirst, South Africa, Zulu*, wood, 13.8 cm h.
393  British Museum (no. 1947 Af19A; computer no. 1949 Af39.1), *Source Miss B Swaine, South Africa, Zulu*, wood, 14 cm h.
394  Johannesburg, private collection, collected pre-1929 in Eshowe, *South Africa, KwaZulu-Natal, Swazi?*, wood, 15 cm h.
395  University of the Witwatersrand Art Galleries, Museum of Ethnology Collection, (no. WME/18), *South Africa, Transvaal* (Limpopo Province), *Swazi(?)*, wood, 14 cm h.
396  Munich, Staatlisches Museum für Völkerkunde (no. 88-188), acquired from Meyer, *South Africa, Natal* (KwaZulu-Natal), *Zulu "Kaffern", Swazi? Zulu?, Isigqiki* (added later), wood, 13 cm h.

397  Tshwane (Pretoria), National Culture History Museum (no. 59.11.2), *South Africa?, Swazi*, wood, 15 cm h.
398  Tshwane (Pretoria), National Culture History Museum (no. 1971.9), *South Africa, Transvaal* (Limpopo Province), *Embuzini, Swazi*, wood, 15.5 cm h.
399  Manchester University Museum (no. SA 9), Clayton Collection, pre-1901, ex-Halifax Museum, *South Africa, Natal* (KwaZulu-Natal) *("Kaffir")*, 'Zulu', wood, 14 cm h.
400  British Museum (no. 2182), *From Kew Botanical Gardens in 1866, South Africa ("Kafirs")*, 'Zulu', wood, 15.2 cm h.
401  British Museum (no. 1934 7-12.6), collected by Major General Sir Reginald Thynne during the Anglo-Zulu War, donated by Lady Baddely (née Thynne), *South Africa, Zulu*, wood, 14 cm h.
402  Manchester University Museum (no. 05156), donated G. S. Thomas, *South Africa, Zulu*, wood, 11.4 cm h.
403  British Museum (no. 1917 11.3.3), *Collected by F. M. Viscount Wolsely in the Anglo Zulu War, Donated by Dowager Viscount Wolsely, South Africa, Zulu*, wood, 15 cm h.
404  British Museum (no. 1898.10-12.6), *acquired from F. E. Foxon* (underside of label reads: *FE Foxon Esq Headrest. S.Africa, Natal*, stamped *Res Magistrate 11 March 87, Umgeni Division*), *South Africa, Zulu*, wood, 19.3 cm h.
405  British Museum (no. 1954 Af23), (Wellcome Collection, no. 76224), *South East Africa, [Zulu]*, wood, 12 cm h.
406  British Museum (no. 1954 Af23), (Wellcome Collection, no. 233043), (on the label appears: *headrest and box, Mashonaland, S. Africa*), *South East Africa, [Zulu]*, wood, 12 cm h.
407  British Museum (no. 1954 Af23), (Wellcome Collection, no. 231238), *South Africa [Zulu]*, wood, 20.1 cm h.
408  British Museum (no. 1954 Af23), (Wellcome Collection, no. 171768), *South Africa [Zulu]*, wood, 12.3 cm h.
409  British Museum (no. 1921.6-16.47), donated by Miss Hirst, *Southern Africa, Matabele?*, wood, 16.4 cm h.
410  British Museum (no. 1954 Af23), (Wellcome Collection, no. 19767), *Southern Rhodesia, Zimbabwe/South Africa?* (sticker on headrests reads *pillow from Zululand*), wood, 12.3 cm h.
411  Tshwane (Pretoria), National Culture History Museum (no. 8342), *South Africa, KwaZulu-Natal Zulu, Hlabisa*, wood, 13 cm h.
412  British Museum (no. 1944 Af4.254), *Collector Mrs A. G. Beasley, South Africa, Natal* (KwaZulu-Natal), *"Bantu"*, wood, 15 cm h.
413  Manchester University Museum (no. 1928.243), *South Africa, Zulu*, wood, 20.2 cm h.
414  Manchester University Museum (no. 1932.301), Speake Collection, 1882–84, *South Africa, Zulu*, wood, 16.4 cm h.
415  Munich, Staatlisches Museum für Völkerkunde (no. 88.530), collected by Wilhelm Joest, *South Africa, Natal* (KwaZulu-Natal), *"Zulu Kaffern"*, wood, pokerwork, 13.6 cm h.
416  Edinburgh, Royal Scottish Museum (no. 1891.2), *South Africa, Natal* (KwaZulu-Natal), *Zulu*, wood, 15 cm h.
417  Tshwane (Pretoria), National Culture History Museum (no. 68.2), *South Africa, KwaZulu-Natal, Mtunzini, Zulu*, wood, 13 cm h.
418  University of the Witwatersrand Art Galleries, Standard Bank African Art Collection (no. SBF 83.31.1), *South Africa, KwaZulu-Natal, Zulu (Attributed to Nominwe Dladla, Msinga)*, wood, 12 cm h.
419  University of the Witwatersrand Art Galleries, Standard Bank African Art Collection (no. SBF 92.49.01), *South Africa, KwaZulu-Natal, Zulu*, wood, 13.6 cm h.
420  University of the Witwatersrand Art Galleries, Standard Bank African Art Collection (no. SBF 83.26.2), *South Africa, KwaZulu-Natal, Zulu*, wood, 12 cm h.
421  Port Elizabeth, private collection of Clive Newmann, King George VI Art Gallery (1999, cat. no. 26), *South Africa, KwaZulu-Natal, Msinga (made by Bhajwa Gcwensa of Emgeni, Msinga, but possibly by Mbhekeni Mzolo c 1935. Owned by Makhashe Hadebe of kwNgubukazi, Msinga Top)*, wood, 14.7 cm h.
422  Berlin, Museum für Völkerkunde (no. III E 7064), collected by Füüllerborn, 1898, *Tanzania, Ngoni, Seat of wood in form of animal*. <u>mlongosi ya muischo</u>, wood, 54.3 cm l.
423  Berlin, Museum für Völkerkunde (no. III E 7124), collected by Füüllerborn, 1898, *Ganderas Town, Tanzania, Ngoni, Seat of wood*, wood, 43 cm l.
424  Berlin, Museum für Völkerkunde (no. III E 16458), collected by Landemann, 1916, *Tanzania, Ngoni, Headrest of wood laterally stretched with stylised animal heads on the ends*, wood, 54 cm l.

425   Berlin, Museum für Völkerkunde (no. III E 12358), collected by Perrot, 1907, *Tanzania, Ngoni, Headrest from Nyassa*, wood, 55 cm l.
426   Tshwane (Pretoria), National Culture History Museum (no. 37.129), *Transvaal* (Limpopo Province), *Sekhukhuneland, Tau*, wood, 14 cm h.
427   Tshwane (Pretoria), National Culture History Museum (no. 37.129), *Transvaal* (Limpopo Province), *North Sotho, Tau*, wood, 15.5 cm h.
428   University of the Witwatersrand Art Galleries, Museum of Ethnology Collection, South Africa, *Transvaal* (Limpopo Province), *Pedi*, wood, 14 cm h.
429   Tshwane (Pretoria), National Culture History Museum (no. 8057), *South Africa, Transvaal* (Limpopo Province), *Sekhukhuneland, Pedi*, wood, 38 cm l.
430   Munich, Staatlisches Museum für Völkerkunde (no. 50.11.19), *South Africa, Transvaal* (Limpopo Province), *Sekhukhuneland, Nkoane's Kraal, Pedi*, wood, 13 cm h.
431   University of the Witwatersrand Art Galleries, Museum of Ethnology postcard collection, collected and donated by N. J. van Warmelo, late 1920s/1930s, *Grandson of Gungunyane*, South Africa.
432   Johannesburg Art Gallery (no. 1987.3.8), collected by A. A. Jaques, pre-1929, *South Africa, Transvaal* (Limpopo Province), *Elim, Swazi*, wood, 13 cm h.

## CHAPTER 8 (pp. 373–385)

433   University of the Witwatersrand Art Galleries, Museum of Ethnology Collection (no. BPC 13.9), taken and donated by William F. P. Burton, late 1920s/1930s, Democratic Republic of the Congo, Mwanza, *Chief Twito Kilukwe*, black and white photograph.
434   University of the Witwatersrand Art Galleries, Museum of Ethnology Collection (no. BPC 13.11), taken and donated by William F. P. Burton, late 1920s/1930s, Democratic Republic of the Congo, *My old Friend, Chief Kajingu with his stool*, black and white photograph.
435   University of the Witwatersrand Art Galleries, Museum of Ethnology Collection (no. BPC 13.8), taken and donated by William F. P. Burton, late 1920s/1930s, Democratic Republic of the Congo, *Chief Twito Kilukwe*, black and white photograph, Mwanza.
436   Johnston (1902, vol. 2, fig. 468), *A Suk, from Lake Sugden Uganda*, nineteenth century.
437   University of the Witwatersrand Art Galleries, Museum of Ethnology Collection (no. WME BPC 12G.27), taken and donated by William F. P. Burton, late 1920s/1930s, Democratic Republic of the Congo, *Hairdresser at Lake Samba*, black and white photograph.
438   University of the Witwatersrand Art Galleries, Museum of Ethnology Collection (no. WME BPC 12G.25), taken and donated by William F. P. Burton, late 1920s/1930s, Democratic Republic of the Congo, *Making a Kilukwe Coiffure*, black and white photograph.
439   University of the Witwatersrand Art Galleries, Museum of Ethnology Collection (no. WME BPC 12G.28, left; 12G.30, right), taken and donated by William F. P. Burton, late 1920s/1930s, Democratic Republic of the Congo, *Bene Munonga hairstyle*, black and white photograph.
440   Powell-Cotton (1904:439), *Man of the Dodinga Hills*, Kenya.
441   University of the Witwatersrand Art Galleries, Museum of Ethnology Collection (no. WME BPC 12G.30), taken and donated by William F. P. Burton, late 1920s/1930s, Democratic Republic of the Congo, *Bulunga hairstyle*, black and white photograph.
442   University of the Witwatersrand Art Galleries, Museum of Ethnology Collection (no. WME BPC 12G.39), taken and donated by William F. P. Burton, late 1920s/1930s, Democratic Republic of the Congo, *Bene Munonga hairstyle*, black and white photograph.
443   Berlin, Museum für Völkerkunde (no. IIIC 19987), purchased from Leo Frobenius, 1904, Democratic Republic of the Congo, *Luba (Shankadi)*, wood, pigment, 18.4 cm h.
444   University of the Witwatersrand Art Galleries, Museum of Ethnology Collection (no. WME BPC 07B.1), taken and donated by William F. P. Burton, late 1920s/1930s, Democratic Republic of the Congo, *A Luban Pillow*, black and white photograph.

445  British Museum (no. Af1954 N23), (Wellcome Collection, no number), Democratic Republic of the Congo, 'Songye', wood, 13.8 cm h.
446  British Museum (no. Af1954 N23), (Wellcome Collection, no. 96827), Democratic Republic of the Congo, 'Songye', wood, 13.8 cm h.
447  Munich, Staatlisches Museum für Völkerkunde (no. 16.16.2), Dietzel, Frobenius, May 1916, Democratic Republic of the Congo *(Kongo Warsch) Kalenga, Katanga*, wood, 15 cm h.
448  British Museum (no. 1949 Af46), Oldman Collection, *Southern Rhodesia*, (Zimbabwe), Shona/Tsonga, wood, 15 cm h.
449  Tshwane (Pretoria), National Culture History Museum (no. 4654), South Africa, *Transvaal* (Limpopo Province), *Pilgrim's Rest, Tsonga*, wood, 15 cm h.
450  Paris, Musée de l'Homme (no. N4 90.65.11), *Southern Africa/Mozambique*, 'Tsonga', wood, 16 cm h.
451  Musée Royal de l'Afrique Central (no. 33170), Democratic Republic of the Congo, *Kwango* (region), *Popokabaka* (district), *Yaka*, wood, 12.2 cm h.
452  British Museum (no. 1949 Af46.351), Oldman Collection, Democratic Republic of the Congo, 'Yaka', wood, 13 cm h.
453  Musée Royal de l'Afrique Central (no. 32833), Democratic Republic of the Congo, *Kwango* (region), *Yaka*, wood, 15.9 cm h.
454  University of the Witwatersrand Art Galleries, Museum of Ethnology Collection, taken by Eileen Krige, 1930s, South Africa, Transvaal (Limpopo Province), *Lobedu Ancestral Shrine and headrest, HaModjadji*, black and white photograph.
455  British Museum (no. 1954 Af23), (Wellcome Collection, no number), *South East Africa*, 'Tsonga', wood, 12 cm h (headrest), *c.* 50 cm l (stick).
456  British Museum (no. 1954 Af23), (Wellcome Collection, no number), *South East Africa*, 'Tsonga', wood, 12 cm h (headrest), 73.5 cm l (gun).
457  University of the Witwatersrand Art Galleries, Museum of Ethnology Collection (no. BPC 05.3), taken and donated by William F. P. Burton, late 1920s/1930s, Democratic Republic of the Congo, *Luba Divination with <u>Kashekesheke</u>*, black and white photograph.
458  Musée Royal de l'Afrique Central (no. 50.13.1), Democratic Republic of the Congo, 'Luba', wood, 18 cm h.
459  University of the Witwatersrand Art Galleries, Museum of Ethnology Collection (no. BPC 21.5), taken and donated by William F. P. Burton, late 1920s/1930s, Democratic Republic of the Congo, *Budya Scarification*, black and white photograph.
460  University of the Witwatersrand Art Galleries, Museum of Ethnology Collection, (no. BPC 12.G. 36), taken and donated by William F. P. Burton, late 1920s/1930s, Democratic Republic of the Congo, *Busanga Woman*, black and white photograph (detail).
461  University of the Witwatersrand Art Galleries, Museum of Ethnology Collection (no. BPC 21.8), taken and donated by William F. P. Burton, late 1920s/1930s, Democratic Republic of the Congo, *Mwanza Scarification*, black and white photograph.
462  University of the Witwatersrand Art Galleries, Museum of Ethnology Collection (no. BPC07A.8), taken and donated by William F. P. Burton, late 1920s/1930s, Democratic Republic of the Congo, *Jealously guarded remains of a stool, which is the sole title deed to Mwanza chieftainship*, black and white photograph.
463  Johannesburg Art Gallery (no. 1987.3.109), collected by A. A. Jaques, pre-1929, *South Africa, Transvaal* (Limpopo Province), *Elim, Tsonga*, wood, 13 cm h.
464  Neuchâtel, Musée de Ville (no. III C 3032), collected by H. P. Junod, 1894, South Africa, *Transvaal* (Limpopo Province), wood, 15 cm h.
465  Leiden, Koninklijke Museum voor Volkerkunde (Müller & Snelleman *c.* 1892, pl. XV, no. 3), South Africa, *Transvaal* (Limpopo Province), wood, 16 cm h.

# Index

abstract headrests
  Luba 134-137
aesthetics 7, 9, 10, 11, 45, 214-216
Acoli 213
Afar 77-82, 190, 197
affinity of form 24
Afmadu 191
Africa(n)
  art 2-3, 8, 9, 29, 31-36, 132, 354
  Bantu languages 246
  headrests 2-21, 31-36, 60, 72
  sculpture 5, 31
Afro-Asiatic (language) 188, 190
*amasumpa* 267, 270
Amhara 205
Amharic languages 72
anatomy of meaning
  useful objects 342-372
ancestors 3, 36, 146, 352, 357, 359, 365, 370
Ancient Egypt 18, 19, 20, 61, 204, 358
  columned headrests 70, 78
Angas, George French 264-265, 266, 269
Anglo-Egyptian Sudan 74, 86
Angola 86-92, 247, 249, 250, 351
angular bases 204-205
arcs 260-263
Arsi 77-82, 199, 201, 202
art
  Africa(n) 2-3, 8, 9, 29, 132, 354
  and headrests 2-21, 31-36
  literature 31-36

Pokot 214-216
primitive 5, 6, 7
styles 26, 132
artefacts 12, 15, 16, 248
articulated supports
  headrests 203-216
artists 214
authentic culture 6
authenticity 3, 67, 71
  Democratic Republic of the Congo 133-159
  and history 132-159
Azande (Neam Neam) 85

Bandiagara Cliffs 36, 358
Bangala District 134
Bankutshu 139
Bantu
  expansion 246-273
  languages/speakers 72, 140, 188, 189, 206, 368
  migration 248
Bari 85-86, 208, 209
Barwe Tonga 202, 253, 262
bases
  headrests 72-73, 203-216
Bashada 207
basic elements
  columned headrests 74-76
Basongo 138, 145
Basongo Meno 139

beads 19, 76, 78, 207, 211, 368
Becker, Rayda 247, 249, 251, 253
Bedaux, Roger MA 36, 38, 39, 40, 41
Belgian Congo 82, 141, 342, 344
Bembe 350
Bent, Theodore 18-19, 20, 70, 74, 157, 254, 256, 262, 347
bent-legged headrests 259-260
Bhabha, Homi 6-7, 8
Biebuyck, D 89, 136
block-form headrests 198-203
Bokala 148
Boni 34, 191, 196, 197
Borana 78, 189
Botswana 93, 150, 202, 249, 260
boundaries
  ethnic 247
  tribal 30
bowls 266, 268
Boyo 350
branch headrests 264
British Museum (London) 12, 13, 16, 20, 76, 79, 85, 86, 136, 157, 192, 194, 203, 208, 265, 267
British Somaliland 84, 197, 198
Brown, Jean 215, 359, 362, 367, 368
Bunianga 148
burial 358, 360
Burton, William FP 70, 142, 144, 342, 343, 349, 350, 363
Bushbuck Ridge 271
Bushong 351

cabinets of curiosities 13, 14
carvers 60, 136, 265
carving(s) 18, 19, 63, 73, 87, 355
categorisation 61, 82
Central Africa 32, 60, 71, 72, 73, 74, 91, 133, 246, 247, 353

Central African variants 250-251
ceramic headrests 144
Charter District 255
Chief Kajingo 343
Chief Kilukwe 342, 343, 344, 345, 353, 356
chronological distribution
  columned headrests 70-94
classification
  ethnic styles 31-32, 35, 43
  geographical 35
  language 35, 43
  material culture 13
  objects 9
  regional 147-149
  taxonomic 32, 35, 43, 63
Clayton, Frederick 268
Cokwe 33, 89, 90, 138, 249, 250, 356, 361, 370
collections 12-16, 20, 61
columned headrests 70-94
  Angola 86-92
  basic elements 74-76
  conical/domed bases 73-94
  Dinka/Bari 85-86
  Democratic Republic of the Congo 86-92
  Ethiopian examples 76-82
  ethnic attribution 71-73
  multiple- 72
  single- 148-149
  Somali versions 82-85
  Southern Africa 93-94, 246
  Sudanese variants 85-86
columns 260-263
Congo 33, 89, 133, 147, 150-152, 246, 261
Congo Free State 138, 143
Congo River 149
conical/domed bases
  headrests 73-94
Cotice 195
craft 4, 11, 12
cross-shape support 257-259

culture(s) 26, 27, 28-29
    authentic 6
    art styles 26
    material 2, 10, 12, 13, 43, 342
Cushitic Boni 34, 192, 196, 197
Cushitic languages 78, 80, 189, 190, 204


Danto, Arthur 11
Darod 190, 191, 192, 195, 196
decoration
    headrests 17, 19, 25, 40, 66, 73, 74, 76-77, 78, 84, 136, 192, 197, 271
Democratic Republic of Congo/DRC 13, 44, 63, 70, 87-92, 132, 133-159, 249, 351, 354
    Luba 134-137, 249
    Lusambo 137-154
    multiple-columned headrests 150-154
    South-East African region 156-159
Dewey, William 84, 88, 93, 135, 149, 152, 190, 191, 196, 214, 249, 251, 253, 345, 366
d'Ibanche 145
Dingiswayo 266
Dinka 85-86, 205, 209, 264
Dir 191, 196
Distant, William 158
divination 246, 357, 361, 362
Djibouti 193
Dogon 36-43, 248, 358
domical bases 205-207
Donne, JB 11, 12
DRC *see* Democratic Republic of Congo
Dumba 348, 351
East Africa 10, 32, 34, 60, 72, 74, 76, 188-216, 264
Egypt 20, 74
Eritrea 80
Ethiopia 34, 71, 72, 74, 75, 78, 132, 190, 198, 199, 200, 206

examples 76-82
Somali versions 82-85
ethnic
    art styles 26
    attribution 71-73, 82, 85
    categories 34, 35
    fixity 3
    groupings 35, 43, 60
    identities 2, 6, 44, 89, 132, 135, 189
    specificity 77-82
    styles 31-32, 36-43, 81, 247
ethnicity 44, 136, 251
Evans-Pritchard, EE 264


Fabian, Johannes 15
Fagg, William 3, 88
Falgayrettes, Christiane 38, 39, 79, 191, 198, 200
Fang 45
female bodies 363, 371
fetishing hair 342-352
figurative
    elements 31, 34, 60, 73, 74
    sculpture 4, 188, 247
figures supporting headrests 352-356
fluting 70, 152, 157, 265, 267, 268, 271
form 24
Foucault, Michel 27, 29
French Somalia 83
Frobenius, Leo 136, 157, 253, 255, 355
Fumu 148, 151
functional objects 9, 10
Fynn, Henry Frances 266

Ganda 189
Geertz, Clifford 9, 10, 12, 26
Gell, Alfred 8-9, 11, 26, 357-358
gender 79, 90, 202
geographical classification 35, 65

geographical distribution
  columned headrests 70-94
Giriama 193
Great International Exhibition (London 1862) 16, 17
Great Zimbabwe 20
Gungunyane 261, 272
Gurage 77-82, 197-198, 199, 201, 368
Gwamba 158, 262

hairstyles 18, 19, 188, 189, 342-352
*hakata (makakata)* 371
Hawkins, Leila 267
headrings 272, 360, 371
headrests
  abstract 134-137
  African 2-21, 31-36, 60
  and art 2-21
  arcs 260-263
  bases 72-73
  bent-legged 259-260
  block-form 198-203
  as bodies 362-372
  branch 264
  Central African variants 250-251
  ceramic 144
  collections 12
  columned 70-94
  columns 260-263
  conical/domed bases 73-94
  cross-shape support 257-259
  decoration 17, 19, 25, 40, 66, 73, 74, 76-77, 78, 84, 136, 192, 197, 271
  East Africa 188-216, 264
  ethnic attribution 71-73
  figures supporting 352-356
  gender 79, 90, 202
  horizontal compositions 263-273
  identity 66
  interlacing 260-263
  iron 38, 40, 41, 62
  ivory 62
  leather-encased supports 208-210
  morphology 65-67
  multiple-columned 72, 150-154
  panel/pillar supports 249-257
  as performance pieces 356-362
  platforms 72
  Shona style nexus 253-257
  single-columned 148-149
  Somali 190-198
  styles 24-25, 31-36
  supports 73
  Tellem/Dogon 36-43
  tied-leg types 72, 210-213
  Tsonga 151-253
  two-legged, tied 210-213
  vertical compositions 248-263
  wood 24-25, 40, 41-42, 62, 80, 136, 198, 200
Hemba 144, 350, 354, 363
High Art 2, 4
Himba 86, 90, 91, 202
history
  and authenticity 132-159
  Bantu expansion 246-273
Holo 88, 89
horizontal compositions 263-273
human
  anatomy/body 211, 252, 362
  figures 353, 367
Hungana 86, 89

iconography 9, 10, 11, 19, 31, 132, 135, 247, 252, 268, 354
  headrests as bodies 362-372

identities
  ethnic 2, 6, 44, 89, 132, 135, 189
  headrests 66
  style 29, 60
Igbo 63
Ingassana (Gaam) 204
Inhambane 156, 252
interlacing 83, 192, 260-263, 271
international exhibitions 266
iron headrests 38, 40, 62
  votive 41
Isambo 138, 139, 145-146, 154
Issa 81, 83, 191, 192, 193, 194
Italian Somalia 192, 195
ivory headrests 62
Jaques, HA 157, 263, 271, 272, 349
Jaques Collection 12, 261, 263, 371
Jebel District 74
Johannesburg Art Gallery 12, 262
Johnston, HH 149, 151, 345
Joss Collection 12, 32, 61, 149
Juba River 191, 196
Jubaland 192, 195
Junod, HP 133, 369

Kalanga 93, 156, 157
Kalenjin 210
Kaltenrieder 263
Kamasia Reserve (Kenya) 210
Kamba 206
Kanyok 354
Kara 206
Karamojong 85, 205, 207, 210, 212, 264, 360
Kasai 92, 133, 134, 136, 138, 139, 140, 142, 146, 149, 150-152, 354
  bent-legged headrests 259-260
Kasai Kapanga 92, 134
Kasfir, Sidney L 26, 29, 44, 60

*kashekesheke* 361
Katanga 75, 92, 133, 134, 136, 142, 146, 150, 258, 342, 355
Kenya 75, 188, 190, 192, 200, 205, 206, 345, 359
Kenya-Uganda 85
Kete 141, 144, 145, 259
Kew Gardens (London) 13, 265
Kikuyu 188
Kinda Kamina 142, 143, 258
Kisalian culture 144, 358
*kolo* scarification 363
Koninklijke Museum voor Volkerkunde (Leiden) 371
Kota 45
Kotokoto 86
Kuba 138, 139, 145-146, 151, 153, 154, 155, 351, 354, 361, 364
  bent-legged headrests 259-260
Kuba Kingdom 138
*kulemba* scarification 365
Kwango region 14, 92, 258, 261
Kwango-Kwilu region 86, 89, 133
KwaZulu-Natal 10, 35, 265, 266, 268

Lake Mweru 135, 136, 155
Lango 213
language groupings 35, 43
Latuka 208
leather-encased supports 208-210
Lele 145
Lewis, IM 80, 81, 190, 191
limitations 60-67
Limpopo 249, 261, 262, 270, 272
literature
  African art 31-36
lobed bases
  headrests 73
Loei 134, 148, 149, 153

Longarum 206
Lualaba region 155
Luba 28, 33, 44, 73, 75, 91, 134, 141, 142, 143, 144, 155, 249, 261, 342-344, 350, 353, 354, 362, 363
  abstract headrests 134-137
Luebo 137, 139, 141, 144, 145, 354
Lulua (Bena) 139, 141, 142, 152, 354, 364
Lulua River 139
Luluabourg 135, 136, 137, 139, 141, 145
Lunda 33, 89, 90, 249, 250, 361
Lusambo 137-154, 155, 259, 354
  variants 141-150

Maes, J 87, 134, 137, 148, 149, 150, 151, 155, 259, 260, 344, 355
  headrest categories 32-33, 148
Maesen, Albert
Malawi 149, 262
Mali 36
Manjacaze 252
Mann, Robert 16-17, 266
Manyika 255
Mashonaland 19, 76, 157, 254, 256, 262
Matabele 270
Matengo 75
material culture 2, 10, 12, 43, 342
  classification 13
Mbala 86, 89, 148, 351, 354
*mboko* 143, 362
meaning
  useful objects 342-372
metal 369
metamorphosis 2, 7
methodology 60-67
Mfinu 147-149, 152
Milundila 142
modernism 6
Mongalla 208

Mongo 148, 149
morphology of headrests 65-67
Moti 192
Mozambique 93, 133, 150, 156, 157, 249, 252, 260, 272
Mpande 264-265, 266, 268, 269
Mswati II 265
multiple-columned headrests 72, 150-154
Mursi 206, 207
Musèe de l'Homme (Paris) 12
Musèe Royal de l'Afrique Central (Tervuren) 12, 32, 33, 38, 39, 77, 79, 87, 89, 92, 192, 362
  DRC headrests 134, 140, 154
Museum für Völkerkunde (Berlin) 12, 135, 144, 271, 355
Museum für Völkerkunde (Frankfurt) 12
Museum für Völkerkunde (Hamburg) 12, 93
MuseumAfrika (Johannesburg) 90
Mutali 262
Mwanza district 142, 144, 342, 350, 353
mythology 30
Mzilikaze 272

Namalengo 75
Namibia 86, 90, 91, 202
natural history museums 13
naturalism 29
Ndau 156, 262
Ndebele 272
Ndembu 363
Ndengese 364
*ndoro* 366
Neam Neam 85
Ngabandi 205
Ngombe 148, 149, 150, 151, 152, 153, 260, 344, 358
Ngongo 89
Ngongo Luteta 138
Ngoni 149, 188, 270, 271, 272, 356, 370
Nguni 263, 265, 268, 269, 359

Nigeria 248
Nilo-Saharan (language) 188, 191, 206
Nilotic-speakers 72, 189, 191, 204, 210, 367
Nkano 89
Nkutshu 139
Nkutu 155, 259
North Sotho 264-273, 356, 367, 370
Nsapo 354
Ntwane 202
Nuba 363
Nuba Hills 74, 75, 86, 204
Nuer 205, 264
Nyangatom 206
*nyora* scarification 365


objects
  classification 9
  functional 9, 10
Ogaden 192, 195, 196
Olbrechts, Frans 3, 146
Omdurman 208
one-tribe-one-style syndrome 25
Oromo 75, 77-82, 197-198, 199, 205, 368


panel/pillar supports 249-257
Pedi 367
Pende 250, 350, 351, 354, 356, 370
performance pieces 356-362
Pitt Rivers Museum 84, 192, 194, 212, 362
planar supports 205-207
platforms
  headrests 72, 203-216
pointille inlay 207
Pokot 85, 202, 206, 207, 210, 212, 247, 264, 345, 358-359
  aesthetics 214-216
polygonal supports 204-205
Popokabaka 92, 155, 258

Portuguese East Africa 254
position 60-67
Powell-Cotton
  Major 83, 189, 192, 194, 204, 345, 359
  Misses 90, 91
  Museum (Birchington on Sea) 84, 192, 193, 194, 195, 346
primitive
  art 5, 6, 7, 13, 15


Rahale 83
regional classification 147-149
Rehanwin 191, 192, 195, 196
Rendille 189
representation 5, 7, 11
reptile skin 209
Rietberg Museum (Zurich) 355


Sab 191, 196
Sanga region 70, 144, 152
Sankuru
  basin 353
  region 136, 259
  River 137, 138, 139
Sapo Kanwamba 92, 134
scarification 348, 363, 365
Schapiro, Meyer 28
sculpture
  african 31, 354
  figural 4
  human figures 350
  primitive 5
  Tellem/Dogon 36, 44
Sekhukhuneland 271
Semitic languages 78
Shaba 92, 133, 140, 142, 143, 342
Shangane 157, 270, 272
Shankadi style 353

Shilluk 209
Shiner, Larry 9
Shona 10, 11, 18, 19, 20, 75, 76, 93, 94, 132, 156, 157, 261, 262, 347, 358, 359, 364, 366, 371
  style nexus 253-257
Sieber, Roy 9, 12
single-columned headrests 148-149
sleeping routines 357, 359
snuff 17, 259, 369
Soga 210
Somali 34, 80, 82, 84, 189, 190-198, 199, 247
  versions 82-85
Somalia 71, 72, 74, 83, 84, 190-198, 199, 200, 203
Songye 91, 92, 138, 141, 144, 152, 259, 354
Sotho 133, 272
South Africa 93, 133, 150, 199, 202, 261, 360
South East African region 156-159
Southern Africa 10, 13, 16, 32, 60, 71, 72, 73, 188, 247, 258, 263
  columned headrests 93-94
Southern-Central African cross-border style 251-253
Spelonken 158, 262
Staatliches Museum für Völkerkunde (Munich) 76, 197
Stanley Pool 134, 151
Steiner, Christopher 5-6, 8
style(s) 3, 24-57, 132
  definition 25-31
  ethnic 31-32, 36-43, 81, 247
  headrests 31-36
  transmission 45
  tribal boundaries 30
stylistic
  analysis 29
  categorisation 82
  identity 60
sub-Saharan Africa 25, 30
Sudan 34, 70, 72, 74, 149, 204, 206, 208, 264
  variants 85-86
Suk 189, 203, 210, 345, 350
Suku 33, 89, 350, 370
supports
  headrests 73, 352-356
Swahili 191, 193
Swayne, Brigadier General Sir Eric 198, 203
Swazi 264-273, 356, 358, 370
Swaziland 252, 271

Tabwa 350, 354, 359, 360, 363, 367
Tanu River 191
Tanzania 75, 188, 193, 197
taxonomic classification 32, 35, 43, 63, 65-67
Teke 73, 86, 87, 88, 89, 92, 134, 147-149, 151, 152, 249, 257, 370
Tellem 36-43, 70, 73, 144, 155, 200, 358
Tempa 141, 145, 155
Tête 254, 256
Tetela 145, 155
Theuws 361
Third World 15
three-dimensional interlacing 260-263
Tiati Pokot 206, 359, 362, 367
tied-leg types 72, 210-213
Tiv 363
Toka 256
Tonga 256
Torday, Emil 86, 135, 137, 145, 348
tourist
  art 62, 83
  market 350
transfiguration 11
Transvaal 133, 252, 369
tribal
  boundaries 30
  model 44
Tsadik, Gebre Wolde 77
Tshwane (Pretoria) 132, 268

Tsonga 93, 94, 132, 133, 148, 156, 157, 158, 258, 261, 272, 358, 361, 364, 369
  Southern-Central African cross-border style 251-253
Tswana 93, 156, 157, 252
Turkana 34, 85, 189, 202, 205, 207, 212
two-legged, tied headrests 210-213

Ubangi region 133, 148, 150-152, 358
Uganda 34, 189, 200, 208
Uganda Kenya 85
University of the Witwatersrand Art Galleries 70, 77, 90, 91, 366
Upemba region 142
Urua 136, 144
useful/utilitarian objects 3, 342-372

Van der Stappen, Xavier 12, 34, 74, 75, 77-82, 191, 199, 200-201
Varnedoe, Kirk 7
Venda 360, 367, 370
vertical compositions 248-263
vessels 265-266
votive headrests 41

Wagowa 75
Waguha 188
Walamo 83
Wanyika 193
Wellcome Collection 91, 135, 145, 152, 193, 204, 209, 265, 269
West Africa 36, 60
Western
  art 2
  cultural norms 349
Wieckmann Collection 13

Wila 86, 90, 91, 351
wood headrests 24-25, 40, 41-42, 62, 80, 136, 198, 200
world art 2

Xhosa 263, 273

Yaka 33, 86, 87, 89, 155, 249, 250, 257, 350, 354, 356, 369, 370
Yansi 147-149, 151
Yoruba 28, 44, 363, 368

Zaire 151
*Zambèze* 35, 254
Zambèze
  Province 254
  region 93, 157
Zambezi 247, 249, 254
Zambia 247, 256
Zanzibar 195
Zappo Zapp 145
*Zeitgeist* 26
Zezeru 255
Zimbabwe 10, 18, 93, 133, 150, 156, 157, 202, 254, 256, 260, 262
Zulu 10, 17, 35, 246, 263, 264-273, 356, 370
Zwgendaba 272

www.ingramcontent.com/pod-product-compliance
Ingram Content Group UK Ltd.
Pitfield, Milton Keynes, MK11 3LW, UK
UKHW050415240426
12048UKWH00021B/1531